SHELVES CLOSETS & CABINETS

From A-Frames to Z-Outs

by Peter Jones

illustrated by
Mary Kornblum, Gary Tong, and Minas Chepikian

Published by Popular Science Books
New York

Distributed to the trade by Sterling Publishing Co., Inc.
New York, New York

Published by
Popular Science Books
Grolier Book Clubs, Inc.

Distributed to the trade by
STERLING PUBLISHING CO., INC.
Two Park Avenue
New York, N.Y. 10016

Library of Congress Catalog Number 77-83698

ISBN 0-943822-96-3

Manufactured in the United States of America

Library of Congress Cataloging in Publication Data (CIP)
Jones, Peter, 1934 –
Shelves, closets & cabinets.
Includes index.
1. Cabinet-work. 2. Clothes closets. 3. Shelving (for books)
1. Title.
TT197.J66 684.1'6 77-83698

Dedicated to

Betty Rice, Florence Hamsher, and Dale Skulnick, whose combined talents and efforts have made this book possible.

Credits

The author wishes to thank Mr. Fritz Koelbel, whose lifelong experiences as a boatbuilder and cabinetmaker rendered him invaluable in his role as technical consultant and project designer for the book. And many thanks to the U.S. Forest Products Laboratory, Forest Service, U.S. Department of Agriculture, for providing the wood grain photographs included in Chapter 3.

Contents

Introduction

Without question, shelves, closets and cabinets in varying forms are an integral part of everyone's day-to-day living. Shelves are so important that nobody ever seems to have enough of them. As for closets and cabinets, ask any woman what she considers most important when she is considering a new place to live, and she will probably tell you, "the kitchen, the bathroom and the storage space."

At first glance a "five-minute" shelf appears to be about as easy to put up as anyone can imagine. It *can* be a very quick and simple project—until you cannot find any studs in the wall, or you are face-to-face with solid brick and no masonry bit. But as easy as a five-minute shelf can be, the art of creating volumes of horizontal storage becomes complicated pretty quickly when you are dealing with small or oddly shaped spaces. From this art have come such innovations as the A-Frame bookcase, which fits under a stairwell, and the Z-Out, which is really three shelf cases hinged together so that they can fold against each other. Collapsed, the Z-Out can be as large as 3′ wide, 7′ high, and 2′ deep. Open, it becomes 9′ long and presents over a hundred feet of totally usable shelf space. It is a great space-saver for any child with a roomful of toys. Yet all it requires is the price of lumber and a day of sawing and nailing.

As for closets, there is the standard, which requires that you fill in two walls with 2′x3′s and sheetrock, then hang some poles and shelves. But there are also movable closets that can be made of plywood and rearranged in all directions to become decorative walls or act as room dividers. The problem most people have with closet space is that they see it as a square, not the cube that it really is. They forget that a closet is not just 4′x4′. It is also 8′ high. So people often waste all that usable space above their clothes when they could be hanging two or more clothes racks, varied-width shelving (each shelf with a specific purpose), drawers, a shoe rack on the inside of the door, and lots of other possibilities.

On top of that, when all this storage space is built and hung, when the open bookshelves float against the living room walls and the bedroom closets are carefully arranged to hold a maximum of possessions, it is the cabinet that becomes the most useful of all construction projects. There are cabinets that fold into themselves to give double the shelf space in half the area. There are cabinets for hanging and storing tools in the garage or basement. There is an endless need for kitchen and bathroom cabinets (it is possible to get the average woman's entire array of cosmetics into one easy-to-build wall cabinet). There are cabinets that stand by themselves and others that hang from the rafters. And you will find how to construct all of these among the projects included in this book.

The secret of effectively utilizing every inch of space, of course, is to know what every shelf, closet or cabinet is to be used for, and to allow room for each of the objects they will contain. Having determined the specific uses for whatever project you are considering, the next step is to plan the project in terms of the space you have to work with. And having carefully organized and worked out every detail, it is essential to keep one's mind open to making changes even during construction. For example, consider the étagère illustrated on the front cover of this book.

It happened that the author was asked to build two étagères to fit in a small apartment. One of them was designed to hold a file drawer and a television set, while the other contained stereo components. The interior designer, Pamela Stern, had a concept of the size and appearance of the finished piece but that was all, so the specific design of the parts and their assembly was left to the builder. After the units were completed, I recalled that the top shelf of each étagère was to hold a stereo speaker. But that would leave the speaker wires dangling down the back of the shelves. Speaker wires, as far as I am concerned, are the opposite of children. They should be heard but never seen. With that idea in mind, I realized that any of the four posts in each unit could easily carry the wires down the étagères to the floor. Since the posts were hollow anyway, it became a simple matter of drilling a ¼″ hole in the back corners of the top shelves so that the wires could be dropped to the floor and pinned along the baseboard to hook up with the stereo receiver. A simple departure, motivated by a constant awareness of the project in progress, and what the étagères were designed to do.

This book includes many projects, each of which has a specific purpose. But no book can answer all of the particular conditions that each one of its readers must deal with. Because it is not the projects themselves that are important, but the ideas behind them, you will find basic plans included for everything from the five-minute shelf to pure furniture that could take months to build, but will offer years of satisfaction. Most of the projects can be completed by anyone with a reasonable complement of power tools. A few of them require the use of such sophisticated instruments as a molder head or dovetail template. All of them demand considerable thinking on the part of the builder before, during and sometimes after he does any physical work. Each project should be considered as nothing more than a general guideline that can be altered to meet the exact needs of the builder.

"How-to" books have one disturbing drawback. They must often reduce very complicated activities to ultra-simple instructions such as: "First, cut a 24″ square from the ¾″ plywood panel." Easy to write, but exceedingly difficult to achieve. Pursuit of the elusive right angle is an awesome endeavor all by itself. The best tool you can use to attain a right angle is a perfectly aligned table saw. Even with that, there is no guarantee you will be able to cut a straight line, let alone two of them that will join together at exactly 90°.

Consider some of the odds against making a perfect right angle: If the wood is slightly warped (and wood usually is), it may rise occasionally as it travels past the saw blade, forcing a cut that is off angle. And who says the average milled board fresh from your local lumberyard is absolutely square to begin with? Measure a few of the boards in your workshop. They are close, but they may be as much as ⅛″ off. As far as thickness is concerned, today's ¾″ planks can be anything from ⅝″ to ¹³⁄₁₆″! Plywood panels are not perfect either; most of them are warped. Sometimes they come from abroad and measure 4′ ⅛″ x 8′ ¼″. That is a blessing because it allows you to use the extra fractions of an inch for your saw kerf and wind up with exactly 4′x4′ or 2′x8′ pieces. But you would be wise to do some measuring first to find out exactly how big the panel really is.

Then there is the human factor. Can you always exert a constant amount of pressure against a given piece of stock when you are ripping it? If you are ripping, say, an 8′ board, it has 96″ worth of opportunity to drift away from the guide fence —and immediately throw 90° out the window.

If the achievement of a right angle seems impossible, the construction of a perfectly square box requires the divine guidance of a Higher Authority. It has occurred to more than one craftsman that his ultimate achievement would be to construct a perfectly square cube which was exactly 90° at every corner, in all directions. Any man who can do that has probably gained the Valhalla of woodworking and might as well hang up his tools forever, because there is nothing more for him to accomplish. But most of us cannot, have not and probably never will achieve that desired level of perfection. Most of us will have to content ourselves with boxes that *look* square, and hope that only we will ever know that, in truth, they are a full ¹⁄₁₆″ less than perfect.

One of the ways to hide the tiny mistakes that creep into even the most carefully executed projects is the use of molding and trim. There are dozens of kinds of molding (see Chapter 7) and thousands of ways to use it for decorative purposes, as well as to effectively hide a bad joint or two. It is molding that can turn a plywood box into a piece of furniture, so it should always be considered as a possible final touch to any project you build.

It is hoped that the discussions of the various ways to conceal imperfections as well as the information on hardware, lumber, tools and the working of wood found on these pages will help you achieve a broader frame of mind when approaching any project. Anyone can pick up a hammer and saw and nail two pieces of wood together. But this book is not for the occasional handyman who puts up a shelf once every three years, if he is pressured to do so. This is a book for the dedicated craftsman: for the person who loves the feel of a smooth edge, who cringes at the idea of hiding an unusual grain under layers of paint. It is for the person who enters his workshop in quest of the perfect right angle, the absolute joint, the person who will gladly spend half a day planning a single cut with his saw so that it will be exactly right. This is a book that aims at giving you, the reader, a sense of the dynamics of designing a project for your own special needs, and then executing it with the highest standards of craftsmanship you can achieve.

There is a way of thinking about projects, of approaching them, that is far more profound than just opening this book to a given page and mindlessly following the instructions.

If you have examined the drawings and read the instructions and have said to yourself, "That's a great idea for a cabinet, but suppose I change this, and do that, and make it look like such-and-such," then you have achieved a new level of satisfaction. You have taken a basic idea and honed it to meet your own personal needs. And when you have completed your task, you will have before you a living thing—a thing that is a part of you, of your time, your energy and your thoughts. If, at that moment, your handiwork commands the full approval of your own discerning eye, you will have stepped from the level of handyman into the realm of master craftsman.

And if the words and pictures in this book help you to achieve that level of satisfaction, then this book—which, after all, is nothing but a closet with some 304 shelves full of ideas and suggestions—will have become a project worthy of both your time and effort, and mine.

—The Author

CHAPTER 1

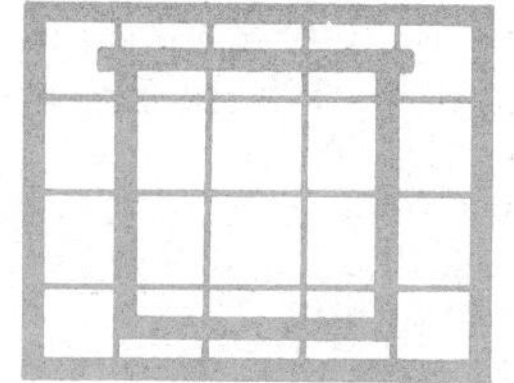

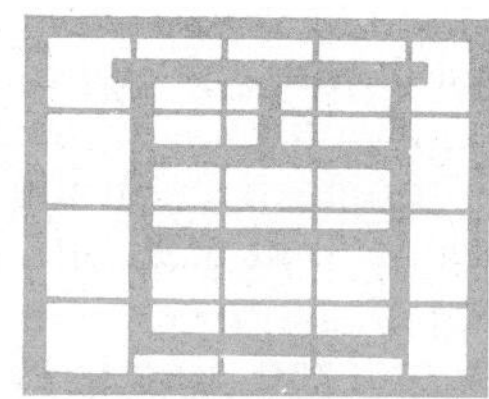
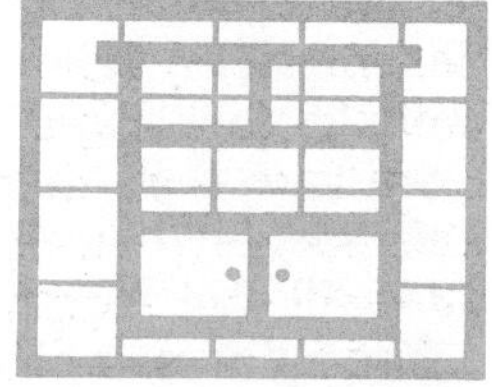

Planning and Utilizing Space

Planning and Utilizing Space

There are three kinds of storage space: dead, live and occasional. Dead storage is where you put belongings that are rarely used, like steamer trunks and old family portraits. Live storage is space for the things used day in and day out, all year long, like salt and underwear. Occasional storage space is an enigma, for this is where you keep objects that are used only some of the time, like galoshes and fishing rods, leaf rakes and egg-nog glasses, insect repellent and snow shovels. You probably could design storage space to hold all these occasional items and still have them accessible, but it would become a centrally located closet of such proportions that it took up more space than it was worth.

Without question, any storage area is more useful if it is designed to hold specific things. But over-compartmentalizing can become as unwieldy as no organization at all. To go about your home building shelves and closets and cabinets for every single item results in more space being consumed for the partitions and platforms than for the objects themselves. Moreover, if you design every compartment to hold a specific item, then discard the item, what do you do with the existing compartment?

During the past quarter century there has been a trend toward built-ins. The rise of plywood as an all-purpose construction material has given builders far more range in what they can do, and designers have had a field day thinking up new ways to bury storage space in the walls, the ceilings and the floors of America's homes. Built-ins *do* have some inherent advantages. They can be very practical, save considerable space, and still be quite attractive. But don't be too quick to assume that the built-in is always an answer, or that it is necessarily more attractive than, say, a veneered chiffonier, which can change the ambience of an entire room just by being placed in a particular spot.

The objectives to remember when planning storage space are:

1. to create more storage within the space you have to work with.
2. to make things convenient to put away and convenient to retrieve.
3. to protect possessions from breakage, moisture, heat, cold or rodents.
4. to do all of the above without detracting from the appearance of your home.

Storage systems divide into three basic forms—shelves, closets and cabinets—which are in turn combined into an infinite variety of hybrids. The shelf is the basic unit. Shelves are everywhere. We store things on shelves. We stand shelves on legs and call them tables. We sit on shelves, sleep on them, walk across them and keep dry under them. We put them in boxes, which are then called cabinets. The cabinets are hung from ceilings, are free-standing, are buried in walls, often have doors and hold drawers (which are really shelves with high sides, unless you want to call them cabinets without tops). And as soon as a cabinet becomes big enough to walk into, we call it a closet. Closets can have all kinds of shelves, including round ones that we can hang our clothes from. They may also contain cabinets, or drawers, or all three. As if that were not enough, we then take our shelves, closets and cabinets and combine them into room dividers, wall units, pieces of furniture and on and on and on. But the purpose of it all is always the same: to create space to store things in, or under, or on, or over.

Shelves

Shelves are not as simple as they appear to be, primarily because a shelf can show up practically anywhere, and therefore in almost any form. Shelves can be fixed between two or more uprights, or be adjustable, slanted, drop-leaf, revolving, sliding, lift-up, recessed, cantilevered, suspended from walls, hung from ceilings, or installed in any number of ways. They can be made out of anything from wood and metal to concrete slabs and laminated plastic, but there are three points of construction that should always be observed:

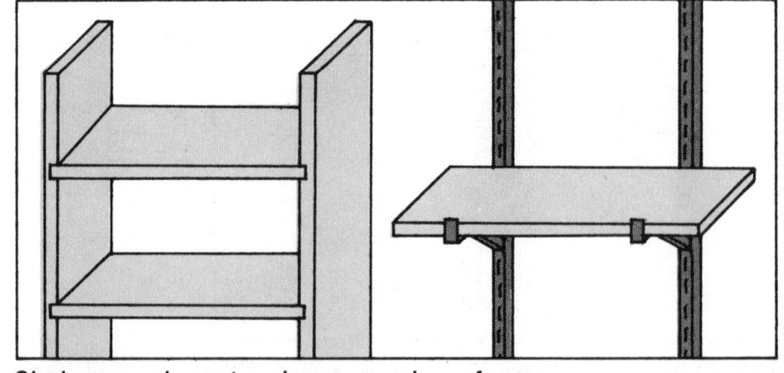

Shelves can be put up in any number of ways.

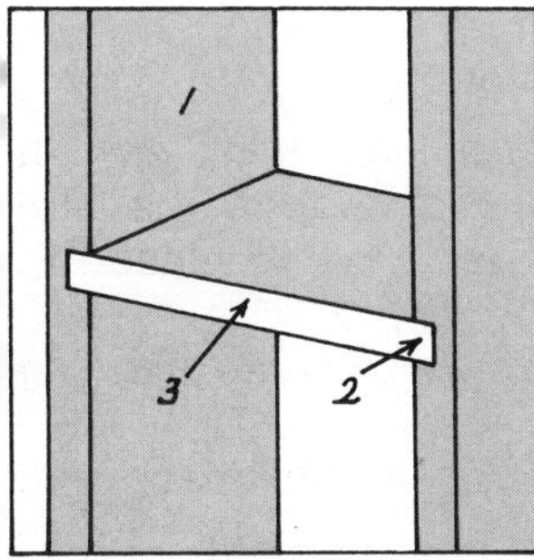

Every shelf must meet three qualifications. 1) It must have steady vertical supports. 2) It should be securely attached to the verticals. 3) It must be strong enough not to sag or break under the weight it will hold.

1) The vertical support for the shelf must be stable. 2) The system for hanging the shelf should be secure. 3) The shelf itself must be strong enough to bear whatever weight it is to hold without sagging.

There are no formulas for determining the kind and size of wood to be used for a given weight. There *is* one widely accepted criterion concerning pine; it is important inasmuch as pine is the material most often used for shelving. A ¾″ pine board can hold the weight of three dozen average books across a 36″ span without sagging. A safer span is 30″, but any pine shelf longer than 3′ should be braced. Half-inch plywood will hold as much weight as ¾″ pine or fir, but because it is thinner, it tends to give more readily, and for the sake of looks should be supported every two feet.

One final element to consider when building a shelf is its finish. Because shelves are flat, horizontal surfaces, they are natural collectors of dust, grease and all manner of residue. Usually, they need some paint or varnish on them, preferably the washable kind. But contact paper, rubber or plastic matting, linoleum, anything that is cleansible, may be used.

Closets

Closets are usually created specifically to hold clothing. Ideally, they are 2′ deep, by 3′ wide, by 8′ high, with a full floor-to-ceiling door. In reality, the height and width are optional. The depth can be shaved to 22″ before it becomes too narrow to hang clothing in, but if it is more than 27″, it begins to waste space.

Closets, of course, can store all kinds of things besides clothes hung on racks. They can have drawers in them, as well as shelves. Shoes can be hung on racks on the inside of a hinged door. Closets can be built into nooks and crannies

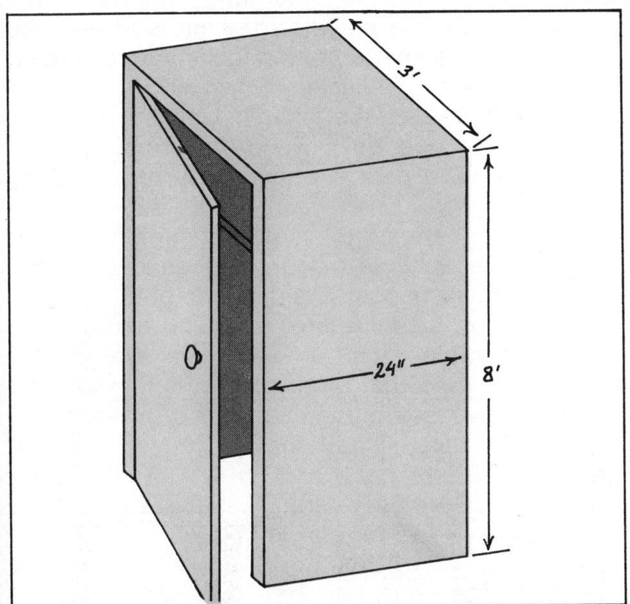

The ideal closet measures 2′x3′x8′ with a ceiling-to-floor door.

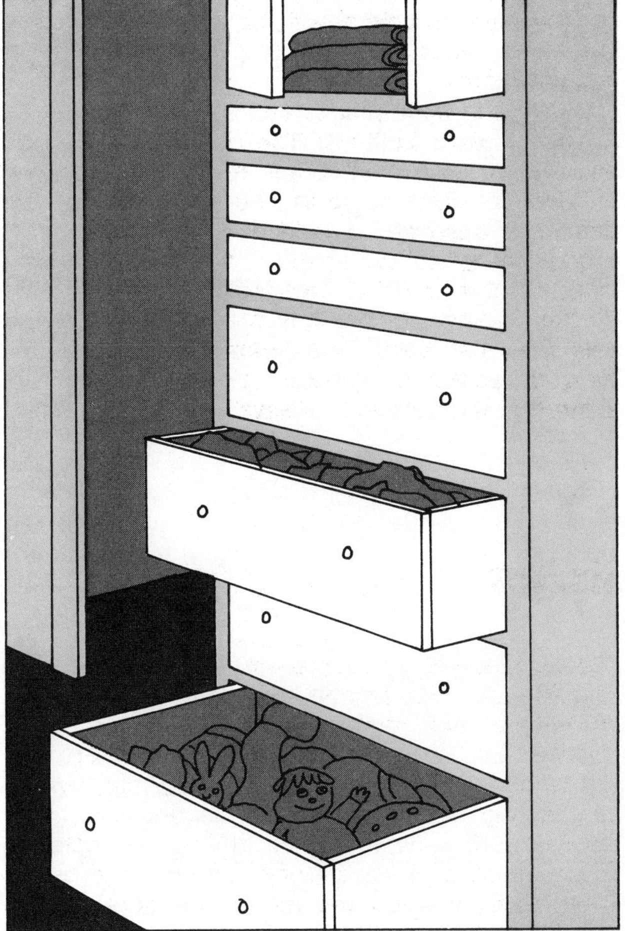

Closets, of course, can store far more than just clothes.

all over the house. They can often be fitted on either side of a window and linked with a dressing table under the window and an overhead storage cabinet above it. In small bedrooms, they can be put up on either side of a bed, or literally become an entire wall. If your front door opens directly into the living room, you can make a closet at right angles to the door and design it as a room divider, giving yourself a bit of privacy in the living room as well as the convenience of a closet next to the door.

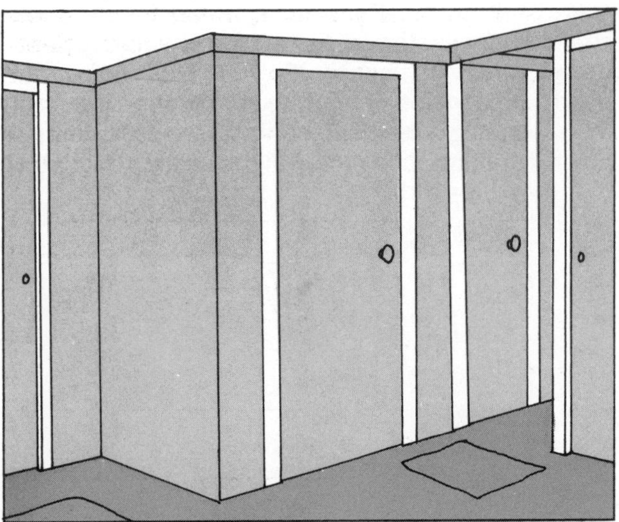

There should be a sizable clothes closet in every bedroom, a coat closet near both the back and front doors, and at least a small closet in any room where guests may spend the night.

Even in houses that seem to be loaded with closets, there are never enough of them, and they are often too small, or in all the wrong rooms. If you are confronted by a closet that is too shallow, you have to look at such variables as its width and height, the location of the door and its dimensions, and so on. Only then can you begin to solve the problem of gaining the depth needed. If a closet is too deep, you can do things such as install swing-out skirt, trouser or tie hangers in front of the clothes rack; hang things from the closet ceiling, or make the opening for the doors

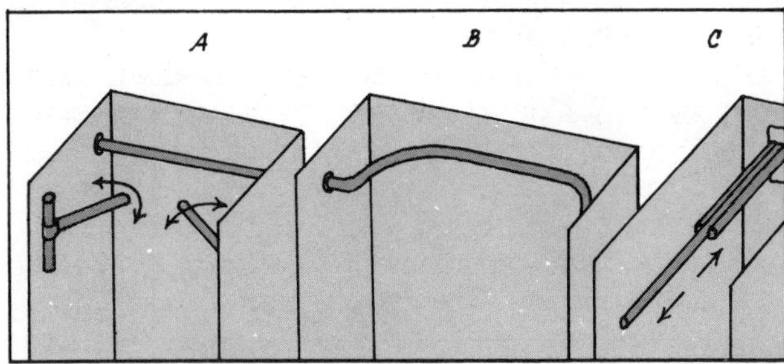

A— Add swing-out racks in front of the clothes pole if the closet is too deep. B— With a closet that is too wide, a U-shaped rack will gain additional hanging space. C— If the closet is too narrow, install a clothes carrier that can bring the clothes to you.

the full size of the closet. If the closet is too wide, try bending a U-shaped clothes rod around the sides and back. A gentle curve at the corners will hold more than right angles will. Deep, narrow closets get the blue ribbon for inconvenience and uselessness. If you cannot make them wider, hang a pull-out carrier down the center so that your belongings will come to you, instead of your having to dive into the darkness after *them.* The carriers operate on ball bearings and can be purchased in lengths of up to 6 feet.

Then there are those luxurious wasters of space, walk-in closets. They enable you to see everything that is stored along their walls; if there is space above the racks for shelves, plenty of other things besides clothes can be stored. If you are lucky and the closet is really big, you can redesign it as a dressing room-closet and take advantage of all the wasted floor space between the racks.

Closet doors are traditionally hinged, but bi-folds require only half the space when open, and sliding doors never swing into the room at all.

Perhaps the most important single element to consider with any closet is its door. With the exception of walk-ins, the door should be the full height of the closet to provide access to all the space above the racks. The traditional closet door is hinged—and for a very good reason. If it is properly hung, it is easier to use and keeps out light, air and insects better than other doors. Better still, a hinged door is really a moving wall that can support cabinets, racks, mirrors, shelves and hooks.

However, there is often not enough space in the room for a hinged door to open completely. The alternative becomes sliding or bi-fold doors. Sliding doors usually are hung in pairs, leaving considerable gaps between them. Worse than not being able to seal off the closet is the fact that you can never see more than half of its contents at any one time, which means you are forever sliding the doors back and forth to get at your belongings. Bi-folds operate reliably and easily, and have the advantage of letting you see into the entire closet when they are open. They have two disadvantages. They are hard to install and, because they are pivot-hinged, the closet can never be effectively sealed.

Cabinets

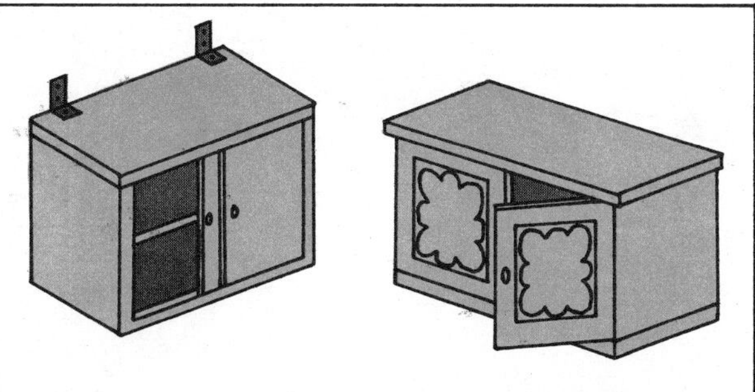

Cabinets can be freestanding, hanging, simple or ornate.

By definition, a cabinet is an enclosed structure accessible through one side. And these are about the only characteristics most cabinets have in common. The majority of them have doors of some kind. Some contain drawers and/or shelves. They can be made from metal, plastic or wood. They can be built-ins, freestanding, hanging, simple or ornate. Cabinets are usually designed for specific purposes, which is why they appear in so many variations.

In most instances, cabinets occupy a passive role in the home. They squat wherever they have been placed, bulging with whatever they are supposed to hold, and have no part in the daily functions of the household, except on demand. In the kitchen, however, storage takes as active and vital a role as the appliances (some of which are cabinets in their own right). Thus, kitchen storage must be properly coordinated with the major appliances and serve the activities that go on around those appliances. In general, cabinets near the range should be designed to contain such things as seasonings, cookware and cooking utensils, as well as serving dishes. Cabinets near the sink should hold the things that have something to do with water, such as non-refrigerated foods, bags, towels, cleaning supplies, everyday china, glassware, coffeepots and tea kettles. The refrigerator is usually the center of food preparation, too, so the storage units around it become repositories for canned and dry goods; measuring, mixing and food preparation equipment; tableware and refrigerator dishes.

In the kitchen, storage takes an active role in the daily functions of living.

The average family has almost as many items to store in a bathroom as it has for the kitchen. But bathrooms almost never have enough storage space.

Bathroom cabinets, or the lack of them, are probably the biggest storage headache in any home. Bathrooms tend to be small, but the list of items logically stored in a bathroom is almost endless. It can include, in addition to medical supplies, such things as cosmetics, cleaning equipment and supplies, towels and sometimes linen, dirty clothes, and a lot of oddball objects like sun lamps, hair dryers and the like. Nobody ever dares face the problem of cramming all the things that ought to be stored in a bathroom into the little or no space that bathrooms afford. Thus, the cab-

Once they appear in a main living center, cabinets begin to take on the qualities of furniture.

inets that can meet the voluminous need of the average bathroom must be ingeniously devised to utilize every inch of available space. Making cabinets for a bathroom may be the biggest challenge of all.

Outside the bathroom and kitchen, cabinets come into focus in cellars and garages, where they tend to be larger, cruder structures for holding tools, equipment and other items of both dead and occasional storage. They also appear in abundance in the main living areas of the home—the living room, dining area and family room. Here, they have a more passive role of holding stereo and television sets, bric-a-brac and miscellaneous items. Here, too, they must be designed in keeping with the decor, and that probably means they must be more carefully built and finished. It is also here that cabinets and shelves often come together to form room dividers or solid walls of decorative storage units that have a variety of functions and uses, all of them specific.

Whether you are building a shelf, a closet or a cabinet, the process begins with a need for more storage, and the dimensions of the area where the project will reside. From those outside measurements, subtract the thickness of the closet or cabinet sides and you have the real dimensions of the storage space. What objects will be kept there? How wide, and fat, and tall are they? Measure them and be sure they will fit where you want them to fit. Can there be more shelves? Or should there be drawers, or perhaps both? Can the cabinet itself be shallower, with a deeper door that has shelves of its own? Can the shelves and drawers and compartments be rearranged so that the project will contain more? Never stop trying to rearrange the inside space; never stop thinking, "There is some better way, if only I can find it."

When all of the questions about dimensions have been asked and answered, turn to the construction itself. What materials will you use? How will the pieces be assembled? Have you the proper tools to make the cuts and joinery it requires? What is the cost in time, effort and money? Can some other, perhaps less expensive, wood be used? Are there alternative joints that are easier to make and just as strong? Draw your plans now, complete with dimensions, saw cuts and joinery. And decide how the face of your project will look. Will the trim be compatible with other furniture in the room? Must the doors match those of other cabinets? Will the hue and the texture of the finish enhance the decor of the room? What hardware is suitable for the project as well as the rest of the room?

When all the plans have been measured and drawn, then remeasure and redraw; when everything there is to know about the project has been considered, it is time to reconsider each minute detail. What more can this project do? What other ways are there of storing things in it? Always there must be that same question: "Is there some better way?" Do not hesitate to undo the thinking and planning you have done, for in the undoing there may come innovations, enhancements, more efficiency, greater beauty.

The making of shelves, closets, and especially cabinets, is not solely a matter of carpentry. It is a process of withdrawing every idea, every thought, every instinct, from the inner resources of your mind and examining each very carefully and open-mindedly, until you are absolutely certain you have chosen all of the correct procedures, techniques and approaches. It is primarily a process of becoming one with the entire project, for what you are doing is molding a thought, giving it form and shape, and ultimately a three-dimensional reality. It is far more difficult to do *that* successfully than it is to saw up some wood and nail it together.

CHAPTER 2

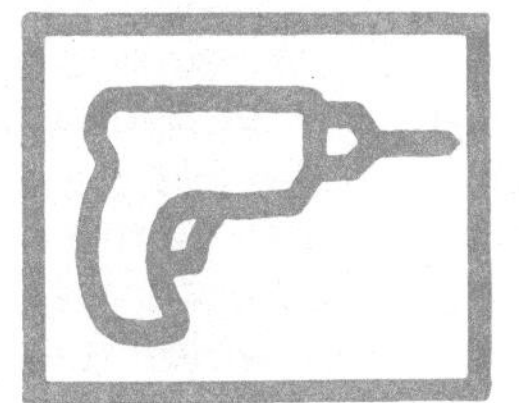
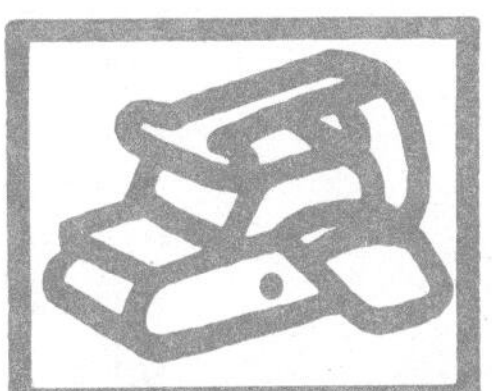

Tools: Extending Their Uses

Tools: Extending Their Uses

Presumably, anyone who is contemplating the construction of a shelf, closet, or particularly a cabinet, already knows how to use a ruler, hammer and screwdriver, and is at least familiar with the functions of most power tools. Consequently, this chapter addresses itself to some ways you can extend the performance of the tools most likely to be found in a home workshop.

As a matter of record, the creation of a basic shelf, closet or cabinet requires the following hand tools and materials:

Tools		
hammer	plane	saw
screwdriver	sander	ruler
chisel	drill and bits	level

Materials		
glue	mollies	screws
nails	sandpaper	

But the real fun—and expertise—comes from getting the most out of any given power tool, be it portable or stationary. All it takes is a little experimentation, some homemade jigs, and a slightly broader view of the tool than is usually found in its owner's manual. Owner's manuals tend to describe a saw, for example, as a saw. Actually, it is a power plant as well as a saw, and as a power plant it may have a variety of applications other than just sawing.

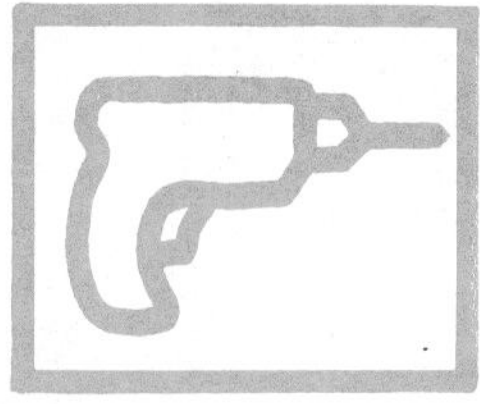

Portable Drill

The most obvious example of the "source of power" concept is the portable drill. The portable drill is blessed with manufacturers who, if we can judge by the number of drill accessories on the market today, consider their products not as holemakers, but as power packs for doing a whole range of things.

A portable drill is usually the first power tool

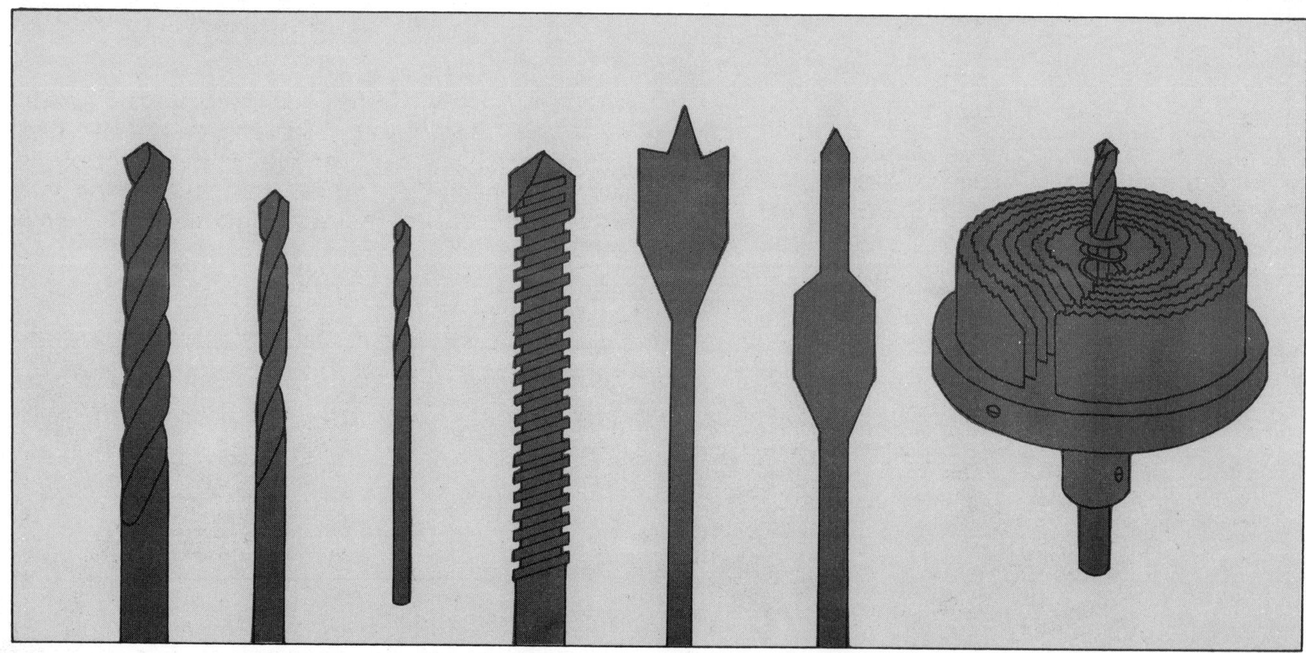

The range of drill bits to be found in almost any hardware store begins with $\frac{1}{16}$" diameter and goes all the way up to the 6" hole saws. Within this size range are high-speed bits for drilling metal, masonry and practically every other material known to man.

people buy, primarily because drilling holes in anything by hand is hard work. True, you can use that little $15 drill to make holes in wood, metal, concrete or anything else. You can also use it to drive sanding discs, polish, turn all kinds of abrasives, mill, shape, mix paint, saw, rout, and even pump water. The inventory of accessories adds up to far more than the cost of the original machine, and the list seems to be almost endless. However, a single-speed ¼" drill is not sturdy enough to handle every one of the accessories available. Anyone with a variety of jobs in mind would be wiser buying a more powerful ⅜" drill with reversibility and variable speed control. In any case, here are some of the accessories that virtually turn the portable drill into an entire home workshop.

Attachments for abrading operations are nearly as numerous as the bits. There are several versions of the perforated disc and drum at the left. Each hole has a sharp cutting edge, making these cheese-graters excellent for removing most materials in a hurry, while the wire wheels can work wonders on rust or paint. The rotary files in the center are useful for carving surfaces and shaping edges, and the flexible sanding disc at the right will convert any drill into a sander-polisher.

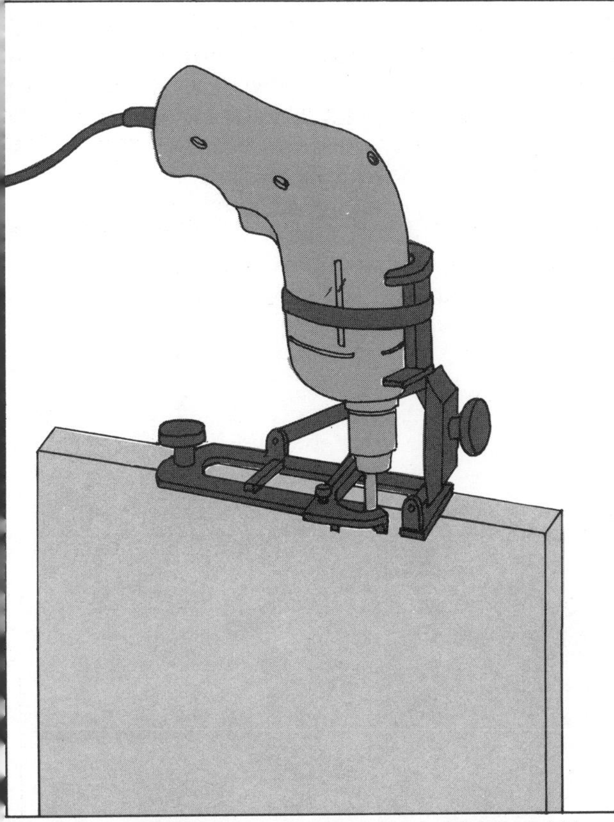

This router-type base plate can accommodate any drill and turn it into a portable shaper. Not only can router bits be used with it, but there are special finishing cutters as well, such as the ones shown above.

For many of the grinding, polishing and sanding operations, this drill stand is a must. It is inexpensive and will hold any drill.

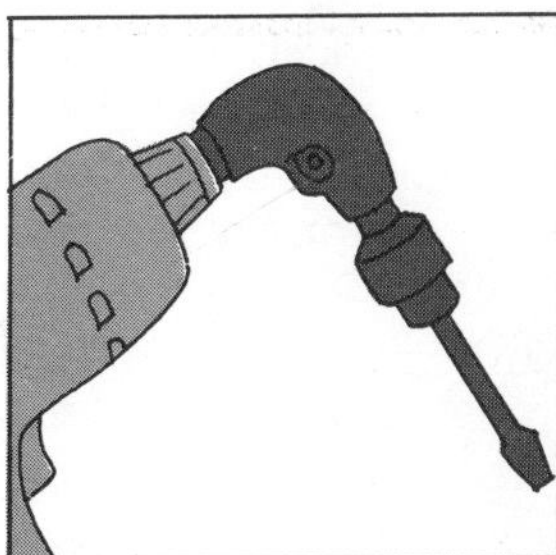

There are right-angle drives, allowing work in tight spaces. The "torque-on" will convert any ⅜" drill into an impact tool. And, if you have a variable speed drill it can be used as a screwdriver par excellence.

The attachment at the left creates a wobble action in a conventional saw blade to cut dadoes and ploughs. You can also buy a jigsaw attachment (center). Or use a common garden hose with the pump attachment (right) to empty 200 gallons an hour.

Routers

The router will let you make fancy edges, trim laminates with ease, and create a variety of joints. Best of all, it produces cuts that are so smooth they rarely need any further attention. The danger with a router is that it is so powerful it is likely to go spinning off in any direction unless it is held firmly in check. Consequently, practically all of the accessories you can buy incorporate some way of holding the machine in control. And when you are not using a specific accessory such as a laminate trimmer or a jamb-and-door butt template, it is wise to clamp at least one guide to your work. It is even better to use two guides and form a channel for the router to travel along.

There is also a router table that can be purchased for holding the router upside down so that it can be used as a stationary shaper, complete with guide. If the manufacturer of your particular router does not offer a ready-made unit, you can build a wooden table that will do the same job.

Another useful router accessory is the dovetail template. It is expensive (about $30) but with it, you can knock off dovetail joints by the thousands without error. The router is ideal for making recessed slots to accept inlay borders, dadoing, rabbeting, and shaping countless designs in wood trim. Now, a pipe and crank arrangement has come onto the market which costs about as much as the router itself. With it, any router can be used as a lathe—which opens up a whole world of possibilities for turning wood.

If you already have a lathe, you can build your own frame to fit over it and allow your router to slide up and down the stock. With the stock locked in place and only the router moving, you can do all kinds of fluting. With a template clamped to the frame top and the router cutting no more than ⅛" at a pass, you can duplicate the same turned piece again, again and again. Or, by adjusting the depth and angle of the router bit, you can create an infinite variety of decorative spindles.

The laminate trimmer accessory has precision settings so that the trimmed edge will be flush with the counter surface.

As long as there is some kind of guide for it to follow, the router will repeat any curve or straight line you require.

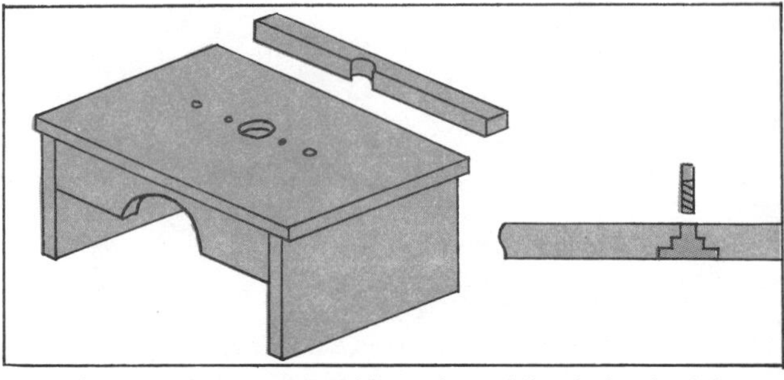

By making the fence removable and providing holes for fulcrum pins, this table can be used for freehand shaping as well as controlled routing. There is nothing to say the table cannot be made large enough to handle bigger pieces than the ready-made unit.

In many ways, using the router in a stand is much easier, since work is fed against the table fence, giving you more control with considerably less clamping, template making and set-up time.

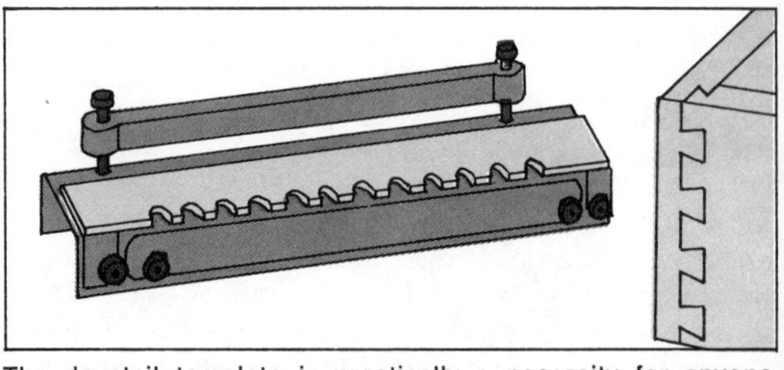

The dovetail template is practically a necessity for anyone doing a lot of jointing. Not only is the dovetail a superb joint that offers multiple glueing faces, but the template makes it one of the fastest and easiest joints to make.

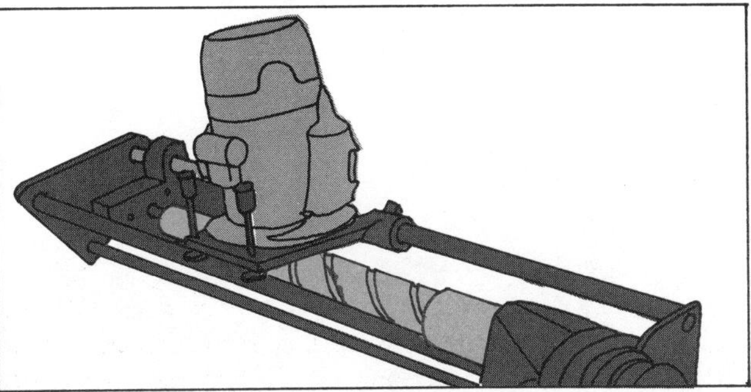

This router-crafter offers some pretty fancy wood-turning capabilities.

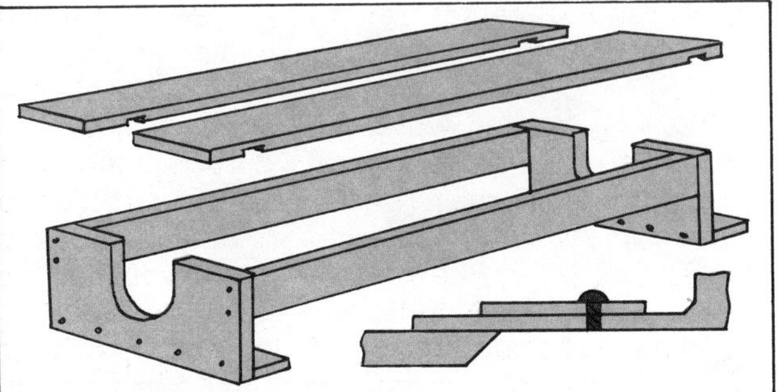

The exact dimensions of this router-lathe jig should be taken from your existing equipment. With it, you can gain the same versatility offered by the router-crafter.

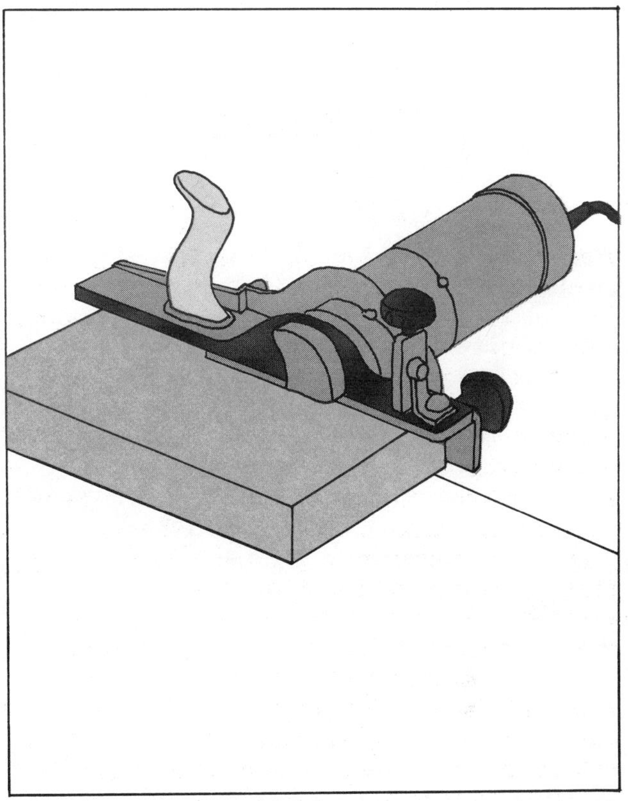

Another useful accessory to consider is the planer attachment.

Belt Sanders

This is the shop workhorse. It can cover large areas in relatively short periods of time and do such things as smooth down undressed lumber, remove old finishes, polish metal, shave the width of a door, and smooth coats of new paint or varnish.

Unlike the old-time belt sanders, the new models are lighter and easier to wield, yet can do all the same jobs their more cumbersome predecessors did. One of the jobs that is easier with the new sanders is edge sanding, although care must always be taken to keep the platen flat against the edge. One trick that practically guarantees a flat edge is to clamp a strip of scrap to each side of the board, broadening the sanding surface. Or, if you have two or more pieces to edge sand, clamp them together and do all of them at the same time.

Most manufacturers offer a stand accessory, which allows the machine to be used either on its side or vertically as a stationary tool. Alternatively, use shims and clamps to hold your machine in place and cut out a workboard to put in front of it.

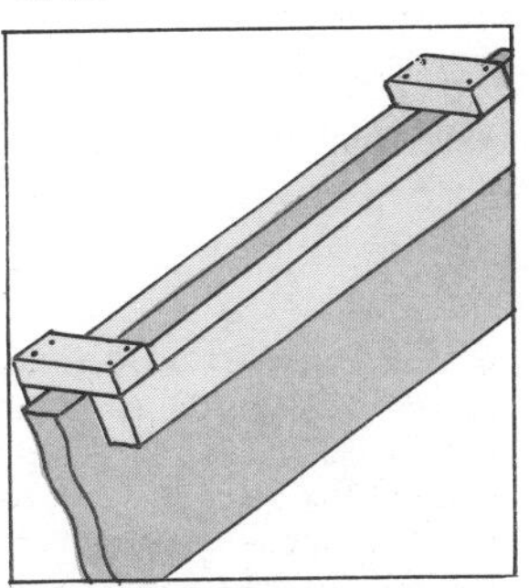

An alternative to clamping scrap around an edge is to nail together a support frame that can slide along the work with your sander.

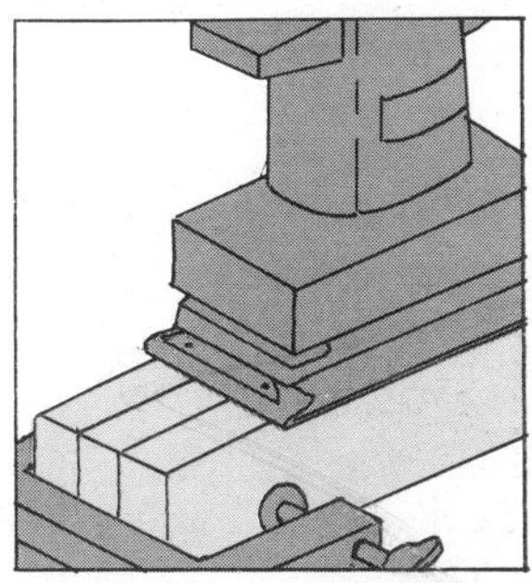

The idea of broadening an edge that must be sanded can be applied when using pad or disc sanders as well as belts.

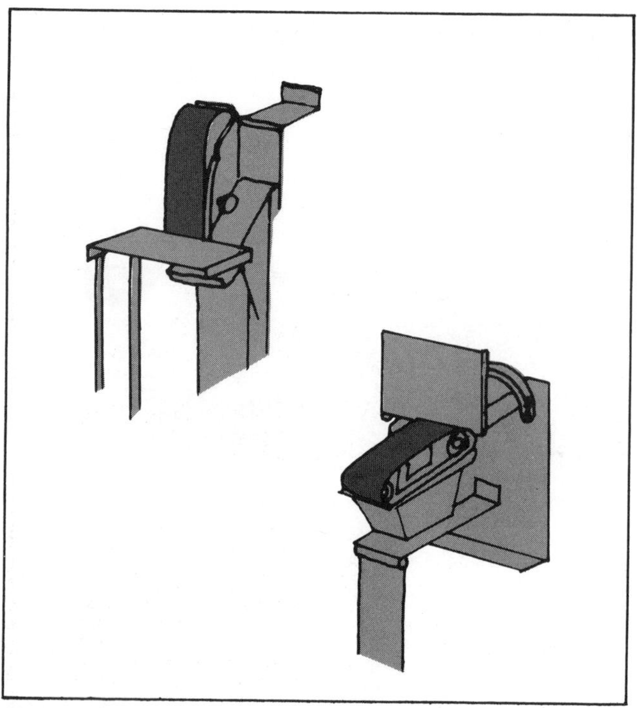

When held horizontal by this metal stand, the belt sander can do a lot of heavy-duty work with less operator fatigue. In the vertical position, touch-ups are a lot easier to accomplish.

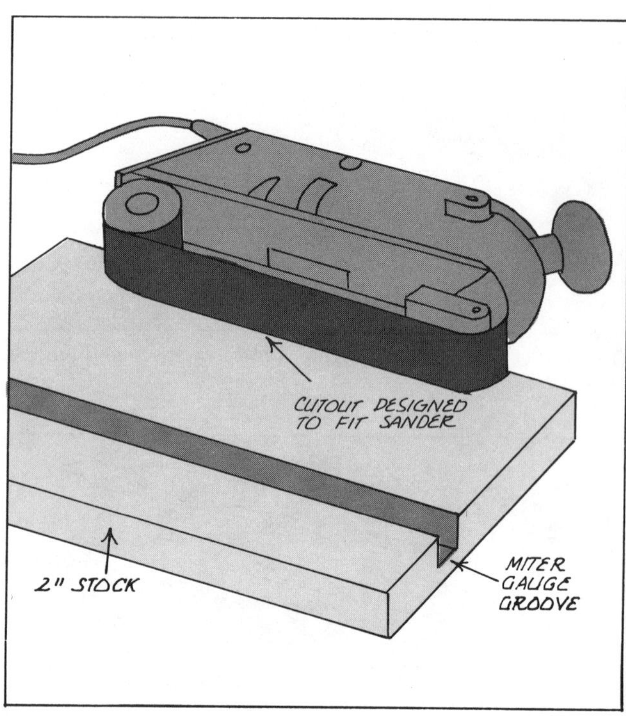

The cutout in this work table should fit the contour of your sander. The groove for a miter gauge is optional, but if you are concerned with precision, a gauge is very handy to have.

Sabre Saws

When the novice handyman begins to look past his portable drill, the second power tool he is likely to reach for is the sabre saw. And a wise choice it is. Even with a full complement of band, jig and table saws in the home shop, there are times when the portability and convenience of the sabre saw make it indispensible. It is possible to mount a sabre saw under a table and use it for controlled fretwork, but by far the best use of the sabre is to cut circles, curves and even straight lines—providing you choose the right blade for each job. Actually, it is blade selection that tells the sabre's whole story of versatility.

In general, a wide blade should be used for straight cuts, and narrow ones for making curves. Blade lengths vary considerably (2½" up to 6"). Always choose the shortest blade that will do the job effectively.

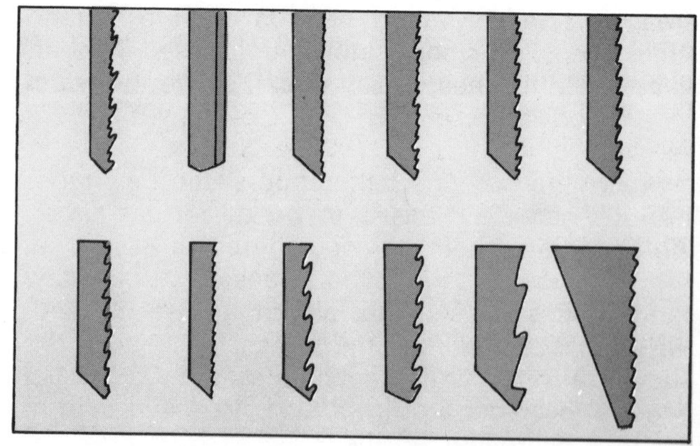

Circles, scrolls and straight lines are all within the capacity of the sabre saw and with the correct blade you can cut anything from hardened steel to Styrofoam.

BLADE CHART

WOOD

teeth per inch	material	uses
3	lumber	Fast, deep angle cuts in lumber up to 6″ thick
5	lumber	Rough general cutting, ripping of stock up to 2″ thick
6	lumber	Same as above, but makes a smoother cut
7, 8	lumber, insulation board	General purpose blades primarily for construction work, produce medium-smooth cuts
10	hardwoods, composition board, plastics	Scrollwork, finish cuts in plywood or veneer. Smoother cuts, but slower
12, 14	plywood, linoleum, rubber tile, hardboards, nylon, plexiglass, fiberglass	Smoothest possible cuts in plywood and fine scrollwork
10	wood with nails, asbestos, laminates	The tempered steel of this blade helps it stand up to nails.
7 flush	lumber	The unusual shape of this blade brings the teeth in front of the base plate so that it can cut through attached moldings or hard-to-reach surfaces.
knife edge	leather, cork, cloth, paper, rubber, cardboard, Styrofoam	Be sure the material being cut is firmly supported.

METAL

teeth per inch	material	uses
6	aluminum, copper, brass, laminates, compositions	Maximum cut in aluminum is ½″
10	same as above	General cutting with a smoother finish
14	aluminum, brass, bronze, copper, laminates, hardboard, steel pipe	General cutting with a smooth finish. Maximum cut in steel is ½″
18	same as above	Generally, this is best with the lighter metals, with a maximum cut of ⅛″
24	sheet metal, light gauge steel, thin-walled tubing, tile, all non-ferrous metals	Wave-set (like a hacksaw blade), does all the same jobs a hacksaw does
32	mild steel rods, pipe, sheet metal	Also wave-set

TUNGSTEN-CARBIDE BLADES

These blades have no teeth. Their cutting edges are particles of tungsten-carbide fused to the blade, and they will cut practically anything. They come with fine, medium and coarse grits and their cutting speed is somewhat slower than toothed blades. When used on wood, they leave an almost sanded cut. They are excellent for cutting ceramic tile or slate, and they produce a minimum of burring in sheet metal.

Circular Saws

This is the granddaddy of portable power tools and is a must for anybody doing on-the-job woodworking. It requires as much as a minute to handsaw a 2″x4″, and then the cut is probably not absolutely true. A portable circular saw takes seconds to do the same job with accuracy. Put a circular saw in the hands of a craftsman for the first time and he will soon find dozens of things it can do, including rabbets, dadoes, bevels and miters. Add a little more experience and some shop-made jigs, and the circular saw is an instrument that comes close to rivaling the bench or radial arm saws.

The most dependable method for achieving a straight rip cut with any portable saw is to clamp or nail a guide to the work being cut. Miters, as well as crosscuts, can be done freehand, but using a miter box or guide guarantees more accuracy more often.

Rabbets involve two passes of the saw. The first cut is a normal rip with the blade at the depth of the rabbet. The second cut requires that the work be placed on end and clamped against

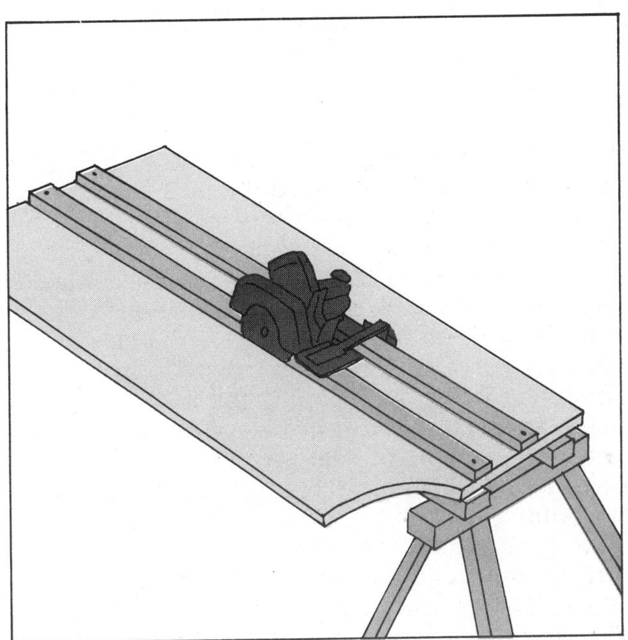

One guide is good. Two are better. In either case, be certain that the guide does not "give" in the middle.

As for any rip cut, some kind of guide should be used.

something that is wide enough to support the base of the saw as well as the guide. Then the saw blade is set deep enough to intersect with the first rip.

Dadoes are produced with repeated cuts, unless you have a set of dado blades. If you are working without the dado blades, use a guide to make the two outside cuts, then rout out the material between them freehand.

Since the circular saw is often used as an on-site tool, it may not always be convenient to use the saw table design shown here. As an alter-

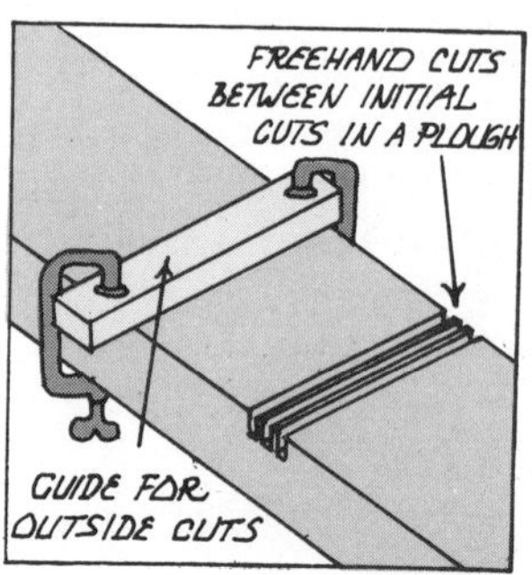

When freehanding cuts between the initial cuts of a plough, be careful to stay inside the channel. When routing plywood, the saw will usually do a quicker, cleaner job than a chisel. In either case, some sanding of the channel may be necessary.

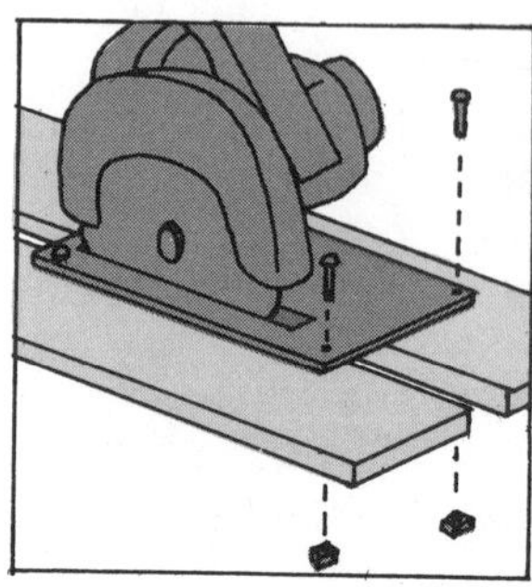

An alternative to clamping the saw to boards is to drill holes in each corner of the saw base plate so that the machine can be bolted or nailed to its support boards.

It is essential that the saw remain steady and at right angles to the first cut, or the rabbet joint will not fit.

Dado blade sets for circular saws are 3½" in diameter and cost about $15. They are well worth the investment.

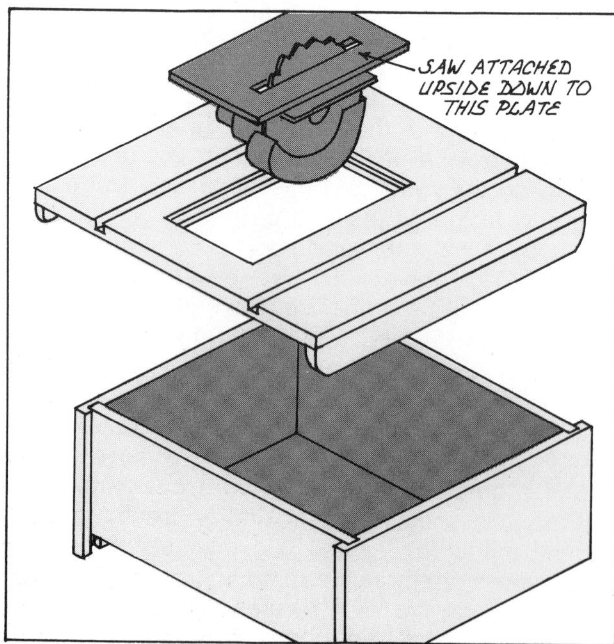

This simple, "flip-top" saw stand should be made small enough to take on site.

native, clamp a board on each side of the saw base plate and suspend the boards between saw horses with the blade facing up. Lock the saw in the "on" position and plug it into an extension cord with a switch. Attach the switch to one of the boards near the saw and use it to turn your "table saw" on and off.

As essential as the circular saw can be on site, it becomes a real boon in a shop to anyone cutting plywood panels. When attached to the panel saw frame shown here, the circular saw will make the first two or three cuts in a panel with more ease and accuracy than any other tool. The panel is stood on edge in the frame and the saw is pulled down its track, slicing the wood into two halves exactly 48"x47$\frac{15}{16}$". No huffing or puffing or cutting crooked lines. Moreover, the plans shown here allow the saw to be rotated so that panels can be ripped lengthwise by locking the saw in place and pushing the panel past the blade. In fact, with a panel saw frame, you can keep cutting at right angles all day long and end up with nothing but nice, square, manageable pieces to handle on your stationary tools.

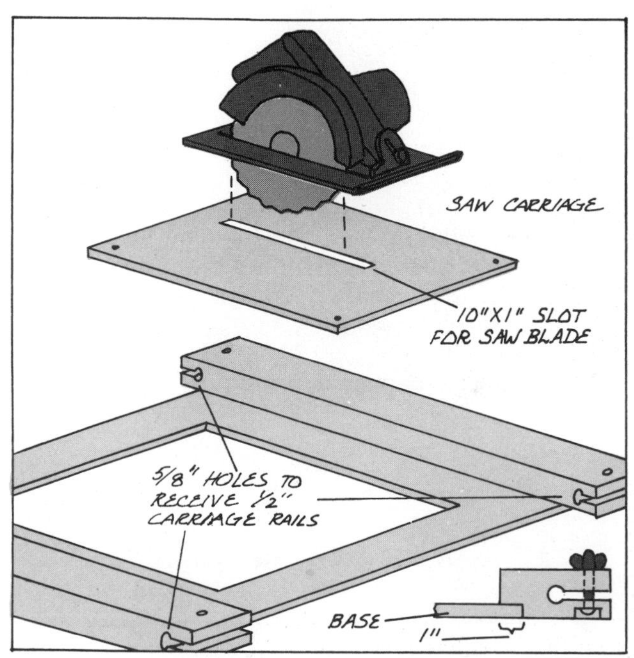

DETAIL OF PANEL SAW CARRIAGE

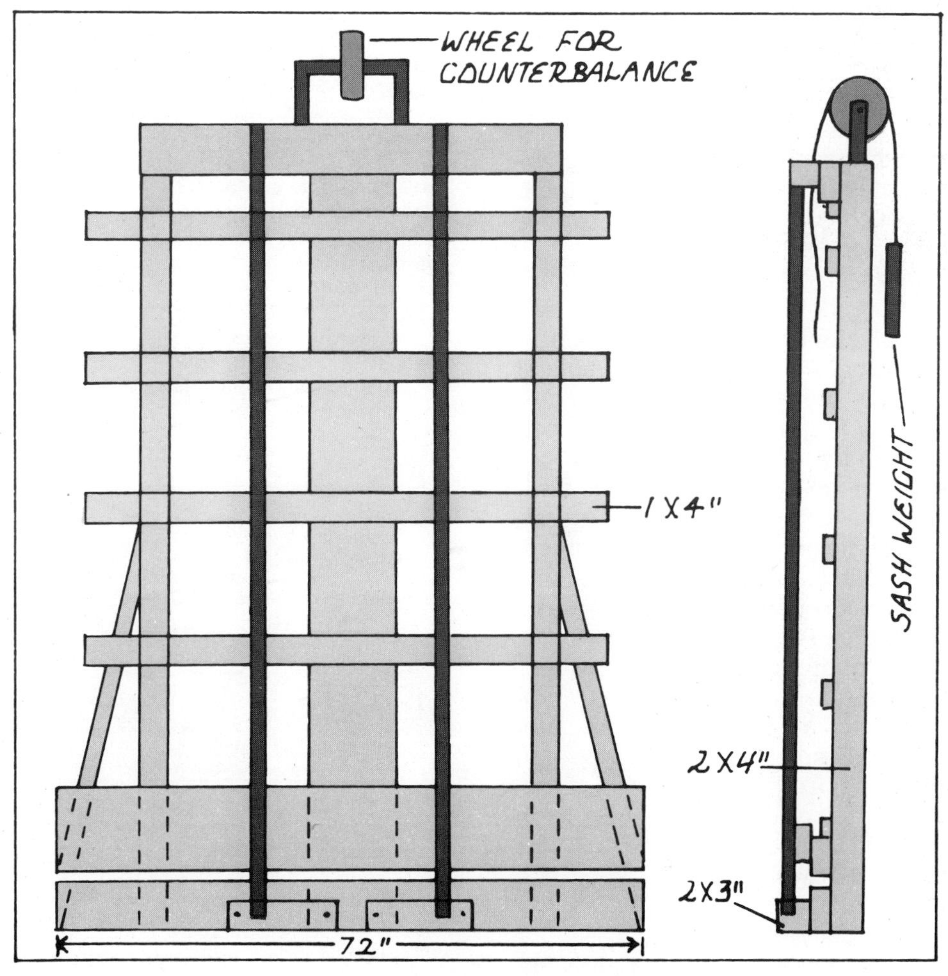

PLANS FOR PANEL SAW FRAME

Stationary Tools

Sooner or later, every carpenter yearns for a table and/or radial arm saw, for he knows that the moment he turns either of them on, he has stepped into the world of the professional. Every kind of saw cut is instantly available to him. Every joint known to man becomes standard procedure. So do routing, planing, molding, shaping and drilling, provided the right accessories are used.

Or you can use jointer-planers, drill presses, shapers, band saws, jigs and lathes to perform the many wood operations that can be done in your workshop. The result is always the same: grow accustomed to the capabilities of almost any stationary tool, and you will forever after feel lost anytime it is not available to you.

Table Saws

There is nothing about straight-cutting wood on a table saw that cannot be found in its manual. Rips, crosscuts, miters, bevels, compounds, camfers, tapers, kerfs and rabbets are all easy and natural operations. With a set of dado blades and a molding head, practically any joint and most shaping becomes about as simple as pushing stock past the blade. But, by adding a few homemade jigs there are even more functions a table saw can perform, such as cutting circles, woodturning and forming decorative designs.

A table saw can do all these things, but sometimes it performs grudgingly. It whines and growls and kicks pieces of stock back at its operator with surprising velocity. It is a dangerous animal that waits with endless patience for the chance to chew off the tip of any finger that strays too close to its bared teeth. The machine is designed to cut with perfect precision no matter what the task, but when you use it never forget that it will literally take its pound of flesh if given the slightest chance. So, the safest way to use a table saw without painful, perhaps mutilating, experience is to always think, *"jig first."*

Obviously, a blade guard should be used whenever possible. But there are many instances when a blade guard is more of a hindrance than a help, particularly when you are working with small pieces. The danger is that the smaller the piece, the closer your fingers are to the blade. So, it is with the close work that you should reach for some kind of support that will keep the saw in line and your hands attached to your wrists. The following pages offer a collection of protective helpmates that at one time or another you might want to consider building.

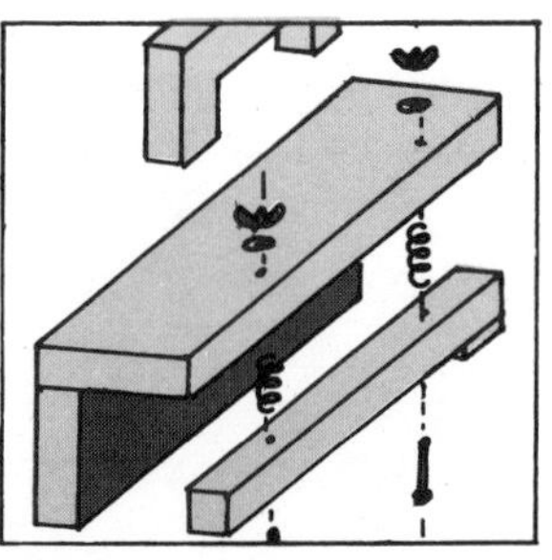

Sometimes the standard push stick will not give enough control over the work. That is the time to go to this spring-loaded hold down. It is built to fit over your rip fence and can be as long as you wish.

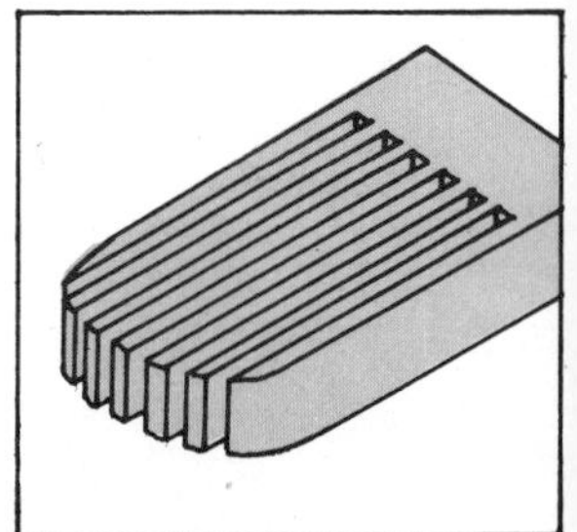

The "spring stick" is a different kind of holder. It is made by kerfing a piece of straight-grained fir or hardwood and is clamped to the saw table so that the work must slide between it and the fence. The "springs" force the work to stay in line with the fence.

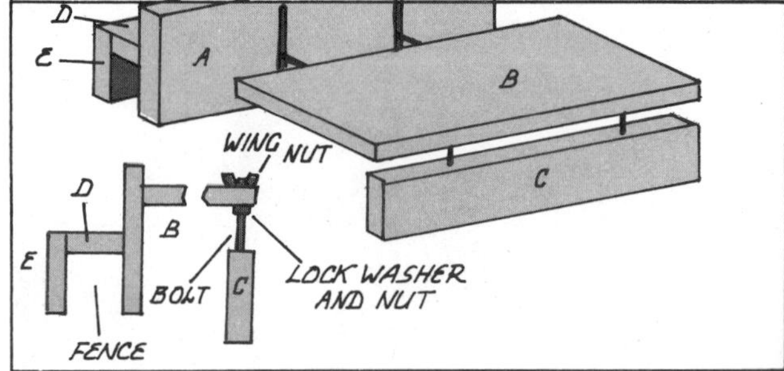

Here is an adjustable trough for handling narrow work that has to be resawed or molded. Sides D and E form a stationary housing over the fence guide. Side A has slots in it to accept the bolts in platform B. B is tightened to A with wing nuts and can be set at whatever height the stock requires. The clamp board (C) is also adjusted with bolts and wing nuts protruding through slots in platform B. The bolts driven into the edge of C should be long enough so that C will touch the tabletop when B is at its highest point against A.

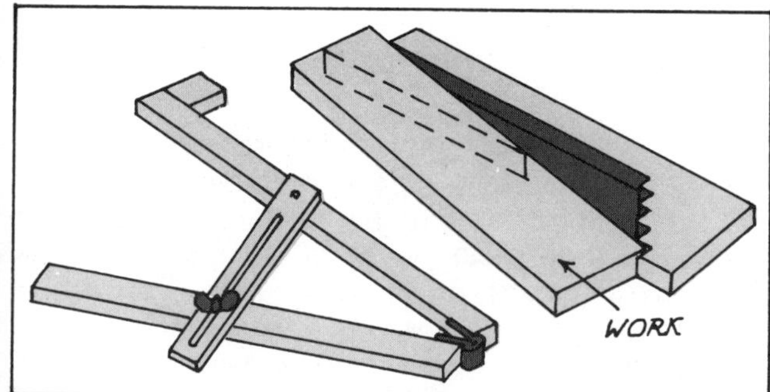

An alternative to the standard taper jig, which can be made or purchased, is the step jig. In either case, the entire jig is slid past the blade with the work.

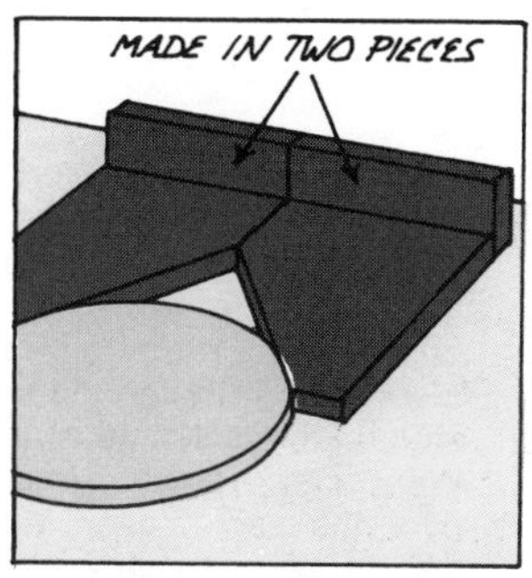

This V-shaped jig is excellent for working on circular stock, whether you are shaping it, routing it or rounding off the curve with a regular blade.

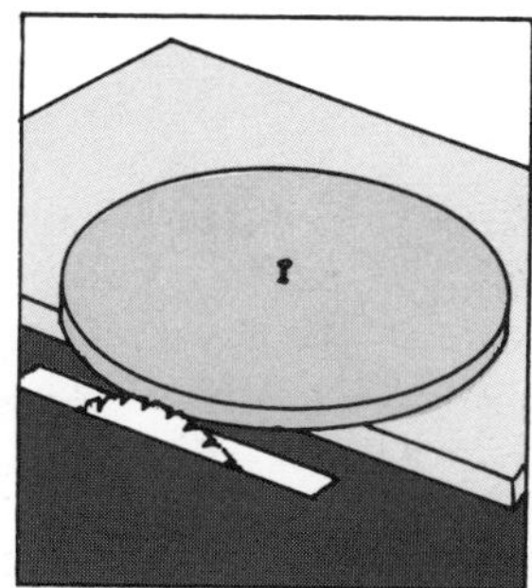

When cutting a circle, clamp a board to the tabletop and drive a nail through the center of the circle to act as a pivot. Then set your blade depth so that it cuts no more than 1/16" and slowly rotate the stock. Continue raising the blade 1/16" at a time until the circle is completely cut. Using this same technique with a dado assembly or molding head, you can do all kinds of routing, dadoing, rabbeting, beveling and camfering.

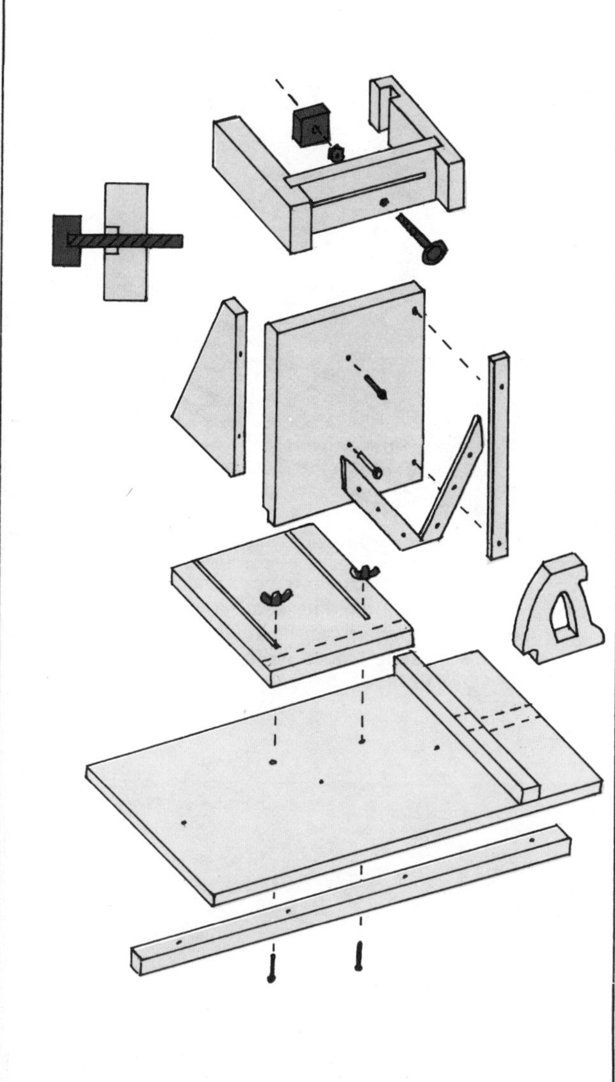

The tenoning jig can come in many forms. No matter how you make it, be certain that the vertical guide is absolutely at right angles to the saw table. Don't try to hold the work against the jig. Clamp it.

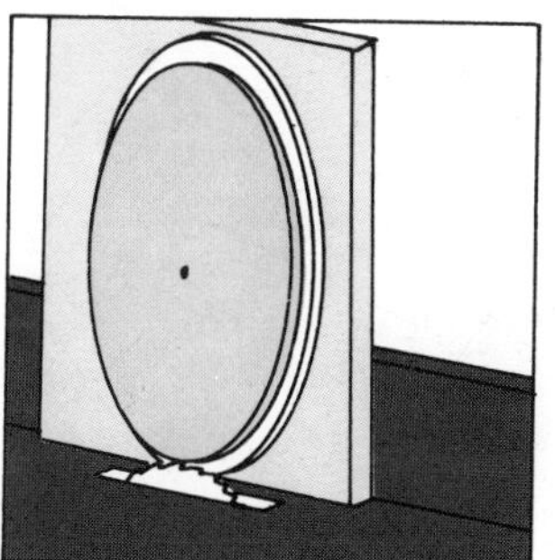

Another way of rabbeting a circle is to nail it against a vertical support and use a molding head. When dealing with curved cuts of any kind, always work very slowly.

Table saw jigs can get to be pretty intricate and must always be constructed carefully so that every angle is accurately measured. On the other hand, the time spent making a jig will save hours of tedious sawing later. Nor is there any end to the kinds of jigs you can make on your own. In designing them, however, bear in mind that the purpose of any jig is (1) to give you a wider margin of safety, and (2) to support the work you are cutting as solidly and accurately as possible. One of the ways to do this is to position blocks on the jig that can ride along the miter gauge slots in the saw table. Another handy design feature to remember is to leave lips here and there in the jig assembly large enough to let you clamp the jig to the fence, table or what have you. Both the clamping edges and miter track blocks are particularly important to the two jigs shown on the next page, since these are designed to help you convert the table saw into a wood-turning machine.

Overhead pivot jig. Work is held in place by drilling a shallow depression in the center of the work with a countersink. Then crank the pivot bolt into the depression until it is seated snugly. Work can now be rotated over the saw blade, which should have no more than 1/16" bite. By working slowly, you can use this jig to hollow out stock. By moving the center of the pivot, a variety of bowl shapes can be made.

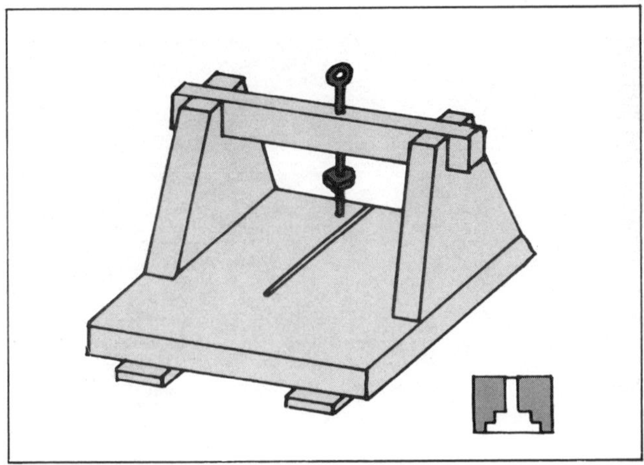

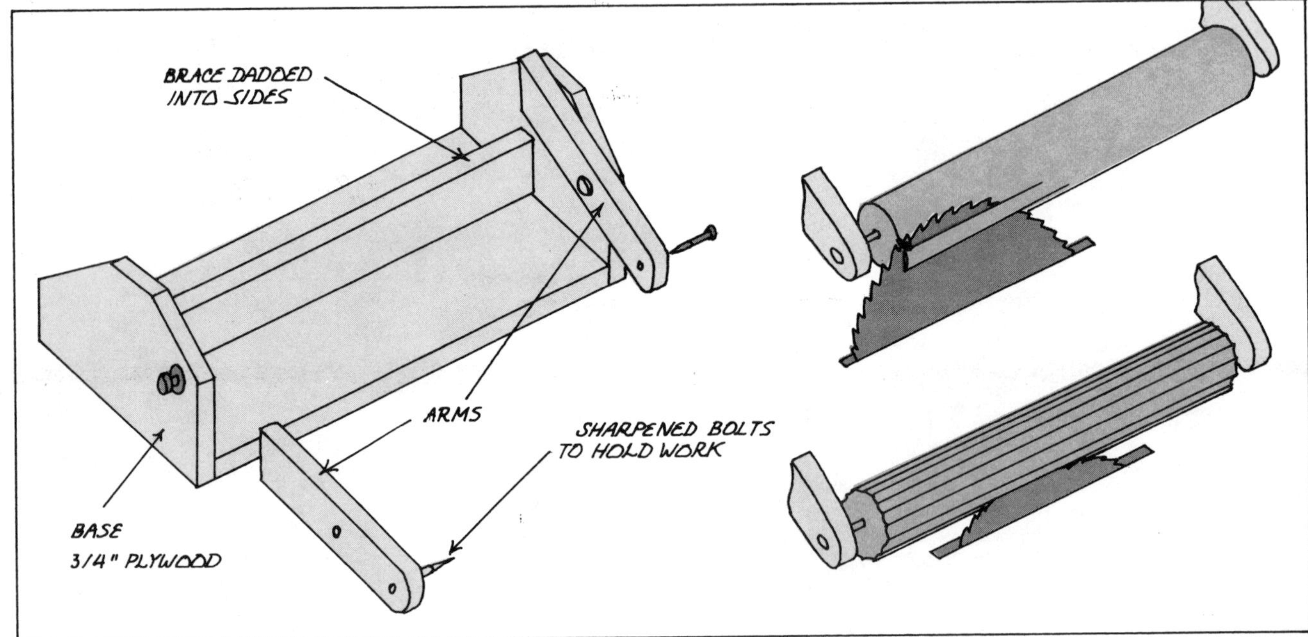

This is a versatile jig for doing circumference work of all kinds. With the movable legs attached, you can "turn" square stock into cylinders as well as tapered dowels. By locking the work in place, the jig actually makes reeding and fluting easier to do than on a lathe. Using a molding head, a variety of beads can be produced, and tapering can be done, while round tenons are best made with dado blades. With a little experimentation, you will find dozens of jobs that can be done on the jig.

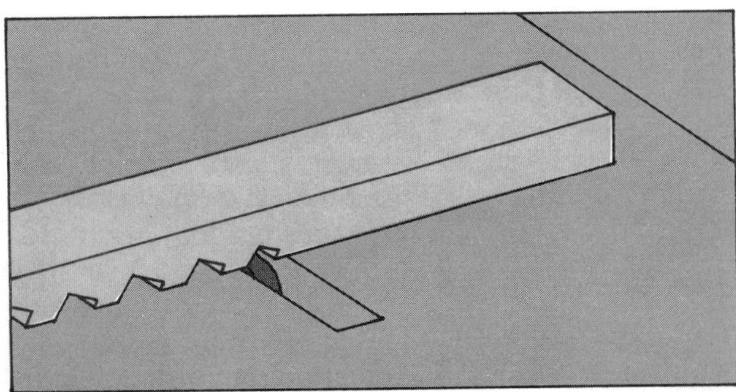

Decorative cuts do not need any particular jig—only some creative thinking. For example, by cutting a 2"x4" with tilted dado blades on one side...

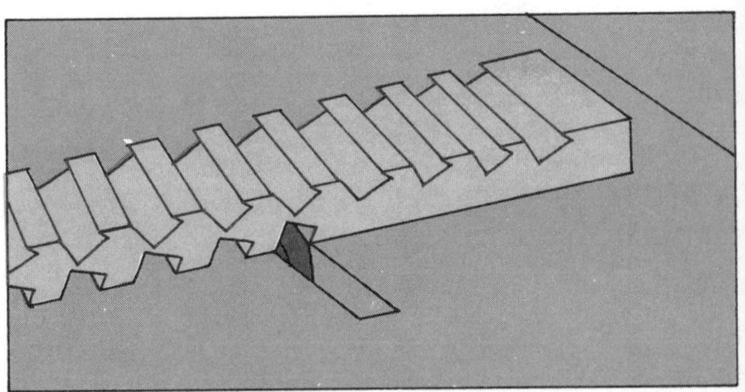

then turning the stock over and making the same cuts on the opposite side...

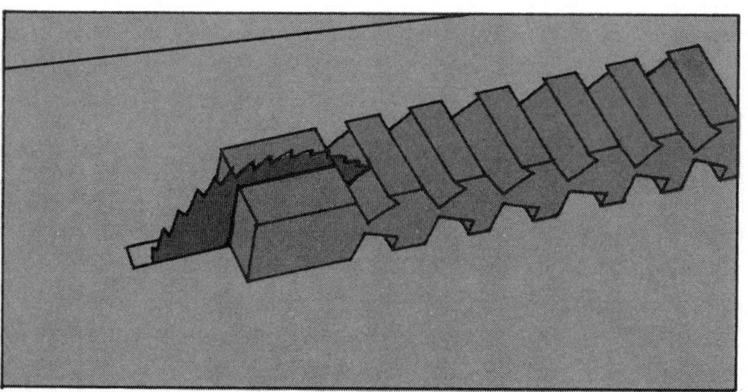

then resawing the board into ¼″-thick strips...

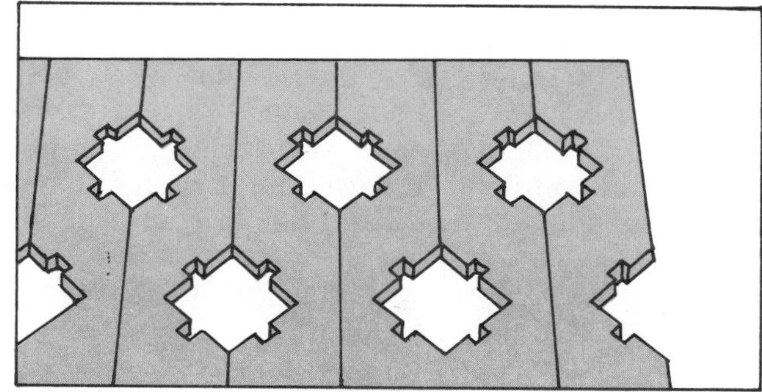

you can achieve a design something like this.

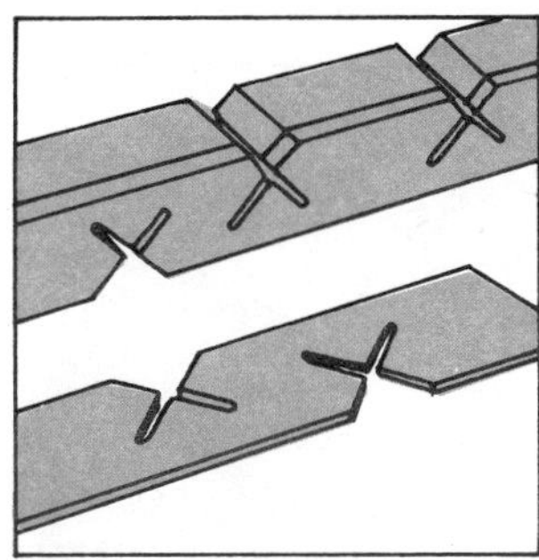

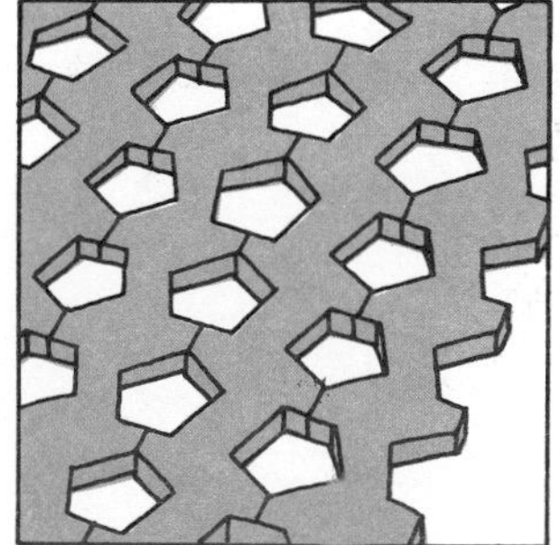

The decorative designs that can be made on a table saw are endless.

Radial Arm Saws

What the table saw has trouble doing easily, the radial arm can do with less effort, and vice-versa. For example, crosscuts, miters and compounds, which usually require relatively intricate setting up and even special jigs on a table saw, are almost instantaneous on a radial arm. Routing and many molding jobs are easier with a radial arm, while ripping is more accurately done on a table saw. Because the radial arm usually has a chuck accessory that can be attached to the back of the motor, it can be used as a drill press or router, which is something the table saw cannot do.

On the other hand, the radial arm has a great many movable parts, all of which are necessary to let the arm rotate 360° and allow the motor to do complete somersaults. This involves a lot of screws and bolts, all of which can loosen up at any time, so the blade alignment must be checked constantly. With nothing movable but the table (or the motor-blade assembly), the table saw demands far less attention paid to its accuracy.

Still, the radial arm is easier and probably more consistently accurate when you are crosscutting or mitering, since it is not that 20′ plank that must be moved, but the saw blade. The advantage of holding the work stationary when crosscutting with a radial arm disappears with ripping operations. The operator must now feed the work from one side of the saw, then reach around the arm and motor to control the stock after it passes the blade. With large boards that is not too much of a problem provided there is good support for the stock on both sides of the saw. But smaller work has a tendency to pull toward the blade and away from the fence. You will have an easier time maintaining control and accuracy if you do your ripping on a table saw.

The ideal arrangement is to have both a radial arm and a table saw. You can rip on one and crosscut on the other, and minimize working time and errors in both operations. In some instances dadoes and rabbets (if they are rip cuts) are better performed on the table saw. Generally, the dado blades and molding heads are easier to gauge and control on the radial arm. The radial has some added capabilities, such as drilling, routing and sanding. Circular sanding discs can be used on either saw, but with the radial arm it is almost mandatory that the elevation table shown here be made and used.

The radial arm can also cut arcs and circles using the pivot method. There is a slight advantage here since the blade is cranked down into the stock (never more than ⅛" at a time) and can be seen at all times, so you are never working "blind." A useful accessory to have when you work with curved pieces is a V-jig such as the one shown on this page, and the turning jig will allow you to perform some very decorative lathe work.

Other jig arrangements may be required from time to time when you work with a radial arm saw. As with any power tool, you should not hesitate to invent arrangements as the need arises.

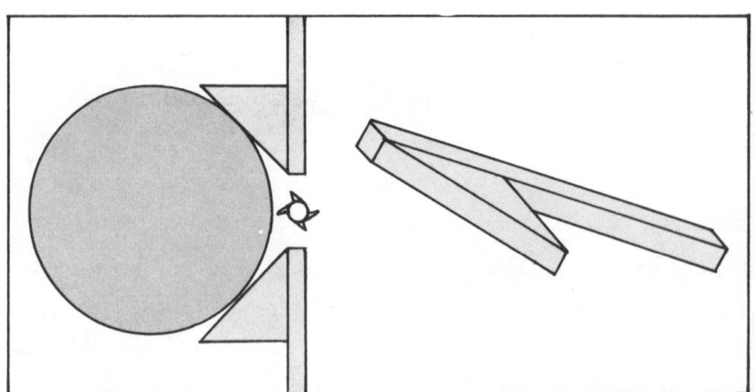

This V-jig is particularly useful for sanding, molding and routing operations.

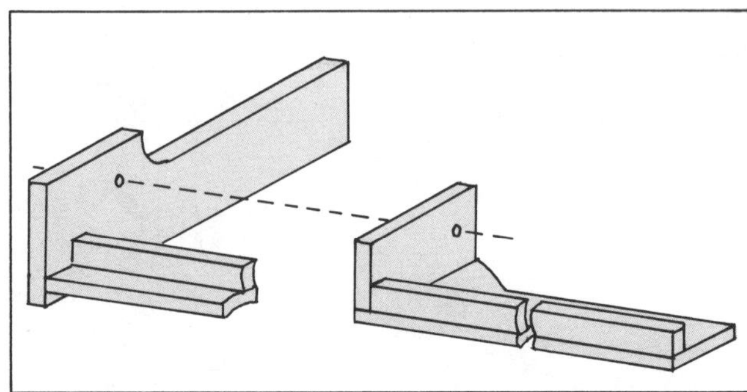

The turning jig permits a variety of decorative work on dowels which can be made with the saw blade from square stock. Then it can continue to hold the work for routing and shaping operations.

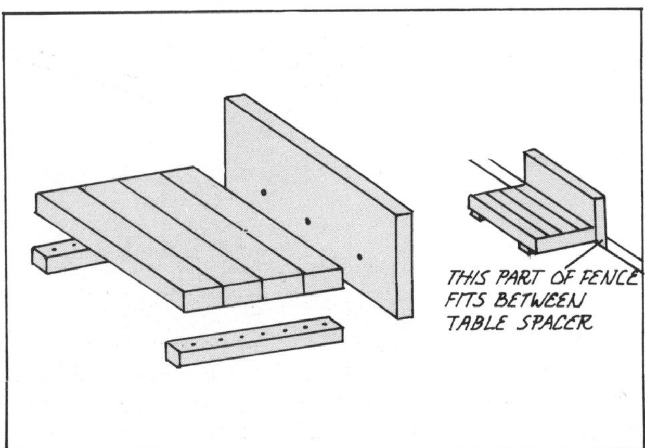

By making two identical tables, you can position them on either side of the motor and use them for end cutting, shaping or molding. Only one table is needed to elevate work sufficiently for disc sanding operations.

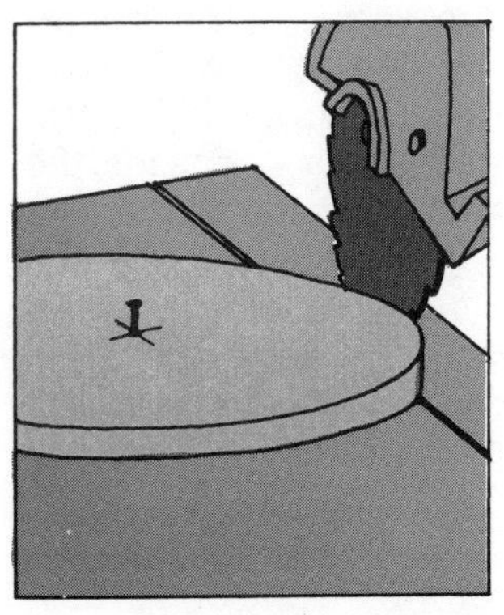

Using a nail driven through the center of the work and into the saw table not only permits you to cut out circles, but also to rout and/or shape them.

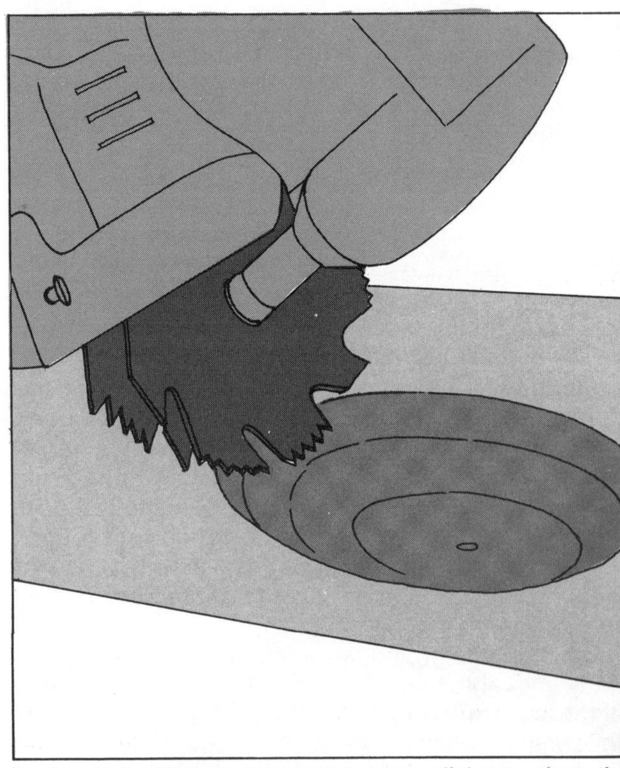

Bowling is particularly successful on a radial arm, since the blade can be rotated as well as angled. The work can be speeded up considerably by using dado blades.

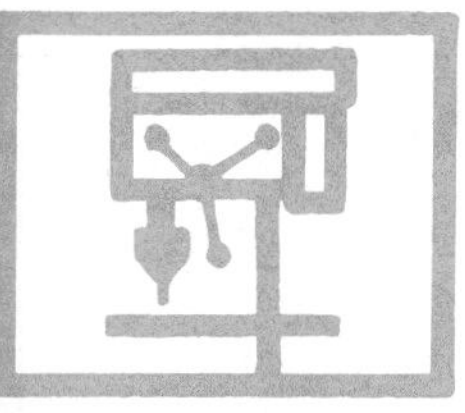

Drill Presses

If all you ever want to do is drill holes, don't waste your money on a drill press. Any hand power drill will do just as well and cost a lot less. But if you intend to do any drum sanding, routing, rasping, shaping, mortising or decorative work, a drill press is the perfect tool to have. It is capable of all these operations, but to do some of them well you may want to make one or two of the accessory tables shown.

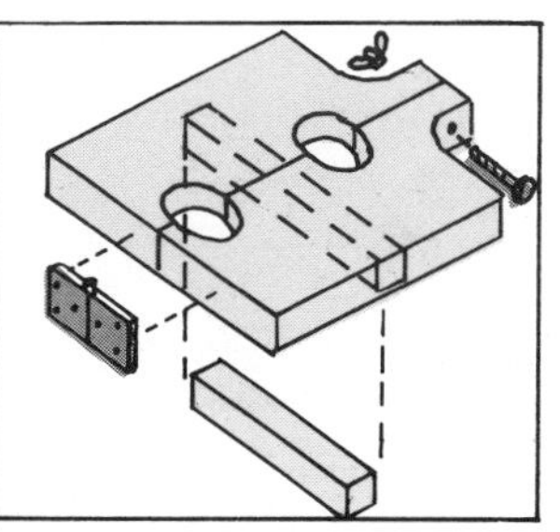

Details of a folding table to be used when drum sanding.

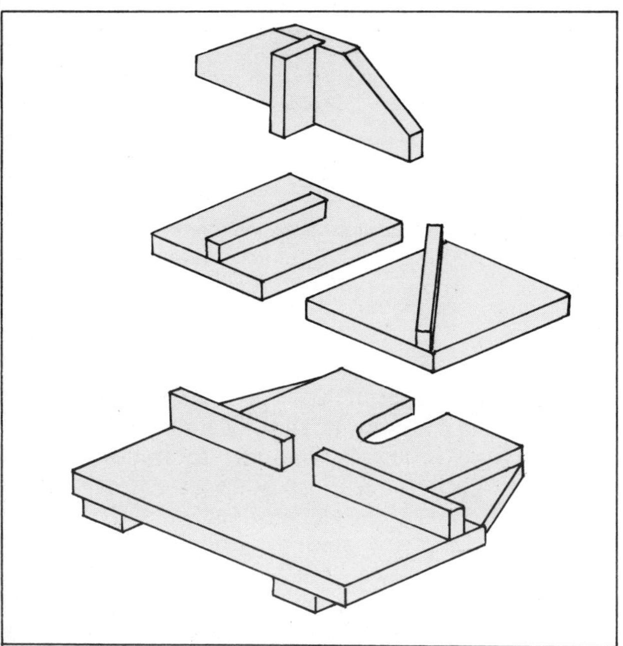

This rotary rasp table can help you achieve some very accurate cutting, especially if you use the auxiliary guides.

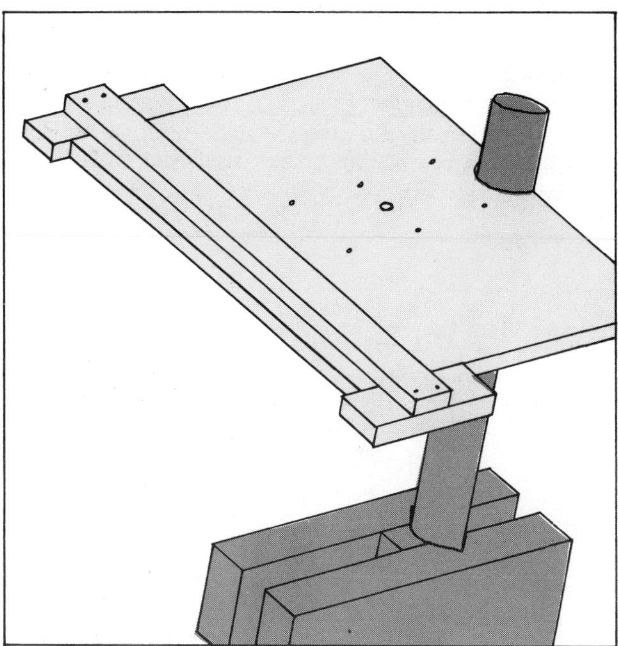

This router table is clamped to the drill press column and can be swung out of the way when not needed and serve as a holding platform for tools.

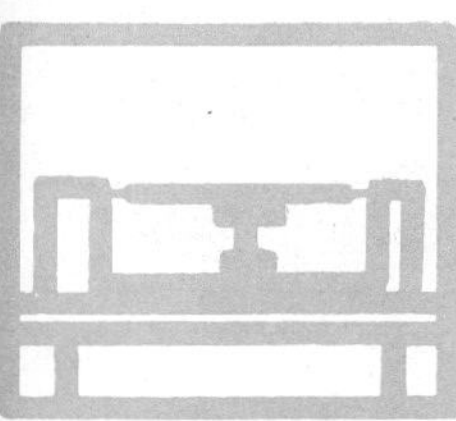

Lathes

The lathe is the only shop tool that produces completely finished work from rough stock, and it can do that in a great many ways using a variety of chisels and knives. But it can also be used as a router, shaper and sander simply by adding chuck adapters to the headstock spindle and using a simple worktable jig.

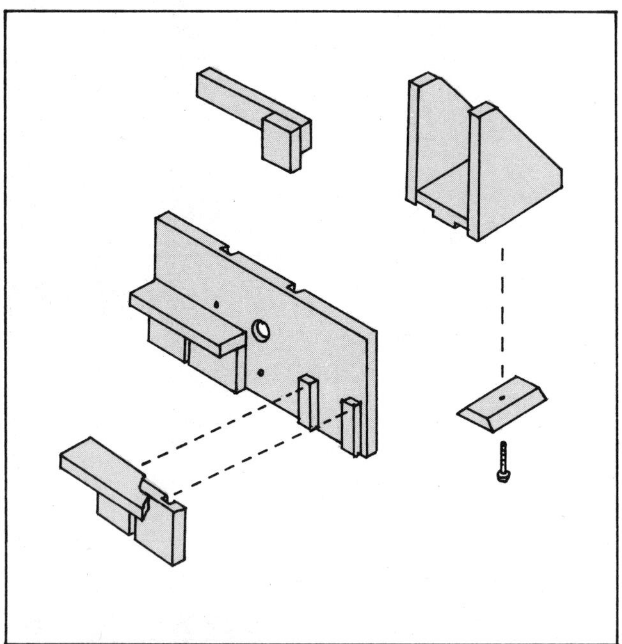

This vertical jig sits on the lathe bed and is ideal for handling small work that requires shaping, drum sanding or routing.

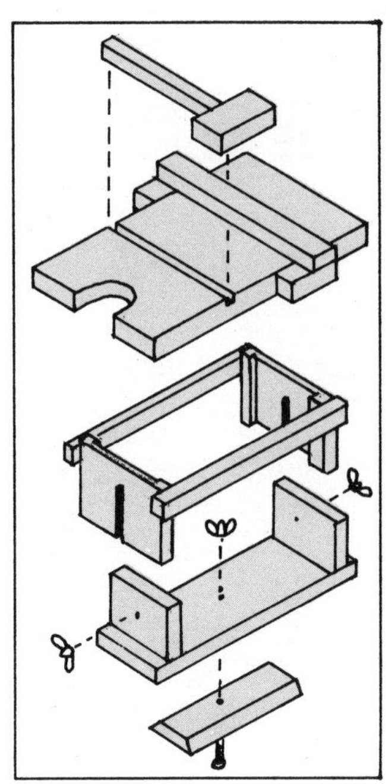

The horizontal table is designed to handle larger pieces when shaping or routing, and as a worktable when using a sanding disc.

Specialty Machines

There are other highly specialized tools that have a place in the home workshop. There is, for example, the jointer, which is a power planer that can also form rabbets, tenons, tapers and bevels, but that is about all.

Shapers shape wood, using the same molding head that can be attached to a drill press, lathe, radial arm saw or table saw. Since the molder blades are all the same, a shaper produces the same results with perhaps a little more efficiency —and that is its only real advantage.

Jig saws cut a variety of fretwork and so do band saws. Both are marvelous machines to have around, particularly if you are cutting a lot of curves. The band saw is slightly more versatile, if only because it is big enough to handle some heavy-duty straight cutting, such as resawing.

Stationary belt and disc sanders sand. They also grind but that is the limit of their functions, important as they may be.

Perhaps the best equipped workshops contain all of the tools discussed. But any shop that boasts a table saw, drill press, band saw and disc-belt sander is more than sufficiently equipped to produce any shelf, closet or cabinet project included in this book.

CHAPTER 3

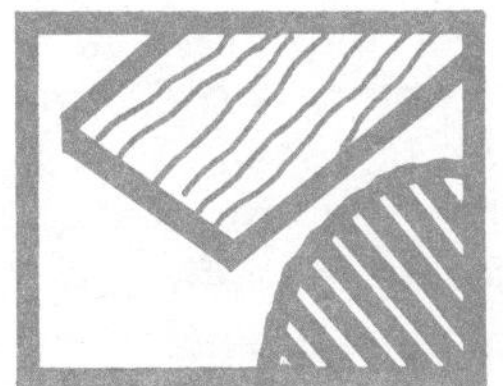
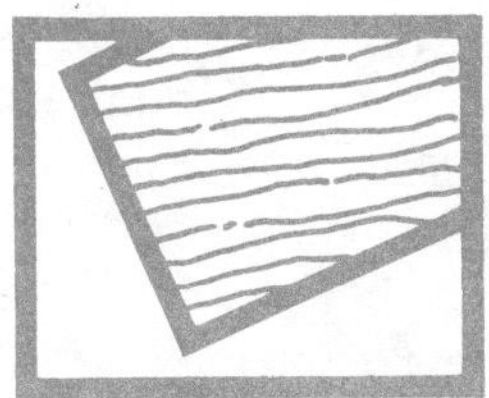

Wood: The Basic Material

Wood: The Basic Material

Deep in the rain forests of Central America, lumberjacks always hew the primavera tree in the dark of a moonless night. The primavera's sap rises and falls, not with the seasons, but with the phases of the moon. If it is felled when the moon is rising, insects will be attracted to its abundance of sap and destroy the logs before they can be brought to market.

The jungles of West Africa are so incredibly dense that the huge African mahogany can only be chopped down by hand. Then sometimes hundreds of men are needed to drag each immense log through the unyielding underbrush to the nearest waterway.

Teak is among the heaviest of all woods, and has the largest leaves of any tree in the world. The leaves average more than two square feet and are so coarse and tough that native cabinetmakers in India use them as sandpaper. The wood itself is so heavy that a newly cut tree will not float. Thus it takes nearly six years for Indian teak to reach America, for in order to harvest the tree it must first be girded, that is, cut completely around the bark and into the heartwood. Then it is left standing for three years or so, until the wood has dried enough to at least float in water. Only then is the teak cut down and the 10- to 15-ton logs hauled by elephant or buffalo to the nearest river.

The red mangrove is a very common tropical tree usually found at the edge of muddy salt flats. Its trunk does not begin at the ground, but is held aloft by hundreds of aerial roots that form a tangled mass of stilts beneath it. There are other trees that have aerial roots, such as the banyan, which drops "stringers" from its lower branches, and they, in turn, take root and grow into separate trees.

Or consider the papaya tree, which has no branches but bears a crown of long, stalked leaves at the top of its trunk. The trunk is made up of a pulpy, pitchlike material, leaving the main support of the entire 30-foot tree to a network of thick-walled fibers in the bark. When the trunk is dried, it becomes a soupy mass; the only solid material left is the meshwork of bark fibers.

If the papaya is too soft to be useful, there are also many trees so hard they have little or no commercial use. On the other hand, there are some woods that have a unique characteristic, such as flexibility, which relegates them to specific commercial uses. The lancewood, or downy serviceberry, for example, is used almost exclusively in the manufacture of flyrods. Then there are all those violinists who absolutely refuse to use any bow not made from beefwood. There are woods such as Burma teak, blue gum and brierroot, which do not burn. In Japan, Burma teak and blue gum are used in building construction to protect against fire, while 10,000 tons of brierroot are consumed each year in the manufacture of tobacco pipes. In Australia, Queensland walnut is valued by the makers of electrical equipment because of its high insulating properties. In every part of the world, trees give man a variety of drugs, oils, glues, confections, cloth, seasonings, fuel and at least 10,000 manufactured products.

There are more than 25,000 different known species of trees in the world today. Of these, 1,182 kinds are found in the United States, with the state of Florida having the most species—314. California boasts the tallest known living tree, a redwood standing 368 feet high with a root system that stretches over an area of three acres. Theoretically, trees are capable of growing indefinitely, and some of the giant sequoias are estimated to be more than 4,000 years old. Then again, the balsa tree must be cut down within seven years or it will deteriorate and become commercially valueless.

Identifying Woods

It is a common notion that the age of a tree can be accurately computed by counting the "annual" rings that appear in the stump. That is true—but only for trees growing in temperate zones where the period of growth and wood production occurs once a year. Elsewhere, there may be numerous interrupted periods of growth each year, producing several layers of wood, and therefore many growth rings annually. In the tropics, where growth is more or less continuous all year long, there are no rings at all in the tree trunks.

To identify any tree it is necessary to examine many more aspects than just its growth rings. No two trees are ever the same, so men have devised numerous categories for the process of identifying wood. The best known—and also the broadest—of these categories are *softwood* and *hardwood*. All conifers, or conebearing trees, such as spruce, pine or cedar, are considered softwoods. All flowering trees, such as oak, maple or mahogany, are hardwoods. But this basic division has its shortcomings since there are softwoods, such as the firs or pine, which are considerably harder than balsa, a tree classified as a hardwood. To eliminate such discrepancies, total classification of any tree involves a consideration of its color, odor, taste, texture, grain, growth rings (if any), resin ducts, pattern and so on. It takes a laboratory and the scientific knowledge of a systematic botanist (or taxonomist, as the scientist who studies trees calls himself) to accurately identify any given piece of wood.

The result of all the work done in classifying trees is that every known species has been given a scientific name chosen according to a strict set of international rules known as the International Code of Botanical Nomenclature. The botanical name is derived from Latin or Greek, so that it will be intelligible to all taxonomists regardless of their native tongue. Each species is, in fact, given two names. The first is its assigned genus. The second is a specific epithet either describing something about the tree, or alluding to the man who discovered the species. Thus, we have *Populus balsamifera. Populus* is the Latin name for poplar. *Balsamifera* means balsam-bearing. The common name for the *Populus balsamifera* is balsam poplar. The scientific name for satinay is *Syncarpia hillii. Syncarpia* means fused fruits, and the species was discovered by a man named Hill.

Besides the botanical nomenclature, trees usually acquire a common name that achieves a broad acceptability. Common names are not subject to international regulation and if a tree is little known or seldom used commercially, it may not have any common name at all. Conversely, many different species may end up with exactly the same popular name, like ironwood. The name ironwood is used for more than 80 different species of trees around the world. It seems that wherever you go, local residents have picked the name ironwood to designate the toughest, meanest, heaviest, orneriest wood in the neighborhood. Fortunately, the taxonomists have their own names for all 80 species, so at least *they* know which tree people are talking about.

How a Tree Is Structured

Under a microscope, and from a battery of scientific tests, it becomes evident that a tree—any tree—is an unbelievably complex structure. It has cells and tissues, chemicals and minerals, crystals of calcium oxalate, sugars, starch grains, oils, fats, resins, tannins and alkaloids. Consider just the cross section of a tree trunk. At the very center is the *pith*, the soft core of the tree, usually darker than the wood around it. Radiating from the pith are vascular *rays* which cut across the layers of wood and through the bark of the tree. The rays are made up of soft tissues, necessary for storing food. The wood at the center of a tree is always darker than the wood nearest the bark, and often a different color. This inner, darker wood is the *heartwood*. The outer ring of lighter colored wood is known as *sapwood*. Heartwood is the main strength of most trees. Its cells are inactive and often clogged with waste materials which give the wood its particular coloring. Heartwood also resists decay better than sapwood. Sapwood is made up of living cells that are busy conducting water and minerals from the root system to the leaves of the tree. The sapwood layer varies between 1½″ and 2″ in width (as much as 6″ in some species). As the tree grows, the inner edge of the sapwood ring becomes inactive and forms heartwood. It is heartwood that provides the lumber you buy; most sapwood is too saturated with moisture to have any commercial value.

Ringing the sapwood, and separating it from the bark of the tree, is a sheath of generative cells

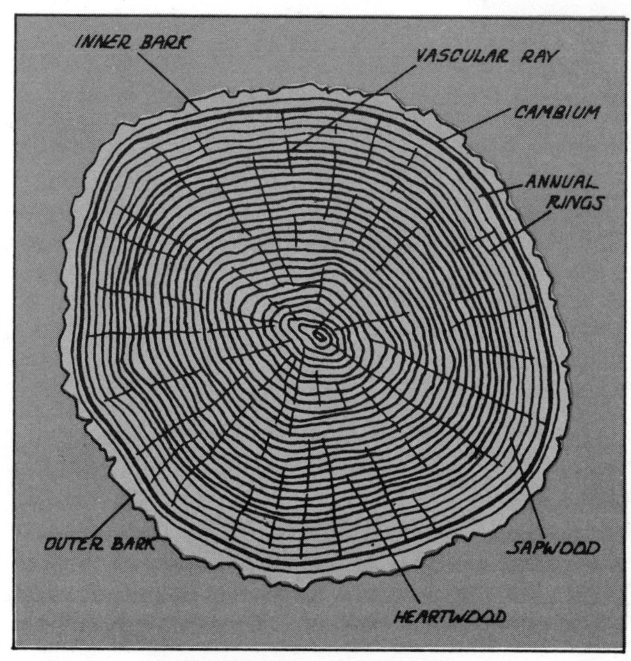

Cross section of a tree trunk.

known as vascular *cambium*. The cambium endlessly produces new cells that add wood to the inside of the tree and more bark to the outside. The inner bark carries food to the living parts of the tree, while the outer bark is made up of dead cells that form its protective shield. It is the cambium that generates the growth rings, which in many climates are divided into two segments. The first ring is formed at the start of the growth season and is called *springwood*, or early wood. The second ring, formed at the end of the growth period, is known as *summerwood*, or late wood.

Wood Cuts and Seasoning

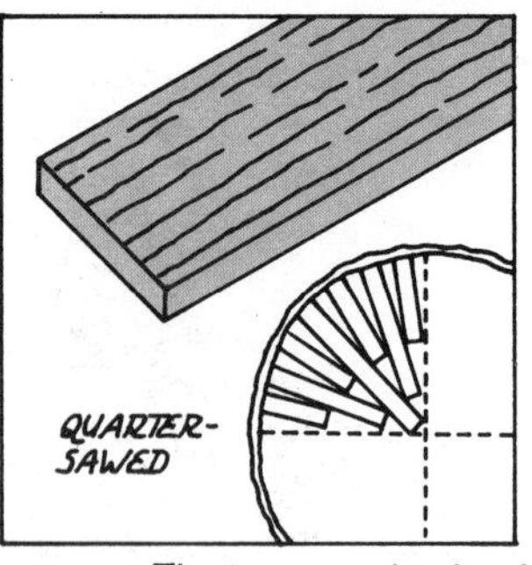

The two ways lumber is most usually sawed.

There are two ways that sawmills cut a tree into lumber. A log that is sliced parallel to the vascular rays has been quartersawed (if it is hardwood), or edge-grained (if it is softwood). When the log is cut perpendicular to the rays it is plainsawed (if it is hardwood), or flat-grained (if it is softwood). You can identify how any board was cut by looking at the growth rings on its ends. If the rings are roughly parallel lines, the board was quartersawed (or edge-grained). If the growth rings form a series of inverted Vs, the board was plainsawed (or flat-grained).

But no log is just cut up at the saw mill. It is also seasoned. All wood has a remarkable amount of moisture in it—anywhere from 30% to three times the weight of the wood. Much of this moisture is "free water" sitting in the cell cavities (it is just floating around between the fibers of the wood). There is also an "absorbed water" content which is especially important because it is this water that affects the shrinkage of the lumber. By definition, "absorbed water" is water that has been absorbed by the wood itself.

After all free water is removed from a piece of lumber, and only the absorbed water is left, the wood is considered to have reached its fiber-saturation point. For most woods, that means 30% of its weight is still moisture, and as this final 30% moisture content is reduced, shrinkage (called seasoning) begins to take place. Shrinkage, by the way, occurs mostly *across* the grain of the wood, so that a board being dried will become narrower, but not much shorter.

The excess moisture in wood is eliminated by one of two seasoning processes. The lumber can be air-dried by stacking it outdoors with spaces left between layers so that air can circulate freely around each piece. The drawback to this obviously economical system is that it takes a long time and in humid, wet or cold climates it is not very practical. So there is kiln drying, which is done in huge ovens where temperature, humidity and air circulation are all strictly controlled. In theory, if the kiln process has been handled properly, the wood will shrink without too many warps, twists, crooks, bows, checks or splits. But anybody who has spent half an hour looking over the merchandise in his local lumberyard knows how far theory can be from reality.

Wood Veneers

Most of the woods that concern the home craftsman are, at one time or another, in one form or another, converted into veneers. Today, depending on the size of the tree they were cut from, veneers come in various dimensions—1/42", 1/40" or 1/28" thick. That sounds simple enough, but it is no easy feat to scrape a less-than-paper-thin sheet of wood from a 10-ton log, even with sophisticated modern equipment.

The art of veneering dates back as far as the time of the ancient Egyptians; it was immensely popular during the Roman Empire for the same reasons it is cherished today. It would be virtually impossible to make furniture from solid pieces of some of the highly patterned woods used as veneers. In some instances, the cost of the solid wood is prohibitive. In other cases, such woods as walnut burl produce a beautiful—but structurally weak—grain that splits and warps when it is used as lumber. Then there are tropical woods like ebony, which is so dense that a small table made from solid stock would be almost too heavy to move. And finally, many of the beautiful patterns that exist as veneers would be totally obscured inside a piece of lumber and never be seen by anyone.

Old as veneering is, it was not until the twentieth century that science and technology provided truly manageable ways of handling veneers. Sharper sawing knives have been developed along with better machinery and more precise cutting and drying techniques. In fact, today veneer can actually be produced in thicknesses of 1/100th of an inch! (See Chapter 7 for some representative photographs of veneers.)

Cutting and Drying Veneers

Veneers are cut at the mills in four different ways. They can be sawed in the old-fashioned way with a circular saw blade, which is really many thin blades bonded together. But the saw wastes considerable stock and about the thinnest veneer it can produce is 1/24". So modern technology has developed three far more efficient ways of slicing off thinner veneers than with a sawing knife. Today, veneers can be peeled from a log by moving it up and down against a stationary blade. They can be rotary cut by putting the log on a huge lathe and rotating it against a knife that "unwinds" the entire piece of wood. Or the logs can be cut in half and then sliced on a veneer lathe, with the flat side serving as an automatic cutoff for each sheet.

No matter how veneer is cut, it must then be dried. This is accomplished by putting each sheet in a dryer consisting of heated plates that move up and down, alternately pressing and freeing the veneers between them. During both the cutting and drying operations, all of the sheets from each log are carefully kept together so that the patterns can be matched by the craftsmen who purchase them. When they come out of the drying machine, each sheet is numbered, measured and crated for shipment.

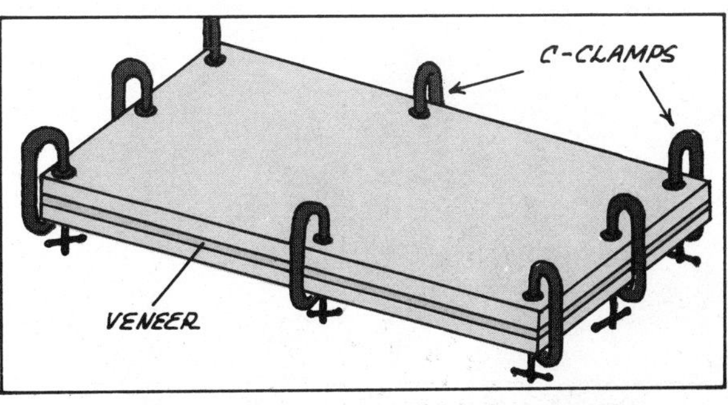

Dampened veneers may be weighted down until they are dry, or clamped between two boards. Be sure the pressure on the veneers is evenly distributed.

Veneers will remain in good condition indefinitely, provided they are laid flat and held down under a light weight. If you should store some veneer at home and it becomes dry and buckles, dip a whisk broom in water and sprinkle the veneer. The damp veneers are then placed under a heavy weight and by the time they are dry, they will be flat and ready for use again.

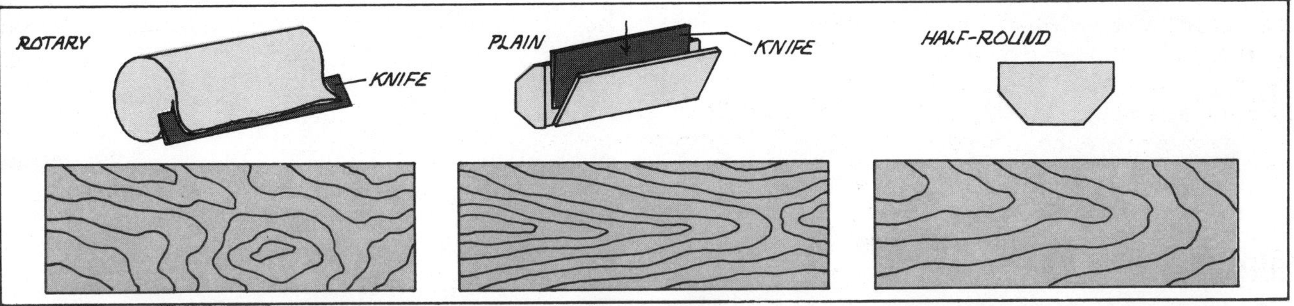

Plain (flat) slicing produces arched configurations called "cathedrals." The rotary cut causes a bolder pattern because no log is completely round and the lathe knife cuts in and out of the annular rings. The half-round cut is across the annular rings and achieves a grain pattern which is a combination of the plain and rotary cuts.

Criteria for Selecting Veneer

The appearance of veneer is described in terms of *grain, pattern, texture, color, odor, taste* and *luster,* although there is considerable misuse of the terms. *Grain,* for example, technically refers to the direction or orientation of wood fibers, and that is all the term refers to. Yet there are six broad categories of grain:

1. *Straight grain* means that the fibers run more

The six major types of wood grain.

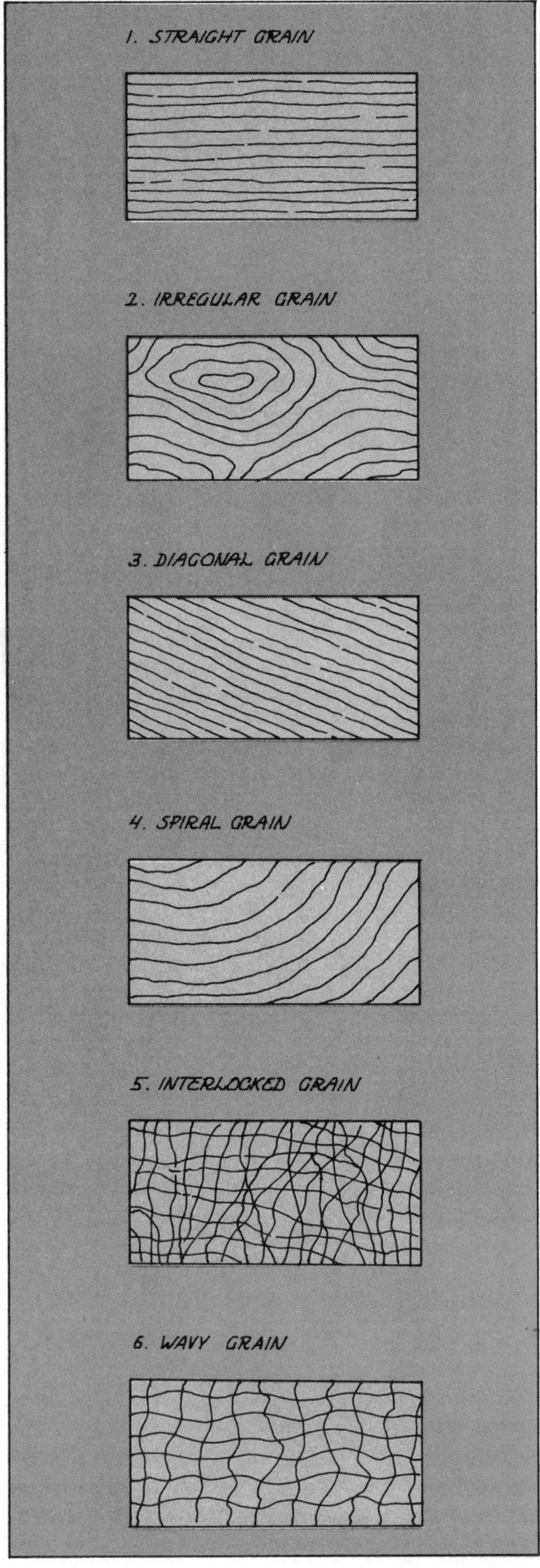

or less parallel to each other along the length of the tree.

2. An *irregular grain* occurs when the fibers vary with the vertical axis of the log. Irregular grains are often restricted to a small portion of the wood, such as around a knot.
3. *Diagonal grains* come from man, not nature. They happen when the person wielding the saw messes up and cuts an otherwise straight grain at an angle.
4. A *spiral grain* is one that twists itself around the tree, like the thread of a screw.
5. *Interlocked grains* come from a spiral going in one direction during one growth layer, then inclining toward the opposite direction in the next layer.
6. A *wavy grain* has the fibers constantly changing directions, and makes the grain look bumpy when it is really flat.

Grain and Pattern

Much of the confusion in terms comes from the difference between grain and pattern. Grain defines the direction of the wood fibers. Pattern refers to the natural configuration seen on the surface of the wood. It is produced by the interaction of several elements in the wood including the growth rings, vascular rays, the grain and what happens to it around knots, burls, crotches and butts, color variations and all kinds of other irregularities.

The grain of the wood has a tremendous effect on its pattern. An irregular grain can create a quilted pattern; interlocked grains often produce a ribbon, or stripe; a wavy grain may generate a fiddleback design. The names for these different configurations go on endlessly because veneer salesmen sometimes think up special names to describe a particular veneer they have on hand. Some of the more familiar patterns are given colorful appellations like mottle, plum-pudding, curly, swirl, crotch, feather-crotch, moonshine crotch, finger-roll, bird's-eye, pigment and burl.

Understanding Texture

The texture of a wood means the feel of it, and is described as fine or coarse. The differences in texture have to do with the size of the wood cells and the width of the vascular rays. If the cells are large and the rays are wide, the texture is said to be coarse (as in oak, ash and chestnut). If the cells are small and the rays narrow, the texture is considered fine (as are most softwoods). Naturally there are plenty of grades in between including moderately coarse (walnut, mahogany), and very fine (European boxwood).

Color in Wood

The colors found in wood range from black to white with practically everything in between. The color of any wood comes from the climate and soil content of the area in which the tree grows. As a result, the color of walnut, for example, varies considerably between France and Italy and even from state to state in the United States. The color is sometimes elusive, too. It may change when the wood is exposed to light, air, moisture or heat, becoming either darker or lighter. It can also be changed chemically: Liming will lighten most woods, while the fumes from ammonia gas will darken wood and remove the pink and red shades. Bleaching can produce some attractive results, and there is a whole industry in Europe dedicated to the dyeing of veneers.

The Fragrance of Wood

Many timbers also have a special scent, particularly when they are freshly cut, although this frequently disappears as the wood is dried. On the other hand, cedar and sandalwood retain their unique aroma, as do camphorwood and pine.

The Importance of Taste

Taste is also a part of wood and has an influential effect on the kinds of lumber used in certain industries. Certain foodstuffs are put in wooden containers that will lend no odor or taste to their contents. Some whiskies and many wines are aged in wooden casks that enhance their taste by imparting a "woody" flavor. Clothes closets and chests are made of cedar because the taste and smell of cedar is repellent to insects.

Luster in Wood

Finally, there is the luster of wood. Luster relies on the wood cells and how they reflect light. As a rule, quartersawed surfaces are more lustrous than flat-sawed ones. If certain patterns such as a fiddleback or stripe are present in a quartersawed board, the pattern will be even more lustrous. It should be kept in mind, however, that luster in wood does not always mean that it will take a good polish.

What Wood for Your Project?

Grain, figure, texture, color, odor and taste are all characteristics of wood that are taken into account by the taxonomists when they set about the task of classifying a tree. More important to the craftsman is which of the 25,000 known species shall he select for a given project? By and large the choice is a matter of personal preference and local availabilities. Given the many woods sold commercially, the choice can also be guided by the "workability" of the lumber. There is not space enough in this volume to describe all of the world's lumber, but the next few pages delineate some of the more readily available woods and present their most usual uses as well as characteristics.

Softwoods

Bald Cypress

Taxodium distichum (having the appearance of *Taxus*, or yew; double-ranked, that is, the leaves are in two rows). Bald cypress is known in various states in the U.S. as black cypress, buck cypress, cow cypress, red cypress, southern cypress, swamp cypress, white cypress and yellow cypress. Found from Delaware to Florida to Texas to Illinois, usually growing in wet lowlands and swamps.

Description. Durable and resists decay. It is medium-hard, strong and fairly heavy. It has a straight, close grain. When rubbed, the wood feels greasy to the touch. Heartwood varies from pale brown to blackish brown, sometimes with a reddish tinge. The heartwood of darker specimens often has a rancid odor but it does not impart taste, odor or color to food products.

Uses. Cypress is everybody's No. 1 choice for durability in the construction of coffins, stadium seats and greenhouses. Because of its decay resistance it is frequently used for posts, beams, roofing, docks, bridges and wooden containers of all kinds. Crotches are sold as veneers under the name *faux satiné*.

Cedar, Western Red

Thuja plicata (an aromatic wood; folded, scale-like leaves). Also known as canoe cedar, giant arbor vitae, Idaho cedar, Pacific red cedar, shinglewood and stinking cedar. Grows from southern Alaska to northern California to Montana and Idaho, primarily in moist soil.

Description. Moderately soft and limber but has extremely high resistance to decay. It has low resistance to nail withdrawal but glues easily and holds paint exceptionally well. Straight-grained, moderately coarse in texture. Easily worked with tools and accepts a good finish. Heartwood is reddish or pinkish brown to dull brown and has characteristic cedar aroma.

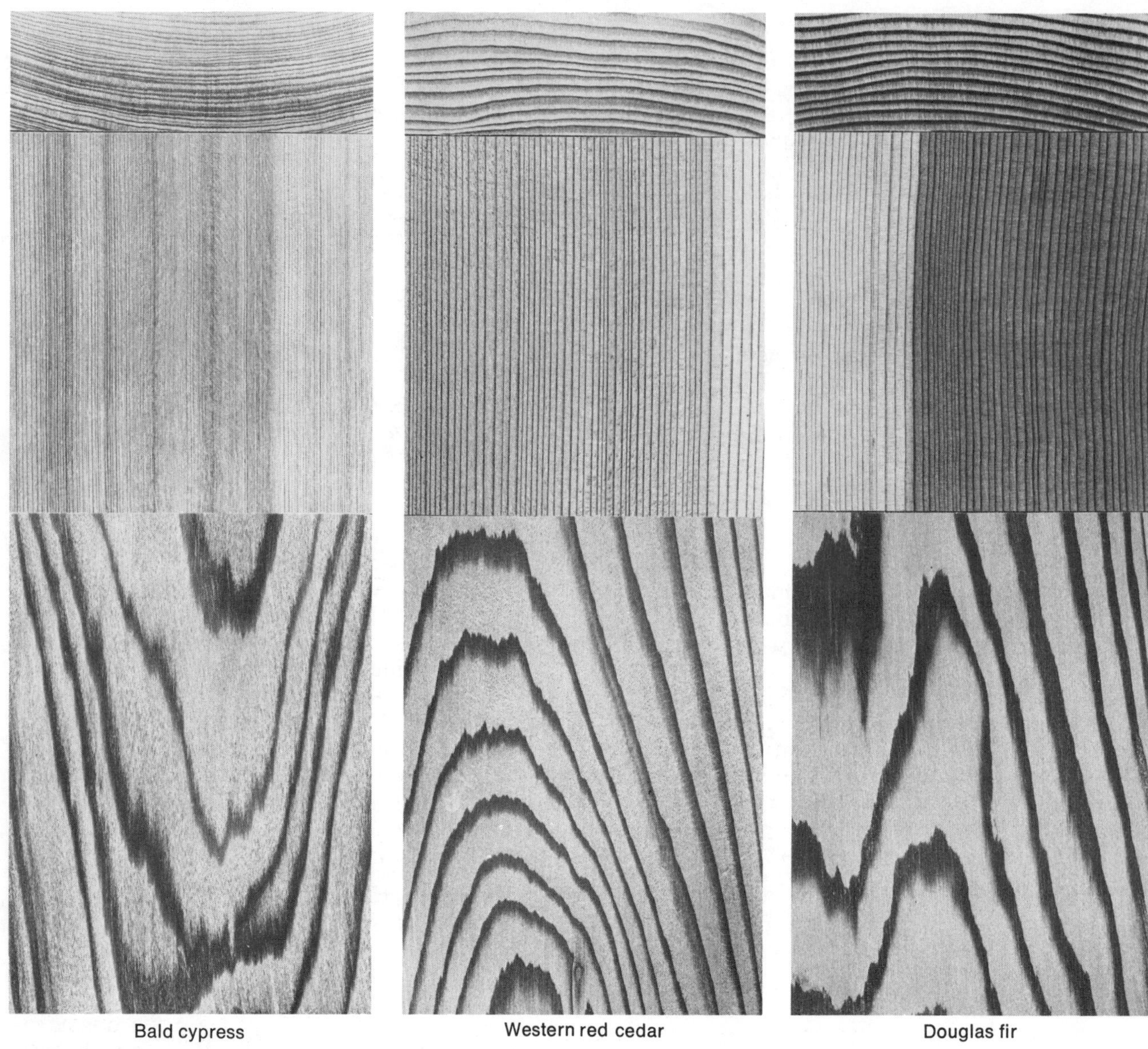

Bald cypress | Western red cedar | Douglas fir

Uses. Shingles, millwork, boatbuilding, poles, posts and house siding. For any outdoor project, this is one of the woods to use.

Fir, Douglas

Pseudotsuga menziesii (false hemlock; after Archibald Menzies, who discovered it in 1791). Also called Douglas spruce, fir, yellow fir, red pine, red spruce, red fir, Oregon pine and a host of other names. Grows all over the western states, from Texas to Canada; sometimes it gets to be pretty fat, as well as over 400′ tall. Its record is 70,000 board feet of high-grade lumber from a single tree.

Description. Moderately heavy and strong, very stiff. Heartwood is dense and relatively hard, with moderate decay resistance. The wood is yellowish and light tan with brownish streaks. It is difficult to work with hand tools but holds fastenings well and can be glued satisfactorily. It is a poor wood to paint since it does not absorb preservatives.

Uses. Douglas fir is primarily used today as a veneer for plywood. It is also used in sashes, doors, boxes, lumber, millwork and as pulp.

Hemlock, Western

Tsuga heterophylla (hemlock; various-leaved). Known also as hemlock spruce, Alaska pine and Pacific hemlock. Grows along the western coast from Alaska to central California and as far east

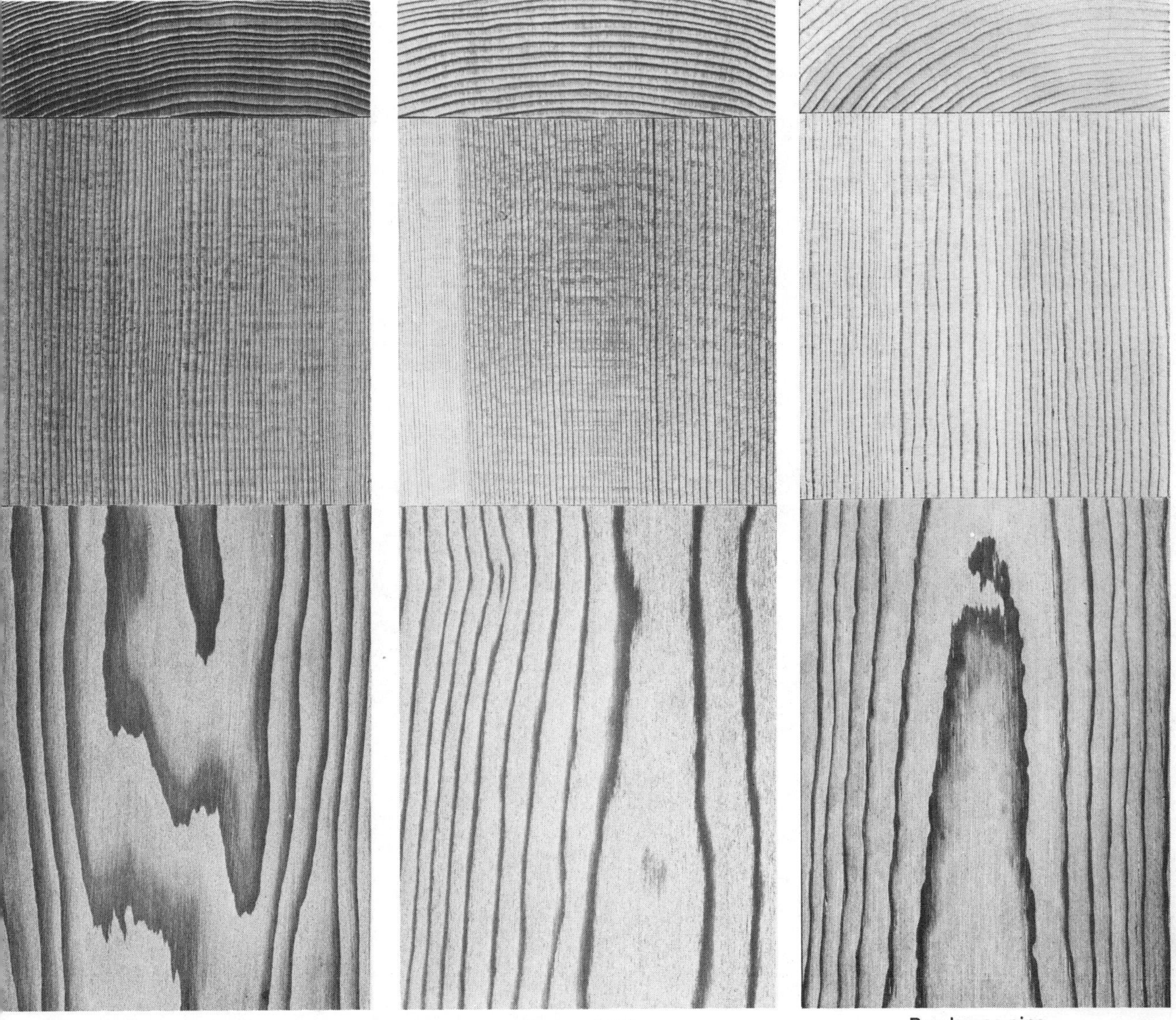

Western hemlock

Western larch

Ponderosa pine

as Montana and Idaho at low mountainous altitudes in those areas.

Description. Heartwood is low in decay resistance but of very fine texture, lightweight and straight-grained. It is light reddish brown, often with a purple cast. Western hemlock cuts easily and produces smooth surfaces.

Uses. Primarily used for pulpwood, containers and plywood core stock. It is also used in lighter construction such as siding, subflooring, joists, studs, planking and rafters.

Larch, Western

Larix occidentalis (the classical name of this species; leaves that fall in autumn). Thrives in Montana and as far north as British Columbia at elevations of 2,000′ to 7,000′.

Description. Heavy and moderately hard, this wood is stiff, strong and reasonably decay-resistant. Ranks high in nail resistance but small or blunt-pointed nails help to reduce splitting. Heartwood is russet brown with no distinctive odor. Will accept a natural or stain finish, but does not hold paint. Hard to work with tools.

Uses. Cheap-grade furniture, poles, railroad ties and structural purposes.

Pine, Ponderosa

Pinus ponderosa (the classical Latin name; heavy). Also called big pine, bird's-eye pine, knotty

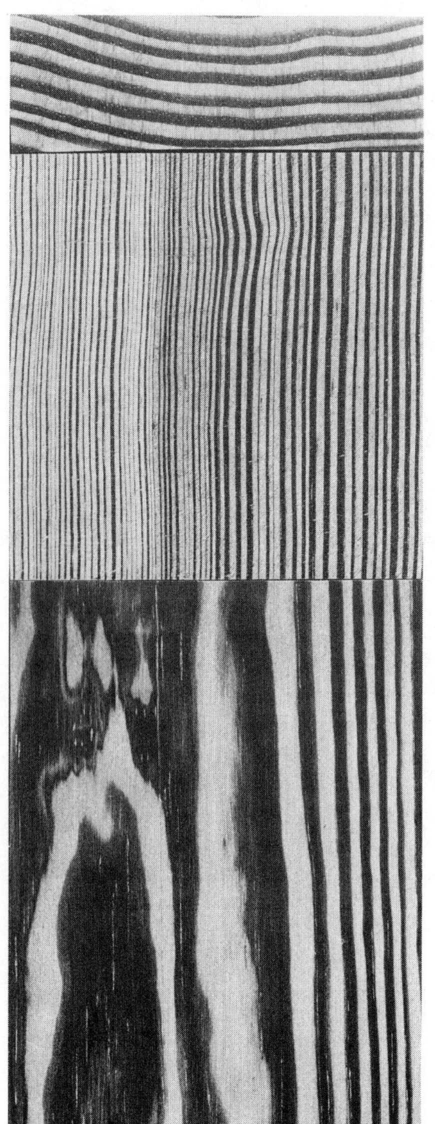
Shortleaf pine

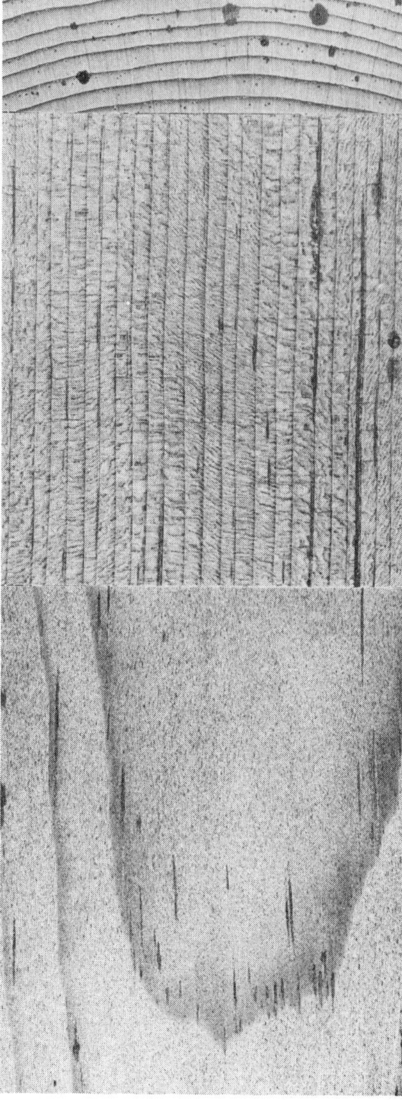
Sugar pine

Western white pine

pine, lodgepole pine, Oregon pine, pitch pine, pole pine and prickly pine. Grows from Alaska to California and as far up the Rockies as 12,000 feet.

Description. Does not warp much but is moderately light, weak, limber and resistant to decay. Heartwood is yellowish to light reddish or orange-brown. A bird's-eye pattern similar to that found in maple is sometimes present.

Uses. Popular for cabinetwork, general millwork, sash, doors and moldings. Inferior grades are used for interior trim, poles, fences, paper pulp and crates.

Pine, Shortleaf

Pinus echinata (Latin name for the species; spiny). Also called Carolina pine, Northern Carolina pine, pitch pine and yellow pine. Grows throughout the southeastern United States.

Description. Moderately heavy, hard, strong, stiff and decay-resistant. Its nail withdrawal resistance ranks with hemlock, spruce and Douglas fir. Heartwood ranges from yellow and orange to reddish brown and tan.

Uses. Principally used in building construction, interior trim and paper pulp, boxes, furniture and telephone poles.

Pine, Sugar

Pinus Lambertiana (Latin name for the species; in honor of Aylmer Bourke Lambert). Other popular names are: big pine, gigantic pine, great sugar pine, shade pine. Ranges from Oregon to lower

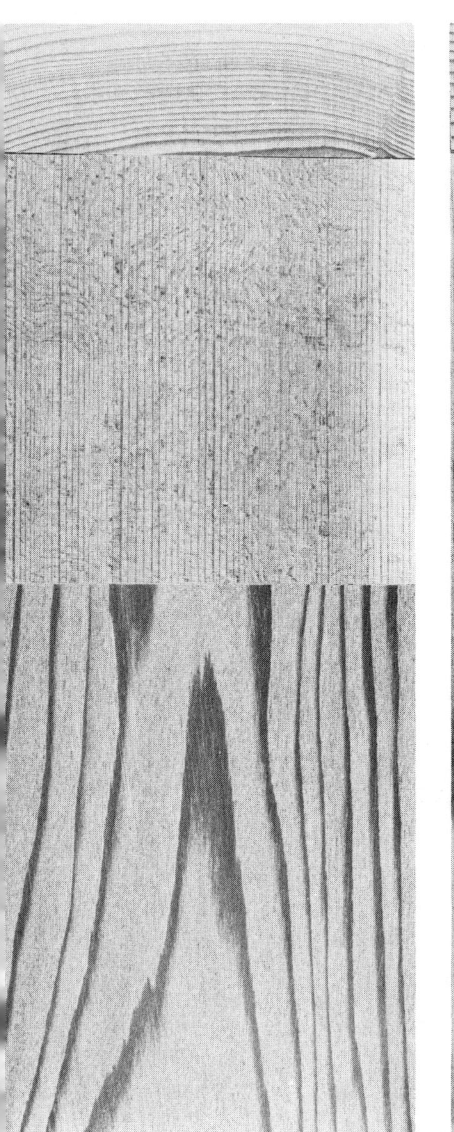
Redwood

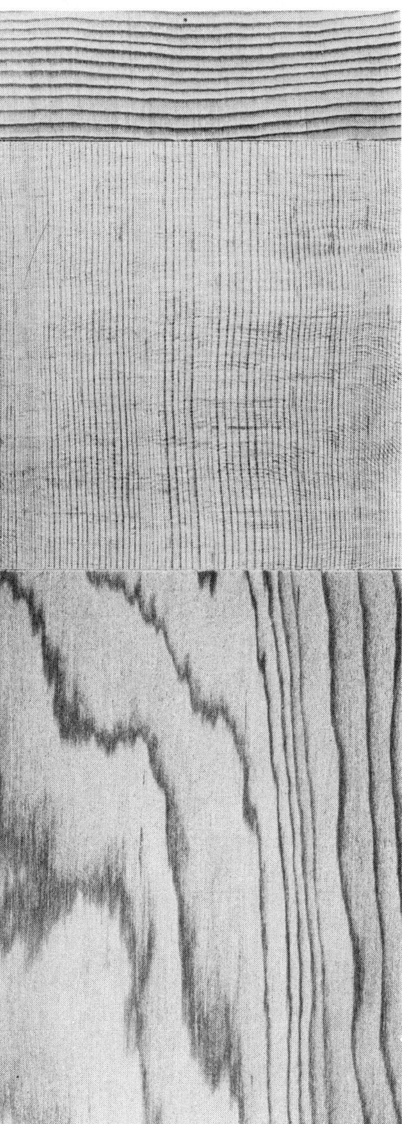
Sitka spruce

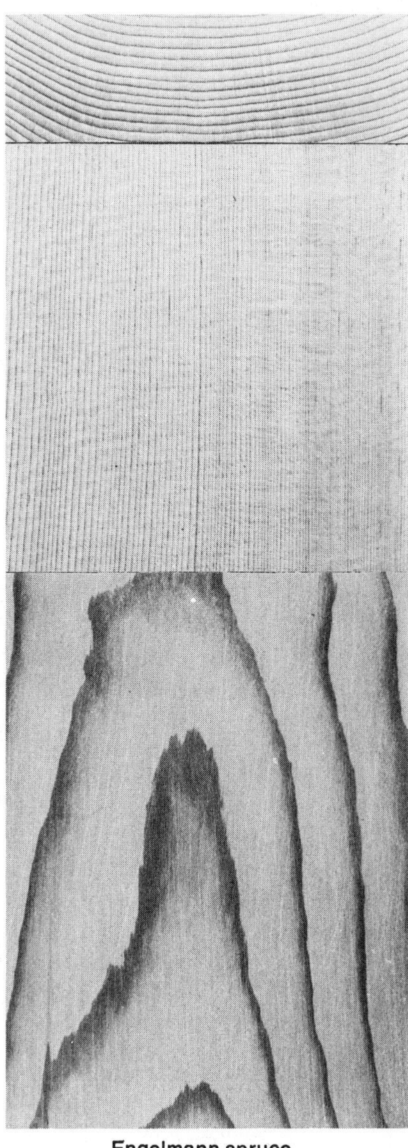
Engelmann spruce

California and Mexico; usually found in the higher altitudes.

Description. Lightweight and moderately soft, this wood is moderately limber and weak, with a low decay resistance. Easy to work with tools, does not split easily and has moderate resistance to nail withdrawal. Heartwood is light brown to a pale reddish brown.

Uses. Suitable for all phases of house construction, millwork, containers and furniture.

Pine, Western White

Pinus monticola (Latin name for the species; of the mountains). Other names include Idaho white pine, mountain pine and silver pine. This species belongs to the northwest—Idaho, Washington, Oregon and British Columbia.

Description. Moderate in weight, softness, and stiffness as well as low in decay resistance. Light cream to reddish brown in color, which darkens with exposure. Works easily with tools and glues readily, does not split easily and has moderate nail-pulling resistance.

Uses. Lumber, three-quarters of it used in construction. After that, planks, millwork, boxes and furniture. It is an all-purpose wood.

Redwood

Sequoia sempervirens (after the Cherokee Indian, Sequoya; always green). The giant redwood is found only in a 35-mile-wide strip that reaches

White ash

Quaking aspen

American basswood

500 miles along the California coast. How big is it? Would you believe a record of 380 feet with a diameter of 26 feet? That made 344,000 board feet of lumber—a little over 65 miles—all from the same tree.

Description. Lightweight, moderately hard, strong and stiff with outstanding decay resistance. Intermediate nail withdrawal resistance but takes paint exceptionally well. Heartwood is a uniform deep reddish brown and has no distinctive odor, taste or feel.

Uses. Framing and construction of houses, millwork, outdoor furniture, trim and molding.

Spruce, Sitka

Picea sitchensis (pitch; of Sitka Island, Alaska). Also called sequoia silver spruce, silver spruce western spruce and West Coast spruce. Grows along the Pacific Coast from Alaska to California but never more than 50 miles inland.

Description. A lightweight wood that is moderately soft, weak and stiff with a low decay resistance. Planed surfaces show a silky sheen but planing produces a woolly grain. Works wel with tools, holds fastenings well. It is not unusua to find large, clear, straight-grained pieces with a uniform texture and almost no defects. Heartwood is light pinkish yellow to pale brown.

Uses. Lumber, cooperage and paper pulp as well as musical instruments. Other major uses include furniture, millwork and crates.

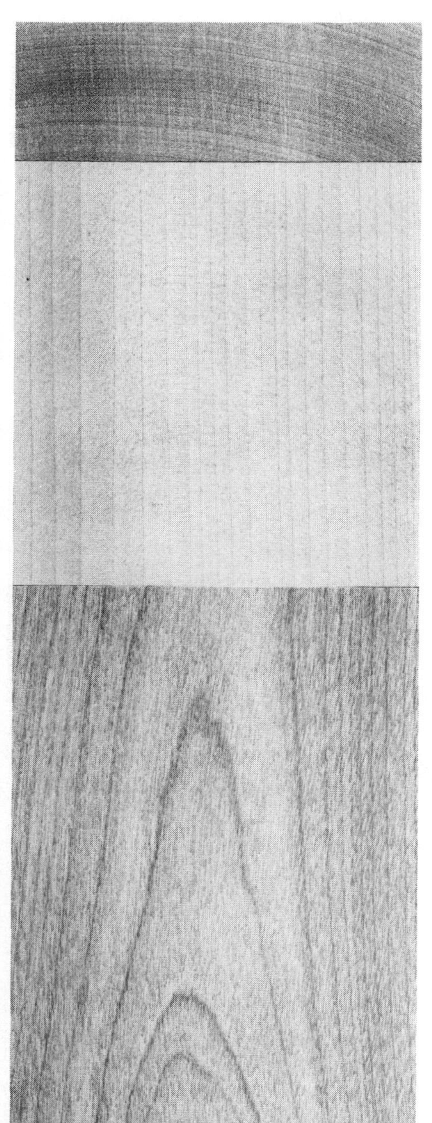
Yellow birch

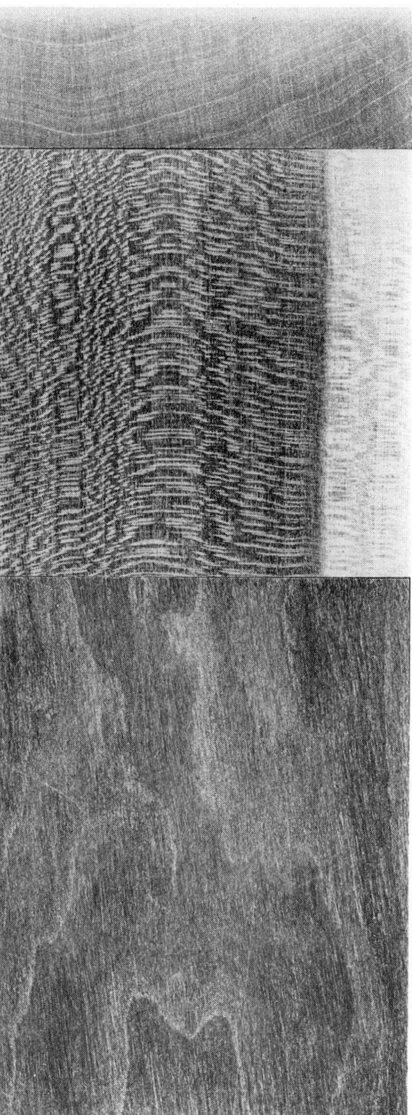
Black cherry

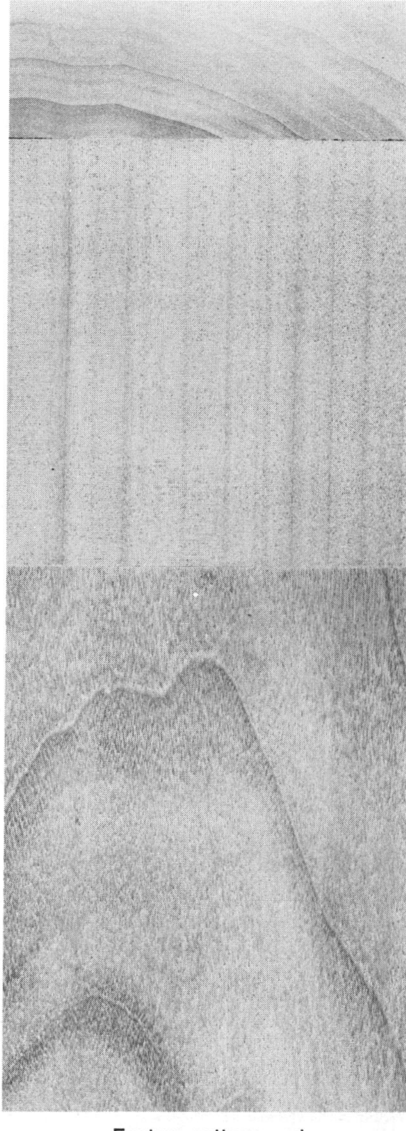
Eastern cottonwood

Spruce, Engelmann

Picea engelmannii (pitch; after George Engelmann, who first identified the species). Found high in the western mountains, ranging from Canada to New Mexico.

Description. Rated as lightweight, it is soft and weak, moderately limber with a low decay resistance. Heartwood is hard to discern from sapwood; both range from white to pale yellowish brown.

Uses. Principally used for lumber, crossties and poles, subflooring, sheathing and studding.

Hardwoods

Ash, White

Fraxinus americana (Latin, meaning ash; of America). Found in most of the states east of the Mississippi.

Description. The wood is strong, stiff and has notable bending qualities. It is moderately rated as to ease of working, tendency to split and ability to hold nails and screws. Heartwood is brown to dark brown, occasionally with a reddish tint. Sometimes confused with hickory, unless viewed through a microscope.

Uses. Handles for everything—shovels, forks, hoes, rakes. Also used for bats and furniture.

Aspen, Quaking

Populus tremuloides (Latin name; resembling the European aspen). Grows throughout the northern and western parts of the United States.

Description. One of the lightweight hardwoods, it is soft, weak, limber and low in decay resistance. Heartwood is light brown to white with occasional brown streaks. Low resistance to nail withdrawal and tends to split under the action of nails or screws. Easily worked with hand or power tools, aspen glues well and can be painted but does not accept stain. Highly patterned logs and some crotches are sold as veneers.

Uses. Principally lumber, pulp, excelsior and matches.

Basswood, American

Tilia americana (Latin name for the species; of America). Also called American linden, bee tree, black lime tree, lime tree, linn, linden, whitewood, wickup and yellow basswood. Found throughout the eastern half of the United States.

Description. Lightweight, weak, moderately stiff with a low resistance to decay. Heartwood is creamy white to a light brown or reddish tint. Easy to work with tools, holds paint well and glues easily. Also resists splitting from nails and has a low resistance to nail withdrawal.

Uses. Most basswood is used for lumber, crates and general millwork. It is popular with furniture manufacturers as a core overlaid with high-grade veneers.

Birch, Yellow

Betula alleghaniensis (Latin name for birch; of the Allegheny Mountains). Also called gray birch, silver birch and swamp birch. Grows from Canada to the Great Lakes and New England; as far south as North Carolina.

Description. Heartwood is heavy, strong, stiff and has a low decay resistance. Creamy brown with tinges of red; a curly or wavy figure is often prominent. The wood works easily with power tools, has a high nail withdrawal resistance and takes a nice finish.

Uses. Primarily used in furniture manufacture, general millwork and woodenware. It is available in both lumber and plywood as well as veneers.

Cherry, Black

Prunus serotina (peach; late maturing). Also referred to as chokecherry, whiskey cherry, rum cherry and wild cherry. Found all over the eastern half of the United States, the black cherry is particularly abundant in New York, Pennsylvania and West Virginia.

Description. Heavy wood, considered hard, stiff and strong, does not require any special saw blades. Sands easily and is capable of holding a highly polished finish. Heartwood is a distinctive light to dark reddish brown.

Uses. The best logs are cut into veneers for cabinetmaking, furniture and musical instruments, but it can also be purchased as lumber.

Cottonwood, Eastern

Populus deltoides (Latin name for the species; triangular leaf shape). The many popular names include aspen cottonwood, Carolina poplar, river poplar, water poplar, yellow cottonwood. Has a wide distribution from the Great Plains to the East Coast; everywhere it thrives best in moist soil.

Description. Reasonably light and soft, wood is limber and has low decay resistance. Heartwood is grayish white to a light grayish brown with occasional streaks of light brown. It has a smooth, even texture and is slightly lustrous. Easily worked with tools, though care must be taken that a chipped or fuzzy grain is not produced. Does not split easily when nailed, has a low nail withdrawal resistance and will glue well if the proper care is taken. Holds paint well.

Uses. Major uses are as lumber and in container and furniture manufacture. It is often used as a core for high-grade veneers and is sold in veneer sizes.

Elm, American

Ulmus americana (Latin name; from America). Found throughout the eastern states except in the Appalachian highlands and southern Florida.

Description. Heavy, moderately hard wood, which is relatively stiff and has a low resistance to decay. Heartwood is brown to dark brown, occasionally with shades of red. Although slightly below average in woodworking properties, elm is excellent for glueing and has an intermediate resistance to nail withdrawal. Also has excellent bending qualities.

Uses. The lumber is a primary material in making containers, furniture, barrels and kegs, principally because it bends so well. Manufactured as veneers for plywood; when quarter-sliced it provides decorative veneers for furniture.

Hickory

Carya ovata (Greek for nut; egg-shaped). There are 16 species and 20 varieties of hickory found in America, most of them growing in the eastern half of the country. True hickories include the shagbark, shellbark, pignut and mockernut. (Not pictured.)

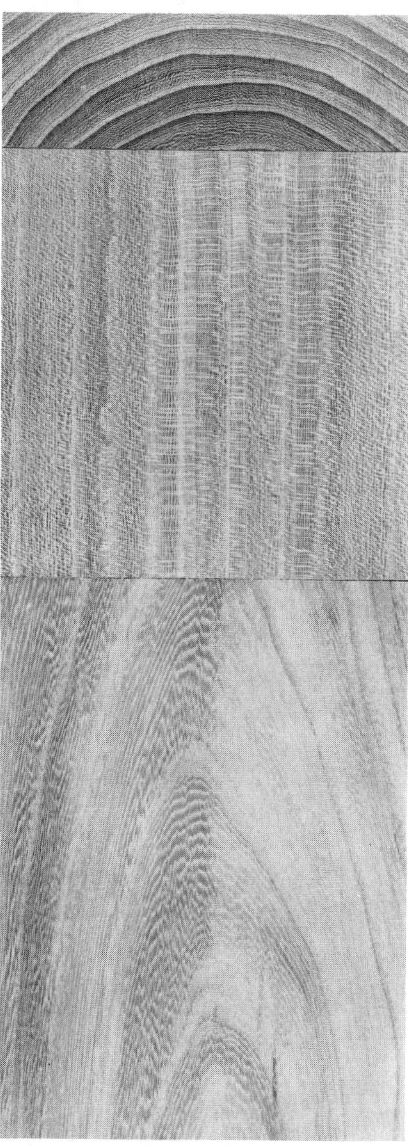

American elm

Sugar maple

Description. The wood of the true hickories is very heavy and very hard. Actually, the combination of strength, hardness, toughness and stiffness found in hickory is unequalled by any other commercial wood. Heartwood is brown to reddish brown and has a low resistance to decay. Can be glued satisfactorily.

Uses. Handles for tools consume 80% of the hickory harvested each year. Other uses include farm implements, outdoor furniture and sports equipment.

Mahogany, African

Khaya ivorensis (after the native name for the tree, Khaye; Latin meaning Ivory Coast). The several species imported from Africa are given names that allude to the ports from which they were exported. Thus they have names such as Lagos, Benin mahogany, Half-Assine, Sekondi mahogany and Grand Bassam. Found all over the west coast of Africa, and there are numerous species grown in Central and South America. (Not pictured.)

Description. Freshly cut African mahogany varies from a light to deep pink, which gradually darkens to shades of light brown to dark reddish brown. Coarser in texture than New World mahogany with less of a tendency to split, although it is not quite as strong. All mahoganies are fairly easy to work with tools, although the grain may rise when it is planed. The interlocked grain of African mahogany produces more patterned logs

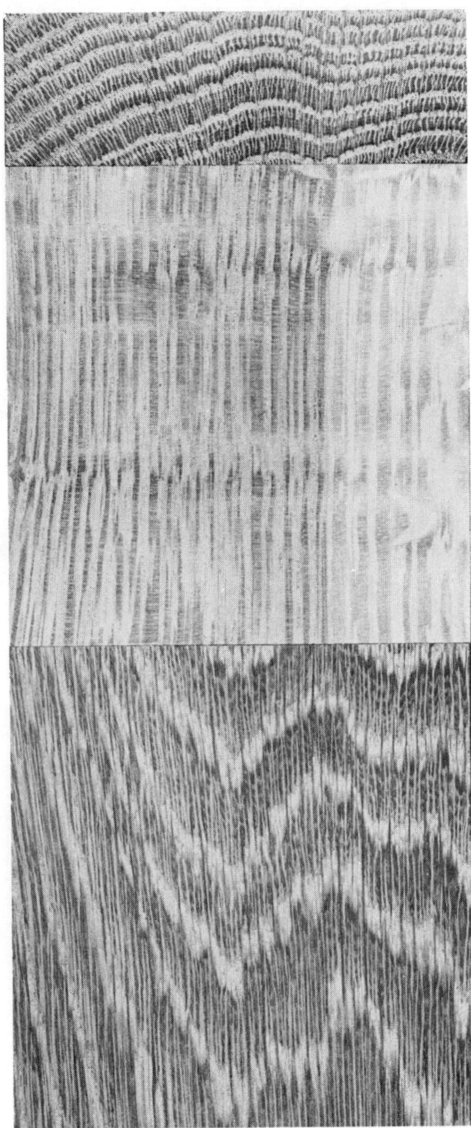

White oak

Yellow poplar

than the New World species, but it is also more likely to warp.

Uses. Premier wood in furniture manufacture. Sold both as lumber and in veneer, some of which is used for making high-grade plywood.

Maple, Sugar

Acer saccharum (Latin name for the species; sugary). Also known as black maple, hard maple, rock maple, sugar-tree maple and white maple. Grows almost everywhere east of the Rockies with the largest quantities found in New England.

Description. Heartwood is a very light tan to reddish brown; it is a heavy, strong wood with an even texture. High nail withdrawal resistance, can be glued and stained, and is capable of a high polish. While usually straight-grained, various patterns can be obtained for veneers including curly, wavy, bird's-eye, fiddleback and a spectacular burl. Sugar maple is easy to work with tools and is excellent for turning.

Uses. Veneer, railroad crossties, musical instruments, lumber, flooring and woodenware.

Oak, White

Quercus alba (Latin for oak; white). Also known as stave oak and forked-leaf white oak. Found all over the eastern parts of Canada and the United States.

Description. Heartwood is light tan to grayish brown. Oak is a heavy, hard wood that is quite decay-resistant. White oak is one of the strongest

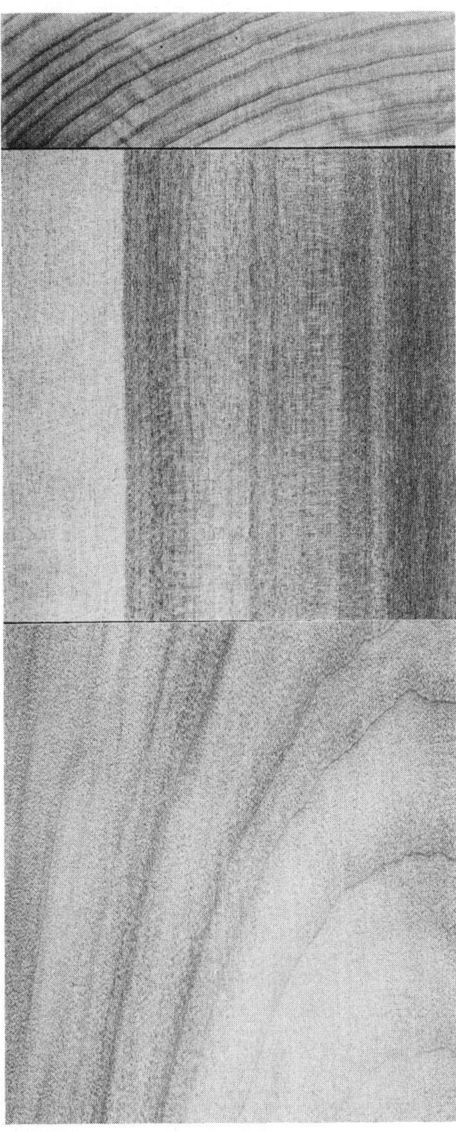

Sweetgum

American sycamore

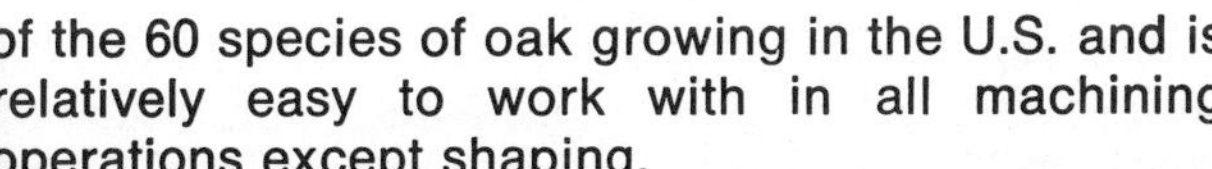

of the 60 species of oak growing in the U.S. and is relatively easy to work with in all machining operations except shaping.

Uses. Most white oak is used in flooring, general millwork, containers and furniture. It is the preferred wood for barrels and kegs and, if people still built wooden ships, it would still be used for that, too. Lots of white oak is sliced into veneers; cut on the quarter it produces a flake pattern; otherwise it gives modern furniture makers the fine straight lines now popular.

Poplar, Yellow

Liriodendron tulipifer (lily tree; tulip bearing). Also referred to as canary wood, canoe wood, poplar, tulip tree and whitewood. Grows throughout the eastern United States, usually in damp locations.

Description. Moderately light, strong and stiff with a low resistance to decay. Heartwood is brownish yellow with a greenish tinge. Sometimes turns to a dark purple or blue as it dries. Although low in nail withdrawal resistance, it will not split during nailing. Will take and hold paint, enamel and stain, and glues satisfactorily.

Uses. Manufactured primarily for veneers, and as lumber for furniture and musical instruments. In veneer form, it is usually used for crossbanding and backs.

Rosewood, Indian

Dalbergia latifolia (after the Swedish physician, Dalberg; broad-leaved). Found in India and Ceylon. (Not pictured.)

Black tupelo

Black walnut

Description. Heavy, with the unique quality of not shrinking. Color of the heartwood is a very light yellow or light rose with both light and dark streaks. Some logs are almost black.

Uses. For over a century, rosewood has been popular in the manufacture of fine furniture. It can be purchased as either lumber or a veneer. It is, however, one of the most expensive woods on the market.

Sweetgum

Liquidambar styraciflua (liquid amber; medicinal storax). Also known as alligator-tree, alligator wood, hazel pine, satin walnut, liquidambar, incense tree, star-leaved gum, red gum and sap gum. Found in the United States from Connecticut to Texas.

Description. Reasonably heavy, moderately stiff, strong and decay-resistant. Rated intermediate in its ability to resist splitting and to hold nails. Heartwood is reddish brown with streaks of darker color and must be specially treated before glueing. Considered above average in turning, boring and steam-bending properties but otherwise is hard to work with.

Uses. Principal uses are for lumber, plywood and veneer. The lumber goes into furniture and millwork.

Sycamore, American

Platanus occidentalis (Latin name for the Oriental plane tree; western). Other names are American plane tree, buttonball, buttonwood, water beech and ghost tree. Grows from Maine to Nebraska and south to Texas and Florida.

Description. Moderately heavy and hard, but cannot resist decay. Heartwood is reddish brown with an interlocking grain that keeps it from splitting. Wood turns well on a lathe and holds its shape after steam-bending.

Uses. The lumber is used in box-making and furniture of all grades. The veneers are popular choices for cabinets.

Tupelo, Black

Nyssa sylvatica (the name of a water nymph; grows in water). Also called blackgum, bowl gum, pepperidge, wild pear tree, yellow gum and stinkwood. Found in every state east of the Mississippi, wherever there is an abundant water supply.

Description. Has a tendency to warp because of its interlocking grain, which also makes the wood difficult to split and nail. Takes a good finish and glues well, although it is below average in machining properties. Heartwood is pale to moderately dark brownish or gray.

Uses. Mainly used as lumber and veneer for furniture.

Walnut, Black

Juglans nigra (Latin for walnut; Jupiter's nut). Found in abundance throughout the eastern half of the United States.

Description. Hard, strong, stiff and exceptionally resistant to decay. Heartwood is chocolate brown with darker (sometimes purplish) streaks. Can be worked easily with hand tools and has excellent machining properties. It finishes, holds paint and stains, and polishes exceptionally well.

Uses. Since Colonial times, black walnut has been one of the most sought-after woods in the country. It produces beautiful butt, crotch, burl, fiddleback, leaf and straight patterns when it is manufactured as veneer. As lumber, it is a first choice among many cabinet and furniture makers. Most gun stocks are made from black walnut.

Man-Made Woods

Particleboard

Also called chipboard, pressboard or flakeboard.

Particleboard is made by mixing wood chips and sawdust with an adhesive and then forming the mixture into panels under intense heat and pressure. The result is a dense, grainless composition board that is extremely stable, rarely warps and is also very heavy.

Excellent for sliding doors, counter- and tabletops, cabinet backs and the like. It is unnecessarily heavy for swinging doors; its edges have a low holding power for screws, let alone nails. Particleboard is, however, ideal for use as a single core for laminates or veneers.

When handling particleboard, bear in mind that it is made with a lot of tough resin, which tends to dull most saw blades quickly. Best assembly method is glue and screw, or at least using glue and screw nails.

Particleboard accepts most paints readily. It is sold in 4'x8' panels in thicknesses of from ¼" to 1⅞".

Hardboard

Hardboard is made by forming refined wood fibers into sheets under heat and pressure. There are two major types, untempered and tempered. Untempered hardboards are used for most indoor applications; tempered panels have a harder, moisture-resistant surface for use outdoors. In its most common form, hardboard has one smooth side and a rougher, furry texture on the back. It also comes channeled, grooved and embossed with different designs, textures and finishes, including some that look like wood, and perforated.

Because hardboard—like pressboard—has no grain, it is equally strong in all directions. It is ideal for drawer bottoms, as sliding doors, cabinet backs, covering benches, tables and countertops, as well as for closet shelving. While hardboard is relatively strong, it has some drawbacks. It should not be expected to span large areas without some kind of support. And it cannot be end-fastened or jointed without blocking behind the corners.

Either nails or screws combined with glue can be used with hardboard. Nails should be driven no closer than ¼" from the edge, and be no more than 4" apart. Nailing should always begin at the center of the panel and work out toward the edges so that the panel will lie flat.

Hardboard will accept most paints, although the surface should first be sealed with a coat of shellac, enamel undercoater or primer-sealer.

The most common sizes sold are 4'x8' in ⅛" and ¼" thicknesses. Larger sheets are available on special order.

Plywood

For durability, strength, versatility, cost and all-round convenience, plywood in its many forms has achieved the ranking of first choice by practically everyone.

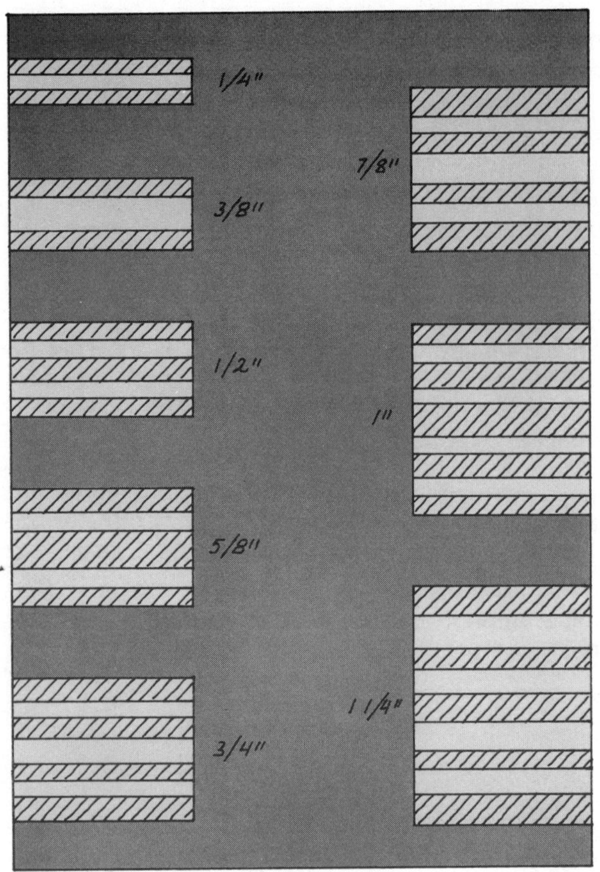

Plywood also comes in thicknesses that are made up of 3, 4, 5, 6, 7 or more veneers.

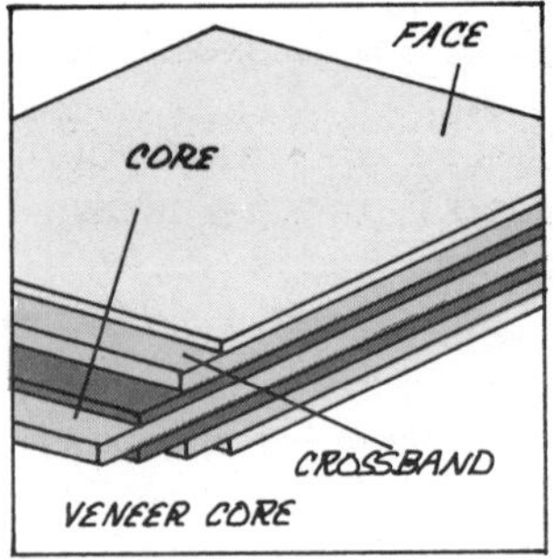

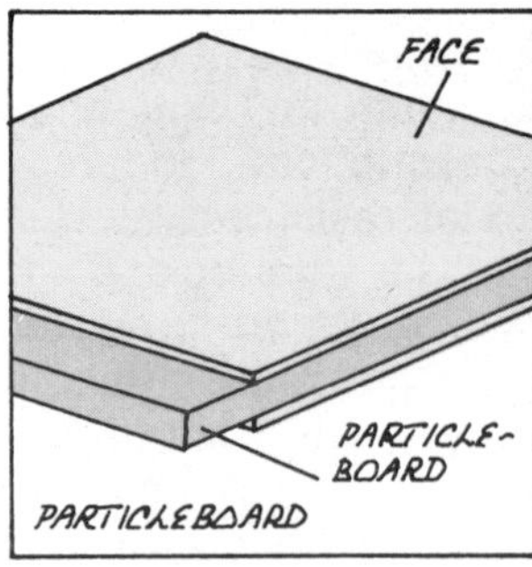

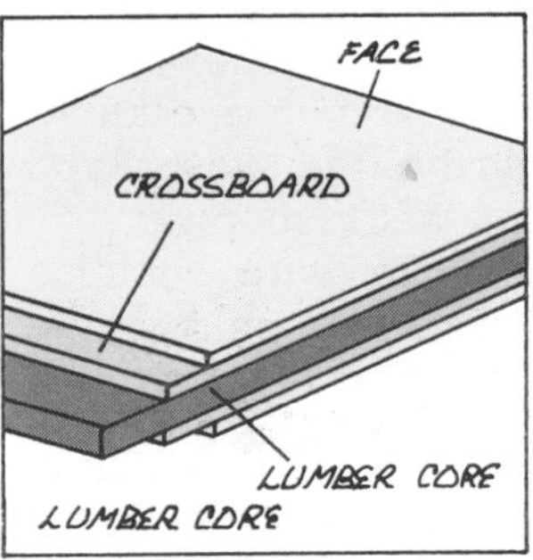

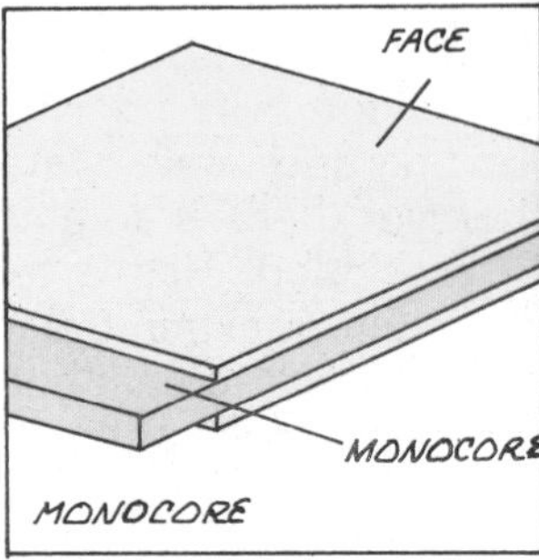

There are four basic plywood constructions, but these can be varied. For example, monocore or particleboard resist bending so well that they can support a veneer on only one side without warping.

Not only is plywood available in thicknesses that go from 1/4" to 1 7/8", but it comes in interior (all-purpose) and exterior (water-resistant) grades, with a host of textured faces (for wall paneling), and sports a variety of hardwood veneers (for decorative work). The most common grades of plywood have either fir or pine faces; the hardwood veneers include birch, mahogany stripe, maple, poplar, plain oak and American walnut. Whatever the need, chances are it can be met with some form of plywood.

By definition, plywood is a large, flat panel usually composed of an odd number of sheets (called plies). Each ply is laid with its grain running at right angles to the ply above and below it; then all are glued to each other under heat and pressure. This cross-lamination of layers spreads the grain strength in all directions, creating a panel that does not split and pound-for-pound is hard to beat for strength. For example, a strip of 1/2" plywood, properly supported to keep it from sagging, will hold more books than a 3/4" pine board of the same dimensions. And at today's prices, it is sometimes cheaper to rip a plywood panel into strips than to buy pine shelving.

To memorize all the grades and classifications for every plywood available is unnecessary. If you walk into your local lumberyard and say you want one good side and one not so good, or two good sides, or junk on both sides, or whatever, they will give it to you. You can inspect it before you buy it and you do not have to worry about A-A, A-B, B-D, C-D grades or any of the other nomen-

PLYWOOD GRADES FOR INTERIOR USE

GRADE	FACE	BACK
A-A	A	A
A-B	A	B
A-D	A	D
B-D	B	D
C-D	C	D

"A" means a clean, smooth side. "B" is almost an "A," but with some minor flaws. "C" is more flawed than "B." "D" may not be sanded, in addition to having splits and knotholes. If these definitions seem somewhat general it is because the standards in the industry have been changing lately. Compare an A-B grade made today with one made 20 years ago and you will be astounded at the difference in quality.

clatures plywood makers have devised to keep score of what they are manufacturing. However, you *do* have to mention the thickness and whether you want an exterior or interior grade. If you are looking for a particular veneer such as birch or hemlock, you have to specify that, too.

No matter what plywood you are working with there are some precautions to observe because of the nature of the material. Practically all of these precautions have to do with the face veneers, which are always very thin, and therefore tend to splinter.

Cutting Plywood. Always use a sharp saw blade. If you are foolish enough to attempt to cut up an entire 4'x8' panel that is more than ¼" thick with a handsaw, it has to be one that can both rip and crosscut (you may be ripping the face ply, but at the same time you are also crosscutting at least one ply underneath) so pick a saw that has 8-11 teeth per inch. Saw with the good side *up* and keep the blade as parallel to the wood as possible. You can further reduce splintering if you tack a piece of scrap under the panel and saw that along with the plywood. If you are ripping all 8' of a ¾" panel, have an extra bowl of Wheaties before you start, because you are in for a long day. When your arm gets tired and you switch to a sabre or portable power saw, turn the good face of the panel *down.* The teeth on both of these tools pull upward and will tear at the top ply facing you. The radial arm and table saw blades rotate their teeth downward, so when cutting plywood with either of them have the good face *up.*

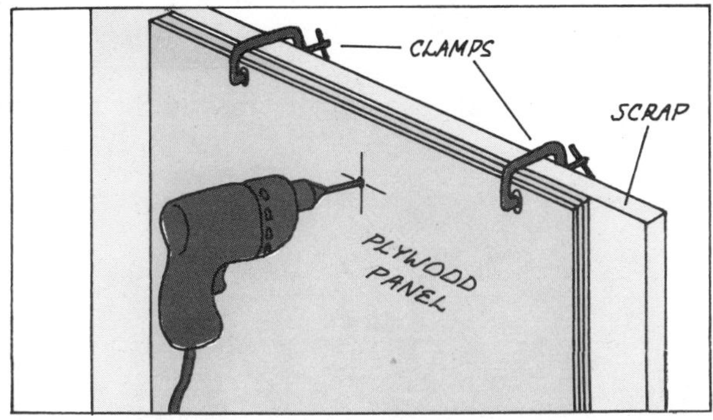

The purpose of clamping scrap behind a plywood panel is to protect the edges around your drill bit or saw blade from lifting away from the panel. So the tighter the scrap is clamped, the more support it will give the veneer.

Drilling, Planing and Sanding. Splintering also occurs whenever you drill plywood. The drill goes in all right, but it will chew up the back of the panel coming out. To avoid this, you can drill the panel until the pilot comes through, then turn it over and complete the hole by drilling from the opposite side. Or, clamp a piece of scrap behind the plywood and drill through both the plywood and the scrap.

The concept to remember is that veneer is very thin, and therefore fragile. Anytime you poke something through the back of it, or scrape against its edges, where it has minimal strength, veneer will chip. This is particularly true when you plane or sand a plywood edge. When you are planing, always work from the outside edge of the veneer toward the center of the panel. Again, use a sharp blade and take very shallow cuts.

The same rule applies when you are working with sandpaper. The faces of plywood seldom need sanding before a primer-sealer is put on, but the edges probably will. In fact, the edges appear to get nice and "hard" after sanding—but don't be fooled: they will still soak up paint like the sponges they really are unless you fill them with spackle, wood putty or wallboard compound first.

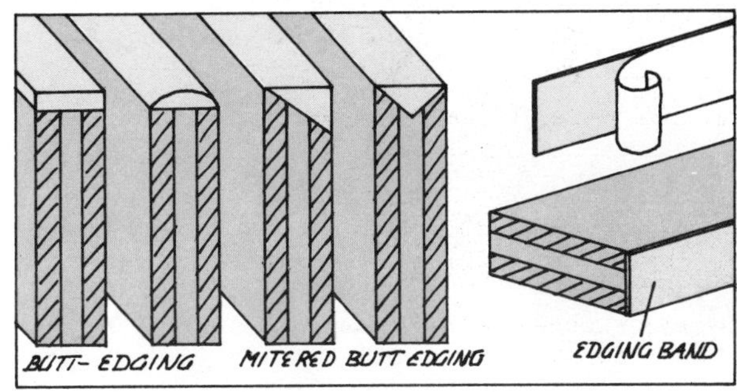

Plywood edges can also be covered with decorative molding, a flat strip of wood, or edge banding sold at hardware stores.

There are some other crafty ways of hiding an unsightly plywood edge. You can tack a piece of molding or trim over it, using glue and nails. You can cut a groove in the edge and fit a piece of plywood or molding into it, although that is a little tricky unless you have a molding head and the proper blades. If you are making a joint, say between the side and top of a cabinet, you can rabbet the exposed side down to about ⅛" thickness and let that act as a veneer for the overlapping edge. Or, you can buy strips of veneer sold as edge banding and glue them to the edge. Some of the edge banding is sold with a pressure-activated adhesive already on it.

Some plywood manufacturers claim you can make any kind of joint with plywood and, if you put it together with glue and nails or screws, it will hold. With thicknesses over ½", that is for the most part true. But remember that with a butt or miter joint you have to nail into the edge of the wood. At best, the edge of any wood has minimal holding power. At worst, a plywood edge ½" or

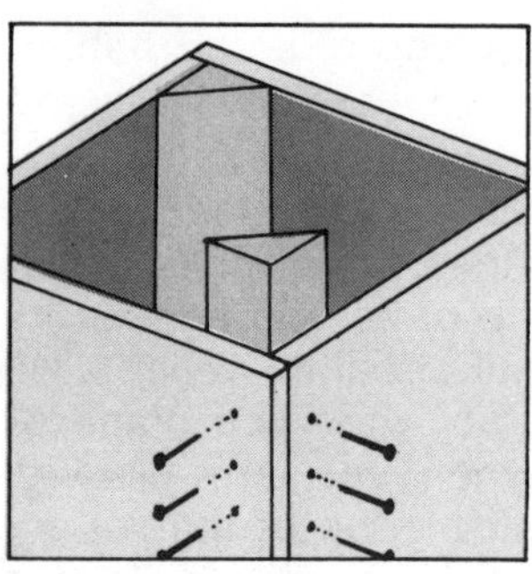

Plywood that is ½" or less in thickness does not have enough edge to support the weight of the wood. Any corner joints that are made should have support blocks glued and nailed or screwed to the sides of the plywood.

less in thickness has practically no grip at all. In other words, if you are joining ½" (or thinner) plywood and have to fasten into an edge, do not trust the joint. Put a corner block behind it and nail into it through the face of the plywood. Or use a glue you can trust.

See Chapter 5 for the proper nail and screw sizes to use with different plywood thicknesses. See Chapter 8 for techniques used in finishing plywood.

CHAPTER 4

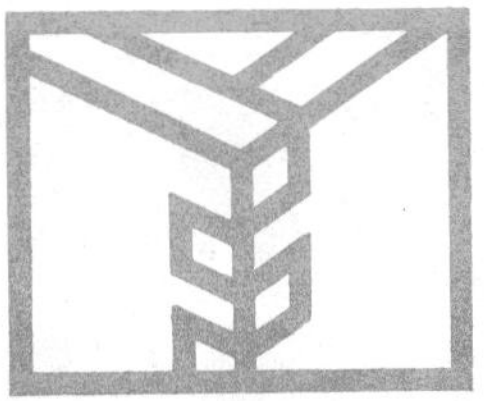

Cuts, Bends and Joints

Cuts, Bends and Joints

There is a time-honored ritual that is always performed before any piece of wood can be sawed. Sometimes, it is an instantaneous act; often, it becomes a painstaking process. But it is a pattern you have probably been repeating for years without ever identifying it as the ancient rite that it really is.

The ritual begins when a piece of stock is selected for cutting. If there are many pieces to choose from, then the decision may be complicated, for such variables as size, strength, purpose and grain must all be taken into account. Once a piece of stock has been chosen, men have been known to spend days examining it, mumbling to themselves, gradually answering a series of questions: Which part of the grain will look best in the finished work? What are the exact dimensions of the finished piece? How can the wood be used to take advantage of its maximum strength? What kinds of saw cuts must be made? Frequently, a precise, measured picture is drawn on the stock using a rule, or a T-square, or a curve. Then it is remeasured and redrawn until it is known to be a perfect design of the shape that will be formed from the raw lumber. Only then is the best available tool "set up" and carefully made ready to perform the cutting that is to be done.

When all this pre-planning is complete, the saw and wood are finally brought together. If it is a particularly beautiful piece of wood and the critical decisions have been hard come by, you may find yourself taking a deep breath, or letting a silent prayer flash through your mind just before the steel teeth of the saw blade bite into the fibers of the wood. Suddenly, the idea of changing the shape of a piece of wood forever more becomes an irrevocable fact.

Saw Cuts and Blades

The decisions that must be made at each step of the pre-cutting ritual are multiple, and not always obvious. There are, for example, only 10 ways of sawing up a piece of lumber—four crosscuts, two end cuts, two edge cuts and two rip cuts. But these ten can be combined into an unlimited number of variations, creating an infinite variety of wood shapes and forms.

Crosscut. A simple, right-angle cut across the grain, with the saw blade set at 90°.

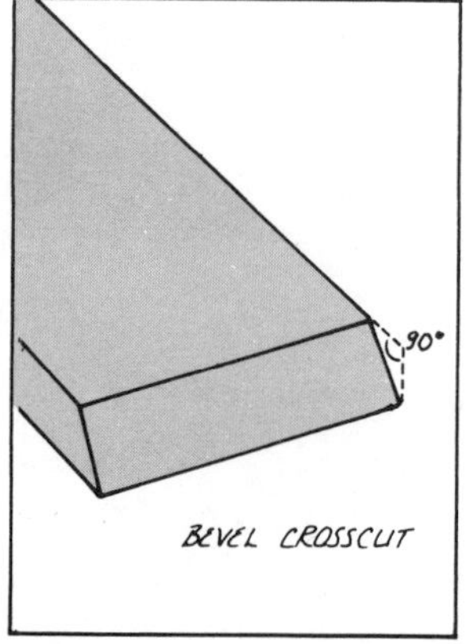

Bevel Crosscut. The same as a crosscut, except that the saw blade is at any angle other than 90°.

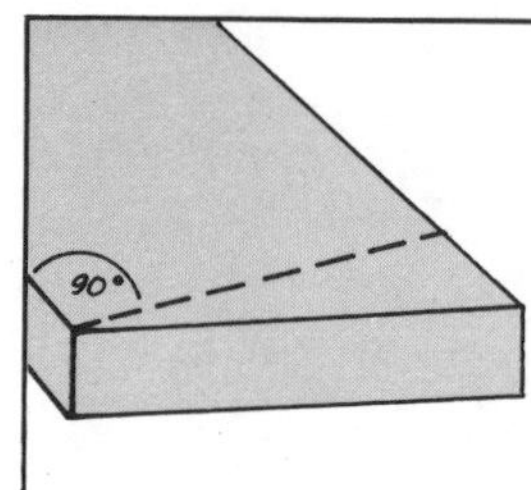

Miter Crosscut. Any angled crosscut with the blade set at 90°. Common usage of the term "miter" assumes that the angle of cut is 45°, but technically it can be anything other than a right angle.

HOW TO COMPUTE MITER AND BEVEL ANGLES

Any closed construction (triangle, square, octagon, etc.) that has all of its sides equal in length requires that the sides all be joined at the same angle. To compute the correct miter or bevel setting for any closed construction, simply divide 360° by the number of sides. Subtract the result from 180° and divide by two. The result is the number of degrees at which the saw blade is set.

Examples

no. sides	angle of miter or bevel setting
3	30°
4	45°
5	54°
6	60°
7	64.3°
8	67.5°
9	70°
10	72°

COMPOUND-ANGLE SETTINGS

PITCH OF SIDE	NUMBER OF SIDES 3	4	5	6	7	8	9	10
0°	B- 0.0° M-60.0°	B- 0.0° M-45.0°	B- 0.0° M-36.0°	B- 0.0° M-30.0°	B- 0.0° M-26.0°	B- 0.0° M-22.5°	B- 0.0° M-20.0°	B- 0.0° M-18.0°
5°	B- 3.5° M-50.0°	B- 3.5° M-45.0°	B- 3.0° M-36.0°	B- 2.5° M-30.0°	B- 2.5° M-25.5°	B- 2.0° M-22.5°	B- 2.0° M-20.0°	B- 2.0° M-18.0°
10°	B- 8.0° M-59.5°	B- 7.0° M-44.5°	B- 6.0° M-35.5°	B- 5.0° M-29.5°	B- 4.5° M-25.5°	B- 4.0° M-22.0°	B- 3.5° M-19.5°	B- 3.0° M-17.5°
15°	B-12.5° M-58.5°	B-10.5° M-44.0°	B- 8.5° M-34.0°	B- 7.5° M-29.0°	B- 6.5° M-25.0°	B- 5.5° M-22.0°	B- 5.0° M-19.5°	B- 4.5° M-17.5°
20°	B-18.5° M-57.5°	B-14.0° M-43.0°	B-11.5° M-34.0°	B-10.0° M-23.5°	B- 8.5° M-24.5°	B- 7.5° M-21.5°	B- 6.5° M-19.0°	B- 6.0° M-17.0°
25°	B-22.0° M-56.0°	B-17.5° M-41.5°	B-14.5° M-33.0°	B-12.0° M-27.5°	B-10.5° M-23.5°	B- 9.0° M-20.5°	B- 8.0° M-18.5°	B- 7.5° M-16.5°
30°	B-26.5° M-53.5°	B-21.0° M-40.0°	B-17.0° M-32.0°	B-14.5° M-26.5°	B-12.5° M-22.5°	B-11.0° M-19.5°	B- 9.5° M-17.5°	B- 8.5° M-16.0°
35°	B-31.0° M-51.5°	B-24.0° M-38.0°	B-19.5° M-30.0°	B-16.5° M-25.0°	B-15.0° M-21.5°	B-12.5° M-19.0°	B-11.0° M-16.5°	B-10.0° M-15.0°
40°	B-35.0° M-48.5°	B-27.0° M-36.0°	B-22.0° M-28.5°	B-18.5° M-23.5°	B-16.0° M-20.0°	B-14.0° M-17.5°	B-12.5° M-15.5°	B-11.5° M-14.0°
45°	B-39.0° M-46.5°	B-30.0° M-33.5°	B-24.5° M-26.5°	B-20.5° M-22.0°	B-17.5° M-19.0°	B-15.5° M-16.5°	B-13.5° M-14.5°	B-12.5° M-13.0°
50°	B-42.5° M-42.0°	B-33.0° M-31.0°	B-27.5° M-24.5°	B-22.0° M-21.5°	B-19.0° M-17.5°	B-16.5° M-15.0°	B-15.0° M-13.5°	B-13.5° M-12.0°
55°	B-46.0° M-38.0°	B-35.5° M-28.0°	B-28.5° M-22.0°	B-23.5° M-18.5°	B-20.5° M-15.5°	B-18.0° M-13.5°	B-16.0° M-12.0°	B-14.5° M-11.0°
60°	B-49.5° M-34.5°	B-37.5° M-24.5°	B-30.5° M-19.5°	B-25.5° M-16.5°	B-21.5° M-14.0°	B-19.0° M-12.0°	B-17.0° M-10.5°	B-15.5° M- 9.5°
65°	B-52.5° M-29.0°	B-39.5° M-21.5°	B-32.0° M-17.0°	B-26.5° M-14.0°	B-23.0° M-12.0°	B-20.0° M-10.5°	B-18.0° M- 9.0°	B-16.5° M- 8.0°
70°	B-55.0° M-24.0°	B-41.5° M-17.5°	B-33.5° M-13.5°	B-28.0° M-11.5°	B-24.0° M- 9.5°	B-21.0° M- 8.5°	B-18.5° M- 7.5°	B-17.0° M- 6.5°
75°	B-57.0° M-18.5°	B-43.0° M-13.0°	B-34.5° M-10.5°	B-29.0° M- 8.5°	B-24.5° M- 7.0°	B-21.5° M- 6.5°	B-19.0° M- 5.5°	B-17.5° M- 5.0°
80°	B-58.5° M-13.0°	B-44.0° M- 9.0°	B-35.5° M- 7.0°	B-29.5° M- 6.0°	B-25.0° M- 5.0°	B-22.0° M- 4.0°	B-19.5° M- 3.5°	B-18.0° M- 4.0°
85°	B-59.5° M- 7.0°	B-44.5° M- 4.5°	B-36.0° M- 3.5°	B-30.0° M- 3.0°	B-25.5° M- 2.5°	B-22.5° M- 2.0°	B-20.0° M- 1.5°	B-18.0° M- 1.5°
90°	B-60.0° M- 0.0°	B-45.0° M- 0.0°	B-36.0° M- 0.0°	B-30.0° M- 0.0°	B-26.0° M- 0.0°	B-22.5° M- 0.0°	B-20.0° M- 0.0°	B-18.0° M- 0.0°

Each B (Bevel) and M (Miter) setting is given to the closest 0.5°.

Compound Crosscut. Neither the angle of the crosscut nor the blade are at 90°. When building a closed structure of three or more sides, the quickest way of computing the proper compound-angle settings is to consult the chart above.

Straight Rip Cut. A right-angle cut in the direction of the grain, with the blade at 90°.

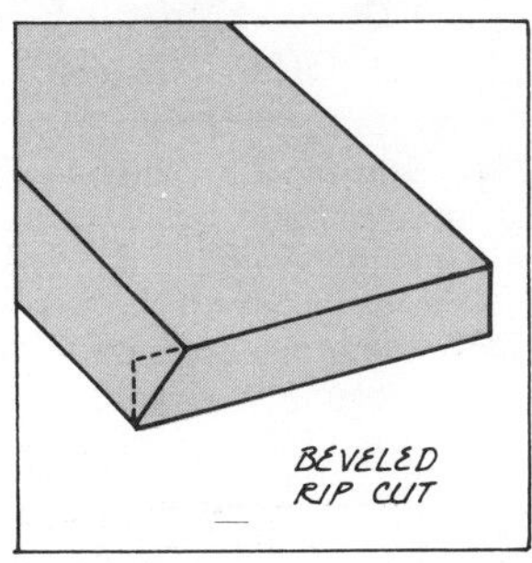

Beveled Rip Cut. The same as a straight rip cut, except that the blade is at any angle other than 90°.

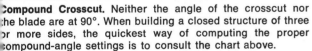

Straight End Cut. This is merely a slice through the end of a board, across the grain.

Straight Edge Cut. The same as an end cut, except that it is made with the grain.

Bevel End Cut. A slice across the grain at any angle other than 90°.

Bevel Edge Cut. A slice with the grain at any angle other than 90°.

Technically, any saw can make all of the basic cuts, including their curved variations. From a practical point of view, there are hand rip saws and crosscut saws to choose from as well as fret saws for cutting curves. The sabre, jig and band saws are designed to handle any curve, while the hand circular, radial arm and table saws are preferable when making straight cuts. Added to this, there are several kinds of circular blades that can be used on the stationary machines and should be taken into consideration whenever a choice of cuts is being made.

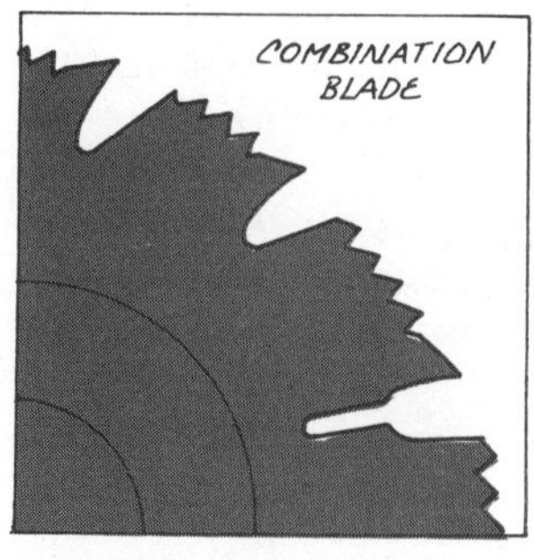

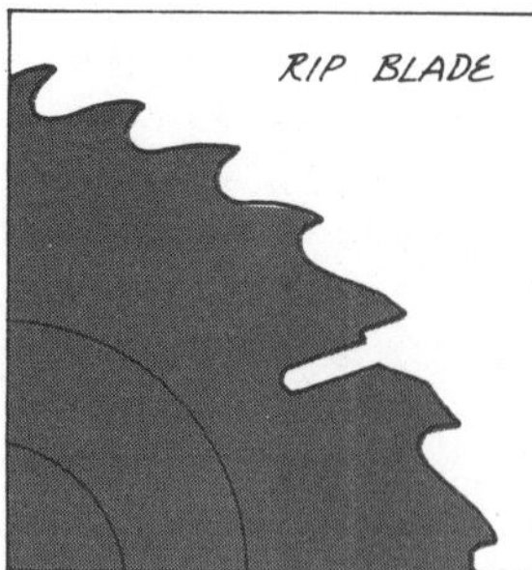

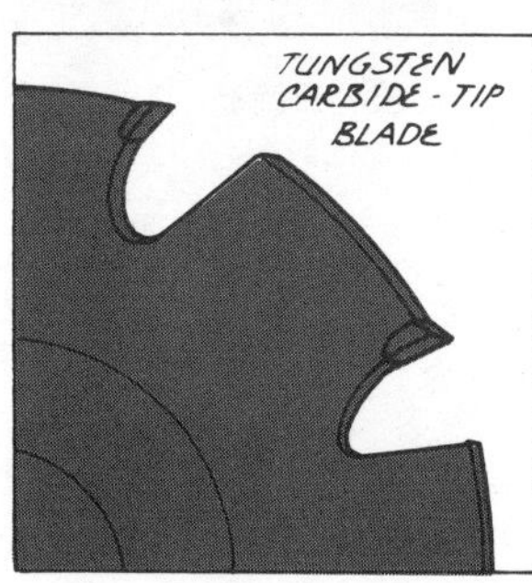

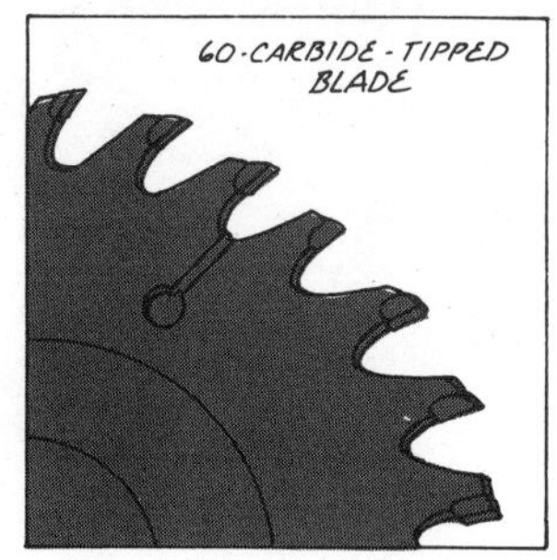

Combination Blade. Distinguished by the expansion slots which help it run true, this kind of blade will handle miters and crosscuts as well as rips.

Rip Blade. This usually has an extra-deep gullet that helps clear sawdust away from the teeth. It will make any kind of cut, but it is designed for ripping.

Plywood and Veneer Blade. Boasting around 200 teeth (in a 10" blade) this is like having a school of piranha fish chomping away at the wood with such tiny bites that it has no chance to splinter. Excellent for laminates, plastics and veneers as well as plywood.

General Purpose Tungsten Carbide-Tip Blade. This has only a dozen or so teeth, but they are made of carbide. Carbide is so strong that it will last five times longer than normal blades before it needs sharpening. The general purpose blades will cut just about anything except ferrous metals and masonry.

60-Carbide-Tipped Blade. With the carbide tips alternately beveled, this will cut anything too. But it does so with almost a satin finish.

Dado Blades. The "dial-a-width" adjustable dado at the left also has carbide tips. It is easier to change the cutting width with this than with the dado set on the right because it does not have to be taken off the saw arbor. Either the blade or the set is a tremendous time- and labor-saver for anyone who is making a lot of joints.

Bending Wood

The magic that can be wrought with a saw extends to still another activity, called kerfing. A kerf is the width of any saw blade (about ⅛"). Kerfing means the multiple use of the blade width to bend a piece of wood. The entire procedure for kerfing is shown in the four drawings on the next page.

Historically, the oldest method of bending wood is with moisture and heat. But that is a tricky game to play, even if you have the right equipment. In the first place, boiling water tends to weaken most wood fibers, so don't run out and fire up that caldron in your back yard. What you need is a large steam oven that can produce a constant supply of steam at a constant pressure for long periods of time. You also have to have a kiln and an assortment of clamping devices, preferably the kind that are hydraulically controlled.

The wood to be bent is first kiln-dried to bring its moisture content down to around 15%, then put in the steam oven. As a rule of thumb, figure one hour of steaming for every inch of board thickness. When the wood is pliable enough to bend, clamp it in the proper shape and let it dry completely.

A far simpler method, which also produces the strongest finished product, is laminating. In this process, several pieces of thin material are bent (one at a time) around the desired curve and then glued to each other. If the curve is not too severe and you want to achieve maximum strength, it is possible to cross-bond the lamination. In this case, every other piece will be glued with its grain running at 90° to the layers above and below it. However, crossbonding makes bending much more difficult and usually requires some heavy clamping.

A smooth layer of glue is applied between each laminate and all of the pieces are then clamped together until the glue is completely dry. If you are dealing with a sharp curve, each laminate may need to be steamed until it is flexible enough to make the bend. Because the pieces are thin, not too much steaming should be necessary, but be certain all of the wood is dry before you do any glueing, or the glue will not hold.

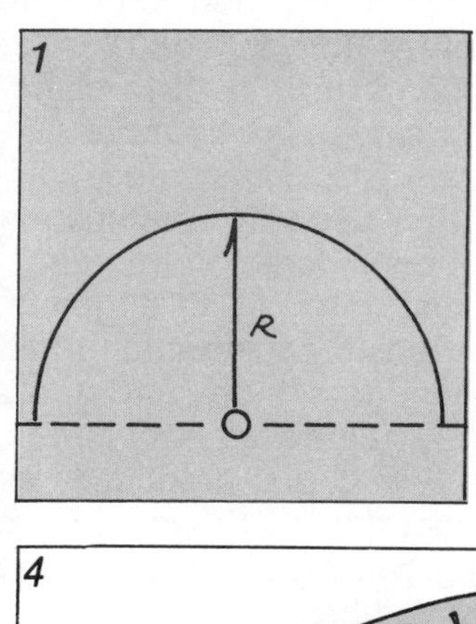

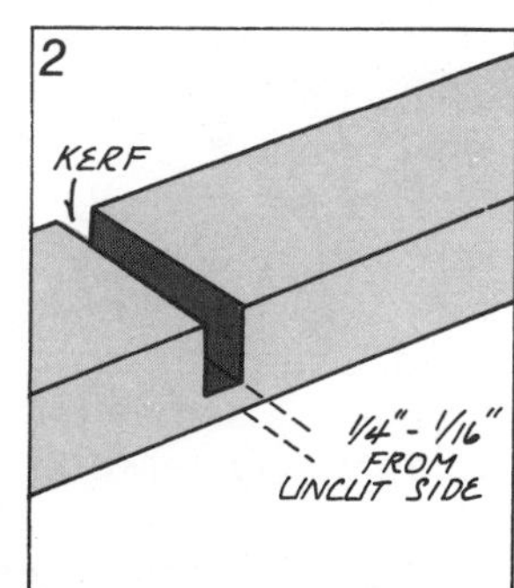

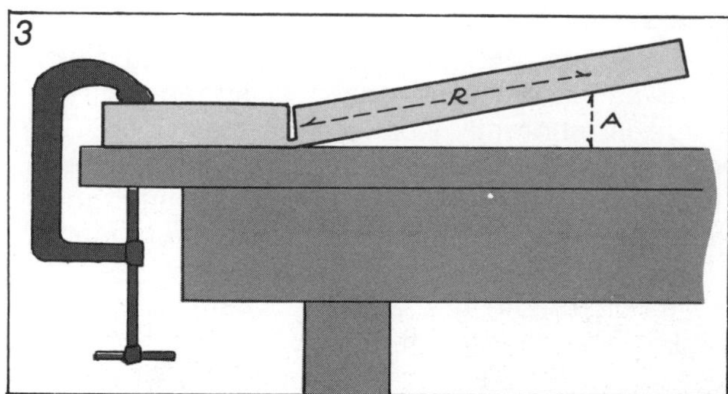

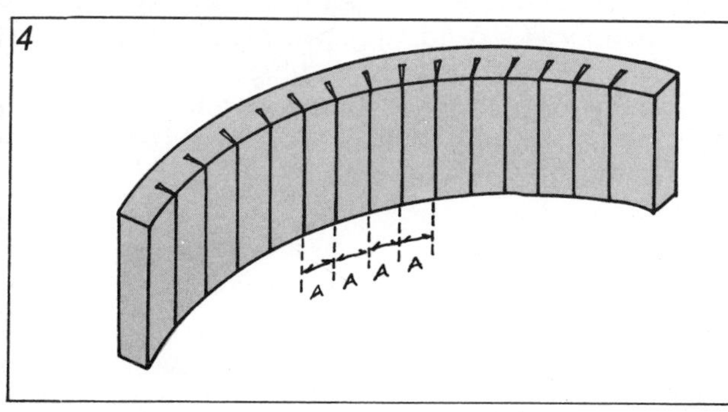

1) Measure the radius of the curve that the bent piece will follow.
2) Cut one kerf in the piece. The kerf should penetrate to between ¼" and $\frac{1}{16}$" of the uncut side of the stock.
3) Clamp one end of the stock to a bench top and bend the other end upward until the kerf is just closed. At a point from the kerf equal to the length of the radius, measure the height of the piece from the tabletop. This measurement (A) becomes the distance between each kerf.
4) Cut a series of kerfs the full length of the piece and fill each one with glue. Bend the piece slowly into place. Kerfing is particularly useful when dealing with plywood, although it will work with any solid stock.
5) While kerfing and steaming both tend to weaken the stock being bent, lamination actually strengthens it.

The Ins and Outs of Joints

Having completed the ritual of cutting pieces of wood to size, the next question is: "How will they be joined?" There are 10 basic wood joints that can be used in cabinetmaking, with at least a score of variations and combinations. The most useful and versatile tool to have when making almost any joint is the dado blade, but many joints can be cut with multiple passes of a normal saw blade. There are also several router bits that can be used to make specific joints, including the dovetail. Therefore, a drill press is handy to have, and a jointer will make rabbets and tenons. The joints themselves have different qualities and applications that are worth noting here.

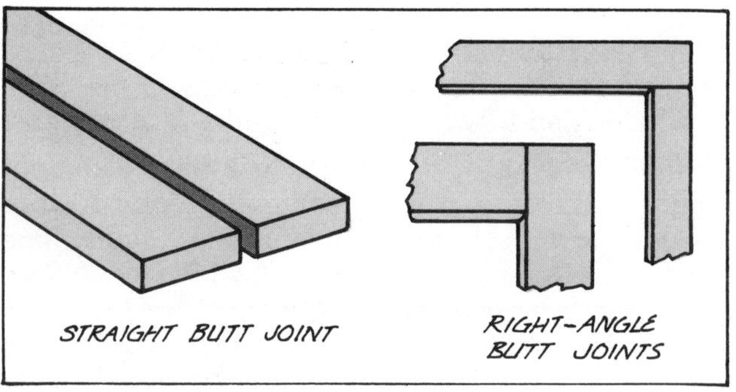

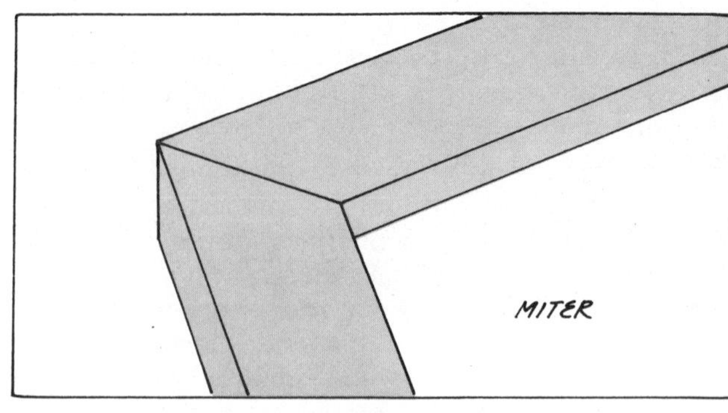

Butt

A butt joint is made when any two edges come together and are held by glue or fasteners. The two pieces can be side by side or they may form a right angle. Because only two surfaces meet, the butt is inherently weaker than most joints.

Uses. Right-angle butt joints are commonly used in framing and making boxes or assembling molding. Straight butt joints are made when boards are laid next to each other, and in putting veneers together to create grain designs.

Assembly. Since the butt is a weak joint, it is most successful when backed by some kind of brace. The two edges coming together should be smooth and should touch at all points. If glue is used, it should be applied evenly over 100% of both edges.

Tools. A butt can be made with any saw. Some sanding or planing may be necessary to assure complete contact.

Miter

Essentially, the miter is an angled butt joint. The angle can be anything other than 90° or 180° (at which point it would become a butt). It is somewhat stronger than a butt since slightly more surface is put into play, owing to the slanted cuts. However, the miter is often used in combination with other joints, giving it considerable strength.

Uses. The miter is the most universal of all joints. It is often used as part of basic construction in all kinds of cabinetwork. Ends, tops, sides and fronts of furniture are frequently joined by 45° miters. They are used in assembling doors, practically all moldings and cabinet decorative work, and it is an effective means of joining two pieces of the same thickness but of different widths.

Assembly. Miter joints should touch at all points and should be glued. They may also be nailed or screwed from both sides.

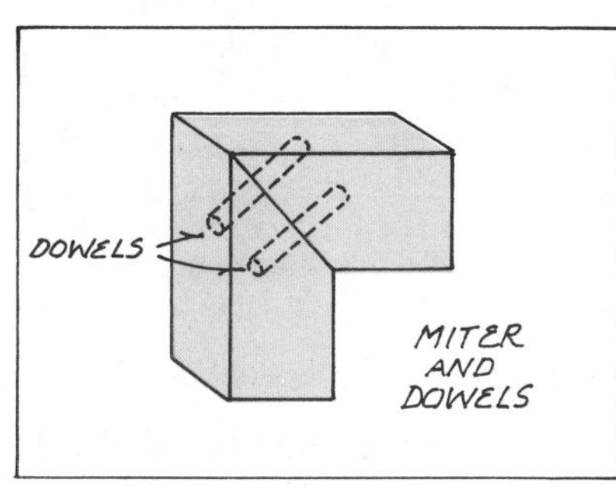

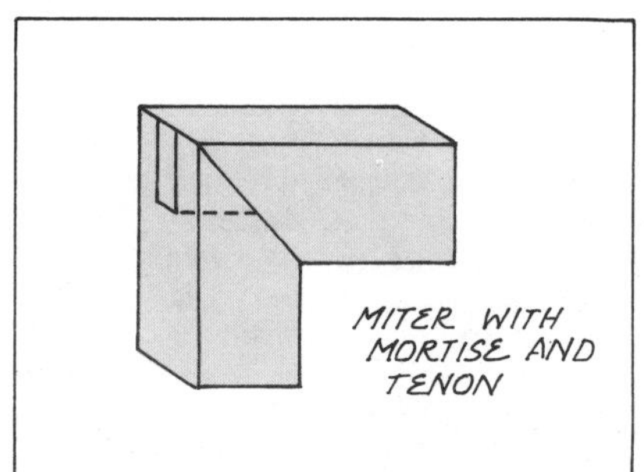

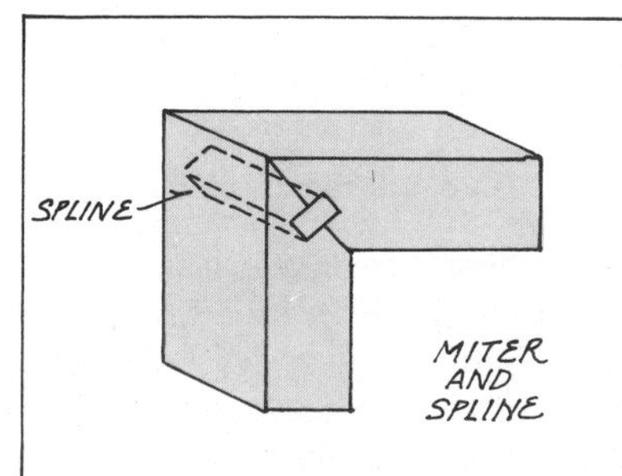

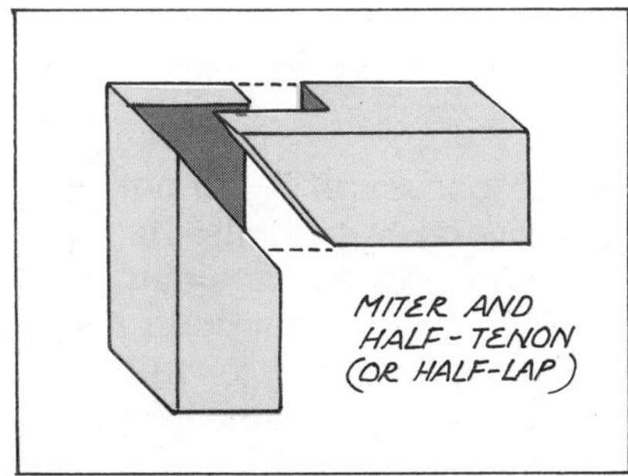

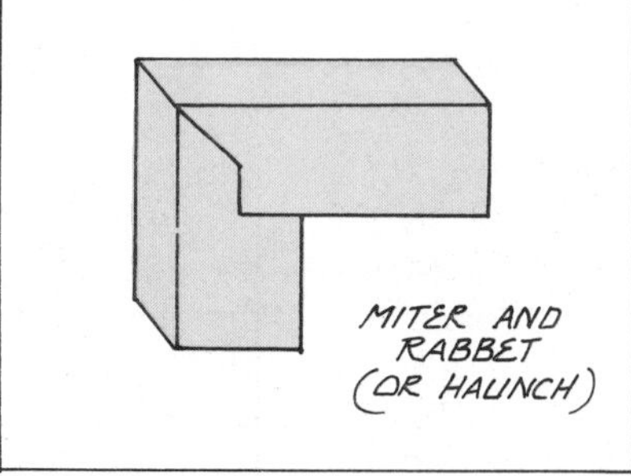

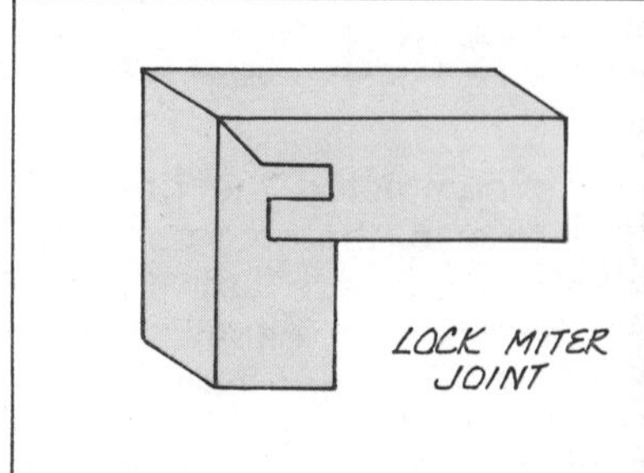

Tools. A miter box provides an essential guide when you are sawing with anything but an aligned table or radial arm saw. Even so, some planing or sanding may be necessary to assure a proper fit between edges.

Variations. The miter can be used with dowels, mortises, splines, half-tenons (or half-laps), rabbets and haunches.

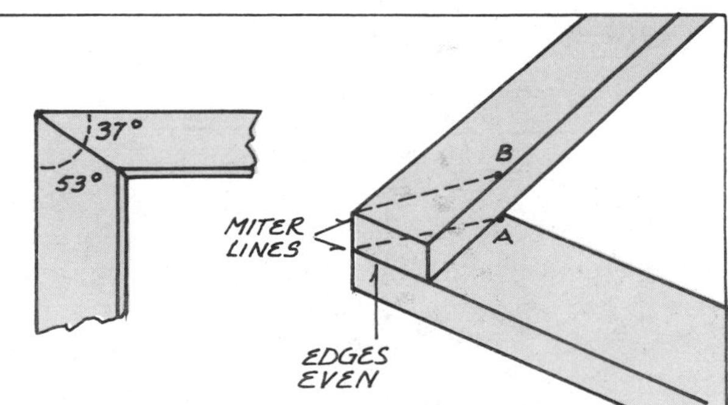

How To Determine A Miter Made Of Varying Widths. Place the narrower piece across the piece it will joint, making sure the outer edges are aligned. Mark the inside corner where the two pieces meet (A). Draw a diagonal from point A to the outside corner of the wide piece. Now reverse the pieces, putting the wider member on top of the narrower one and marking the inside corner (B). Draw a diagonal from point B to the outside corner of the narrower piece. The two diagonals are the miter lines. When they are cut and joined, the two pieces will form a right angle, even though the miter lines do not follow the same angle.

Dado

The strongest of all wood joints, this is essentially a trough cut out of one piece of wood that matches the dimensions of the piece fitted into it. The stock that is dadoed is weakened, but as soon as the slot is filled and glued, it is re-strengthened. If the dado is cut with the grain, it is called a plough.

Uses. Dadoes are primarily used in shelf assembly. A dado not only holds the shelf in place, but helps the entire project to establish its right angles. Dadoes are also used for recessing hardware (such as hinges) and as slots (or ploughs) to accept a panel in the center of door frames.

Assembly. The joint should be made with glue and usually nails can be toed into it, or driven from the outside.

Tools. The dado blade is made specifically for dadoes and ploughs, and can be used with any circular power saw. Multiple passes of a regular saw blade, a router, dado chipping tool, handsaw and chisel will all make dadoes.

Variations. When used as a half-lap, the dado is ideal for joining leg braces, while the housed dado joint provides an extra surface that can add stability. The stopped dado is a decorative feature used when there are to be no facings on the cabinet. The dado can also be used in its various forms to make box or drawer corners.

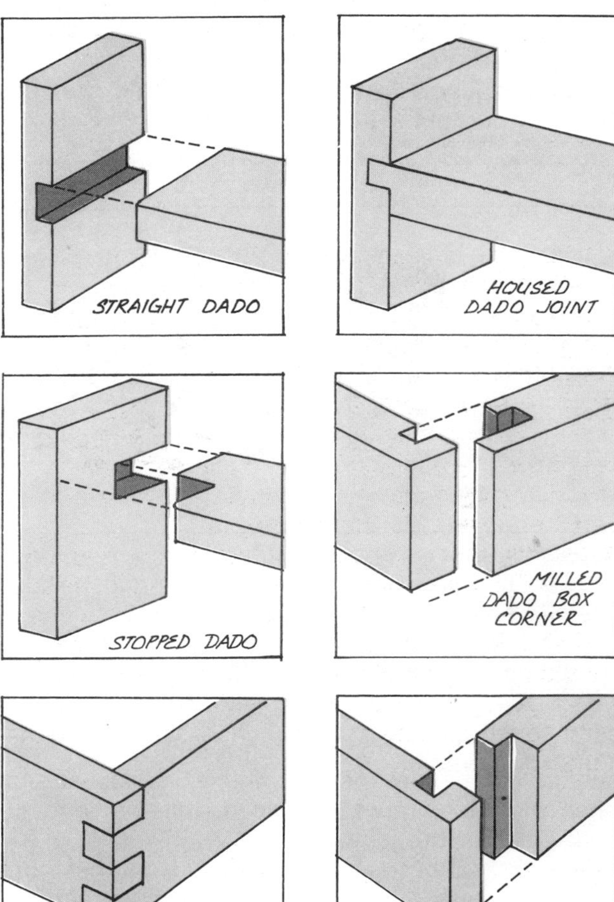

Spline (Feather or Tongue)

The spline is a thin strip of wood used to reinforce joints. It is a modified tongue and groove with both sides of the joint grooved to accept the spline as a tongue.

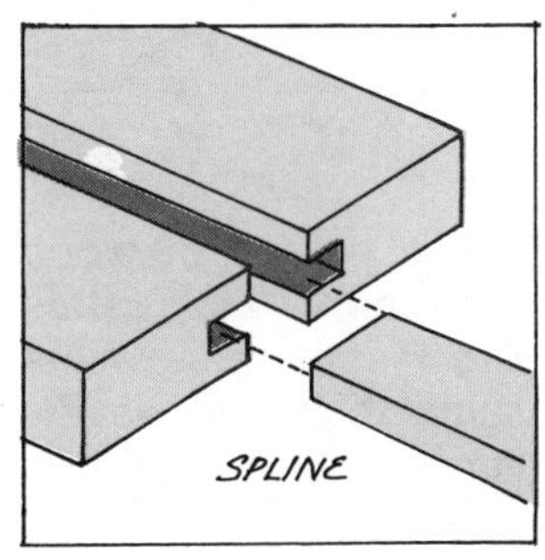

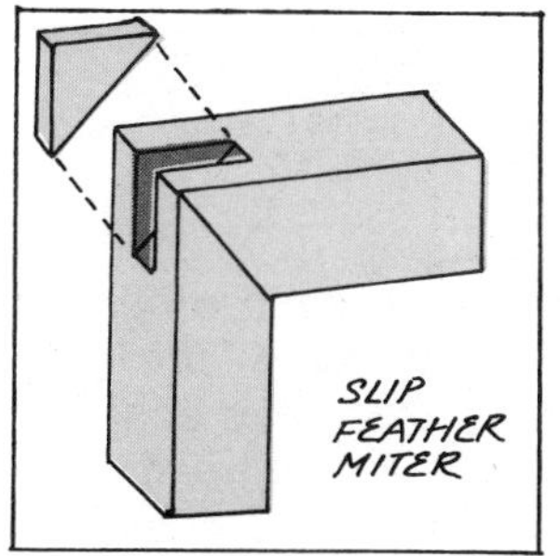

Uses. To strengthen such joints as the miter and butt.
Assembly. Grooves are cut into both joint edges. Both grooves are given a coat of glue and the spline is then forced into them.
Tools. A dado blade is preferable for cutting the grooves, although multiple passes with a normal blade will do the job.
Variations. The slip feather is a triangle that fits into only part of the joint.

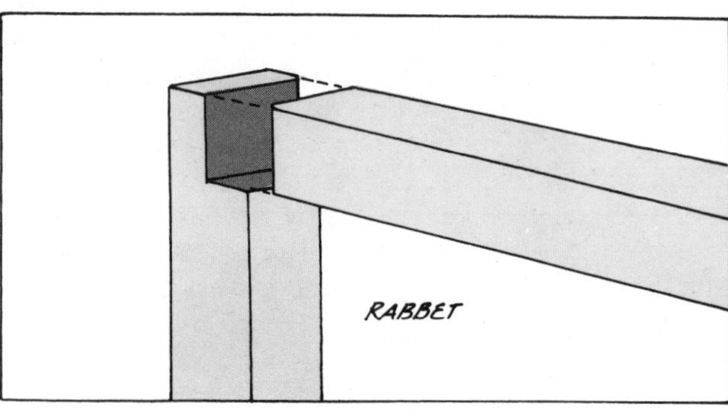

Rabbet

A notch cut out of either the length or width of a piece which conforms to the thickness of the stock that will join it. It amounts to a square slot, or dado, that ran out of space and fell off the edge of the work. It is stronger than a butt joint, if only because it has two extra glueing surfaces and often nails or screws can be driven into one or both sides of the joint.
Uses. The rabbet is widely used in cabinet corners, to recess the backs of cabinets, in window frames, and to join the top piece of a box to its sides.
Assembly. To assure a smooth outer edge, set the dado blade slightly wider than the rabbet and let it overhang the work. Glue, as well as nails or screws, should always be used with a rabbet joint.
Tools. The easiest way of making a rabbet is with dado blades, but it can also be cut with two intersecting passes of a regular saw blade. Jointers, routers and shapers will all make excellent rabbets.
Variations. See miter section for rabbet miter joint.

Lap

A lap joint is formed when two pieces of wood overlap each other. Usually, the term "lap" refers to reducing the overlapping sections so that together they achieve the same thickness as the stock being used. It is the simplest of all joints to make and is often combined with other joints.

Uses. Excellent for supports and to strengthen corners.
Assembly. Matching edges of the joint should be smooth and entirely covered with glue.
Tools. Any saw, dado blade, jointer, plane, chisel—even a sander—can be used to make a lap joint.
Variations. If you do not see one you like illustrated here, make up your own. The lap is extremely accommodating when it comes to combining with other joints.

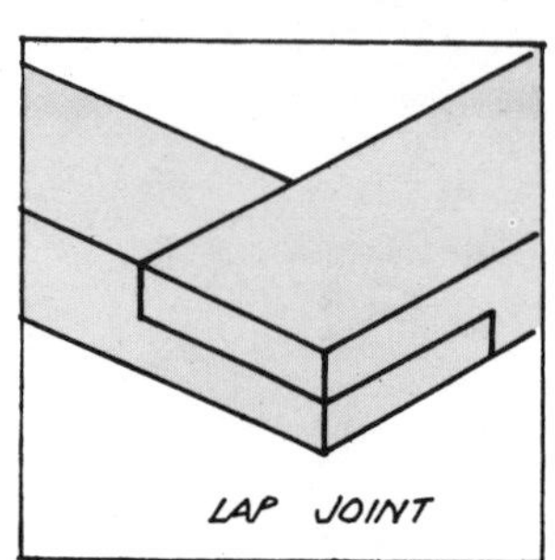

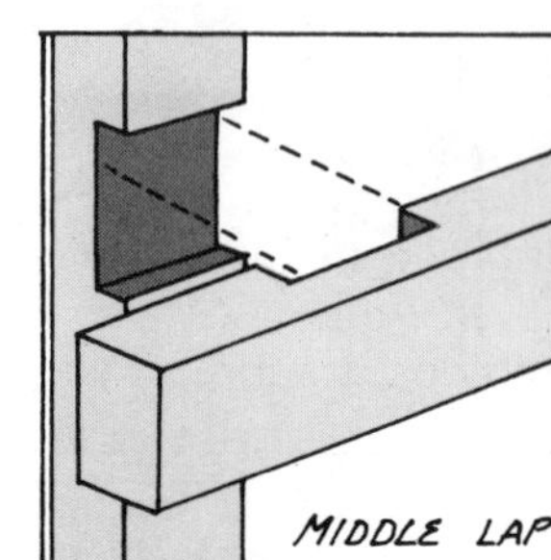

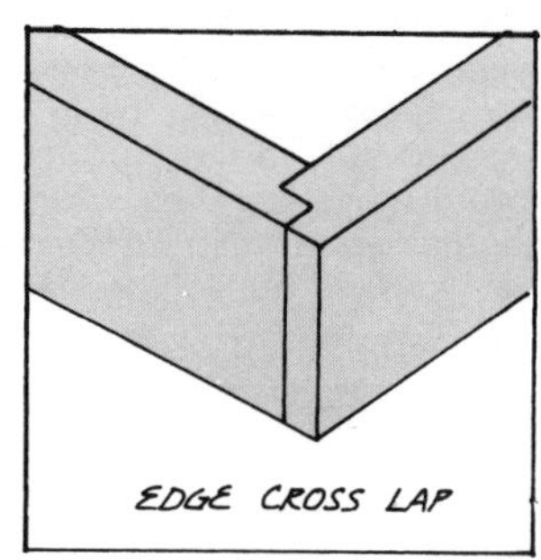

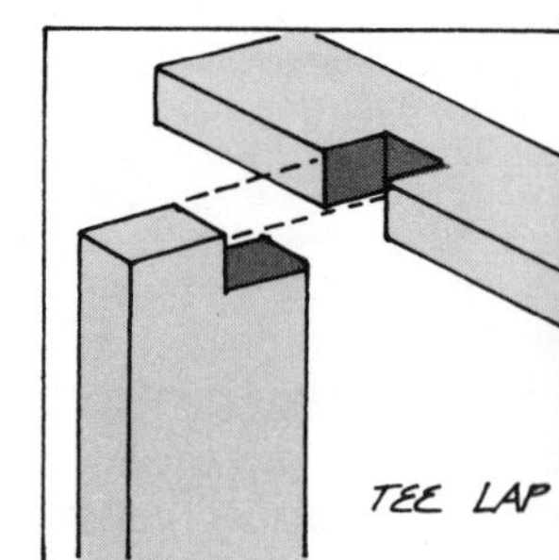

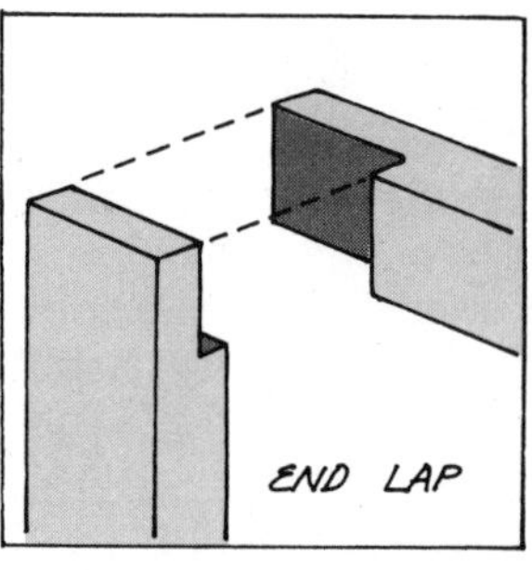

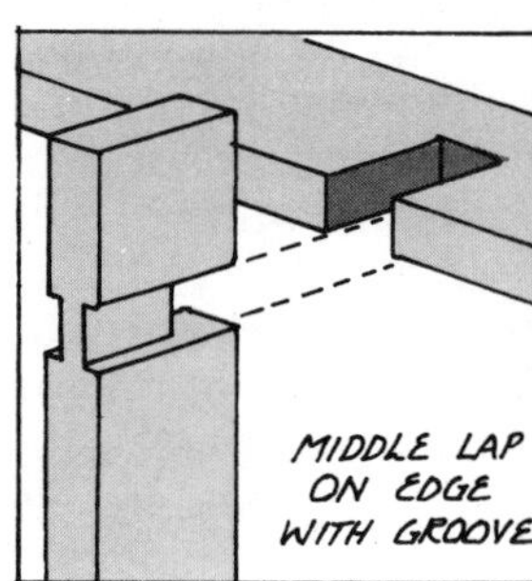

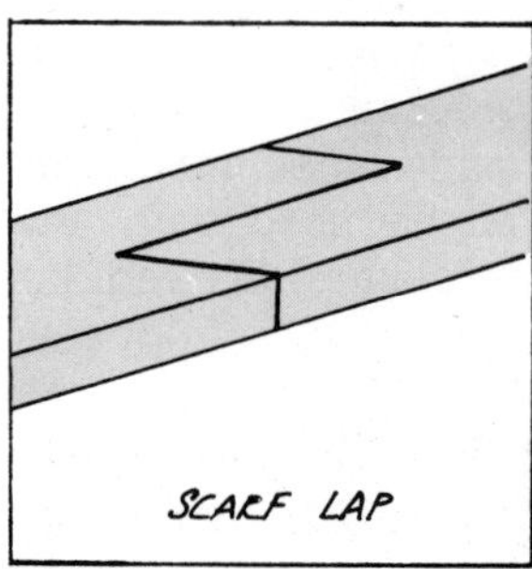

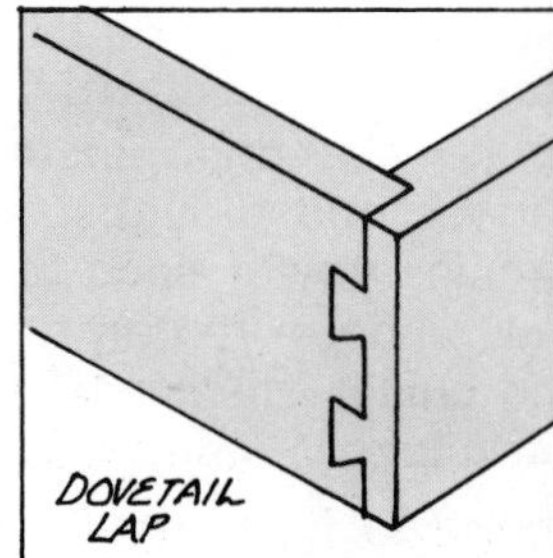

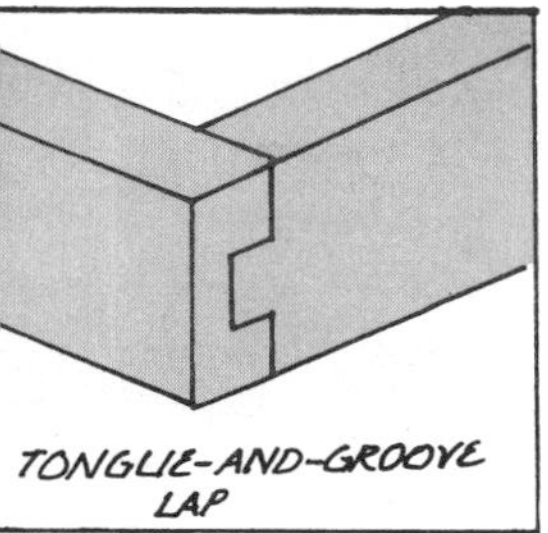

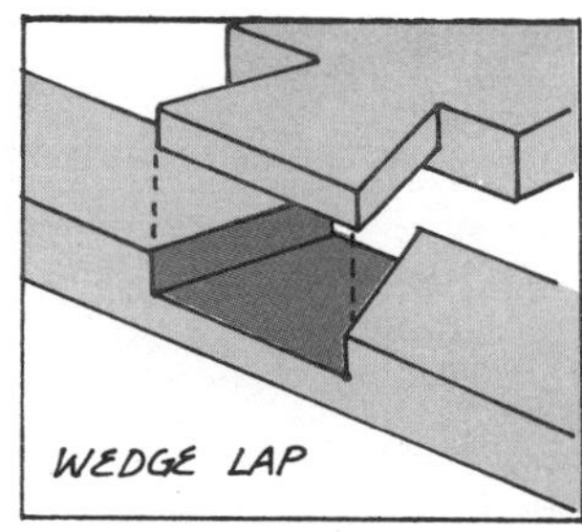

Tongue and Groove

effect, the tongue and groove is an open mor-se and tenon, with one edge grooved to accept tongue cut out of the joining edge.

ses. The best known use of tongue and groove is flooring, but it is an excellent joint for assem-ling two or more boards in almost any project. It also useful for holding the lips of cabinets or abletops, or the edging on plywood.

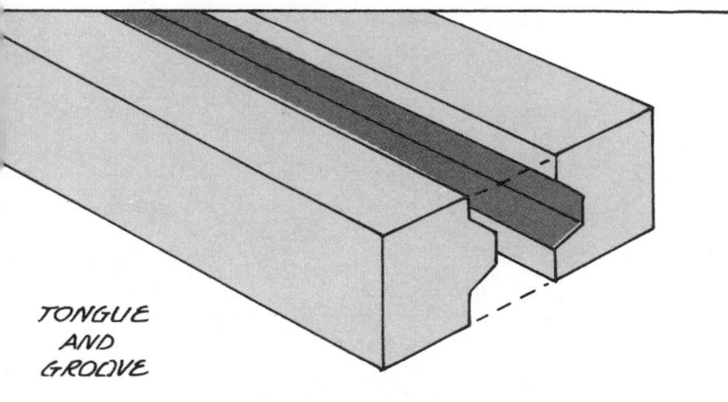

ssembly. The tongue must fit snugly in its match-g groove and still allow space for glueing.

ools. The easiest, most accurate way of making a ongue-and-groove joint is to use a molder head ith tongue-and-groove blades. If a molder head, r the stationary power saws to run it, are not vailable, a dado blade will do almost as well. A outer or drill press can also make the tongue and roove.

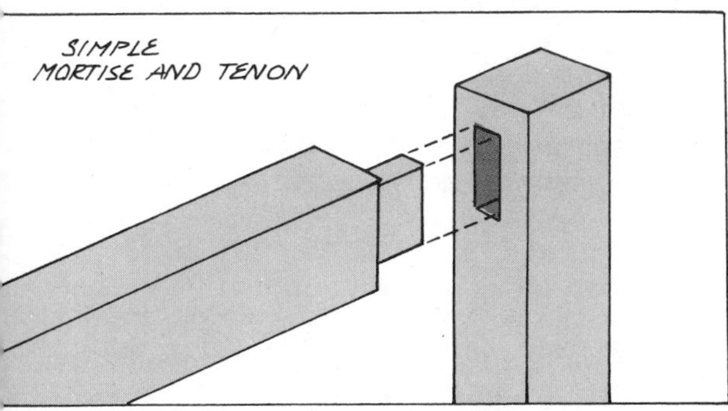

Mortise and Tenon

his is perhaps the most secure of all joints, tight nough to hold together—provided the pieces fit snugly—without glue or nails. With them, it is practically indestructible. The mortise is a rectangular hole bored in one of the joining pieces. The tenon is a rectangular peg carved from the opposite piece.

Uses. Cabinet facings, furniture rungs and door frames almost always use some form of the mortise and tenon. Nearly any situation that requires exceptional stability and squaring is a candidate for this joint.

Assembly. Care must be taken to be sure that the mortise and tenon are exactly in alignment. Whether glue and nails or screws are used depends on how the joint is being used.

Tools. The mortise can be made with augurs, router bits or drills. All of these make the holes. A chisel is needed to square off the round corners. A simpler way to make the mortise is to use a mortise machine, except practically no one short of a furniture manufacturer has one. However, there is a mortise attachment that can be used on a power drill that is economically feasible, and designed to cut square holes.

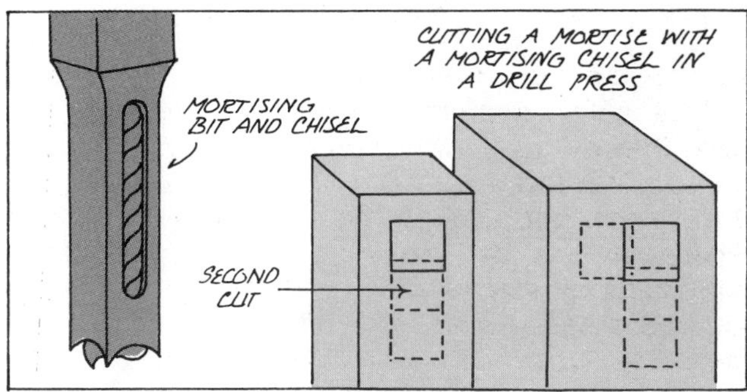

The tenon can be made with a dado blade or with multiple passes of a regular blade. A hand saw and chisel can also be used.

Variations. You can be about as creative inventing mortise and tenons as you can making lap joints. Some of the possibilities are illustrated here and on the following page.

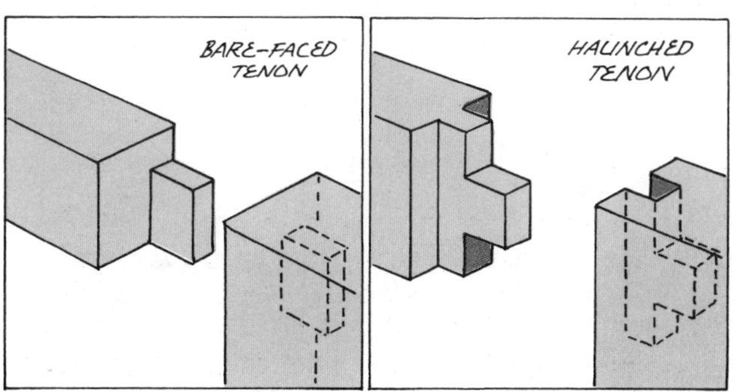

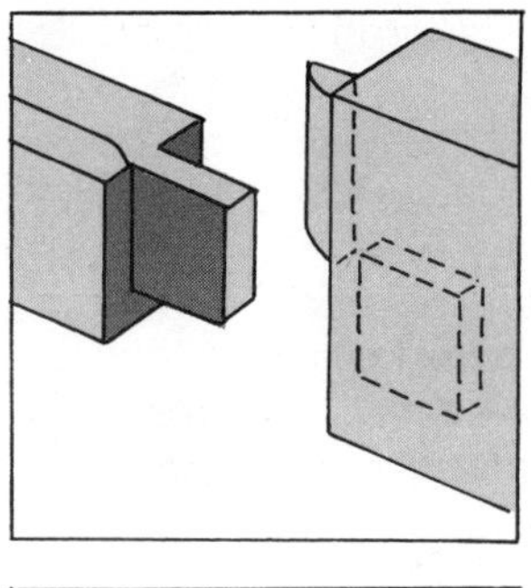

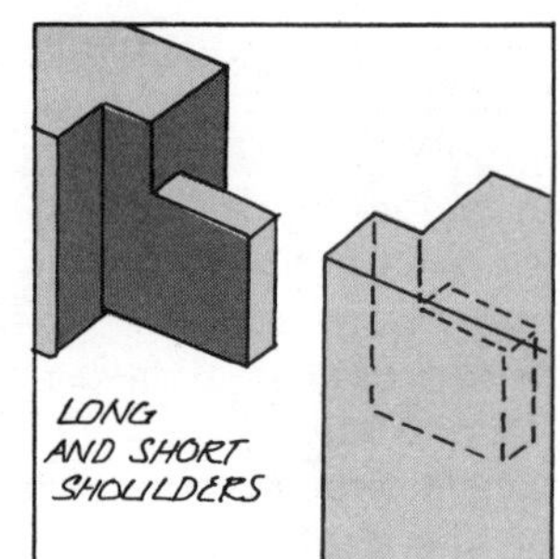

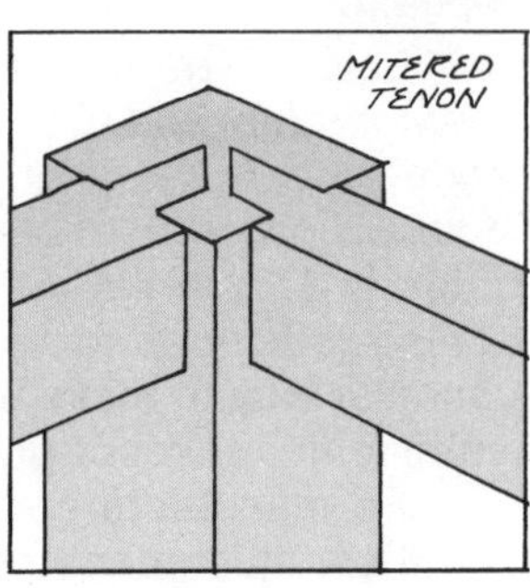

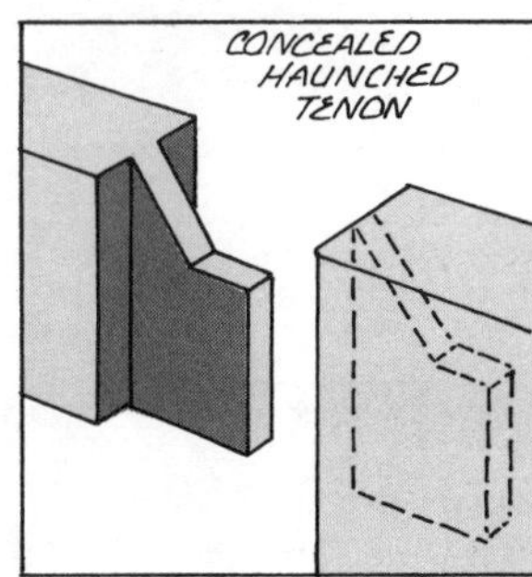

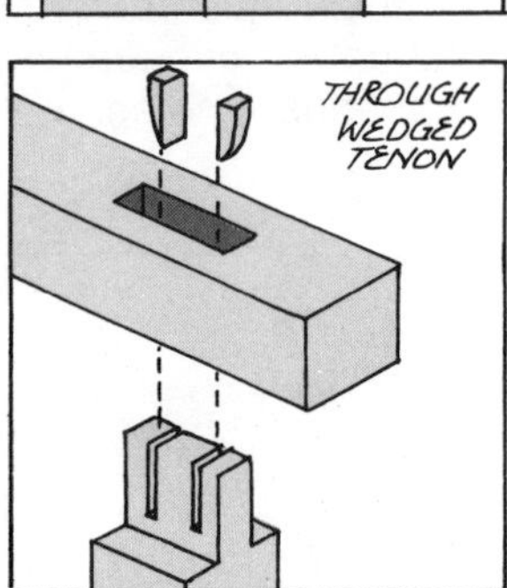

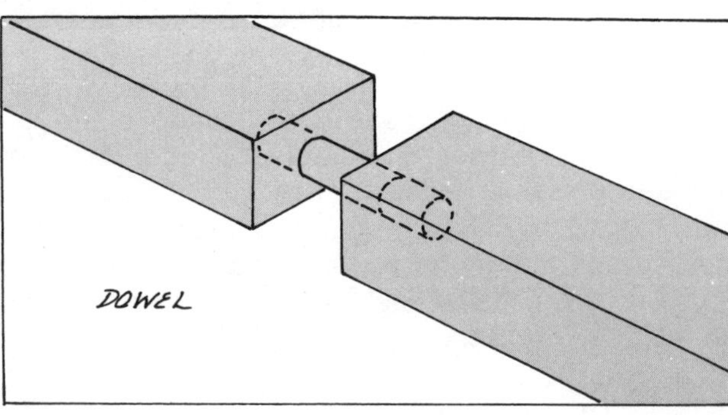

Dowel

Dowels are added to a butt or miter joint as a means of strengthening it. The dowel itself is a round peg inserted in a round hole. Two of them placed in the center of an end butt joint will make it about as strong as a mortise and tenon.

Uses. Excellent for putting two boards next to each other and keeping them together. Doweling has extensive use in all furniture and cabinet-making.

Assembly. The critical problem in doweling is to line up the holes with the pegs so that the joint comes out flush. Dowels are usually made of a hardwood such as maple or oak, but pine dowels are more readily available at lumberyards and in most cases are quite acceptable if properly fitted and glued. If you are working with a softwood dowel, cut a spiral groove around the barrel. This will allow excess glue in the hole to escape, as well as provide more glueing surface inside the joint.

Tools. A drill. The bit should be only slightly larger than the diameter of the dowel. Dowel centering pins are extremely useful for determining where the opposite hole should be drilled, and a dowel centering attachment tool is even more accurate.

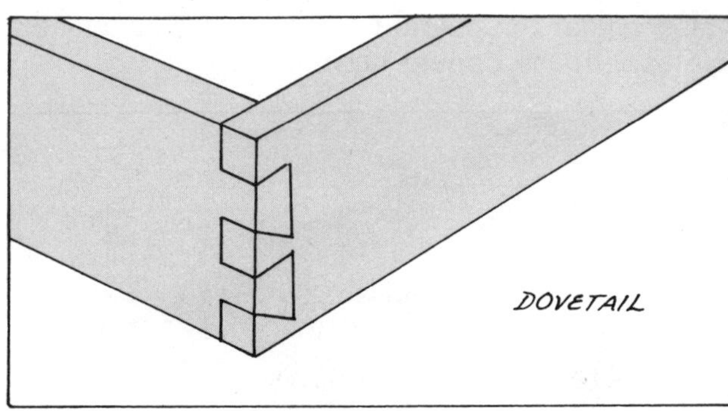

Dovetail

This is the time-honored drawer joint. It has been made by hand for centuries and some of those dovetails have withstood the test of thousands of years of time without the aid of any glue. As it has always been, both pieces of the dovetail have a series of evenly spaced, slightly triangular shaped tenons which fit into corresponding holes in the matching piece.

Uses. The major use of the dovetail is to join the sides of drawers and small boxes. But there is no reason why it cannot be used on larger projects.

Assembly. The joints should be glued, but because of the flared design of the tenons, they will probably hold anyway. By rounding the edges of the tenons and drilling a hole all the way through the joint for a dowel, the dovetail can be used as a hinge.

Tools. It makes no sense to make a dovetail by hand, when for about $35 you can buy a dovetail template. The template holds both pieces of wood together while a dovetail router bit cuts the tenons and mortises simultaneously. It takes about 60 seconds to make an average-sized drawer corner.

Variations. There are a number of different kinds of dovetails that can be made. A few of them are shown here and on the following page.

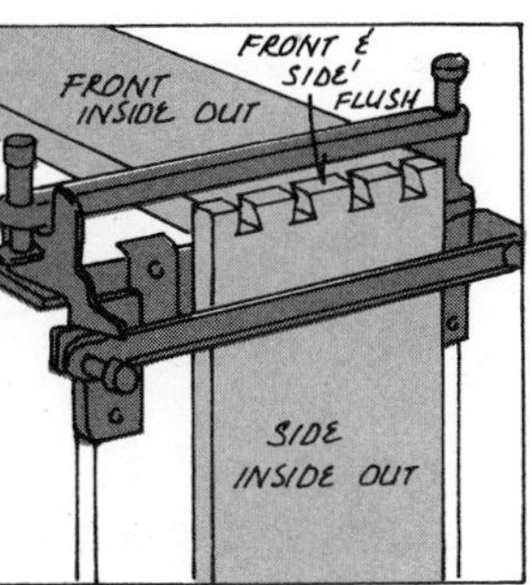
FRONT & SIDE' FLUSH
FRONT INSIDE OUT
SIDE INSIDE OUT

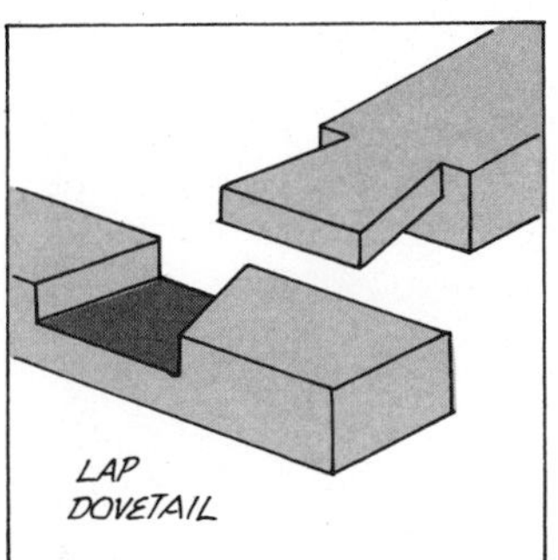
LAP DOVETAIL

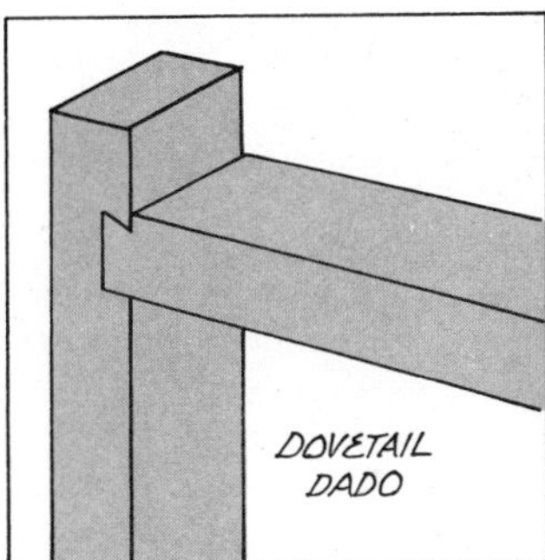
DOVETAIL DADO

THRU SINGLE DOVETAIL

SECRET DOVETAIL

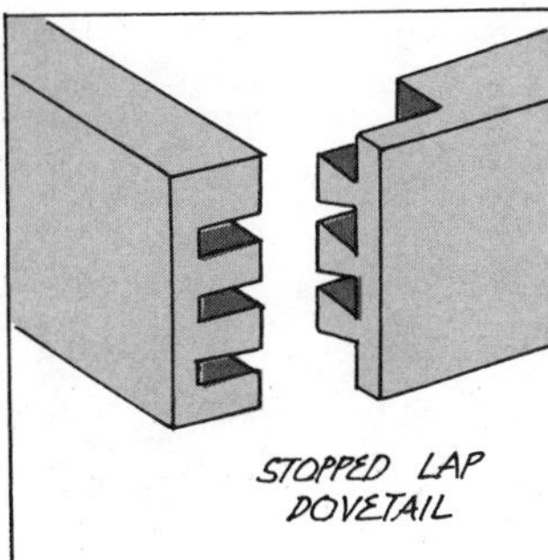
STOPPED LAP DOVETAIL

THRU MULTIPLE DOVETAIL

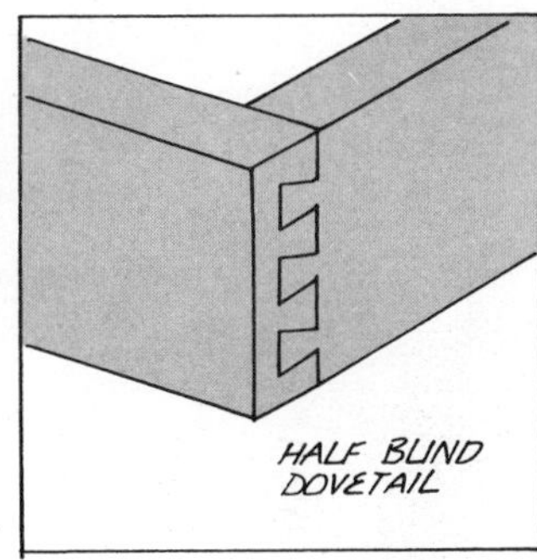
HALF BLIND DOVETAIL

CHAPTER 5

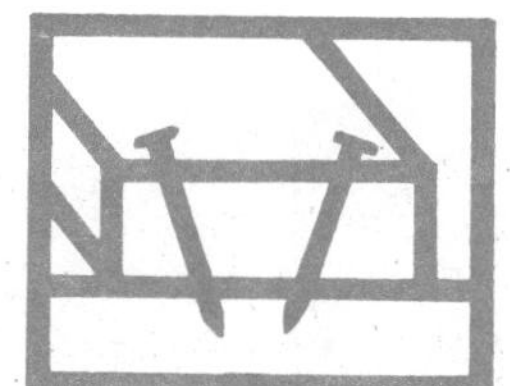

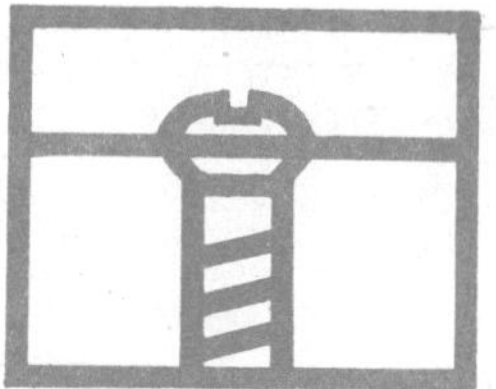

Fasteners: Assembling the Parts

Fasteners: Assembling the Parts

The wood is cut and the joints fit to perfection. But what holds it all together? Nails and screws, bolts and glue, all of which come under the heading, "fasteners." Without question, nails are the quickest, most practical way of fastening two pieces of wood together. Glue makes a better-looking joint. Screws are stronger. Either or both of the latter, when used in conjunction with a well-fitting joint, will create a stronger union than nails. Still, for ease and quickness, nothing beats that ugly old common nail.

Spikes, Brads and Pieces of Wire

There are more than a hundred different kinds of nails made of steel wire, iron, copper, zinc and brass, and each of them comes in a full assortment of sizes. They range from railroad and boat spikes that need a sledge hammer to drive them all the way down to wire brads so thin that it takes more than a thousand (count 'em) to make a pound. However, only a dozen or so of all the nails available are practical when you are making shelves, closets or cabinets.

Selecting the Right Nail for the Job

Two rules prevail when using nails: 1) choose the right nail for the wood and 2) drive it in correctly. A nail does its job via the friction produced by the pressure of the wood against the nail's shank. How well the nail holds depends on three things: 1) the condition of the wood, 2) the shape and texture of the nail and 3) the size of the nail in relation to the thickness and type of the wood.

If the wood is soft, the nail will readily go into and through it—but it will pull out just as easily. Conversely, the harder the wood, the harder the nail goes in, and the harder it will come out. If the wood is so hard that it bends the nail you have chosen, try one with a thicker shank. However, there comes a point when a nail thick enough not to bend will proceed to split the wood. The only recourse then is to drill a tiny pilot hole for each nail, but if you have to drill holes, you might as well use screws. There is one other alternative, but it is questionable. Dry wood splits more readily than wet, and if you soak any board long enough, it will not split at all. The trouble with wet wood is that when it dries, it shrinks. And that will leave the nails in it rattling around in expanded holes.

The shape and texture of a nail is also of primary consideration. The more nail surface touching the wood, the better it will hold. "More nail surface" can come in the guise of a long, thin nail, or a short, thick one. A long, thin, pointed nail goes in more easily than does a thick, blunt one. However, it is more likely to split the wood. A blunt-pointed nail (you can blunt any nail with a hammer before driving it) has less splitting action and even better holding power. That may sound like, "always use the biggest, thickest, bluntest nail you can find," but a better compromise is to use nails with a diamond-shaped point.

Another way of getting more nail surface against the wood is to use any of the many types that have ridges or spirals along their shanks. These nails have to be driven in more slowly, because while they have excellent holding power they also increase the chances of splitting.

There are three rules of thumb that may help in choosing the proper nail size for your project.

1. Select a nail that is no more than three times as long as the thickness of the first piece of wood it must enter.

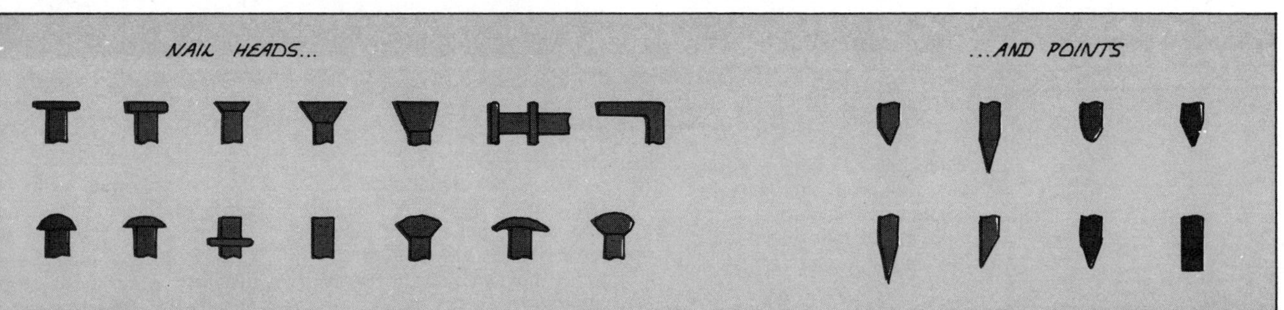

Nails come with all sorts of heads and points.

2. If the wood is very dry, use a coated box nail instead of a common nail of the same length.

3. If you are nailing a thin board to a thick one, the nail should go only two-thirds through the thicker piece. The one exception to this rule is when you are nailing molding and trim. Nearly all trim is cut from soft wood, for which long, thin finishing nails are usually in order. There is rarely any pressure or weight brought to bear on molding or trim, so lighter nails that will not split the wood are sufficient.

Driving a Nail Properly

Where and how you drive a nail is another important consideration. Driving *across* the grain (through any of the sides of a board) provides more holding power and the wood is less likely to split. Driving *along* the grain (into the board ends) leaves the nail easy to pull out. Furthermore, any shearing stress on the nail is liable to split the wood. Whenever possible, set each nail at a different angle, particularly if you are going into the end of the board. This way, the nails can reinforce each other as well as carry the load at least partially along their shear lines. A nail should always be sited so that the strain against it is across its shank, not along its length. The rule to follow is: situate the nail so that any live load on it will either drive it in deeper, or force the load against its shear angle. Anytime you cannot follow the rule, consider alternative ways of fastening the joint, such as angle irons, straps, bolts or screws.

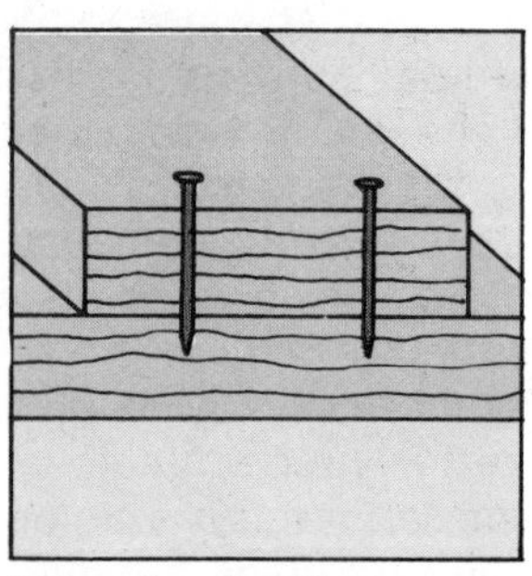

Although nails driven across the grain can always be pulled out, they have far more holding power than when they are driven into the end of a board.

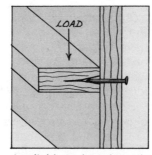

A nail driven along the grain (into the end of a board) may well split the wood. It is also extremely easy to remove since it has almost no holding power.

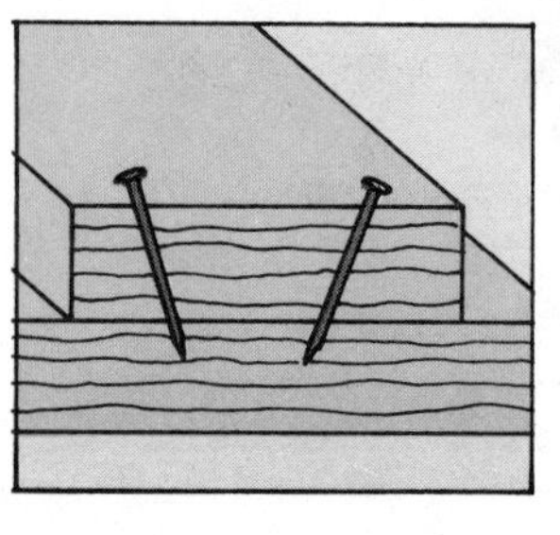

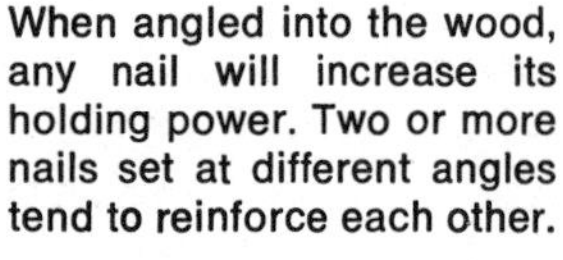

When angled into the wood, any nail will increase its holding power. Two or more nails set at different angles tend to reinforce each other.

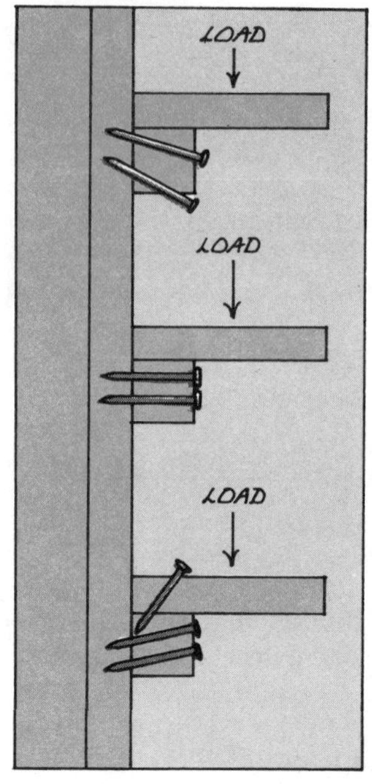

Any load put on the shelf at the top of the picture will steadily push the nails out of their holes. The nails holding the middle shelf are able to take the shelf load across their shear lines and will hold much better. The three nails in the bottom shelf have all been driven from the direction the weight will be on them. As a result, the more weight they have to carry, the deeper they will be pushed into their positions, and the less likely the joint has of coming apart.

Common and box nails are driven until thei heads are flush with the wood. Finishing and casin nails are driven until the heads are flush with th surface, then a nail set is used to pound the below the surface. Old-timers like to brag that the can drive any nail flush with a softwood boar and never leave a hammer dent. Try it sometime preferably on scrap. Set up six common and si finishing nails and pound them in, absolutely flus with the board. If you have left a single hamme dent in the wood, you fail. When you are workin on a project that has to be unmarred when completed, it is safer to plan on using a nail set wit finishing nails.

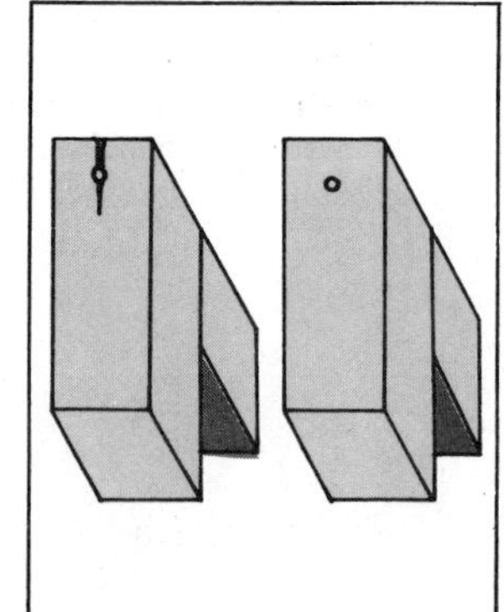

A nail driven too close to the edge of a board may split the wood, but in any case, one nail is not enough to hold the two boards tightly together.

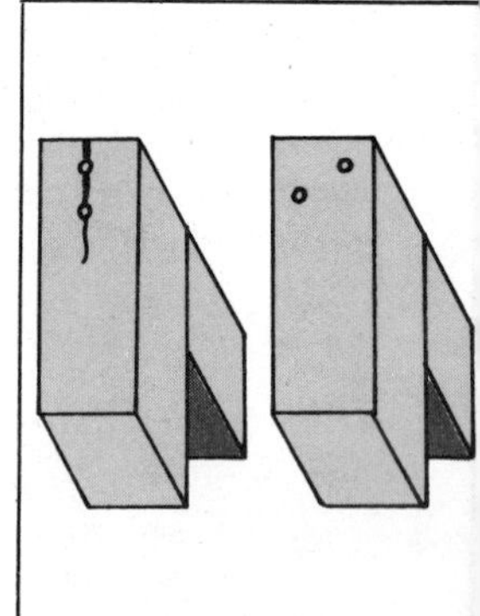

Two nails driven into th same grain line will almos guarantee that the wood wi split. With the nails set i different grain lines, ther can be very little movemen in the joint and no splitting

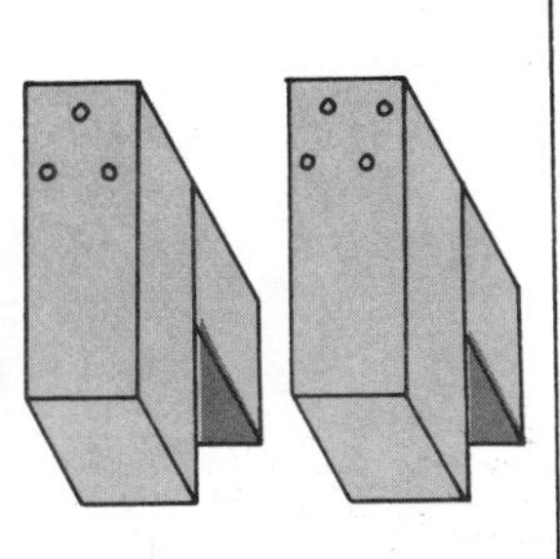

Three or even four nails, as long as they are in different grain lines, and particularly if they have been driven in at different angles, should be sufficient to hold the joint together for a long, long time.

Types of Nails and Their Uses

Common and box nails are sold in similar lengths. The common nail, of course, is used in all kinds of rough carpentry. The box nail has a thinner wire shank and is excellent for toenailing because it is less likely to split the wood.

Finishing nails are made of finer wire than are the commons, and have smaller heads. A *casing nail* is like a finishing nail, but with a conical head. Both are used in finishing work since their heads can be driven below the surface of the wood and filled over. Generally, the casing nail holds better than the finishing.

Annular thread nails have a broad twist around the shank that provides good holding power where there is no lateral load on the nail. It is not particularly resourceful at holding end grains, plywood, hardboard or particleboard.

The spiral thread nail has a shank that makes it look like a screw. It has excellent holding power both laterally and vertically and can be used to advantage in end grains, but flunks the test of strength in plywood. However, it does work well on hardboard.

Screw thread nails will hold anything except end grains and plywood edges.

Painted panel nails are fairly new on the market.

Nail sizes are only designated by length, which is referred to as the "penny." The "penny" size is written as a number and the small letter "d". Thus, a box of tenpenny nails is marked "10d," which, as anyone who has worked with nails knows, refers to nails that are 3" long.

The penny "d" used to stand for the price of the nail per hundred, so in the old days a 10d nail meant that the cost was 10¢ per 100. In Great Britain, the small "d" is still used as a symbol for the English penny, which is where this symbol came from in the first place. Today, in this country, the "d" refers only to the length of a given nail, no matter what kind of nail it may happen to be. When ordering nails, you say, "10d common," or "8d finish," so that you will get the right length with the right kind of head. The charts shown here tell you what length each of the pennies stands for.

The gauge of the nail (that is, its diameter) has no bearing when you order nails. The gauge is really only important if you are splitting wood and want to go to a thicker or thinner nail, or if you need to drill pilot holes. The pilot hole should always be at least half the diameter of the nail, and smaller still, if circumstances allow.

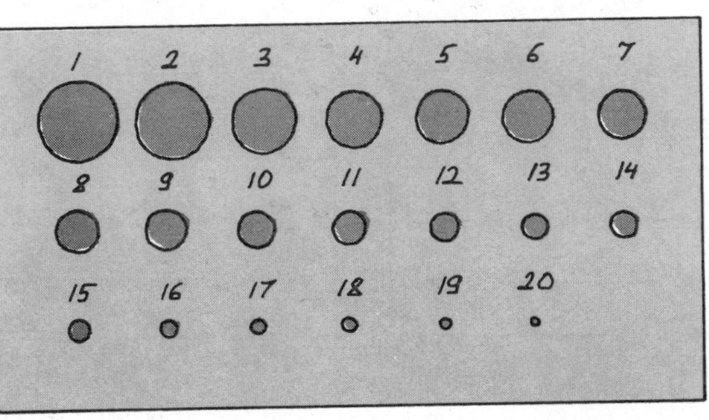

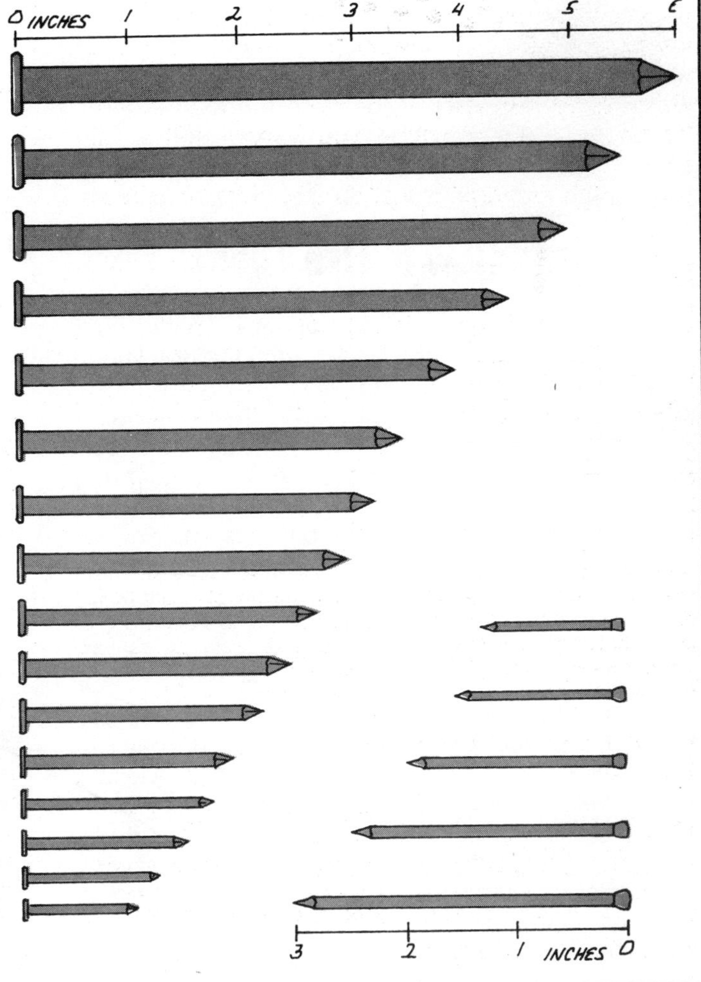

The plywood manufacturers have determined the best nail sizes to use for each thickness of the plywood. They recommend that glue be used with the nails shown here to produce strong joints.

NAIL SIZES USED WITH PLYWOOD

thickness of plywood	casing nail	finish nail
¾"	6d	8d or 10d
⅝"	6d	8d
½"	4d	6d
⅜"	3d	4d
¼"	¾-1"	3d

1" blue lath nails may be used if there is no objection to the heads showing.

They come with screw-type shafts and they are very tough. If you put one into plywood and then try to get it out, you will probably mess up the wood long before the nail comes free. They are ideal for putting small projects such as drawers together. They come in all sorts of colors, but in only one diameter; they are between 1" and 2½ in length. So don't expect them to hold an 8'x8'x8 plywood closet together. Inch for inch, however they are a tough, reliable asset. They are so tough in fact, that it takes a very sharp hacksaw blade to cut off any points that stick out the back of your work.

Knurled thread nails have nearly straight flutes along their shafts. They are designed to hold in masonry, and that they will do. They are the nail to remember when you are hanging bookshelves or cabinets on a brick wall.

Cement-coated nails come in both screw and unthreaded versions. They are covered with a rosin which is an adhesive that melts and lubricates the nail as it heats up while being driven. As the nail cools down, the rosin forms a tight bond with the wood. When using them, never leave one partially driven home or it will "freeze" and you will never be able to move it.

The corrugated nail is a handy weapon to have when you need to strengthen a straight butt joint or miter. They are, however, hard to drive home evenly, and even harder to get below the wood surface and fill over.

Screws— Where and How to Use Them

Wood screws demand more work than nails, but they are preferred for most cabinetwork. They make a neater union, and will "draw" a joint tighter, then hold better and longer than any nail. They are a necessity if the work is likely to be taken apart for repair at some future date, when greater holding power is needed at a joint, or when it is important to have a job that is unmarred.

Screws are made from steel, brass, copper or bronze and should always be used when the pull of the load is to be along the length of the fastening. In other words, if you are faced with a situation in which a nail might pull out, use screws.

A screw has two dimensions: The diameter of the shank just below the head (the part that is ungrooved) has a code number, and the overall length, which is given in fractions of an inch. The shank diameters are designated by numbers that have no relation to anything, but that start at "0" for the smallest and go up to No. 24. Actually, there are diameters larger than 24, but they are bigger than any cabinet will ever require. Each of these coded numbers comes in a full range of lengths, so when buying a screw you have to give both dimensions by saying, for example, "A dozen No. 14s, 2½ inches long."

The length of a screw is determined by measuring from its pointed tip to the area of its head. Flathead screws are measured from the point to the *top* of the head. Oval head screws are figured to the *rim* of the head. The length of the round-head types ends at the *underside* of the head.

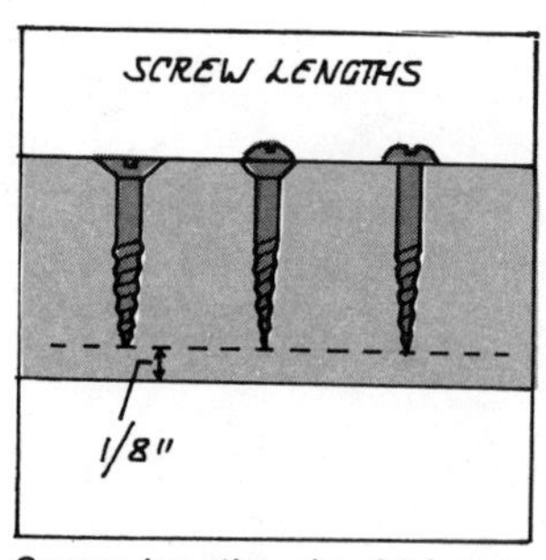

Screw lengths should be at least ⅛" shorter than the combined thickness of the wood being joined.

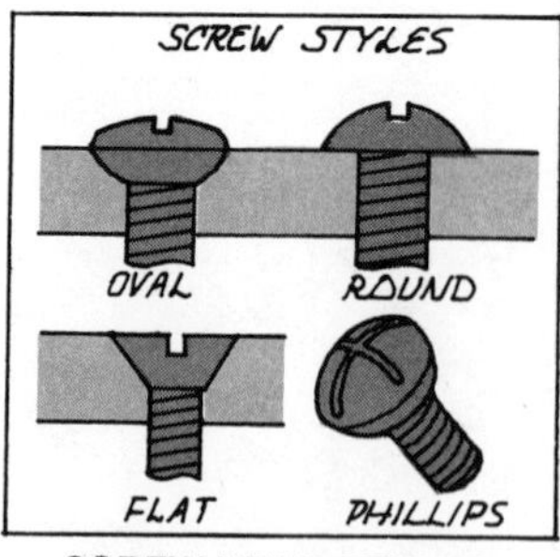

SCREW HEAD STYLES

What Screw for What Job?

To decide which kind of screw you need for a given situation, start with the head. Round and oval heads will remain exposed, and can be used as part of the project's decoration. Or, they can be put where they are unobtrusive. Flat heads can either be countersunk and filled over, or left flush with the wood.

Next, consider the kind of wood you are working with. Use a thin screw (and therefore a lower code number) in hardwoods and thicker screws (higher code number) for softwoods. Nevertheless, remember that the thicker a screw, the stronger it is, so always pick the maximum diameters practical for the job.

Finally, determine a length that will not exceed the combined thickness of the wood you are joining. If you plan to countersink the screws, remember to include the depth of the countersink when you are figuring the screw length.

Standard wood screws have a single, straight-across slot which will accept a standard-blade screwdriver. There are also Phillips-head screws which have a crossed slot and, obviously, require a Phillips-head screwdriver. Because the Phillips blade does not overhang the screw, many cabinetmakers prefer Phillips-head screws, on the grounds that there is less chance of marring the work. This is particularly important when dealing with plywood, since the thin edges of ply around a screw hole are subject to easy damage.

The plywood manufacturers have some suggestions about screw sizes, too. The lengths shown here are minimal. Any time you can use a longer length, do it.

Plywood Thickness	Screw Length	Screw Size	Drill Size for Shank	Drill Size for Thread
3/4″ 5/8″	1½″ 1¼″	#8	11/64″	1/8″ (9/64″)
1/2″ 3/8″	1¼″ 1″	#6	9/64″	3/32″ (7/64″)
1/4″	1″	#4	7/64″	1/16″ (5/64″)

If you are drilling near an edge and it splits, increase the shank drill size by 2/64″, as shown in the parentheses.

Some Hints About Screws and Screwdriving

Charts are all very nice—if you can find them when you need them. The next time you have a screw in one hand, a box of drill bits in the other and no chart in sight, there is another way of determining proper bit size. Hold a bit in front of the threaded portion of the screw. If you *cannot* see the screw threads above and below the bit, the bit is too large. Keep trying smaller bits until you can see the threads.

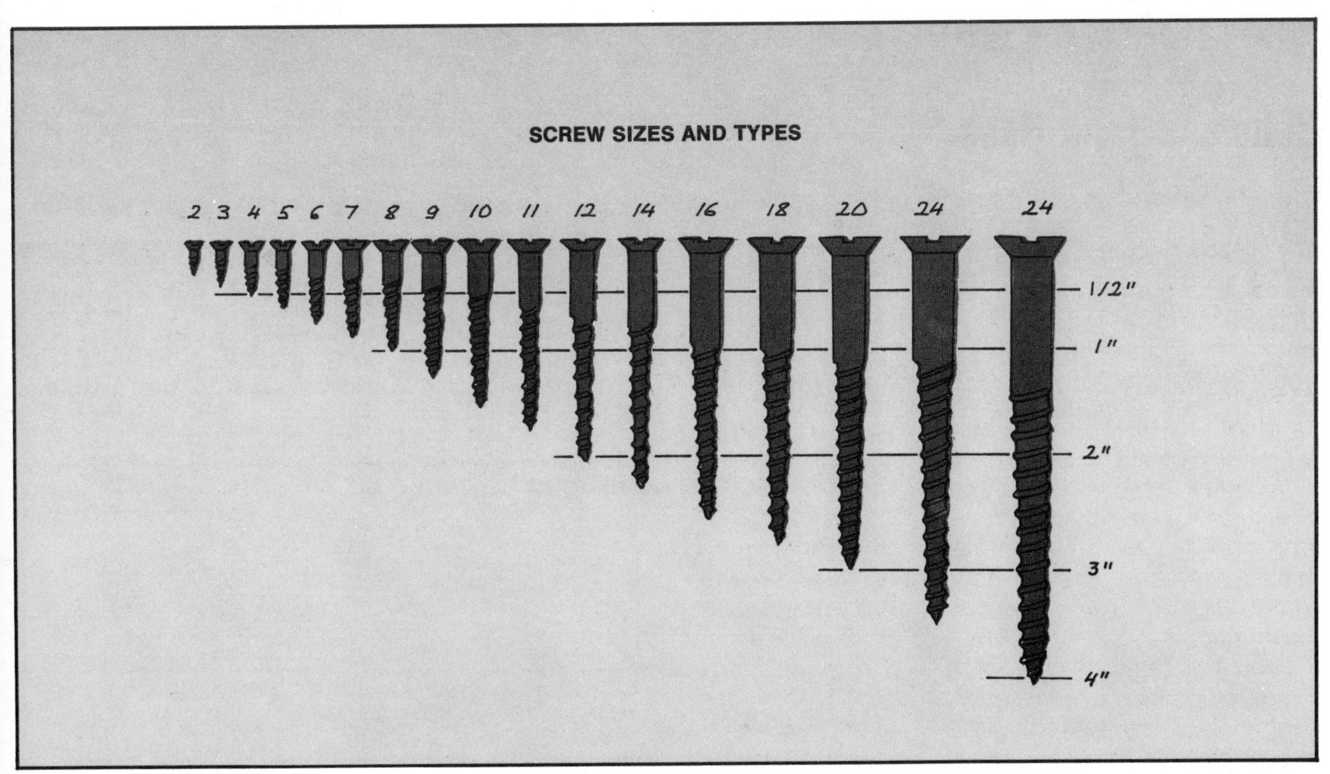

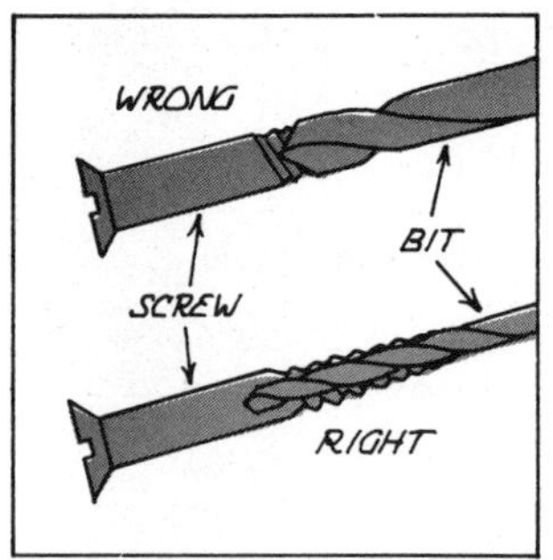

In the top picture, the bit is too large for the screw. In the bottom picture, the threads of the screw can be seen both above and below the bit. The bit is the correct size for drilling a pilot hole for this screw.

It is only the threads of a screw that actually hold it in place, and only the threads need to bite into any wood. If you think a screw is going to be "in tighter" because you had to grunt and strain and develop blisters putting it in, you are wasting your time and energy. A hole the size of the shaft, less the height of the threads, will make life much easier; driving in screws will be infinitely quicker.

When working with softwoods, it is usually only necessary to make a small indentation as a pilot for the screw. For hardwoods, drill a hole as deep as the screw is long. If you need an exceptionally large screw you will risk splitting wood if you do not drill a hole that is the same diameter as and depth of the unthreaded part of the screw shaft. The smooth end of the shaft has relatively little holding power, so why fight it through the wood?

There is an old wives' tale about putting soap on the threads of a screw to make it easier to drive. The old wives were right. But it is better to use graphite or candle wax because, over the years, soap turns into a sort of glue and cements the screw into its hole; it also rusts steel screws and corrodes brass ones. The result is that trying to get a soaped screw out of the wood can become an impossible task. Do not try oil as a loosening agent either; it will penetrate most wood and stain the grain.

In driving a screw, use a screwdriver with the longest barrel you can, and be sure the blade fits snugly in the screw slot. The longer the screwdriver, the more leverage you have to work with. The looser the fit of the blade in the slot, the more chance you run of chewing up the slot. If the slot does become battered, it may be possible to fix it somewhat with a hacksaw or metal file, but that is a lot of work and there is no guarantee that you can save the screw.

There are two "tricks of the trade" for removing a tight screw. If turning the screw counterclockwise does not loosen it, give the screw a twist in the opposite direction. Then try loosening it again. Keep repeating this tightening-loosening action until the screw loosens. If that fails, hold a hot soldering iron against the screw head. The heat will expand the metal and, as it cools, shrink it away from whatever is bonding it.

Bolts and Their Uses

There are three types of bolts that are useful when making shelves, closets or cabinets.

Lag bolts are really heavy-duty versions of the wood screw and are available up to an inch in diameter and 16″ long. They have square or hexagonal heads and are driven in with a wrench. If you are hanging a wall cabinet and you know where the studs are, a lag bolt is about as strong a hanger as you could find.

Carriage bolts have round heads and coarse threads. The head can be either flat or conical, which allows it to be countersunk.

Hanger bolts are oddly shaped, but handy. The pointed end is a wood screw and the headless

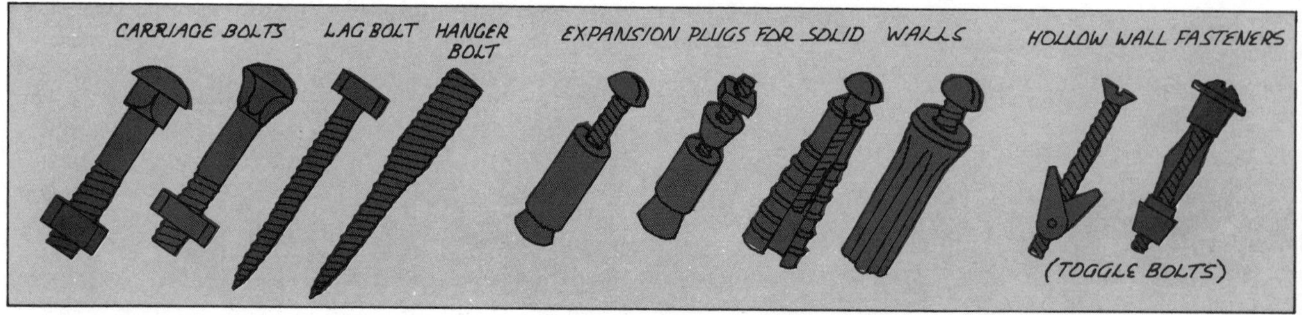

shaft is machined to accept a nut.

Aside from the masonry nails discussed earlier, there are several kinds of anchor devices that will fasten objects to both hollow and solid walls. Some of these are lead or plastic plugs that are fitted into a drilled hole; they will expand against the sides of the opening when a screw or nail is driven into them.

Another kind of anchor, known as a molly, or toggle, travels through the hole that has been drilled through a hollow wall, then opens up behind it. A few of the types that can be purchased in almost any hardware store are shown on the preceding page. But whatever the design (and designs vary widely) the principle of holding is always the same, and it works.

Adhesives

In recent years, home craftsmen have grown accustomed to reaching for the white glues every time they want to stick something together. Actually, there are a lot of alternatives to white glue, and the first of them is cream-colored glue. For sheer strength, the cream-coloreds, or *aliphatic resin glues,* set faster than the whites, and will hold longer under constant pressure.

Then there is old-fashioned *hide glue*. Hide glue is sold in liquid form these days, as well as a powder and in chips. For things like furniture repair, hide glue in any form remains unsurpassed. Over a period of time, furniture joints are put under considerable stress and inevitably they will open up. At that point, it is nice to be able to clean the old glue out and put new glue in, and the hide glues can all be dissolved in hot water. So if a project is not about to be subjected to the great outdoors, hide glue is an excellent choice, even though it requires at least 3 to 4 hours of clamping time.

But there are other adhesives to choose from, and nearly all of them are stronger and easier to work with than anything our predecessors ever had. The important rule to observe when using any modern glue is: Follow the manufacturer's directions precisely. Furthermore, be sure you are using the correct glue for your particular project. Some adhesives are waterproof. Others are heat-resistant. Some need clamping, others do not. Some are inflammable, others are toxic. All of them will do the specific job they are manufactured to do.

Applying Adhesives

Contact cement is applied to both surfaces with a brush or spreader and allowed to set until dry to the touch (10-20 minutes). When the pieces are brought together, the glue bonds immediately. The contacts are widely used in veneering and for putting laminates on countertops. But don't expect them to hold parquet floors, or do a very commendable job on joints.

Liquid resins (white) are made with a polyvinyl emulsion which is not waterproof. The whites are suitable for wood, cork and leather. They are pretty good in joints, especially when used with nails or screws.

Plastic resin glues come as a powder to be mixed with water. They are resistant to water, mold and rot, so they work well on wood, particleboard, veneers and the like. They must always be clamped for drying.

Powdered casein glue is made from milk curd and is a strong, water-resistant glue that is excellent for oily woods such as teak. It is mixed with water and sets best at low temperatures. Caution: The caseins may stain some woods.

Resorcinal. Waterproof and strong. It comes as a powder catalyst and a liquid resin that have to be mixed. Usually a dark red in color, it requires clamping.

Epoxies have two liquid components (a resin and a catalyst) which must be mixed. They should be clamped because they dry slowly, but they will hold anything and are resistant to both heat and moisture.

Hot melt glues come in round 2″-2½″ long sticks which are inserted into an electric glue gun. The glue melts at 380°F. and squirts out the nozzle of the gun. It dries with 90% of its strength in 60 seconds. You use up a lot of glue sticks quickly, but there is hardly anything the hot melts cannot hold together, including the frame of a heavy wooden door, upholstery, ceramics, formica and leather furring strips. With a one-minute setting time, it is easier to just hold two pieces together than to clamp them. The drawback is that only small areas can be worked on at a time.

Clamps You Can Rely On

If you choose the right glue and have the right clamps, the glueing job can still go wrong if your preparation is inadequate. Glueing is a series of tiny steps that must be made in one continuous motion. So when getting ready to glue, make certain that all the parts, and all of the clamps needed to hold them together, are near at hand. The wood to be glued must be dry and free of oil or dust.

Run a trial assembly to make sure all the parts fit properly and also to set your clamps at approximately the openings they will be needed at. Have scrap blocks nearby to keep the clamps from marring the wood.

Completely assemble the project, checking to be sure the joints are all tight and that no light shows through any of them. If you see light, the joint should be re-jointed or re-cut.

If the glue you are using must be mixed, do tha just before you are ready to use it, not ahead c time. Glue should be spread over both surface (in most cases), then smoothed so that it penetrates every pore of the wood. When glueing en grains, let a layer of glue soak in (and dry), the apply a second coat.

One final caution. Some craftsmen are unde the impression that the more clamp pressure pu on a joint, the stronger it will be. They are wrong There should be only enough clamp pressure t shut out any light in the joint. Too much pressure will squeeze the glue out of the joint altogether. Not enough pressure, and nothing wi stick together. The rule is: Make the wood snug and nothing more.

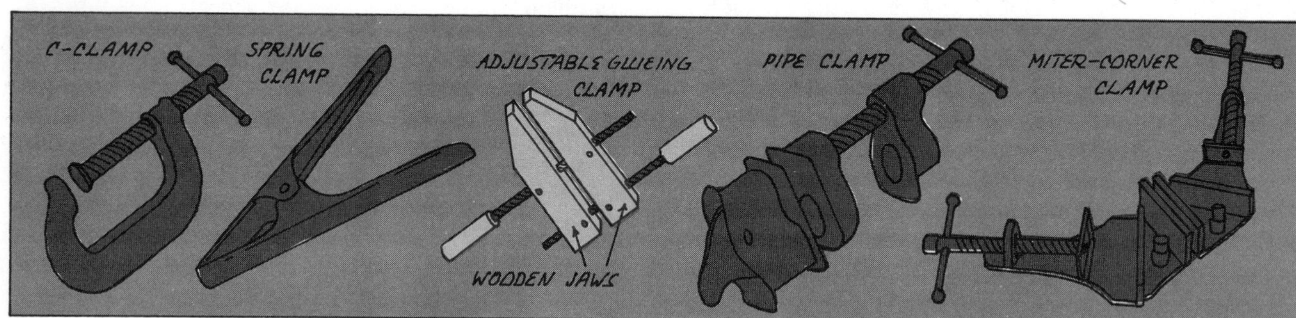

Some handy clamps to have. The bar or pipe clamps are ideal for holding a whole project together. Wood screw clamps are useful with smaller projects; in most instances, the jaws must be parallel to each other. C-clamps will tend to mar the wood, so use scrap blocks whenever possible. Corner clamps are a boon if you are putting a box with beveled edges together. Spring clamps are used for light jobs, or to hold a joint in place while screws or nails are driven into the wood.

CHAPTER 6

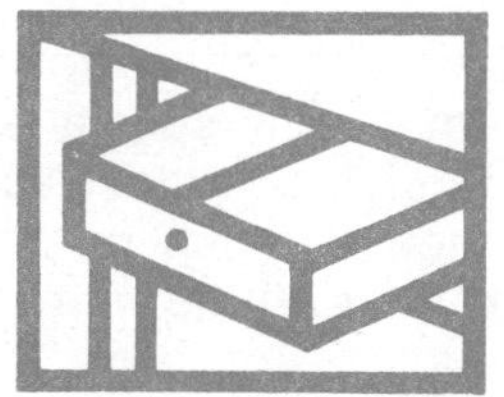

Drawers, Doors and Frames

Drawers, Doors and Frames

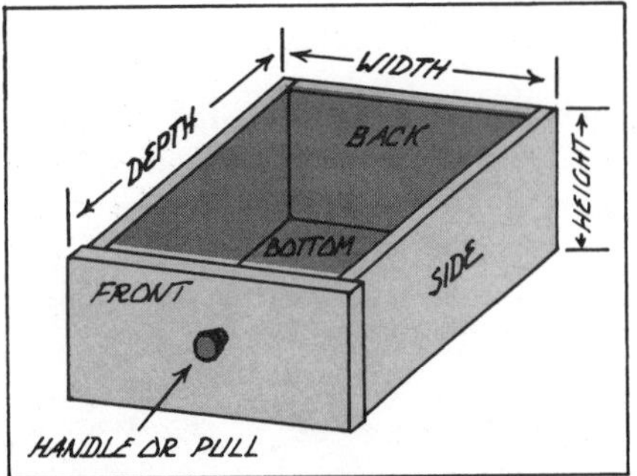

Nomenclature of a drawer.

Drawers are like discreet, well-trained servants. They appear at your bidding, withstand your closest scrutiny, then disappear from sight when they have fulfilled your needs. To take full advantage of the convenience they offer, drawers should always be positioned low enough so the average person can see all the way inside them, and there should be enough space in front of them so that anyone can stand directly before them and still pull them completely open.

All that may sound rather obvious. But there are drawers so high they must be reached by a ladder. There are drawers so deep that when they are filled, no one can find the bottom. There are drawers so big that, when they are pulled all the way out, their weight threatens to topple the cabinets holding them. There are drawers so wide that no one can reach both handles at the same time. There are also a great many drawers so short that they are continually being jerked right out of their frames.

There are no maximum or minimum dimensions for the ideal drawer, for the size of every drawer rests squarely on the uses it was designed to fulfill. There are, however, a few guidelines to bear in mind:

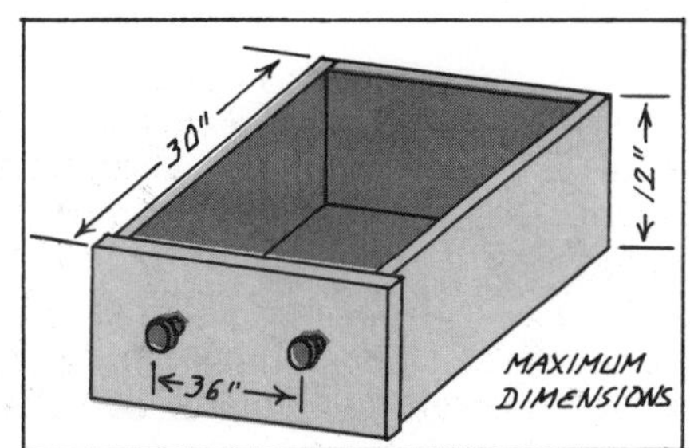

Recommended maximum drawer dimensions.

1. Try to make your drawers no more than 12" high or 30" deep (about the length of a long arm).
2. Place the handles no more than 36" apart, so that anyone can reach both of them and still have full pulling power.
3. Do not install a large, heavy drawer at the top of a cabinet where its loaded weight may tip everything over (as happens with many an office filing cabinet).
4. Be sure the drawer has a stop, so that it will not come popping out unexpectedly into someone's arms.

When you come down to it, every drawer is just an open box. So if the drawer you are making does not require any special appearance, it is as simple and quick a project as there is. If it is to have a particular finish or decorative front, you will want to take a little more time and care with its construction.

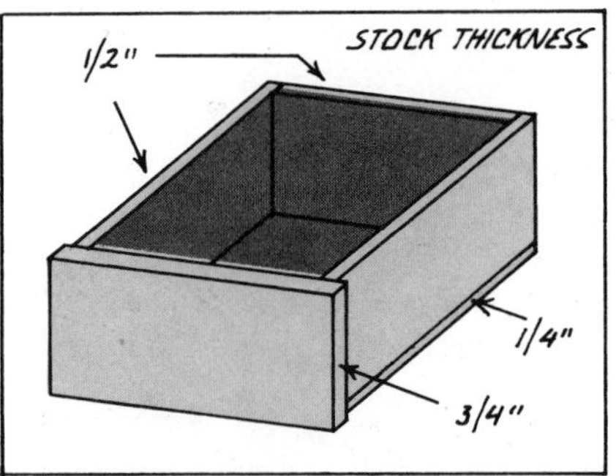

The average drawer is made from ½" stock for the back and sides, ¾" stock for the front and ¼" stock for the bottom.

A drawer can be made from any stock, although plywood is especially good for the sides back and bottom since thinner pieces can be used with no loss in strength. Most drawers are made in thicknesses that range between ⅜" and ¾". Usually, they are ½" stock. The bottom is normally ¼" stock, but it could be as much as ¾". Fronts are anything from ¾" to 1½" thick.

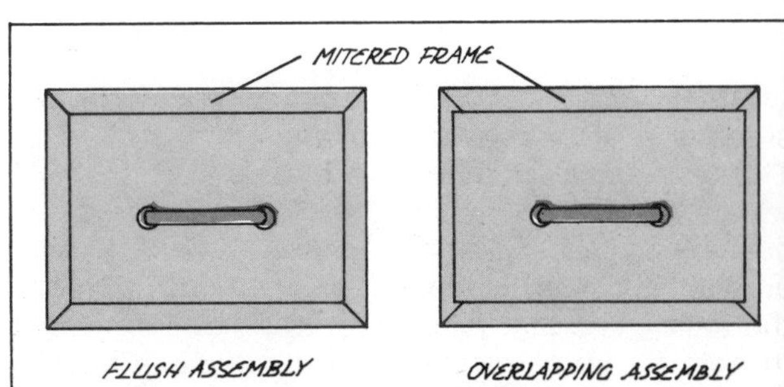

"Flush" assembly means that the front of the drawer will fit inside the drawer frame and be flush with the front of the cabinet. An "overlapping" assembly means that the drawer front overlaps the frame around it.

Drawer assembly is classified as either flush or overlapping. The flush drawer demands more accuracy in construction since it must fit exactly inside its frame with all of its edges clearly visible. Overlapping drawers conceal the spaces between the drawer sides and the frame.

By definition, a drawer is destined to carry considerable weight and to withstand a variety of pressures. As a result, the joints used in making any drawer should be carefully chosen for their ability to endure endless pulling and pushing.

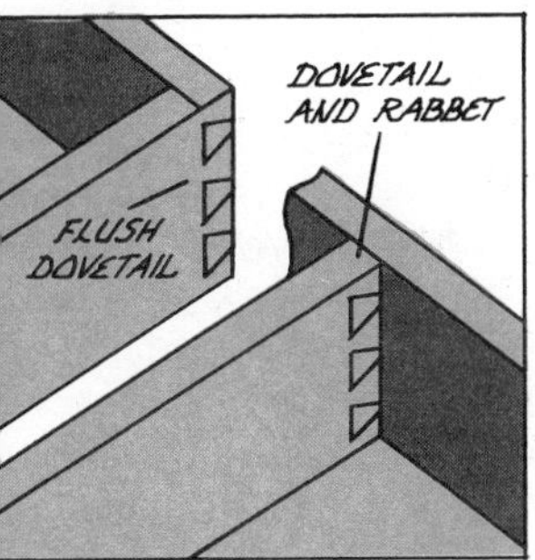

The dovetail joint can be made flush or inside a rabbet. Either way, the dovetail is ideal for all corners of any drawer.

The ideal joint, the one that meets all of the drawer's requirements of stress and strain, is the dovetail. If you have a dovetail template and tools for routing, the choice is obvious for all the corners of any drawer you make.

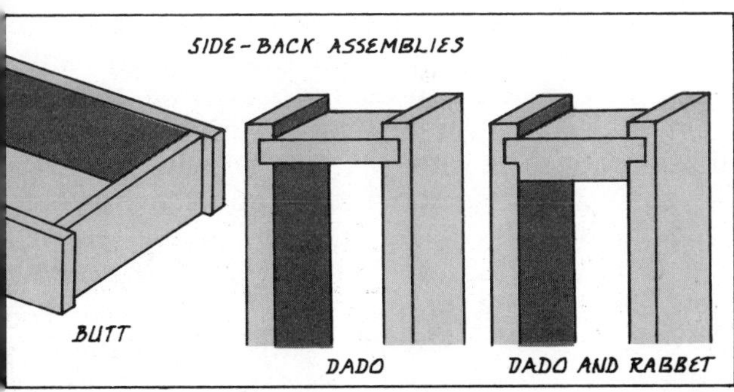

The back of a drawer should always be placed between the sides so that whatever is in the drawer cannot force the side-back joints apart.

Other than the dovetail, joining the back and sides of a drawer can fall to any of several joints. The most usual ones are the butt, dado, and dado with rabbet. The two dadoes are excellent because they allow the load in the drawer to slam against the back without ever knocking it free of the sides. The butt joint, even with nails or screws to help it, cannot promise as much durability.

Joining the sides to the front becomes slightly more complicated, if only because the front is usually larger than the side-back-bottom assembly in order to hide the space between the sides and the frame. Furthermore, the entire weight of the drawer and its load is literally hauled back and forth by the front.

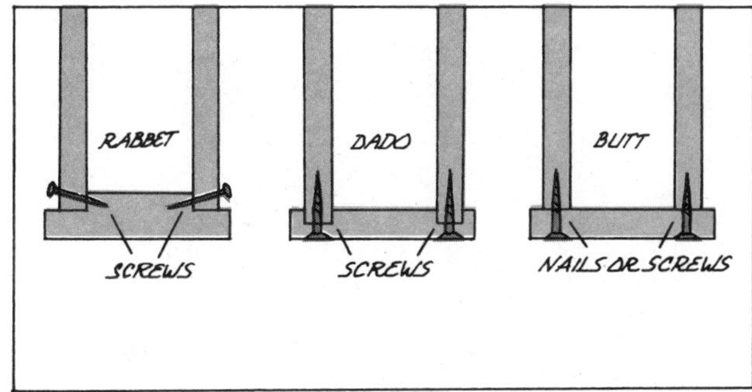

The most trustworthy method of assembling the front and sides is with a rabbet joint. Any fastener used with either the butt or dado must go into the ends of the sides and will have a minimum of holding power.

The easiest way of joining the front and sides is with a dado or butt joint and, because so much stress will be concentrated at these joints, they should not only be glued but also screwed together. Nails will never work because the load is concentrated along their length and they will have no holding power. A better arrangement is to rabbet the back of the front piece at each end. This allows either nails or screws to be placed at right angles to the load so that the pull against them is across their shear.

The "paste-a-face" drawer front is an alternative to rabbeting. Be sure the nails or screws used to attach the face are short enough not to come through the face.

Rabbeted drawer fronts are not always routed out of a single piece of wood. The front of the drawer can be made flush with the sides and then the lip added as a separate face. This "paste-a-face" technique is helpful if you are planning to veneer the drawer front or make it decorative in any way and want to work on it separately. The face is glued to the front and screws are driven into it from the inside of the drawer.

Drawer bottoms can be glued and screwed flush to the bottom edges of the front, back and sides. They can be set into a rabbet cut on all four edges. They can be inserted into a dado

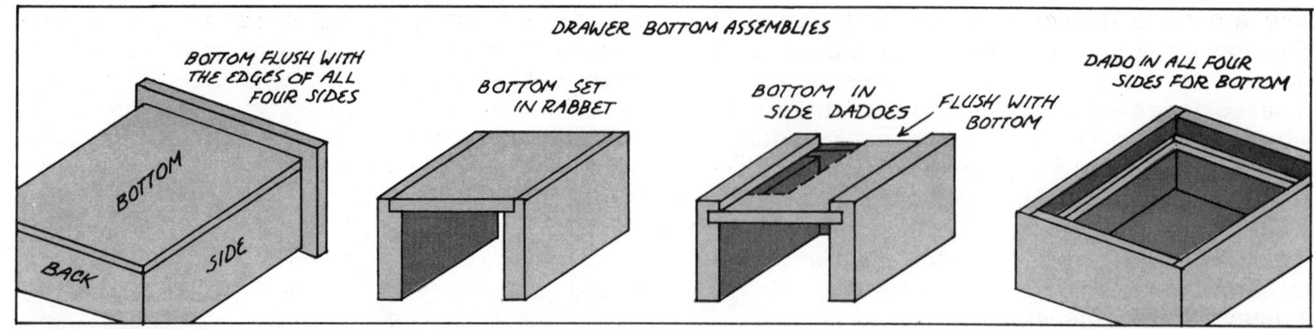

Bear in mind that if you nail or screw a drawer bottom flush, or even in a rabbet, to the bottom edges of the drawer, it will have minimum holding power. The fasteners will be going in the direction of the load, which in turn has every opportunity to push them out of their holes.

that is cut in any two, three, or all four sides. The 4-sided dado is by far the best, since the bottom has two important functions. It must carry the full load of whatever is put in the drawer, and it guarantees the squareness of the entire project. Because it is boxed into the dado, the bottom can be left unglued so that it will have room to expand or contract without splitting.

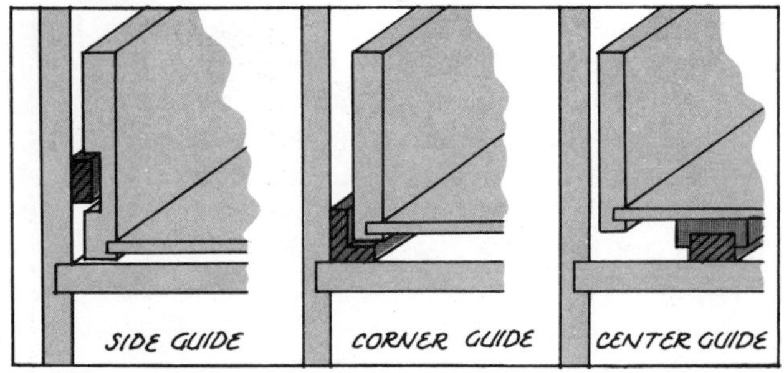

If at all possible, wooden drawer guides should be made from hardwood stock and attached with both glue and screws.

There are four ways of attaching drawer guides—at the sides, in the bottom corners, along the center bottom, or with hardware. The side guide consists of square pieces of wood, or rails, attached to the drawer frame on both sides of the drawer. The rails extend into dadoes routed out of the sides of the drawer. Thus, the entire weight of the drawer rests on the rails, so make sure they are well-anchored to the frame. The reverse is also possible, with the dadoes cut into the frame and the guides glued and screwed to the sides of the drawer.

The corner guide has a pair of L-shaped strips that support the drawer on the bottom edges of its sides. This is a less risky arrangement in that the weight of the drawer is fully supported by the frame and there is little chance of a rail giving way under pressure.

The center guide is a grooved strip of wood attached to the center of the drawer bottom, which rides over a rail nailed to the frame. If the drawer is particularly large, two guides will provide more stable drawer action.

There are a variety of metal and plastic drawer slides and guides that can be purchased at almost any hardware store. They all come with manufacturers' instructions which consistently make their installation sound easy. And some of them are. But if you decide to install a set of drawer slides, beware! Most metal slides require ½" space between the drawer and the frame to accommodate the metal track and slide. Less than that ½" and the drawer will not move. More than that, and the drawer will fall off its tracks. And heaven help you if the sides of the frame and the sides of the drawer are not absolutely parallel! However, if you do get everything exactly right, you will have a free-wheeling drawer with more sliding action than you could ever duplicate with wooden parts. Installing metal slides can exhaust your patience, but they are well worth the trouble.

Drawer Frames

It is urgently recommended that whenever possible, you build the frame for any drawer *after* the drawer is made. If you try building the frame *before,* your measurements can be accurate, the assembly correct in every detail—and when you get the frame together, you will discover a fraction of an inch difference somewhere that prevents the drawer from working. You can get into this same bind consistently, with drawer after drawer, frame after frame, no matter how careful you are. And you will never figure out how you do it, either. Mistakes can happen when you build the ame around a drawer, too, but it is easier to djust loose pieces of a frame than it is the drawer self.

The easiest kind of frame to work with is a avity which completely houses the drawer, and between 1/16" and 1/8" larger all around it. The ox frame, however, is an unnecessary consumpon of wood, and if you are putting half a dozen rawers in a cabinet, all that extra wood will make our project inordinately heavy. Extremely stable, ut heavy—and expensive.

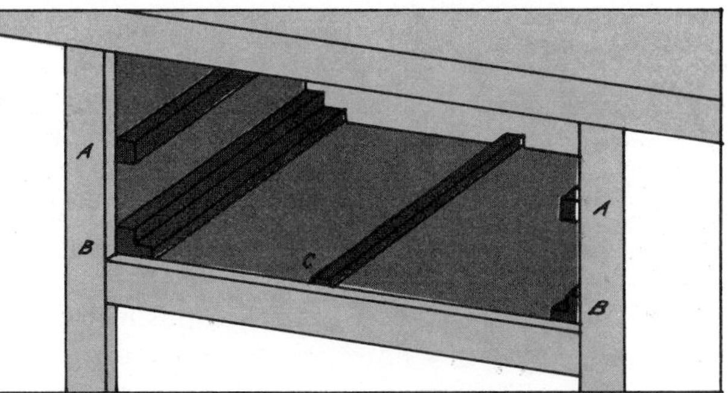

he picture shows the relative position of the side (A), corner 3) and center (C) rails in a box frame. Obviously, only one rrangement is necessary for any given drawer.

A box-frame construction does have certain dvantages. The guide rails are easier to attach ecause no matter where the drawer needs them, here is always solid wood to support them. If netal drawer slides are being used, you can imply put a slide on one side of the frame, attach he drawer, then bring the opposite side against he drawer and insert the other slide. Move everyhing around until the drawer is aligned properly nd attach the free slide in place with a pair of crews. Try the drawer out and keep adjusting he tracks until it works perfectly. Only then do ou put the loose frame side in place. This process s not so bad with one drawer, but if you have, say, three of them in a tier, it can be a time-consuming procedure to get all of them in perfect alignment. If the drawers are overlapping assemblies, the task is eased somewhat because you can make up for many discrepancies with the face trim of the cabinet. If the drawers are to be flush, you will need a little luck. But at least the face frame can be twisted and joggled around the drawer fronts before they are attached permanently (looking perfectly square, one hopes).

nchor the interior side of the box frame only after the metal lrawer slides are perfectly aligned and the drawer is working roperly.

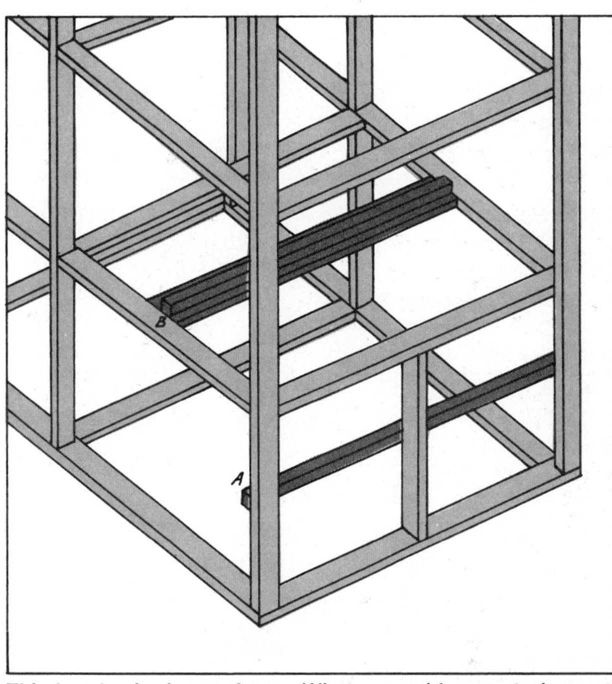

This is a basic drawer frame. Whatever guides are to be used should be braced near their centers to keep them from sagging. Corner guides will sit on the horizontal frames and be fully supported. Side rail guides will need a vertical support (A), as well as metal slides. If center guides are required, each horizontal frame should have a center piece (B) under the rail.

The other way of making a frame is to assemble a series of vertical and horizontal rectangles. The risk with this arrangement comes from all those right angles going in all directions. Using mortise and tenon joints will help square everything up, but if you are using 1"x2" (or smaller) stock, the wood may not be absolutely straight to begin with.

The frame construction permits any of the wooden guides and even metal slides to be used, but again it helps if you are working around already built drawers. Consider how ticklish it could become when six drawers all have to line up in two directions and also fit perfectly in those funny oblong holes that are permanently attached to each other, and you will see why it is easier, and probably quicker, to make the drawers first.

Doors and Door Frames

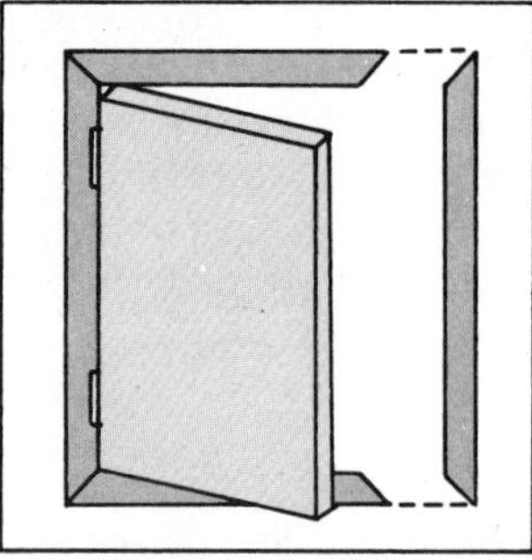

It is not critical that door frames be built around cabinet doors. But it is easier to make a perfect fit, particularly if the door must seat inside the frame.

It is also easier to construct a door frame around an already existing door than the other way around. However, doors are easier to fit into a frame than are drawers because they are rarely more than an inch or two thick. Further, they do not have to fit into a deep well, but merely seat within the enclosure of four pieces of wood.

The most sensible way of fitting a door is to put the hinge side of the frame in place and hang the door. Then build the rest of the frame. The miter joint is usually in order here, because it is more decorative and, if cut true, it can help square the frame.

Sliding Doors

There are two types of cabinet doors: sliding and hinged. Sliding doors can be made of wood, plywood, plastic, glass, hardboard, pressboard or metal. As a rule there are at least two of them, each with its own track to slide in. The tracks are either routed out of the top and bottom of the cabinet, or they can be purchased separately from hardware stores and lumberyards. Either way, the track that runs under the top of the cabinet is usually ⅜" deep. The track in the bottom of the cabinet is 3/16" deep. The doors are cut 3/16" shorter than the height between the bottoms of the two tracks. They are installed by shoving them upward into the top track, swinging them inward over the lower track, then allowing them to drop into the lower track.

Tracks are available for ⅛", ¼", ½", and ¾" thick doors. If the doors are to be thicker than the track, they will have to be rabbeted at the top and bottom to fit into the tracks, as shown in the picture.

With large closet doors that slide, the door will move more readily if it is hung from an aluminum track and travels on wheels. The track, wheels and floor guides all come in the same package of hardware along with instructions for installing. When making a door of this size, bear in mind that a solid piece of wood, even plywood, is subject to humidity change and therefore warping. If the door is not too large, a good material to use is pressboard or chipboard. It will be heavy, but will not warp. The drawback is getting the screws to hold the wheels to the top of the pressboard. Instead of screws, try attaching the wheels with small bolts that are countersunk and filled over. An alternative to the weight and warping problem is to construct a frame and panel door, as is discussed a little later in this chapter.

Bi-folds

Bi-folds, which are normally hollow-core or louver doors, also require special hardware sets to in

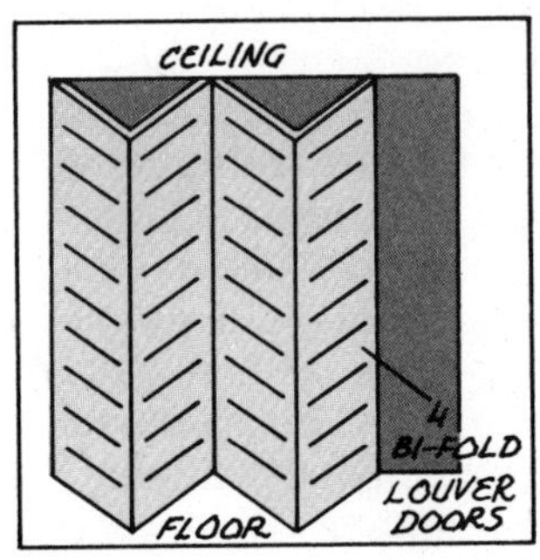

The trouble with bi-folds i that they have to close o a large area, and they ca only function within the con fines of an absolutely squar frame. The trouble with th frame is that one side of is the floor, which rarel makes a right angle with an wall, to say nothing abou whether it is parallel wit the ceiling.

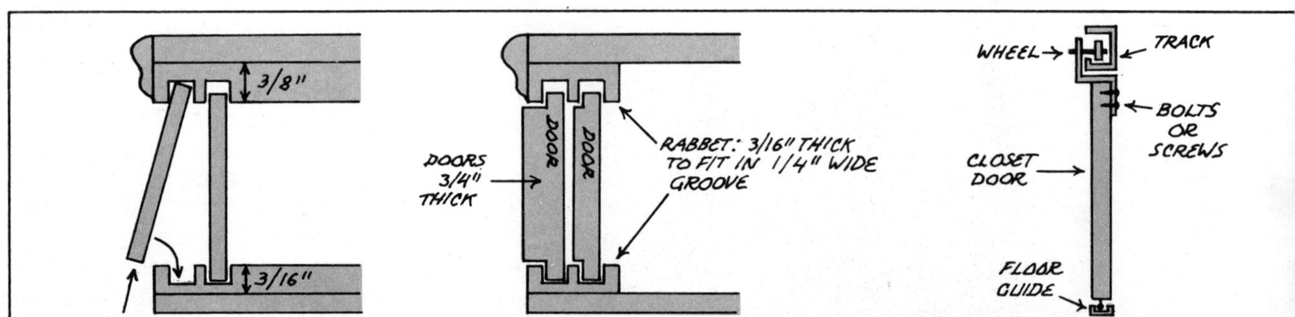

Sliding doors are cut ⅜" narrower than the distance between the bottom of the track grooves so that they can be inserted in the tracks and will have ample "sliding" room.

By rabbeting the top and bottom, a thicker door can be made to work in any of the pre-cut tracks sold at lumberyards.

Sliding doors for closets must be hun from an aluminum track. A solid woode door this large is liable to warp. It is safe to make it out of pressboard, or use frame-and-panel construction.

tall. The hardware consists of pivot hinges, a guide track and wheels. If you absolutely insist on hanging a set of bi-folds, pay careful attention to the manufacturer's instructions. If you are a glutton for punishment and are thinking about hanging a double set of bi-folds (four doors in all), be forewarned: The top of the door frame must be level; both sides *and the floor* must all meet at right angles. If you cannot make the entire frame absolutely square, find another way of closing the closet. Even under optimum conditions, double bi-folds are likely to need hours of shimming, drilling, screwing and unscrewing, planing, rehinging and general puttering around before you can make them open and close properly.

Hinged Doors

Hinged doors can be of a hollow-core, solid wood, or frame-and-panel construction. No matter how they are made, they will be hinged in one of three ways—lipped, full overlapped, or flush.

Lipped doors are the easiest to fit, since they are rabbeted along their inner edges and hinged to cover all sides of the face frame with no cracks showing. If the frame is too small, the rabbet can be made wide enough to include it and no one will be the wiser.

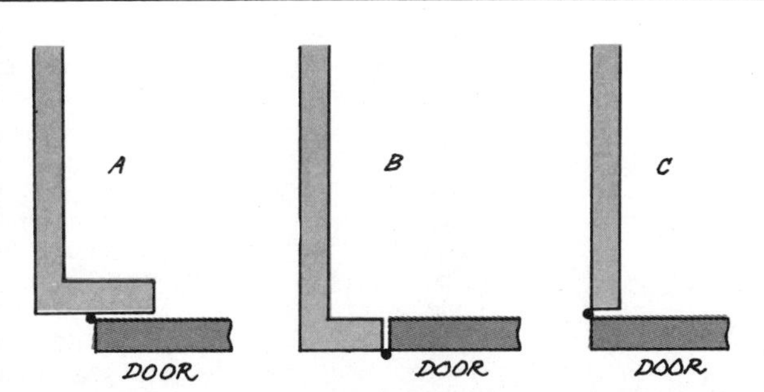

There are three ways of hinging a door—lipped (A), flush (B) and full overlapping (C).

By definition, a full overlapped door has no rabbets, but closes flush against its frame. Actually, this door can overlap two, three, or all four sides of the frame and is hung with either a pin, or pivot hinges.

Flush doors must be fitted into their frame (just like room doors), and they require a back stop and some careful measuring so that they fit properly. The stop can be the front edge of a shelf behind the door, or strips of wood tacked to the inside edges of the frame. There should be no more than 1/8" of space between the door and its frame at any point.

A solid wooden door, if it is small enough, will give years of service and probably not warp too much. Although it is safer to make a solid door out of pressboard, a carefully selected piece of unwarped plywood will also work well. If you use a single, wide piece of solid wood you are asking for trouble, particularly if it is softwood. There is less chance of warping if you make a solid wood door by joining narrow strips using butt, spline, or rabbet joints. Better still, add a crossbrace or two and/or a diagonal to at least one side of the assembly.

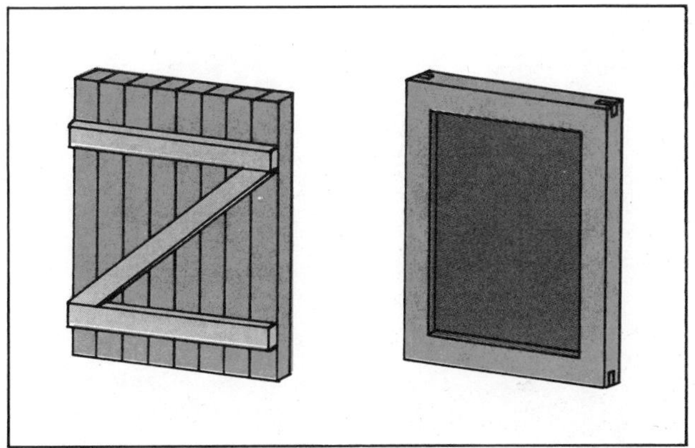

A door made of solid wood has less chance of warping if it is constructed from narrow pieces and braced. The frame-and-panel construction takes time and effort to build, but it nearly eliminates any chance of warping or splitting over years of use.

The best way to minimize warping is with a frame-and-panel construction. It takes more time and care to build, but if the door is to go on a decorative cabinet, it is well worth the labor. The idea behind the frame and panel is to produce a lightweight, sturdy door that can resist warping and splitting, no matter how large it is. Historically, the frame and panel has not been confined to small doors, either. It has long been used to make closet doors and cabinet end panels as well as dust covers between drawers.

The frame and panel can be made in any number of creative ways, but all of them will be variations on the four basic construction methods shown on this page—the butt joint, dado-mortise and tenon, dowel, and rabbet-mortise and tenon.

Essentially, the frame and panel is a frame made of one thickness, while the middle of that frame is filled with wood of a lesser thickness. Panels usually range from 1/8" to 1/2" thick; the frame can be as much as 2 1/2" thick.

In making the frame and panel, begin by cutting the frame pieces to size. Then make whatever joints you have chosen. Test-assemble the frame to make sure all of the joints are correct and that the frame fits properly in the cabinet. Now, rout the inside edges of the frame to accept the panel. Cut the panel and be sure it fits inside the frame without forcing any of the joints apart.

If the panel is to have any decorative work done on it, such as camfering or veneering, complete all necessary procedures before glueing the panel and frame together. If the door is to be rabbeted along its inside edges, also do that before you assemble it.

If you do not want to dado the frame, the panel can be inserted by using any number of molding arrangements, such as those shown below.

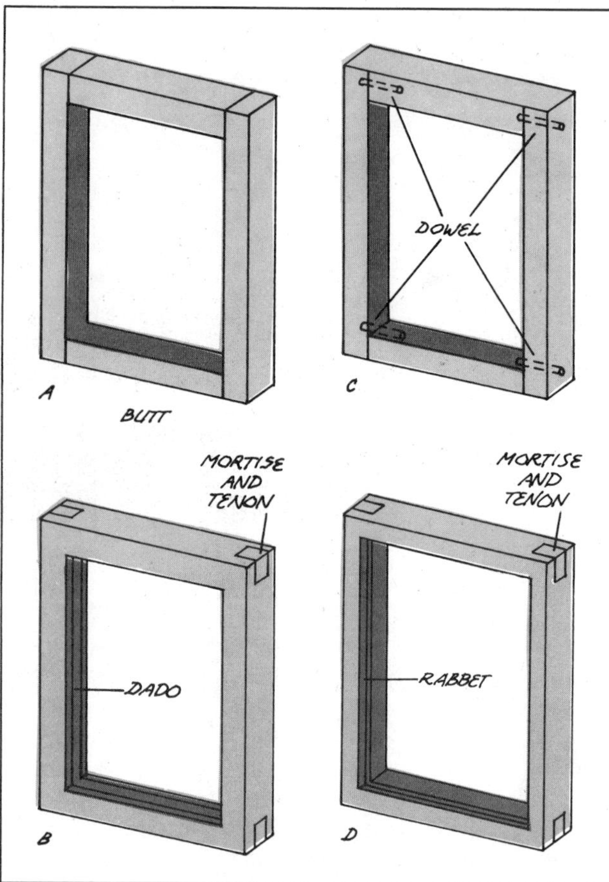

The butt joint, the dado-mortise and tenon, dowel, and rabbet-mortise and tenon are four of the joinery combinations that can be used to make a frame and panel.

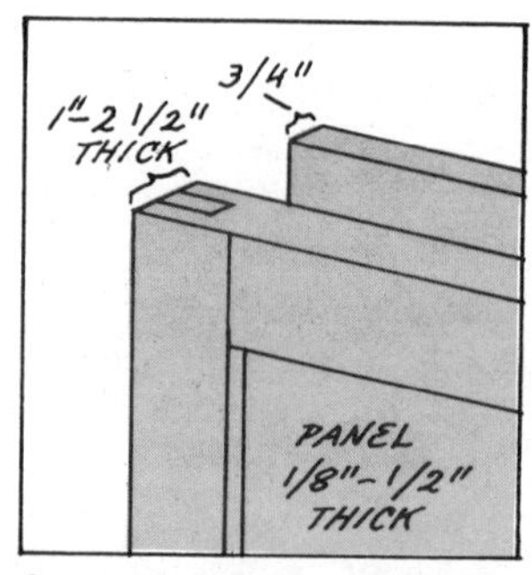

Square inch for square inch, a frame 2½" thick with a panel ½" thick will be lighter and sturdier than a door the same size made from ¾" solid wood.

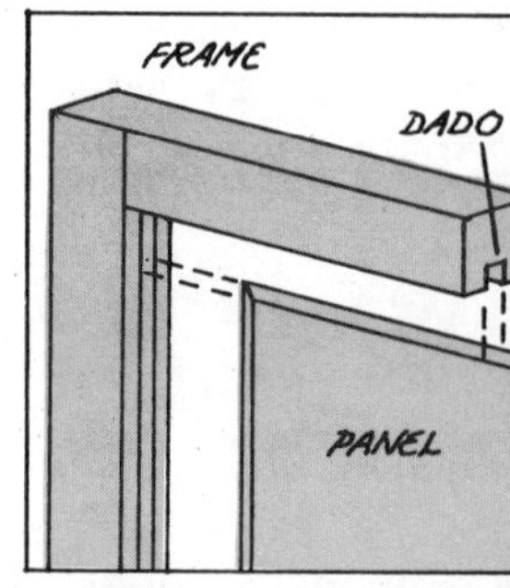

The panel need not be glue in its dado slot. If the door to spend most of its exis ence in a humid climat glueing will deter the pan from expanding and cor tracting, making it vulne able to splitting.

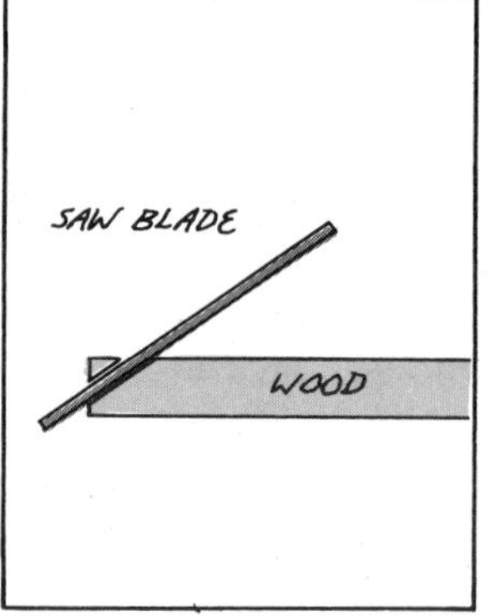

Camfering a ½"-thick panel is best done with either a table or a radial arm saw.

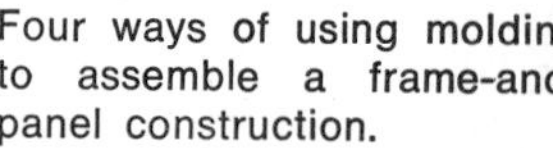

Four ways of using moldin to assemble a frame-and panel construction.

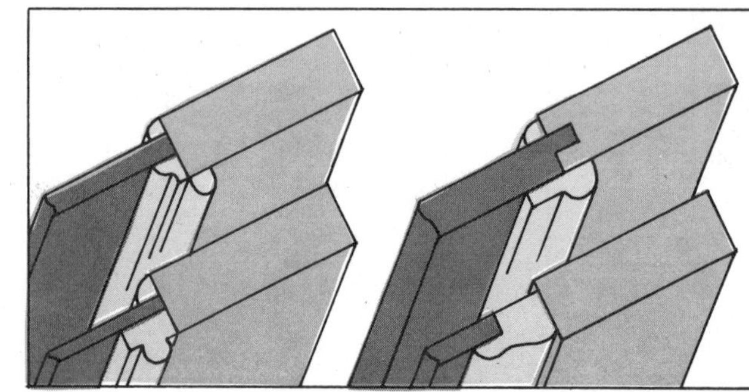

CHAPTER 7

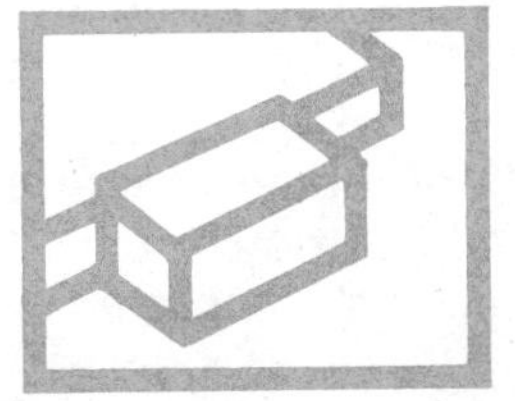

Veneering, Molding and Trim

Veneering, Molding and Trim

More than 3,500 years ago the Egyptians were producing intricate inlaid and veneered chests, tables and cabinets. The Egyptians were lucky. They had access to copper mines and knew how to make bronze tools that could retain a sharp edge. They figured out how to peel veneers that were ¼" thick (more or less) from a log, and they developed stone-grinders to smooth these veneers even thinner. Thus, the Egyptians developed the two basic steps in veneering: cutting wood in paper-thin sheets, and glueing these sheets to other wood.

Centuries later, all of Rome fell in love with veneered furniture, and the rich spent fortunes to acquire tables and chests decorated with it. It was the Romans who invented the hand plane and bow saw, which enabled them to cut their veneer even thinner, and then smooth it far better than the veneer produced by the Egyptians. Then came the Dark Ages and, like most of the other advances by mankind, veneering became an obscure, seldom practiced art.

Finally, in 1805, the English invented the first powered circular saw. It was not particularly good at cutting veneers, but it heralded the coming of powered knife-slicers in 1880, which brought veneering back to popularity. Then, at the turn of the 20th century, there occurred the biggest advance of all. People started glueing thin plies of wood together with the wood grains running at right angles to each other—and a new material called plywood was born.

Advanced techniques are used for cutting, handling, glueing, clamping and repairing veneers. The veneers are thinner, more even, and sometimes sold with a special backing that makes their natural brittleness more manageable; modern glues are stronger, quicker, and cleaner than ever before. Because of these technical advances when a craftsman turns to the art of veneering he is not really venturing into a very deep abyss. After 3,500 years of evolution veneering is still nothing more than glueing some thin pieces of wood to thicker, stronger, less attractive pieces. But you get it all polished up and—presto! From the cocoon of a wormy wooden box there emerges a butterfly of furniture.

Veneering

Like anything else that appears simple at first glance, there are some intricacies to veneering that should be noted. Everything you do in veneering has to be very precise. Measuring, cutting, joining, glueing, repairing and finishing must all be exact, because it is the veneer that people look at and there is no way of hiding a mistake the way a structural error can be hidden.

Still, the biggest problem with veneering a cabinet is to decide what face veneer to use. There are well over 250 kinds of wood sold as veneers, and each of these is likely to produce anything from straight stripes to bee's-wing, rope, curly, mottle, burl, peanut, leaf, flake, quilted, circles, waves, bird's-eye or waterfall to name just a few of the patterns available. (See this chapter for a few representative photographs.) And no two sheets are ever alike, either. Even when they are cut from the same tree, veneers differ from each other. As a result, it is wise to do all your shopping at once because veneer-buying is not like going to a supermarket. You cannot go back next week and get more of the same pattern you have at home and expect it to be identical.

Face veneers are sold in either 1/40" or 1/42" thicknesses with their lengths and widths determined by the size of the tree they were cut from. Veneers which are not highly patterned are marketed as "crossband" in thicknesses between 1/28" and 1/8". Crossband is used either to back a particularly fragile face veneer, or as part of the core of a panel. Poplar is the veneer customarily selected for crossband, although sycamore and mahogany are also frequently used.

When selecting a face veneer, you want to consider the grain and color in terms of how it will look when finished. You want to take into account the shock-resistance and warping tendencies of the wood itself, and the effect of light reflection as well as the pure design of the pattern. Technical knowledge could play a part in your choice, but all that becomes irrelevant the moment you fall in love with a particular pattern. So just buy what you like and worry about working with it when you get home.

Relatively speaking, veneer is not expensive. It costs between 25¢ and $1.50 a square foot. For a moderate-sized cabinet, measuring 60"x30"x20", you could buy a veneer costing $1.50 per square foot and spend under $30 to cover the sides, top nd front. Despite its comparatively inexpensive ost, however, you never want to waste veneer ecause each piece is literally one of a kind. here is no other exactly like it anywhere in the niverse, and it should be treated accordingly.

A FEW OF THE MANY VENEERS AVAILABLE TO CABINETMAKERS

ASH (USA) cream with brown; stripes.

ASPEN (USA) white to yellow with pale brown; mottle, crotch, straight stripe.

AVODIRE (Africa) white-yellow to gold; plain, stripe, mottle.

BENGE (Africa) light to dark brown with red-brown stripes.

BUBINGA (Africa) pinkish with wavy purple lines.

BUTTERNUT (USA) pale brown; superimposed cathedral pattern.

CARPATHIAN ELM BURL (England, France) red to tan; circles and central eyes in pattern.

CHERRY (USA) light red-brown; open wavy pattern.

EBONY, GABOON (Africa) black; little visible pattern.

FAUX SATINE (USA) yellow-brown; straight stripe.

GONCALO ALVES (Brazil) dark brown with tan streaks.

KELOBRA (Mexico) brown with greenish cast; streaked, broad wavy lines.

LACEWOOD (Australia) pinkish, flecked with brown.

MADRONE BURL (USA) reddish brown, pinkish.

MAKORI (Africa) pinkish to reddish brown; various degrees of ripple crossfire.

ORIENTALWOOD (Australia) greyish brown to pinkish; straight stripes.

PADAUK (Burma) golden brown with red-violet stripes.

PALDAO (Philippines) gray to reddish brown; wild, irregular-striped pattern.

PRIMAVERA (Central America) pale yellow to brown; wavy stripes, mottle has a changing sheen that varies with light reflection.

ROSEWOOD (Brazil) tan, golden brown to almost black; striped, wavy pattern.

ROSEWOOD (East Indies) dark purple to ebony with streaks of red or yellow; straight stripe.

ROSEWOOD (Honduras) orange-brown to dark brown; irregular stripe.

SAPELE (Africa) dark red-brown; striped with crossfire flecks that sparkle.

SATINWOOD (Ceylon) gold to deep yellow; straight, wavy, rippled, mottle, bee's-wing mottle.

TAMO (Japan) tan with wavy brown grain; leaf, narrow wavy stripes plus a small, peanut-shell pattern.

THUYA BURL (Africa) golden to reddish brown with dark brown streaks; twists, swirls, numerous eyes.

ZEBRAWOOD (Africa) straw color; straight dark brown stripes.

Preparing Veneer for Use

Veneers do not always come ready to cut and glue, either. They are fragile, often brittle pieces of wood and if they have been subjected to a lot of handling, storage, humidity changes and transportation, they may need some preliminary repair work.

Sometimes the wood splits, usually along the grain at the ends, although butts, burls and crotches are apt to develop cracks anywhere in the vicinity of their eyes and pinholes. Repairing these splits is standard practice among people who do veneering all the time. The edges of the split are carefully butted together again and held in place with a strip of veneer tape stuck to the *right* side of the sheet, the side that will *not be* glued. By the time the veneer is glued to the cabinet and the tape is peeled off, no one, including you, will ever notice there was ever any split at all.

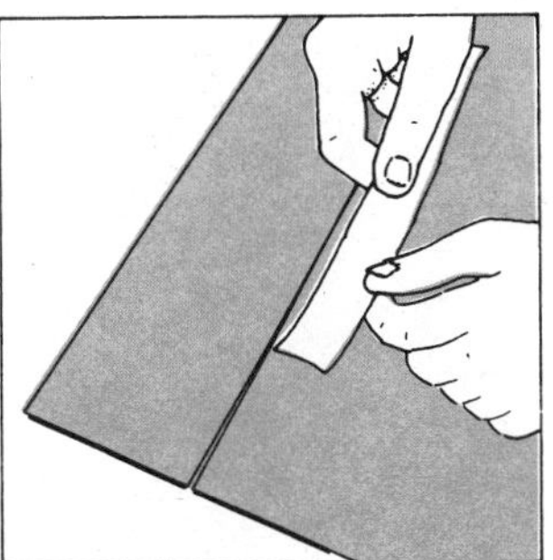

Transparent stationery tape may be substituted for veneer tape.

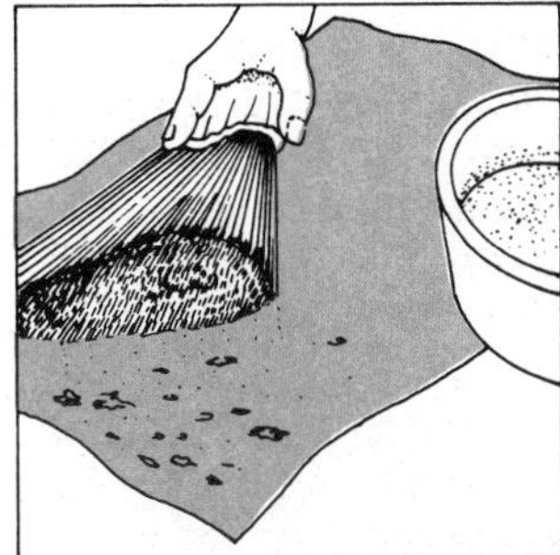

Be very sparing with the amount of water sprinkled on any veneer that must be flattened.

Veneers also curl or warp in funny ripples that make them unruly to handle. Fortunately, flattening veneer is a simple matter. Sprinkle some water on the curled sheet and flatten it out evenly under weights. When the wood dries it should be flat. If it isn't, dampen it again. Experts prescribe nothing more than dipping a whisk broom in water and spanking it against your hand once or twice over the veneer. That will produce splashes of water here and there, but that is all you really need.

If you are flattening more than one veneer at a time, sandwich each sheet between brown paper.

When flattening more than one veneer at a time, each sheet may be sandwiched between sheets of brown paper. Try to keep the veneer edges aligned so they will have less chance of breaking.

A Few Representative Veneers

Zebrano

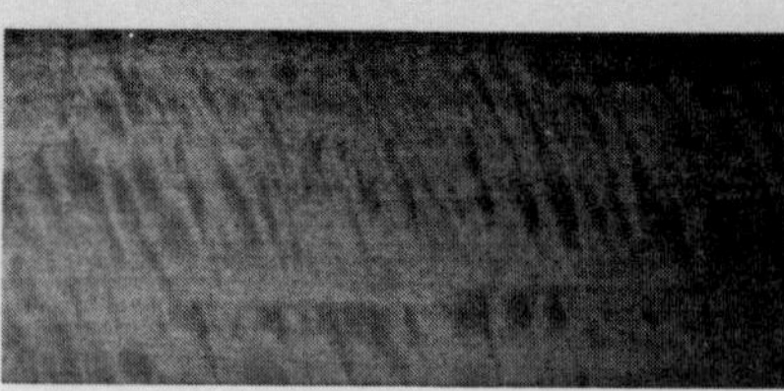
Primavera

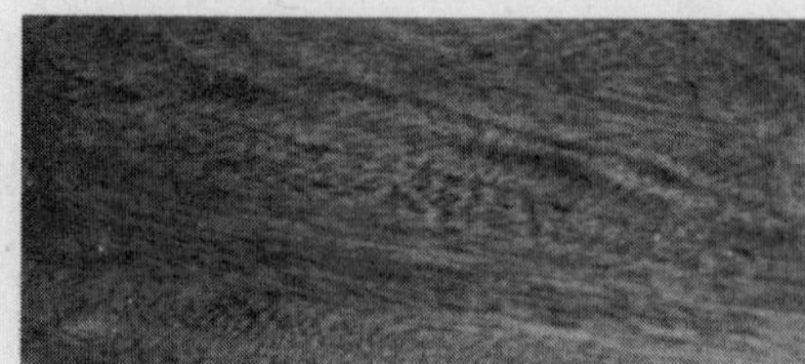
Honduras Mahogany

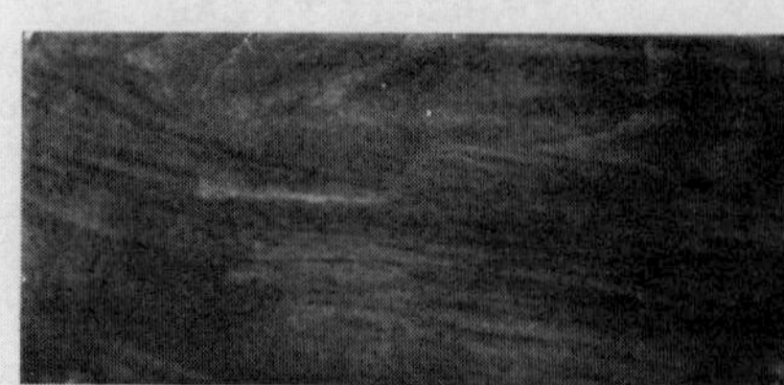
Butternut

China Wood

Rosewood

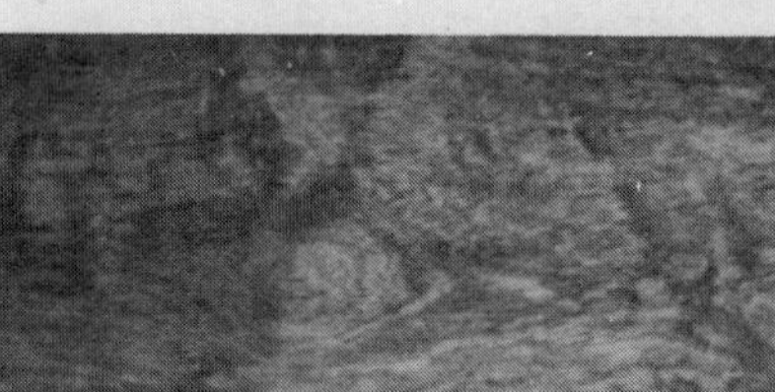
East Indian Laurel

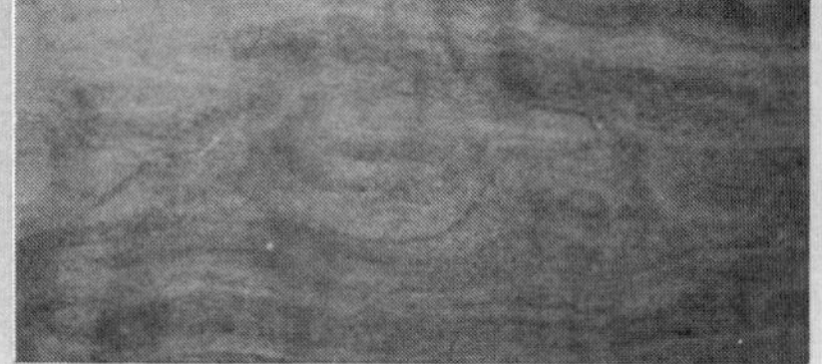
Aspen

Sycamore

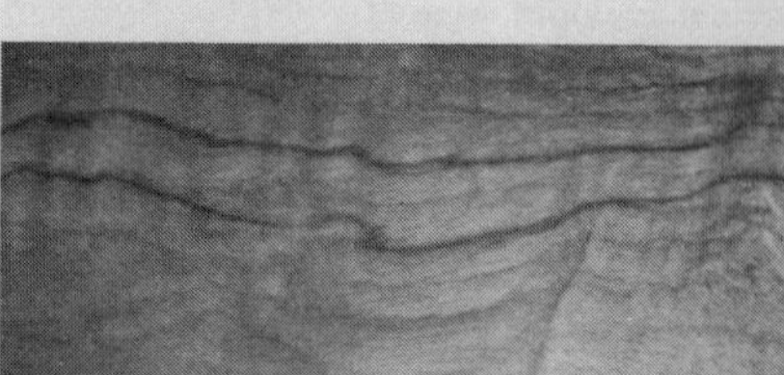
Teak

Black Walnut

Narra

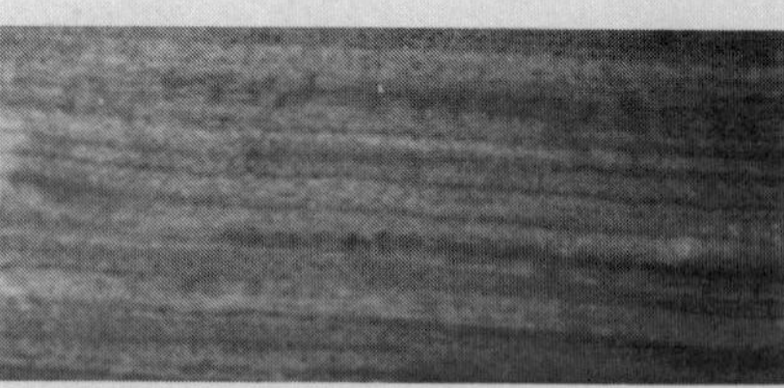
Oriental Wood

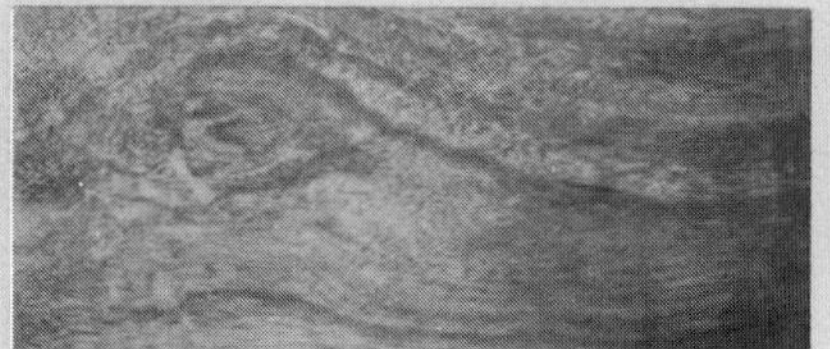
Benge

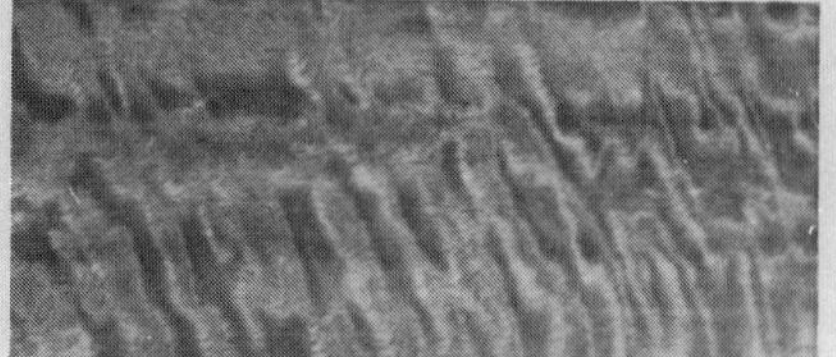
Eucalyptus

Red Cedar

The most readily available brown paper is a grocery bag, but when you cut it open, get rid of the seams. Do not use newspaper, or anything with printing on it; the ink rubs off on the wood. Stack the veneer and brown paper on a flat surface and put a flat panel (like plywood scrap) over the pile. Gradually place heavy weights (stones, scrap metal, bricks, anything heavy) evenly on top of the panel. The more weight the better. Let the veneer stand for 24 hours, then change the paper padding and put the veneer back under its weights. In fact, keep them there until you are ready to cut and glue the veneer. One day is mandatory. Three days are ideal. Anything after that is a bonus. The veneer must be absolutely dry when you work with it. Glueing moist veneer will only make it split as it dries. Besides, the glue will not hold very well. All of which means: Do your flattening well in advance of the day you plan to use the veneer.

Backing Veneer

Once in a great while (like one out of 100 times) you will run into an ornery piece of warped veneer that just will not get unbuckled. This is liable to be something like a sheet of burl or crotch, and the answer is to glue it to another piece of veneer. There are also a few veneers, such as aspen crotch and thuya burl, that are so delicate they need backing no matter what condition they are in, because as the humidity changes they will develop cracks. There is one other situation when backing is necessary, and that is when you are veneering fir or fir plywood. Fir has an uneven grain and any face veneer glued to it will tend to follow the peaks and valleys of the grain. Consequently, fir should always have a sheet of poplar or sycamore crossbanded between it and the face veneer.

There is roughly a 50-50 division among professionals over whether veneer grains should go with or at right angles to each other when they are being backed. If you choose to have the grains going in the same direction, use plain mahogany veneer for the backing material. If you prefer to crossband, poplar or sycamore are good choices. They are a little less stable than mahogany so their grains should run at a 90° angle to the grain of the face veneer.

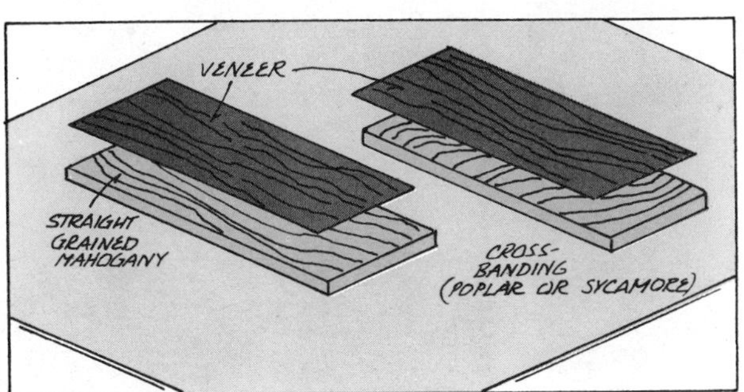

When crossbanding, use poplar or sycamore. If the grain of the face veneer and its backing are to go in the same direction, use plain (straight grained) mahogany.

Veneering Tools and Equipment

All the equipment one needs to do veneering is shown on this and the next page. It includes such items as an old hacksaw blade, a craft knife, razor blades and emery boards, gummed veneer tape and a veneer saw. These are the basic tools, and all are inexpensive. You also need T-squares, rulers, a glue-spreader and assorted rolling devices such as are used for baking and hanging wallpaper. You will also need an awl, a hand plane, and probably a few more clamps than you already have.

The veneer saw is a neat little gadget. Its teeth have no set, so they leave a narrow kerf and they are not sidetracked by the pull of a testy grain, the way a craft knife can be. Nor do they chip the edges along the cut. The craft knife has a definite place, however, especially if you are cutting across a regular grain or making a curve. And there are some rules to follow in cutting veneer: Always use a sharp, pointed, tapering blade. Always cut from an edge toward the center. If you are smart, you will always use a straight edge as a cutting guide. If you are *really* smart, you will always put transparent tape on the underside of a cut to minimize chipping.

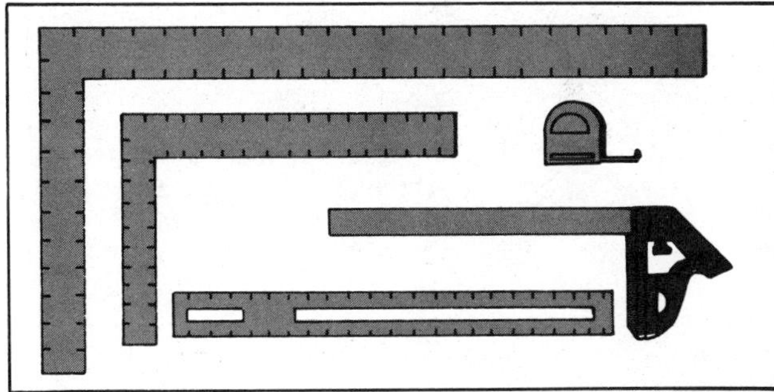

Tools to measure with include a ruler, T-square, steel square and a 6′ measure. Except for the 6′ rule, all of these can double as cutting guides.

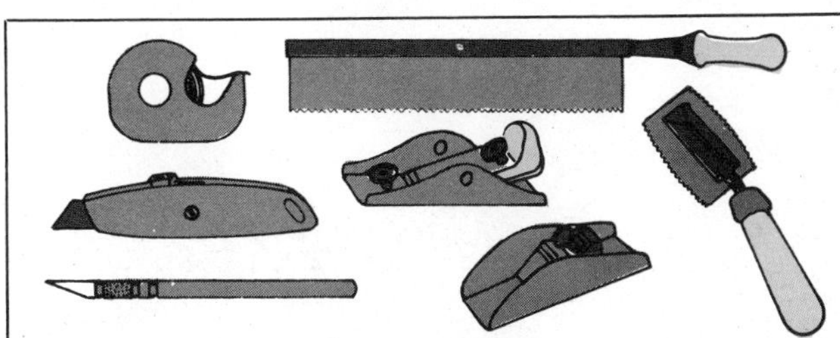

Cutting tools include gummed tape, hack saws, razor blades, craft knives, small hand planes, emery boards and a veneer saw.

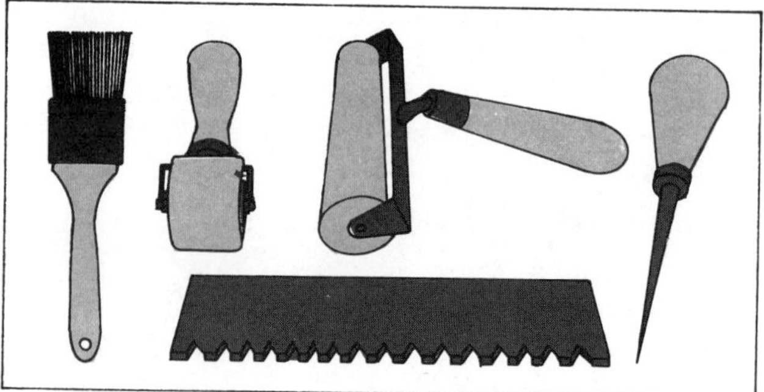

The tools needed for glueing include brushes for moving glue to the edges of your work, various sizes of rollers, an awl for holding veneer down when glueing, a notched board or two to act as glue spreaders, and masking tape.

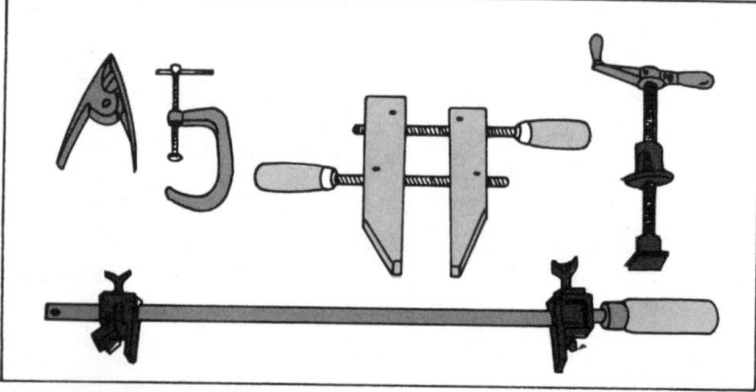

The bar and C-clamps may be the most useful clamping devices when veneering a cabinet. But the spring clamps and hand screws are extremely helpful. Plans for building a veneer press frame that utilizes the veneer press screw are shown on page 9.

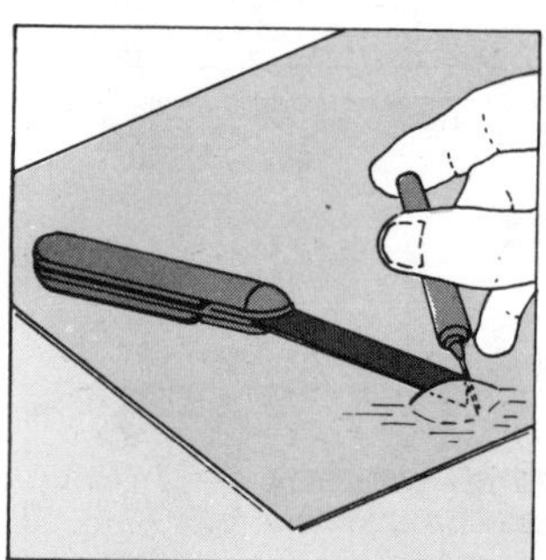

Aside from clamps, the art of repairing veneer requires a glue injector (about $2), an eye dropper, a thin-bladed spatula ($2.50), a sharp chisel and an assortment of shaded shellac sticks.

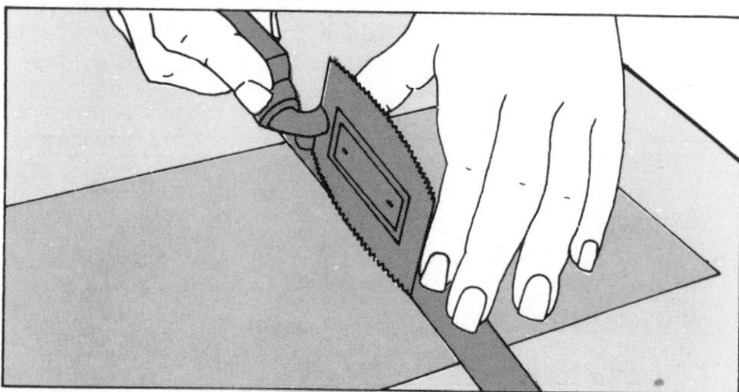

The veneer saw is indispensable because it has a narrow kerf and is not influenced by the pull of a tough grain. The craft knife is ideal for cutting end grains and curves as well as small cuts.

Matching Patterns

Veneer sheets are scrupulously kept in order from the moment they are cut at the sawmill to the moment they are sold in a lumberyard. As a result, you can buy two or more sheets from the same log that will form a design simply by butting their edges. This is called book-matching because the pieces look like an open book—one of countless ways that veneer can be arranged into designs.

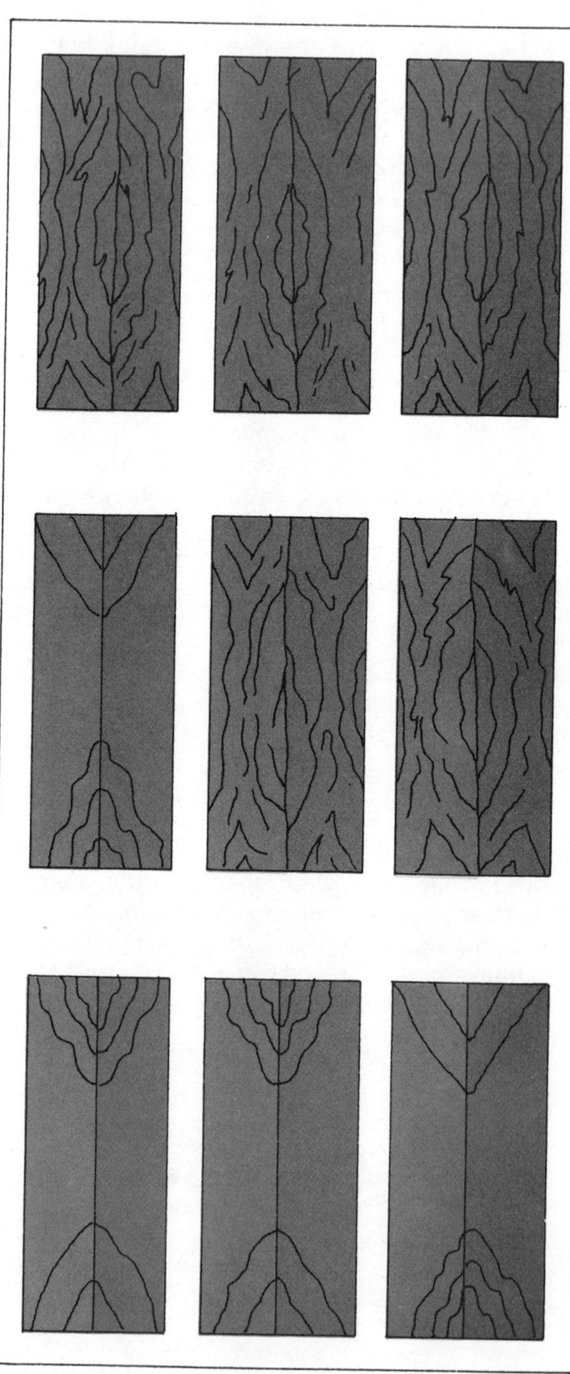

By doing nothing more than assembling consecutive sheets of veneer cut from the same tree, you can create any number of fancy designs.

The problem in matching and joining veneer sheets lies in the joint. It has to be a perfectly straight line, which means both edges must be absolutely true. The solution is to cut both edges at the same time. Line up the two pieces and hold them under the pressure of a cutting guide such as one leg of a steel square. Now saw through both sheets at the same time and you will have a pretty good matching cut. Pretty good, but not good enough.

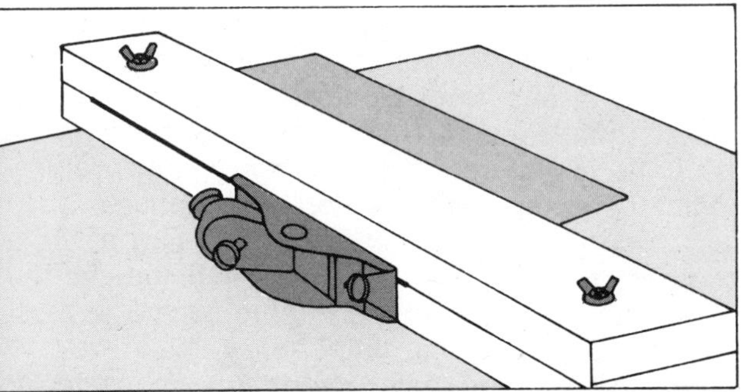

A simple but effective jointing jig can be made from two pieces of hardwood such as maple or oak. The pieces are approximately 1½"x3"x24" and are bored for two carriage bolts and wing nuts. Both pieces of a veneer joint are clamped in the jig and planed or sanded flush.

Next, clamp the two sheets together in the jointing jig shown on this page and plane them, using a shallow blade set that barely bites the wood. Keep planing until you can no longer feel any protrusions. If you have a jointer-planer, the jig can be easily run over that, since planing the jig down evenly will not impair its efficiency.

At this point, you should have a joint that matches when the sheets are laid next to each other on a flat surface. Try to make the figures come together at all points, and when you have done the best you can, attach the two sheets with veneer tape. Turn the sheets over and bend the joint slightly open. Run a bead of cream glue down into the joint and lay the work flat to dry. From here on, treat the joined pieces as a single sheet of veneer; when it has been glued in place and thoroughly dried and the veneer tape removed, it will be.

Measuring Veneer

The surest way of measuring veneer is to lay it under the piece it is to cover and make a tracing on the sheet. Then cut the veneer a little wider than your pencil lines. An alternative is to cut two adjacent edges exactly along the pencil lines and leave the other two sides with extra veneer. Whichever system you use, it is always safer to have veneer to trim off, so that you will never be caught with a short edge somewhere.

SOME RULES FOR STORING VENEER

1) Never store veneer on end.
2) Keep veneers on a flat surface with a light weight such as a plywood panel on top of them.
3) Keep the edges of the sheets as even as possible so that they can support each other.
4) A cool, even mildly damp, basement is a better place to store veneers than a hot attic or furnace room.

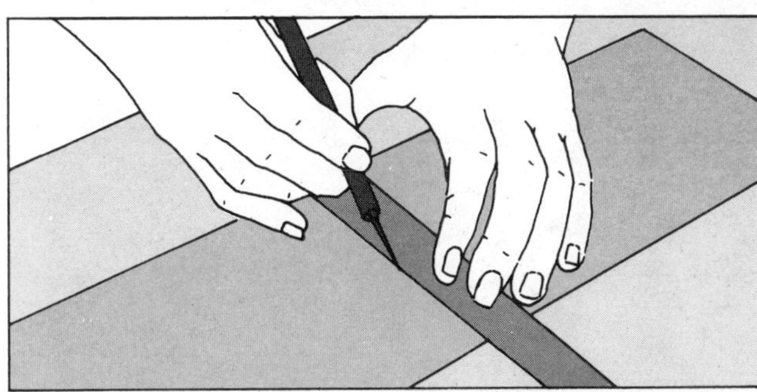

After tracing off the dimensions of a veneer piece, you can either cut around the lines, leaving an overhang on each edge, or cut two adjacent sides exactly and leave an overhang on the remaining sides.

Glueing and Glues

You may be wondering which is the "right" side of a 1/42" thick sheet of veneer. The side which is tight, of course. Glue is always applied to the soft side. The way to tell which side is which is to rub a finger over the edge of the end grain. One side of the veneer will chip more readily than the other; that is the soft side, the one which you glue to your project.

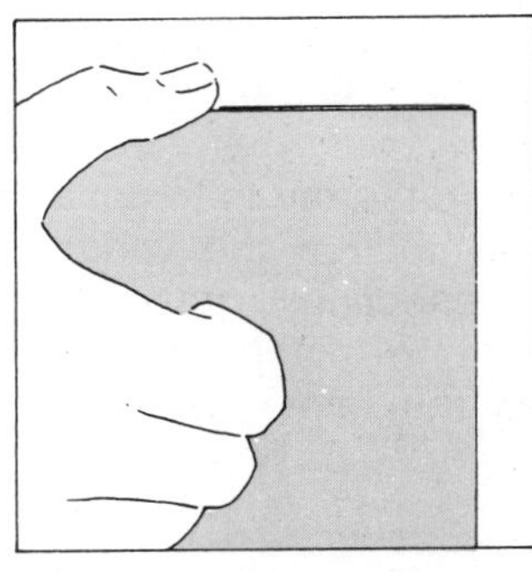

"Thumbing" the end grain of a piece of veneer will produce chipping on one side. The chipped side is the soft side, the side that should be glued.

There are two exceptions to this rule. If you are matching consecutive panels to create a matched design, every other sheet will have to be glued with the right side down. The other exception is bird's-eye maple, which looks like a burl but is not. The eyes on one side of bird's-eye maple feel like bumpy peaks. On the other side you can see, but not really feel, tiny craters at the points of the eyes. It is always the underside (soft side) with the peaks that is glued down. If you glue bird's-eye maple with the right side down the eyes will pop out.

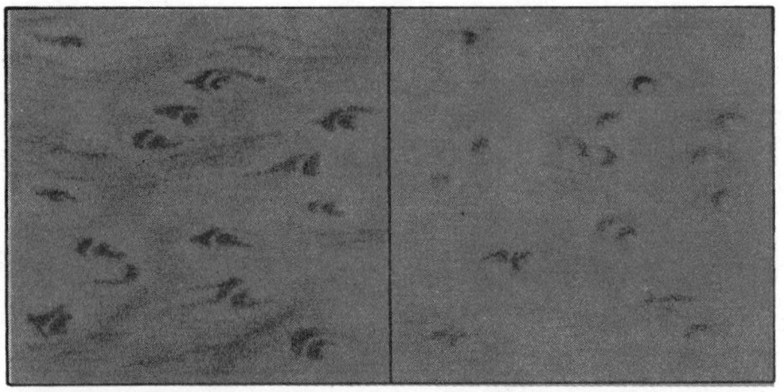

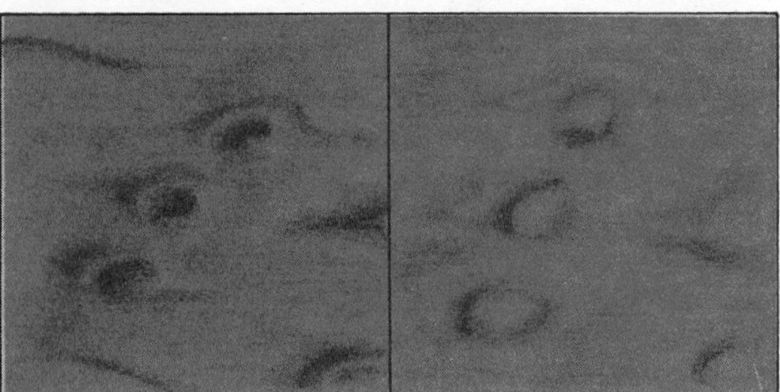

With bird's-eye maple, there is only one side you should glue down—the side with the peaks.

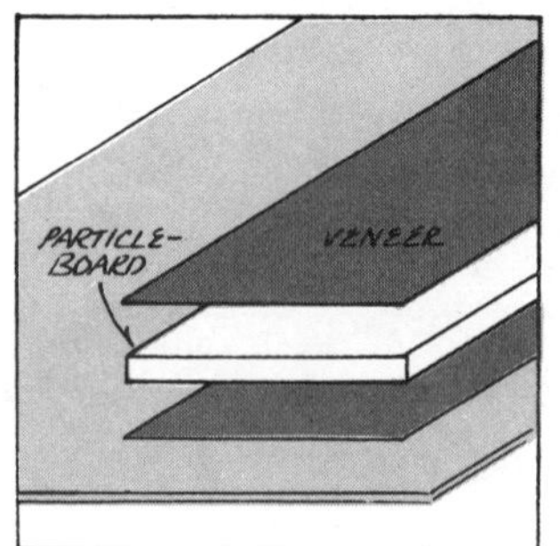

Particleboard is as porous as veneer, so it makes an excellent core. Hardboard must be scratched with a craft knife so that glue will adhere to it properly.

There are three modern glues used in veneering: white (polyvinyl resin), cream (aliphatic emulsion) and contact cement. In general, the white glues are used for small projects or those in which you are laying down several small pieces and need time for assembly. The cream glues develop tack faster than the whites and are somewhat stronger, so the creams are excellent for larger, less intricate assembly. The contacts need a long time to set, so they are ideal for large projects, such as covering a cabinet. However, they bond on contact and do not require clamping, which makes them a favorite for almost any project.

The job of any glue used in veneering is to cover every square inch of surface so that the veneer will not develop blisters. Veneer by nature is porous, which gives glue plenty of places to seep in and grip. Veneer is also thin, so it is absolutely vital that all glueing surfaces be free of dust or foreign matter. Small as they are, dust particles can break up the adhesion of glue when you are dealing with sheets of wood that are porous and thinner than paper. In addition, glue hardens by losing its moisture. Some of that moisture immediately enters the veneer and causes it to warp. Consequently, when you are using a white or cream glue, apply it to the panel, not to the veneer. Above all, any type of glue coverage must be total, even, and a little heavy. One way to judge whether you have used enough white or cream glue is by squeeze-out. If there is no squeeze-out at the edges, you did not use enough glue. It is always better to have to clean a little glue off the edges than not have enough adhesive where the veneer is most vulnerable to moisture and lift-up.

When you are using contact, cover both glueing surfaces. In fact, contact should always have two coats, with the second coat coming about an hour after the first. The surfaces are ready to go together when a sheet of brown or wax paper will slide over the surfaces without sticking. Place the paper over the panel, leaving about ½" at one end. Align the veneer with the panel and press the unpapered edges into place. Now slide the paper back an inch or two at a time, constantly working your fingers against the veneer, pressing it into place. As soon as the paper is removed, roller the entire surface. It is not a bad idea to clamp or weight the project for about half an hour "just to make sure."

CHARACTERISTICS OF GLUES USED IN VENEERING

Glue	Size Of Project	Temp.	Application	Clamp Time	When To Trim Edge	Glue Line	Blister Repair	Setting Time	Spreader	Clamps Weights	Clean Up	Comments
WHITE (polyvinyl resin)	small	70°	heavy, even	1 to 12 hrs.	12 hrs.	thin	use	delayed	comb, brush	a must	use warm water at once	wait 3-10 min. after application & before assembly
CREAM (aliphatic emulsion)	medium	75°	heavy, even	1 to 12 hrs.	12 hrs.	none	possible uses	stiffens faster than white	comb, brush	a must	use warm water at once	preferable for non-porous woods and hardboard
CONTACT	large	70°-90°	2 coats 1 hr. apart	none ½ hr. recommended	at once	none	none	after 2nd coat, bond within 2 hrs.	comb, brush	optional	warm water, lacquer thinner	can be used on any project

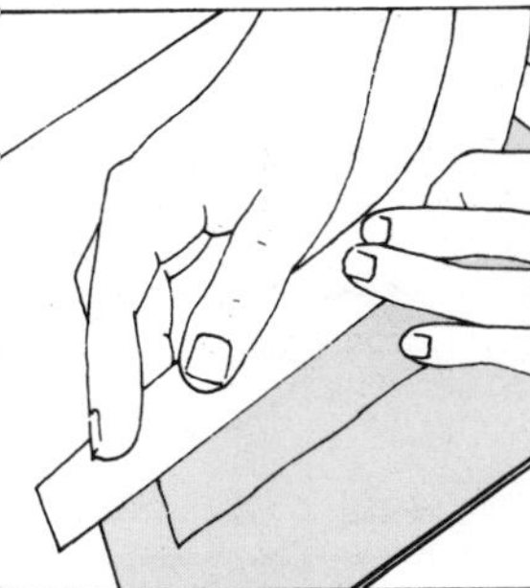

Contact glue bonds on contact. Work a slip sheet of either brown or wax paper between the panel and the veneer so they can be aligned properly.

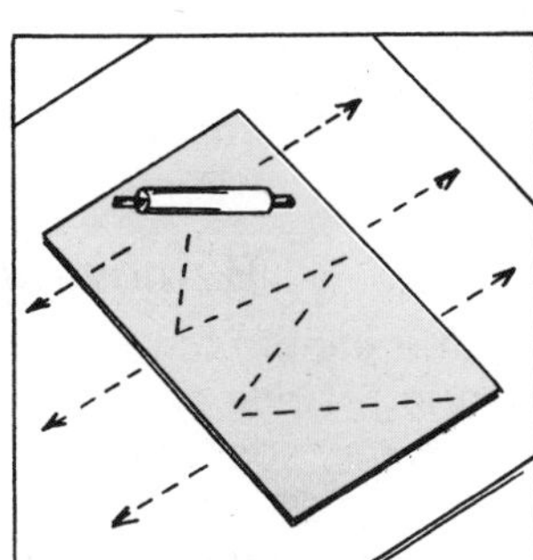

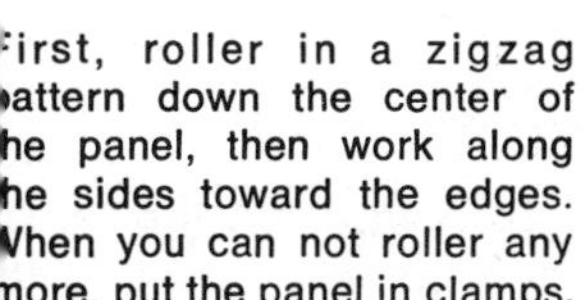

'irst, roller in a zigzag pattern down the center of he panel, then work along he sides toward the edges. Vhen you can not roller any nore, put the panel in clamps.

Rollering may be the most important part of eneering. The object is the same as with any butt oint—to get all points of both glueing surfaces to neet. So lean on your rolling pin, or wallpaper oller, and zigzag your way down the center of the anel. Then go down each side, pushing your way ut to the edges. Do not stop rollering until your rms feel as though they are about to fall off, then ut a plywood panel over the veneer and either lamp it or pile weights on it. With contact glue he clamping is not necessary. If you used either white or cream glue, wait at least 12 hours for he glue to harden.

Clamps have already been discussed in Chapter . When you are veneering, they operate under he same principles as any other clamping operation. Just remember that you want to put pressure

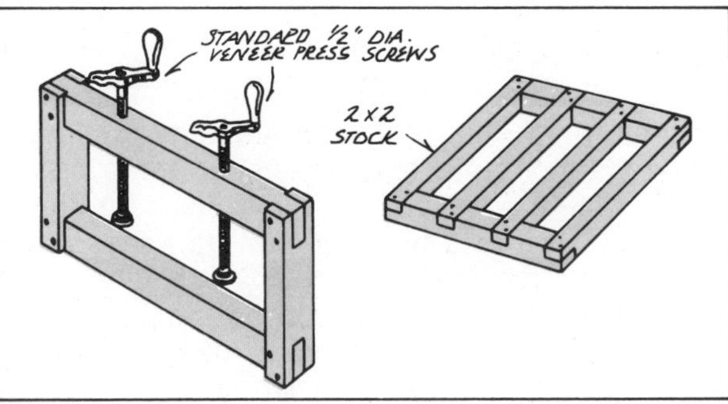

'ou can make this drill press as long as you wish, with s many veneer press screws as you need. Besides the press ed, you should have at least two frames.

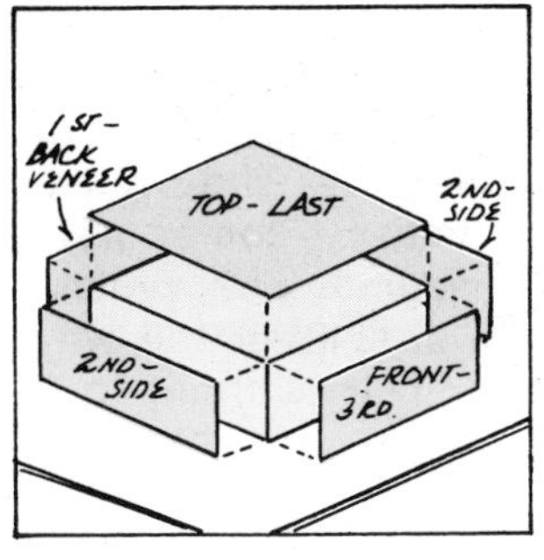

When veneering a cabinet, put the back on first, then the ends, the front and finally the top, so that you will cover as many edge grains as possible.

on every part of the veneer, so use them every few inches. There is a special little item called a press screw, which is, quite simply, a screw with a handle on it. If you buy a few of these you can make some veneer presses like the ones shown here, and they will effectively hold your panels under an even pressure while they are drying. Otherwise, put clamps wherever you can and when there is no place for them to grip, use bricks and cinder blocks to hold glued-together surfaces flat.

Attaching and Repairs

The order in which you attach veneer to a project is always the same: Put the veneer you will see first on last. Hence, with a cabinet you veneer the back first, then the ends, the front, and finally the top. By following this procedure, you can be sure of always covering as many veneer end grains as possible.

However, each veneer project is bound to need some repairs made as you go along, and these ought to be done before you continue glueing since you may have to put the clamps back on for another day or so after they are completed. You will have to trim the edges, peel off tape, fill in dents, correct blisters and refasten edges which have lifted. With the exception of trimming the edges, all of those activities require putting the work back under pressure. If there are not too many such repairs, you may be able to make all of them at once and then clamp the work only one time. But if that is inconvenient or awkward, clamp separately after each operation. From now on, everything you do is directed at protecting the veneer for a lifetime of use, and there are no advantages in trying to save a day or two of waiting time.

Trimming and Sanding

When the glue is dry, run transparent tape along the overhanging edges, on the face side of the veneer. Turn the panel over so that it is face down on a flat, hard surface and trim off the excess edges with a veneer saw or craft knife. The tape will reduce splintering and chipping, but cut around the core very lightly anyway. Then make deeper cuts until the excess material comes free. Do not try to lop off thin veneer in one whack; even with a tape backing it will splinter the way plywood does when you drill it without any backing.

Always use a sanding block, and always sand by pushing the sandpaper away from the edge.

All trimmed edges must be sanded, too. But lightly. And always with a sanding block, so that the edges of the sandpaper won't pick up slivers of wood and rip the whole veneer. Again, because the veneer can easily chip, sand by pushing—*never pulling*—the sandpaper away from the edge. As for power sanding, forget it. If you choose not to forget it and want to risk all that long, hard work you have just put in, take the finest grit you can buy and sand something with it. When the paper is worn down, put it on a vibrating sander and use the machine very briefly, with a very light touch.

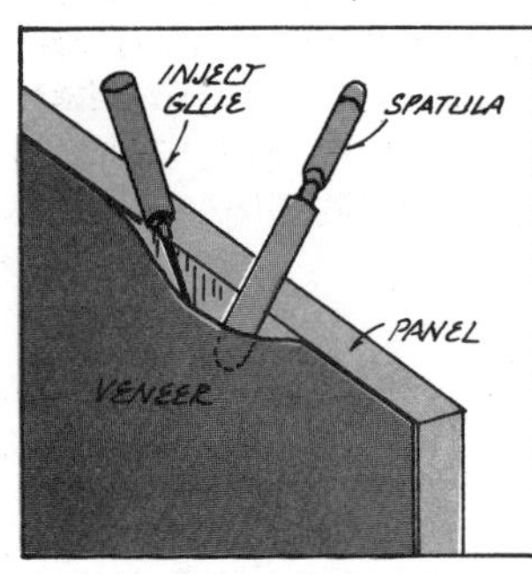

Pull the loose edge away from the core and inject white or cream glue into the split, then clamp for 12 hours.

In the course of sanding, you will discover places where the edges have lifted away from the panel. Pull the edge back gently with the tip of your spatula and insert white glue with a glue injector. Then clamp the edge in place. White glue is preferred because it will settle into the crack more readily than cream glue. Contact will not run at all, even if you could hold the split open long enough for it to dry.

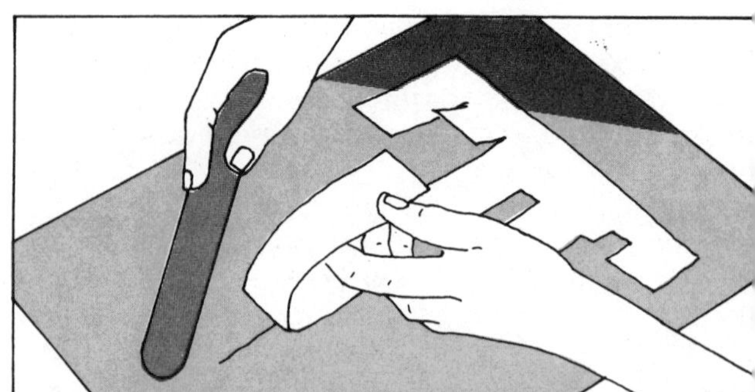

Get as little water on the raw veneer as possible when moistening the back of tape. Use the thin blade of a spatula carefully as you lift the tape.

Removing the Tape

Lay the panel face up and go to work on the tape, covering joints, splits and the trimmed edges. With a wet cellulose sponge, *very carefully* dampen only the tape. Water is a natural enemy of wood, and wood as thin as veneer is particularly vulnerable to it. So be especially careful not to allow water to touch unfinished veneer when all you want to do is loosen the gummed tape. When the tape is damp, work around its edges with the blade of a thin-edged spatula or very dull kitchen knife. Work carefully and deliberately, and eventually you will be able to peel off the tape.

Actually, the tape will split apart and leave a fuzzy layer adhering to the wood. Moisten this, too, but to a much lesser degree than the tape, and keep peeling. At this point, a sharp chisel or cabinet scraper held at right angles to the veneer and pulled toward you under pressure can be a helpful tool.

After the tape has been completely removed, check the entire panel for any dents or nicks in the veneer surface. Using an eye dropper, dampen each depression with hot water. After subjecting your veneer to all that water, clamp or weight the panel for 24 hours; at least let the wet wood dry overnight.

Minor Defects

Blisters are the result of not enough glue under the area, or a change in the humidity, or insufficient rollering. Note that two out of three causes are your fault, not Nature's. First, just try rollering the blister. If it is a big one, test its edges gently with the roller to see if the blister gives any indication that it will go down. Do not pounce on the middle of a big blister with your roller or you may split the veneer. If the roller works on the edges, work your way gradually toward the center; when the veneer is flat, weight it down for a day or so. If rollering does not work, try heat.

If you are sure there was plenty of glue under he blister lay a sheet of aluminum foil over it and ress it with a moderately warm electric iron. troke it a little, then roller the veneer again. Keep his up until you get the blister down flat, then lamp it in place for a few hours.

If there is inadequate glue under the blister r all else has failed, slit the veneer along the rain on both sides of the bump with a craft knife. ift the edge of the cut with the knife point, inject little white glue under one slit and press the blis-er down hard to spread it. Repeat the treatment long the other slit, then place a wood block over he blister and weight it down for at least 12 hours. , after all that, the blister rises again, go back to he hot-iron technique. At least now you know here is sufficient glue under the blister.

Another way of flattening blisters is to iron them with a moderately warm iron. Put aluminum foil between the iron and the veneer.

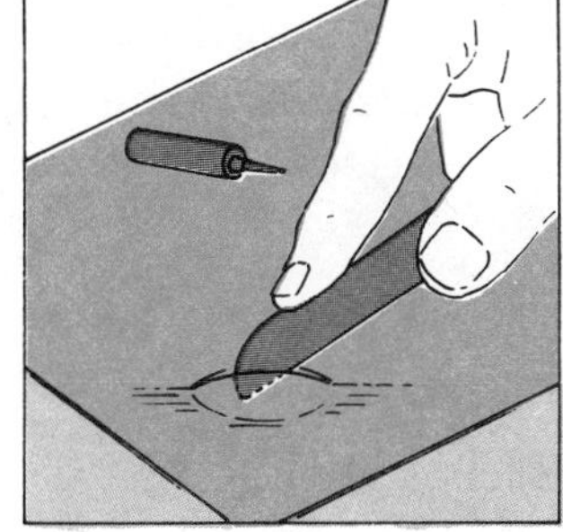

Slit the blister on both sides by cutting along the grain, then inject white or cream glue under the slits; clamp.

Heat the blade of a spatula, rub it against the end of a shellac stick, then push the shellac into the crack.

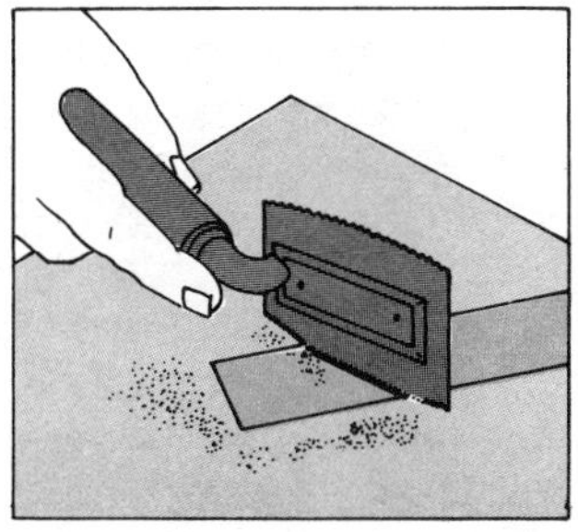

t first, use more glue than sawdust. As you reach the top of the crack, mix more saw-dust than glue.

There may also be some cracks in the veneer, as well as joints that are more visible than you would like. The best way to fill these is with a shellac stick. The sticks come in a variety of shades including mahogany, walnut, cherry, ebony, holly and maple as well as transparent. When you have two shades that are close, but not exactly the color you want, always use the lighter shade. You can also mix the colors as you put them on the veneer.

Heat the blade of a spatula and rub it against the shellac stick, then press the warm wax into the crack. Continue doing this until shellac has built up over the edges of the crack. Allow it to harden overnight, then use a chisel held in a vertical position to scrape off the extra shellac; sand the veneer lightly.

If you cannot come close to the wood color with any of the shellac shades you can make your own filler. Scrape sawdust from a scrap of the veneer with a veneer saw. Next, pile the sawdust on a piece of wax paper beside a puddle of white glue. Collect some glue on your spatula, add slightly less sawdust, and begin to fill the crack or joint. As you reach the top of the crack, use less glue and more sawdust to "top off" the work. Allow to dry for at least 24 hours, then scrape away all excess glue and sawdust. Sand lightly. There is only one rule to remember when you are filling cracks. Always work *with* the grain, but try to be as irregular as possible so that the filler appears to be a part of the pattern. This is one time when your craftsmanship is measured not by what you do, but by how little of what you have done can be seen.

As soon as your project has been glued and inspected and repaired, clamp or weight it until you are ready to put a final finish on it. And remember that the sooner you get a finish over that raw wood, the less chance humidity will have to make it expand, contract, and develop new cracks.

Finishing

There are, of course, numerous ways of finishing a veneered project. You may want to stain it first. Open-pored woods such as mahogany, walnut, oak, lacewood and any of the burls require a wood filler to bring out the grain. Filler will also enrich a stain, if you have used one.

You can rub lemon, linseed or tung oil into a veneer, cover it with shellac, or varnish, or both. Or you can use a urethane varnish. The urethanes come in high gloss, satin, or dull finishes and they can be either brushed or sprayed on. Their advantages are that they are easy to use and do a marvelous job of sealing any veneer under an almost indestructible finish.

There is a wide variety of carvings that can be purchased at the same lumberyard where you get your veneer.

Inlays

Sometime you may want to inlay a cabinet with any of the many different carvings now available on the market. You could just paste them on the veneer, but the purists will frown on you for taking the easy way out. You are expected to cut a hole out of the veneer and fit the carving inside it.

You have two options for cutting a hole in veneer. You can lay the carving on the veneer, trace its outline with a pencil, then cut out the hole with a craft knife. Be careful; you are risking splinters and an uneven cut because the grain will pull at the knife.

Your other choice is a balsa wood sandwich. Put the veneer between two sheets of balsa wood and tape all three sheets together. It helps if the balsa is exactly the same size as the veneer, so that you can be precise about marking the hole and, in addition, protect the veneer edges. Mark off the hole you want to cut on the top balsa sheet and drill through the three sheets. Set your fret saw in the hole and saw away. When the hole is complete, sand the edges before you remove the veneer from the balsa. If the hole still has any imperfections between it and the carving they

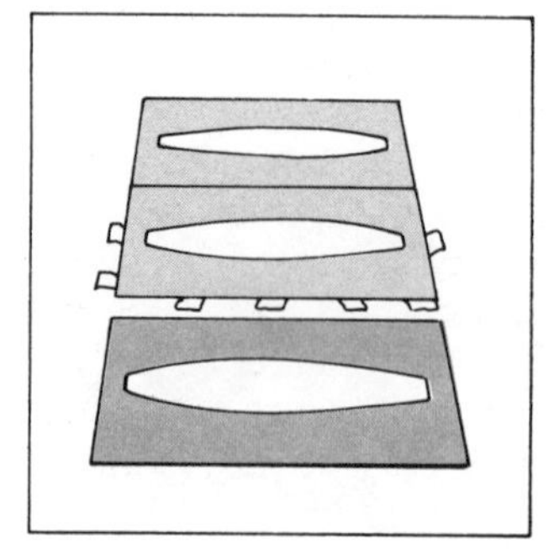

The balsa wood sandwich is held together with tape. If you work the fret saw carefully, there should be no chipping to contend with after the hole is cut.

The inlaid borders shown here are actual widths. Their colors range from black to pale yellow.

can be filled in after the veneer and carving have been glued to the project.

All those pretty inlaid borders you see on old furniture can now be purchased ready for glueing. They come in a variety of patterns and widths and are usually sold in 3′ lengths for something around 20¢ to 30¢ a strip. They are so inexpensive they are normally sold a dozen strips at a time—so spend the $3.00. It's worth it. The widths range from 1/32″ to 1¼″ and the thickness is 1/28″.

Inlays can be put down in the middle of a piece, or around its edges as a border. At first glance, it may seem reasonable to lay a short piece of veneer in the center of a panel and then glue the border around its edges. Don't try it. It is almost impossible to get a large piece of veneer absolutely square on a panel and end up with, say, exactly 3/16″ on all sides.

Perhaps the clearest way of demonstrating the technique of inlaying is to describe a specific project step by step. Suppose you are veneering a cabinet top with a 3/16″ inlay border around the outside edge, and another 1/2″ band three inches inside the edges. The procedure is this:

1. On the core panel, mark off exactly where the band and border edge will be.

2. Measure the rectangle inside the banding route and cut the veneer for that section. Two sides are cut exactly. The other two are allowed a 1/4″ overhang.

3. Measure and cut the four 3/16″ band strips, leaving an inch or so at each end for overlapping at the corners to allow for mitering.

4. Measure and cut the four veneer strips between the band and the edging. Cut them full length so that the corners will overlap, giving you

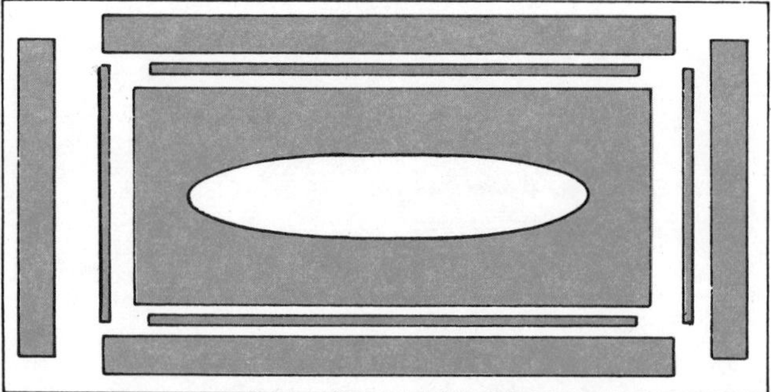

The banding and edge border should be marked on the panel exactly where you want them. All veneer pieces are cut to fit inside the lines which overhang on at least two sides of each piece.

plenty of room for mitering. The strips should be slightly wider than the band and edge lines so that one side can be trimmed.

5. Measure and cut the 1/2″ edge strips, leaving enough length for overlapping and mitering.

6. Pre-assemble all of the parts to make certain everything fits properly.

7. Lay narrow masking tape around the entire edge of the top, making certain that it does not extend beyond the inside pencil line. Also tape over the two sides of the band that will initially be covered by overhang of the center piece.

8. With a project this size, contact glue is in order. Begin by putting glue on the center piece and the middle of the top. After you have applied the second coat of glue, remove the masking tape covering the banding lines.

9. Now, line the "exact" edges of the center veneer along the banding lines and roller the center piece into place.

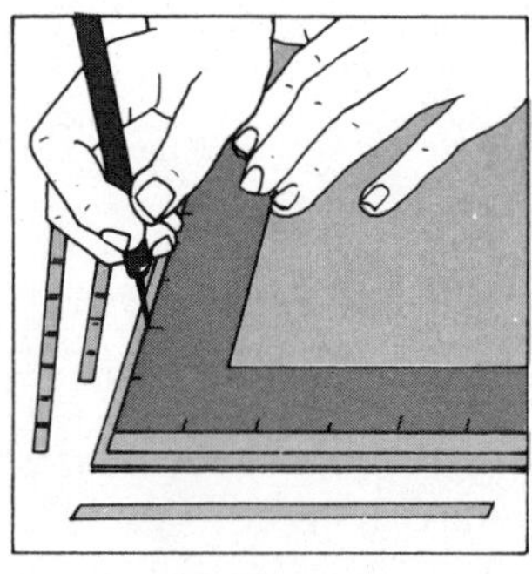

Cover the edges and two of the banding routs with masking tape so that glue will not get on the panel. The tape can be removed as soon as the second coat of glue has been painted on the panel, since glue on only one side of a joint will not stick to anything.

10. Carefully trim the overhanging edges to conform with the banding rout.

11. Apply glue to the 3/16″ banding strips and the banding rout between the edge of the center veneer and the outside pencil line. When the second coat of glue is dry, place a strip of wax paper at each corner where the bands will meet.

12. Glue the bands around the center piece, allowing their ends to overlap at the corners, on top of the wax paper. Be very careful that the

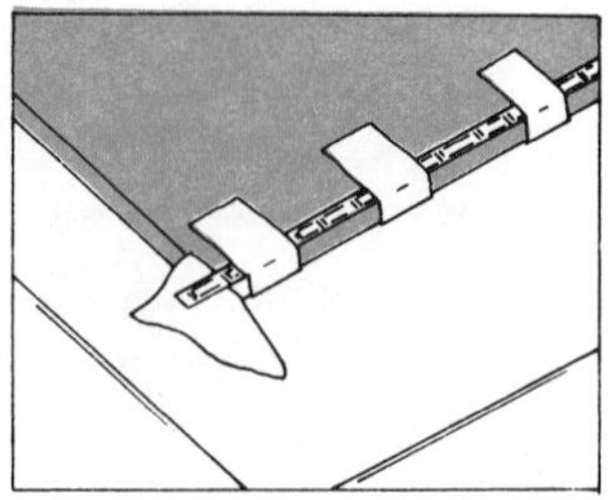

When glueing the bands press them as tightly as possible against the edges of the center veneer piece. The wax paper under the banding corners is removed as soon as the miter angle is cut.

bands butt tightly against the edges of the center veneer.

13. Next, cut a miter joint at each corner with a craft knife. When you have cut through both overlapping bands, remove the wax paper and roller the joints.

14. Again place wax paper under the strips at each corner until the miter angle has been cut. Glue the four strips around the band, making sure that each of them is as tight against the band as possible.

An alternative way of handling the masking tape is to leave it until you have trimmed the overhang, letting it act as a protection against splintering.

15. When the strips are in place, trim their outside edges to accept the 1/2″ border. When you have completely sawed through the overhanging veneer, you should be able to remove it from the panel by peeling off the masking tape around the edge.

16. Glue the edge border in place, again allowing for overhang at the ends so that you can make mitered corners.

17. Clamp and weight the entire piece for half an hour and then repair any dents, blisters or lift-up edges.

18. When all repairs have been made successfully, sand the border and banding down until it is flush with the veneer.

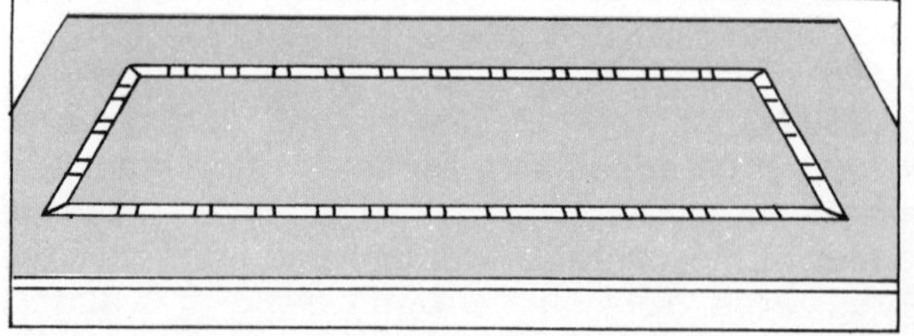

When all repairs have been made on the veneer, sand down the banding and edge border until they are flush with the veneer.

Molding and Trim

After the veneering is done, and before you finish a project, molding and trim should be given serious consideration. A veneer all by itself lifts any cabinet into the realm of furniture. But it is still a box with straight lines and square angles, and no relief in sight. The visual relief in any furniture (other than modern) comes from the occasional curve of whatever molding or trim you place on it as decoration.

Molding is often used on doors and it is a natural cover-up around the edges of a top, particularly if you would otherwise be looking at the raw edges of plywood. The kind of molding and trim you select, and where you put it, is strictly a matter of the builder's taste. There is plenty to choose from and if you don't like what is available at your local lumberyard, get a molding head and set of blades and invent your own.

Shown on these two pages are some of the molding shapes you can buy, as well as a delineation of the most common molding blades and how they can be combined to make an almost infinite variety of decorative shapes. But first, consider the simple box cabinet on this page and note how different it can look, just by changing the molding and trim that decorates it.

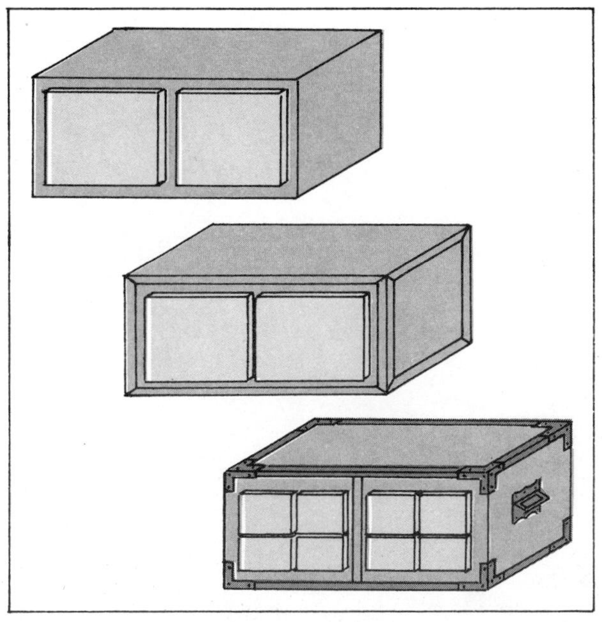

A few molding variations can change the look of the same basic cabinet. The possibilities are endless; use whatever moldings blend best with your decor.

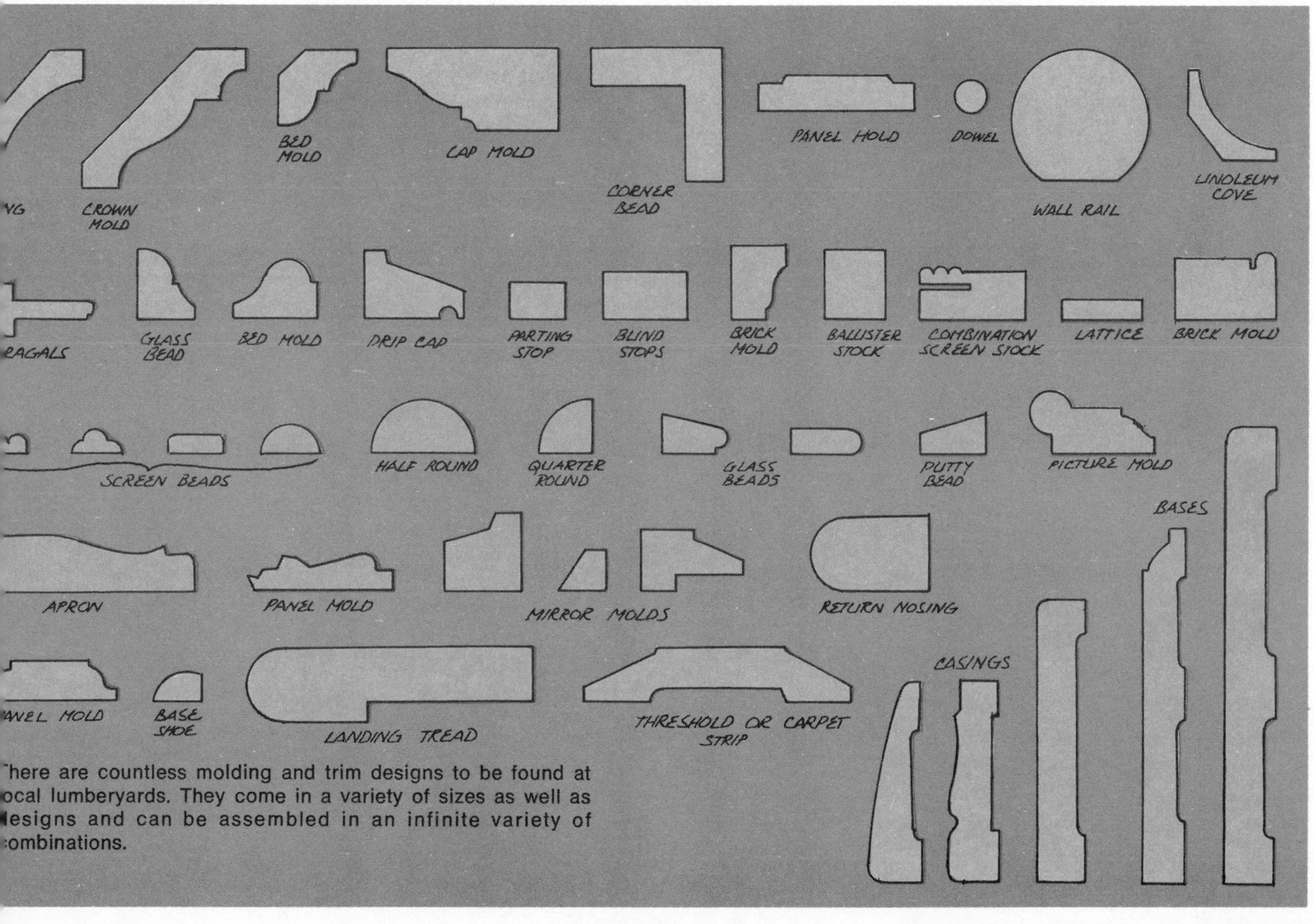

CROWN MOLD
BED MOLD
CAP MOLD
CORNER BEAD
PANEL MOLD
DOWEL
WALL RAIL
LINOLEUM COVE
GLASS BEAD
BED MOLD
DRIP CAP
PARTING STOP
BLIND STOPS
BRICK MOLD
BALLUSTER STOCK
COMBINATION SCREEN STOCK
LATTICE
BRICK MOLD
SCREEN BEADS
HALF ROUND
QUARTER ROUND
GLASS BEADS
PUTTY BEAD
PICTURE MOLD
BASES
APRON
PANEL MOLD
MIRROR MOLDS
RETURN NOSING
CASINGS
PANEL MOLD
BASE SHOE
LANDING TREAD
THRESHOLD OR CARPET STRIP

There are countless molding and trim designs to be found at local lumberyards. They come in a variety of sizes as well as designs and can be assembled in an infinite variety of combinations.

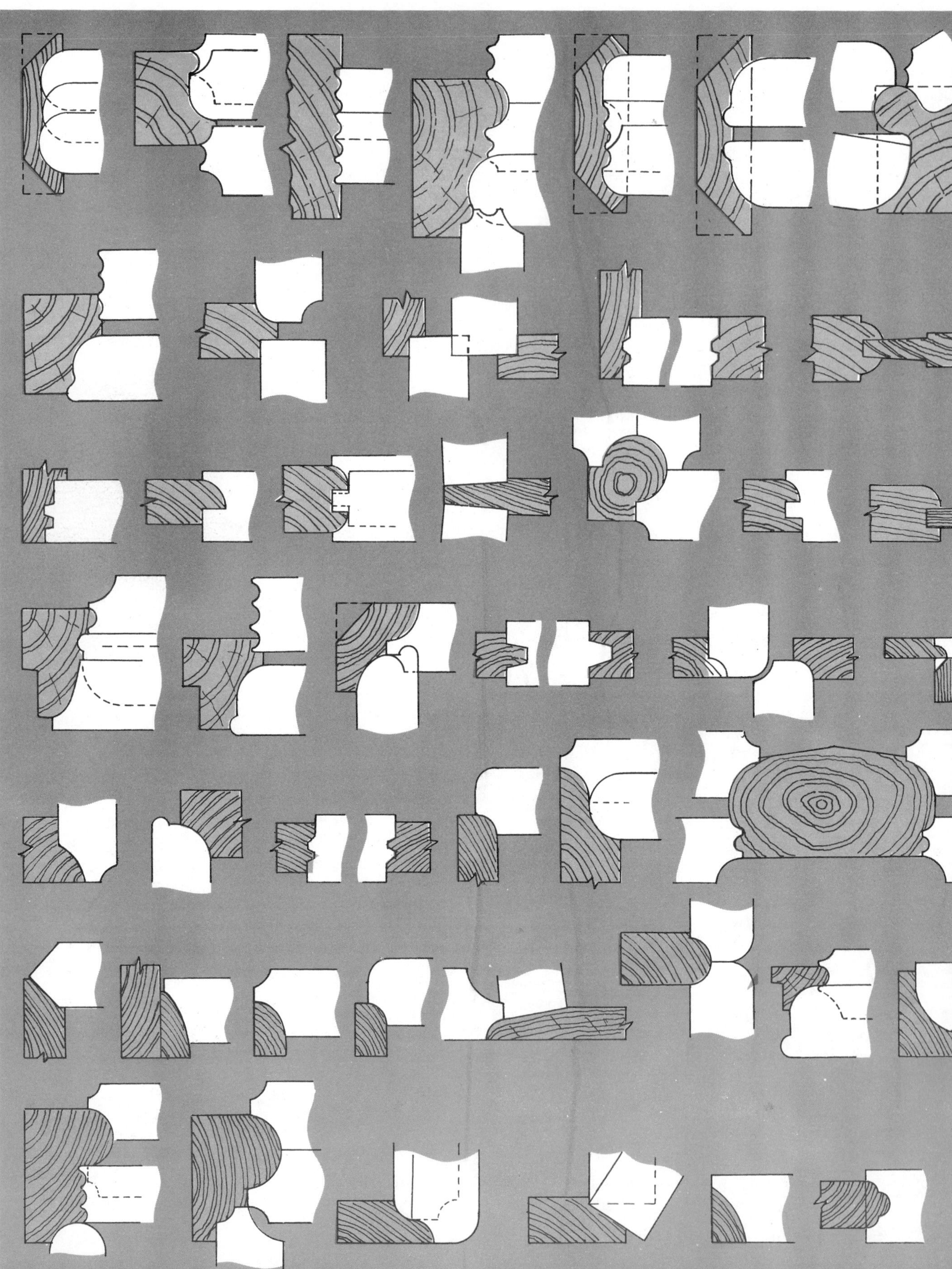

The molding blades shown above can be used in combination to create all the designs shown here, as well as a great many other configurations.

CHAPTER 8

Some Finishing Touches

Some Finishing Touches

It is very human to keep saying all through a project, "I'll cover that mistake later." Mis-measurements can be allowed for when the wood is cut. Cuts that are slightly off can be hidden by clever joinery. Ill-fitting joints will surely disappear under wood filler. Dents and gouges will no doubt vanish with a little extra sanding and some heavy paint goobered into them—except the paint somehow never really hides them.

In fact, paint rarely hides much of anything, and clear finishes tend to illuminate practically every flaw, including some that may not have been noticed before it was applied. A finish protects, enhances, glorifies, preserves for posterity. But no finish is ever any better than the surface it covers. Besides, mistakes can be made in applying paint or varnish, even when it is applied to a perfect surface.

Filling and Sanding

A perfect finishing surface is smooth. It is even, with no dents or gouges, scratches or imperfections. Its cracks and holes have been filled to blend into the wood; the filler is neither higher nor lower than the surface around it. Arriving at so flawless a surface is no easy chore. A man can easily spend days filling and smoothing a piece of wood that looks no different when he finishes than it did when he began. It only *feels* different.

And fill and sand you must. You do it until the sight of sandpaper makes you weary. Then you do it some more. First you sand with a medium grit. Then you graduate to a fine, and from there to a superfine. If you are machine-sanding, there is a step-by-step procedure to follow too. With a medium-grit paper, a circular sander will do some heavy-duty digging at really rough spots or "highs." But the circular sander leaves deep, curved marks in the wood that cannot readily be covered by any finish. Then there is the belt sander. This is great for covering large areas but be sure the machine is running before it touches the project and keep it moving all the time. Sand only with the grain; never use a belt sander across the grain. Although the tendency is to lean on those circular sander scratches, *don't.* You may erase the circular scratches, but at the expense of "dishing" a part of the surface. The belt sander can be used with medium and fine grits, but the fine grit that comes on sanding belts is not even close to the fineness you ultimately need. After the belt sander, go to the vibrator with fine and superfine grades. And finally finish the whole thing off by hand with a superfine grit wrapped around an old-fashioned sanding block.

Exactly when to stop sanding is not something that can be spelled out on paper. The complete surface should be smooth to the touch, and only by touching the wood can you decide whether it is smooth enough. There is a point, however, when further sanding is a waste of time.

Plywood is sanded by its manufacturer, and in most instances it requires nothing more than the use of fine and superfine grit. Fir plywood has long, high ridges in the grain that will always be long, high ridges. Grind them down and as soon as they are painted or varnished, they will rise again. The plywood edges, of course, are another matter. They will sand down with a surprisingly small amount of work, especially with a belt sander. But they are porous and must always be filled, or covered with an edging veneer, unless they are to be hidden under molding or trim.

As the sanding drones on, hour after hour, you can break the tedium by stopping to fill gouges, edges and dents with wood filler. Wood can be

SANDPAPER GRIT CHART

There are three natural minerals, flint, emery and garnet, and two synthetics, aluminum oxide and silicone carbide, used in making sandpaper. The composition of the paper is always marked on the back of each sheet, along with the grade, or degree of roughness.

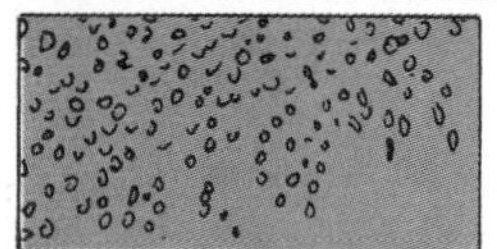
Flint is quartz and is white in color.

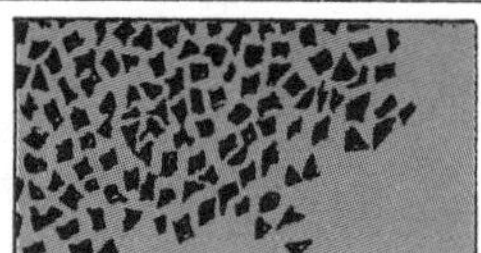
Emery is black and very hard.

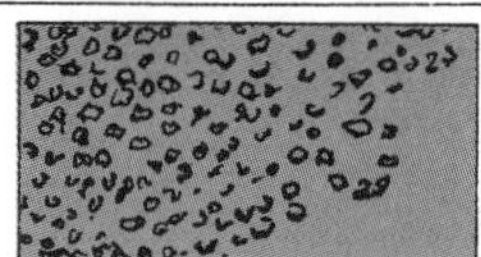
Garnet is a reddish brown mineral and provides a medium hardness but with excellent cutting edges.

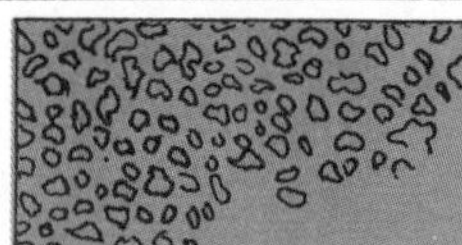
Aluminum oxide is a synthetic mineral and extremely hard as well as durable. It is off-white to gray in color.

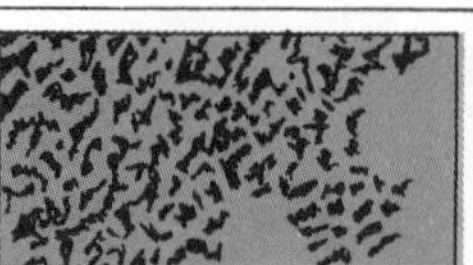
Silicone carbide is a synthetic. It is shiny, black and has sharp cutting slivers.

filled with all kinds of materials. There is wood putty, which comes as a powder to be mixed with water. Homogenized wallboard compound is easier to work with and will sand magnificently but it will not take too much of a beating. Plastic wood is the quickest-drying and hardest of all. The most consistent problem when filling wood is screw holes. It seems as if no matter how much filler is put into a screw hole, when it dries there is always a sag in the middle of the hole. Sometimes the sag never appears, but assume it will and figure on at least two applications of filler. The first round is stuffed into the hole and immediately wiped flush with the surface of the wood. After the filler is completely dry the second application is pushed down onto the first until the surface of the filled-in area is higher than the surrounding wood. When that is dry, sand it flush. Aside from screw holes, there can be scratches and gouges and hammer dents. The scratches and gouges can be filled and sanded, and so can the dents. But before you fill a dent (particularly in plywood), try covering it with a damp blotter and pressing with a warm steam iron. Often (but not always) this will raise the wood.

When filling and sanding is completed, all dust must be carefully wiped off the project. A dry rag will not get all the dust particles, and a damp one is not much better. Use a tack rag, which can be purchased either at stores that handle wood finishes, or be homemade. Any piece of lint-free cotton cloth can be used as a tack rag. The cloth is sprinkled (not soaked) with varnish that has been diluted by about 25% with turpentine. In a pinch, you can do without the varnish but turpentine alone is not as efficient. Fold the cloth tightly and wring it almost dry. Then wipe the wood thoroughly.

Bleaching

If the color of the wood is too dark, or if it has stains that are undesirable, it can be lightened with any full-strength chlorine bleach available at most grocery stores. First, heat the wood. Either stand it in the sunlight, or put it under a spotlight for about an hour. Then soak the dark area with undiluted bleach and keep wetting it until the discoloration vanishes. Do not let the bleach dry between applications. When the stain is gone, wash the still-wet bleach off the wood and wipe it dry. Allow the area to air-dry for an hour or so before sanding it lightly with a fine sandpaper to remove the raised grain. Be careful not to sand any deeper than the bleach has penetrated.

Sealing

Many wood-finishing experts recommend putting a clear sealer on everything, no matter what the wood is, or what the finish will be. Wood itself is never perfect. Even the hardest teak or ebony will have "soft" spots that soak up a little more of the finishing material than elsewhere, and leave a flat or even rough area. Wood sealer is made to fill in those "soft" spots. Any sealer will do, but the clear lacquer sanding sealers are particularly effective. They go on easily with a brush or rag and dry within minutes, although it is better to let the sealer stand for a day before sanding. Best of all, a very light sanding will produce a satiny touch to the wood. Obviously, under lacquer, the lacquer sealers are ideal. But they work just as well with anything else, including a stain.

There is nothing like a coat of something wet on wood to show up all the places the sandpaper missed, as well as every scratch and gouge that was never filled. So if the something wet is a clear sealer, there is still plenty of time to make the appropriate repairs after it is dry. That sends you back to the wood putty and sandpaper but it is better to discover those sandpaper "skips" now than after the final coat of finish is applied.

Finishing Materials

If at all possible, do not have a deadline for completing the finish on any project. Having done all the work necessary to build your project, do not destroy its completed appearance with even one careless swish of a brush wielded under the pressure of little or no time. Now is the time when nothing should be hurried. The wood must be carefully and meticulously prepared for the first coat of finishing material. Each coat must have its proper amount of drying time. Then it must be thoroughly prepared to receive the next coat.

Nor is this the place to save money on materials

or equipment. Use high-grade silicone carbide, or open-coat aluminum oxide sandpaper, not the cheaper grades. Select the best quality paint or varnish you can find. Use top-grade brushes or rollers. And, just as important, put yourself in the patient state of mind which assumes it is going to take at least two coats of finish (with sanding in between) and maybe more, even if you have used a sealer and a primer coat. Craftsmen have never had better finishing materials to work with than those available today. They are so good they have reduced the toil of finishing to less than a third of what it used to be. But there are still no real "one-coat" finishes.

Painting

When it comes to painting a utility cabinet, in almost every case the paint should be an enamel, which is really just a varnish with a pigment in it. The selection of paint over a clear finish is, of course, determined by the project and its ultimate uses, as well as the wood. If the wood pattern and grain do not have much character, you might as well paint it.

The procedure for painting is simple and tedious, but to omit any of the steps will diminish the effect of the ultimate finish. Sand the wood and wipe it clean with a tack rag. When it is dry, put on the wood filler, particularly if the piece is a softwood, or an open-grained hardwood such as oak, walnut, mahogany or chestnut. The filler, when it is dry, will require only a light hand-sanding; using machines at this point would only grind away more wood than is necessary. Next, put on a primer coat. It doesn't have to be a perfect paint job, but don't leave any globs or unpainted spots, either. When the primer is dry, sand it and wipe off *all* of the dust. Now come the finishing coats with a light sanding after each one. It is boring but necessary. Normally, two or three coats of a high-grade furniture enamel are enough, but only you can decide the number of coats. Finally, after the last coat has had a month or so to dry, it can be given a coating of furniture wax to protect it.

The paint brush through all of this should be of a good quality—that means expensive. Before using it, hold it under running water and pull at the bristles. You may get the loose ones to come out in your hand, instead of on your project. When using enamel, as with varnish, never dip the brush more than a third of its length into the paint, and always flow the paint liberally with a minimum of strokes and without bending the bristles any more than necessary. Then cross-stroke immediately at right angles to the original direction, using a very light touch and very little paint on the tip of the brush. This will fill in the ridges left by the brush and provide a smooth finish.

Staining

The purpose of a stain is to soak *into* the fibers of the wood and accentuate the grain as well as color it. (Paint and varnish, on the other hand, sit on top of the wood and to one degree or another cover the grain.) A wide range of tinted stains are offered on the market and these can be mixed to produce even more colors. If the stain is too dark, it can be lightened by thinning it with turpentine or mineral spirits. Usually, the commercial stains have to be darkened, either by adding color or by putting several coats on the wood.

There are also stains that have wax, or varnish, or even wood sealer in them. They are not much better than regular stains at staining, or waxing, or varnishing, or sealing. With the combination stains, the manufacturer is trying to make a one-coat finishing product but winds up producing nothing more than a colored wash. There is a salvation from the commercial stains. It costs less in the long run, is more satisfying to use, and is unquestionably a more precise way of getting the color *you* want the wood to have. The salvation is to mix your own.

Buy a can of *penetrating oil stain* at any large paint store. Also buy a tube of burnt umber artist's oil, and another tube of burnt sienna. The umber is a dark brown. The sienna is reddish. Properly mixed, they can create almost any shade in the brown family. If you do not like any of those, add any other oil color you want and keep mixing until you have the color you want. Pour enough of the oil stain to cover your project into a dish and mix in the artist's oils. By itself, the oil stain looks golden brown, but actually it has no color of its own, so you are giving it all the hue it will ever have.

When you attain the color you want, dip a clean, lintless rag into it and rub the stain into the wood. Let it stand for an hour or two and then rub off the excess oil that remains on the surface of the wood.

If you do not remove the excess stain, the wood will continue changing color, so actually you can just wait around and watch it penetrate until it reaches the tone you want and then arrest its action by wiping it. If the color is too dark, thin it with turpentine. If it ends up too light, give the project a second coat. After a 24-hour drying period, a coat or two of varnish will give the stained wood a high gloss. If you want a semigloss, put on one or two coats of stain varnish. You can also give it a coat of wax, or rub boiled linseed oil into it.

A caution about making your own stain: It is pure penetrating oil formulated to soak into the wood and darken it during the drying process. So watch it carefully and wipe it off at the exact moment it attains the color you want. With not very much practice, any color can be achieved. Realize in advance, however, that after you have created the precise color of mahogany and applied it to that exquisite pine cabinet, the wood will be very handsome, but it will still look like orangeish pine, not mahogany.

Stain can sometimes come out blotchy because of imperfections in the wood. The best way to avoid, or at least minimize, this unevenness is to give the wood a coat of sealer first, providing it is not a straight-grained hardwood. Then stain it. It is also wise to test-stain on a scrap of the wood you are covering. Usually, the color is a shade or two different after it is applied from the shade it appears to be in the mixing dish.

Shellacking

Shellac comes in two colors: orange for dark woods and white for light woods. It is a good primer-sealer on plywood that is going to be painted. It can also be used under varnish, but be forewarned that it will darken the wood it is applied to. Shellac is made from the resinous secretions from an Asian insect known as the lac. The secretion is made into a powder and mixed with denatured alcohol to produce shellac. How much lac is in a given solution is indicated by the "cut" of the mix. A 2-lb. cut, for example, means that two pounds of lac was mixed with one gallon of alcohol. A 3-lb. cut would be three pounds of lac per gallon of alcohol.

Because of the alcohol, shellac evaporates quickly, so don't buy any more than you are likely to need within a relatively short time. The cut you buy is immaterial, but dilute it to at least a 3-lb. cut by adding the appropriate amount of denatured alcohol. There is usually a thinning chart printed on the shellac can label.

Do not shake shellac. Stir it, because shaking causes bubbles that will get on the brush and stay on the wood. Ideally, a new brush should be used for each coat you apply but brushes can be cleaned between coats with alcohol and then a mild solution of household ammonia and warm water. And by this time you know that you should thoroughly wipe your project with a tack rag before even touching it with the shellac.

Brush the shellac into the wood with long, even strokes, overlapping each stroke slightly. With shellac, it is possible to brush in any direction because the strokes will normally fade as the shellac dries. If the shellac has been cut to a 3-lb. or thinner consistency, the first coat will dry within two hours and can be rubbed down with a fine-grade steel wool pad. After this, wipe the surface clean with a tack rag and apply the next coat. If this is the final coat, and the gloss is too high, a light rubbing with fine steel wool will give it a satiny sheen. If varnish is to go over the shellac, two coats of shellac are usually enough to provide a solid base. If you are not varnishing, you may want to give your project several coats of shellac, steel-wooling and wiping clean after each coat.

Varnishing

Now available in high and medium glosses, satin finish and flat, varnishes have, for centuries, been resistant to spilled liquids and easy to apply. They are made of resins, linseed oil, drying agents and enough turpentine to make them flow. Until recently, the bewildering array of varnishes on the market were all more or less alike. They dried slowly, and while their finish was harder than any other, heat could blister them and some liquids left hard-to-remove stains.

Then came polyurethane. The urethanes are varnishes. They are easier to apply than regular varnish, dry faster, are impervious to water, alcohol, dirt and the onslaught of active children. Furthermore, they are truly clear and barely darken the wood they protect. There are some restrictions with the urethanes, however. Generally, they cannot be used over shellac, lacquer or most of the sander-fillers.

All varnishes have a tendency to accumulate

specks of dust while they are drying. As a result, they should be applied in as dust-free an environment as possible. It also helps if you select a fast-drying varnish. There is no real advantage in the slow dryers anyway, and the longer the varnish is wet, the more dust will collect on it.

The surface of the wood must be absolutely free of any foreign matter, so wipe it thoroughly with a tack rag immediately prior to varnishing. The varnish should be flowed over the wood with either a high-grade brush, a rag or a foam rubber pad. The foam rubber pads are especially good since they are disposable, hold a good load of varnish, and leave no brush stroke. Therefore, much of the delicacy needed to apply varnish with a brush is eliminated.

When brushing, use a minimum of strokes and finish off by stroking lightly along the grain with the tip of the brush, using almost no varnish. When you get the hang of just "kissing" the finish, you will discover you can eliminate any sign of a brush stroke and achieve a uniform finish. To remove excess varnish from the brush, tap the bristles lightly against the inside of the container. Never drag the brush over the rim of the can; dragging causes tiny bubbles to form in the varnish which make it almost impossible to achieve a smooth finish. *For this same reason, as with shellac, always stir varnish; never shake it.*

To wipe varnish on with a cloth pad, fold the cloth and dip it into the varnish, soaking it generously. Spread the varnish with long strokes applied parallel with the grain. Do not rub hard, and do not try to work the varnish into the surface. Keep an eye out for runs and wipe them up as soon as you see them, because varnish does not level itself and any globs you miss will be there to stay.

Most projects require at least two coats of varnish. Each coat should be sanded lightly to the point where all of its sheen has been dulled. Do not scrub the finish; just smooth it to a uniform satiny-smooth texture with no "shiny" spots. Then wipe thoroughly with a tack rag and apply the next coat. Some experts recommend that a very fine grade of aluminum oxide paper be used after the first coat, and Superfine #400 waterproof paper with soapy water as a lubricant be used on the second coat. As an alternative, a very fine grade of steel wool can also be used on varnish.

If the project has been stained, the varnish may streak the color unless it is first sealed into the wood. A thin coat or two of shellac will seal the stain and also serve as a solid base for the varnish, as well as reduce the number of varnish coats to no more than two.

No matter how careful you are, there will be some specks of dust on the final coat of varnish. Or there will be tiny bumps, or it may have too much gloss, particularly for a tabletop. So there can be no final coat of varnish as such. You could go on sanding down coats and applying "final coats" until doomsday and still not get a perfect finish. So don't try. Rub the last coat instead.

Rubbing is done only after the last coat has had at least a week to dry and harden. Mix a paste of powdered pumice stone and motor oil (never linseed or any drying oils). Dip a heavy, folded cloth pad into the mixture and "sand" the surface with long, straight strokes, always going with the grain, and using a moderate pressure. By the time you have achieved a smooth texture to the finish, you will have also dulled its luster considerably. If you wish to restore the luster, mix a modicum of powdered rottenstone and crude oil into a paste and rub that against the surface. This is a much finer mixture than pumice and when the excess paste is wiped off the varnish, it should leave the desired luster. Continue wiping paste off the wood using clean cloths until the surface "squeaks."

Tung Oil

Perhaps the most important ingredient in the best varnishes is tung oil, which happens to be one of the oldest wood preservatives known to man. Tung oil was used to weatherproof clothing, shoes, boats and houses in China for centuries before Marco Polo introduced it to Europe in the 13th century. Most of the world's tung oil is still produced in China, but among other nations, the United States now produces about 50 million pounds of the oil annually. Eighty percent of that oil goes into the making of the best house paints and varnishes, both exterior and interior. The spar varnishes in particular need tung oil because of its water resistance and weather durability. Food and beer cans are treated with it, and so is the protective lining in tank cars. Heat will not affect it or "draw it out" of the wood, and it is an excellent sealer for wood, metal, concrete and brick.

Many professionals insist that tung oil provides a better finish than linseed oil, lacquer, varnish or shellac because it will not darken with age, mildew, or bleed excessively. The oil is rubbed into wood using either a cotton pad or the bare palm of a hand. Continue rubbing until the oil is completely worked into the fibers of the wood, then let it dry overnight. The result will be a low luster finish. To achieve a satin sheen, or medium luster, apply a second coat. For a high gloss, keep rubbing in coats until you get the degree of gloss you want. Allow each coat to dry thoroughly before putting on the next one, and always apply it on a dry, warm day, or in a heated room.

Tung oil will solidify into a jelly if it is exposed to air for very long, and no matter how tightly you seal the can, it will be exposed to enough air to make it congeal. Any time you want to store tung oil that is less than three quarters of a can, either put it in a smaller container, or fill the can with stones until there is no room left in it for any air.

Linseed Oil

If you have six months, or a year (or forever) to spend finishing a project, the finish to use is *boiled* linseed oil, not raw linseed oil. The can has to be labeled "boiled," which it is not, by the way. "Boiled" in this case means the manufacturer has added drying agents. The raw oil hardly ever dries, which makes it fine for exterior uses where it must combat the elements.

There are numerous ways of applying linseed oil and everybody who does much of it seems to have his own method. Generally, the procedure is to mix two parts linseed oil with one part turpentine or mineral spirits in an *open* can and place it on the stove in boiling water. When it is hot, dip a rag in the oil and apply it to the wood. Now the fun starts—with both hands. Rub the oil into the wood, working only a small area at a time. About 15 or 20 minutes of hard hand-rubbing either with the cloth or bare palms should be enough for the wood to become saturated. Then wipe away any excess oil with a clean rag and move on to the next section (you will have to reheat the linseed oil every once in a while), and the next, until the project is completely saturated. Then wipe clean. Be sure to dig any excess oil out of the corners and crevices because it will harden or, worse yet, become sticky.

If you rub the oil into the wood hard enough, you can get away with putting on a new coat every 24 hours. But a week's drying time is the usual recommendation. Linseed oil produces a beautiful, mellow luster. The more coats applied, the more lustrous will be the finish, and there should be at least three coats. The finish is not particularly water-resistant, but it can withstand mild heat and is less likely to show scratches than varnish. And, of course, it should be given another coat or two every six months or year during the lifetime of the finished piece.

There is one danger with linseed oil and it lies in the rags you use. Burn them. Store them in water. Get rid of them somehow, but do not leave them lying around. They are highly combustible. And never boil the oil in a closed can, either. It will probably explode.

French Polish

A centuries-old variation on the linseed oil finish is really a technique called French Polish. It produces the kind of high polish that homemakers today are forever trying to achieve when they assiduously polish furniture.

To achieve this high gloss, make a wad about the size of a baseball from lint-free rags and saturate the wad with hot boiled linseed oil. Then squeeze it dry, dip it into a dish of 1-lb. cut shellac and rub it into the wood.

Do not just slap the cloth on the wood, but handle it like a belt sander. Have it in motion before you touch the surface and keep it moving. Wipe fairly hard in a circular motion, forcing the shellac and linseed oil into the pores of the wood, but not with so much pressure that the pad sticks or stops. When the pad begins drying, work your way to the edge of the wood and off it, without stopping until the pad is completely clear of the surface.

When the entire project is saturated, allow it to dry for 24 hours, then apply the next coat. With the French Polish technique, each coat contributes to a high sheen gloss and you stop applying coats only when the finish is as glossy as you wish. If you go too far and it gets too glossy, you can dull it by rubbing it with a pumice-oil paste.

Lacquer

Lacquer can be applied with a brush or a spray gun. And make sure you are working in a well ventilated area; lacquer is extremely toxic. Spraying is by far the better technique since lacquer was originally developed to be sprayed on production-line furniture. It is akin to shellac in composition except that acetone is used instead of denatured alcohol. It comes in colors as well as clear, and both versions are very quick-drying. In fact, lacquer is dry almost before it hits the wood and is hard enough to sand within 1 to 1½ hours. When you buy lacquer, buy twice as much thinner. The lacquer must be thinned on a one-to-one basis, and you will need the rest of the thinner for cleaning up. And don't forget a can of lacquer sander-filler. Lacquer goes down in thin coats and must have an even base beneath it. Each coat must be sanded and wiped clean with a tack rag, and when you have enough coats the project should be given the same pumice-and-rottenstone paste treatment as varnish.

If you *must* use a brush, it should have natural bristles because acetone eats nylon bristles. Work with long, even strokes with only a slight overlapping and be very delicate—and swift—about any touching up you do.

With spraying, start the gun aimed away from the project and keep it moving over the wood. It is better to spray on a thin coat that has a few bare spots than to go back and try to cover them. Sand and clean each coat and do not take the chance of building up too much lacquer in any one spot. It will only become too thick, and therefore gummy.

When applied correctly, lacquer produces a hard, beautiful finish. But you will pay the price for it in labor and the tension of having to work with no room for error.

Waxing

Ever since World War II Americans have busily waxed up their furniture on an average of once a month. The furniture dutifully looks shiny for a few weeks—until the dirt, grease, body oils and general air pollution settle on the wax polish and dull its gloss. So more wax is piled on top of the grime, shining it up and sealing it to the furniture. Over the years, the wax (and dirt) build up, and the furniture turns dark. Glasses, doilies and fingerprints start sticking to the gummy wax surface, leaving ugly scars, while the real finish beneath it begins to crack and chip. The finish cracks because the wood expands and contracts from moisture, be it from a wet glass, wet wax polish or the weather.

Still, newer wax-laden polishes encourage people to shine up their old furniture "like new." "Like new" may well have been a low luster, hand-rubbed sheen. What most of the labels on these polishing agents fail to specify is that they should be applied *only after the old wax has been cleaned off.* One logical explanation for this omission would seem to be that the users might shy away from a product w ıich necessitated first scrubbing their furniture clean before performing their weekly or monthly ritual of wax-polishing.

Lemon Oil

Wax is nice, one coat at a time. But a better way of preserving your cabinet project is with pure lemon oil. *Pure,* not lemon oil with beeswax, linseed oil or silicones added. Every month or so dampen a rag with pure lemon oil and rub it into the finish. It is not greasy, but any excess must be wiped away because it will not evaporate. Nor should you put any more of it on the project than the wood will absorb. You will find that it is a very small amount. Best of all, the lemon oil picks up the dirt on the furniture and deposits it on the cloth, rather than sealing it into the wood.

Lemon oil cannot be put over wax, so the furniture must be cleaned first, but from then on it will keep the furniture clean. And it has been amply demonstrated that a clean finish will last between four and five times longer than one that is laden with wax. The lemon oil works into the wood and prevents it from absorbing moisture, so it is a good idea to put some of it on the undersides of a project once or twice a year to protect the wood.

Hardware

There is a seemingly endless array of cabinet hardware to be found in all sorts of stores, from pharmacies to discount chains to lumberyards. Some types, like hinges or leg braces, are primarily functional. Some are purely decorative, such as brass corners and joint plates. Most serve the dual function of making the moving parts of a cabinet work properly, in addition to setting the tone of the project's appearance.

Without attempting to compile a catalog of all the hardware sold in the United States today, the next few pages define the types of fixtures to be found. The reader should be familiar with what is available and should take all of the possibilities into consideration at the time he is designing any project. It is, after all, the way a shelf, closet or cabinet is to look when it is completed that most determines the design of its assembly.

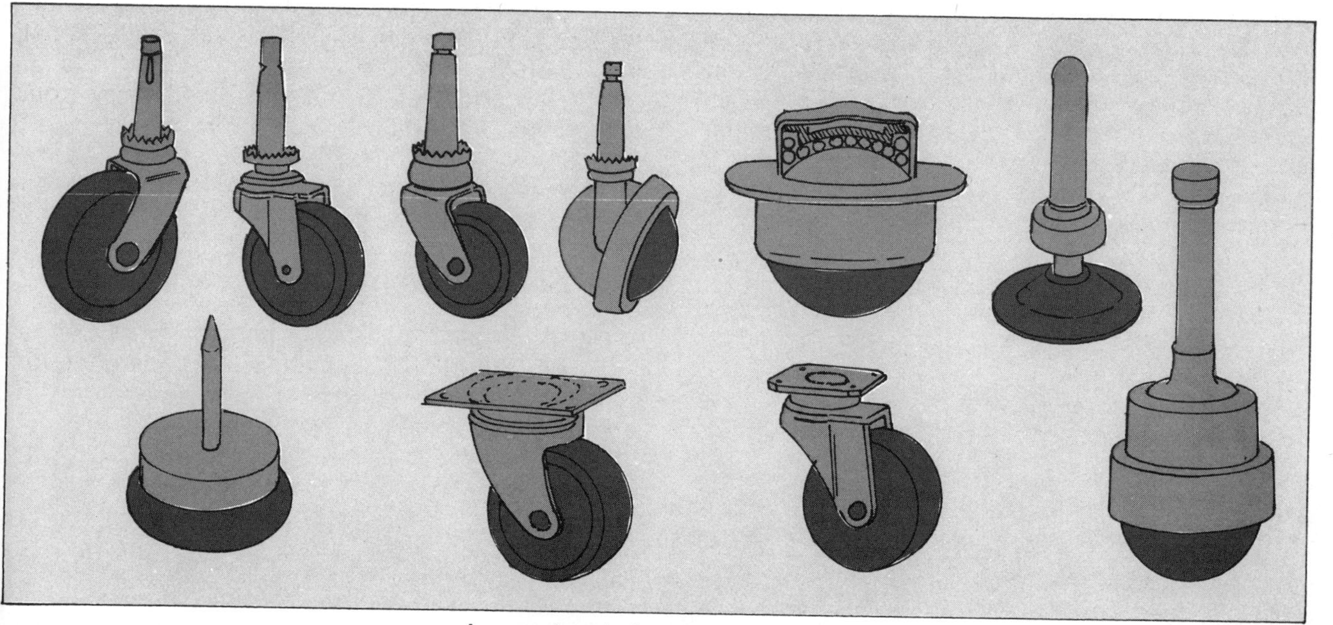

An assortment of casters and glides.

Casters and Glides

To begin at the bottom, so to speak, there are a surprising number of ways to make a simple wheel, or caster as it is called if it is supposed to go under a piece of furniture. Casters are usually not more than 6″ in diameter, but they can be very fat, or even in the shape of a ball. They can have stems or base plates; they may or may not swivel; they may come with or without ball bearings. They can be made of plastic, wood, rubberized compounds or metal. The round casters, particularly the ones with an angled rubber tread, are excellent for heavy cabinet doors because they can spin as well as rotate and therefore follow the arc of the door swing more easily than a straight swivel wheel.

There are no special advantages to using a stemmed caster as opposed to one with a base plate. The stemmed caster has to have holes drilled into the bottom of the cabinet, and the one with a base plate is screwed or bolted in place. In either case, most of the caster and its mechanism can be hidden by attaching it to a brace recessed inside the cabinet base, or by adding a skirt around the bottom of a project; the skirt comes down to within a quarter of an inch of the floor.

If casters are not appropriate, the alternative is a glide. Glides may be plastic, rubber, metal or wood, and usually have a nail in their center which is driven into the bottom of the cabinet. They do not move; they only raise the piece an eighth of an inch or so off the floor. There is one variation of the glide which is adjustable. The glide is attached to a threaded bolt, so that it can be raised or lowered to level the project wherever it is standing.

Legs, Leg Braces and Shelf Supports

Anyone who has wandered into a reasonably sized lumberyard lately knows how many different kinds of wooden legs can be purchased. There are carved ones and turned ones, long ones and short ones. You can have colonial, Roman, Greek, European and plain tapered designs. The problem is how to attach them to whatever you are building.

Within the category of hidden metal products that have little or no decorative function are such things as braces and supports. Some legs come with a bolt stuck in their base which threads into a metal plate screwed to the bottom of the project. The plate may have only one bolt hole, but some of these plates offer both a perpendicular and a slightly angled leg position. However, the base of a leg will take plenty of beating from all directions, so whenever possible it should be supported by something more than a single ¼″ bolt. This means that it should be forced into its corner and held there by some sort of corner brace. The brace could be made of wood. It could also be metal in any number of forms that have been worked out to give any leg it holds the full support needed.

When contemplating a folding-leg arrangement for something like a hidden table, remember that there are several folding-leg brackets, some of which are accompanied by a locking brace mechanism like the kind used on card tables. Similar to these braces are the dropleaf supports which

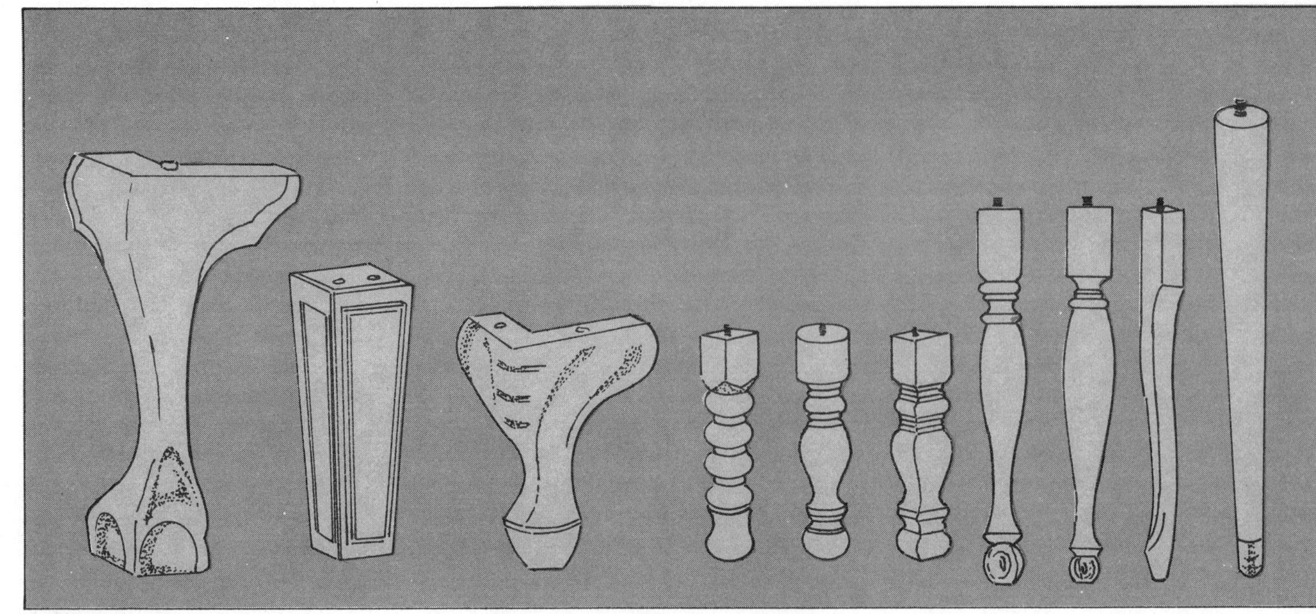

A representative selection of furniture legs.

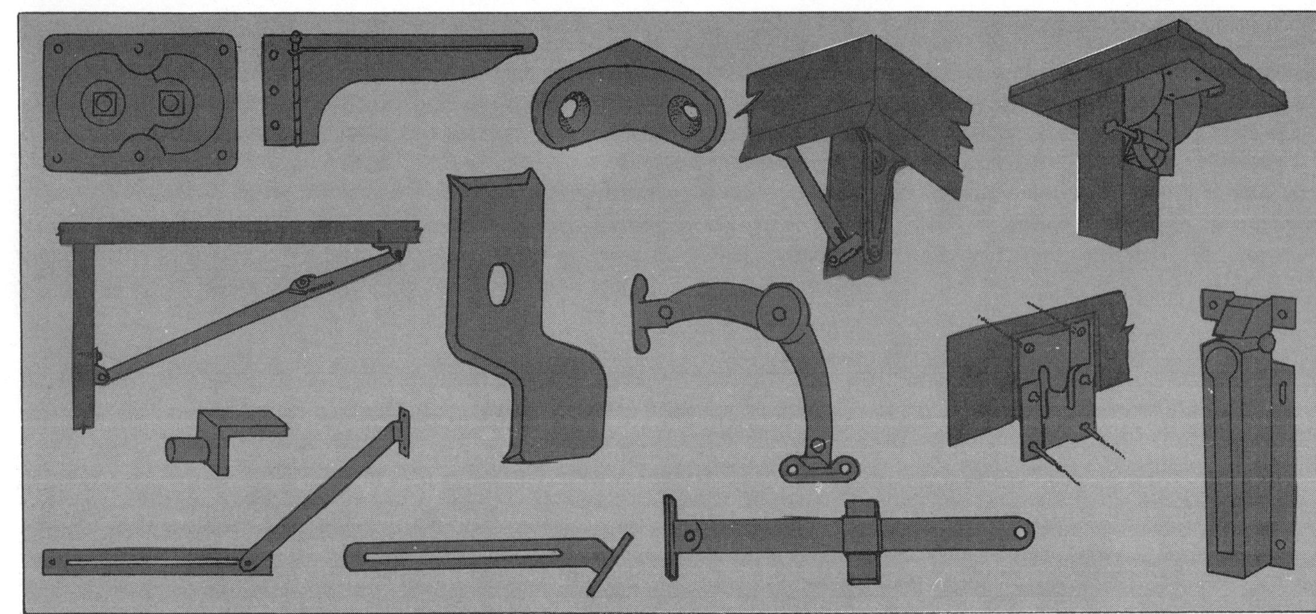

Various leg braces and shelf supports.

allow a shelf or leaf to be folded downward, but which then lock when opened to hold the shelf horizontal.

Finally, there are the lid supports. These usually consist of a thin metal strip with a slot in its center. The support slides up and down on a knob inserted in the slot which can be tightened to hold the lid open at any point.

Hinges

Perhaps the largest single collection of utility hardware are hinges. They come in all sizes from 8′ long piano hinges on down. There are special cabinet hinges that can be completely hidden There are pivot hinges, double-action hinges fo folding doors, no-mortise hinges and door butts There is also an enormous range of decorative styles and designs that can turn the hinge into a very desirable highlight of the completed project Hinges have to be seen before they are chosen but a few of the many, many designs are shown here as a broad guide to selection.

Catches, Latches and Locks

There are countless different kinds of catches and latches too. And even more variety when it comes

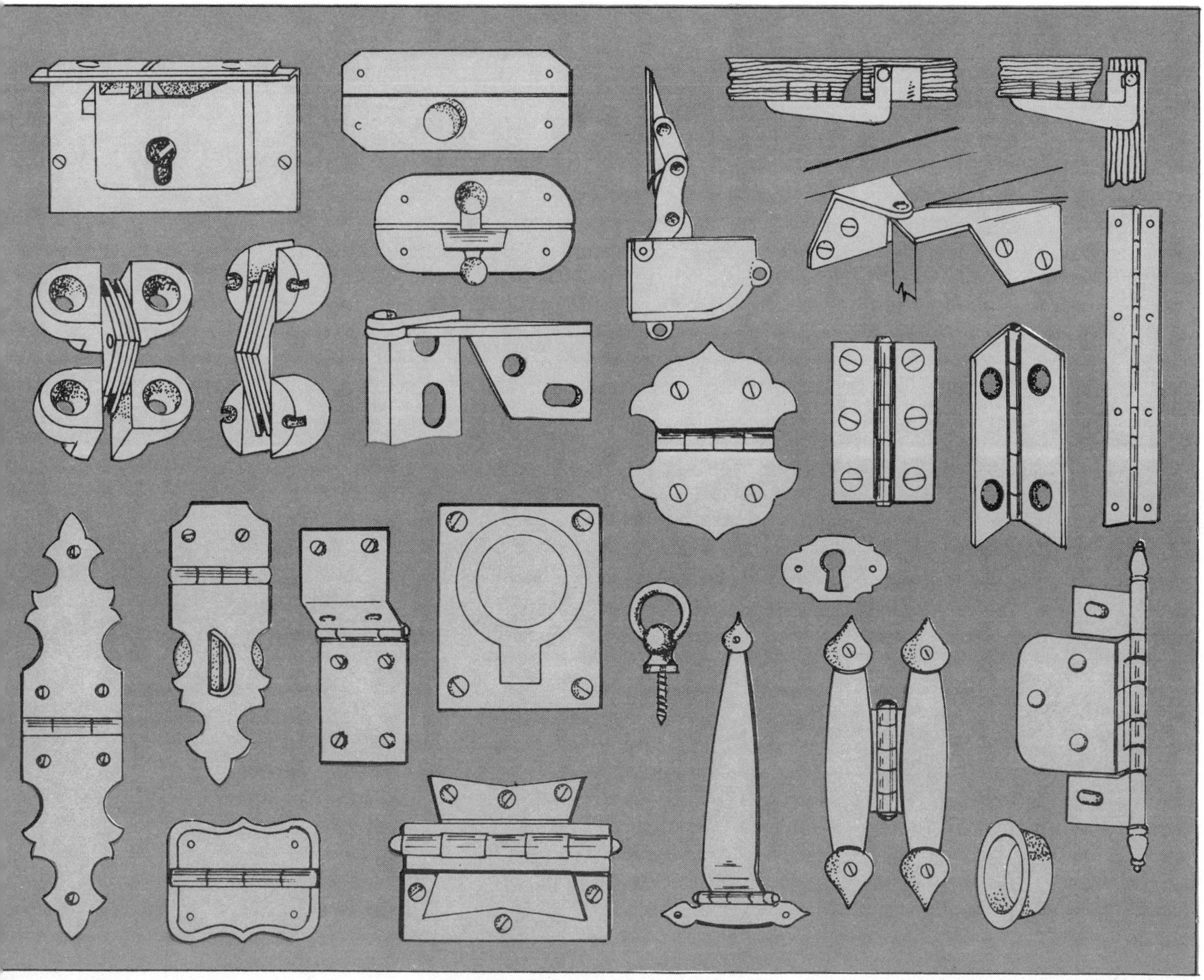

Some of the many hinges available.

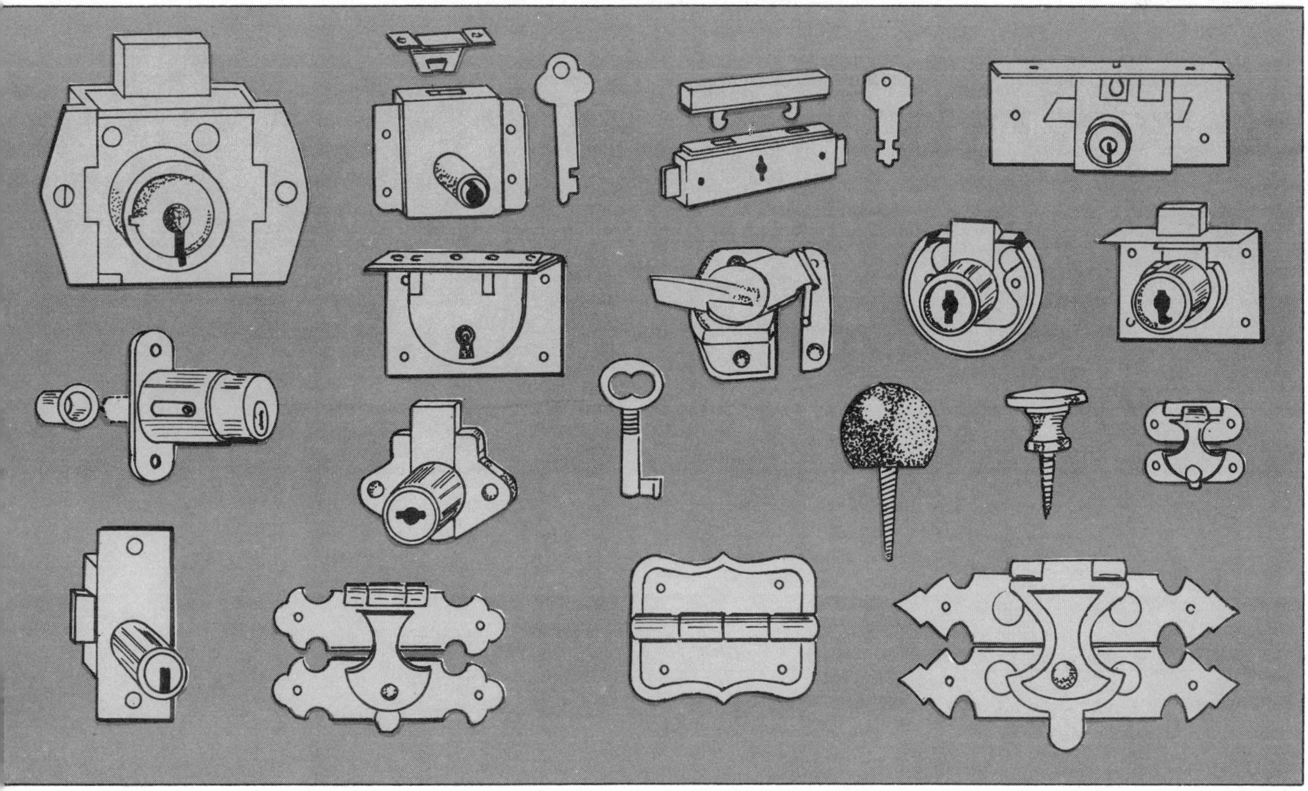

Shown here is an assortment of catches, latches and locks.

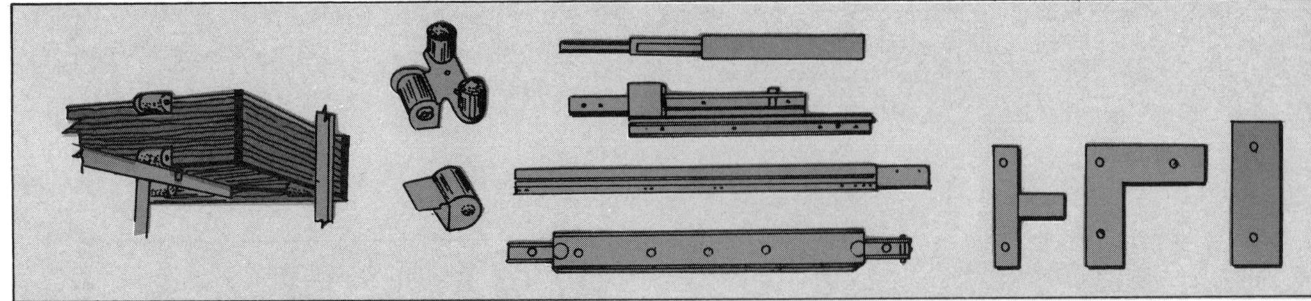

A selection of different types of drawer glides and guides.

to locks. Cabinets which have a light, ¾″ thick door usually incorporate a magnetic catch, but there are a variety of these to choose from, and all of them have their mechanical counterparts. If a lock is preferred, there are untold numbers of them, too. They can be either hidden, or out in plain view where they may—or may not—add to the decor of the cabinet.

Drawer Glides and Guides

Drawer glides vary according to how much you want to pay. Essentially, they all have a pair of slides attached to the sides of the drawer which roll inside guides mounted to the cabinet walls. Sometimes, the guide units have ball bearings. Sometimes, they incorporate extensions that permit the drawer to come out beyond the cabinet

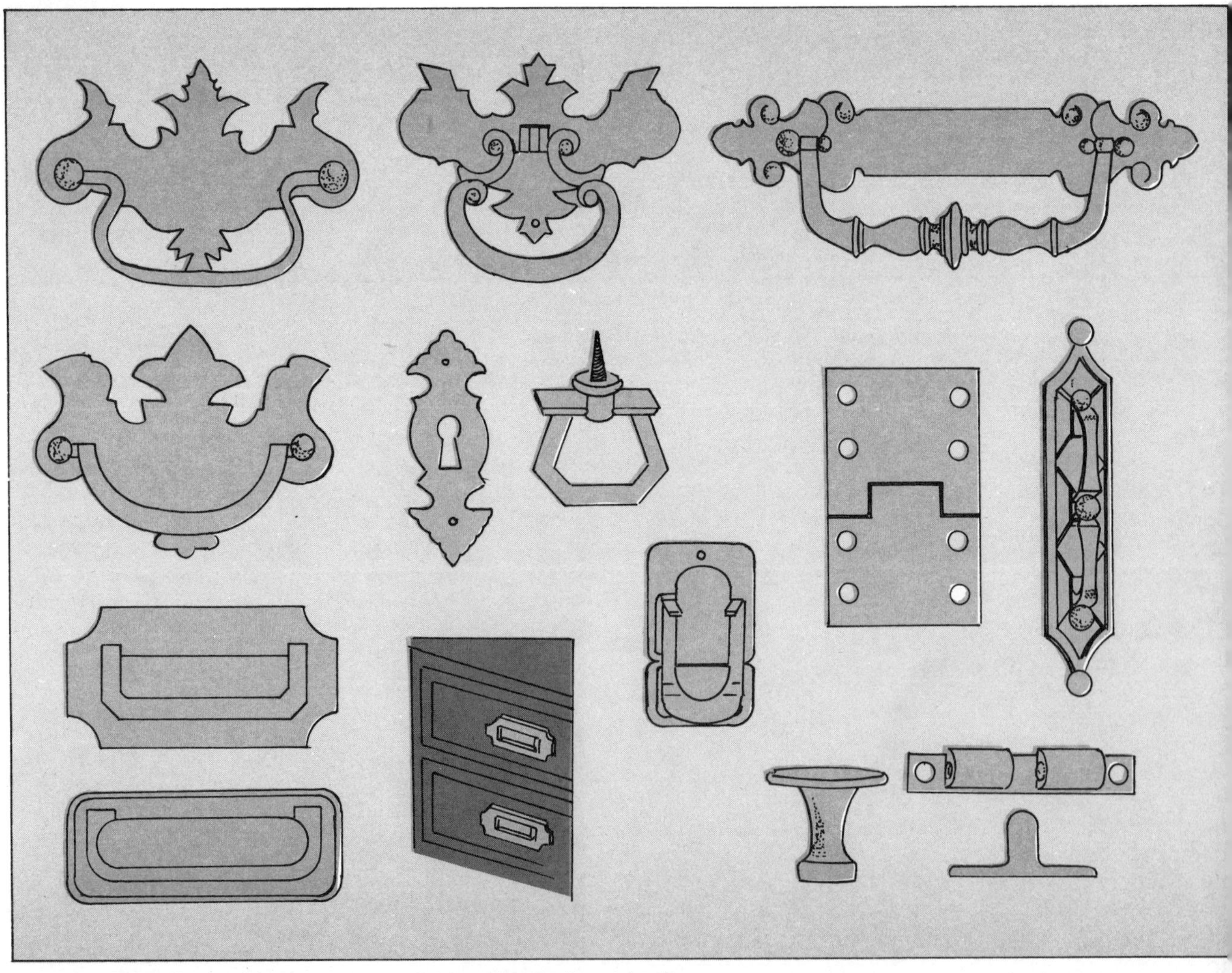

You can choose from a tremendous range of handles, knobs and pulls.

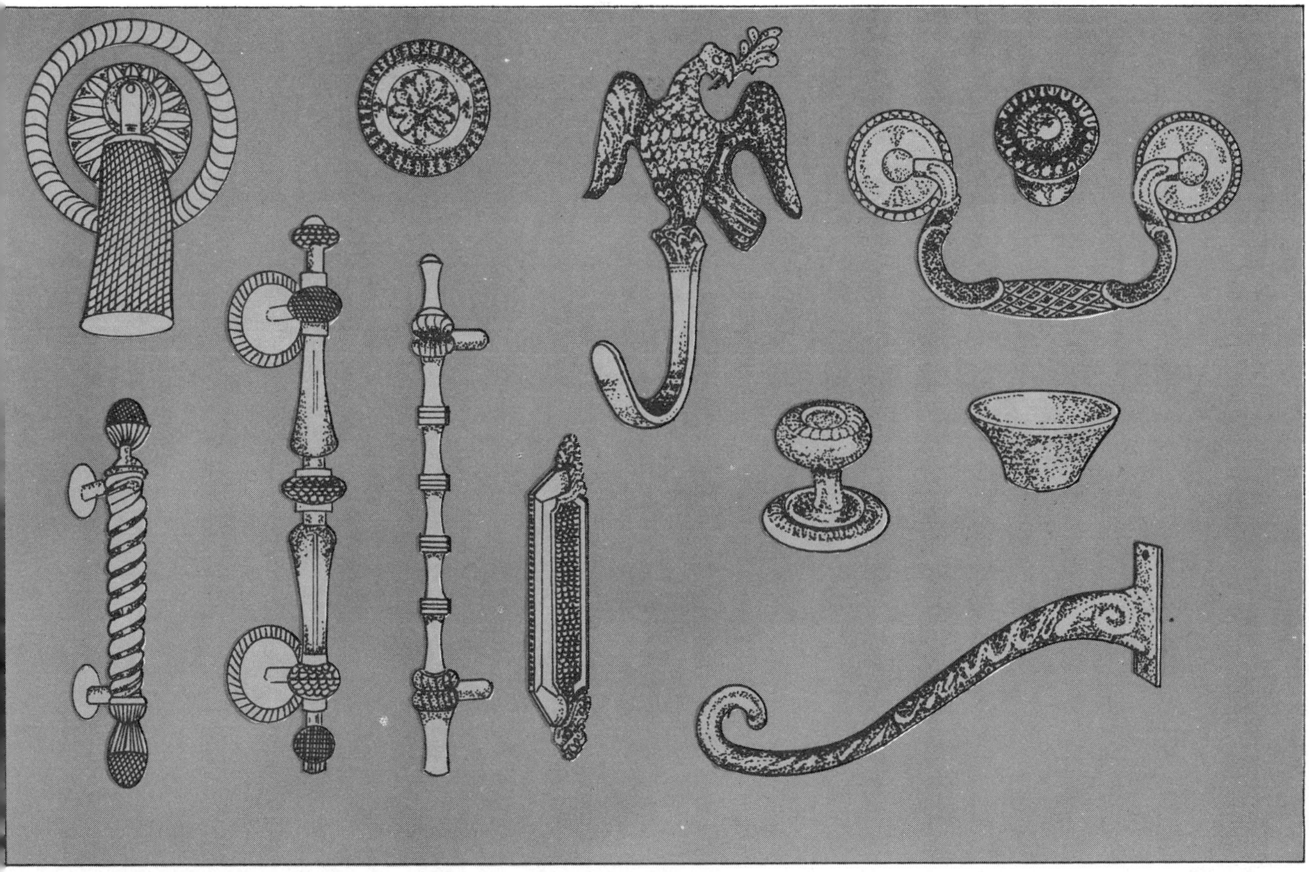

The variety of decorative hardware available is practically unlimited.

itself. Once they are installed—which can be a time-consuming experience in itself—they offer a truly easy drawer action that is worth the effort.

Handles, Knobs and Pulls

The hardware used to pull open cabinet and closet doors has so many variations that the purchaser can almost literally dream up any far-fetched design he wants, and then go out and buy it. There are traditional furniture pulls, recessed handles, Early American decorative knobs, modern creations made of wood, metal, glass, rhinestones, seashells, and every other material known to man.

Decorative Hardware

In addition to the primarily functional hardware described above, you can also buy purely decorative L- and T-shaped strips of brass or steel to put across joints on the front of a cabinet. Then there are the metal corners which are tacked onto the corners of a chest. They are attractive but have no real strength to lend a well made project.

Specialty Hardware

The manufacturers have begun to turn their attention to special needs, and as a result there is now available a range of specialty metal and plastic items on the market suitable for use on certain out-of-the-ordinary projects. For example, there are sliding pot racks, disappearing wastebasket holders and clothing carriers. The way to discover these unusual items is to look through the assortment offered by any store you are in. The assortment for sale is constantly changing. They keep cropping up in the marketplace and, because they are so specialized, they sometimes disappear as suddenly as they appeared.

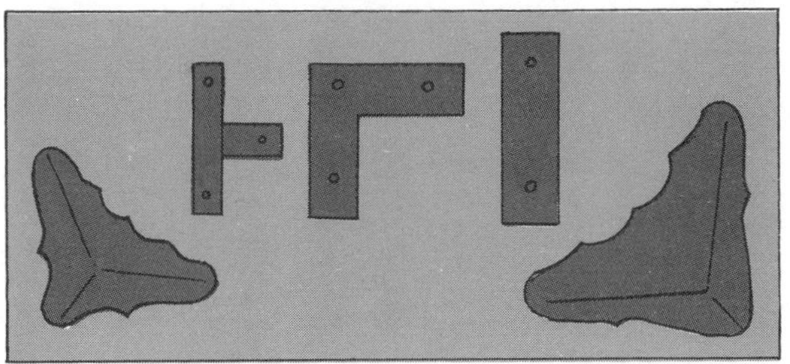

A few of the many kinds of specialty hardware to be found today.

CHAPTER 9

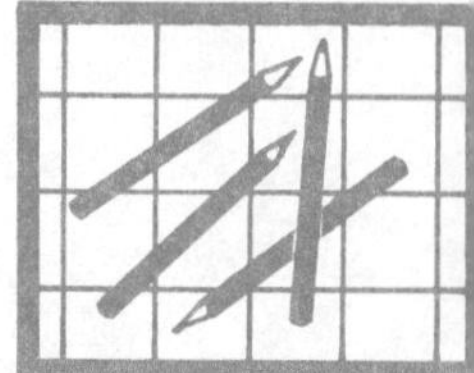

Planning Projects

Planning Projects

The next four chapters contain the plans for numerous shelves, closets and cabinets that can be constructed in the average workshop with a reasonable complement of hand and power tools. But not one of these projects, as presented, is guaranteed to be suitable for any reader's particular needs without some modifications.

Contained in these chapters are drawings, dimensions and descriptions of assembly procedures. There are even suggestions as to how specific projects can be altered to suit different needs and tastes. Still, the odds are that they will not meet any one builder's individual requirements. So what this chapter is all about is how to modify these projects to suit *you.*

To begin with, there is the matter of space—or lack of it. If you find a cabinet on these pages that more or less strikes your fancy, chances are the dimensions will be all wrong. These projects are laid out using ideal measurements. Nobody lives in ideal surroundings. So, first you take the idea. Then you measure the space you want to put it in. Then you recalculate the whole project according to *your* dimensions. That part is easy, because an inch is an inch, and you either have it to use, or you don't.

The best fun in redesigning something comes after the basics are settled. You know the cabinet cannot be 2'x4'x3'. It has to be 1½'x3'x2½'. It is an attractive cabinet, with three drawers and two doors which close on a tier of shelves. But you want to store your stereo equipment in it. That means the inside has to be completely redesigned to accommodate a receiver, record changer and, if you can get them in, a couple of hundred records. You will have to discard the drawers, perhaps replace them with a sliding tray for the record changer. You will need a shelf somewhere for the receiver, and at least 13" below that for the records.

Then there is the outside of the cabinet. In the book, it is perhaps a modern Danish design. But your living room is antique Spanish. Therefore, some flourishes will have to be added, heavier molding, perhaps, a darker stain, and maybe more ornate doors.

The design of a project must spring from the need it is to fulfill. The need is always for more storage space in a limited area, and this need can always be met if the craftsman approaches whatever space he has with his mind open to change. See your space not as a square alone, but as a cubic area that can hold certain possessions. For example, a food storage closet need be no deeper than the largest box of cereal it will be required to hold. Its door space should be at least 4" wide in order to hold dozens of cans and small containers. This way, the closet will hold more of everything than would a straight 8"-deep set of shelves with a hollow-core door. A stereo unit requires only a sliding tray 15" or 16" wide and 10" or 12" deep to hold the changer. Give it any more than that, and precious space that could be used for other things will be lost.

With the orderliness that comes from first determining the specific needs that a shelf, closet or cabinet must fill, there comes a direct and simple project flow chart that divides into three major stages: Construction, Prefinishing and Finishing. There are sub-sections, of course, so the entire chart looks like this:

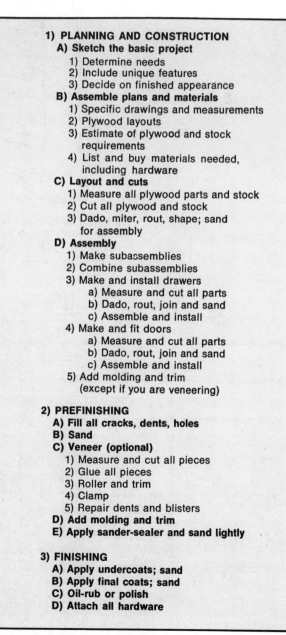

1) PLANNING AND CONSTRUCTION
- **A) Sketch the basic project**
  - 1) Determine needs
  - 2) Include unique features
  - 3) Decide on finished appearance
- **B) Assemble plans and materials**
  - 1) Specific drawings and measurements
  - 2) Plywood layouts
  - 3) Estimate of plywood and stock requirements
  - 4) List and buy materials needed, including hardware
- **C) Layout and cuts**
  - 1) Measure all plywood parts and stock
  - 2) Cut all plywood and stock
  - 3) Dado, miter, rout, shape; sand for assembly
- **D) Assembly**
  - 1) Make subassemblies
  - 2) Combine subassemblies
  - 3) Make and install drawers
    - a) Measure and cut all parts
    - b) Dado, rout, join and sand
    - c) Assemble and install
  - 4) Make and fit doors
    - a) Measure and cut all parts
    - b) Dado, rout, join and sand
    - c) Assemble and install
  - 5) Add molding and trim (except if you are veneering)

2) PREFINISHING
- **A) Fill all cracks, dents, holes**
- **B) Sand**
- **C) Veneer (optional)**
  - 1) Measure and cut all pieces
  - 2) Glue all pieces
  - 3) Roller and trim
  - 4) Clamp
  - 5) Repair dents and blisters
- **D) Add molding and trim**
- **E) Apply sander-sealer and sand lightly**

3) FINISHING
- **A) Apply undercoats; sand**
- **B) Apply final coats; sand**
- **C) Oil-rub or polish**
- **D) Attach all hardware**

Some of the steps are self-explanatory. Others perhaps need annotation:

Sketch the basic project. Start with the space that is to be filled and measure it exactly, its depth, width and height. Try to imagine the objects you want to keep there already hanging or sitting on shelves, or however they can best be stored. As you imagine them floating there in space, all neatly arranged, begin to rearrange them. Can you get more into the space these objects do not take up? If so, should this space be filled with shelves, or hooks, or what?

After you get everything fitted into the space, in your mind's eye begin adding the supports, the walls, the shelves, the uprights. You can begin doodling on paper at this point, putting down a gridwork of verticals and horizontals. And don't forget the doors. Doors are just movable walls that conceivably can hold all sorts of things. That

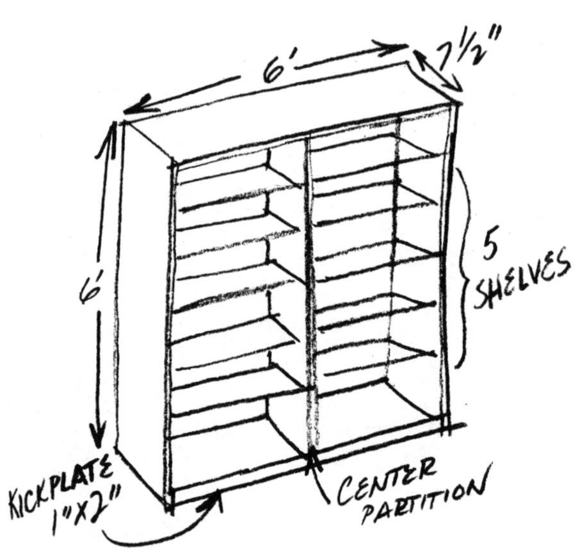

You do not have to be a talented artist to sketch a project. No one but you need ever see your drawings. They are only to help you fix in your mind exactly how you expect the finished project to look.

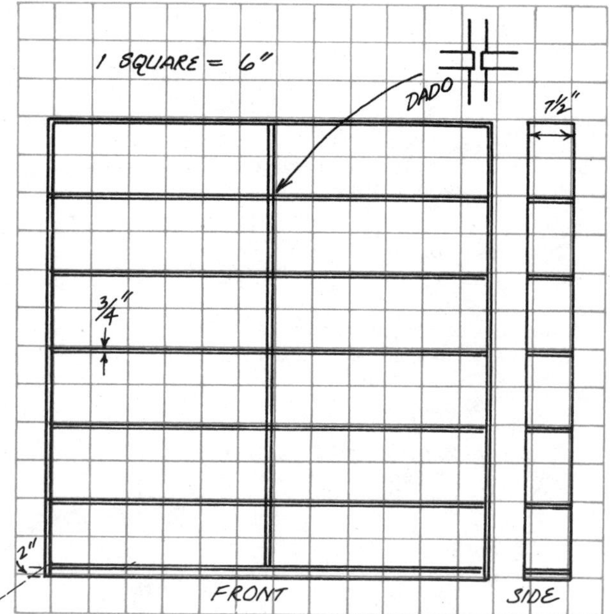

The formal drawings are easier to make on grid paper. Any special details—molding configurations, joints, curves, should be noted here, complete with exact dimensions.

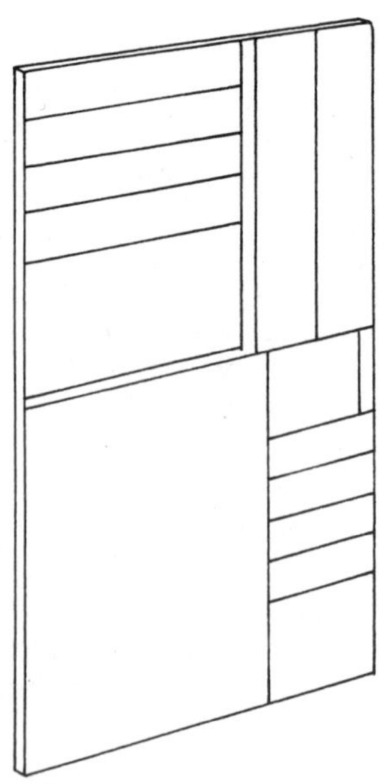

One way to allow for the saw kerf is to use a carpenter's pencil when marking the plywood. The wide lead allows you to make ⅛" lines.

s an unusual feature, so make a note of that, too.

When you have as many of the basics of the project as you can think of for the moment, sketch the front of it, how it will look when it is closed. What molding should it have to be in keeping with other objects in the room? What kind of hardware is compatible with the design? Should the piece be veneered, or varnished, or painted?

It takes a while to do the drawings. Some projects may result in a few restless nights before they are complete in your mind. Somehow, new ideas like to come in the night, so keep your drawings on the night table and jot down any new ideas that jolt you awake as you are dropping off. That sounds strange, but the worth of every project is directly proportional to how much of yourself you are willing to put into it, how much care you take in its completion.

Assemble materials. When you have a rough sketch of what your project is going to look like, do the formal drawings. One good material to use for this process is grid paper, which can be purchased at any stationery store. The grids are usually ½" square. You can mark off a 4"x8" rectangle and immediately have an accurate, scaled drawing of a plywood panel. Next, you have to play around with the rectangle, fitting as many pieces of the project as possible into it, until you have determined how many panels you will need, and how you will cut each of them. At the same time, you can estimate the amount of stock you require and the length of molding and trim, even decide what hardware you wish to use. Finally, make a complete shopping list of all the materials and supplies needed to complete the project. The list should include everything: wood, hardware,

Linear/Metric Conversions

1 inch = 25.4 millimeters
1 inch = 2.54 centimeters
1 foot = 304.8 millimeters
1 foot = 30.48 centimeters
1 foot = 0.305 meter
1 yard = 0.915 meter
1 mile = 1609.34 meters
1 mile = 1.609 kilometers
1 square inch = 645.16 square millimeters
1 square inch = 6.45 square centimeters
1 square foot = 929.03 square centimeters
1 square foot = 0.093 square meter
1 cubic inch = 16.38 cubic centimeters
1 cubic inch = 0.016 liter
1 cubic foot = 28.32 liters
1 liquid quart = 0.9475 liter
1 liquid gallon = 3.79 liters

Metric/Linear Conversions

1 millimeter = 0.0394 inch
1 centimeter = 0.394 inch
1 centimeter = 0.033 foot
1 meter = 39.37 inches
1 meter = 3.28 feet
1 kilometer = 3280.83 feet
1 kilometer = 0.621 mile
1 square centimeter = 0.155 square inch
1 square centimeter = 0.0011 square foot
1 square meter = 10.764 square feet
1 square meter = 1.2 square yards
1 cubic centimeter = 0.061 cubic inch
1 liter = 61.02 cubic inches
1 liter = 0.035 cubic feet
1 liter = 1.056 liquid quart
1 liter = 0.264 liquid gallon

nails and screws, glue, finishing materials, etc. If costs concern you, call your local lumberyard and ask about current prices. Wood prices these days are on a yo-yo string and last month's bill will not necessarily reflect this week's prices.

Layout and cut. When the wood is in your workshop, go over the plywood panels and rule off your cuts, bearing in mind the width of your saw kerf (probably 1/8"), and that the first cut or two should reduce the panel to a manageable stack of pieces. Mark off the stock, too. Mark off everything you possibly can except the drawer and door parts. Those are better left until their cavities have been assembled and they can be built to exact measurement. Now, cut everything. When that is done, change the blade on your saw and do the dadoes, miters, whatever joinery and shaping must be done.

Assembly. First, preassemble the frames for drawers and doors, the basic box, and so on. Then put them together, using whatever glue-nail-screw combinations you have chosen to hold the project together.

Drawers and doors. Whenever possible, build the drawers and doors before their frames exist; then fit the frames around them. Measure and cut all the pieces, do the joinery work, and assembly. Then install them. You can add the trim and molding now, except at the areas where you are planning to veneer, if you have elected to do that.

Prefinishing. Fill all cracks, dents, gouges and joints and begin sanding, starting with medium grits and working down to the super smooth. If you are veneering, the sanding is minimal.

Veneering. Measure and cut all veneer pieces. Glue and roller, then trim the edges and clamp the veneer to dry. Then repair any imperfections and attach the molding and trim. Give the project a final, light sanding, then a coat of sealer-filler, if that is included in your plans. Sand the sealer.

Finishing. Give the project its undercoats and sandings. Then put on the final coats, sanding in between, and finally do the oil-rubbing. Last, fasten all the drawer pulls and catches, latches, knobs and casters in position.

The procedure for constructing any project is the same, progressing from a need to an idea, to drawings, to cutting and assembling and the process of finishing. Only the work flow is identical from project to project. The ideas are invariably different. The needs always vary, and so does the space. And that is why the purpose of the projects included in this book is to stimulate your own creative abilities, to give you hints that you, and you alone, can use to develop effective solutions to the storage problems you wish to solve.

CHAPTER 10

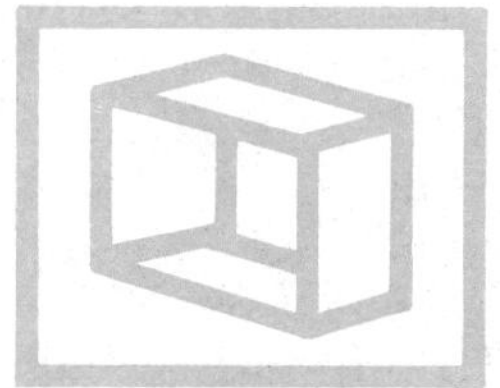
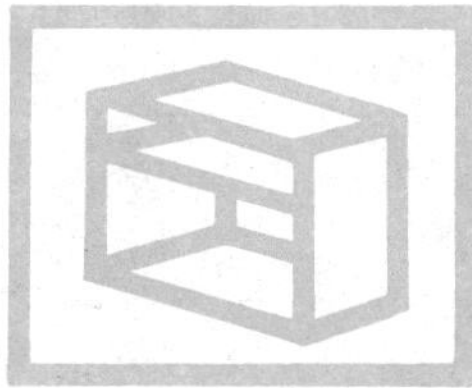

Shelves

Shelves

The secret to a successful shelf is stability; it must always be constructed as securely as possible, no matter where it is, or how it is attached. It is fair to say that shelves can literally be installed almost anywhere, and held in place by a wide variety of methods. By and large, however, the most secure support for a shelf is a vertical support of some sort. Therefore, any discussion of shelves has to begin with a consideration of the uprights that support them, and how secure *they* are.

Not too many years ago, manufacturers developed a track-and-brace system for holding shelves; it immediately became a boon to householders all over the country. Today, shelf tracks and braces can be purchased almost anywhere, and attached to almost any wall. The tracks are U-shaped and have slots as well as screw holes in the bottom of the "U." The buyer usually has to drill holes in the wall for lead plugs or toggle bolts, and the tracks have to be hung no more than 3′ apart (because of the shelf itself, not the tracks). But once the braces have been locked into the slots along the track, the shelves will hold hundreds of books until the wall crumbles. The wall, then is a sturdy upright that supports vertically installed tracks. The tracks hold narrow horizontals (the brackets), which, in turn, hold a wider horizontal: the shelf. The easiest way to hang vertical shelf tracks is to drill for the highest screw in the track and all but tighten the track to the wall.

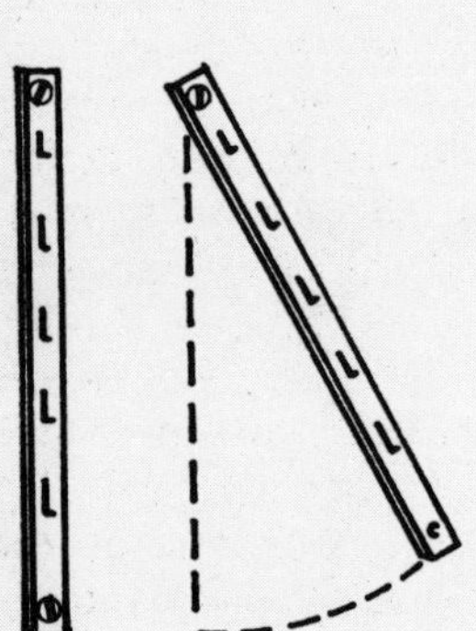

Hang shelf tracks loosely from their top screw and allow the track to seek its own plumb.

No matter how you join four boards, they will still be rickety without added support.

A diagonal back brace is an excellent way of stabilizing a set of shelves.

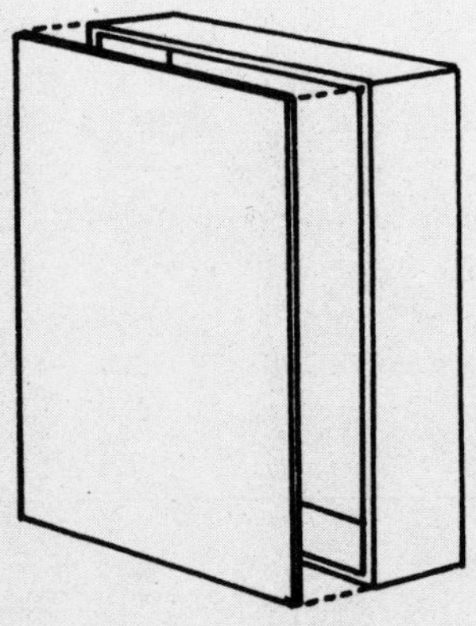

A full back, glue-nailed to every member of a shelf case, will make the unit about as solid as it can be.

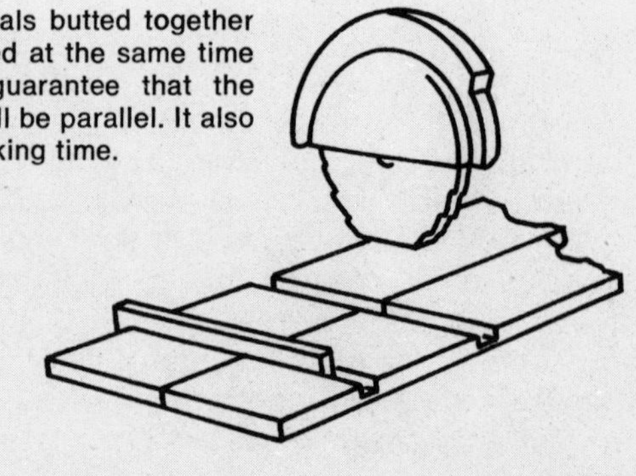

Two verticals butted together and dadoed at the same time at least guarantee that the shelves will be parallel. It also saves working time.

If it can swing freely, the track will act like a plumb line and settle into a vertical position. Then press it tightly against the wall and mark the other screw holes. Before drilling the holes, step back and look at the track. It may be vertical all right, but it may also look crooked because the wall is not straight. You might want to set the track off center so that it *looks* straight.

Start with two vertical pieces of wood, held parallel at each end by two horizontal wood pieces, and you have a box consisting of two shelves with two uprights. It will probably be rather rickety, even if the joinery is as intricate as, say, dovetails. Install more shelves and the unit becomes more stable between the uprights—the more shelves, the more stable the unit. Still, it is liable to continue swaying back and forth, even if each shelf is cleated or dadoed in place.

As long as the unit wobbles in any way, the requirement of stability in the shelves has not been met. The unit could be stabilized by attaching it to a solid upright, such as a wall. A diagonal reaching from one top corner to its opposite bottom corner is effective, a full back spanning the entire unit even better. Cut square, the full back serves to guide the parallel of the sides and shelves, and if glue-nailed to the back of each shelf, the entire unit will be secure enough to almost guarantee no shifting at all.

One of the problems often encountered when making a simple set of bookshelves is getting all of them parallel. The time to solve this problem is at the joining stage. When dadoeing two vertical supports for a shelf, make the dado in both sides at the same time. Under ideal conditions, crosscut dadoeing is done with a radial arm saw and a dado blade. Start at any of the dadoes, align the two verticals, butt them side by side, and make the first dado through both of them with one pass of the saw. Then insert a piece of scrap that spans both boards and fits tightly enough into both dadoes to hold the boards together. In this way, you not only have a handle for moving the boards around, but they will not become misaligned. You can go ahead and do whatever dadoeing you want with the knowledge that the shelves will be parallel. The alternative to this procedure is to measure and mark the cutting points for each dado on both verticals, then cut them separately. Remember, however, that the more measurements you take, the more opportunities for error.

Even when you *know* the shelves are parallel with each other, once they are assembled and standing they still may not be horizontal to anything but themselves and the floor. If the shelves are a built-in unit they can be leveled, and the kick plate need only be cut at whatever odd angle the floor appears to be lying. A freestanding project presents a completely different situation; it must be shimmed, braced or held steady as well as level by some device, even if you have to invent one.

Assembling a set of shelves and securing them solidly is only the beginning. After that come the decorative touches that distinguish an arrangement of bare horizontals from an attractive, pleasing piece of furniture. The variations that can be applied to a shelf for decorative effect are almost limitless.

The most obvious enhancement of a simple, unadorned bookcase is a straight rail that crosses under the front of the case top and is repeated in a parallel rail along the bottom, under the bottom shelf. This "basic framing" idea can be extended to include both sides of the case as well. And if there are partitions, they too can have stiles against their front edges. Starting with a bookcase made with ¾" stock, the frame can easily be 1"x2" stock which is either left square at the edges, or rounded off. The frame itself can be given a quite different look simply by mitering the corners. It might also be given strips of trim down the face of the stiles, or tacked to the inside of their edges.

If the idea of 1"x2" stock seems too bulky for the case, thinner stock can be used, or the frame can be made from any of several moldings beginning with cove and half-round. The molding will look out of place, however, if it is confined only to the verticals, so when putting it along the edges of the case, consider adding it to the front edges of the shelves as well. Most molding, of course, should be mitered at all corners.

The next possibility for enhancing a shelf case that should be considered is the top of the unit. The top can be made flush with the sides or can extend beyond them by ½" or ¾". It can hang over just the sides or just the front, or all four—top, sides and front. The top can be left as a straight overhang, its edges can be trimmed with molding, or a cove molding can be fitted under the overhang for a designer's touch.

In almost every instance, the square box (which a standing shelf case is) has to be

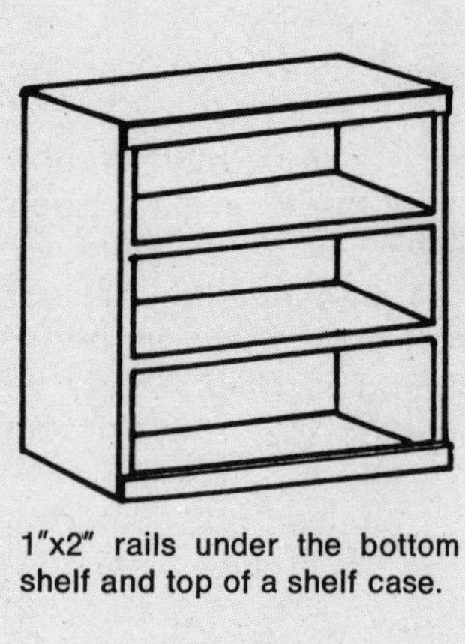

1"x2" rails under the bottom shelf and top of a shelf case.

An entire case can be framed.

Instead of 1"x2" stock, a case can be trimmed with molding.

A case top can overhang the front and sides.

Overhanging tops are enhanced with trim tacked under the lips.

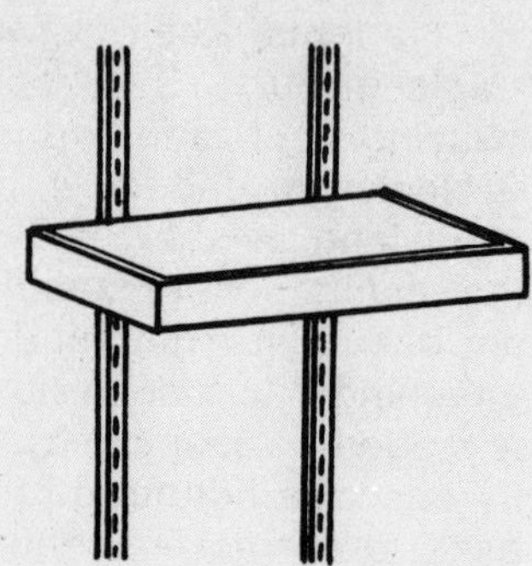

A shelf with a simple, wide lip.

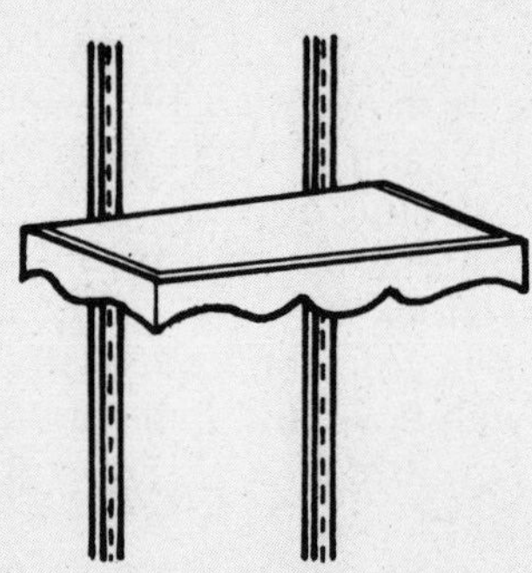

Shelf and scrolled skirt.

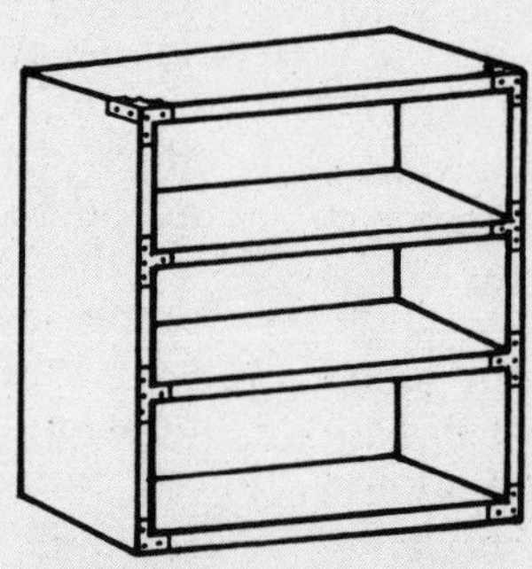

Cases have a quite different look when decorated with interesting hardware.

Bases can also be enhanced with trim.

built from ¾" stock and there is a thick solidness about the look of wood ¾" thick. It appears heavy, sometimes ponderous, particularly if its edges are all squared off. This ponderous look is made more so by the solidity of the case itself. Suddenly a project that seemed "delicate" in the mind's eye and even in the preliminary drawings, becomes cumbersome in appearance because of the size of the wood and the squareness of the box. And the eye, startled by this thick, square look, immediately looks for some way to provide visual relief. Molding and trim offer that visual relief because of their curves. Even if the trim is nothing more than a ¼" beading glued down the center of a ¾" edge of a board, it immediately breaks up the monotony of squareness throughout the unit.

And there are other ways to offset the rigidity of straight right angles. Sometimes, it is effective to thicken a shelf dramatically by giving it a wide lip, or skirt. In a number of instances, the wideness of a shelf may highlight the decor of an entire room. One of the projects in this section suggests a set of such shelves reaching up to the ceiling between great, towering pillars that are 1′ thick. Pillared shelves are not a project to be attempted in a small room, but in a room with a 12′ or 14′ ceiling, they can become especially effective, simply because they are so big.

The thick-lipped shelf need not be just a wide facing made up of straight lines. The lip could easily become a decorative valance with, again, curves along its underside to relieve the sameness of a vertical and horizontal construction. The valance motif can also be repeated either identically, or in a modified form, along the front edge of the shelves. Scrollwork, whenever it is attached to a shelf, has the ability to break down that straight, flat look so inherent in any horizontal construction.

Sometimes, however, the straight, flat look is precisely the appearance the unit is supposed to have, as in the military chest shown in the final chapter of this book. But the chest is decorated with brass angles. Nothing says the corners of a shelf cannot be treated in the same way. The decorative possibilities of hardware, therefore, should never be ignored when planning any shelf project.

Then, there is the base of a shelf case. The base can be given a kick plate. But it might also have a baseboard that surrounds the sides and front of the unit. And there are any number of ways to decorate a baseboard. It can be merely a 1″x4″ plate nailed to the bottom of the case. It can also have a crown molding along its top edge. It might also be made from a combination of boards, plates, trims and moldings. The base itself can be a straight board; it might be scrolled with feet at each corner.

The feet of the sides of the case are cut out of the bottom edge of each side, then the baseboard is scrolled. Boards for both the front and the sides are cut and mitered. The side boards are glue-nailed or glue-screwed in place, and the face board is attached to the front of the bottom shelf and the front edges of both sides. Made in this manner, the base serves no purpose other than to decorate the bottom of the case.

Alternatively, the base can hold the entire unit. To do this, a heavy cleat must be glue-screwed around the underside of the sides and front of the bottom shelf. The cleat should be at least 1″x1″, and it will hold the weight of the unit better if it is made of hardwood rather than plywood or a softwood. The cleat becomes the major support for the base—and the unit—since the base is glue-screwed to it and extends down below the cleat to the floor. Often, bases made in this manner are shaped pieces of wood with fluting, coves or some other type of curves and carvings. It is not a difficult way to mold the base plates, but it is time-consuming and probably not worth the extra effort unless the project is to be used as a piece of furniture.

With shelf cases, as well as cabinets, it is often desirable to have the unit stand flush against the wall. The difficulty encountered in achieving this comes from the baseboard running along the joint between the floor and the wall. In modern homes, the baseboard may not be more than 3″ or so; in older homes it has been known to go as high as 2′, although 6″ is perhaps the average. The baseboard usually has some ornamentation of its own, such as a trim along its top edge, and often a ¼″ round at its base that is nailed to the floor. Presuming the baseboard is ¾″ stock, plus the ¾″ quarter-round at the floor, this configuration presents an obstruction 6″ high and 1½″ wide at its base, which keeps a shelf case standing at least that far from the wall. The question is how to get around this rather inconvenient obstacle.

With cabinets, the sides can sometimes be extended 1½″ beyond the back and then notched to fit around the baseboard. But with a shelf case, the depth usually is not enough to allow the luxury of wasting 1″ or 1½″ of the shelves just to get around 1½″x6″ of wood at the bottom of the unit. If this is the situation, let the top of the unit overhang the back until it touches the wall.

Another solution is to match the depth of the bottom shelf to the thickness of the baseboard. For example, if the shelves in a case are 8½″ deep and the baseboard is 1½″ thick, the bottom shelf becomes 7″ wide and the sides of the case are notched to fit around the base plate.

A third way of dealing with baseboards, if the board is only 3″ or 4″ high, is to position the bottom shelf at a level above the baseboard. The sides of the unit are then notched below the back edge of the board.

Still another way is to build the unit on a frame high enough to allow its bottom shelf to be installed at a level above the top of the baseboards.

No matter how you get around the base-

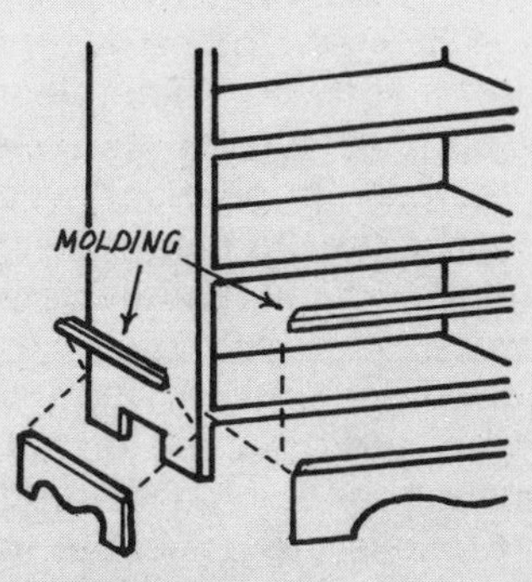

The base need not have a straight bottom edge, but can also be scrolled.

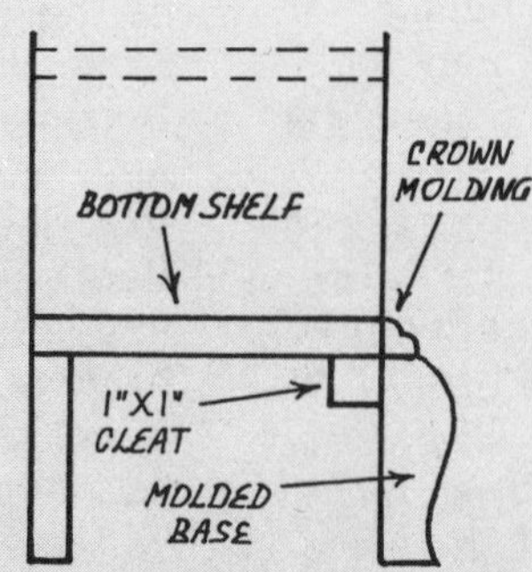

Assembly of an add-on base.

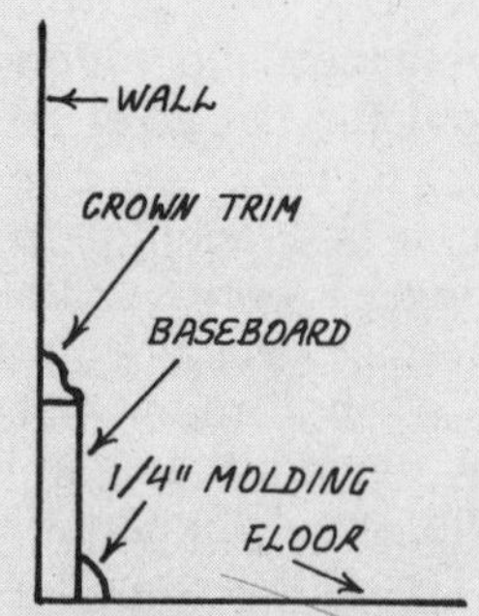

Baseboards can be as much as 1½" thick.

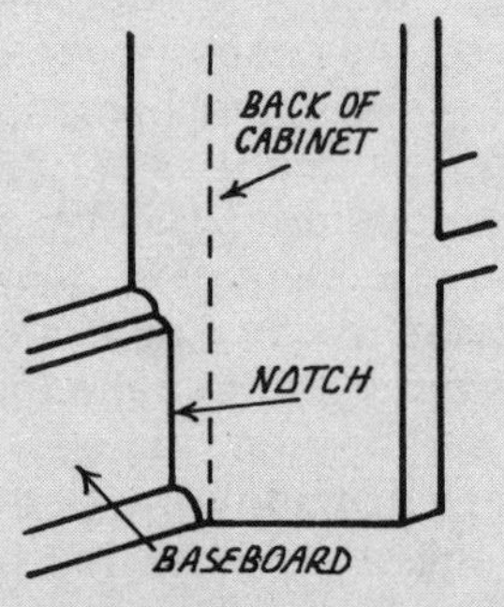

A baseboard notch may take up too much shelf width if the back of the unit is inset.

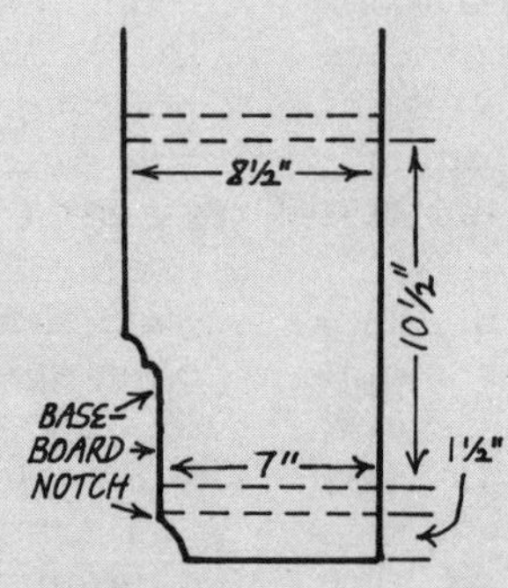

The bottom shelf can be made narrower by the thickness of the baseboard.

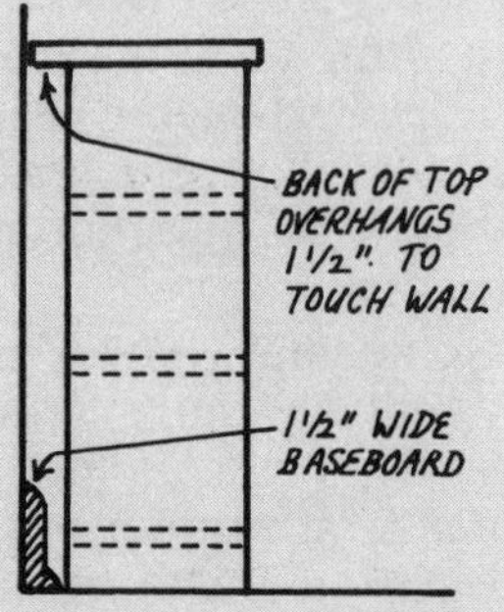

The case top can be extended at the back by the thickness of the baseboard.

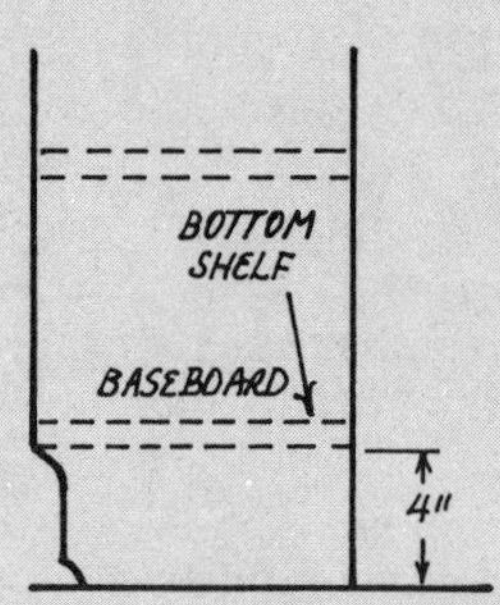

Sometimes the bottom shelf can serve as the top of the kick plate and also be above the baseboard.

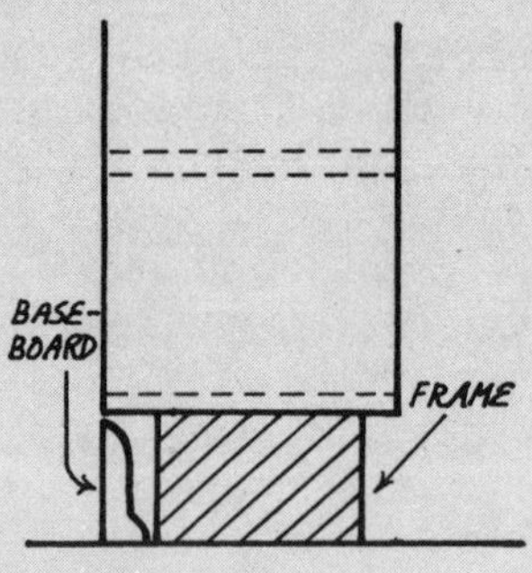

The case can simply sit on a frame.

board problem, there will be a more or less unsightly recession in the back of the case. It is debatable whether or not there is an advantage to cutting the notch to exactly fit the contours of the baseboard. If the unit is ever moved to another room, its notch may not fit in its new location. On the other hand, if it is not moved, it certainly looks neater if the entire unit stands snugly against the baseboard and wall. Perhaps, with certain units, some decorative type of scroll can be made in the back of the sides which is a part of the overall design of the shelf case and, at the same time, hides the fact that the unit has been constructed around an awkward baseboard.

In any case, when approaching a shelf project, the sense of design must always be present. Into that design must go thoughts about the baseboard and what to do about it. The kick plate should also be considered, as well as the top, and the moldings or trim that will be included. It may be that after due consideration of all these elements, the builder will settle on just a plain, straight shelf. That is fine. Plain, straight shelves have been serving mankind for centuries. Still, all of the possibilities should be evaluated in terms of the room where the shelves will be used, and the furniture around them. If the unit is to be built in to, say, an alcove, you may well want it to be as unobtrusive as possible. Then, the only considerations are its length, depth and proper support for the shelf every 3′ or so. But if the shelves are to blend into the atmosphere of an ornately furnished room, then the unit must have some enhancing features. These can be trim, or scrollwork, or can be achieved through the judicious use of a molder head or router bit applied to the edges.

The projects presented in this section all offer the craftsman endless possibilities for adding decorative touches. For the most part, they are simple in their construction, but they have each been chosen first for their usefulness as storage units, and then for the opportunities of enhancement that they offer. Because they are shelves, and not particularly complicated to put together, they are not what one would call challenges in themselves. They only become a challenge if they represent a new venture for the builder, a new approach, or design, or technique that he can experiment with and develop—or discard. But if the experimentation is to be along the lines of decoration, they are all excellent projects on which to try a new approach, to hone an old skill, to test out a different visual effect that may then be developed to some more pronounced degree in the construction of a closet, or cabinet, or piece of furniture.

Basic Bookshelves

This fundamental bookcase, with a few variations, can provide a useful project in both construction and wood-finishing. The drawings show a unit, 7½" deep x 6' wide x 6' high, but it could be any size. The only thing to remember is that pine boards, the most commonly used shelving material in the United States, need to be supported every 30" to 36" if the shelves are required to hold anything as heavy as books.

Materials for Basic Bookshelves

Quantity	Description
60'	1"x7½" pine shelving for the shelves and case
2 pieces	¼"x3'x6' Masonite for back
6'	1"x2" for kick plate

Sides (Fig. A). In the design shown, the verticals are rabbeted to the top of the case, so they are cut 5′ 11⅝″ long and rabbeted at one end. The rabbet is half the thickness of the wood, or ⅜″ deep. The shelves are held in dadoes which are 11″ apart and ⅜″ deep. The bottom dado is 1½″ from the bottom of the sides, so that the 1½″-wide kick plate can fit under the bottom shelf.

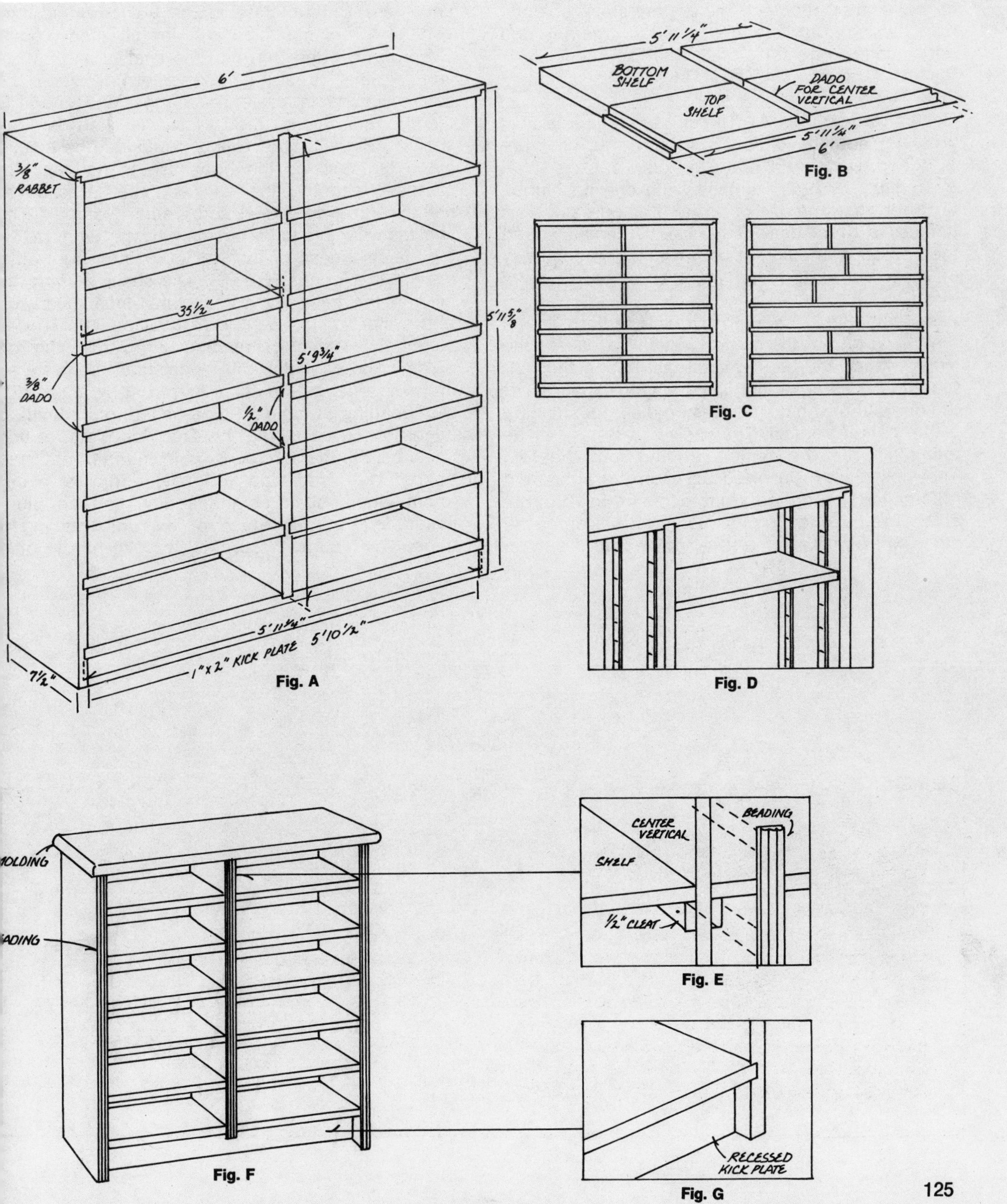

Fig. A

Fig. B

Fig. C

Fig. D

Fig. E

Fig. F

Fig. G

Horizontals (Fig. A). All ten shelves are cut 35½″ long. The top of the case is 6′ long and rabbeted at both ends. The bottom shelf is 5′ 11¼″ long, and, when laid next to the top shelf, should exactly match the length between the back edges of the rabbets (Fig. B). If it does not, measurements for either the rabbets or the bottom shelf, or both, were wrong. Butt the two shelves together and dado them on center (36″ for the top shelf; 35⅜″ for the bottom). The 1″x2″ kick plate is cut 5′ 10½″ long.

Center vertical (Fig. A). The center vertical is 7½″ x5′ 9¾″, and the dadoes on each side of it are ¼″ deep. Dadoing a board on both sides so that every slot is *exactly* aligned, with one no higher, or lower, than the one opposite it, is no easy task. It takes a great deal of care and precision, and the operation should not be hurried. The accuracy of the results, however, make it all worth extra effort.

Assembly (Fig. A). Begin by glue-nailing five of the shelves from the center vertical to *one* of the sides. Attach the bottom shelf last, fitting the bottom of the center vertical into its dado. Now repeat the operation with the shelves on the opposite side of the center vertical. The shelves will have to be toenailed into the center vertical from the *top.* The kick plate is inserted between the sides and glue-nailed under the front edge of the bottom shelf. The case top is glue-nailed to the top of the sides, with the center vertical fitting into the dado in its center. Stabilize the unit by glue-nailing two 3′x6′ strips of ¼″ Masonite to the back of the shelves, butting them at the back of the center vertical. Bevel the edges of the Masonite 45° with a sander or router.

Variations. Shown is a sampling of the types and sizes of bookcase units. For example, the vertical center could be a series of wood pieces 11″ high, inserted between the shelves in either a vertical line, or staggered somewhat along the center line. It is easier to stagger the supports than to get them exactly lined up between the shelves (Fig. C). The vertical could also be a solid piece that divides the bookcase in half and instead of dadoing the shelves, shelf tracks are nailed onto the sides and center vertical. The shelves will have to be cut slightly shorter, to allow for the thickness of the tracks, unless the tracks are set in ploughs (Fig. D). The shelves could be held in the case with cleats; half-inch cleats on either side of the center vertical can be hidden behind 2″ molding or beading (Fig. E). Or, the top piece could be wider and longer than the case, so that it overhangs the sides and front by about ½″ with beading or molding glue-nailed to the leading edges of the case (Fig. F). The kick plate, in this instance, can be recessed ½″ from the front of the bottom shelf and sides (Fig. G). Strips of a different wood, such as mahogany, can be glue-nailed to all front edges of the unit, making it appear as though the project is solid hardwood.

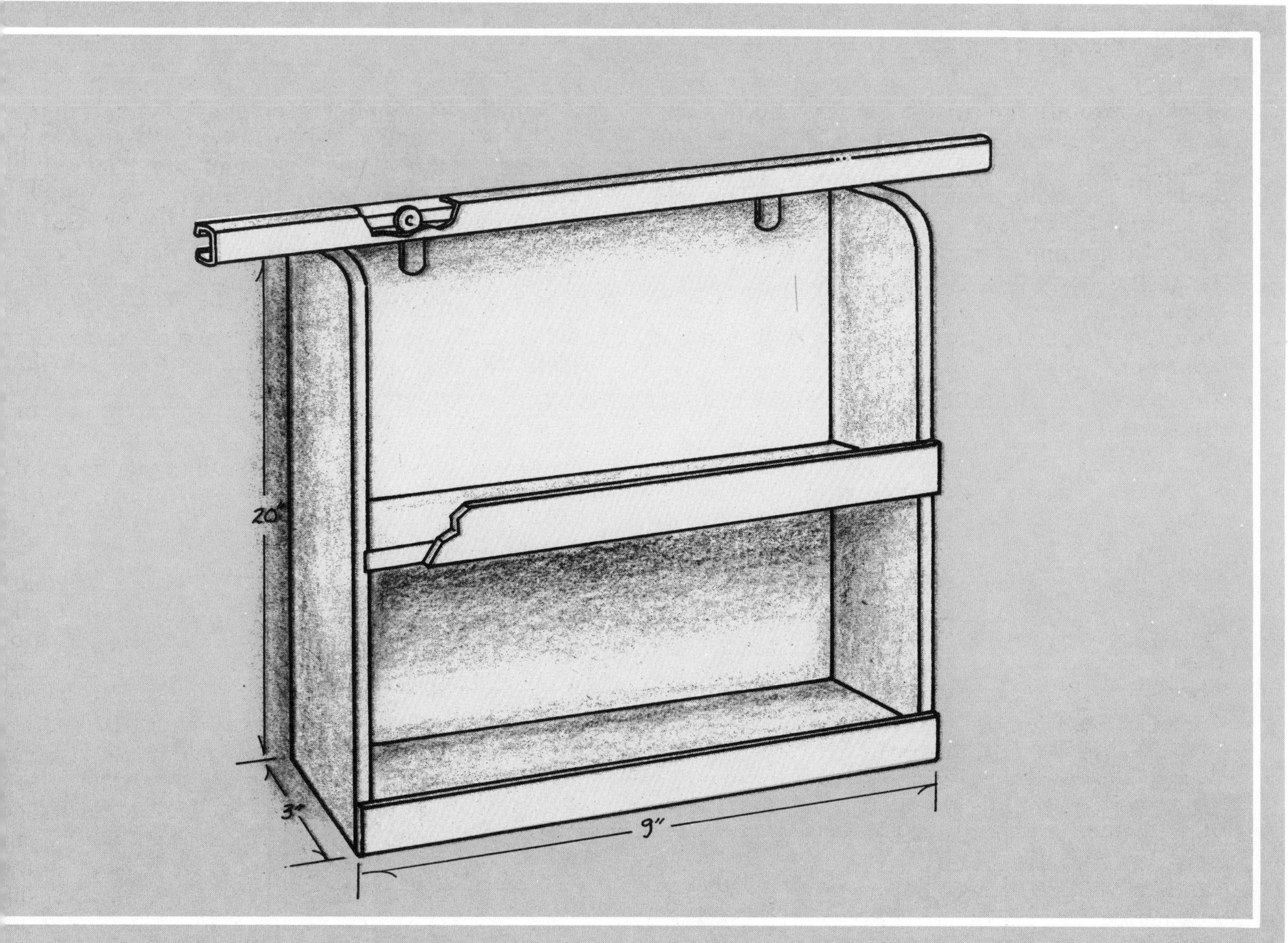

Sliding Shelf Rack

One of the common problems with shelf storage occurs when the shelves are too deep. A shelf that is deeper than necessary to hold the things stored on it is an open invitation for people to stuff objects at the back—where they are promptly lost from sight, and forgotten. Still, if the storage space is there, it is a sore temptation to use. And it should be used.

The sliding shelf rack is one solution to the too-deep shelf problem. It is ideal for storing such things as medicine, spices or cosmetics. It can also be used any place that must hold a combination of objects, both small and large. The cosmetic-medicine chest shown here is an example. The cabinet shelves are 9½" deep by 10½" high; the shelf behind the rack has been narrowed to 6", which is deep enough to hold boxes of cotton, large bottles and so on. The sliding rack, then, has 3" of storage space, which is more than enough to handle small medicine bottles and cosmetics. The size of the rack itself should never be more than one-half the width of the cabinet (in this case, 18") so there will be full access to the objects stored behind it.

Materials for Sliding Shelf Rack

Quantity	**Description**
1	track-and-glide set to match length of shelves
58"	½"x3" stock for sides and shelves
1	¼"x9"x20" luan or Masonite for back
18"	¼"x1½"x9" strip of luan or Masonite for shelf lips

Sides. These are cut from ½″ stock, and measure 3″x20″. They are dadoed ¼″ deep at the 10″ mark to accept the center shelf.
Shelves. The bottom shelf is ½″x3″x9″. The middle shelf is ½″x3″x8½″. (There could be one more shelf, if each one is made 6½″ deep.)
Back. The back is a ¼″x9″x20″ piece of luan or Masonite.
Lips. The lips are both ½″x1½″x9″ luan or Masonite.

Assembly. Glue-nail the center shelf into its dadoe on the sides and butt-join the bottom shelf to th bottom of the sides. Glue-nail the back to th shelves and sides, and attach two track glides t the top edge. Glue-nail the lips to the front of th sides, making lips flush with the bottom c the shelves.

Screw an aluminum or plastic track to unde side of the shelf above the sliding rack. Con plete by hanging the sliding shelf from the track

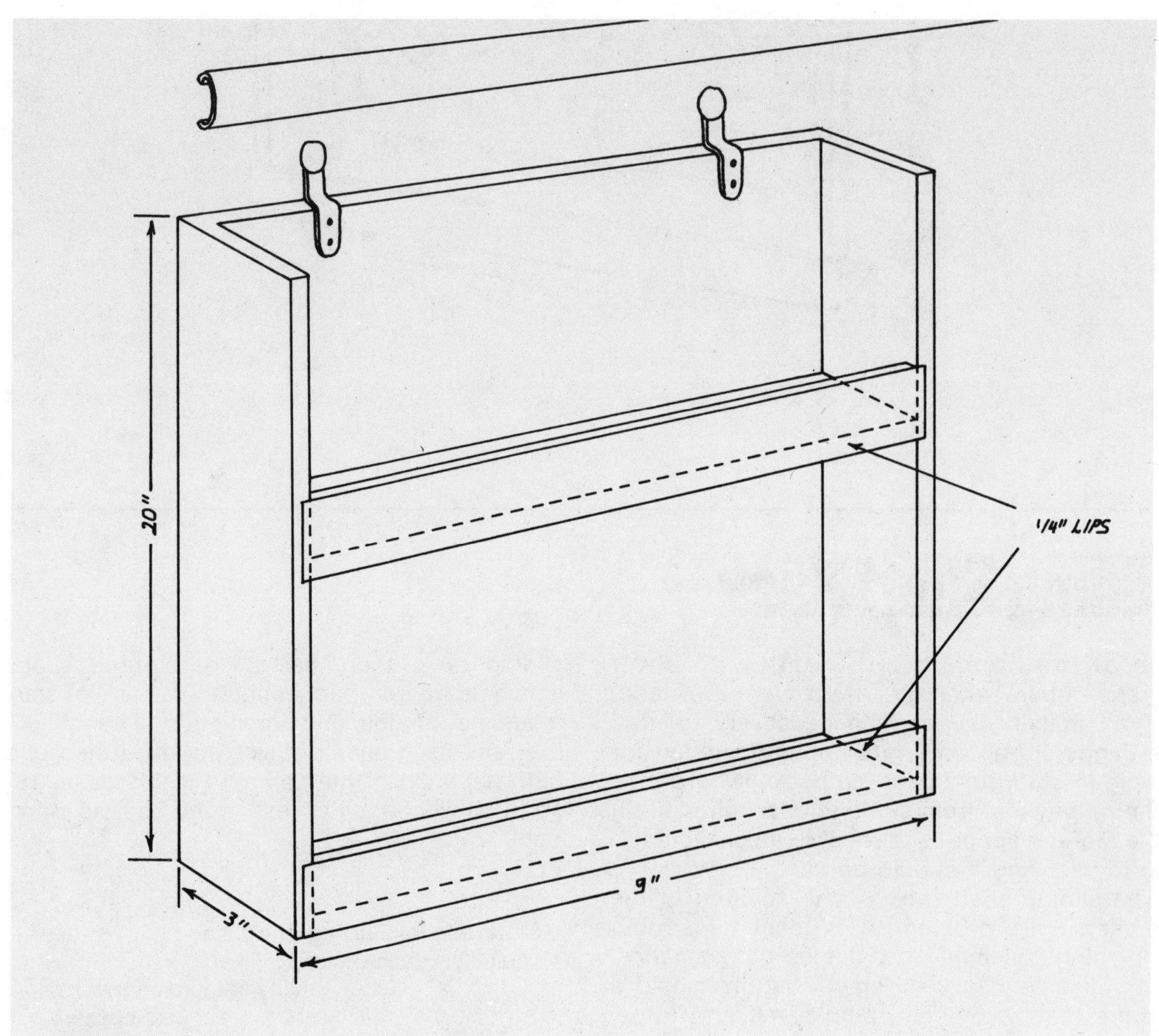

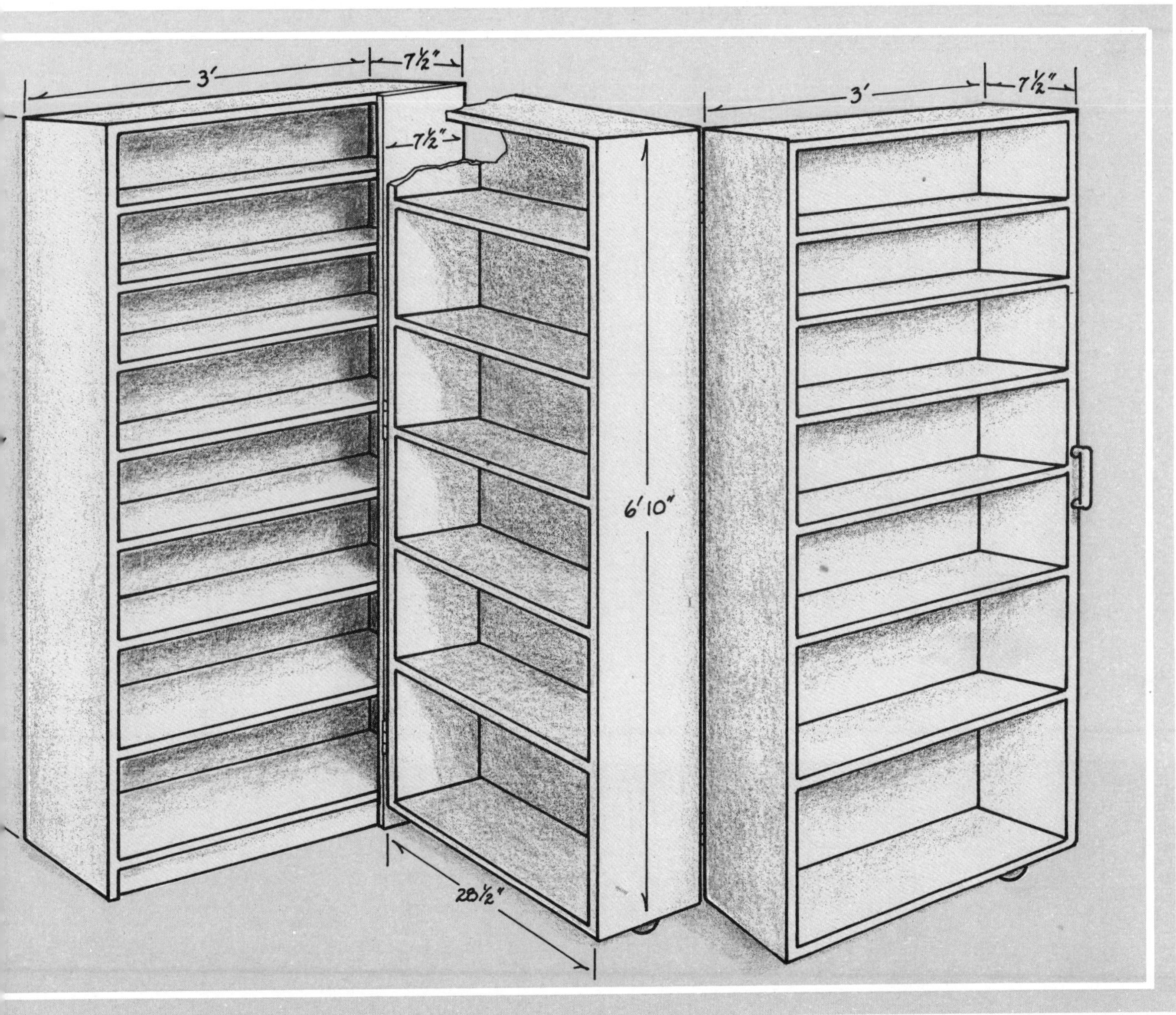

Z-Out Shelves

The Z-Out is so simple and quick to assemble that its efficiency as a storage unit comes almost as a surprise. It literally can be built in under four hours and is ideal for filling a corner with all a child's toys. In the version shown here, the three hinged shelf units are all the same depth, but they could easily be of varying dimensions. It is recommended that the front and middle units not exceed 3′ in width, or they will become too cumbersome for children to handle. They will also have more opportunity to warp. Because there are so many shelves in the Z-Out, it may be less expensive to buy plywood and rip it. But it is quicker to purchase pine shelving in whatever widths you have chosen for the three units.

Materials for Z-Out Shelves

Quantity	Description
72′	1″x8″ pine shelving for shelves
42′	1″x8″ pine shelving for verticals
2	⅛″x3′x7′ luan for center and front unit backs
3′	1″x2″ firring for rear unit kick plate
7′	1″x8″ pine shelving for rear unit faceplate
6	3½″ door butts to attach center and front shelf units
2	2″ casters with treads for center and front units
2	large handles

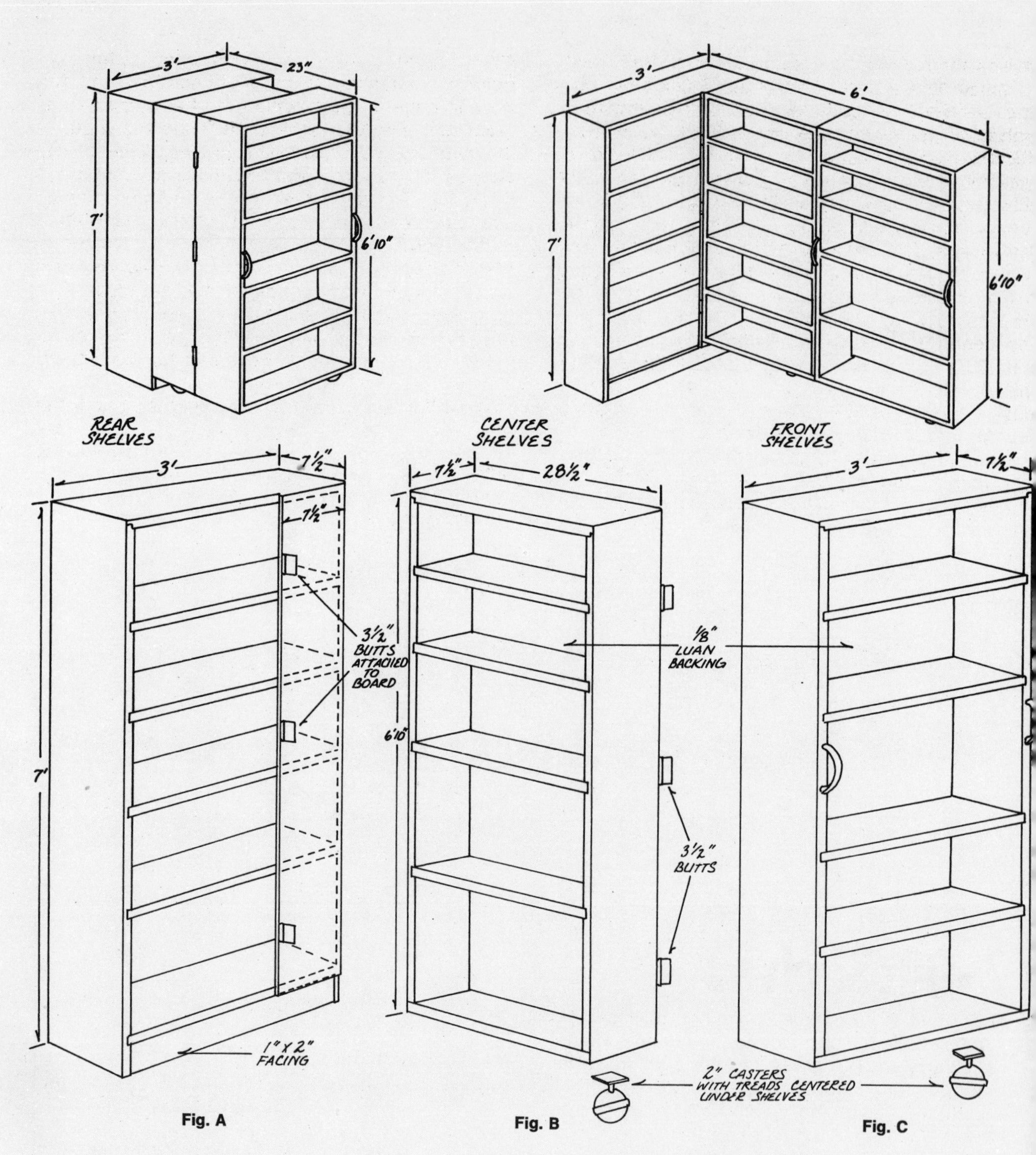

Fig. A

Fig. B

Fig. C

Rear shelf unit (Fig. A). Cut the two verticals 7′ in length and dado them for the shelves. Higher shelves should be on the bottom, and should range from between 15″ and 18″ to 8″ near the top. The top shelf is rabbeted. The bottom shelf is positioned 1½″ from the bottom of the verticals and is supported by a 1″ x 2″ kick plate. A board that is the width of the center shelves (in this case 7½″) i glue-nailed to the front right corner of the shelve to accept the three 3½″ butts that hold the cente shelves (see Fig. D). If you choose a left-han swing (Fig. E), then the front plate is glue-naile down the left side of the shelves. Eighth-inch lua or Masonite can be glue-nailed to the back of th shelves for stability, but since the rear unit *must* be nailed to the wall to keep the Z-Out from tipping, the back is optional. *Do not* nail the rear shelves in place until the entire Z-Out is assembled. The wall and floor probably do not make a right angle and exactly how vertical the rear unit will stand depends on whether the casters under the front two units roll properly.

Center unit (Fig. B). The center shelves are their own width shorter than the rear unit. For example, in Fig. B, the center shelves are 28½" wide by 7½" deep, while the rear shelves are 36" wide. The center unit is also 2" shorter than the rear unit (6'10") to allow for a 2" treaded caster. The shelves are dadoed in place and must have at least a ⅛" luan back. The top shelf is rabbeted, but the bottom shelf, which must support the entire weight of the unit, is butted against the bottom ends of the verticals. The treaded caster is situated under the swing end of the shelves, about 4" in from the edge. In a right-hand swing, the butts are attached to the right vertical and the leading edge of the faceplate on the rear shelves.

Front unit (Fig. C). These shelves are the width of the rear shelves (3') and the height of the center shelves (6'10"), and must also have at least a ⅛" back. They are assembled in exactly the same way as the center unit, with the bottom shelf butt-joined to the bottom of the verticals, and the caster at the end opposite from the butts. The handles are placed in the front edges of the verticals. The hinges in a right-hand swing are attached to the left rear of the unit and the front left side of the center shelves. They are reversed for a left-hand swing.

When the Z-Out is finished, stand it against the wall and swing the front units open. The rear shelves will probably have to be shimmed so that the casters can always touch the floor.

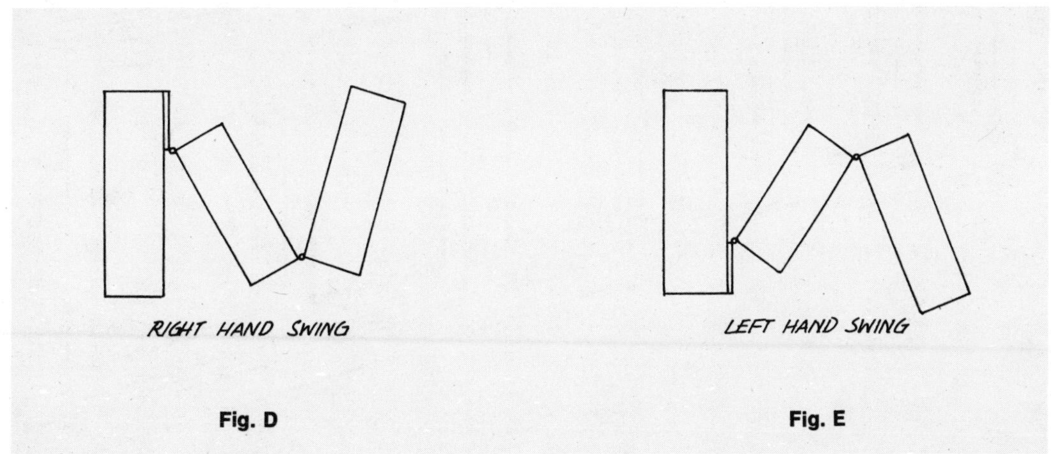

Fig. D

Fig. E

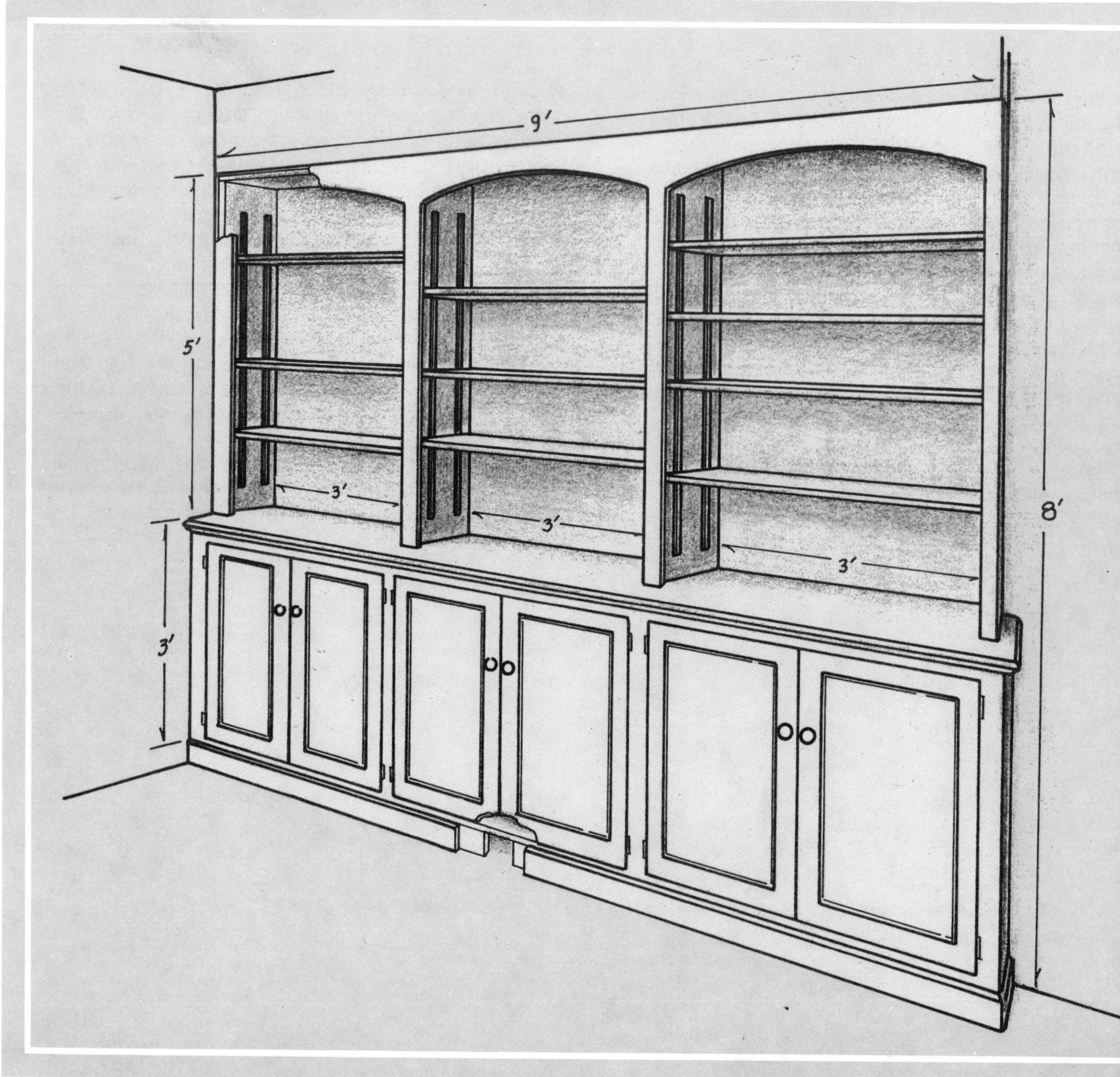

Built-In Bookcase

The basic built-in bookcase can be constructed in any number of ways, but what makes the difference between a box with shelves and a piece of furniture, are the additional touches that give the project the finished look of fine furniture. The cabinet bookcase shown here is an example, yet it could be refined even more with a bolder use of both molding and trim.

Materials for Built-In Bookcase

Quantity	Description
55′	1″x8″ stock for bookshelves and partitions
10′	1″x12″ stock for deck
50′	1″x11″ stock for cabinet shelves, partitions and sides
86′	1″x2″ clear pine stock for trim and cabinet doors
96′	shelf track and support pins
2	¼″ plywood panels good on both sides for cabinet doors
11′	1″x3″ stock for kick plate molding (as needed)

utting. The two case ends are 1"x11" stock, 8' ng. Five feet is ripped to a width of 7¾", with e remaining 3' left 10¾" wide. The shelves, par-ions and top plate are all 1"x8" stock. The deck 1"x12" stock cut 9'3½" long, with a 1½"x7¾" otch at each end, as shown in Fig. A. The cabinet artitions and bottom shelf are cut from 1"x11" ock (see Fig. A).

ssembly. A ¾"x2"x10¾" cleat is nailed to the ottom edge of each side, to support the bottom abinet shelf. Assemble the top, bottom, ends, eck and all partitions. The partitions are placed on center. If you decide to stabilize the case ith a back, use ¼" plywood nailed to the rear dges of the frame.

There can be as many shelves as needed, and e quickest, most versatile way of putting them in ny cabinet is with adjustable shelf tracks. The tracks should be installed in both the shelf and cabinet portions of the project and all shelves will need to be cut 34¼" long, to fit between the tracks.

Variations. Now come those added touches. The arched façade of the bookcase could be any kind of decorative curve cut from ½" or ¾" plywood. Rather than leave the curved area blank, a variety of decorative molding could be added to it. The 1"x2" clear pine stock nailed to the front of the partitions and sides could be fluted molding, or any other decorative facing. The same type molding could be fastened to the 1"x2" stock. The front edge of the deck has two pieces of molding around it, mitered at the corners. The curved strip under the decorative edging could be something more or less ornate, depending on your personal taste. The under molding is attached to 1"x2" stock nailed under the length of the deck. 1"x2"

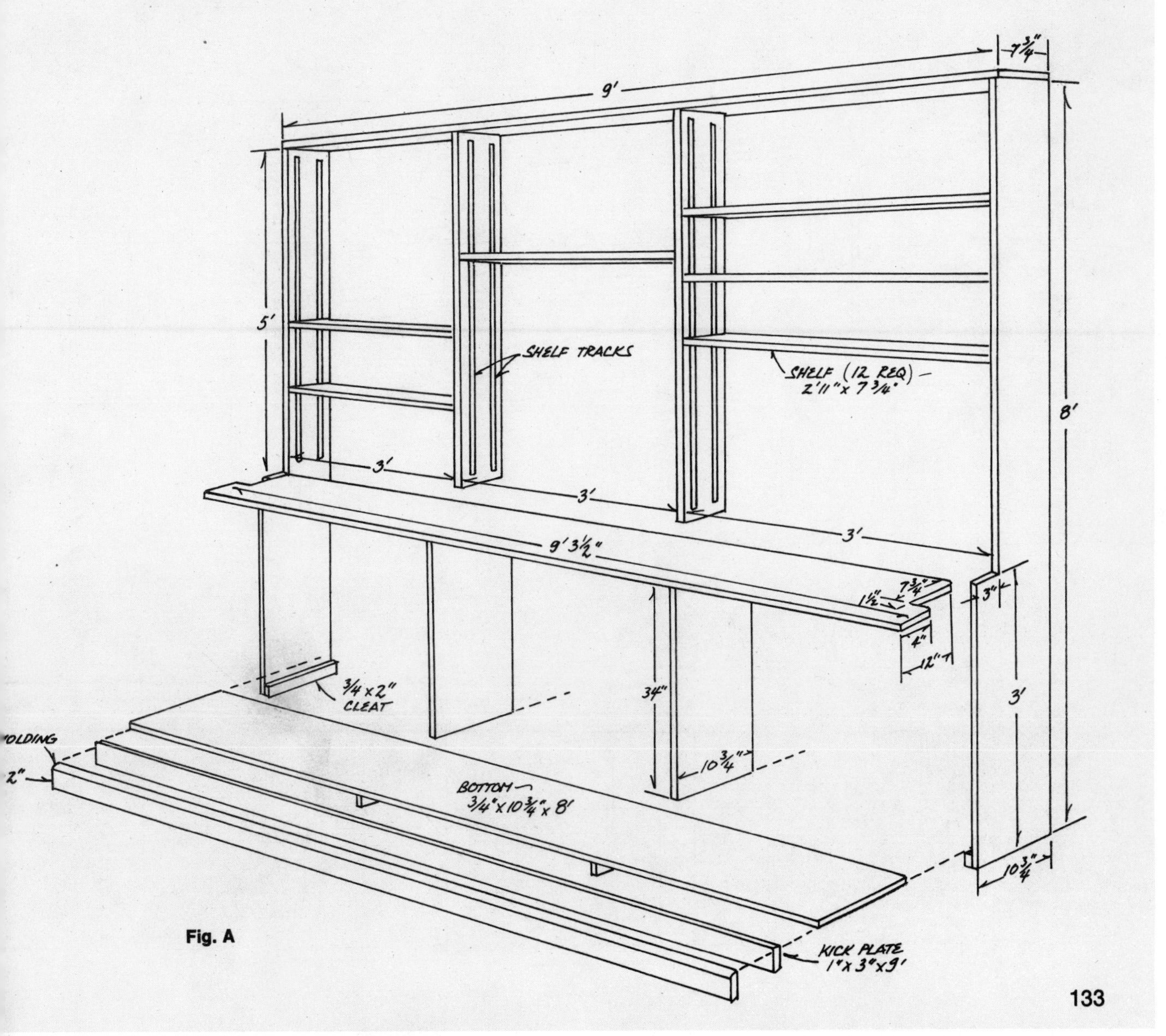

Fig. A

stock is also used to face the cabinet partitions and sides, but again, these could be molding. The kick plate is 1"x3"x9' stock, faced with a 1"x2" strip (Fig. A). The 1¼" difference between the two boards is filled with curved molding, a motif which might also be duplicated around the top of the bookshelves, above the arches.

Doors. The simplest way of making the six cabinet doors is to cut ¼" plywood into 32½"x32¾" pieces. Then miter 1"x2" stock to form a frame which is glue-nailed flush with the outside edge c the squares (Fig. B). The inside edges of th frame can simply be rounded. Or they could b curved with any of several router bits, or they coul be finished with strips of molding.

When the doors are hung and all of your deco rative touches are in place, the completed built-i bookcase can be finished in any manner tha blends with or matches the decor of the roor where it will stand.

Fig.

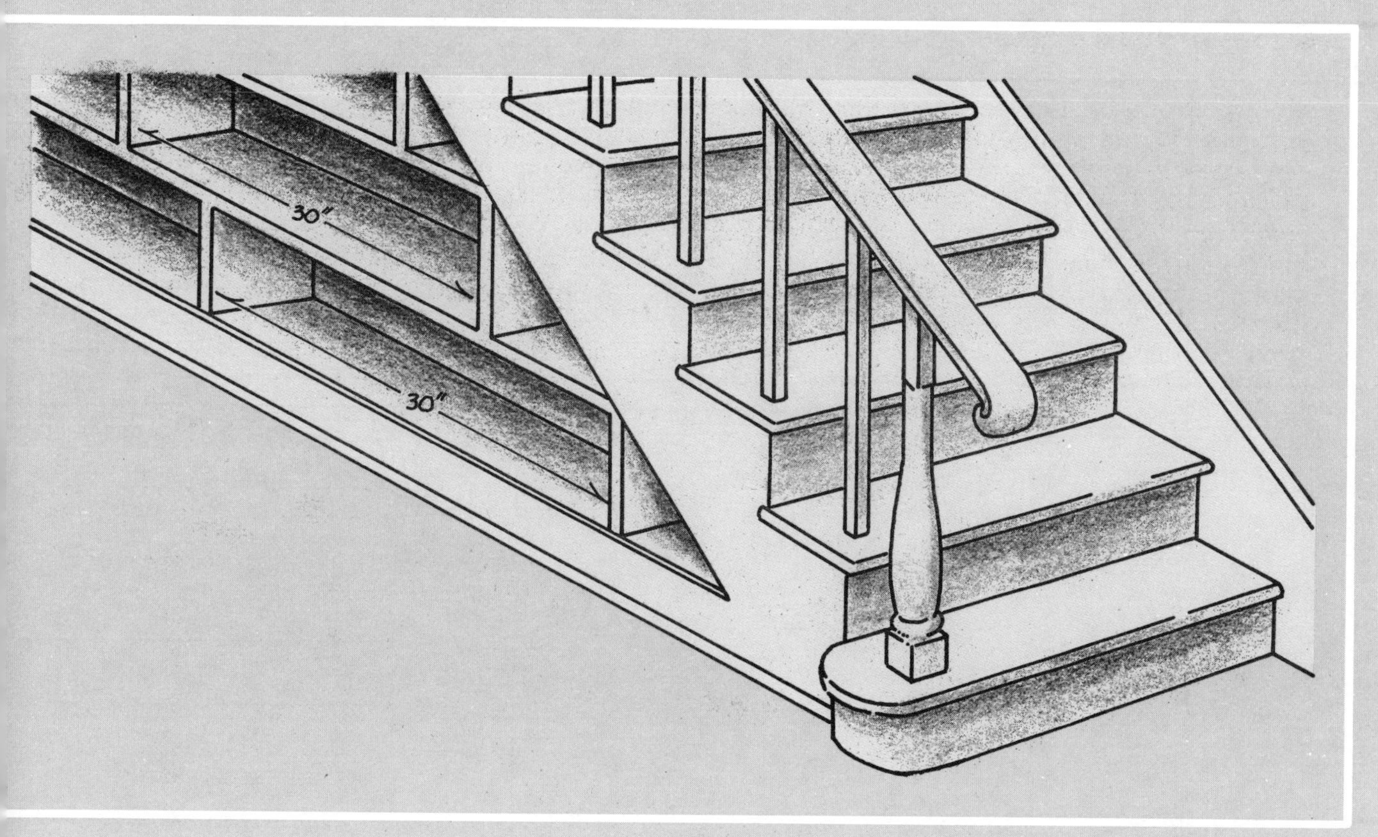

A-Frames

The area under a flight of stairs often presents a volume of A-shaped space that is more or less wasted. It may already be taken up with a shallow, almost inaccessible closet, but that is its major problem—it is too shallow, and too hard to use. The thing to remember about stairways (and under the eaves in an attic) is that you are dealing with a triangle that inherently has a large, but inaccessible, corner. The solution, therefore, is to transform that elusive triangular corner into space that can be better utilized. Here are a few of the ways that can be done:

A-frame bookshelves (Fig. A). Stairs are normally between 8″ and 9″ high, which is too low for most books unless they are paperbacks, so a bookshelf arrangement will not be able to "extend" the stairs. Essentially, each shelf is beveled at the stair end and nailed to the bottom of the stair stringer, then braced by a vertical support. The shelves can be as long as desired, but should be supported every 30″ to 36″. The triangular corners immediately under the stairway can be used to hold small knickknacks or short books. The shelves themselves can be either flush with the outside of the stairway, or recessed against the wall.

Bookcase and roll-out shelves (Fig. B). If the shelves built under a stairway are flush with the outside of the stairs, they will normally be 7½″ deep. If the stairs are 30″ wide, there is still an unused space 22½″ wide behind the bookcase. This could become a closet, or another set of shelves, or it could hold roll-out shelves such as shown in Fig. D.

Shelves and cubbyhole desk (Fig. C). If the stairway is 36″ or wider, a set of 7½″-wide shelves can be extended under it, and the space behind them might be taken up with a 28″-wide writing desk. The desk can have shelves above it as well as

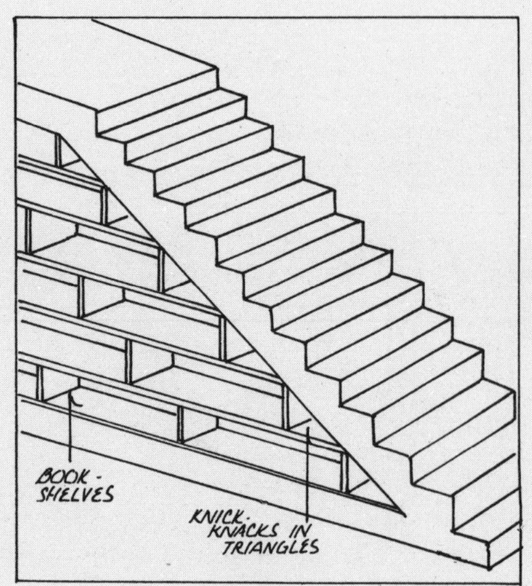

Fig. A

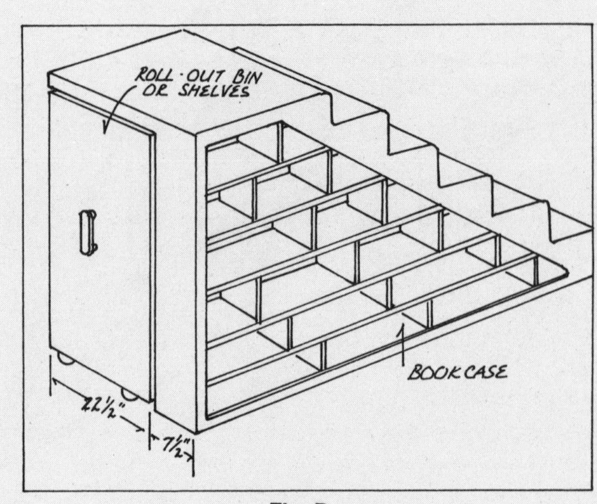

Fig. B

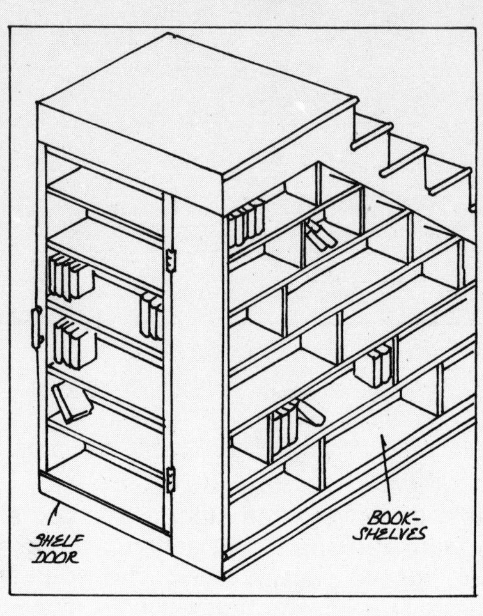

28"
DESK
BOOKSHELVES
SHELF
DOOR
7½"

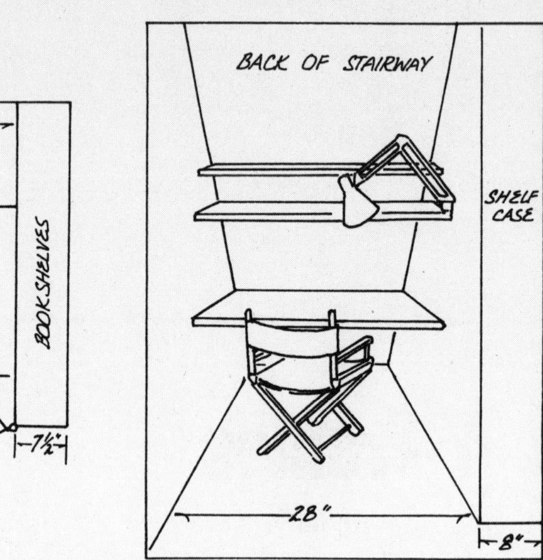

Fig. C

ROLL-OUT
SHELVES
28"
½" PLYWOOD
7'
¾"
PLYWOOD
6'
18"
CASTERS
2x2 OR 2x3
POST

Fig. D

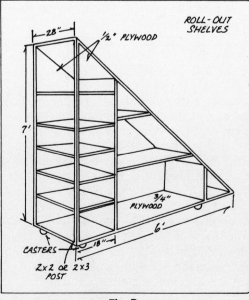

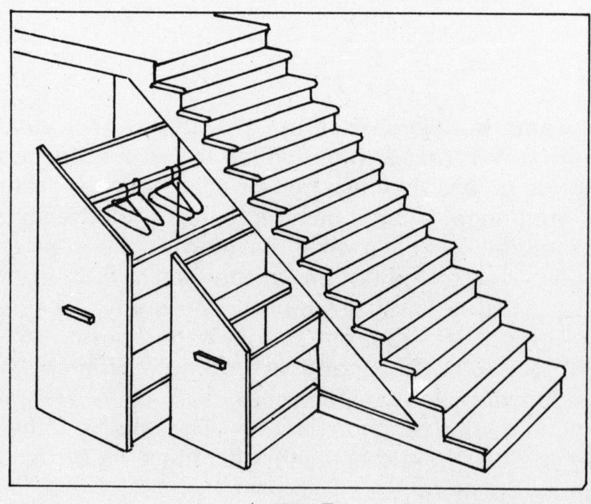

Fig. E

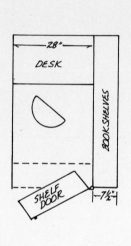

drawers, and will have to be provided with a light. An ingenious way of closing off the "office" is to give it a door which is also a bookcase. If this arrangement is to be used, consider *not* putting a back on the shelves so that whoever sits in the cubbyhole doesn't get claustrophobia.

A-frame roll-out shelves (Fig. D). Often, the wall below a stairway has been extended to the floor to form a closet, which winds up having a huge, unusable triangle at the back. The roll-out shelves fit exactly into the closet, but can be pulled out to reach any of the objects stored at the back. The dimensions given in Fig. D are hypothetical, since the shelves should be designed to fit precisely in the space that exists. Construction could be with metal shelf standards as well as wood. When using wood, the shelves and bottom plate are ¾″ plywood, while the hypoteneuse and back of the unit are ½″ plywood. A 2″x3″ can be used at the open front corner of the shelves.

A-frame roll-out bins (Fig. E). These can be in any number and any size. They are as long as the stairs are wide, and can have any number of designs. As simple boxes, they will store all kinds of things. Or, if they are high enough, a clothes pole can be installed at the top (Fig. E) to hold off-season garments. The bins can also be designed to hold specific objects, such as sports equipment or foul-weather gear (Fig. F). However designed, they should rest on a ¾″ plywood base and have four casters for easy maneuverability. The faceplate should be decorated to be compatible with the surrounding room decor and can be extended to within ¼″ of the floor to hide the casters.

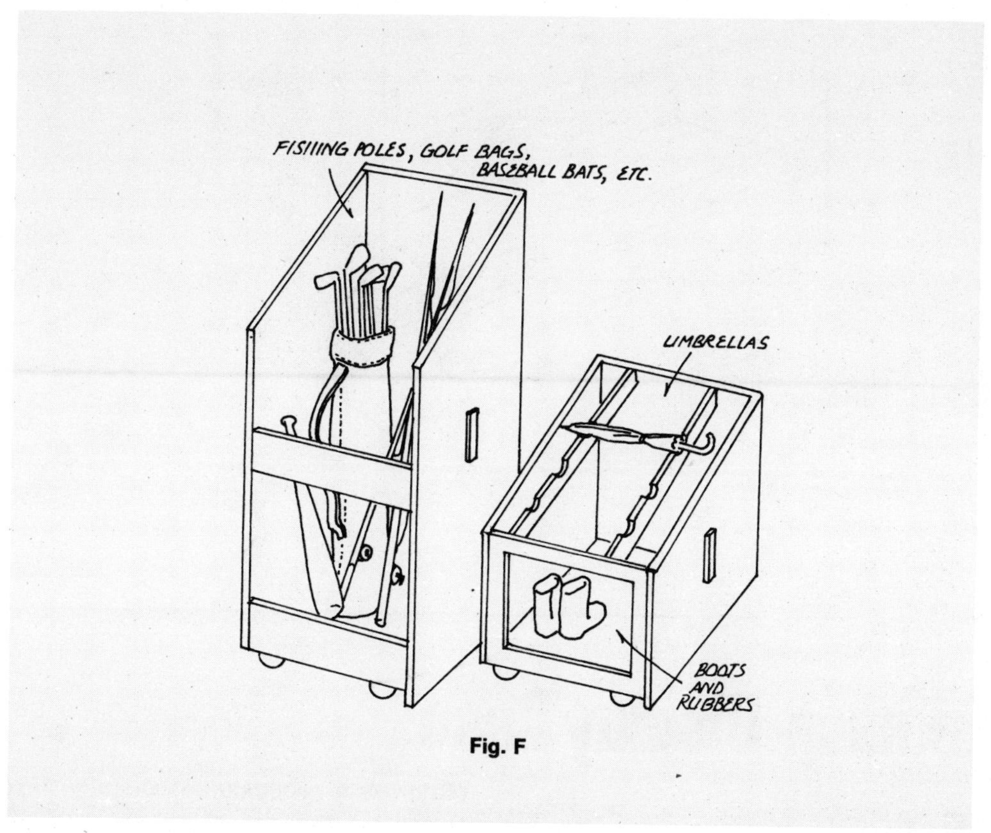

Fig. F

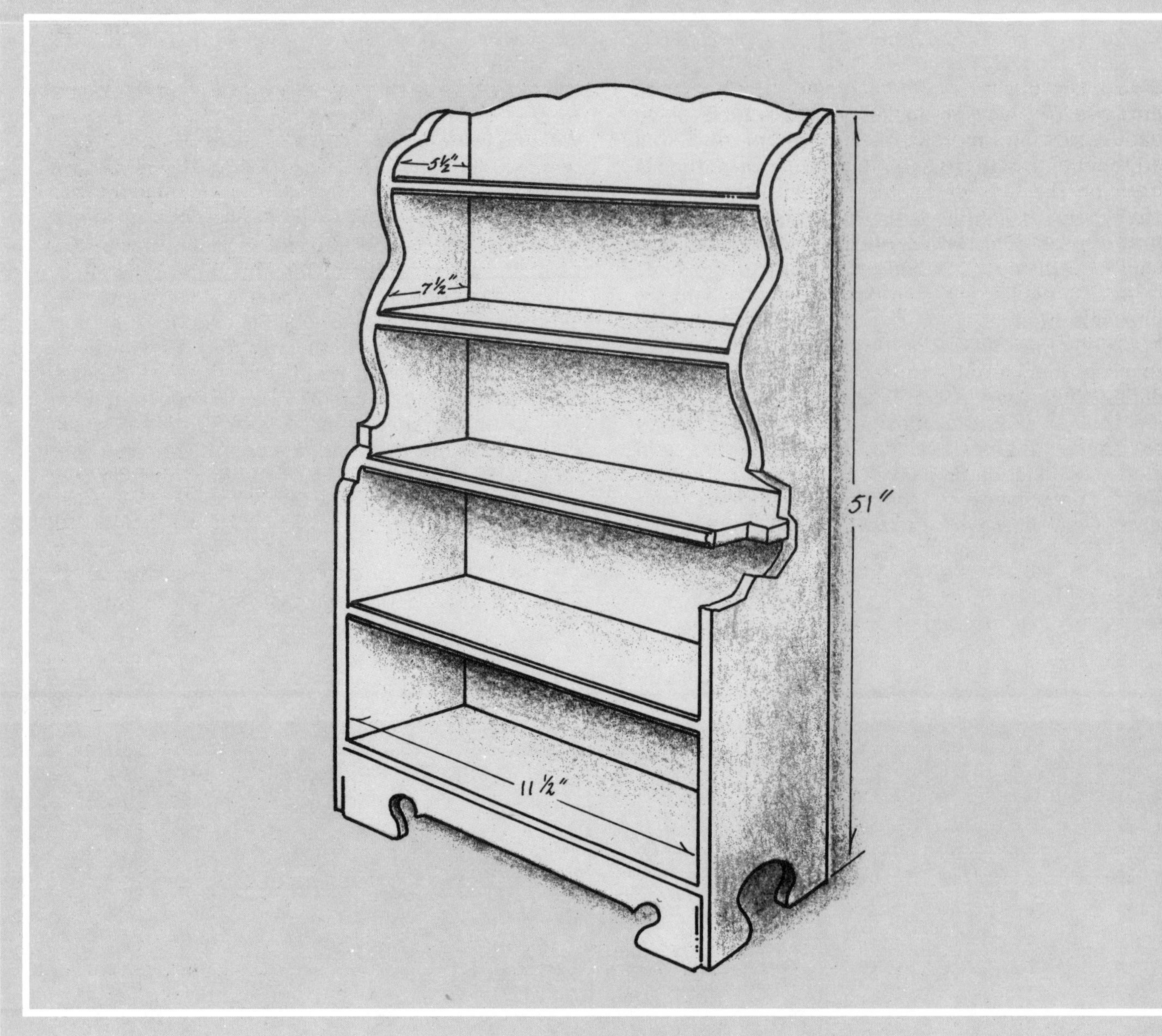

Knickknack Display Case

A decorative shelf case can be made from any wood, but if plywood is the choice, there will eventually be a lot of edges that have to be filled or hidden. The project can be veneered, or a good cabinet wood might be selected and then carefully finished. The dimensions shown here can all be changed, and any curve design can be used.

Materials for Knickknack Display Case

Quantity	Description
2	¾"x11½"x51" stock for sides (pine, plywood or any cabinet wood)
8'	¾"x11½" stock for three bottom shelves
32"	¾"x7½" stock for 4th shelf
32"	¾"x5½" stock for 5th shelf
1	¼"x32"x51" piece for back (or several narrower pieces)
1	½"x4½"x32" stock for kick plate

Sides. The sides are 51″ high and 11½″ wide at the base. The shelves are blind dadoed with each dado stopping approximately 2″ from the front edge. The top of the bottom shelf is placed 4½″ from the bottom of the feet and each shelf is 10½″ high, with 2½″ left above the fifth shelf to form its back. The curves above the first three shelves and between the feet are cut with a band or sabre saw in any configuration, so long as they are consistent.

Shelves. The three bottom shelves are 11½″ wide by 31¼″ long, with a ¼″x2″ notch cut from both ends of the front edges to form a blind dado. The fourth shelf is 7½″ wide, the top shelf 5½″ wide. Both are notched for blind dadoes. The front edges of the shelves may be left square, or all but the first shelf can be rounded off by sanding, or they can be given a designed curve using a molder or router. The first shelf, however, must remain square so that the kick plate can be attached to it.

Front plate. The feet are cut from ¼″x4½″x32″ stock, using either a band or sabre saw. The curve should be compatible with the other curves in the project.

Back. The back is ¼″ stock measuring 32″x51″ with curves cut into the top edge. If you cannot find an appropriate piece of stock in the correct size, narrower boards can be rabbeted together to form the required dimensions, or a plywood sheet can be covered with a veneer compatible with the cabinet wood used for the rest of the project.

Assembly. If the project is to be veneered, it should be done after assembly. If the project is being made of a good cabinet wood and will not be veneered, tight dadoes plus a strong cream glue will hold firmly without screws. The shelves are glued into place first. The back should be glue-screwed to the frame and shelves. The front plate can be attached to the bottom shelf and glue-screwed from the inside using glue blocks placed under the front edge of the bottom shelf and down the corners made by the front legs.

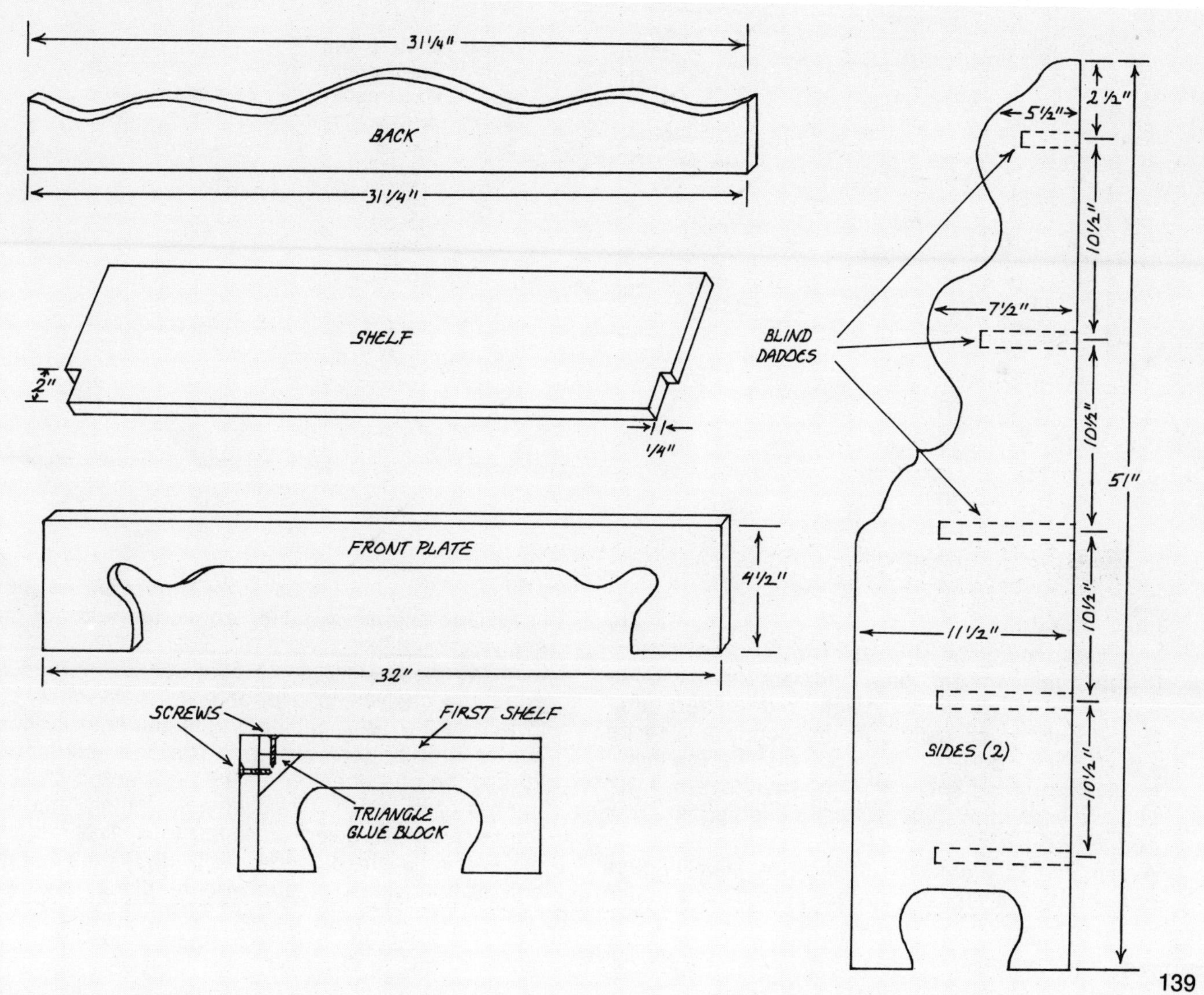

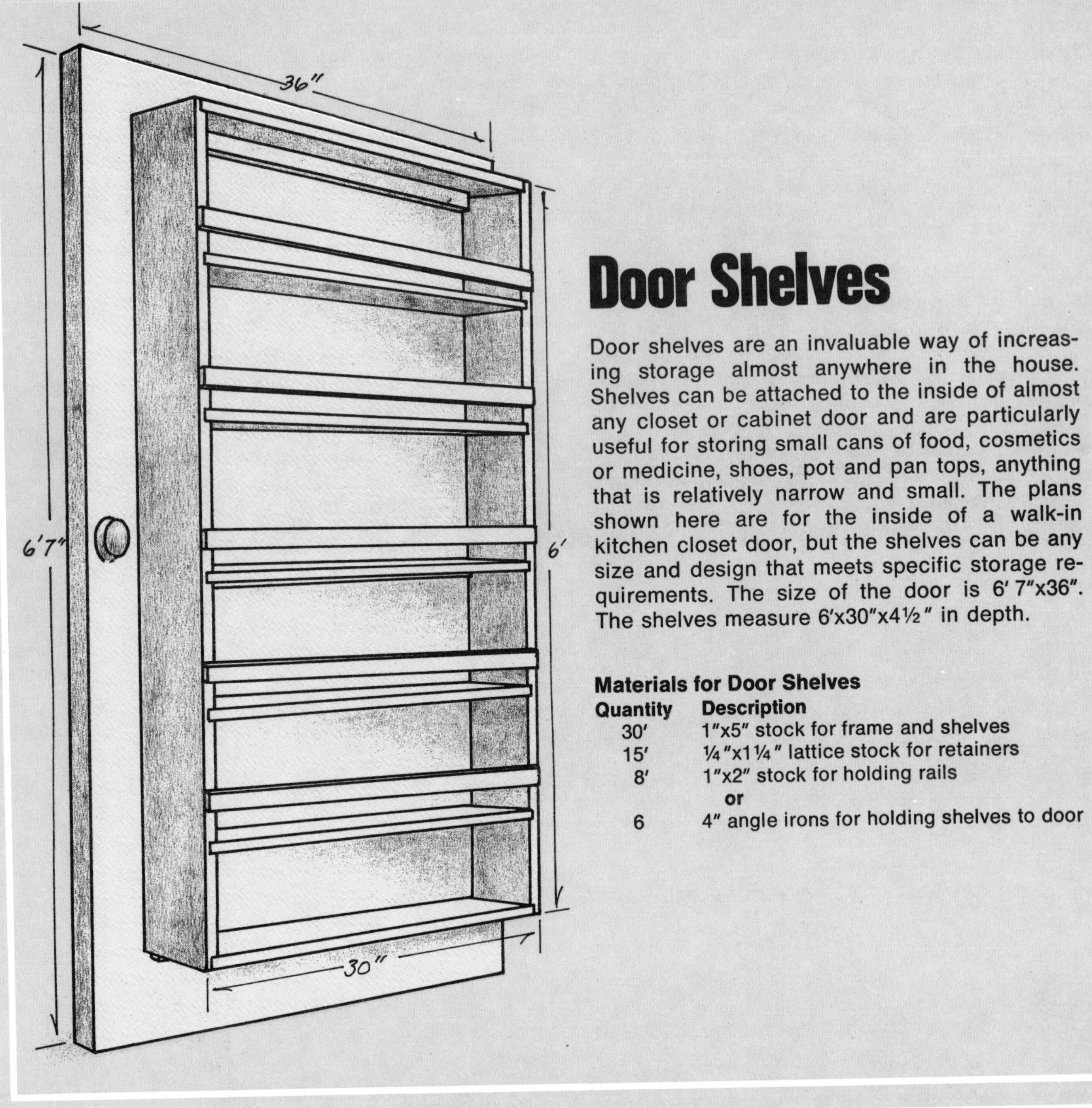

Door Shelves

Door shelves are an invaluable way of increasing storage almost anywhere in the house. Shelves can be attached to the inside of almost any closet or cabinet door and are particularly useful for storing small cans of food, cosmetics or medicine, shoes, pot and pan tops, anything that is relatively narrow and small. The plans shown here are for the inside of a walk-in kitchen closet door, but the shelves can be any size and design that meets specific storage requirements. The size of the door is 6' 7"x36". The shelves measure 6'x30"x4½" in depth.

Materials for Door Shelves

Quantity	Description
30'	1"x5" stock for frame and shelves
15'	¼"x1¼" lattice stock for retainers
8'	1"x2" stock for holding rails
	or
6	4" angle irons for holding shelves to door

Cutting. The 6' sides are cut from 1"x5" stock. They are rabbeted at both ends, and dadoed every 11½" to accept the shelves. The top and bottom of the frame are 30" long, and rabbeted at each end. Shelves can be any height and desired number. If only small cans and dry goods are to be stored on the door, for example, the shelves might easily be placed every 6". The shelves are 1"x5" x29¼", while the ¼"x1¼" lattice strips are cut 30" long.

Assembly. Assemble the shelves in their dadoes and attach the top and bottom pieces. The lattice retainers are glue-nailed across the front of each shelf, approximately 1-1½" above the edge of the shelves.

Installation. The simplest, most secure method of attaching shelves to a door is to glue-screw 1"x 2" rails to the door, positioning them under the top, center and bottom shelves. The top rail is cut 28½" long and attached to the door about 4" from the top of the door. The shelves are then hung on the rails and screwed or nailed to it. The remaining two rails are placed snugly under the center and bottom shelves, screwed in place, and the rack nailed to them. The alternative to this method is to use a pair of metal angles under each of the same three shelves.

However, if the shelves are to be attached to a hollow core door, the rails or angle irons must be so situated that they have solid wood to attach to. There is usually a 6″ wide center brace across the center of a hollow core door, in the area where the handle is placed. The top and bottom frames are also about 6″ wide. Before building shelves for a hollow core door, tap a small nail into the top and bottom of the door to determine how long the shelf frame must be to reach from the top to bottom braces.

Variations. If the shelves are to hold the tops to pots and pans, the shelves will vary in height from 6″ to 15″ (Fig. B), and the lattice retainers must be placed slightly above the center line of the tops. The shelves, themselves, usually need be no wider than 2½″. If the shelves are to store cosmetics and medicines (Fig. C), the lattice retainers should be flush with the shelf tops so that small articles cannot roll under them and off the shelves. If the shelves are to hold shoes, the retainers can become ¾″ dowels placed at the height of the instep of the shoes (Fig. D).

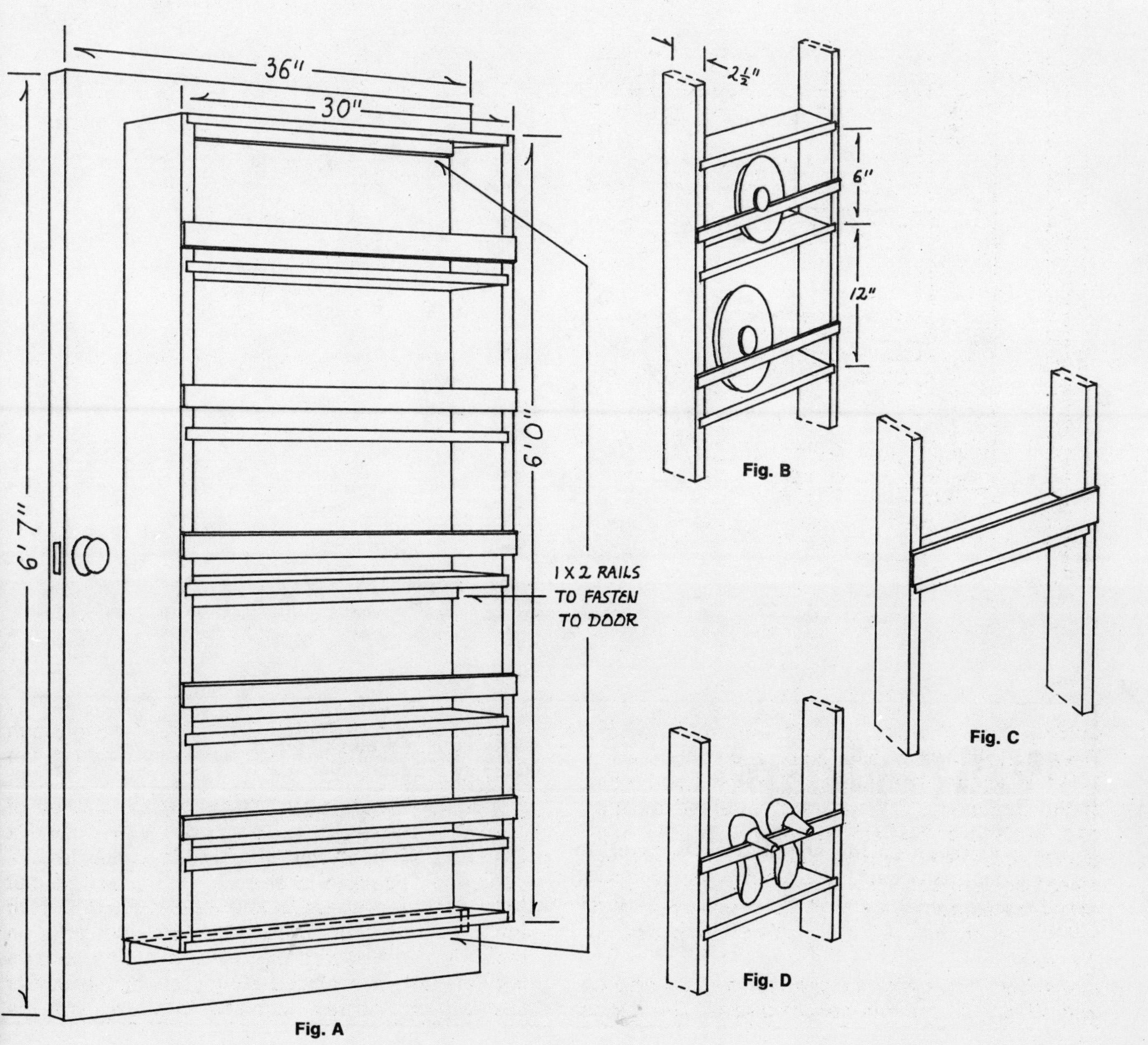

Fig. A

Fig. B

Fig. C

Fig. D

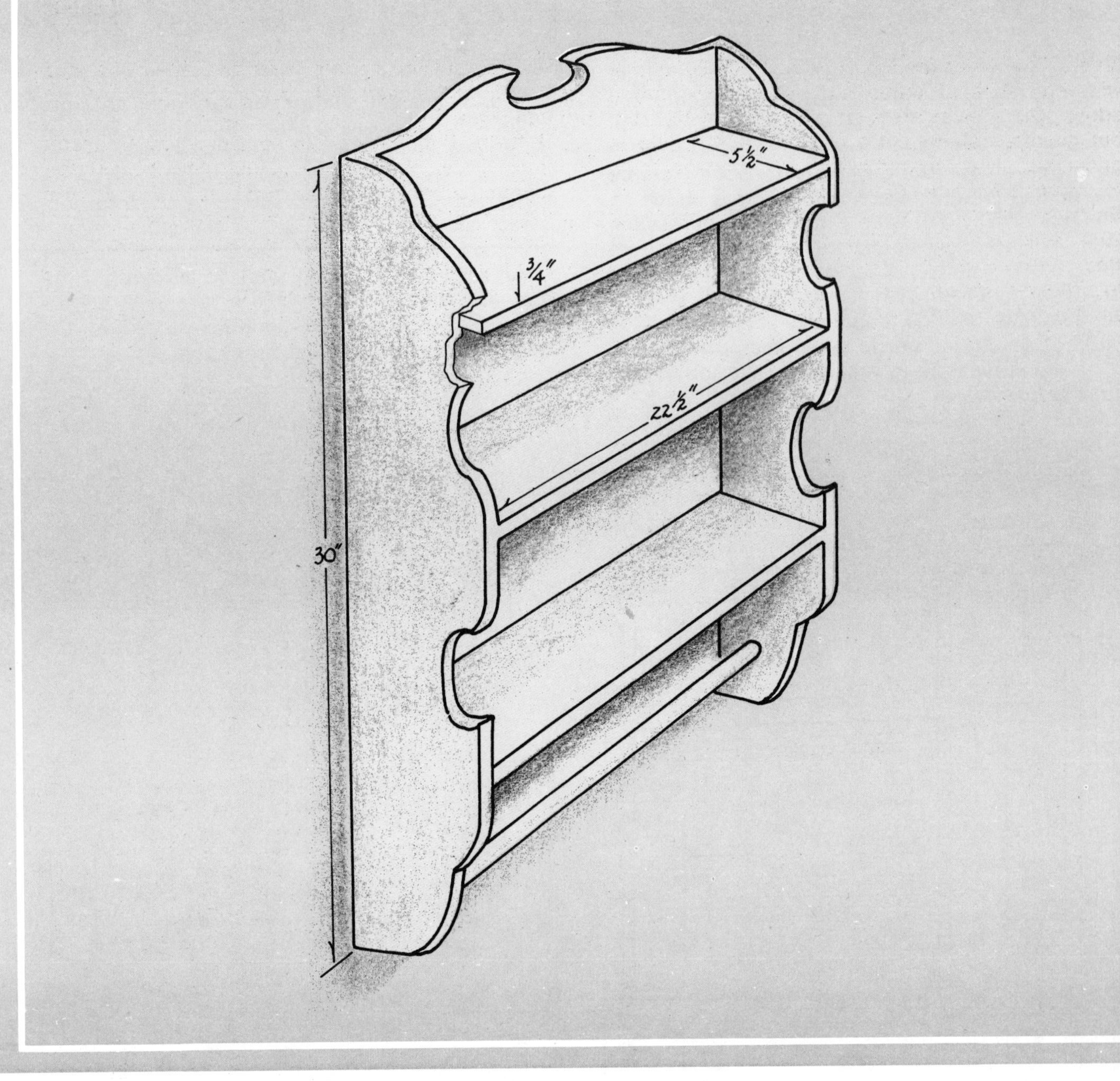

Wall Cupboard

As a variation on the standing shelf case, the wall cupboard can be any style and any size. The drawing here shows one design. The drawings in Fig. A are for a second version 24"x 30", and from there on, there are countless other variations.

Materials for Wall Cupboard

Quantity	Description
Case	
2	1"x6"x30" stock for sides
3	1"x6"x23¼" stock for shelves
1	½" or ¼"x30"x24" plywood or rabbeted stock for back
Drawers	
2'	½"x3" stock for drawer sides, front and back
1	¼"x6"x6" stock for drawer bottom

Sides. The sides in Fig. A are 1"x6"x30" stock with any style of curve cut out of the leading edges. The shelves are spaced in any way desired, but all three shelves are dadoed. A ¾" hole is drilled deeply enough into the bottom of each side to accept a ¾" dowel towel rack.

Shelves. The three shelves are 1"x6" stock, cut 29¼" long.

Back. This can be ½" or ¾" thick stock, rabbeted together as shown in the picture, or it can be a solid piece of ¼" or ½" plywood which begins at the back of the bottom shelf and extends above the top of the sides, with scrollwork cut out of the top edge.

Drawers. If drawers are to be used, they are made from ½" stock, and are loose-fitting boxes partitioned under the bottom shelf, as in Fig. B. See Chapter 6 for drawer assembly suggestions.

Assembly. Glue-screw the shelves and dowel them into their dadoes. Glue-screw the back to the back edges of the sides and shelves.

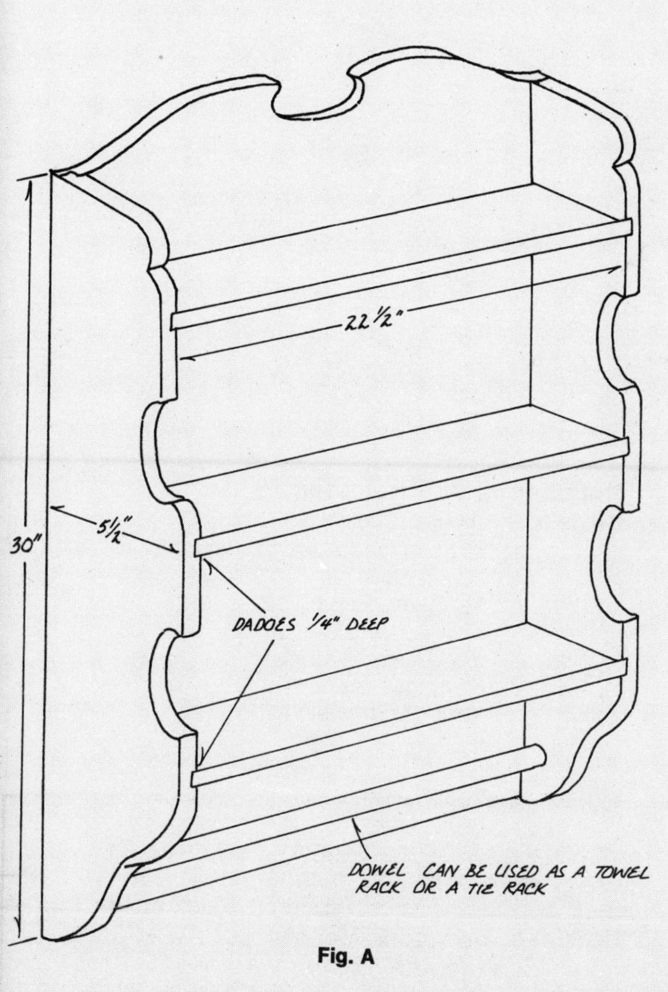

Fig. A

Fig. B

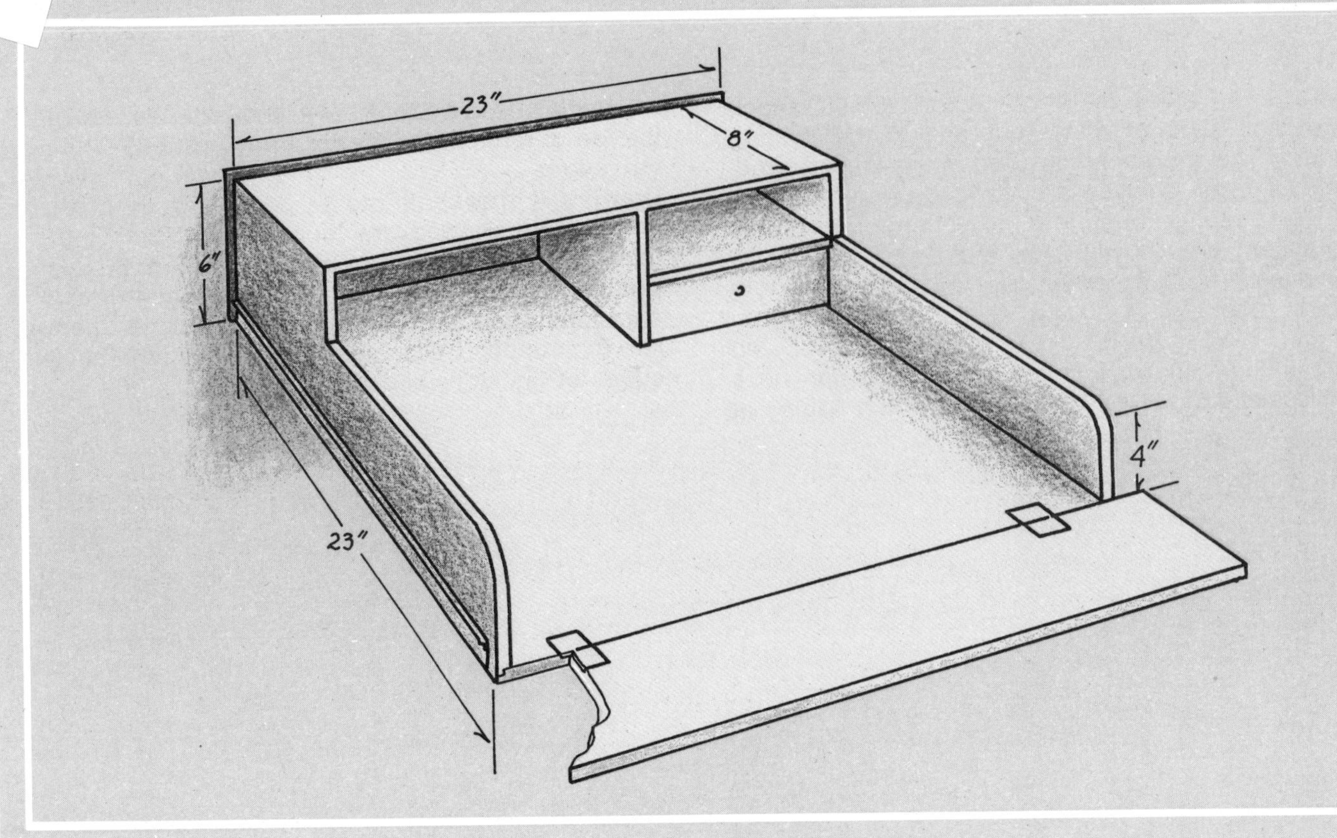

Pop-Out Writing Shelf

The plans here are for a desk that might pull out of a kitchen counter. It could be hidden in a buffet, be designed as a child's study area, or be part of a bedroom closet/bureau arrangement—anywhere in the house where it is needed. What a desk requires is a space from 28″ to 30″ above the floor, in a cabinet, counter or wall that is roughly 24″ deep. The accompanying drawings provide for a writing surface of 22″ square.

Materials for Pop-Out Writing Shelf

Quantity	Description
½	¾″ plywood panel for desk top, sides and door
¼	½″ plywood panel for partition, dust-cover and drawer
1 set	24″ drawer guides
3	3″ hinges for door
1	knob for drawer

Sides. These are 23″ long with an 8″ section, 6″ high at the back, rabbeted to fit the cabinet top as shown in Fig. A. The front 15″ section is 4″ high with the top front corner curved on a 3″ diameter. A ¾″x⅜″ plough runs the length of both sides, ¾″ above their bottom edges to accept the desk top. The right side also has a ½″x¼″ plough for the drawer dustcover, as shown in Fig. B. The back is ¾″x21½″x6″. The top edge is rabbeted ⅜″, and is dadoed for the desk partition (Fig. B).

Top. The top of the cabinet is 8″x23″, with its back and side edges rabbeted to meet the top of the sides. Its underside has a ¼″x½″ dado for the partition (see Fig. B).

Cabinet partition. This is 6⅞″x8″, with a ¼″x ½″ plough positioned 3¼″ up from its bottom edge (Fig. B) for the drawer dustcover.

Drawer. The drawer, made from ½″ stock, is 8″ long by 8″ wide with 3″ sides (see Chapter 6 for assembly suggestions). It fits into the lower right corner of the desk cabinet. A dustcover, ½″x8″

x8½", is inserted over it, between the cabinet partition and right side of the desk.

Desk top. This can be made from plywood, preferably with a hardwood face, such as birch or maple. It is 22¼" wide by 23" long. The underside of its front edge has a ⅜"x⅜" rabbet. A plough, ½"x8", runs from the back edge, and is 8⅜" from the right side (see Fig. B).

Desk door. The door is 6" wide by 24" long with a ⅜"x⅜" rabbet along its inside bottom edge (Fig. B), to match the rabbet under the front edge of the desk top. The face of the door is given a design compatible with the other doors in the counter.

Assembly. The desk top is dadoed into the sides and glue-screwed in place. The back fits between the sides and on top of the desk top. The cabinet center position is glued into its plough in the desk top, then the drawer dustcover is inserted into its dadoes on the partition and right side of the desk. The cabinet top is glue-screwed into the rabbeted sides and back of the desk. Drawer guides are attached along the bottom edge of the sides. The door is attached to the front edge of the desk with three 3" hinges, mortised so they are flush with the desk top and the back side of the door. The door extends ½" beyond the sides of the desk to hide the drawer tracks. The drawer is assembled and inserted into the lower right corner of the cabinet.

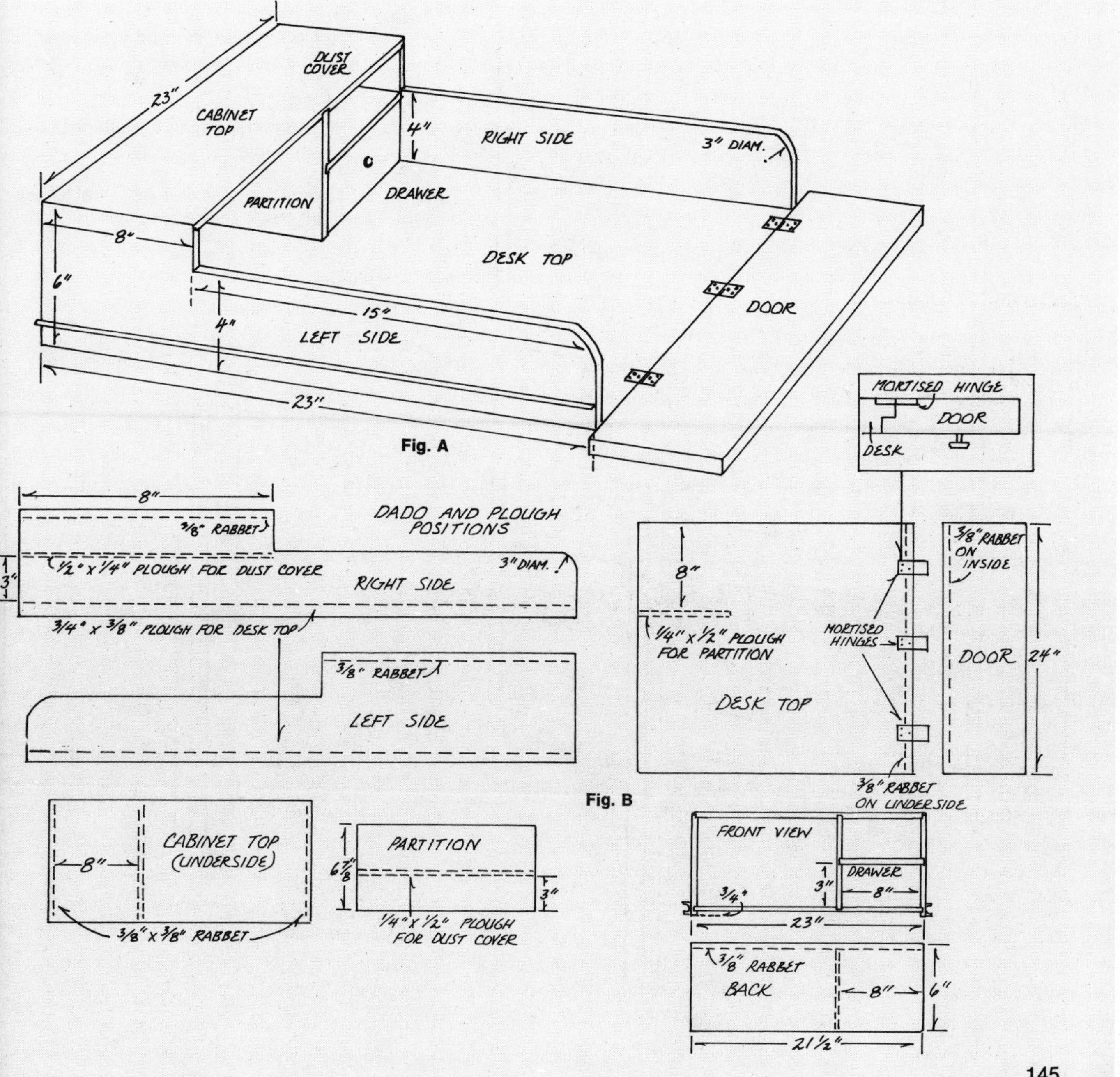

Fig. A

Fig. B

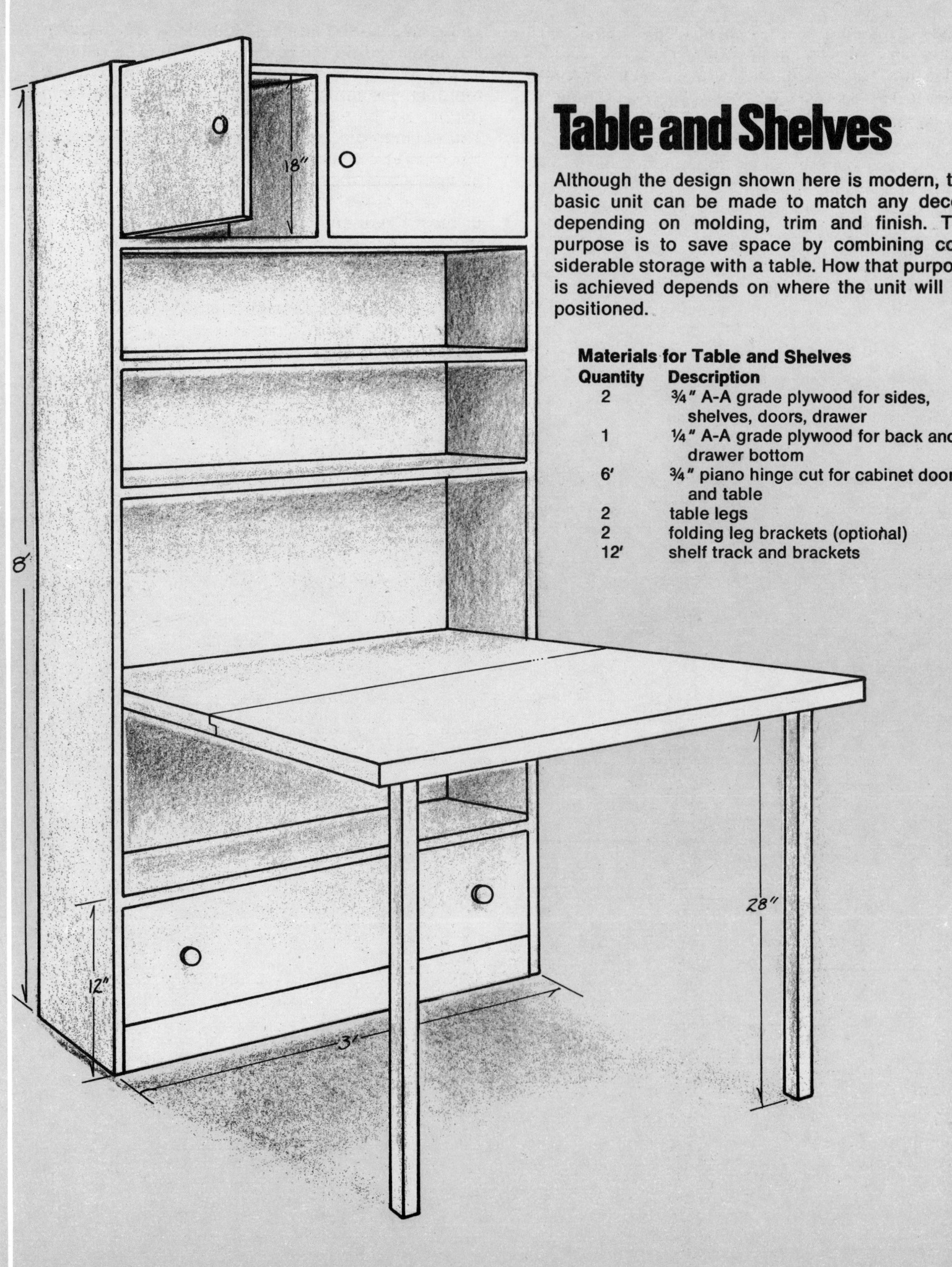

Table and Shelves

Although the design shown here is modern, th basic unit can be made to match any deco depending on molding, trim and finish. Th purpose is to save space by combining co siderable storage with a table. How that purpos is achieved depends on where the unit will b positioned.

Materials for Table and Shelves

Quantity	**Description**
2	¾" A-A grade plywood for sides, shelves, doors, drawer
1	¼" A-A grade plywood for back and drawer bottom
6'	¾" piano hinge cut for cabinet doors and table
2	table legs
2	folding leg brackets (optional)
12'	shelf track and brackets

Sides. Assuming an enamel or lacquer finish, the entire unit can be made from ¾″ plywood. The sides are 12″x8′, with rabbets at both ends and dadoes 18″ from the top and 12″ from the bottom.

Horizontals. The top and bottoms are 12″x36″ and rabbeted at both ends. The horizontals that fit into the dadoes are 12″x35¼″. Since shelf tracks are to be used, the shelves are cut 12″x24″x9½″. There can be as many of them as desired.

Drawer and doors. (See Chapter 6.) The drawer which fits into the base of the cabinet can be assembled any way the builder wishes and can be partitioned to store linen, silverware and the like. The cabinet doors, as shown, are ¾″x18″x18″ plywood squares attached with piano hinges. But the could be panel-and-frame construction, decorated in any manner.

Back. A back is necessary primarily because of the unit's size. It should be made of ¼″ plywood or Masonite.

Table. There are at least two choices of type. If there is no particular space problem, the table might be solid-assembly, 34½″ wide by any length, and positioned from 28″ to 30″ from the floor (Fig. B). The table itself might be ¾″ plywood with a 2″ lip framed around it, and solid metal or wooden legs. The table could also be hinged to the back of the cabinet and to the center, with folding legs that tuck under the leaf (Fig. C).

Assembly. Glue-nail the rabbeted top and bottom to the sides and the two dadoed horizontals between the sides. Glue-nail the back to the frame. Measure, cut and assemble the drawer to fit in the drawer recess. Assemble and hang the doors. Attach the shelf tracks between the tabletop and the bottom of the cabinet. Add the table and hide all visible plywood edges.

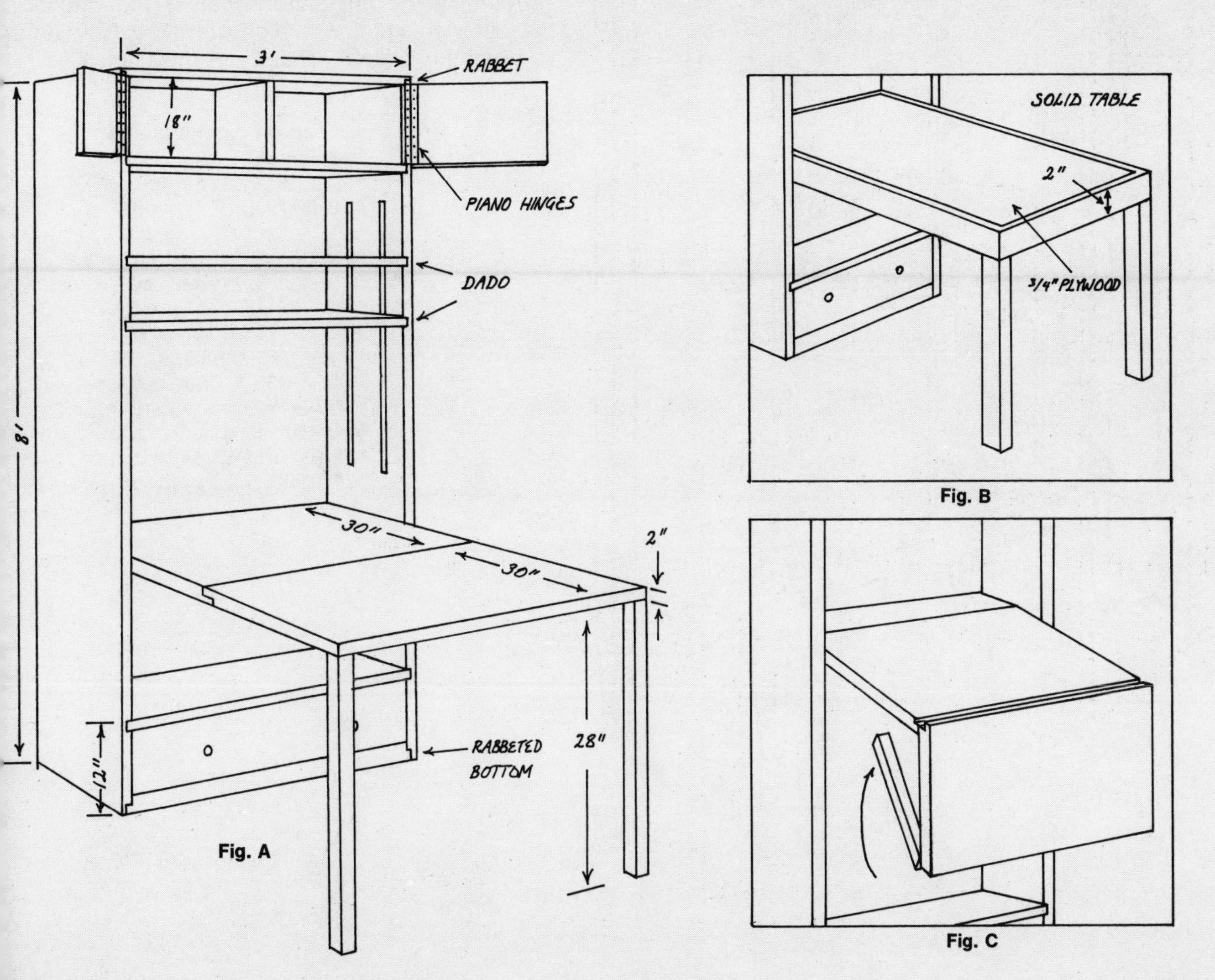

Fig. A

Fig. B

Fig. C

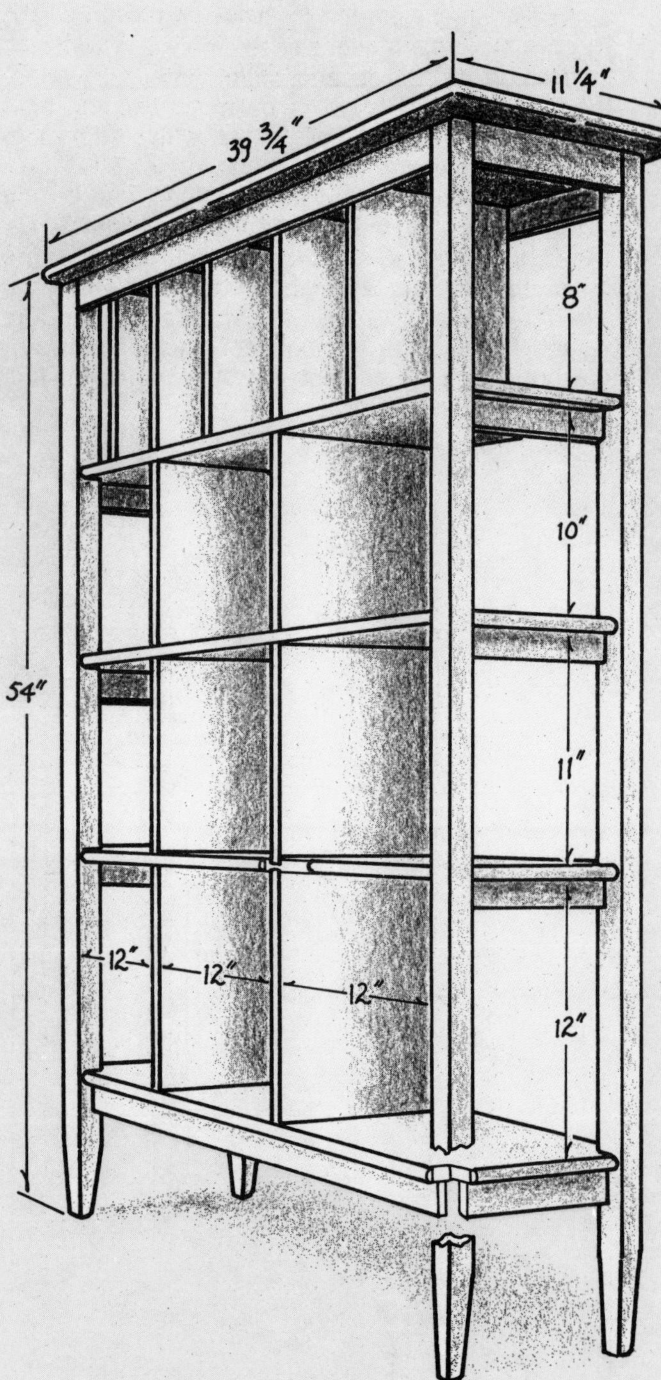

Elegant Bookshelves

The secret to the elegant appearance of this bookcase lies in the apparent delicacy of its structure. And yet, it is as stable and strong as any design to be found. Whether the selection of material is pine or a high-grade cabinet wood, it demands a rich, grain-enhancing finish.

Materials for Elegant Bookshelves

Quantity	Description
4	1⅛"x1⅛"x53¼" legs
2	¾"x1½"x36½" top rails
8	¾"x1½"x8" shelf rails
2	¾"x2¼"x36½" bottom rails
2	¾"x2¼"x8" bottom rails
1	¾"x11¼"x39¾" case top
4	¾"x9¼"x37¾" shelves
8	¼"x¾"x8" end caps
8	⅜"x¾"x36½" face caps
5	¼"x9¼"x9¾" top partitions
2	¼"x9¼"x10½" partitions
2	¼"x9¼"x11½" partitions
2	¼"x9¼"x12½" partitions

erticals. The legs are rectangular posts, 53¼" ng x 1⅛" x 1⅛", slightly rounded along their utside edges. The feet are tapered gradually to "x¾" along the last 5" to accommodate brass eeves and casters.

The five shelf-spacers between the top shelf nd the top of the case are 9¼"x9¾". The two pacers between the third and fourth shelves are ¼" wide by 10½" high. The two spacers between ne third and second shelves are 9¼" wide by 1½" high. The two spacers between the bottom nd second shelves are 9¼" wide by 12½" high. ll of the spacers are cut from ¼"-thick stock.

orizontals. The top of the case is ¾"x11¼"x 9¾"; each of the four shelves is ¾"x9½"x 37¾". The ¼"x¼" dadoes, made in the top and bottom of the middle two shelves, are set 12" in from the ends (see Fig. B). The bottom and top shelf are dadoed in the same positions with the top shelf having a ¼"x¼" dado every 6". The underside of the top of the case is routed in the same positions as the top of the top shelf (see Fig. B). All of the shelves have a ⅝"x⅝" notch cut in each corner to accommodate the verticals.

The top of the case has two rails, ¾"x1½"x 36½", under its front and back edges, plus ¾"x 1½"x8" rails at each end. The bottom shelf is supported at front and back by two rails, ¾"x2¼"x 36½", and by two end rails, ¾"x2¼"x8". The other three shelves have ¾"x2½"x8" rails under

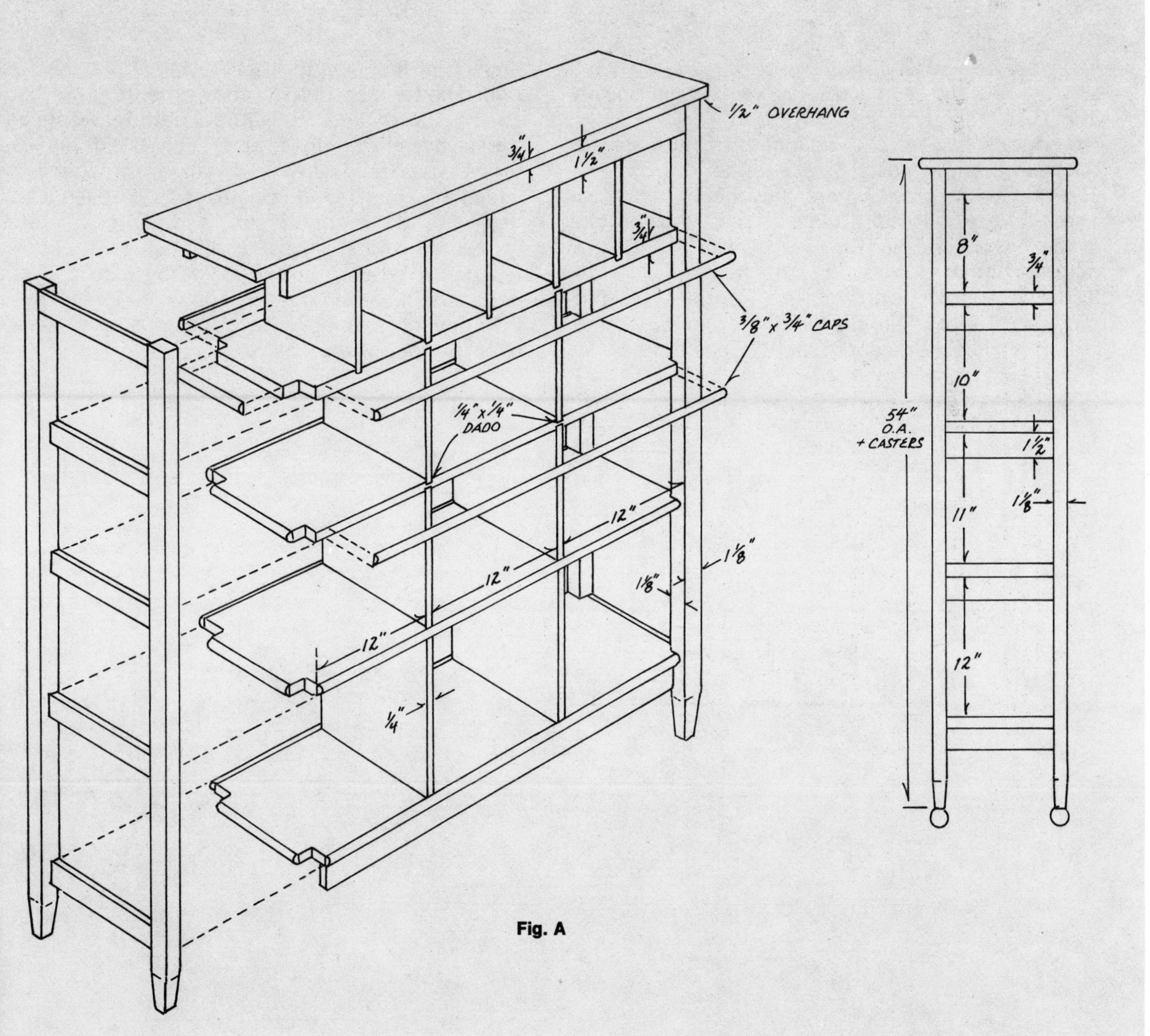

Fig. A

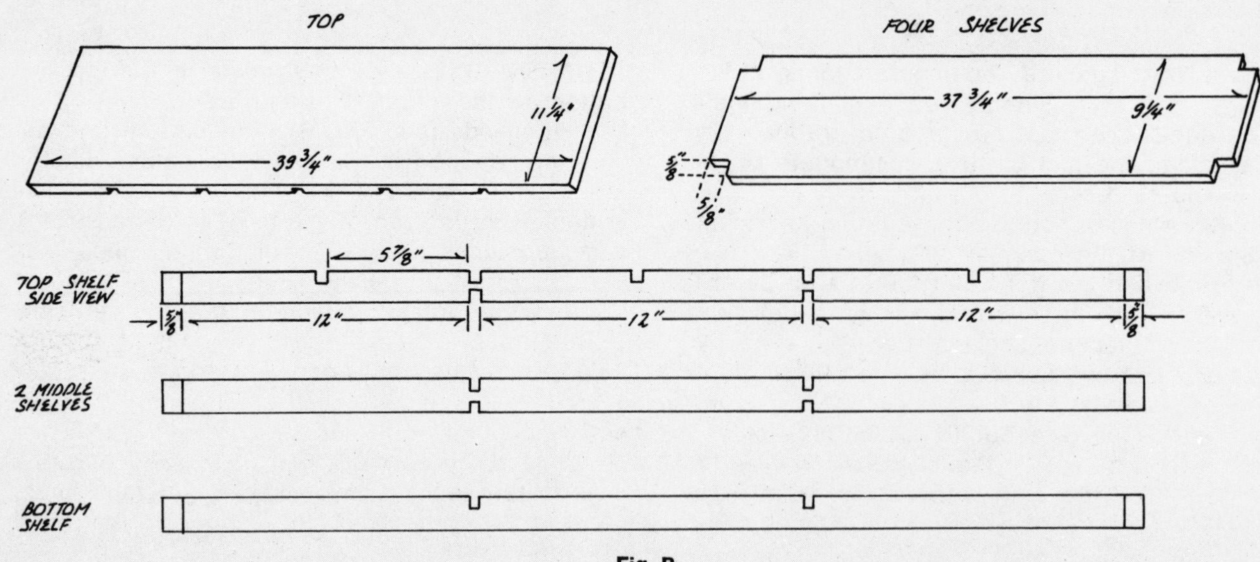

Fig. B

each end. Each shelf has two face caps, ⅜"x¾" x36½", and two end caps, ¼"x¾"x8" as shown in Fig. A.

Assembly. The four 2¼" bottom shelf rails are set between the four posts, 5" above the foot of each vertical, at the point where they begin tapering. The 1½" top rails are attached flush with the top of the posts (see Fig. E). As shown in Fig. D, the rails are either doweled, or attached with 2" #10 flathead screws, which are countersunk and plugged. The bottom shelf is fitted on top of the bottom rails. The second shelf is positioned 12" above the first, the third shelf, 11" above the second. The top shelf is 10" above the third. As each shelf is assembled, the vertical partitions between the shelves are glued and each fitted into the proper dadoes. The 8" end rails are attached between the posts under both ends of each shelf, using dowels or countersunk and plugged screws.

The top of the case is positioned so that there is a ½" overhang on all sides. The face and end caps are attached to the edges of the shelves, then the brass sleeves and casters are inserted over the feet of the posts.

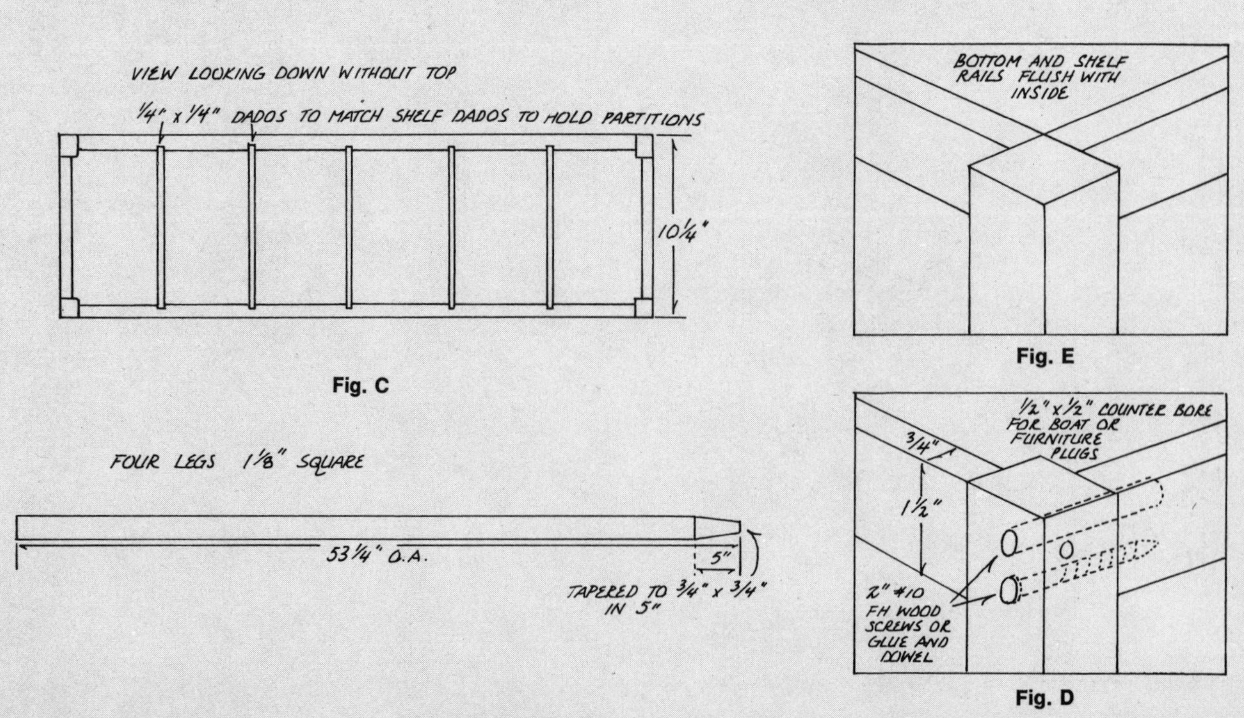

Fig. C

Fig. E

Fig. D

CHAPTER 11

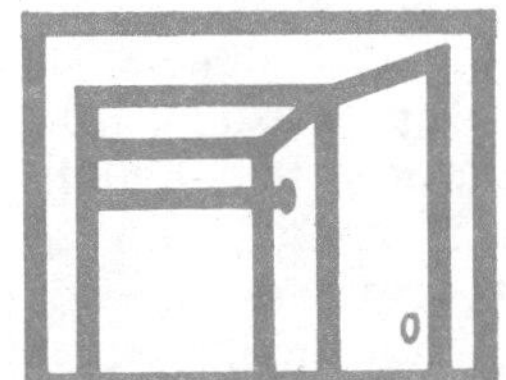

Closets

Closets

A closet is a small room. Into that room can go all types of storage features from shelves to poles to cabinets to drawers. Which combinations of these you choose depends on what is to be stored in a given closet, whether it is clothing, equipment or a hodgepodge of items there is nowhere else to put.

But closets, more than any other kind of storage, require painstaking planning if the maximum use of minimum space is to be achieved. For example, part of a woman's closet can be divided into shelves and dividers with compartments for hats, handbags, dozens of pairs of shoes, scarves and other accessories. Men's accoutrements are even easier to compartmentalize within a closet, for most men tend to own fewer "unessentials." Space can be allowed for shirts, and for hanging trousers as well as jackets. There can be drawers for underwear, socks and handkerchiefs, and shelves for work clothes, sweaters and shoes, all in a relatively small space.

There are some simple expedients that can immediately improve the usefulness of a small closet. Any closet that is at least 8' high can handle double clothes poles; there are no rules that say all clothing must hang at the same height, nor that it cannot clear the floor by only an inch. For small children, there can be high shelves and poles for out-of-season garments, and a lower pole placed so that they can reach the clothing they use day to day. With narrow closets, if the door is nearly ceiling height, a shelf can be placed above the top clothes pole, be the full depth of the closet, and still be both accessible and utilitarian.

People often ask what are the most practical locations for closets in their homes. There should be one sizable closet in every bedroom, and a clothes closet near the front and back doors. There should be some kind of clothes closet in any room that might be used by guests. And it is a good idea to have a closet for athletic equipment or work clothes near one of the outside doors.

All of these closets can be divided and subdivided with shelves, drawers and cabinets. They can be built from almost any material, although the usual combination for erecting a closet wall is 2"x3" studs and wallboard. Nevertheless, plywood, paneling and pressboard can also be used.

Within the walls of any closet, the arrangement of modular storage areas can be whatever meets your needs. There may be pipes to build around, or to be concealed in such a way that the enclosure is an added advantage rather than a hindrance. The closet itself may be an odd size that presents a headache in interior design, and a challenge to the builder's ingenuity. The door may be too low to allow the full use of the closet's height. One way of overcoming that problem, if the closet is deep enough, is to construct a shelf case that hangs from the ceiling of the closet with a block-and-tackle system (see the hoist-up catchall project in the cabinet section). The unit can then be raised or lowered, making any of the shelves readily accessible.

Then again, an enclosure may turn out to be a little too big for a closet, and yet not be big enough to serve as a room. In this case, perhaps a wall can be knocked down and the area combined with the room adjacent to it.

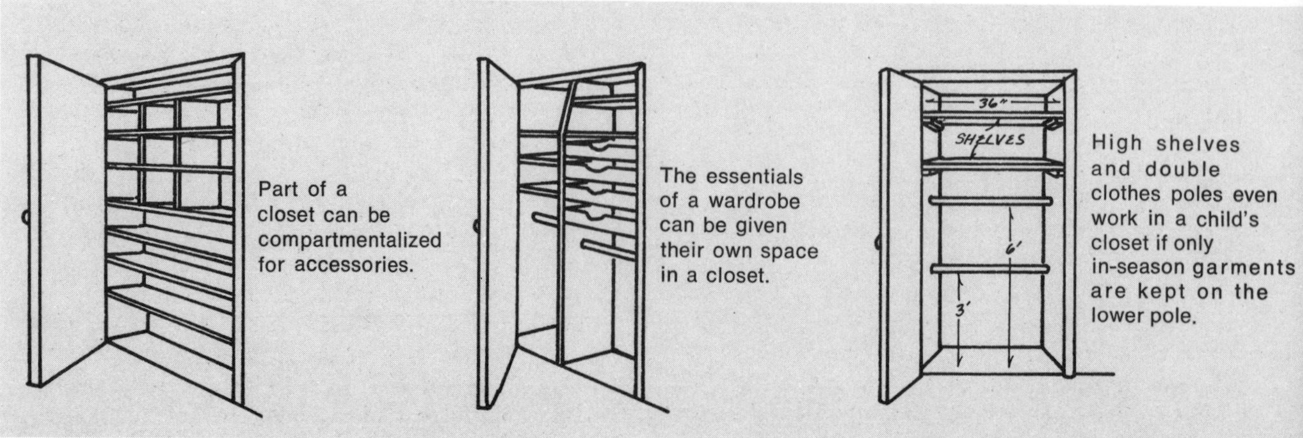

Part of a closet can be compartmentalized for accessories.

The essentials of a wardrobe can be given their own space in a closet.

High shelves and double clothes poles even work in a child's closet if only in-season garments are kept on the lower pole.

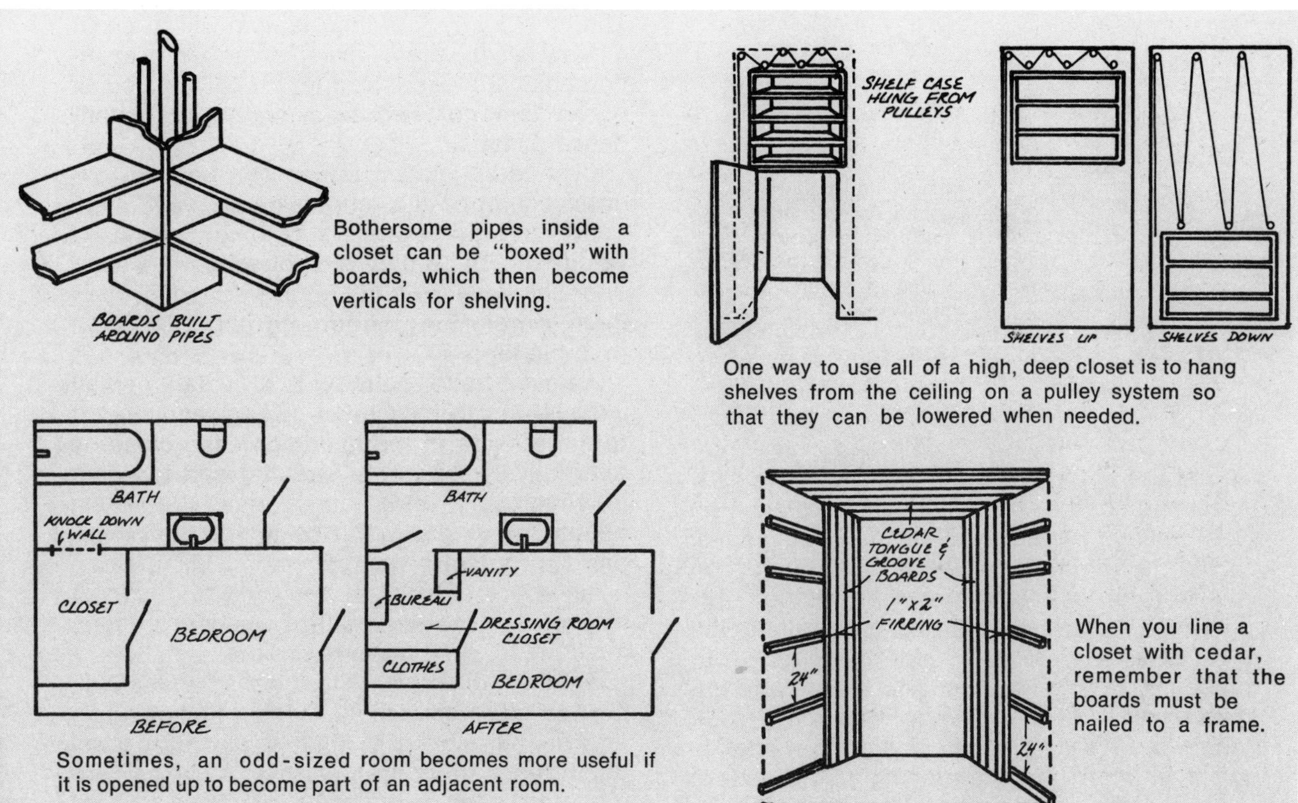

Bothersome pipes inside a closet can be "boxed" with boards, which then become verticals for shelving.

One way to use all of a high, deep closet is to hang shelves from the ceiling on a pulley system so that they can be lowered when needed.

Sometimes, an odd-sized room becomes more useful if it is opened up to become part of an adjacent room.

When you line a closet with cedar, remember that the boards must be nailed to a frame.

This space conversion could become ideal if the "closet" were between a bedroom and bath, for it might well be transformed into a closet dressing area.

The insides of clothes closets are often short-changed so far as their decor is concerned. Sometimes there is no inner wall as such, merely bare studs. These, of course, are a handyman's delight because they offer innumerable opportunities for supporting cabinets, shelves, racks and hooks. At other times, the interior of a closet is left unpainted with all of its rough construction exposed. The closet could—and should—be decorated in all sorts of ways if it is large enough for people to enter and stay more than a few minutes. There is an old-fashioned way of decorating a closet, too, and that is to sheath the inside with tongue-and-groove cedar or redwood. Cedar planks are brittle and will split easily, however, so when lining a closet with them, first nail 1"x2" firring strips the full width of each wall. The strips should be positioned along the ceiling and floor, with spacers nailed a maximum of every 24" in between. The ceiling is also framed and is the first section to be paneled. Toenail each board, driving the nails into the top edge of the tenon side at a 45° to 55° angle and then countersink them, so that the groove of the next plank will fit over the tongue. The only difference between nailing cedar planks and laying a hardwood tongue-and-groove floor is the brittleness of the cedar, so great care must be taken when nailing it.

But no matter what the inside of a closet looks like, it should still be well lighted, and perhaps ventilated. A light is almost a necessity in any closet big enough to enter, as well as in any closet that is deep enough to remain in partial darkness even with its door open. Normally, a naked 75-watt bulb screwed into a porcelain lamp base is all that is necessary. The lamp base should be properly connected to a house branch circuit or plugged into a normal outlet. Jury-rigging a light inside a closet may be quick and easy, but think what could happen to a closet full of garments if that bulb dangling from an extension cord should somehow cause a fire.

The positioning of a single bulb is also important. Its purpose for being inside the closet is to illuminate the contents of the enclosure. So don't tuck it high up on the ceil-

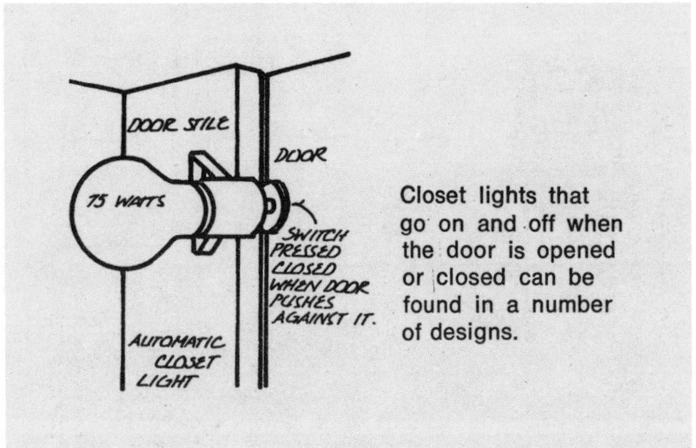

Closet lights that go on and off when the door is opened or closed can be found in a number of designs.

ing at the back of a wide shelf that shields it from most of the room. It should be placed on the ceiling, well forward of the shelf edges. If that is not possible, it can be mounted on the front of, or even under, the top shelf.

The best arrangement for controlling the light is with a switch outside the closet, but this, too, is not always possible. One alternative to an outside switch is a switch or pull chain on the lamp itself. Or, the light can be what is known as a closet light; this fixture has a large button at its back (which is against the door). The light goes off when the door is closed and goes on when it is opened. The automatic closet light works fine with hinged, as well as sliding or bi-fold doors. But unless one light is installed on each side of a sliding or bi-fold door, the door with the light must always be opened—often at considerable inconvenience for whoever is entering the closet. If there is difficulty in bringing electrical power inside a closet, there are also cordless lights available that operate on flashlight batteries.

During hot, damp weather, the contents of a clothes closet are liable to experience that persistent nuisance, mildew. Mildew can spread through an entire wardrobe in no time, given the right percentage of humidity. There are all kinds of products on the market to help protect clothing from mildew, as well as to clean it off. But a simpler method is to keep a 75-watt incandescent bulb burning in the closet during humid weather. In a small closet of less than 6 square feet, one constantly burning bulb is enough. Thereafter, add a 40-watt bulb for every extra 3 square feet. However, when more than two bulbs are used, install half of them near the floor and the other half on the ceiling. The lower bulbs are placed about 1′ above the floor, and should be encased in heavy wire mesh so that neither clothes nor feet can touch them. The constantly burning lamps will prevent mildew all by themselves; a further precaution against closet mustiness is to link a small ozone lamp or two to each of the incandescent bulbs.

Closets situated in attics can become excessively hot, and ought to be ventilated. Louvered doors are an automatic form of ventilation, but if they are not suitable, a solid door can have rows of 1″ holes drilled through them 1′ from the bottom and about 6″ down from the top.

An even better solution is to install a small exhaust fan in the closet ceiling, and duct it to the outside of the building. If the closet is alternatively too hot in summer and too cold in winter, try installing a small bathroom heater/fan fixture in the ceiling. In fact, there are bathroom fixtures that come with a heater, a fan and a light all in one unit; this type of fixture can also serve all of a closet's needs for lighting, heating and cooling.

Another dilemma with clothes closets is how to store shoes. All kinds of shoe racks can be purchased in almost any hardware, department or home-fixture store. Most are made to hang from walls or the inside of doors where their contents can easily be seen and found. There are also shoe holders with pockets for each shoe. These can be hung anywhere and have the advantage of keeping dust from settling on the shoes, or at least their toes. Included in this section are designs for making shoe holders, drawers, shelves and compartments out of wood. But note: It is rarely suggested that shoes be stored directly on the floor of any closet. When left on a floor, shoes have a peculiar habit of getting kicked around and disappearing into the darkest corners of the closet. In deep closets, where space is not at a premium, the shoes can be stored on long shelves, but they should still be elevated above the floor. The shoe shelves can be one of two designs:

One version of such a shoe shelf is simply a raised platform about 12″ deep. This can be a 1″x12″ pine board, or made of ½″, even ¼″ plywood, but it should be elevated from the floor by a 1″x2″ frame. If the stock used is ¾″, it need have only a 1″x2″ rail at the front, back and sides; if thinner stock is used, it should be supported by spacers in the frame every 2′. Another way of constructing the elevated shoe shelf is to make it between 15″ and 18″ wide and angle it up the wall. A strip of ¾″x¾″ stock is then nailed the length of the shelf at about the three-quarters mark of

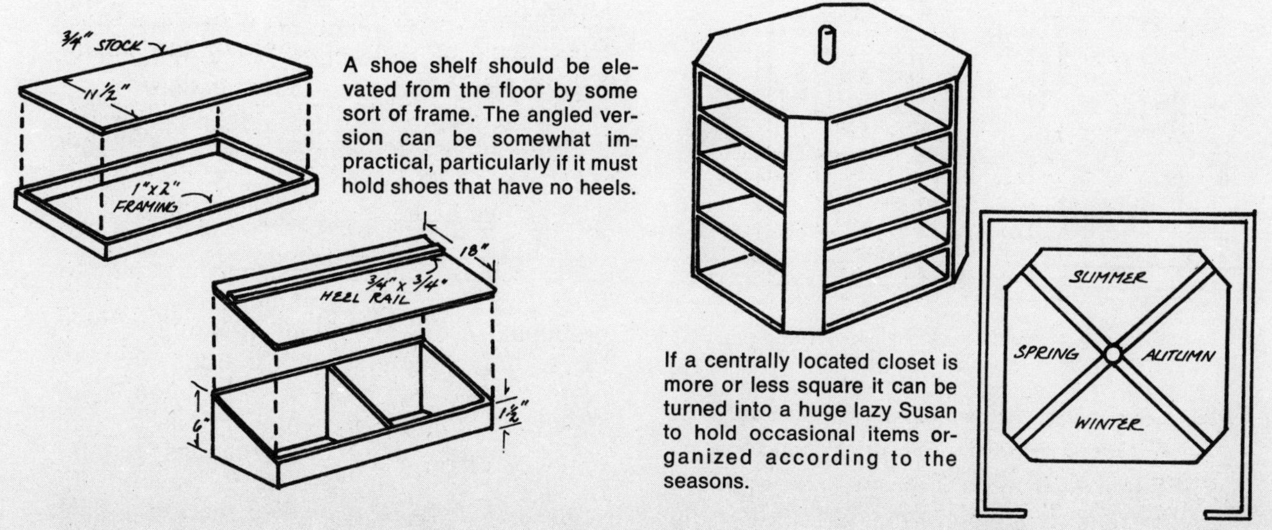

A shoe shelf should be elevated from the floor by some sort of frame. The angled version can be somewhat impractical, particularly if it must hold shoes that have no heels.

If a centrally located closet is more or less square it can be turned into a huge lazy Susan to hold occasional items organized according to the seasons.

the depth of the shelf, to catch the heels of the shoes. This is a more complicated structure and it looks a little more custom-made, but apart from being more trouble to build, it offers no special advantages over a flat shelf. In fact, the shoes may not always stay put on a slanted shelf and the heel-catching strip gets in the way of moccasins, sandals, sneakers and any other footwear that does not have a heel for it to catch.

For the most part, the closets suggested in this section of projects are oriented to storing clothes, but in a house full of nooks and crannies that might be closed off, a closet can also become an outsized, built-in cabinet for storing numerous items. An example of this is the bar closet project, which extends the idea of a huge, stand-in cabinet and functions as a storage area as well as a center of activity. In that particular project, you will find a hint of interior closet decor, simply because a bar closet would not normally be hidden away in a secluded corner of the house. But the bar closet is only one kind of specialty closet. Another kind would be the traditional china closet, which presents a series of shelves deep enough to hold china and glassware, but not much more. People have been known to turn a really narrow closet into bookshelves, and devote slightly deeper ones to linens. A shallow closet can be turned into a stereo unit with space for holding records as well as equipment.

There was mention earlier in this book of putting all of a household's occasional storage in one centrally located unit, and while such a closet is perhaps desirable, it is also likely to be impractical. If a large, walk-in closet exists in a central room of the house, it would be a logical place for such storage, for it could have shelves and compartments lining all of its walls, each designed to hold the particular objects to be stored. If the available storage space were less than a walk-in size and more or less square, conceivably, the lazy Susan unit shown here could be made to work almost as well. The dimensions depend on the size of the closet; the configurations of shelves, compartments and cabinets depend on what is to be stored. The objects used in winter are kept on one side of the lazy Susan octagon; summer things are stored on another, with the spring and fall things each kept in their own sides of the octagon. The unit, obviously, is revolved to present the storage appropriate to the season.

A second possibility, if the storage space is very high and narrow, and has a relatively low doorway, is to assemble four hoist-up shelf cases, each of which is partitioned to store the different objects needed for different seasons of the year. These are then hung from the ceiling with a block-and-tackle system, so that there is about 6′ of space underneath them. Shelves can be put around the sides of the closet anywhere they will not interfere with the units, as they are raised or lowered according to the season and the contents of the cabinets.

Whether or not the interior of a closet is

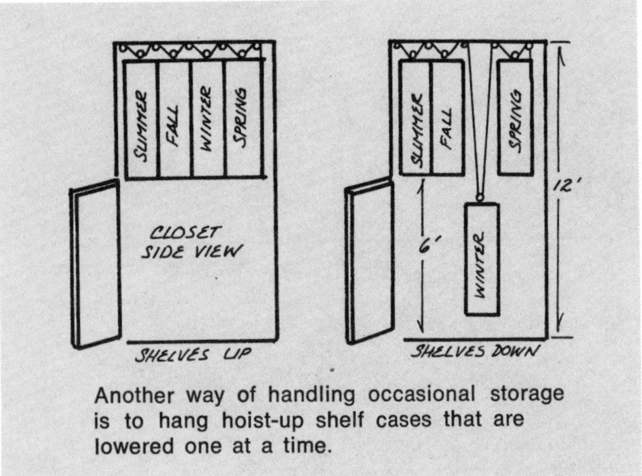

Another way of handling occasional storage is to hang hoist-up shelf cases that are lowered one at a time.

decorative may not be terribly important to the life-style of the family that uses it. But the exterior should blend with the decor of the room where it is located. This means that the top of the closet's outside walls may require some compatible crown or molding that carries the motif of the rest of the room. There should also be a baseboard decorated in the same way. The closet door may also require compatible treatment. In a bedroom this could mean nothing more than an unadorned piece of plywood or a piece of matching trim or molding. The decor of a kitchen closet may well have to include fancy molding, or even a frame-and-panel construction.

The hardware, too, should be taken into consideration. The hinges and knobs, even the catches, may—and should—be chosen with an eye as to how they will fit in with the rest of the room.

All of these possibilities, and many more, exist and must be carefully studied in approaching a closet project. It would be nice to be able to say that all of the combinations have in some way been touched upon in the 10 closet projects presented in this section, but to include all of the situations and the variations on their themes is beyond the scope of this book. However, consider each and all of the ideas shown here whenever you set about the design of any closet. Buried here and there in each of the projects are ideas that can be compounded and put to some specialized use, that can be turned around, or reshaped, and redesigned, to solve that difficult closet problem that exists in your home.

Lumber and Wallboard Closet

The most obvious way of building a closet occurs when there are two or three walls that merely need to be filled in. And the traditional way of filling them is with a lumber and wallboard construction.

There is an old myth that says studs have to be 2"x4"s set 16" on center. But wallboard manufacturers, most professional carpenters and practically everyone else, agree that framing is cheaper and easier to handle—and just as sturdy—if it is made with 2"x3" studs set 24" on center. In fact, even that rule can be stretched if there are enough braces between the studs. Thus, a 32" wall can be made with two 2"x3" studs supported at the top and bottom, and cross-braced every 2'.

For the sake of simplicity, suppose you have a corner 6' long on one side and 3' on the other, with a ceiling 8' high, and have decided that this will form the back and one side of a closet 6' long by 2' deep by 8' high.

Materials for Lumber and Wallboard Closet

Quantity	Description
62'	2"x3" stock for framing
4	4'x8' wallboard panels
5 lb.	10d common nails
2 lb.	wallboard nails
1	roll wallboard tape
1 gal.	wallboard compound
1	30"x6'8" hollow core door
1	set 3½" butts
1	doorknob set
17'	door trim
17'	doorstop
16'	1¼" dowels for clothes poles
	Lumber as needed for shelves

Frame. Mark off the walls of the closet on the floor, and nail the 2"x3" soleplate to the floor, with 10d nails every 2'. It is easier to achieve a straight line if the soleplate is first laid down, the location of the doorway marked off and then the plate cut away. But, for the moment, just mark off the door (Fig. A).

The door width should be increased 1" to each side for the jambs, plus 1⅝" on each side for the short studs, which will be added to the rough framework. Thus, a door, 30" wide, will have a space of 35¼" between the two initial studs.

Now secure the top plate to the ceiling, exactly above the soleplate. Positioning must be done with a plumb line, or by standing a stud upright and trueing it with a level. Mark the position where the top plate is to be attached, and nail it to the ceiling. If the closet wall is running across the joists, there will be no problem finding wood to nail into (it will probably be every 16"). If the wall is running parallel to the joists, and the ceiling is fairly secure, use toggle (molly) bolts. If the ceiling structure is not strong, the "experts" say move the wall until the top plate can run under a joist. In actual fact, when you are dealing with a short wall, it is possible to simply ram the top plate against the ceiling with the studs. If the studs are really tight against the plate, with the additional assurance that the two end studs will be secured against some other surface, the plate will hold quite adequately.

The studs are cut a fraction of an inch long and hammered into position at 16" (if you are a wealthy purist), 20" or 24" intervals. There are two tricks for putting up studs alone that make an aggravating chore much simpler. The studs must be toe-nailed into the soleplate and top plate on all four sides, and they must be on center, or you will never be able to find them behind the wallboard. The first trick is to drill pilot holes through all four sides of both ends of each stud. That reduces the amount of sliding off-center that the stud does as the first two nails are driven in. It also reduces the amount of hammering. The second trick is to cut a piece of scrap 1½" shorter than the spacing you want between studs. Hold the spacer against the previous stud, butt the new stud against it, then nail. Every stud will come out on center, and you will not have to measure any of them.

Begin by putting the first stud against the wall

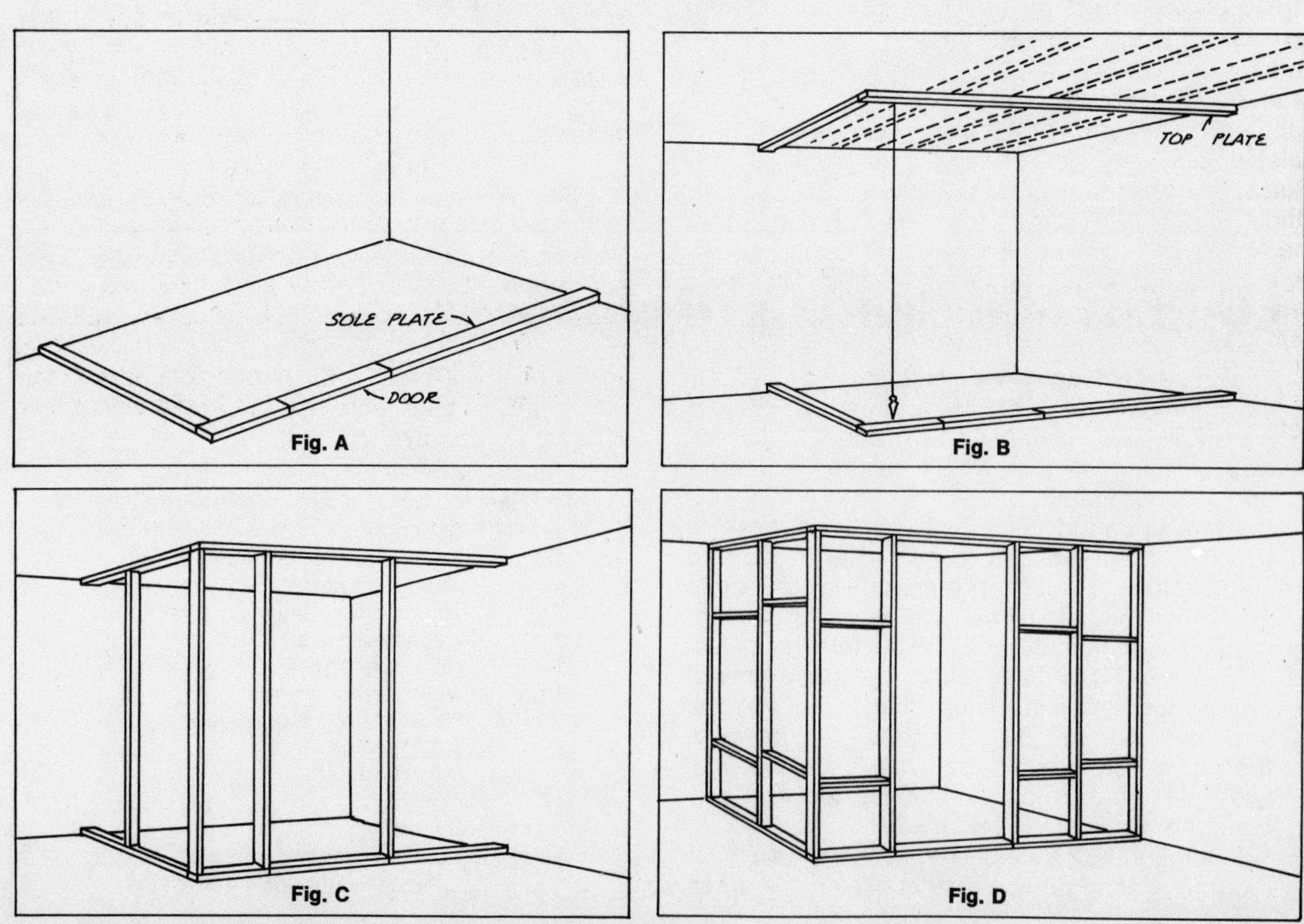

Fig. A

Fig. B

Fig. C

Fig. D

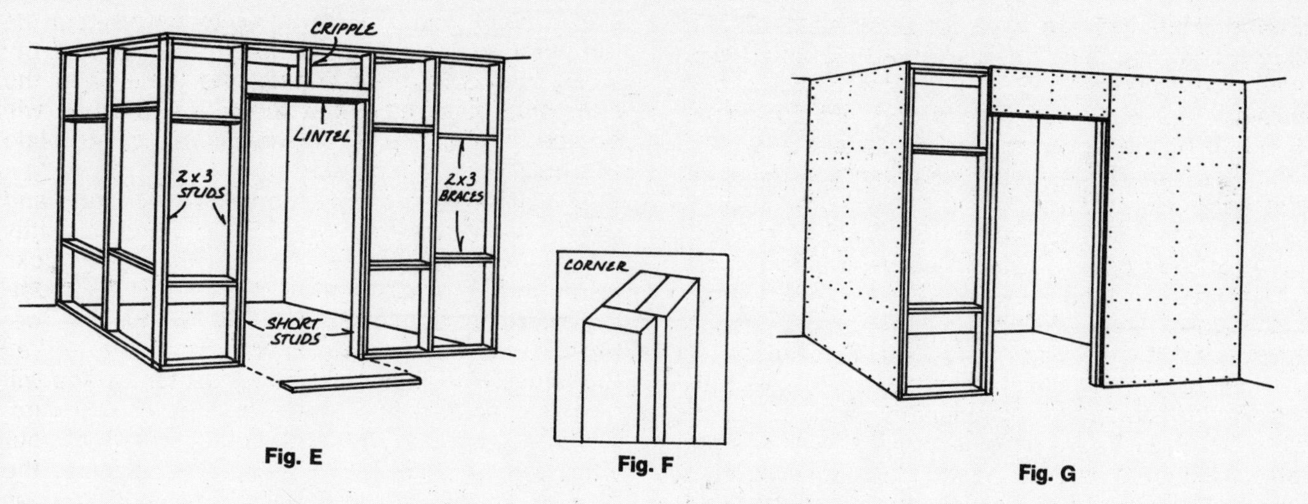

Fig. E

Fig. F

Fig. G

and toenailing it to the top and soleplates. Then continue down the wall until all of the studs are in place. For further support, nail cross-braces between studs (Fig. D). An average wall, 8′ high, will require two braces, more or less evenly spaced between each stud.

For the average short wall, an outside corner consists of three studs nailed together as shown in Fig. F, if the inside is to be covered. If it is not to be covered, two studs in the form of an "L" will suffice.

Framing the door. The door should have a stud at each end of where the soleplate was marked. The soleplate can now be sawed at the base of the studs. Two short studs are nailed to the face of the studs (Fig. E). The short studs are 1″ longer than the height of the door, plus 1″ more if there is to be a threshold. (The soleplate, removed from between the studs, is nailed to a second 2″x3″ the same length. The two pieces are nailed to the top of the short studs with their narrow sides vertical to form a lintel. A short stud, or "cripple," is nailed between the top plate and the lintel, at the center of the doorway. The door jambs and the door may then be hung in place.

The framing is now complete, but if there are any built-ins to be installed, or if shelving is to be supported in any way by the studs, the braces should be added now, along with vents, wiring or any other structural component that will go inside the closet.

Wallboarding. Start with the inside of the closet. Begin at one corner and work along both walls, unless you are putting in a ceiling as well, in which case, start with that. Always begin nailing at the center of the panel (there should be a stud right down the middle of it if they were put up 24″ on center). Nails should be spaced every 6″ and are never placed closer than ⅜″ from the edges. When the wallboard is in place (Fig. G), cover the joints with tape and three coats of wallboard compound.

Inside the closet. The clothes poles and shelves are positioned after the final coat of compound has been sanded. Complete any detail work around the door or elsewhere, then finish to blend with decor of room.

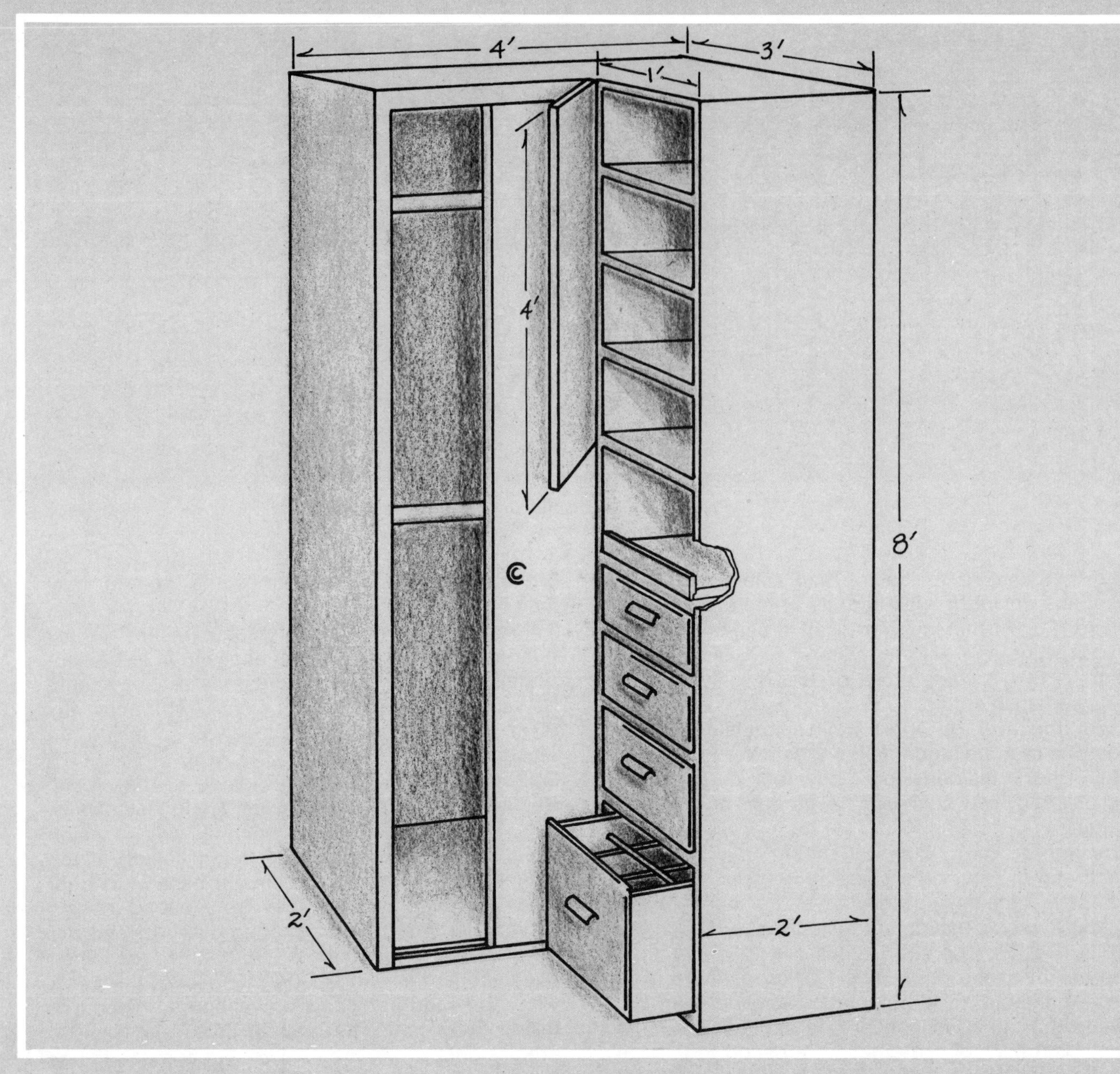

Corner Clothes Closet

The problem is a "dead" corner, 4'x3'. There are probably half a dozen effective ways of utilizing such a space for storage. You might square off the whole corner to make a 3'x4' walk-in, install a double bank of shelves, design a kitty-corner arrangement. Or, you could knock down one or both walls and start over again, etc. Another possibility is to combine a clothes closet, 24" deep, with a set of drawers and shelves, 12" wide.

Materials for Corner Clothes Closet

Quantity	Description
Closet	
52'	2"x3" stock for framing
1½	⅜"x4'x8' wallboard panel for short wall
8'	1¼" dowel for clothes poles
½	¾" A-B grade plywood panel for sliding door
1	4' sliding door track and door hardware kit
1	36" threshold saddle
Bureau	
2	½" A-B grade plywood panels for sides, shelves, drawers
½	¾" A-B grade plywood panel for shelf door, drawer fronts, bottom
20'	1"x2" stock for drawer rails and spacers
6'	½" dowel for shoe drawer dividers
¼	¼" plywood panel for bureau back

The closet. This could be an all-plywood construction, but panels, 8′ high by ¾″ thick, have to be braced by a 2″x3″ frame anyway. Since a frame must be put up, it is cheaper to cover them with wallboard. As shown in Fig. A, the short 24″ wall is set at right angles to the 4′ wall. Then a double-header is nailed to the joists to form the front top of the closet. It is supported at the 3′ wall end by a 2″x3″, which is shimmed until it is absolutely true. A metal sliding door track is screwed to the underside of the header, and a sliding door, ¾″x 22″x91¾″, is hung from the track. Make sure the door moves easily and stops snugly against the studs at each end of its track before you go any further. When it does, rip a threshold saddle in half and nail it to the floor inside the closet so that the door roller guide touches it at all points. The other half of the saddle will be added later. In setting the braces between the 2″x3″ framing, place them in position to support both a high and a low clothes pole. Either wallboard both sides of the frame, or nail plywood paneling to the outside of the closet.

The bureau (Fig. B). The bureau is 12″ wide by 24″ deep by 8′ high, made entirely of ½″ plywood. The sides are 23⅞″ wide by 8′ high and are attached to a ¼″ plywood back 12″x8′. The top half of the bureau contains four shelves for work

Fig. A

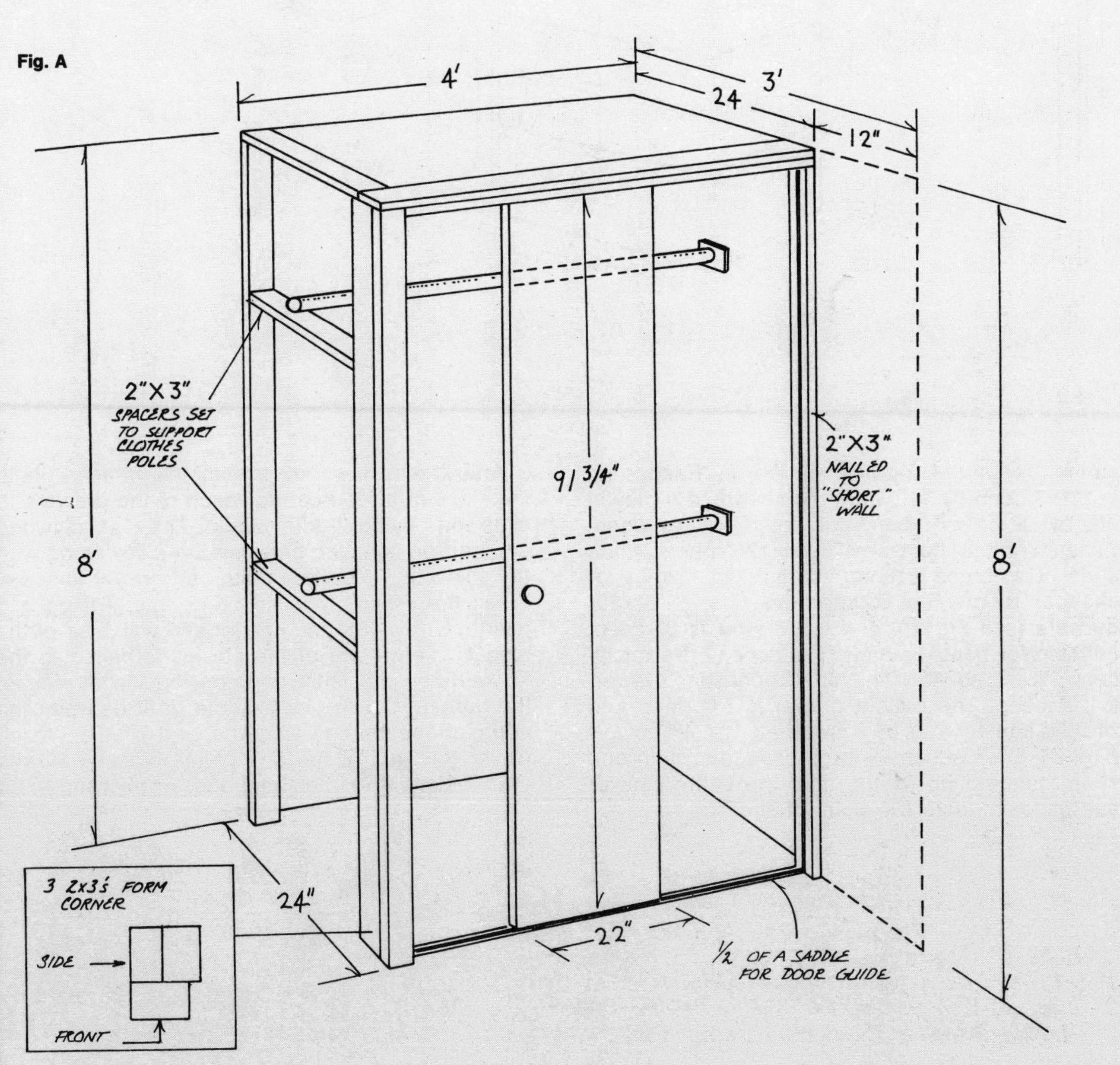

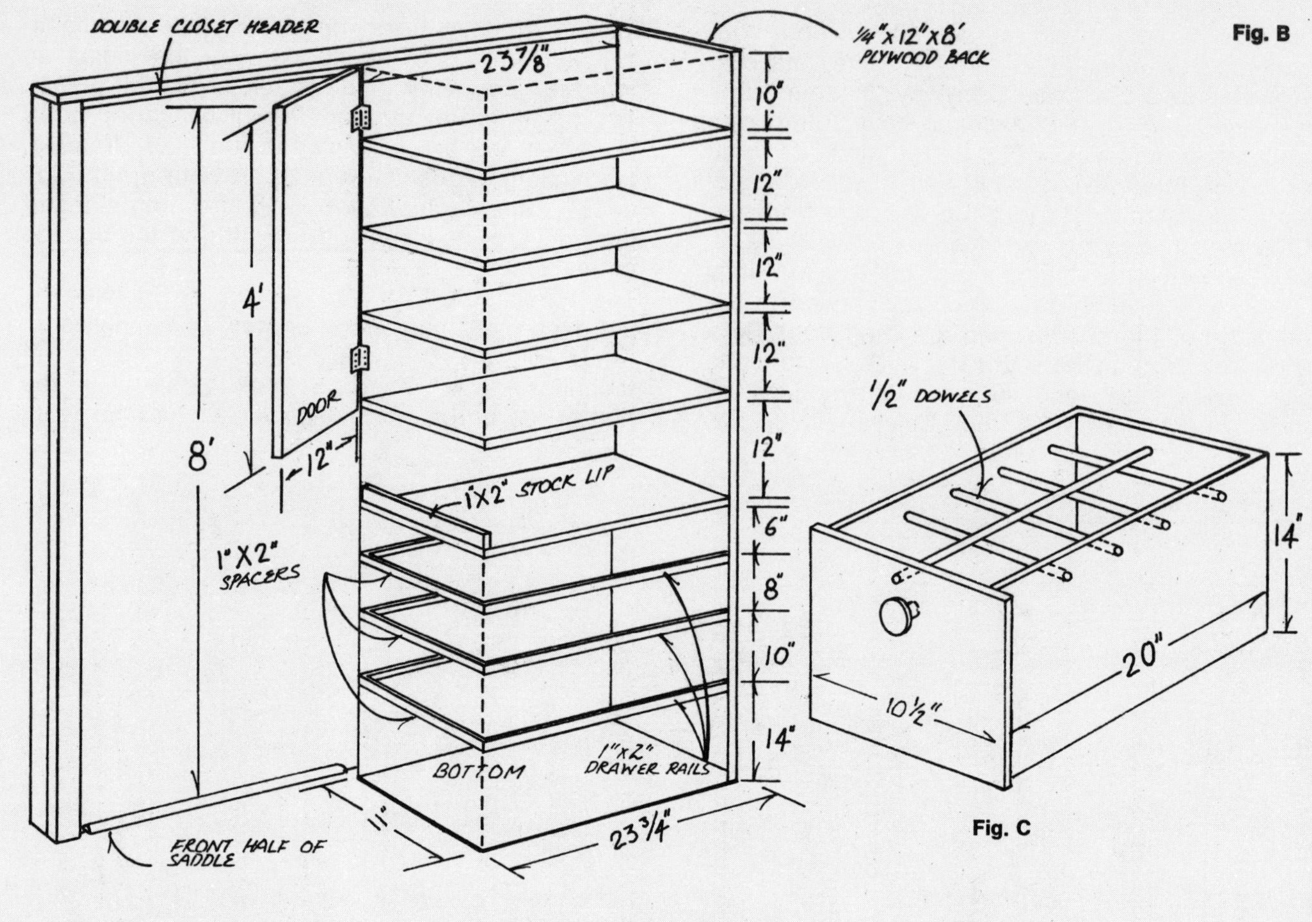

clothes, sweaters, T-shirts and so on. Each shelf is 23¾" deep by 11" wide; the shelves are closed off by a 12"x4' door cut from ¾" plywood. Beneath the bottom shelf is a 12" space which ends at a lipped counter for holding jewelry or change. Below the counter are four 10½"x20" drawers (see Fig. B). The top drawer is 6" deep, suitable for handkerchiefs. The second drawer, 8" deep, is for socks. The third, underwear drawer, is 10" deep. The bottom drawer is 14" deep and divided into squares by a crosshatch of ½" dowels (Fig. C). Each square is large enough to hold one shoe standing on its toe, and the entire drawer can accommodate five pairs of shoes.

After the drawers are assembled, attach rails to the sides of the bureau for each of the drawers to slide on, using 1"x2" stock. The ½" plywood counter top is nailed between the sides along with the shelves, ¾" bottom plate and drawer spacers. When the assembly is complete, stand it up and nail the left wall to the header and wall stud of the closet. The bottom of the bureau is nailed to the floor. Hinge the shelf door on the closet side of the bureau. Cut the half-saddle to fit between the edge of the bureau and the end of the closet. Cover the stud at the end of the closet wall and the header with either wallboard or plywood.

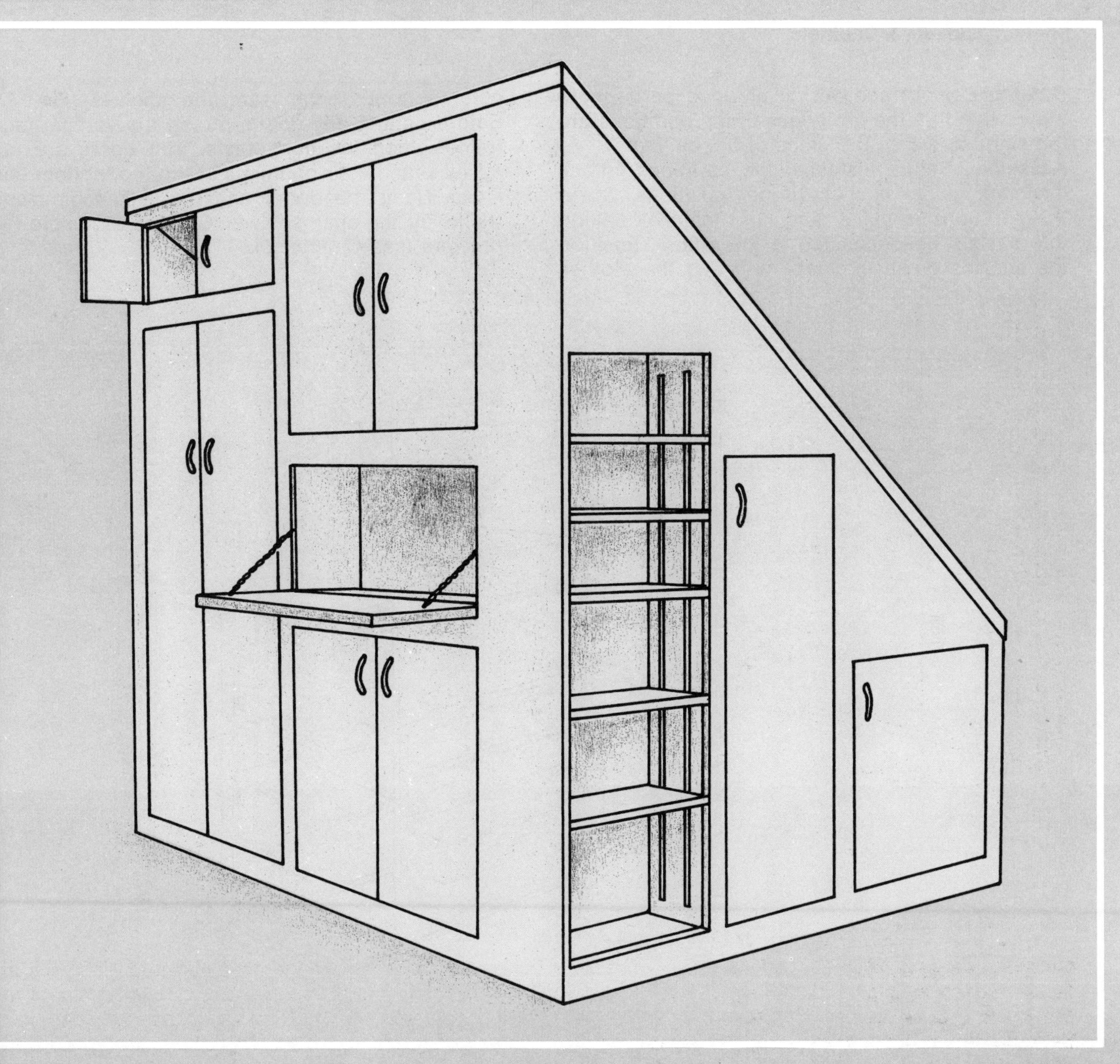

Under-the-Eaves Closet

The sloping ceiling under the eaves of a house that provide no headroom can be transformed from wasted space into a useful storage area by boxing it in and dividing the box into shelves and drawers. The divisions can be in any combination and should be dictated by the objects to be stored. The version shown here is 7′ high at the front and 6′ 11½″ wide. The depth is 37½″ from the front to the back of the door behind the open shelves, but the unit could be continued all the way to the corner where the wall meets the floor.

Materials for Under-the-Eaves Closet

Quantity	Description
7	¾″ B-D plywood panels for partitions, doors, floor, shelves, fronts and backs
2	½″ B-D for interior partitions, and drawers
1	¼″x4′x4′ plywood for drawer bottoms
1¼″	3′ dowel for clothes pole
12′	1x2 stock for framing
44′	1x1 stock for shelf cleats
	Pulls, hinges, etc., as needed

Cutting. Lay out and cut all plywood parts, making certain that the top edges of the partitions are the same angle as the slope of the ceiling.

Assembly. Before installing the partitions, attach the shelf cleats in their proper positions. Stand the partitions in place, and hold them by nailing into a 1"x2" header nailed to the rafters. Position the shelves on their cleats, and add the clothes pole in front of the wardrobe shelves (Fig. A). Before cutting any doors, attach the vertical face frames, then the horizontals. The doors are cut 1/16" less than their openings at the top, bottom and sides. Hang the doors and the adjustable shelf tracks for the open shelves. Cut and assemble the drawers (see Chapter 6).

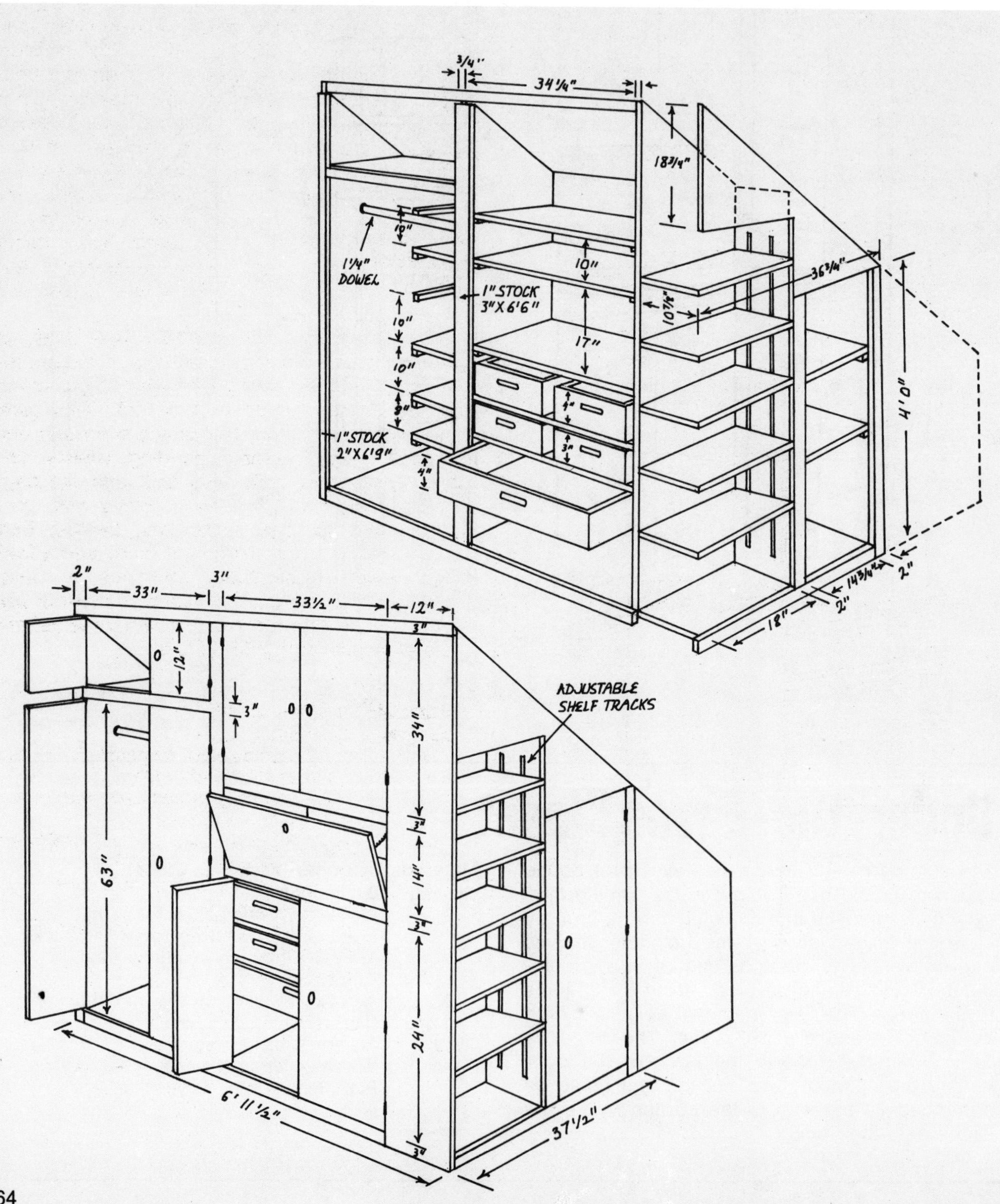

Linen Closet

Bathrooms are usually tight on space, so any closet that is added must be especially well organized to get the maximum use of every square inch. As a result, the planning of a linen closet begins with considerable measuring and mentally organizing all the items to be stored in it. Then the closet must be designed to hold them all. More than just organizing, the most-used possessions should be at eye level; the top section should hold the least-used things; the bottom should be for large, bulky items, such as bedding and cleaning supplies. And each of the three divisions ought to be separately accessible.

The linen closet suggested here has, of course, almost limitless variations in design, depending upon the items it is to hold. This closet is 36″ wide by 24″ deep by 8′ high. That takes up a lot of space, but that space will hold: out-of-season and in-season bedding, window and shower curtains, bath mats and rugs, ice bags and heating pads, towels of every size, bed linens and spreads, large jars, bottles, bath salts, tissues, soap, extra light bulbs and a folding ladder. Construction of such a closet amounts to assembling a goodly number of plywood pieces into a maze of compartments, and it is probably best built on site.

Materials for Linen Closet

Quantity	Description
2	¾″ A-D grade plywood panels for sides, top, shelves and dividers
1	¾″ A-B grade plywood panel for doors and pull-out shelves
1	½″ A-B grade plywood panel for shelves and dividers
1	¼″ plywood panel for closet back
16	22″ shelf guides
12	3″ hinges for folding and solid doors
6	door pulls
7	shelf pulls

Cutting. Cut all parts of the closet according to the five diagrams shown in Fig. A. For the sake of simplicity, all joinery consists of glue-nailed butt joints. If you prefer to dado, the dimensions shown will have to be adjusted accordingly.

Assembly. Glue-nail the top (B) to sides (A) and (J), then add back (Z). Position fixed shelves (M), (R), (S) and (C), as shown in Figs. B and C. Put in place stiffeners (D) and (E), then insert dividers (V), (O), (P), three (Us), two (Ts) and (G) between

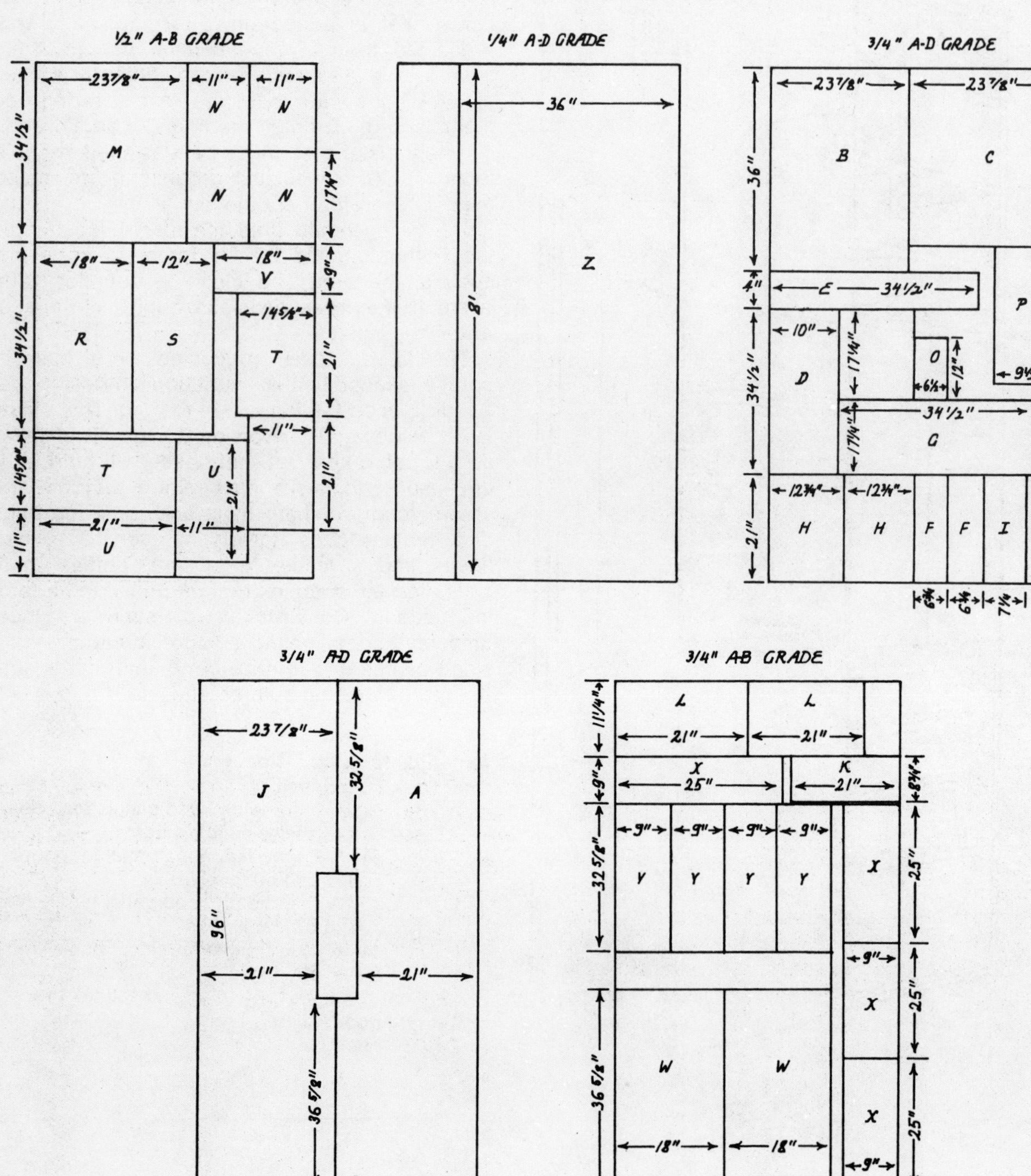

Fig. A

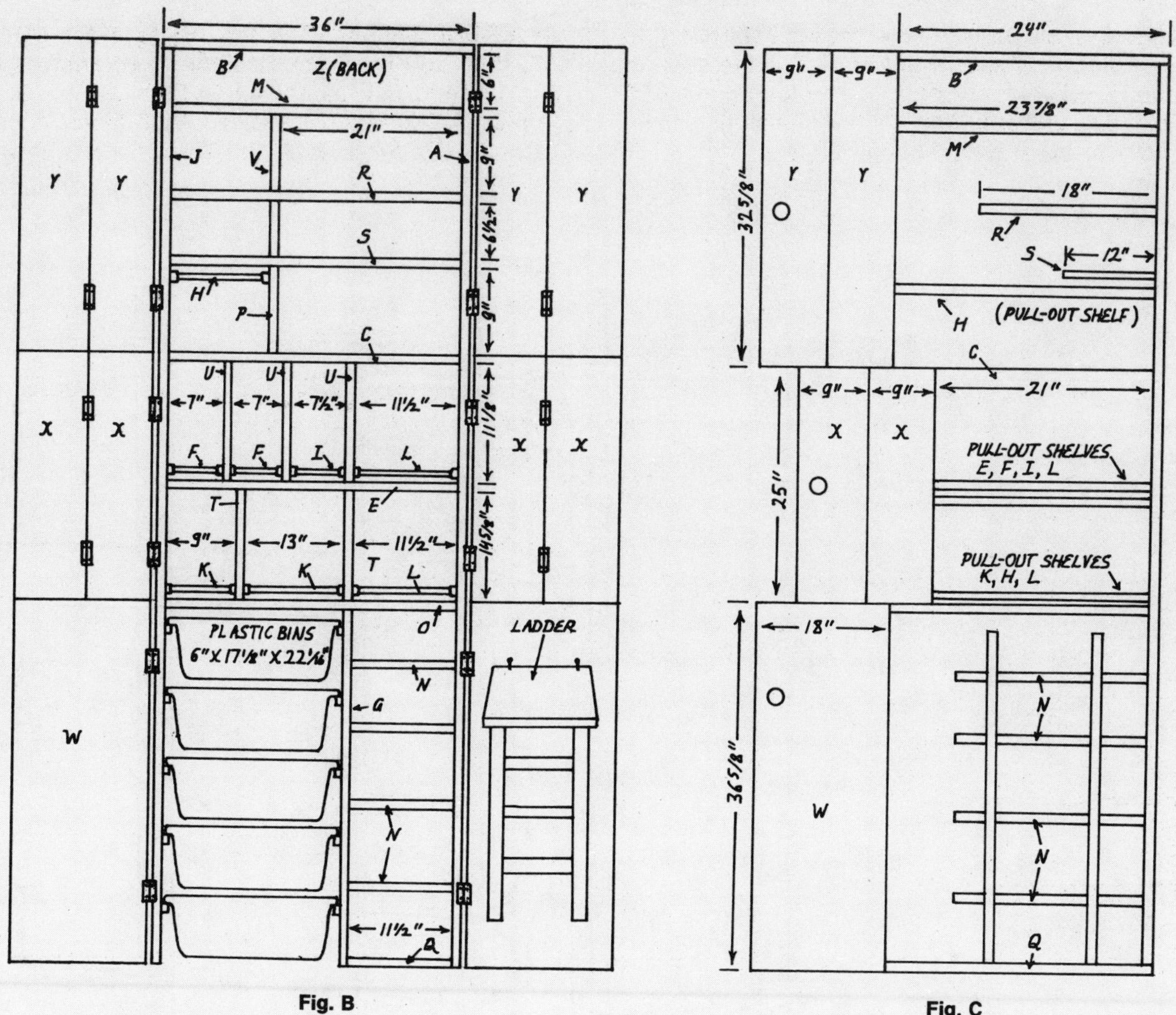

Fig. B

Fig. C

the shelves. The bottom of (G) is glue-nailed to bottom (Q). Shelf guides are attached to both sides of the three (U) and two (T) dividers and the left side of (P). Attach the guide slides to shelves (I), (K), two (Ls), two (Fs) and two (Hs). Attach the adjustable shelf tracks on divider (G) and side (A), and put the four (N) shelves in place. The six plastic bins that hang between (G) and side (J) are 6"x17⅛"x22¹⁄₁₆" and are held in place by strips of ¾" round molding nailed to the sides of their recess. Hinge the (X) and (Y) doors, and hang them with door (W) as shown in Fig. B. The doors are held shut by magnetic catches; a set of hooks are added to the inside of the right side (W) door to hold a small folding stepladder. The face of the doors is finished according to the decor in the rest of the room.

His-and-Hers Wall Closet

Take any wall. This one is 14′ long and 8′ high. Divide it in half, add shelves, drawers, pull-out shoe racks and clothes poles hidden behind four 3′ doors, and you will probably solve a lot of storage needs.

Materials for His-and-Hers Wall Closet

Quantity	Description
3	¾"x23½"x45½" for sides
1	¾"x23½"x36" for top
3	½" for round edging
2	¾"x1½"x45½" for face stiles
4	¾"x1½"x21" for rails
1	¾"x3½"x21" for rail
2	¾"x2¾"x22½" for back rails
2	¾"x1½"x11¼" for top rails
2	¾"x1½"x11¼" for bottom rails
24	½"x¾"x22" for shelf guides
6	¾"x11⅛"x22¼" for pull-out shelves
2	¾"x14"x34½" for short partition
2	¾"x½" round x 40' for partition edges
8	¾"x1¼"x22" for drawer slide mounting blocks
Drawers	
4	1¼"x9½"x21½" for front
4	½"x8½"x19½" for back
8	½"x8½"x22½" for sides
4	¼"x21½"x19½" for bottom
1 set	22" drawer slides

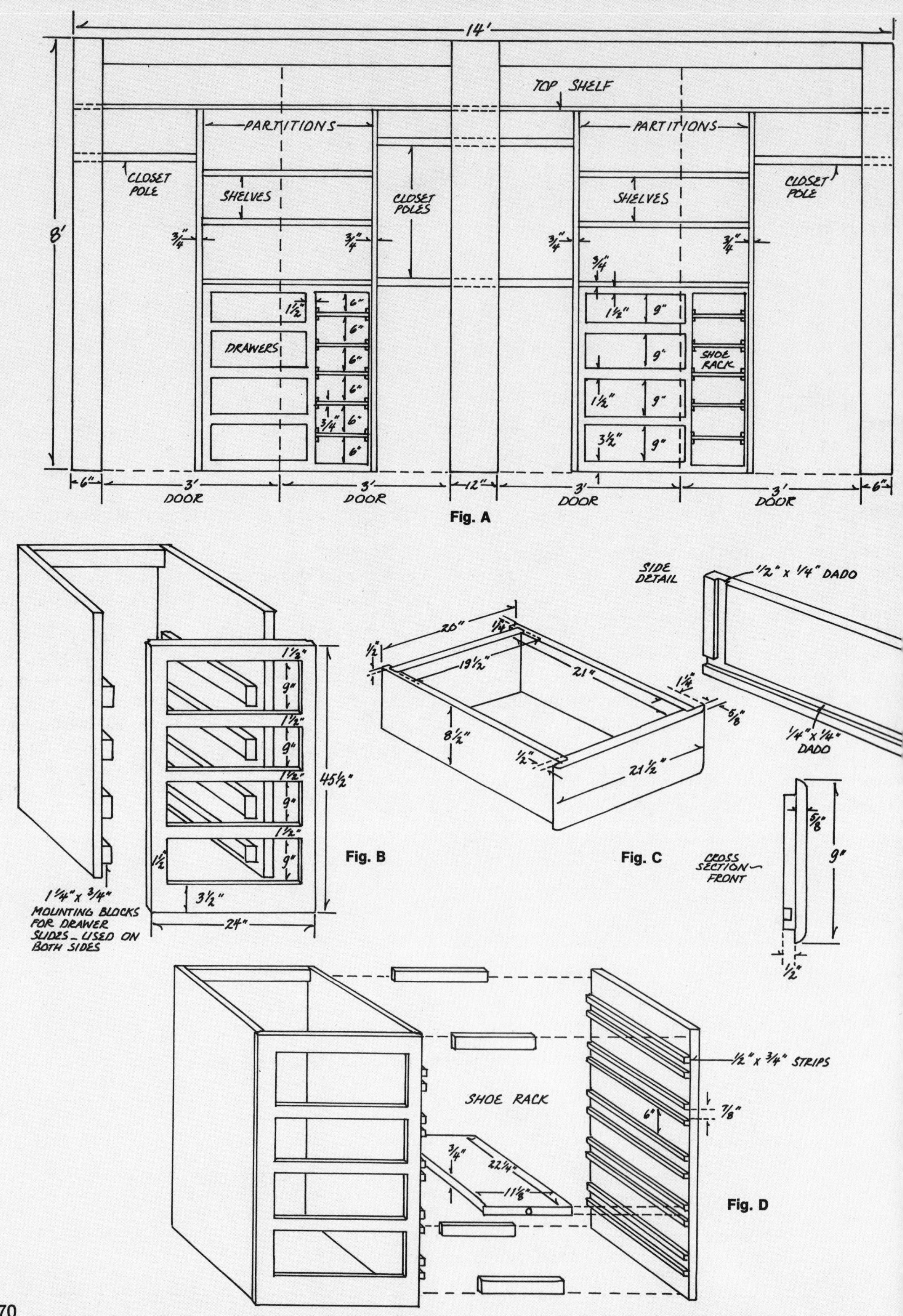
14'
TOP SHELF
PARTITIONS
PARTITIONS
CLOSET POLE
SHELVES
CLOSET POLES
SHELVES
CLOSET POLE
8'
3/4"
3/4"
3/4"
3/4"
3/4"
1 1/2"
6"
DRAWERS
3/4"
1 1/2"
9"
SHOE RACK
1 1/2"
3 1/2"
6"
3'
DOOR
3'
DOOR
12"
3'
DOOR
3'
DOOR
6"
Fig. A
1 1/2"
9"
45 1/2"
3 1/2"
24"
1 1/4" x 3/4"
MOUNTING BLOCKS FOR DRAWER SLIDES _ USED ON BOTH SIDES
Fig. B
20"
1/4"
1/2"
19 1/2"
21"
1 1/4"
5/8"
8 1/2"
1/2"
21 1/2"
Fig. C
SIDE DETAIL
1/2" x 1/4" DADO
1/4" x 1/4" DADO
CROSS SECTION FRONT
5/8"
9"
1/2"
SHOE RACK
1/2" x 3/4" STRIPS
6"
7/8"
3/4"
22 1/4"
11 1/8"
Fig. D

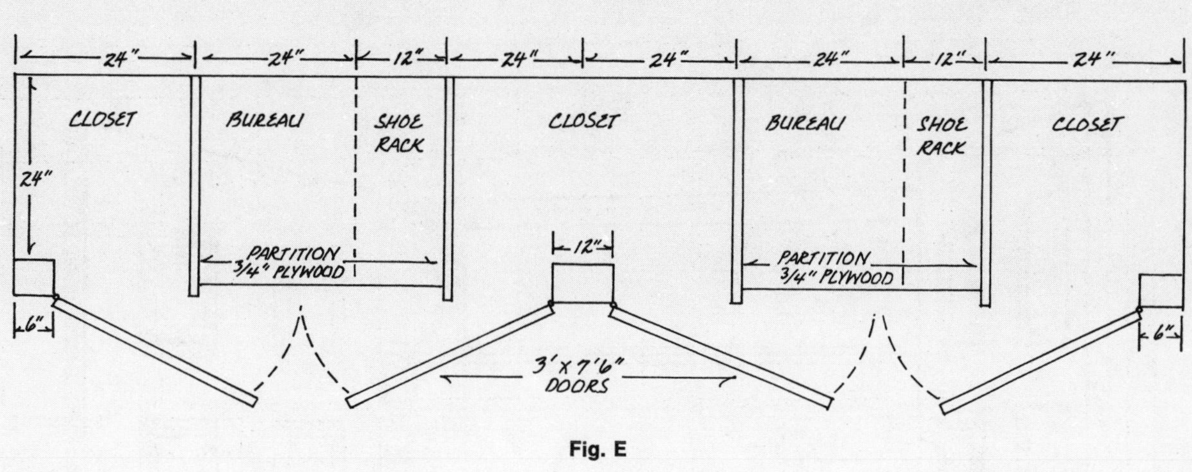

Fig. E

Frames and doors. Assuming that an entire wall is being encased, use a standard 2"x3" or 2"x4" frame construction up the side walls and across the ceiling (Fig. A). The outside doors are hung from a 6"-wide wall frame. The middle doors are hinged to a 12" center post that bisects the wall.

Doors. The 3' x 7'6" doors will warp if they are single pieces of plywood. They must be either hollow core, or frame-and-panel construction.

Shelving. Any arrangement can be made. A single 18"-wide shelf can run the length of the back wall at about the 7' level, and can be supported along the wall as well as by the partitions. The partitions can also support a variety of shelf configurations over the bureaus.

Partitions. The partitions are simply 2'-wide, ¾" plywood and should divide the two end closets from their adjacent bureaus and again between the bureaus and the center closet.

Drawers and bureau. (See Chapter 6.) The drawers and bureau are any size required. Fig. B shows an assembly for a four-drawer bureau which will hold the drawers shown in Fig. C.

Shoe racks. The shoe racks are pieces of ¾" stock 11⅛" wide by 22¼" long with ½" x ¾" strips glue-nailed to the sides of the partitions ⅞" apart. (See Fig. D.) The racks slide between the strips and are each wide enough to hold two pairs of shoes.

Assembly. Erect the 2" x 4" (or 2" x 3") door frame and hang the doors as shown in Figs. A and E. Put up the ¾" panels, attaching them to the bottom of the top shelf. Attach shelves between the partitions over the bureaus. Assemble the bureaus and shoe racks and put them in place. Double poles can be hung in the closet areas and any raw plywood edges can be covered with ¾" half round.

Bar Closet

Given a conveniently located enclosure that measures at least 22"x4', you have an opportunity to convert that space into a compact serving bar that also holds all of the glasses and other equipment needed for a good-sized party. Because the space is likely to be cramped, the cabinet should be built on-site.

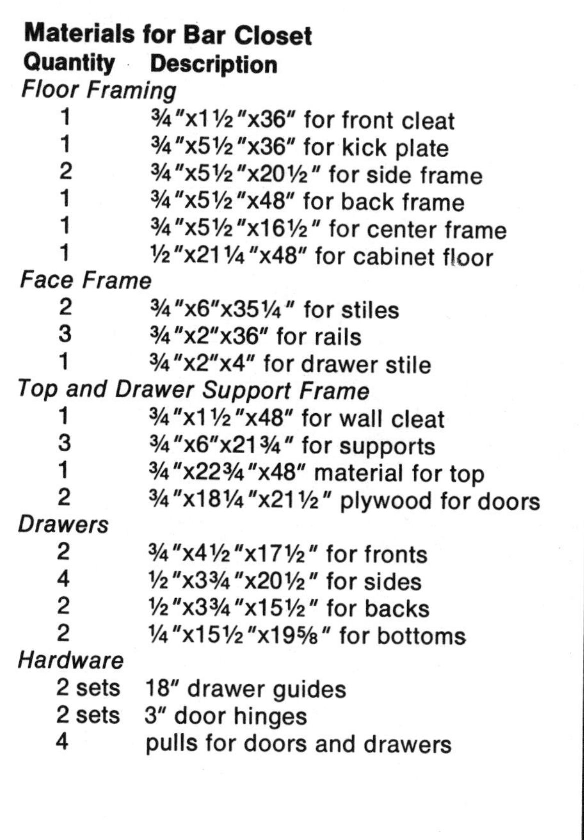

Materials for Bar Closet

Quantity	Description
Floor Framing	
1	¾"x1½"x36" for front cleat
1	¾"x5½"x36" for kick plate
2	¾"x5½"x20½" for side frame
1	¾"x5½"x48" for back frame
1	¾"x5½"x16½" for center frame
1	½"x21¼"x48" for cabinet floor
Face Frame	
2	¾"x6"x35¼" for stiles
3	¾"x2"x36" for rails
1	¾"x2"x4" for drawer stile
Top and Drawer Support Frame	
1	¾"x1½"x48" for wall cleat
3	¾"x6"x21¾" for supports
1	¾"x22¾"x48" material for top
2	¾"x18¼"x21½" plywood for doors
Drawers	
2	¾"x4½"x17½" for fronts
4	½"x3¾"x20½" for sides
2	½"x3¾"x15½" for backs
2	¼"x15½"x19⅝" for bottoms
Hardware	
2 sets	18" drawer guides
2 sets	3" door hinges
4	pulls for doors and drawers

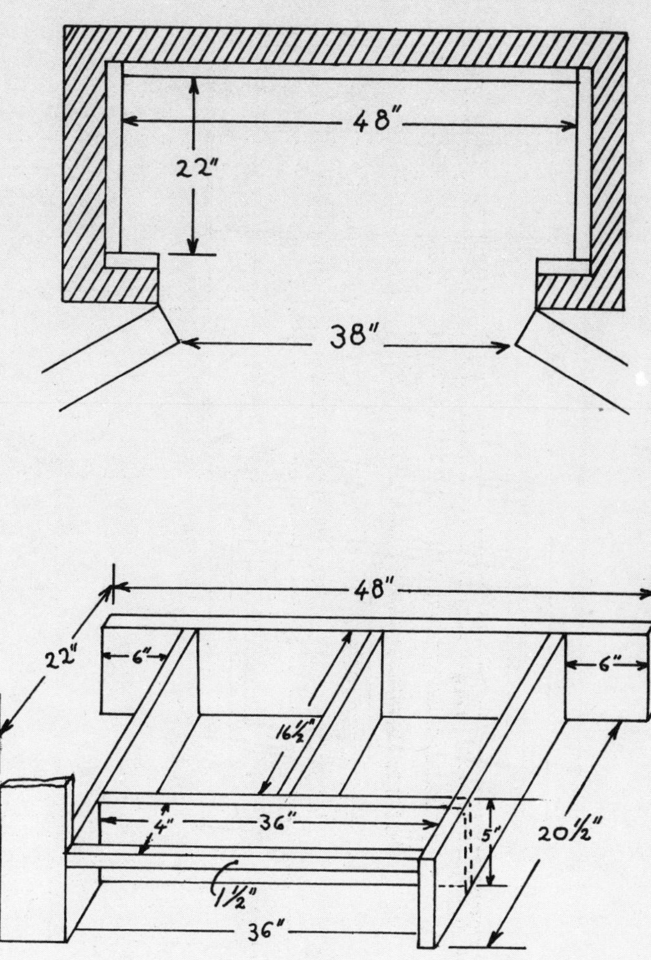

Fig. A

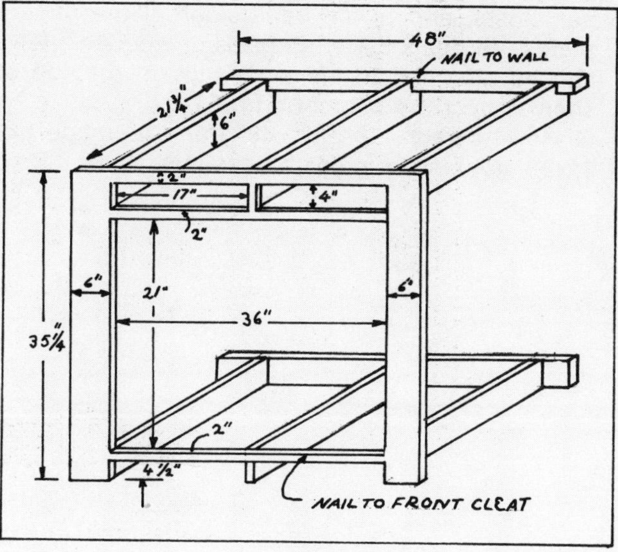

Fig. B

Assembly. Nail the 5½"x48" back floor frame member to the floor and rear wall of the enclosure. Toenail the 20½" side frames and the 16½" center frame members in place as shown in Fig. A. The 5½"x36" kick plate fits across the front of the center frame brace. The ¾"x1½"x36" front cleat is 4" in front of the frame brace. Nail the ½" x21½"x48" cabinet floor to the top of the frame. Erect the 6"x35¼" side faceplates (Fig. B), and connect them with the three 2"-wide face frame rails to form the door and drawer frames. The drawers are divided by a ¾"x2"x4" stile. The 1"x2" back-wall cleat is nailed to the rear wall. Before securing it, be certain that it is level in both directions with the front cabinet frame. When the cleat is in place, notch the three 6"x21¾" supports and nail them between the cleat and the face frame as shown in Fig. B.

The 22¾"x48" top can be pressboard or plywood, but in either case should be laminated, since the material used will probably have to withstand considerable spillage during the lifetime of the unit. An alternative to a laminated top might be butcher block, slate or marble.

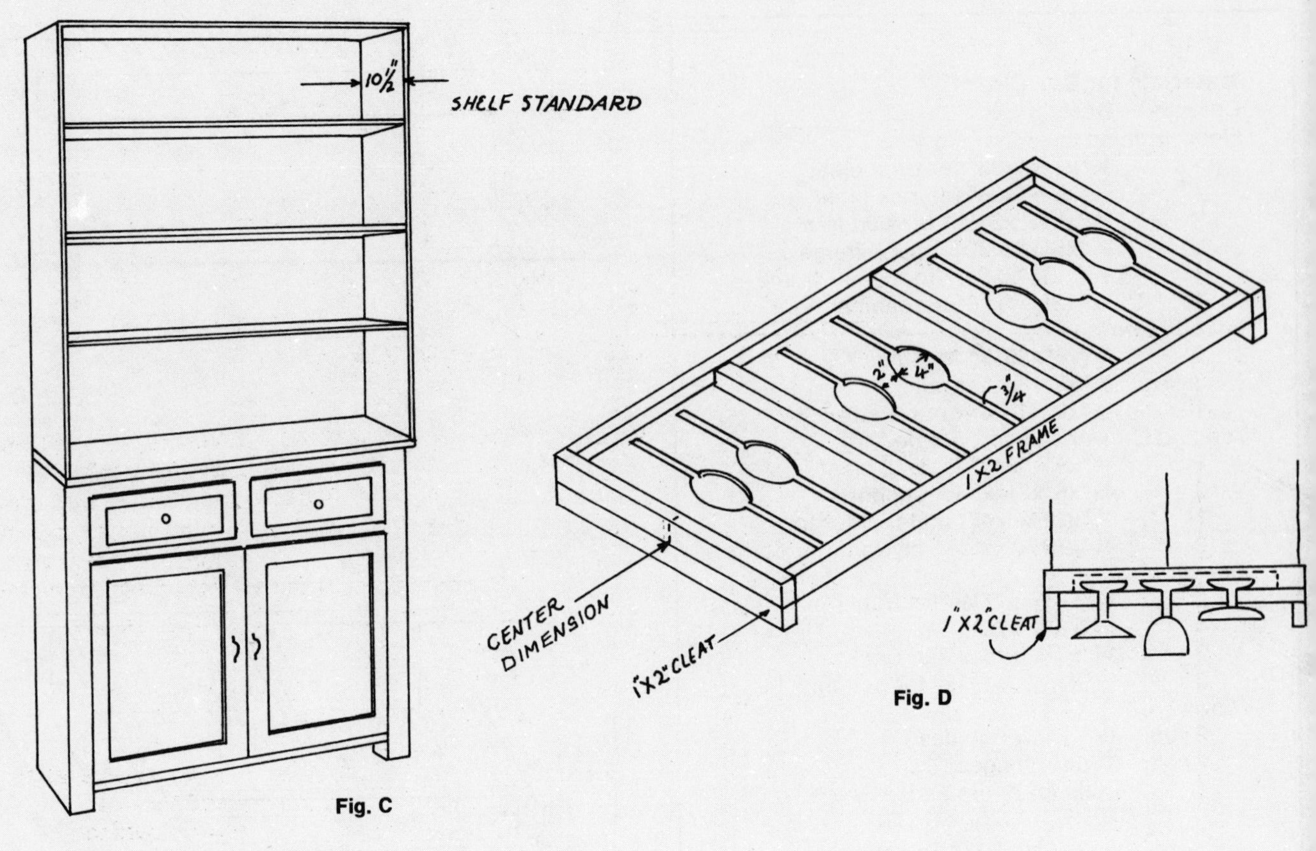

The drawers and doors can be any construction desired, and decorated in any manner. Adjustable shelf tracks are attached to the rear wall of the bar closet, and to the back sides of the 6″ face-plates. Verticals for either glass or wooden shelves can be attached to the side walls to provide 48″ shelves over the cabinet (Fig. C).

Glassware rack. The 22″x48″ frame is made from 1″x2″ stock with cross-braces set every 16″ on center (Fig. D). A piece of ¼″x22″x48″ plywood is then glue-nailed to the underside of the frame. A row of circles 4″ in diameter is cut out of the plywood along its center line, with 2″ left between each circle; each circle has a ¾″-wide slot extending to within 2″ of the front and back frame members. The rack is suspended above the cabinet by resting it on 1″x2″ cleats nailed to the closet walls under the sides and back of the frame.

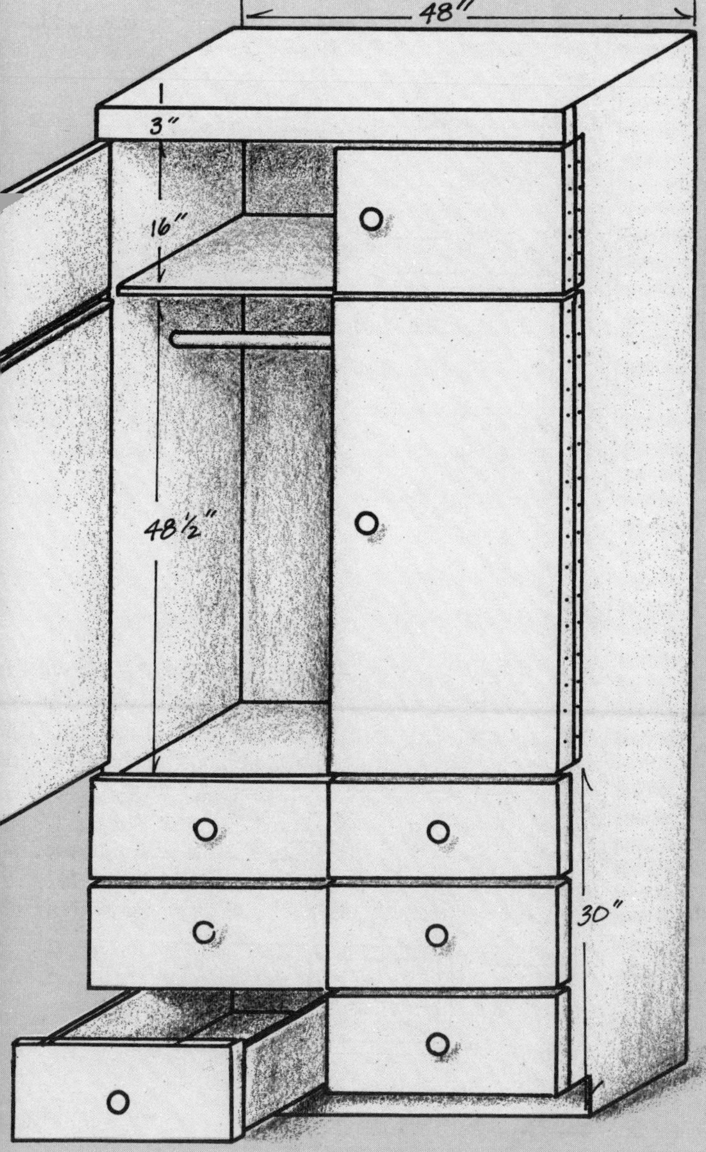

Wardrobe

The idea of a freestanding wardrobe is a time-honored way of providing closet space for a small guest room. This type of unit can also become the "his" half of a complex of closets in a master bedroom. In general, the wardrobe shown here is 8′ high by 24¾" deep by 48" wide, and is easier to assemble on-site.

Materials for Wardrobe

Quantity	**Description**
2	¾"x24"x8′ sides, notched for kick plate
3	¾"x24"x47" for top and shelves
1	¾"x24"x29½" for drawer partition
1	¾"x16½"x24" for top partition
1	¾"x3"x48" for kick plate
1	¾"x2"x46½" for wall rail
2	¾"x1¾"x46½" for floor cleats
1	¾"x3"x4′ for valance
2	¾"x2½"x65" hinge stiles, notched for shelves
Accessory Box	
2	½"x16"x23½" for top and bottom
3	½"x9½"x16" for sides and partition
Doors	
2	¾"x23$\frac{15}{16}$"x48½" for main doors
2	¾"x23$\frac{15}{16}$"x14½" for top cabinet doors
Drawers	
6	¾"x8¾"x23$\frac{15}{16}$" for drawer fronts
12	½"x8"x21½" for backs and inside fronts
12	½"x8"x22½" for sides
6	¼"x21"x21½" for bottoms
10′	crown or cove molding for top trim
6 pr.	22" metal drawer guides
12′	¾" piano hinge

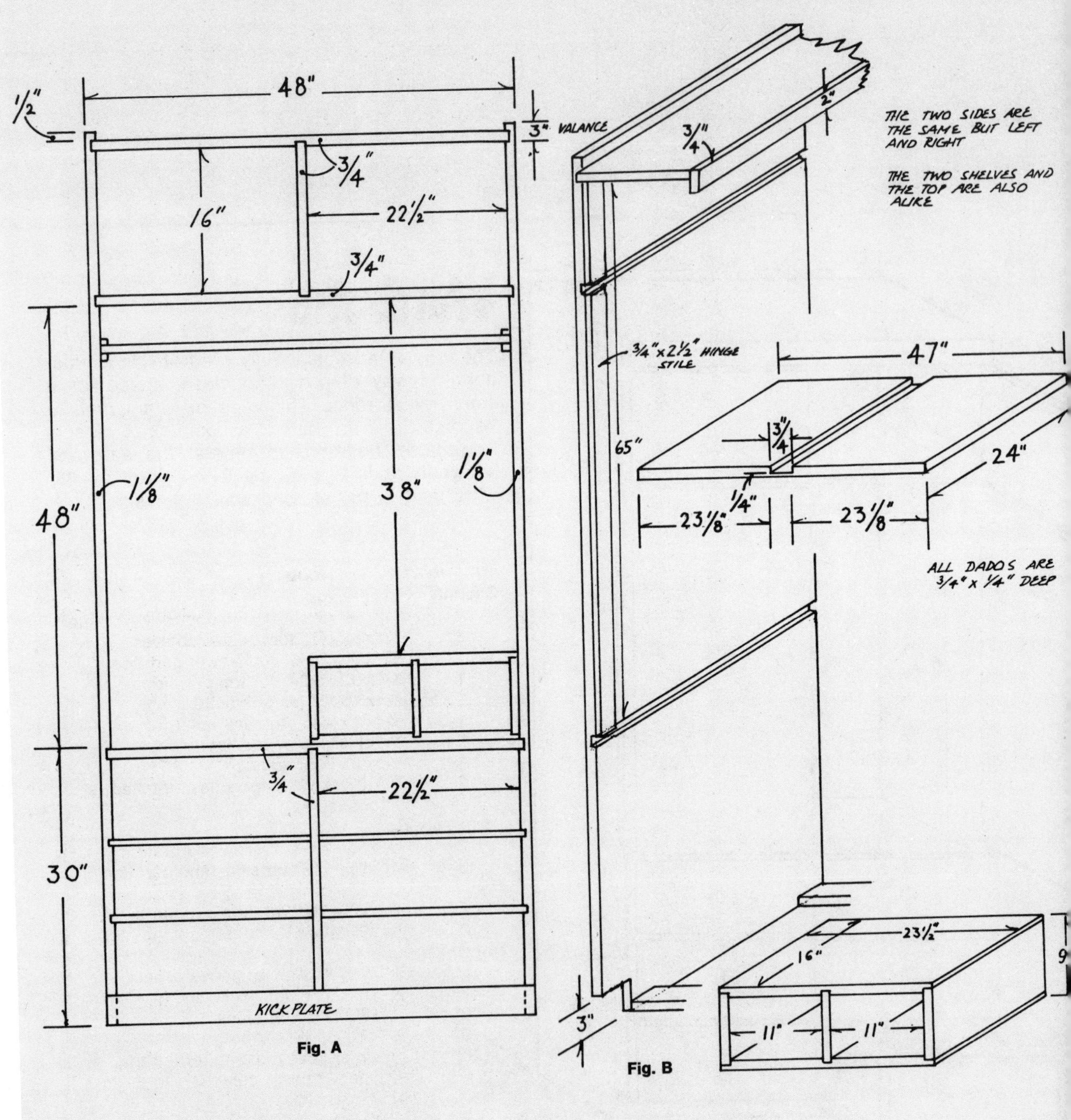

Fig. A

Fig. B

Assembly. Cut all pieces included in the materials list from ¾" plywood or pressboard. The sides are dadoed for the top shelf, drawer dustcovers and bottom (Fig. A). The top shelf and cabinet top are dadoed on center for the top center partition; the lower partition is dadoed for each of the shelf dustcovers. Assemble the shelves and partitions to the sides, and glue-nail a ¼"x4'x7' Masonite panel to the back edges of the unit. The 3"-wide valance is glue-nailed across the front of the cabinet top (Figs. A and D). The 23½"x10" accessory box (Fig. A) is assembled and glue-nailed to the right side and top drawer dustcover of the cabinet. The base of the unit has ¾"x1½" cleats, butted between the front and back edges of the sides (Fig. B); the drawer partition is notched (Fig. C) to fit over the cleats. The 3" kick plate is glue-nailed to the back of the 3¾"x3" kick plate notch cut from the bottom front corners of the sides and drawer partition.

Drawers and doors. The drawers are assembled as shown in Fig. D and rest on metal drawer guides. All four doors are cut from ¾" plywood (see materials list), and are attached to ¾"x2½"x 65" hinge stiles glue-nailed to the sides of the cabinet with piano hinges. The clothes pole is either an expandable metal clothes hanger, or a 1¼" dowel set in chocks glue-nailed to the insides of the unit.

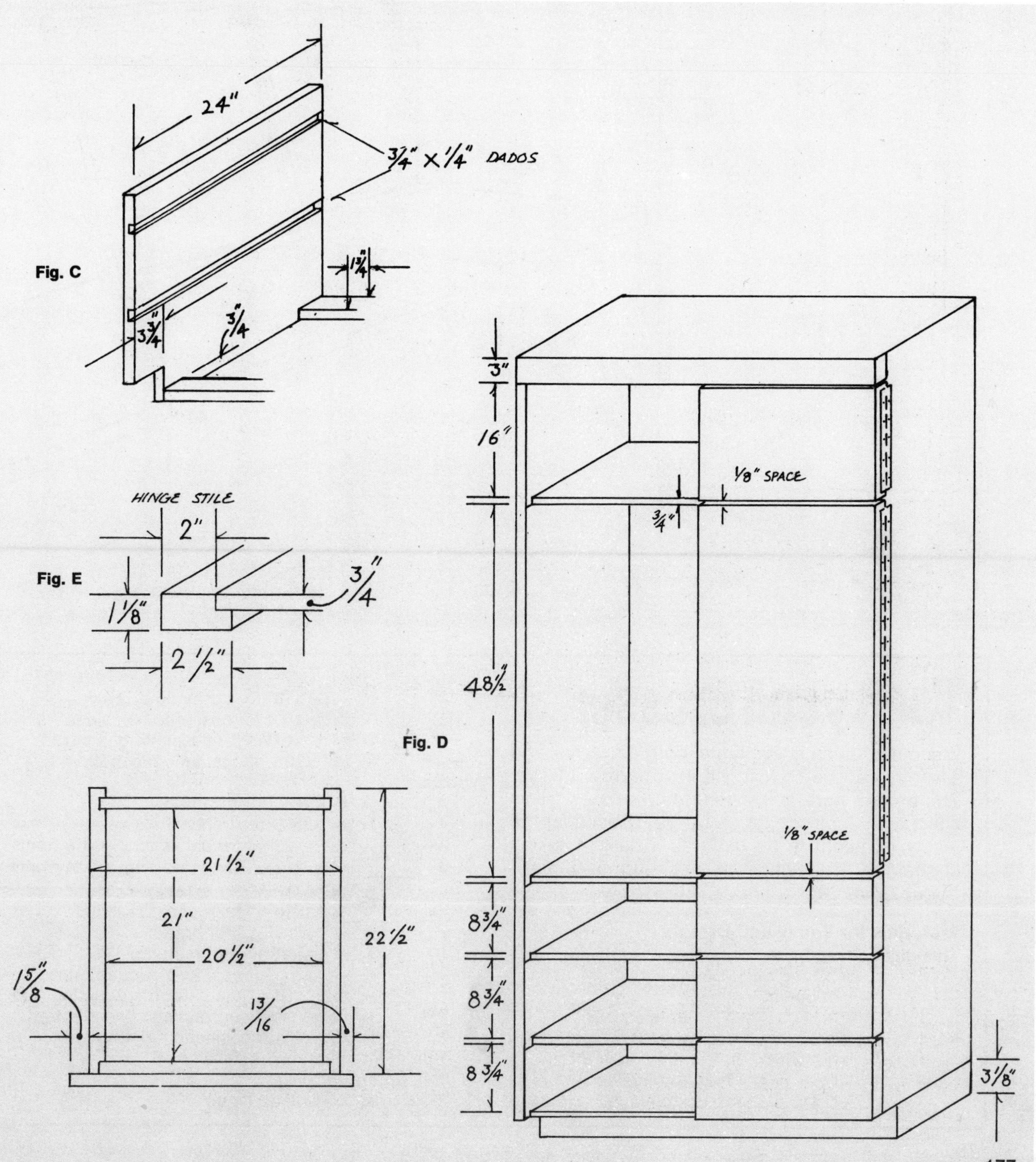

Fig. C

Fig. E

Fig. D

Vanity and Dresser

If enough space is available, both a dresser and a vanity can be built to fill in a narrow alcove. The project here is 8′4″ long, but it could be as short as 4′ or longer than 12′. Because the vanity is meant to be used as a desk, the unit should be no higher than a normal table—about 29″ or 30″.

Materials for Vanity and Dresser

Quantity	**Description**
3	¾″x17¼″x29¼″ for partition and ends of bureau
1	¾″x1¾″x48¾″ for top cleat
1	¾″x3½″x100″ for back top support
1	¾″x2″x48¾″ for front top support
2	¾″x1¾″x48¾″ for floor cleats
1	¾″x4″x50½″ for kick plate
2	¾″x4⅞″x18″ for cosmetic box sides
2	¾″x4⅞″x50″ for cosmetic box sides
1	¾″x4⅞″x17¼″ for cosmetic box partition
1	½″x17″x50″ for cosmetic box bottom
Drawers	
4	¾″x10″x25 1/16″ for fronts
4	¾″x4″x25 1/16″ for fronts
8	½″x9½″x22½″ for backs and inside fronts
6	½″x3½″x22½″ for backs and inside fronts
8	½″x9½″x16½″ for sides
6	½″x3½″x16½″ for sides
7	½″x15½″x22½″ for bottoms
1	¾″x19″x50½″ for bureau top
2	¾″x15″x24″ for cosmetic section tops
1	¾″x1½″x50½″ stock for top doubling
7′	¾″x1½″ stock for framing cosmetic top
1	¾″x3″x24″ for cosmetic top hinge rail
7 pr.	metal drawer guides
8	drawer pulls
2′	¾″x¾″ piano hinge

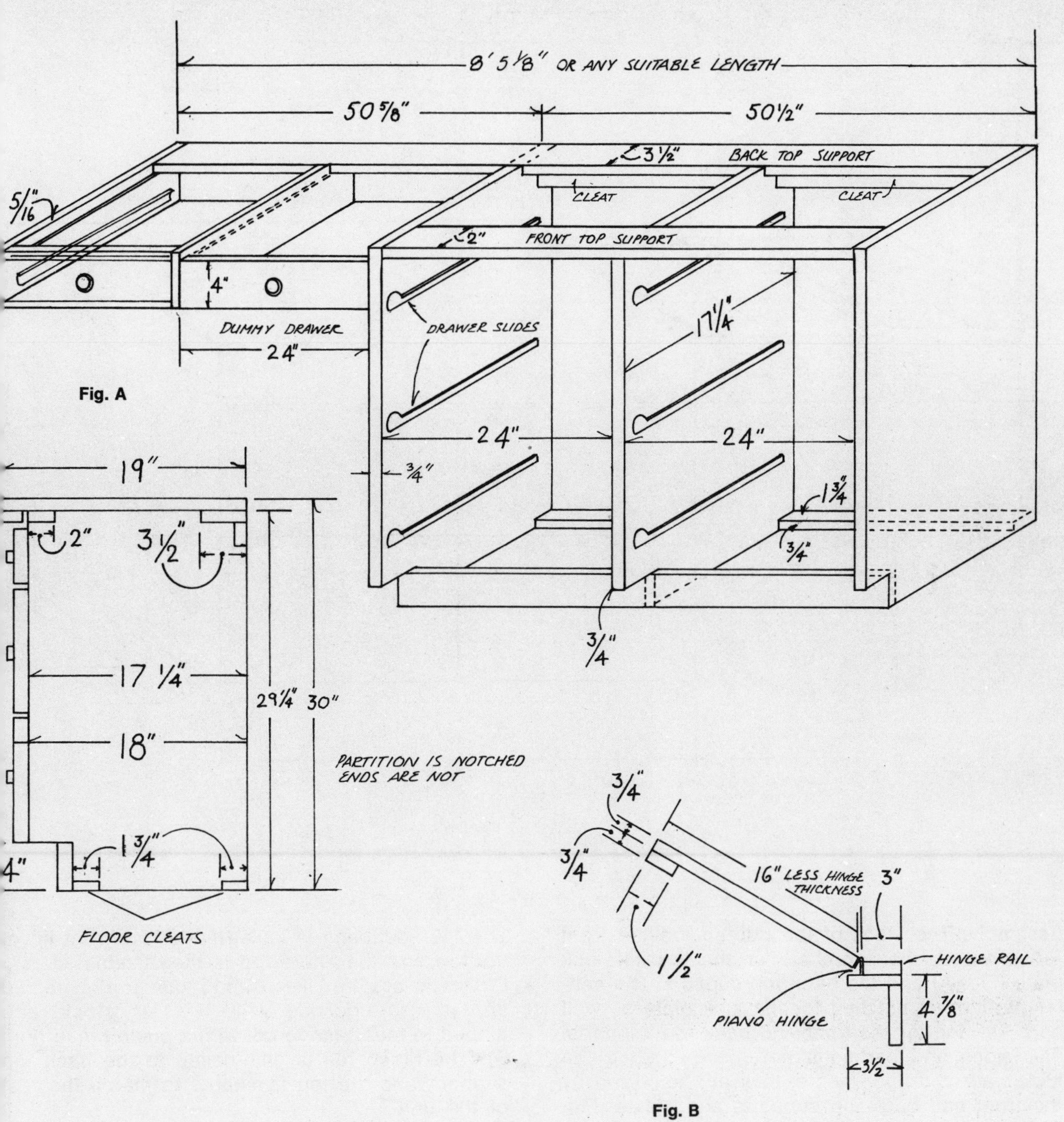

Fig. A

Fig. B

24" 24" 50 1/2"

3"

48 1/8"

19"

1 1/2"

1/8" FOR CLEARANCE
SPLIT IN THREE SPACES

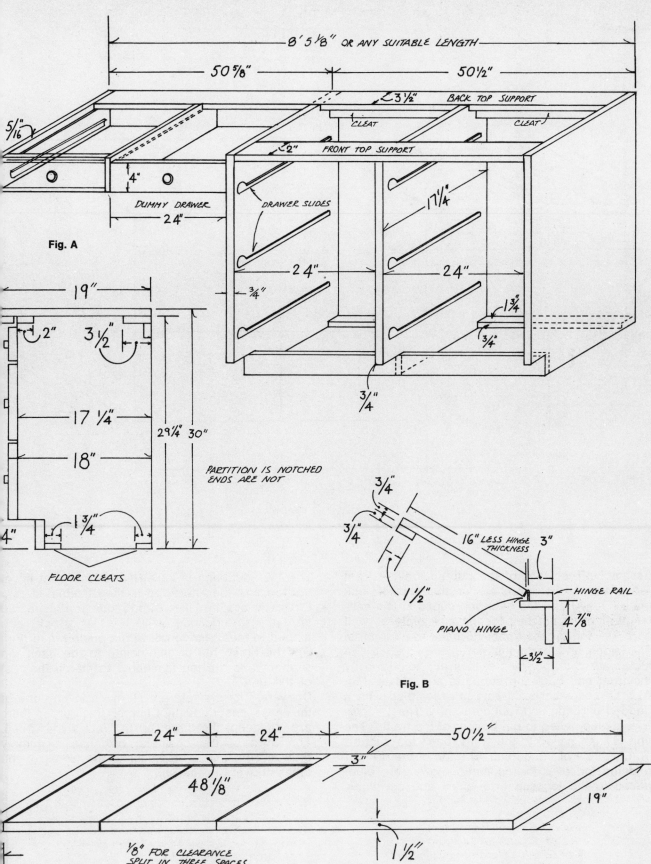

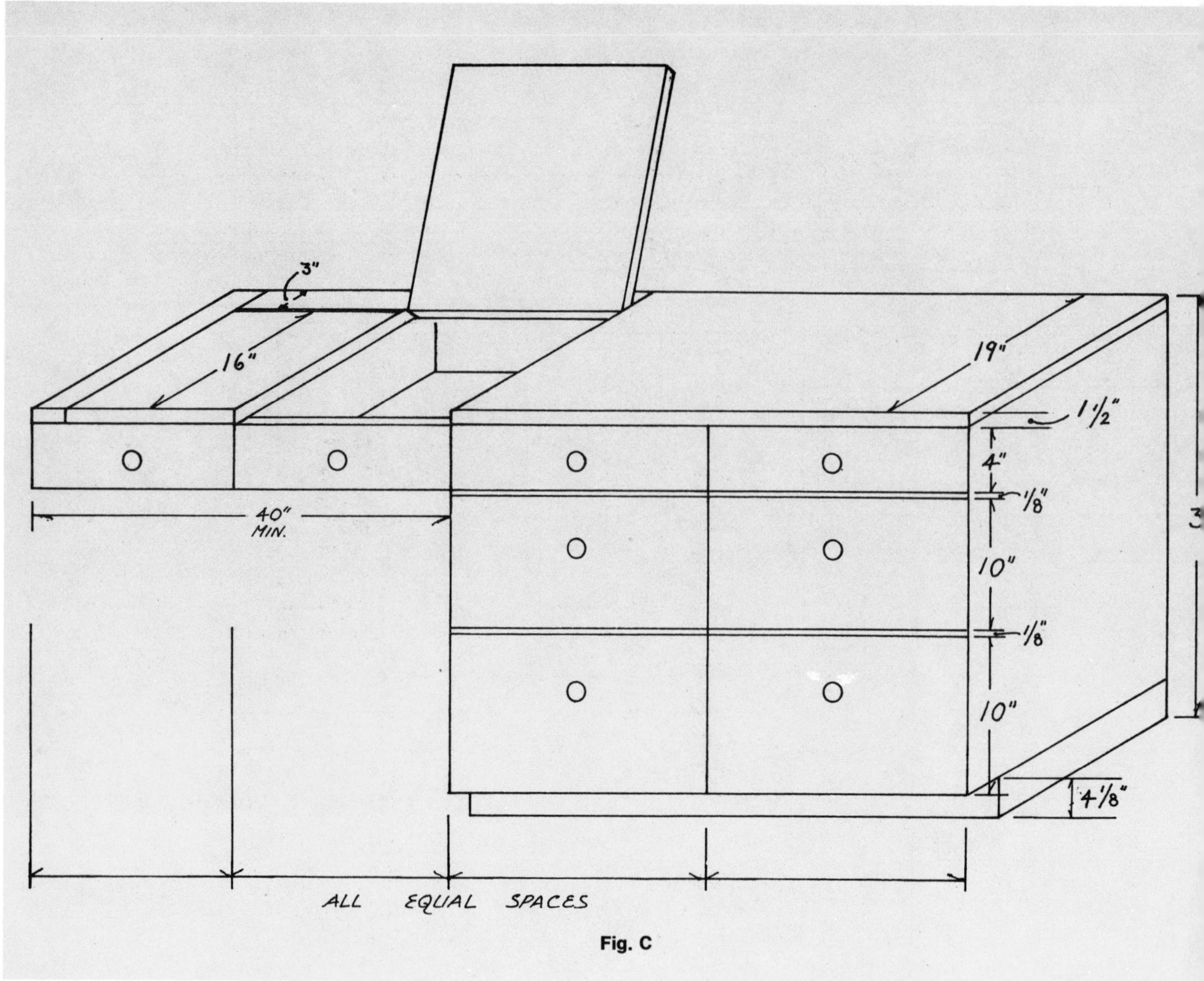

Fig. C

Assembly. The sides of the bureau are cut from ¾" plywood, then notched for the 3½"x4" kick plate (Fig. A) and the back top support. The center partition is notched for the kick plate as well as at the top for the front and back top supports. The sides and partitions are glue-nailed to the kick plate and floor cleats; they are stabilized by the front and back top supports and cleats (Fig. A). The cosmetic box frame is assembled with a dadoed partition and rabbeted ends. The ½" bottom is glue-nailed to the bottom of the frame. The unit is then nailed to the walls, back top support and left side of the bureau. The top of the dresser and the top over the cosmetic drawer are glue-nailed to the top supports, sides and partitions. The 1½" doubling is nailed under the front lip of the top and the entire top is then laminated.

Cosmetic box top. The ¾"x15"x24" top is framed around its underside with ¾"x1½" stock, and hinged to the 3" hinge rail with a piano hinge (Fig. B). The hinge rail is glue-nailed to the back top support, and the top laminated to match the rest of the unit.

Drawers. The drawers are all made in any one of the ways described in Chapter 6. Four of them are 10" deep; the three top drawers are 4" deep. The front of the cosmetic box has a dummy drawer front that is identical to the fronts of the other drawers in the unit.

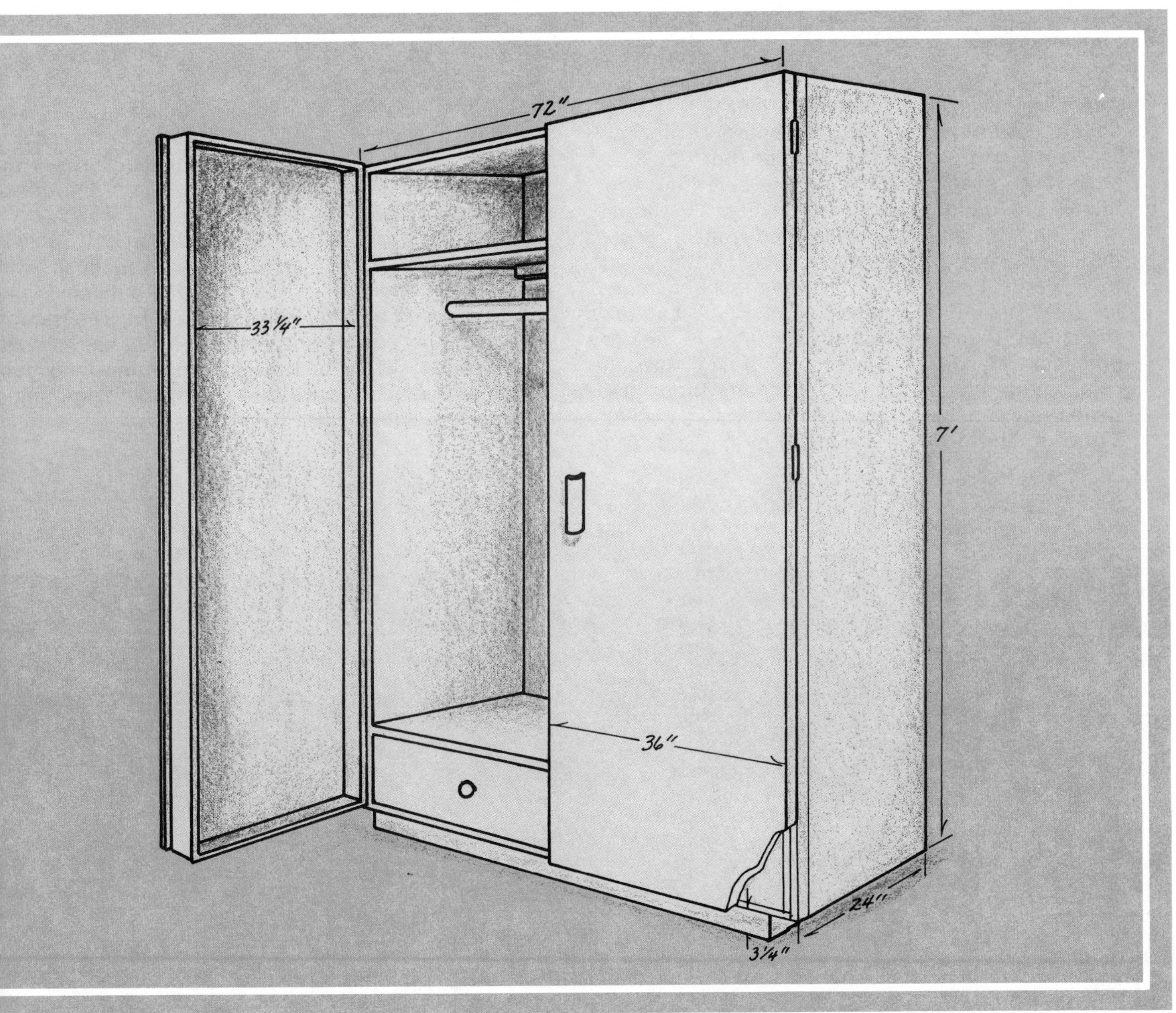

Master Bedroom Closet

Another way of providing a closet area without putting up drywalls is to build a separate unit like the one suggested here. It should be the height of the ceiling, or at least 7' high by 26½" deep by 6' wide, but it could take up the length of an entire wall, if more sections were added.

Materials for Master Bedroom Closet

Quantity	Description
2	¾"x22"x84" for closet sides
2	¾"x24"x71" for top and bottom
1	¾"x24"x83" for partition
4	¾"x24"x35⅜" for shelves
2	1⅛"x2½"x84" for hinge stiles
2	¼"x3'x84" for backs
21'	¾"x3¼" stock for base
2	¾"x2"x34⅞" for securing rails
Drawers	
38'	¾"x10½" stock for fronts, backs and sides
4	¼"x22"x31¾" for bottoms
Doors	
2	½"x36"x84" for door faces
4	1⅛"x2"x84" for door frame sides
4	1⅛"x2"x34" for door frame tops and bottoms
3 pr.	3½"x3½" for door butts
2	expandable clothing rods
4 pr.	drawer pulls

Assembly. All parts described in the materials list are cut from either ¾" pressboard or plywood. The base is a simple frame made from ¾"x3½" stock and measures 66"x23". The sides and partitions are dadoed as shown in Fig. B, and assembled with glue and nails. The front edges of the sides are faced by nailing a ¾"x2" hinge stile to a ¾"x2½" support rail, which has been routed for the front of the shelves (Fig. B). A back for the closet is optional, but it will certainly give the unit more stability if two pieces of ¼" Masonite are butted at the center partition, then glue-nailed to the back edges of the sides and shelves.

Drawers. The drawers are made by any construction method desired; each face measures 34½"x 10½". However, the ¾"x2½" stile supports require that the guides on the outside of the drawers be attached to ¾" spacers, so the width of the drawers becomes 32" (Fig. D).

Doors. Both doors are ½" plywood, cut 36"x84" and backed by a 2"-wide frame fitted flush with the top, bottom and hinged side, but leaving a ½" overhang on the latch side (Fig. E). The frames can support narrow shelves, dowels to hold shoes, full-length mirrors or hooks for hanging long garments. Both doors are hung from the hinge stiles using 3½"x3½" door butts.

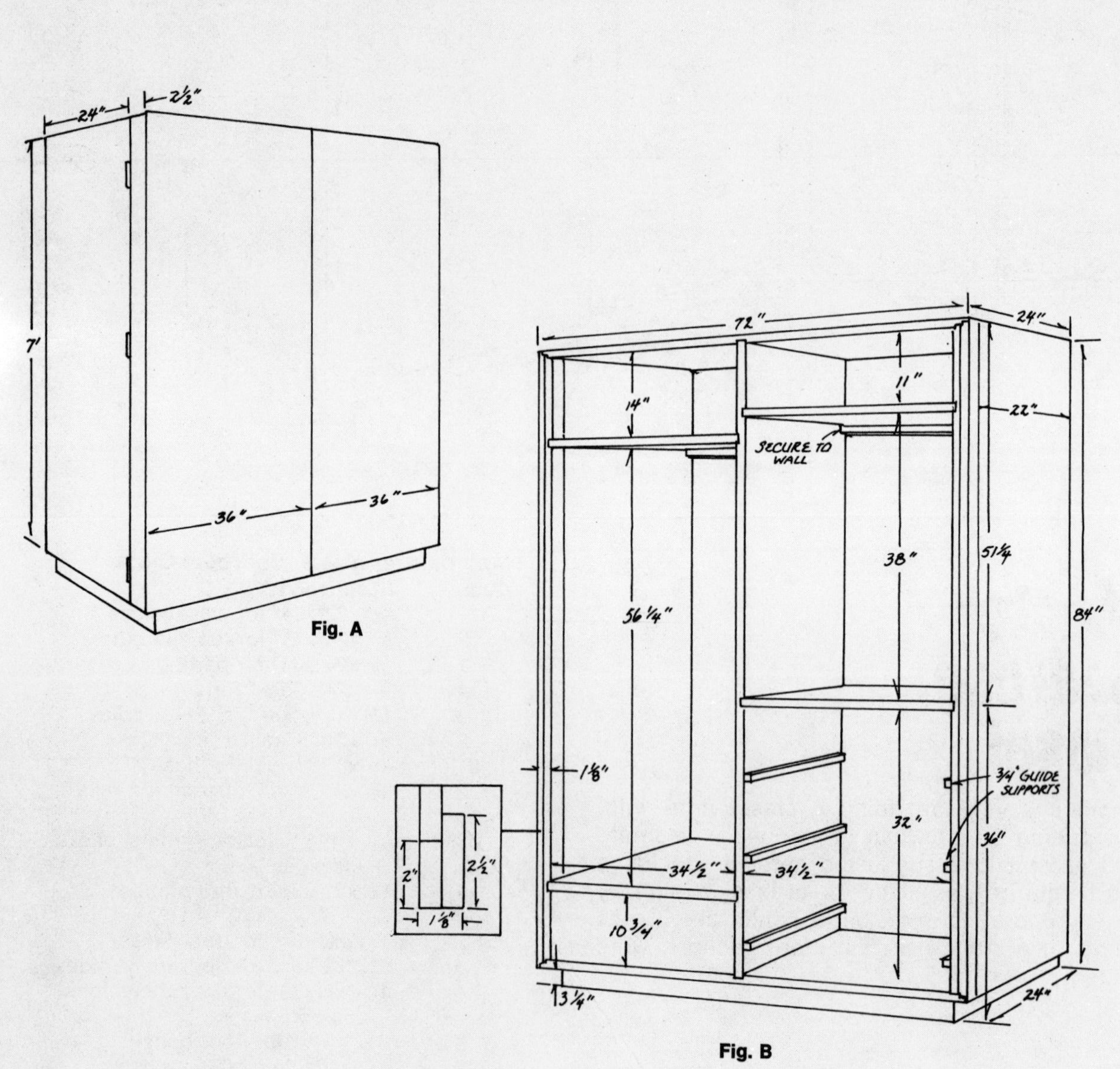

Fig. A

Fig. B

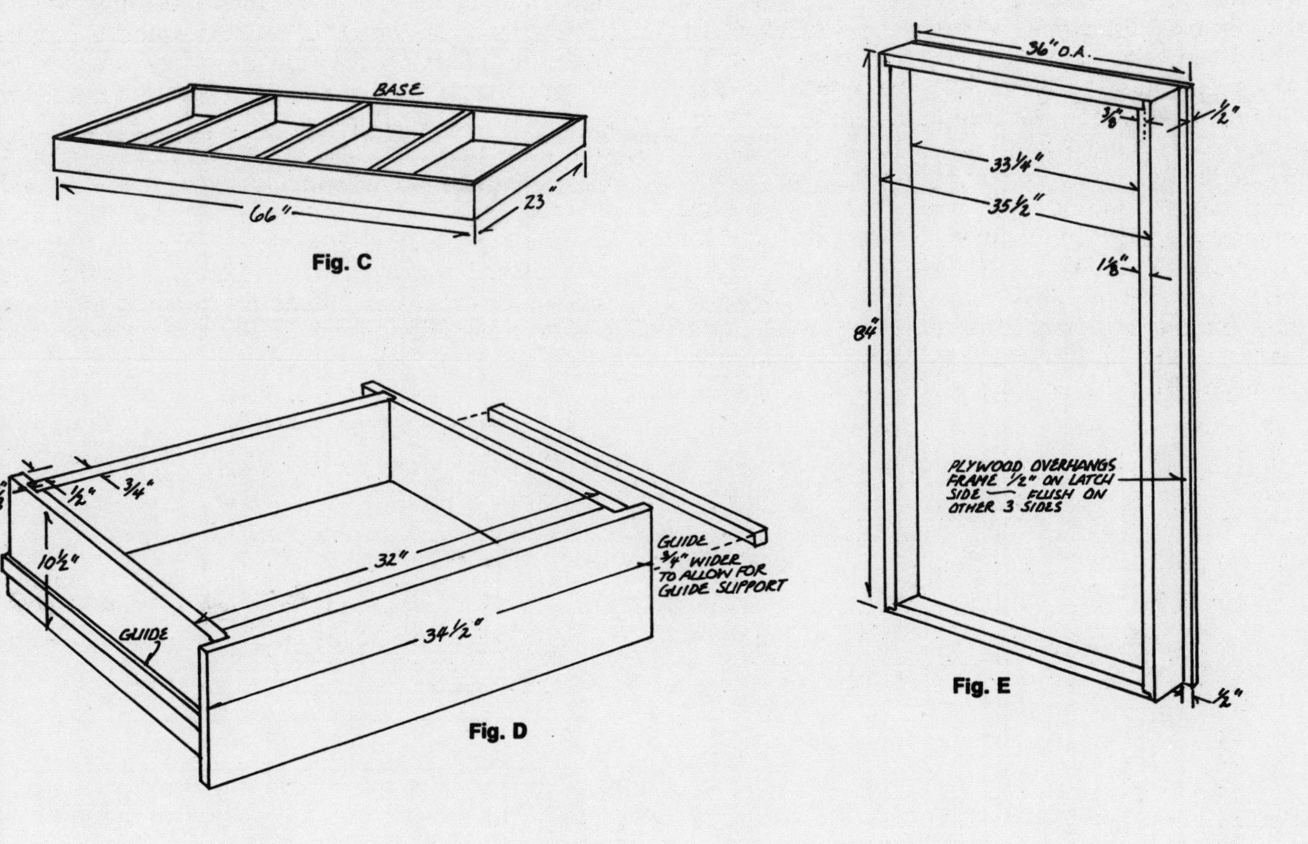
BASE
66"
23"
Fig. C
1/2"
3/4"
10 1/2"
32"
34 1/2"
GUIDE
GUIDE
3/4" WIDER TO ALLOW FOR GUIDE SUPPORT
Fig. D
36" O.A.
3/8"
1/2"
33 1/4"
35 1/2"
1 1/8"
84"
PLYWOOD OVERHANGS FRAME 1/2" ON LATCH SIDE — FLUSH ON OTHER 3 SIDES
Fig. E
1/2"

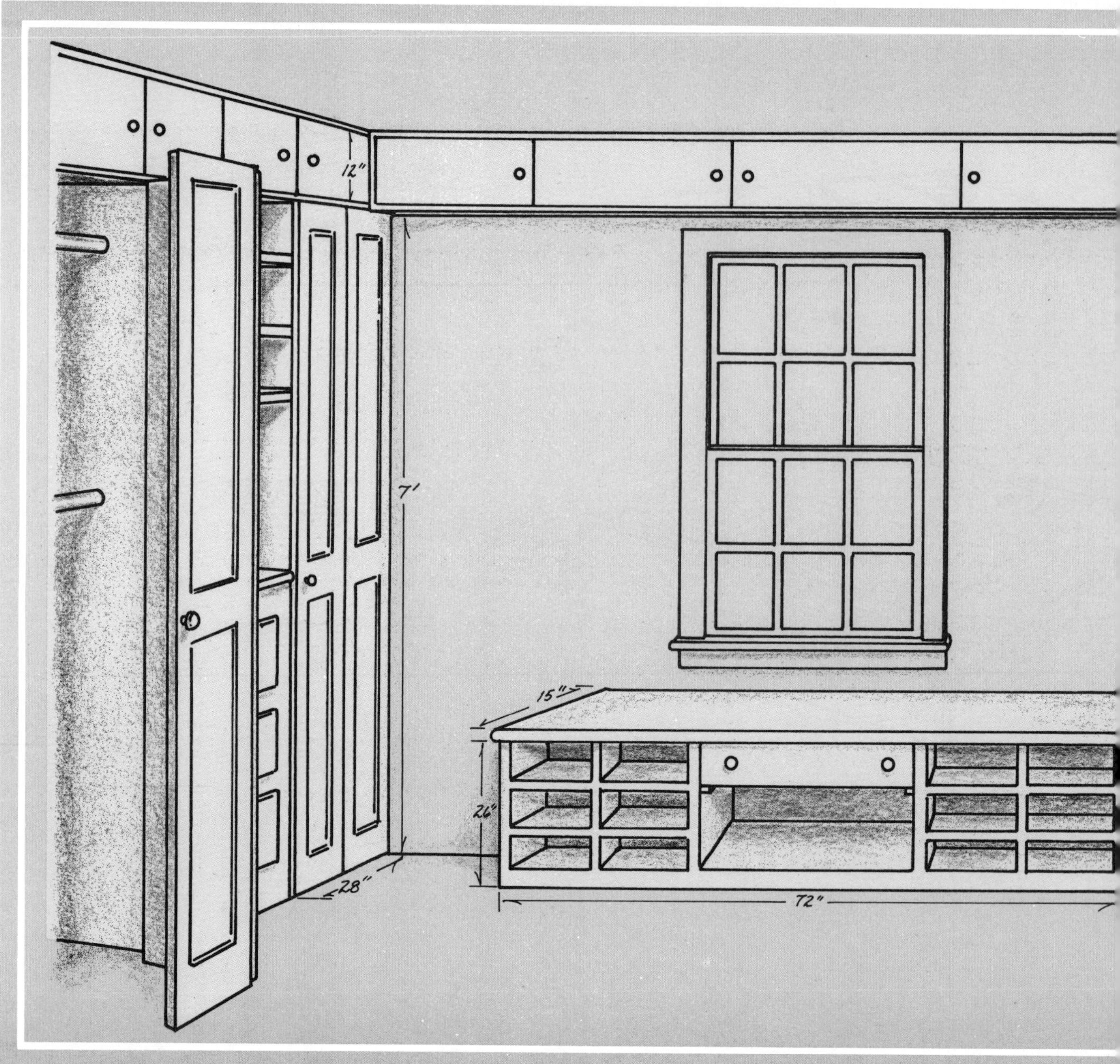

Walk-In Closet

Given enough space, a walk-in closet becomes not only a storage area, but a dressing room as well. For example, a small room measuring 7' wide by 8' high by 12' on its window side, can accommodate the complete haberdashery of two people, and still leave space for them to dress without bumping elbows.

Materials for Walk-In Closet

Quantity	**Description**
Window Seat	
1	¾"x16"x72" plywood for seat top
2	¾"x15"x26" for seat sides
2	¾"x15"x20¼" for partitions
4	¾"x15"x23¼" for shelves
6	¾"x6½"x15" for shelf partitions
1	¾"x16"x71" for bottom
1	¾"x3½"x70½" for kick plate
9'	¾"x½" cove or quarter round molding for top trim
Drawer	
1	¾"x6"x24" for front
1	½"x5½"x22" for back
1	¼"x22"x15½" for bottom
2	½"x5½"x15" for sides
1	14" set drawer tracks

One-side assembly (Figs. A and B). The partitions could be stud-and-wallboard walls, but it is easier and saves space if the walls are merely ¾" plywood panels divided in half. The two dividers are nailed to the floor 28" on center, and support a ¾"x24"x7' shelf that butts across their top edges, and is cleated at each end to the walls. A 1"x2" frame faces the front of the shelf, and is divided by verticals every 21". Three-quarter-inch plywood doors are hinged to the frame to close off the top shelf.

Double clothes poles are placed in the left closet for hanging shirts and jackets. The right closet has a single high pole for trousers with a shelf above the pole. Both closets may have hollow-core, louvered or plywood doors. Adjustable shelf tracks, 4' long, are attached to the partitions to hold ¾"x24"x28" shelves over the bureau. Construct a drawer face-frame between the partitions and make three drawers to fit.

Other side assembly (Figs. A and C). Again, ¾"x 16" plywood partitions are erected 30" from each wall, with 24" between them. Four-foot adjustable shelf tracks are attached to the partitions and a three-drawer bureau, 30" wide, is built under the shelves. The clothes closets are placed at right angles to the bureau and shelves. On the window side, the closet is 22"x48" (Figs. C and A) with two shelves above the single clothes pole. The doors are either sliding, or bi-fold louvers. The opposite

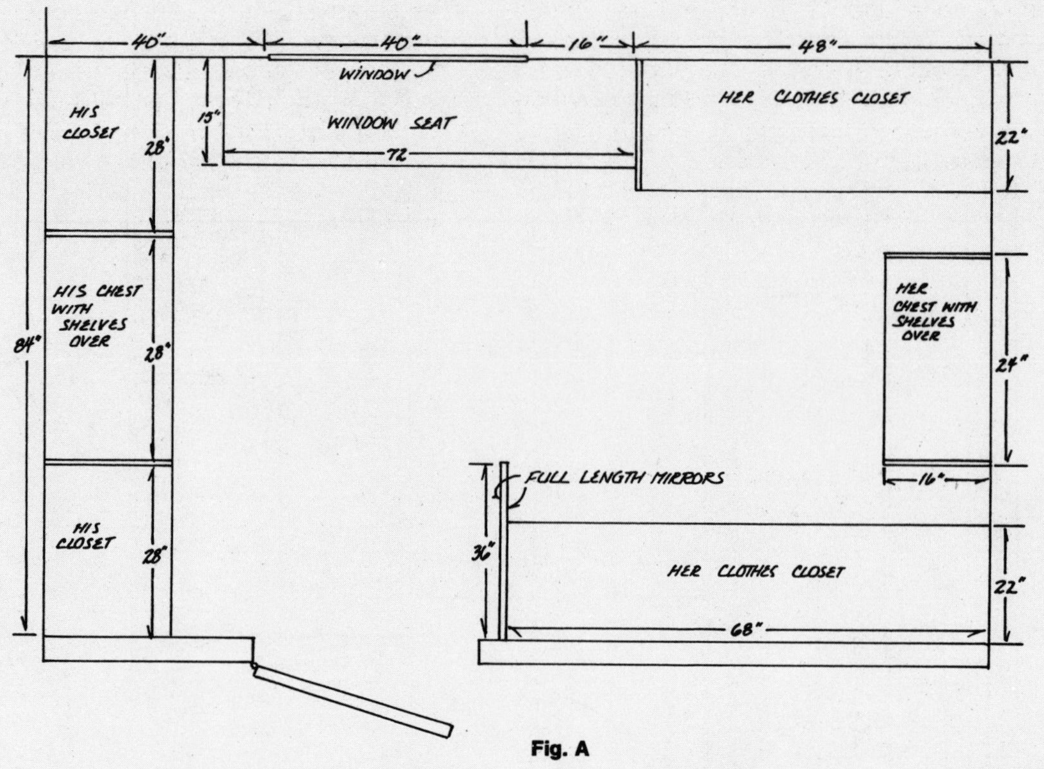

Fig. A

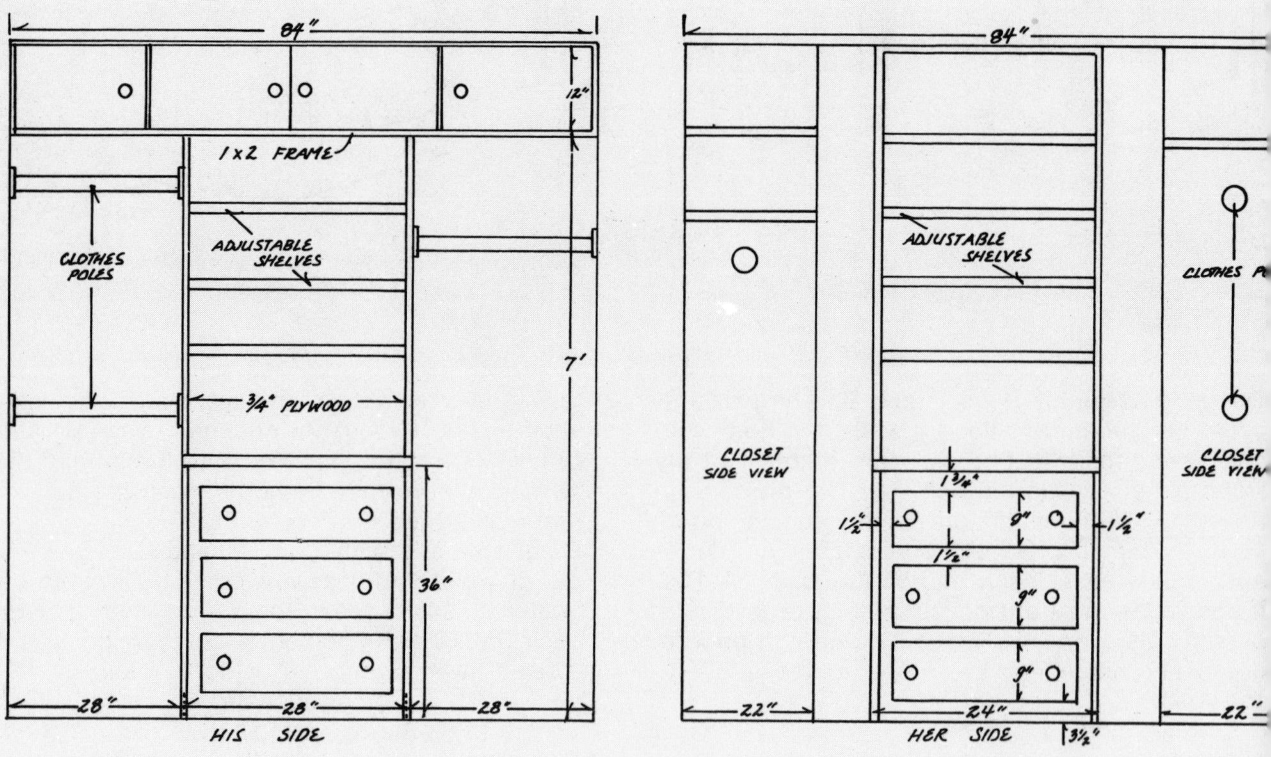

Fig. B

Fig. C

loset is 68″ long and 22″ deep, and has double lothes poles. This closet has doors compatible vith other closets in the room. The partition at the loset entrance end (Fig. A) is ¾″x36″x8′ plywood. 3oth sides of the partition hold full-length mirrors. **Vindow seat assembly** (Figs. A and D). The window)etween the two closets has a seat under which is ontained a drawer and compartments for shoes. he entire unit is constructed from ¾″ plywood as shown in Fig. E. All partitions are dadoed for the shelves. The 22½″x15″x6″ drawer is suspended by drawer guides and is used for shoe polish, brushes, etc. Three-quarter-inch molding is attached around the front and sides of the seat top.

A shelf is attached to the wall over the window (Figs. A and D), and is face-framed to accept sliding doors.

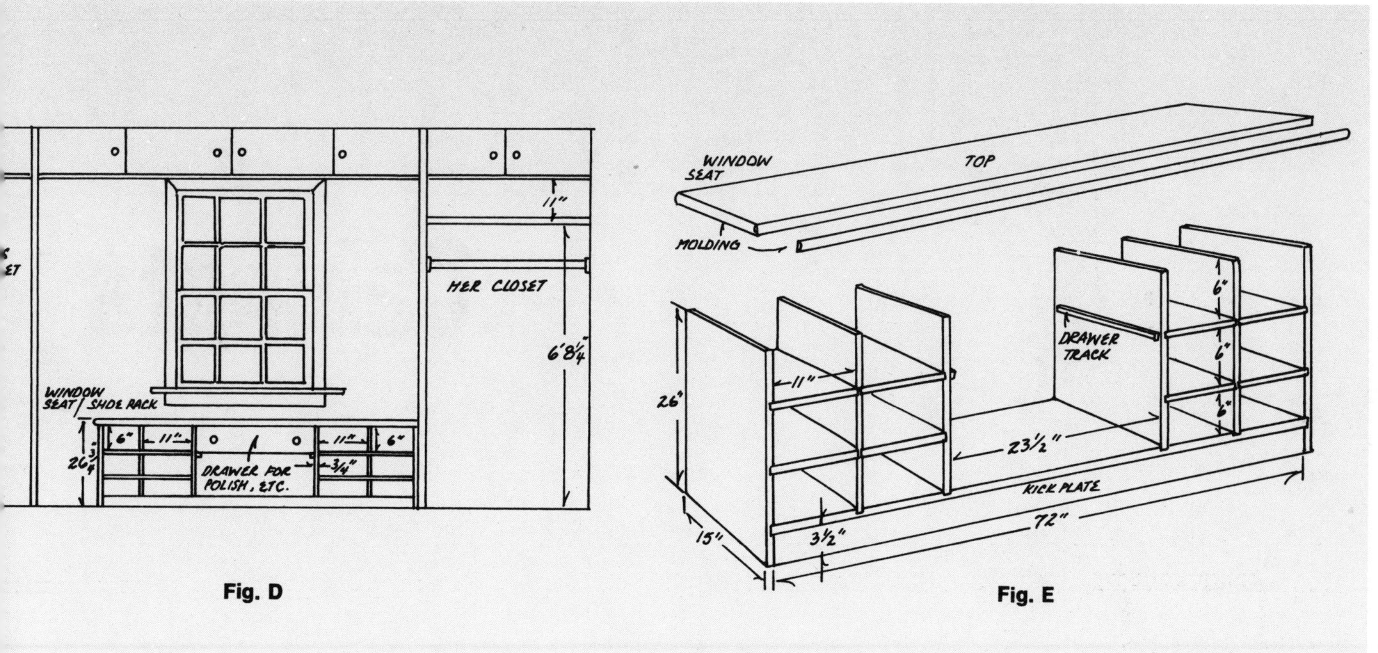

Fig. D

Fig. E

CHAPTER 12

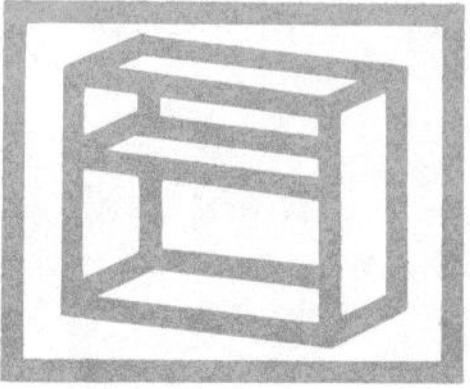
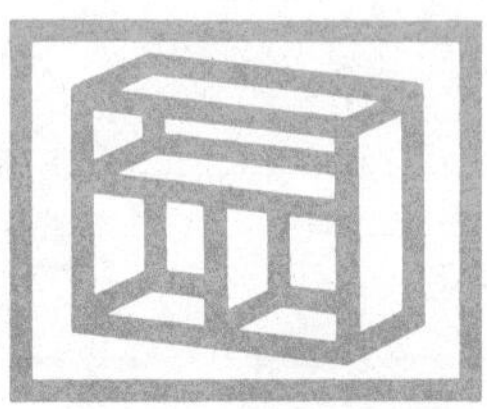
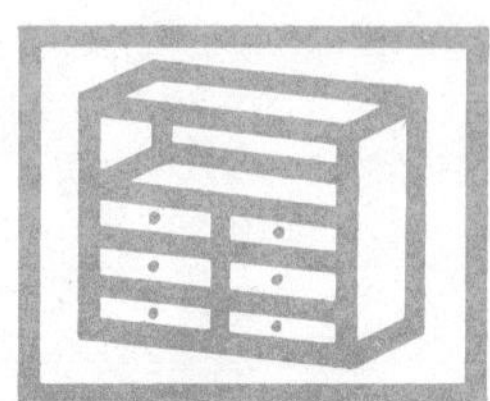

Cabinets

Cabinets

Cabinets come in many sizes and shapes, only a few of which are demonstrated by the projects included in this chapter. They can be a part of a separate piece of furniture, they can be built directly into a wall, or they can be freestanding. Very often, cabinets are hung on a wall or from a ceiling, and there are several methods for hanging a cabinet. Nevertheless, how a cabinet is hung is considerably influenced by the wall or the ceiling itself, its composition and general condition.

Angle irons. These can be the big, bracket-type of L-shaped support that extends down the wall, well below the bottom of the cabinet. They are decorative, but tend to have some spring in them. To keep the unit from bouncing every time anyone passes by it, attach a small angle iron to the top of the unit. If you do not want the angle irons to show, use smaller ones both under the bottom and attached to the top of the unit.

Rails. If the cabinet does not have a back, or if there is at least a 1½" or 2" space directly under the top, a rail made from 1"x2" stock can be solidly attached to the wall. The cabinet can then slide over the rail and be secured by screws driven into it through the top.

Shelf tracks. Shelf tracks are made for shelves, but they are certainly strong enough to hold some types of cabinets. Track braces can be purchased up to 18" in length, so a reasonably deep cabinet can be placed on them.

Solid back. If you plan to attach a cabinet directly to a wall and let all of its weight be held by the back, it is best to make the back out of ¾" stock. With a back that strong, you can drill through it for screws, mollies or lead plugs, even nail it to the wall.

Joist hangers. When hanging a cabinet from a ceiling, locate the joists and use them for support. You can hang the cabinet from chains, metal straps or rods, but all of these should be attached to the *side* of the joist, not to its bottom edge. Another method is to

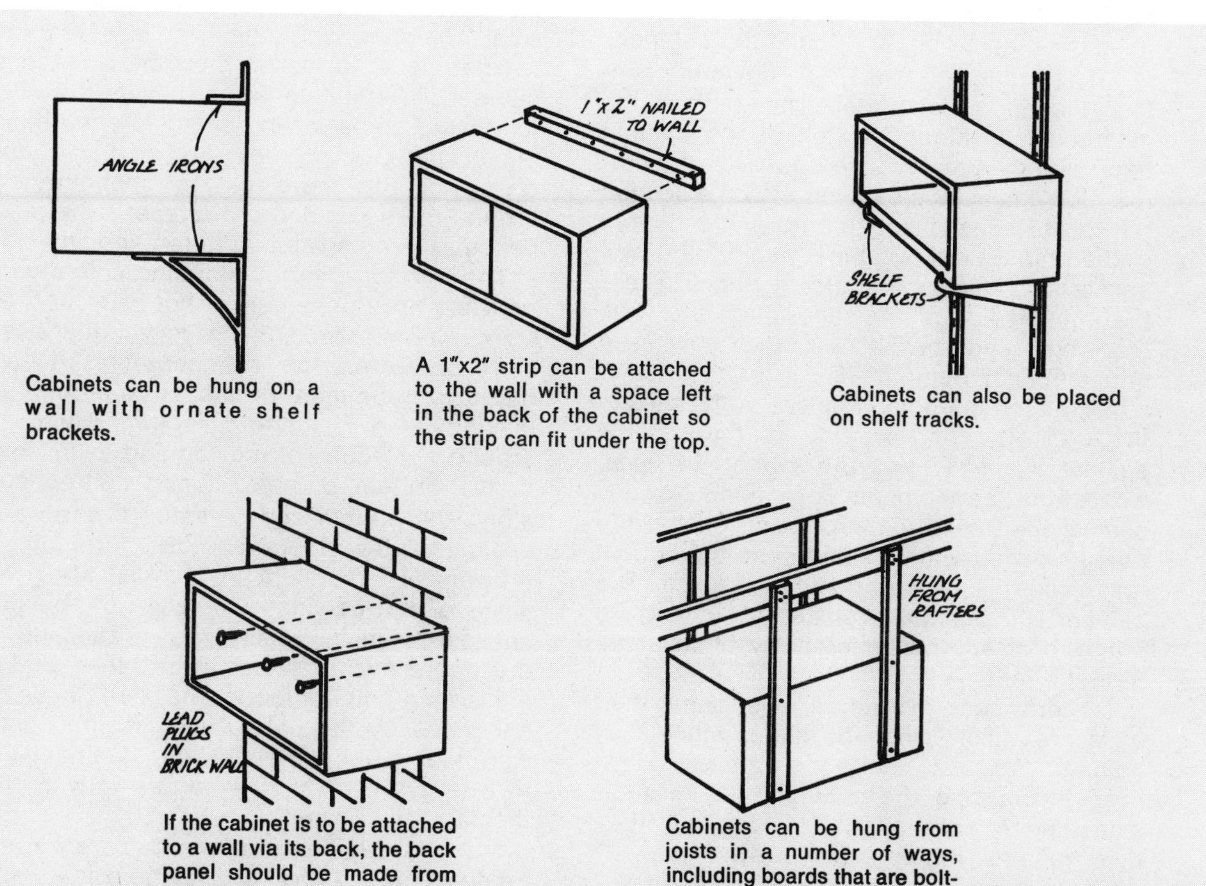

Cabinets can be hung on a wall with ornate shelf brackets.

A 1"x2" strip can be attached to the wall with a space left in the back of the cabinet so the strip can fit under the top.

Cabinets can also be placed on shelf tracks.

If the cabinet is to be attached to a wall via its back, the back panel should be made from ¾" stock.

Cabinets can be hung from joists in a number of ways, including boards that are bolted to the joist and cabinet.

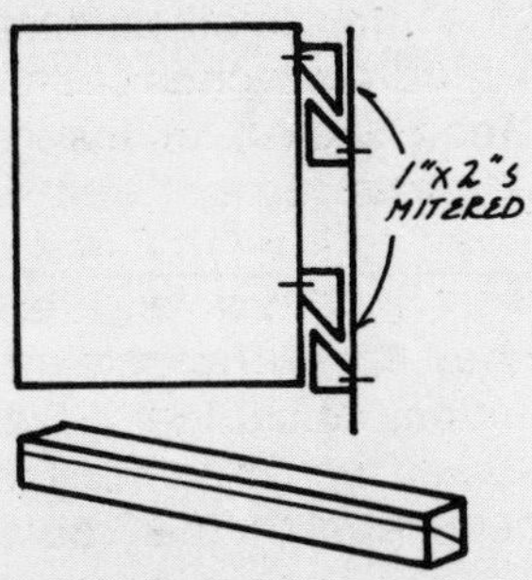

1"x2" strips are cut down the center at a 45° angle. The top half of the pieces are attached to the back of the cabinet and the bottom half to the wall.

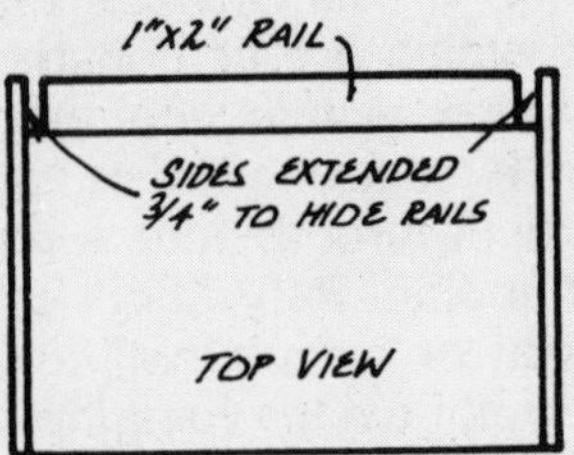

In order to hide the 1"x2" hanging rails, inset the cabinet back ¾".

bolt strips of ¾"-thick wood to the joists and the sides of the cabinet. To do this, however, the dimensions of the cabinet will have to approximate the measurements of the space between the joists. That distance will probably be 16" or a multiple of 16". Make certain by measuring the space between the joists before you begin to build the cabinet.

Mitered rails. Rip two 1"x2"s down the center at a 45° miter. Attach one-half of the mitered stock along the top of the cabinet back with the pointed side down and the narrow side against the cabinet. Attach a second rail in the same manner across the bottom of the unit. Hold the cabinet against the wall and level it, then mark with a pencil where the pointed tips of the rails touch the wall. Mark both ends of the rails (they may be a little crooked). Using nails, screws, toggles or plugs, attach the bottom halves of the rails to the wall. The narrow side of the rails is against the walls and the top of the side, where the bevel begins, is lined exactly against the pencil marks. Now slide the top rails (attached to the cabinet) into the bottom rails. You will be surprised how solidly the cabinet will remain in place. Yet it can be removed at any time merely by lifting it up from the rails on the wall.

The drawback to mitered rails is that their ends are visible from the sides, since they hold the cabinet ¾" away from the wall. However, by building the cabinet with its sides extending ¾" past the back, you can effectively hide the rail ends from view.

The nature of a cabinet is such that it usually presents an appearance somewhat different from that of shelves, or a shelf case. For one thing, a cabinet usually has doors, and, at first glance, seems to be a completely enclosed box. Here again, there is a need to break the visual monotony of a basically square, flat-edged unit. And there are plenty of ways to provide this curved relief. With a small, hanging unit, the trim used can be smaller, less obtrusive, than on a standing cabinet. A ¼" beading that covers the edge joints and corners can do wonders in changing the look of any box. Add to this simple curve slightly more ornate configurations around the doors and drawers, and the piece becomes a completely different-looking unit.

The trim for a larger, standing unit, can be heavier, more prominent in both size and design. In other words, the larger the piece, the more ornate can be the decoration. It does not have to be more ornate, but the option of making it so is there. This trim can come around the edges of the top and even down to the bottom corners. It can be repeated along the bottom and reflected in the panel design of the doors and the face of the drawers. There might be scrolls, and even some of the carvings that can now be purchased in many lumberyards, attached to the doors and drawers; these alone are an interesting point of focus. They can be further enhanced by the careful use of good hardware that is both functional and distinguished in the style in which it carries forward the theme of the design.

Often, a cabinet is dramatic merely by its presence in a room, or by where it is positioned. In this case, it becomes almost superfluous for the unit to be anything other than a simple box. A case in point is the kitchen hanger project in this section. The hanger is meant to hang from the ceiling above a peninsula or island. There it is, right in the middle of the ceiling, and with solid doors or thick shelves, it will have the effect of a wall divider, severing the room into separate compartments. Build it with glass shelves, or at least thinner, ½"-thick shelving, and give it glass doors on both sides (or no doors at all), and it becomes a decorative, although still functional, addition to the room as a whole. So, before slapping yards of ogees, crowns, casings and coves all over a cabinet, think about where the unit will be located, and the effect it will have on the entire room just by being there. It is also a good idea to build a cabinet and install it for a few days without any trim or enhancements, then live with it for a time until you can decide whether you like it the way it is, or whether it needs something to make it look better, or different.

All of the trim suggestions that apply to shelves and shelf cases are applicable to cabinets (see the introductory comments for Chapter 10—*Shelves*). With freestanding cabinets, the kick plates can be constructed in the same manner as they are with shelf cases, and so can the baseboard notches. There is, however, a slightly different problem when making a baseboard-notch for cabinets.

The base of a cabinet, for any number of reasons, may need to fully cover the back edges of the cabinet. This means that if the unit must also fit around a baseboard, some maneuvering will have to be done at the bottom rear edge of the unit. Cabinets do have the advantage of being deeper than most shelf cases; it is therefore possible to simply inset the back in dadoes so that the back extends all the way to the floor *in front* of the molding, then notch the backs to go around the baseboard. If this arrangement is undesirable, the notch must first be cut in the sides and it should be made deep enough to include the thickness of the back. Thus, if the baseboard is ¾" thick, and the back of the cabinet is ¼" plywood, the notch must be 1" in depth. Presuming that the height of the baseboard is 6", the notch will also be 6". But the backing must be as long as the cabinet is wide, and 6¾" high. The top corners of the back are then notched so that the top ¾" of wood will extend up inside the cabinet, ¾" above the notch. The upper part of the back is cut only wide enough to meet the top side of the notch. When the cabinet is assembled, the bottom piece is fitted from side to side with its ¾" tab overlapping the bottom edge of the top half of the back. The space between the two backs is filled with a strip of wood ¾" square.

That is a lot of work just to get around a piece of baseboard, but there is no avoiding it if the cabinet is to have a full back. If it does not need a back at the baseboard level, the backing can merely stop at the top of the

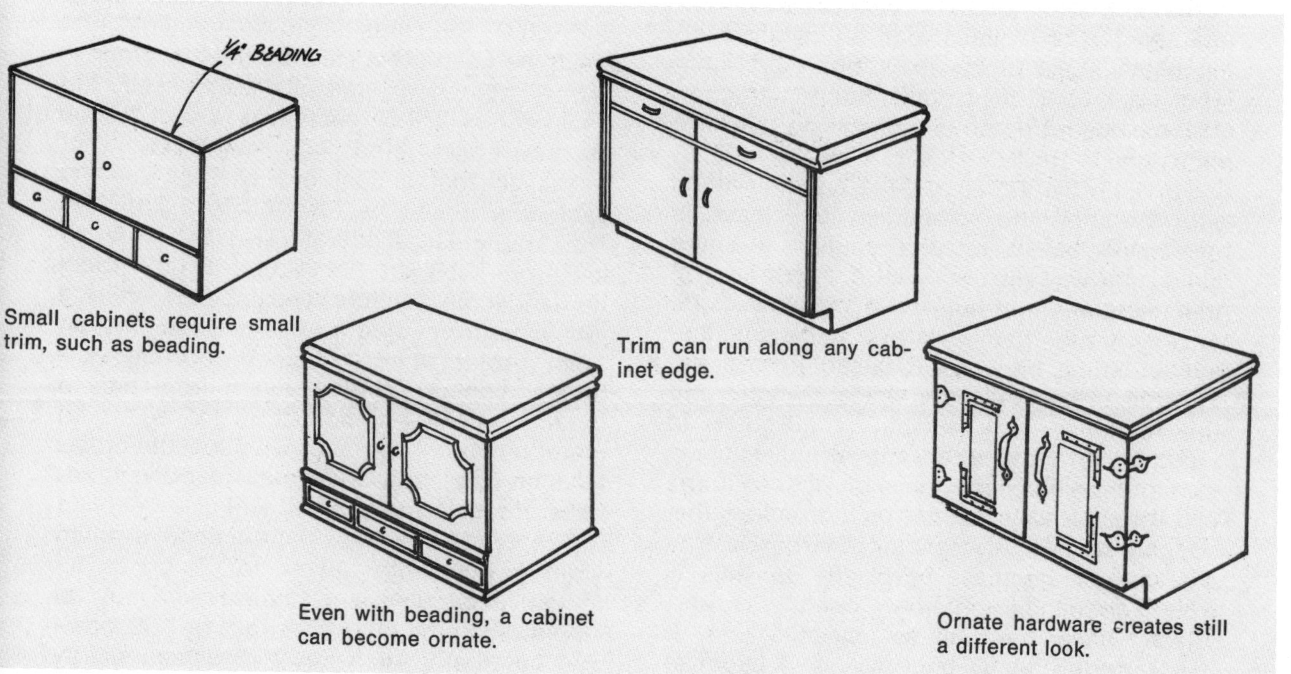

Small cabinets require small trim, such as beading.

Even with beading, a cabinet can become ornate.

Trim can run along any cabinet edge.

Ornate hardware creates still a different look.

Cabinets can be hung from joists; they almost seem to "float."

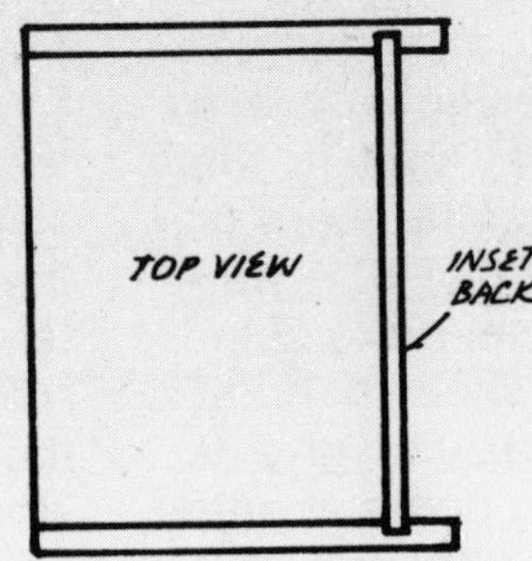

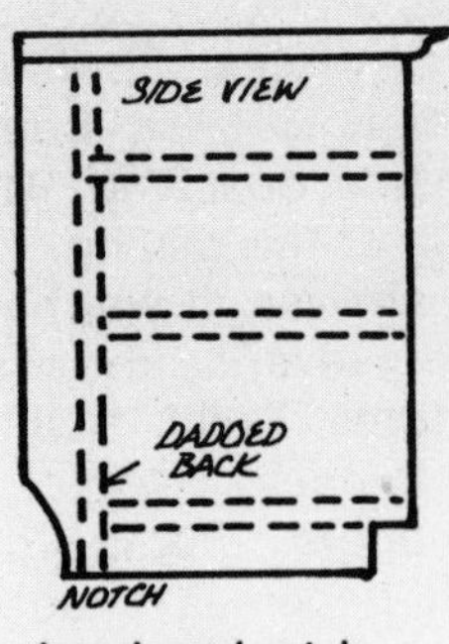

Backs can be inset to allow for the baseboard notch.

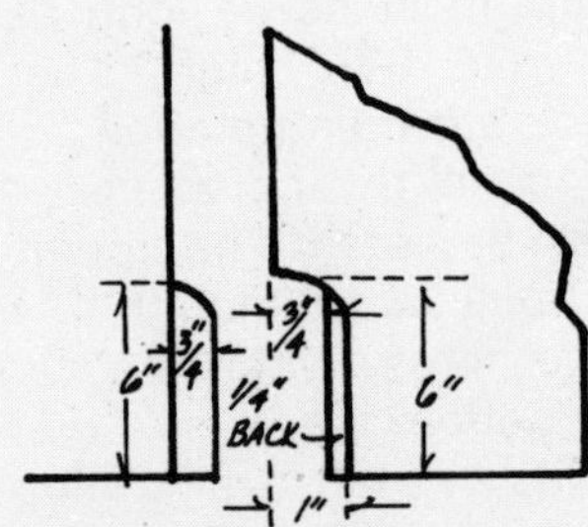

Notches can be cut to fit exactly around the particular baseboard.

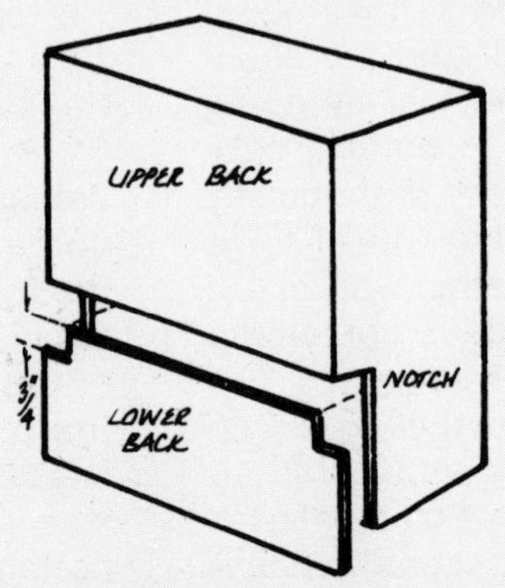

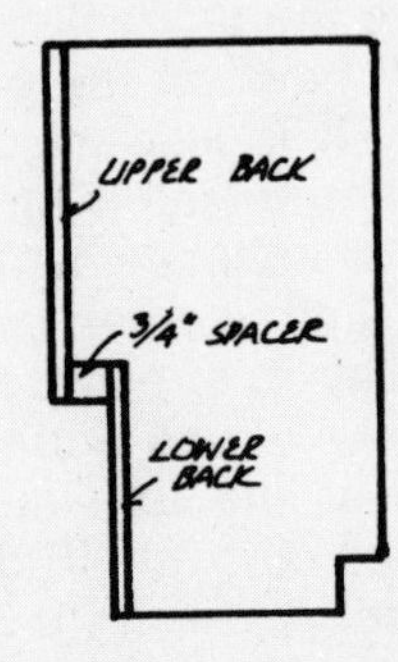

A baseboard assembly can be constructed by attaching two backs between a spacer.

notch and the rest of the unit be left open. This might happen in a situation where the baseboard is less than 4" high and the bottom shelf of the cabinet can be installed immediately above it as well as form the bottom of the kick plate. Essentially, the construction of a baseboard notch is identical to that of a kick plate.

For all of its variations, the cabinet, along with the shelf and sometimes the closet, is but one element of that unique structure called the wall divider. Wall dividers can be thin partitions that support a piece of cloth, or they can be half-walls of a more substantial structure. They are devised from metal and plastic as well as wood and cloth, and they can have any number of purposes in addition to that of attractively dividing a room. Some dividers can be purchased in the form of pipes which in turn hold brackets that support either shelves or small cabinets. The shelves can be glass or plastic as well as wood, depending on how "open" the purchaser wishes the room to appear.

A room divider is normally used because the space it separates is a large one. If it is large enough, the divider becomes an opportunity to provide different kinds of storage and, given the three basic components of a shelf, a closet and a cabinet, there are countless combinations that can be devised. The final project in this section is a wall divider that is constructed with adjustable shelf tracks so that almost any type of shelf or cabinet unit can be inserted in the divider. That particular divider is also 24" wide, allowing it to be used on either, or both, sides for handsome furniture-type cabinets, shelves, tables, drawers and so on. It is an "adjustable" project that is planned so changes in its components can be made from time to time. However, it could just as well be a complete, unchangeable unit with specific places for a stereo and television, bookshelves, perhaps a desk and even a closet.

The construction of a permanent wall divider begins with the same principles followed in building any dry wall. In must be framed in some manner, either by solid vertical members, or with 2"x3" framing; the

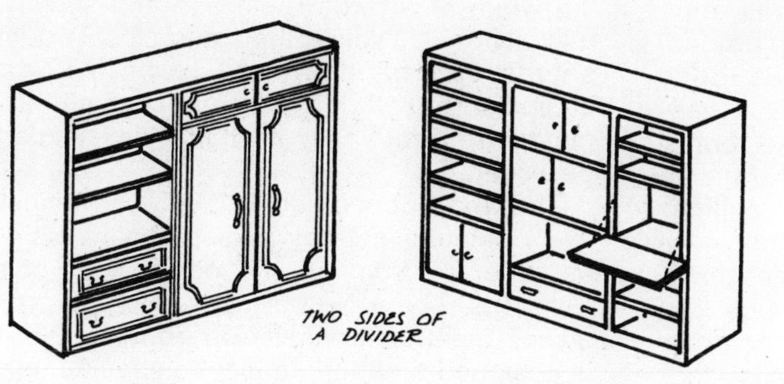

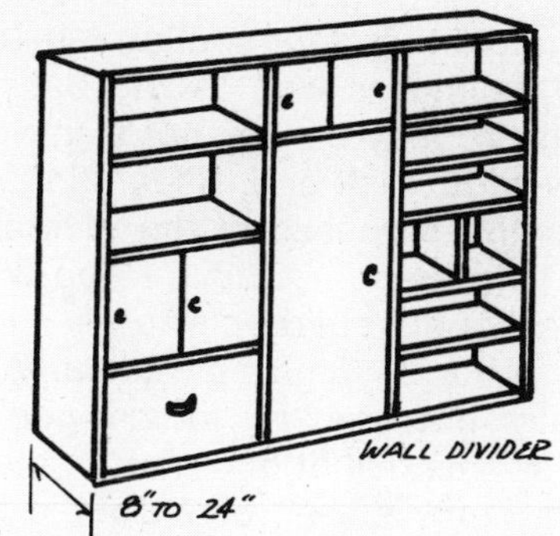

Wall dividers can be subdivided to hold practically anything.

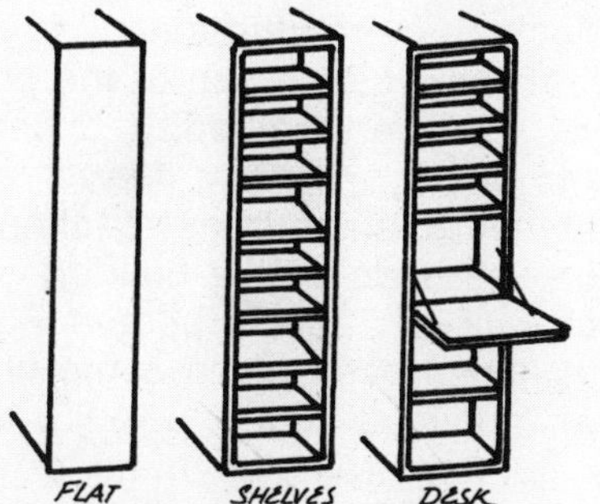

The end of a wall divider offers useful space that can be employed in many ways.

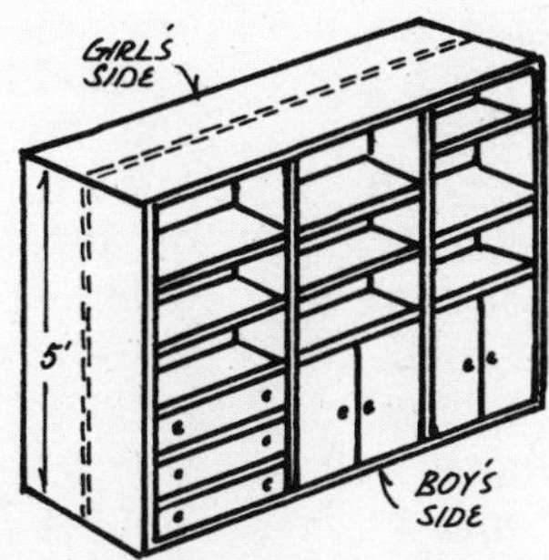

A child's room can be sectioned with a wall divider that offers separate storage units for each youngster.

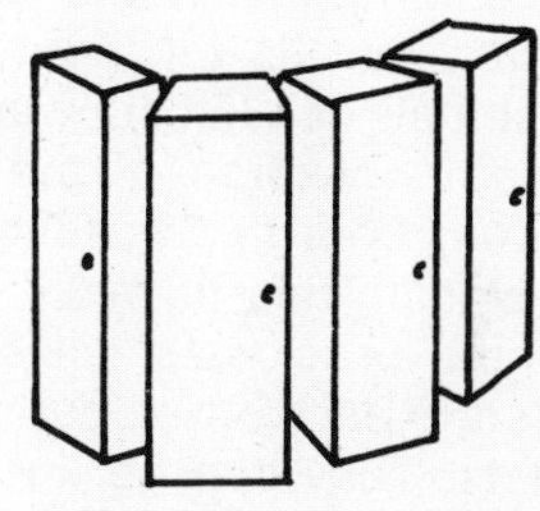

Room dividers can even be separate units hinged together to form several different configurations.

verticals are united by rigid horizontal rails at the floor and the ceiling and, if possible, somewhere in the middle. The width of the divider is optional but if it is to serve as a bookcase, it will need to be at least 8" deep. For cabinets, the depth must be from 12" to 24". If there is to be a clothes closet, the minimum interior depth has to be 22".

Having determined the height by the distance from the floor and the ceiling (assuming the divider is room height), and the depth by what components will be fitted into the divider, nothing changes. If the unit has shelves, they are assembled in the same manner as for any large bookcase. If it is to contain cabinets, each one must be cut and fitted in the same way cabinets are always assembled. Their doors will still be made and hinged in the time-honored way doors and drawers are always made. The closet will need a partition or two; there must be clothes poles and perhaps even shelves, but it is made just as if it were any standing unit.

The finished appearance of the divider is vital to the entire room. Conceivably, one side of the unit could have, say, the formality of a house entranceway, while the other side reflects the casual atmosphere of a family room. It is not outlandish to consider two entirely different forms of trim and molding for the opposite sides of a wall divider. It is, after all, at least a half a wall and as with walls everywhere, its opposite sides can easily face quite different room decors. One side might support kitchen cabinets, faced with a light, airy molding, while the other side continues the heavy Spanish design of the dining room. The problem of coordinating the two arises in the middle of the free end of the divider, where the decoration of one room ends, and that of the other begins.

Usually, the very end of a divider is treated as if it were a doorway and is left pretty much as a flat, unobtrusive if rather narrow, wall (or very wide half an archway). Under certain circumstances, it might be used as an end closet, or serve to support a small fold-down writing desk, or even be a narrow tier of shelves.

But no matter what the decor of the rooms

it divides may be, a room divider—if it is a floor-to-ceiling unit—constitutes a wall, and it should therefore continue the crown around the ceiling as well as the baseboards. Both of these may or may not transverse that narrow-width wall end, depending on the rooms and the purposes of the divider.

Dividers do not have to be floor to ceiling. In a double children's room, they might only be 5′ or 6′ high, particularly if the unit's main purpose is to provide storage for toys. This height of 5′ or 6′ is also a good one if the unit is used as a double bookcase that separates conversational areas in a living room. In a kitchen, dining or family area, the divider can itself be divided with its bottom half ending at around 36″ to serve as a counter, and its top portion becoming a set of cabinets for kitchenware.

Another version of the room divider that has considerable versatility is the hinged cabinet-closet. This is really a series of narrow cabinets or closets, all with doors, and all hinged to each other, but standing at different heights. They can be lined up along a wall. They can be set in a circle and become a pillar of storage. They can be placed at odd angles to each other and partially divide a room. They can be stretched partway across the width of a large room and still successfully divide it. The cabinets and closets themselves can be designed to hold sports equipment, a wine cellar, a bar, clothing, glassware, practically anything that needs to be stored.

The world of cabinets is infinite. Practically every cabinet that any person constructs will be different from all the others that come from the home workshop—which is what makes them so gratifying to construct. Each is designed and built to meet a specific need.

Here again, in this section the projects offered are meant to be suggestions to the builder who is thrashing out a storage problem and needs "one more little touch" to the cabinet he wants to create. Each of the projects that follow can be modified, and decorated in dozens of ways. And so they should be, for the cabinet is, aside from its inherent utility, a statement made by the builder. And that statement can only have a personal signature on it if it has been given some final, very particular individual touch, a touch that stamps it as coming from the hand of the builder and displays his particular talent as a cabinetmaker.

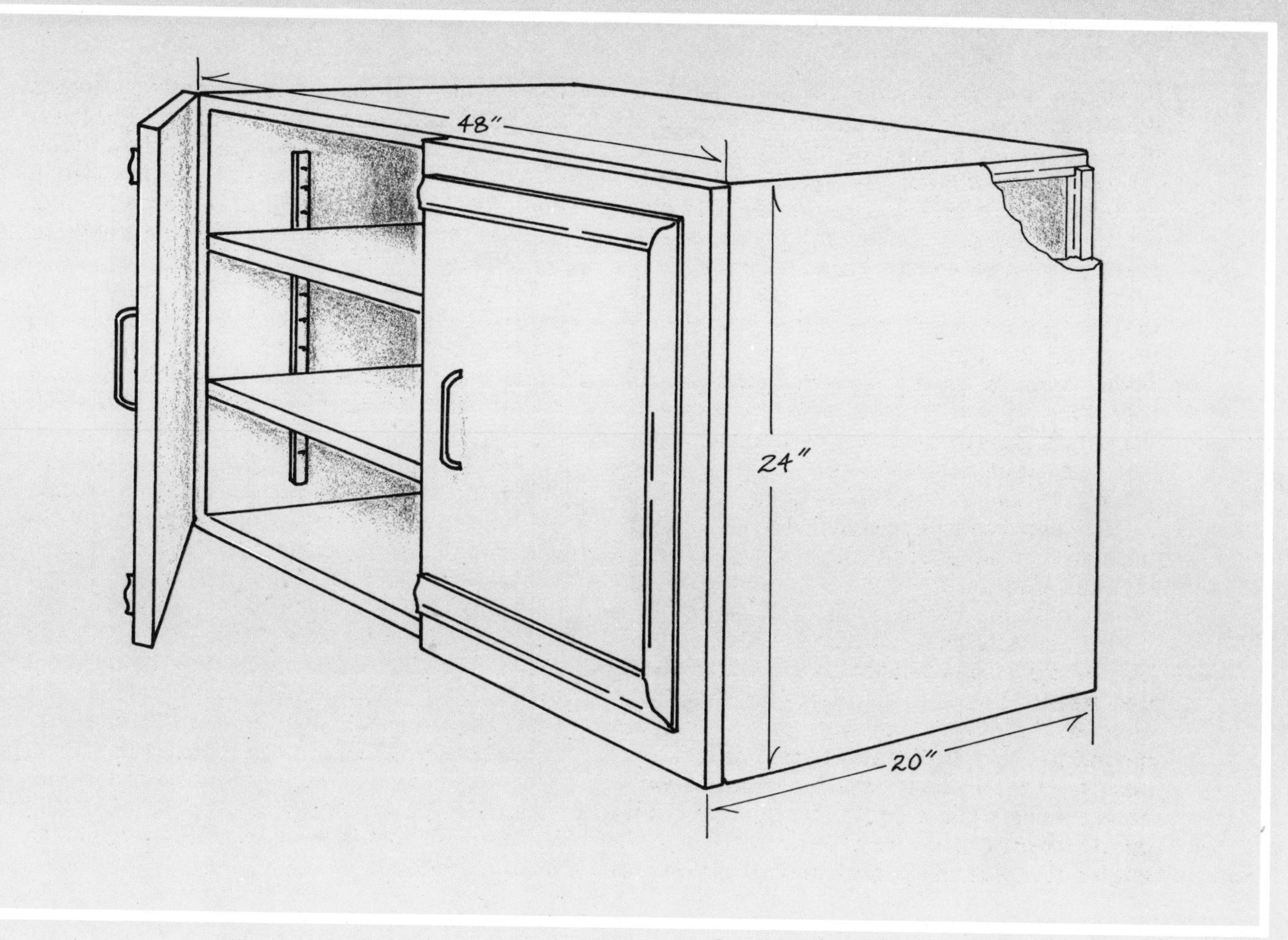

Basic Cabinet

There are numerous variations of the basic cabinet demonstrated throughout this book; sometimes the value of a simple box as a storage medium becomes lost within all its guises. A cabinet can be longer, or narrower, or wider than the one shown here, but essentially they should all be constructed in the same manner.

Materials for Basic Cabinet

Quantity	Description
½	¾" plywood panel for sides, shelves and partition
½	¼" plywood panel for doors and back
1	4′-long set of door tracks
12′	adjustable shelf tracks
	Door hinges and pulls (as needed)

Cutting. A cabinet can, of course, be made from any wood. This one is 20" deep by 24" high by 4′ long, so ½" or ¾" plywood is in order. The top and bottom are cut 4′ long by 20" wide, and are rabbeted at each end. The sides are 24"x20", and are also rabbeted top and bottom. The center partition is 18½"x23¼", and fits into ⅜" dadoes cut on center across the top and bottom. The back is 24"x48". Its thickness can be ⅛", ¼" or ½". If the cabinet is to be hung on a brick wall, however, the back should be ¾" stock. The sliding doors are 25" long by 23" high.

Assembly. The top and bottom are glue-nailed to the dadoed partition and rabbeted to the two sides. Then the back is glue-nailed to the frame and divider. Adjustable shelf tracks are attached to both sides of the partition and to the cabinet sides. The shelves can also be dadoed in place.

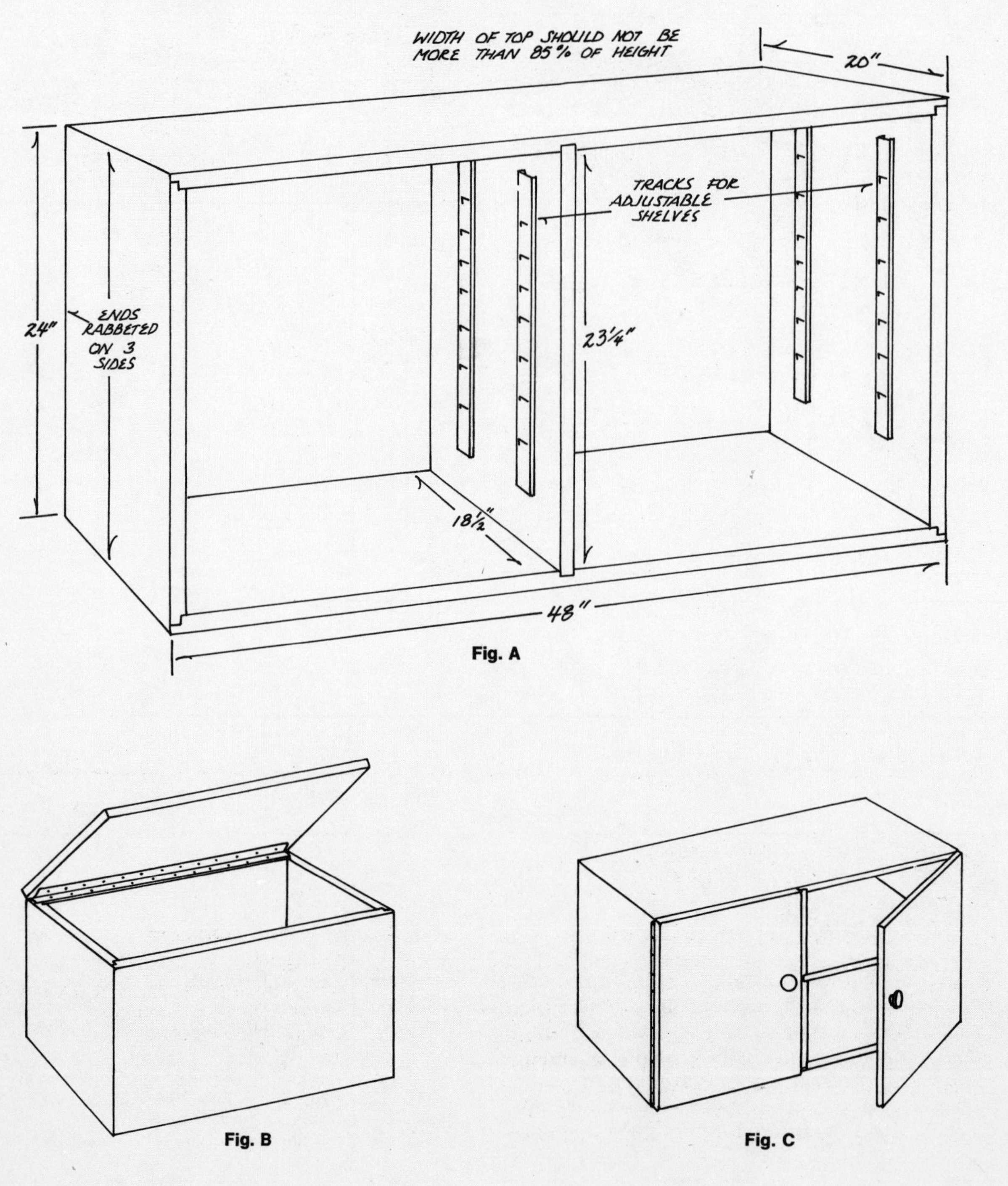

Fig. A

Fig. B

Fig. C

Some variations. The cabinet can be placed on its back (Fig. B) and the doors replaced by a hinged top. Singed doors can be used instead. The unit can be put on legs, hung on walls or stood on end. It can be painted, varnished, veneered, left unadorned or crowned with all kinds of molding, trim and decoration.

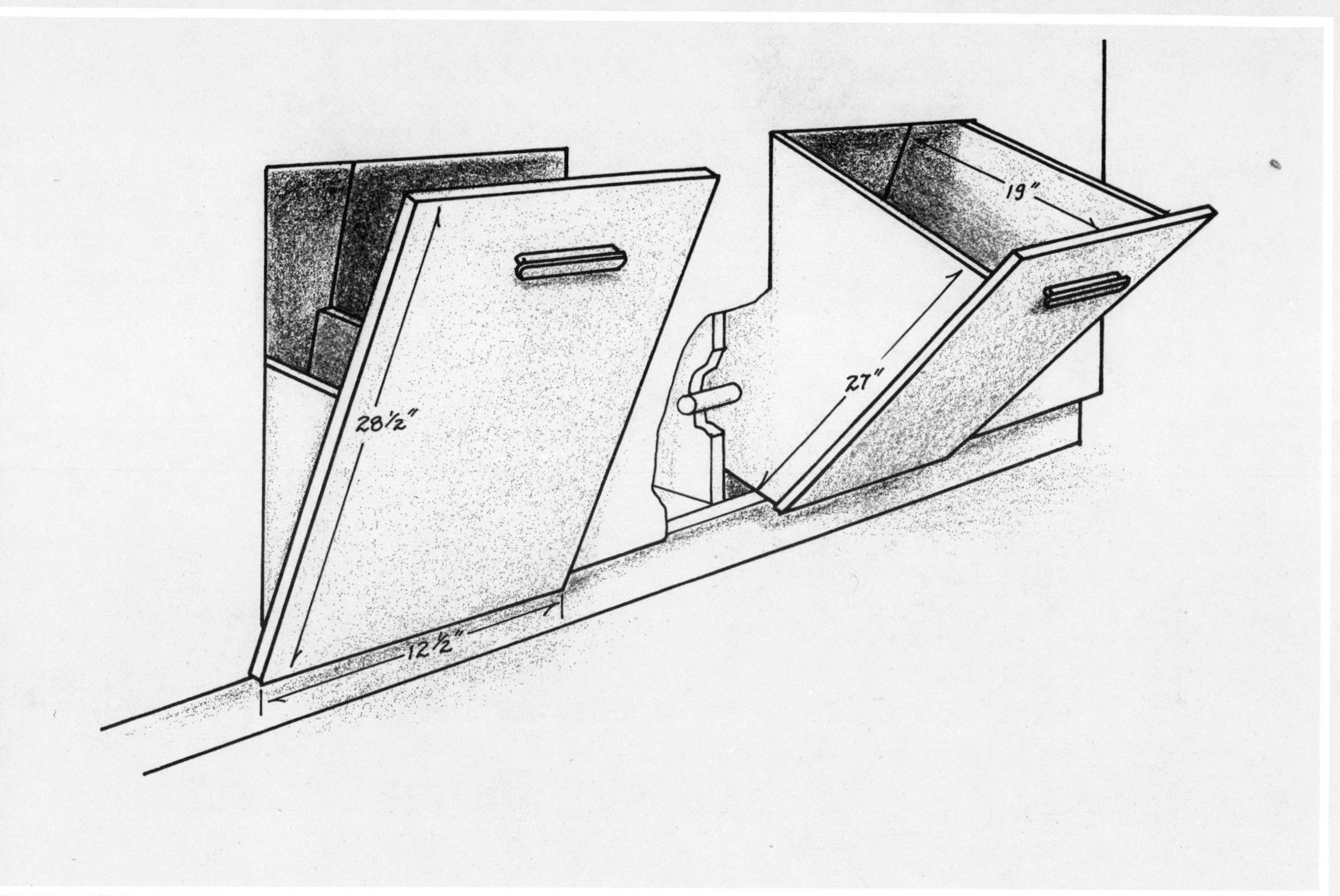

Built-In Hampers

Hampers can be made in at least two forms—tip-open, and pull-out. They might be defined as drawers, but then a drawer is a kind of cabinet anyway and the basics of hamper construction are about the same as any drawer or cabinet. They are nothing more than boxes with unusual angles, but it is the angles that must be carefully determined for each project. The drawings here show a basic, beside-the-sink clothes hamper, made from ¾" plywood.

Materials for Built-In Hampers

Quantity	Description
1	¾" plywood panel for front, back, sides and bottom of hamper
1	1" dowel for pivot rod
	or
1 set	drawer guides
1	handle

Front. 12½" wide by 28½" long, which will make the top of the front 1½" higher than the sides so that it can act as a stop when the hamper is closed.
Sides. Both are 24" high at the back and 27" at the front. The 15" bottom forms a right angle with the back and front. The 19" top edge is angled upward to meet the 27" front edge. A 1⅛" pivot hole is drilled in the lower front corner, as shown in Fig. A.
Back. This is 12½" wide by 26" high. It will extend 2" above the back of the sides so that it can act as a stop for the unit when it is opened.
Bottom. 12½" wide by 15" long.
Assembly. The front, back, sides and bottom are

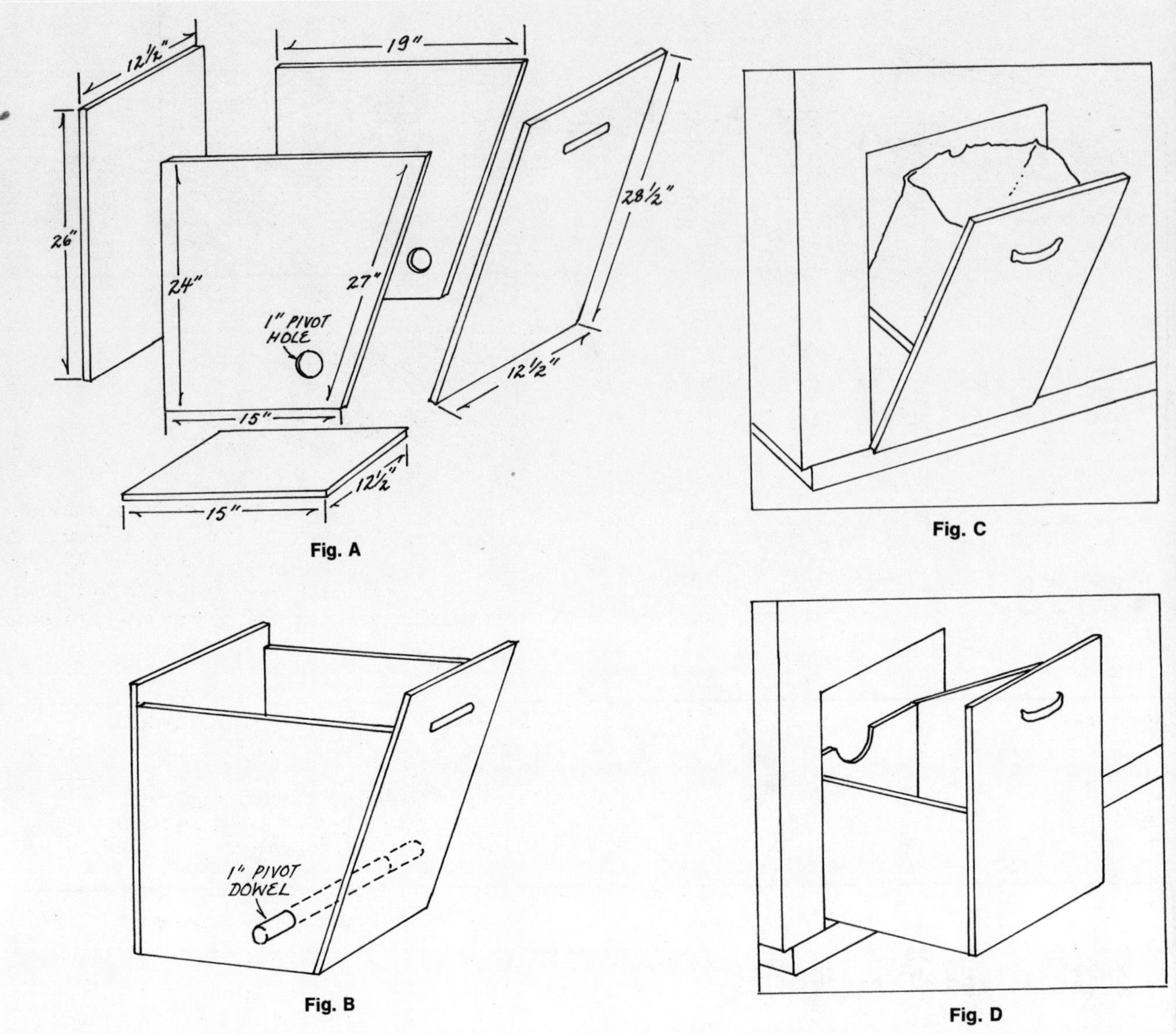

Fig. A

Fig. B

Fig. C

Fig. D

all glue-screwed together using any joinery. The back of the unit will be 3" lower than the front, and both the front and back plates will extend above the tops of the sides.

Installation. The hamper is suspended no less than 1" above the floor so that it has enough room to tip forward. The simplest way of hinging it is to drill 1⅛" holes through the sides of the unit and into the walls of the cavity to hold a 1" dowel (Fig. B). One side of the cavity will have to be drilled completely through, so that the dowel can be inserted from the outside, through the hamper, and into the opposite wall. A cross-beam (1" x 2") is attached to the top of the cavity so that it can stop both the front and back of the hamper when it opens or closes.

Variations. The schematics show a clothes hamper. But Fig. C is for a garbage pail or bag which fits into a wooden pocket constructed against the bottom of the front plate. A chain can be attached to the cavity to prevent it from opening too far, or the back of the pocket can be extended 1" on each side to stop the hamper when it reaches the cabinet walls. Note that the entire front of the unit is lipped to conform with other cabinets in the kitchen.

Fig. D is still another version which has odd-sized sides and a notched back, allowing it to fit around various pipes under a sink. In this case, the hamper probably will not be able to tip because of the pipes, so it is mounted on metal guides that allow it to be pulled straight out, like any drawer.

Children's Storage Boxes

For the frustrated parent who wants the children to pick up their own toys, there are a number of ways to make "putting away" a game. The fun in this kind of project really comes from the finishing, rather than construction of what amounts to a box on wheels.

Materials for Children's Storage Boxes

Quantity	**Description**
Storage Truck	
1	¾" plywood panel
4'	2"x2" stock for wheel supports
1 set	3" hinges for cab top
Refrigerator	
1	¾" plywood panel
16'	1"x1" stock for shelf cleats
5	3½" hinges for doors
Range	
½	¾" plywood panel
2	3½" hinges
28"	brass chain for oven door
Noah's Ark	
1½	¾" plywood panels
3	4" hinges for ramp-side
Camel, Elephant or Swan	
½	¾" plywood panel for each animal
4	nuts and bolts for wheels

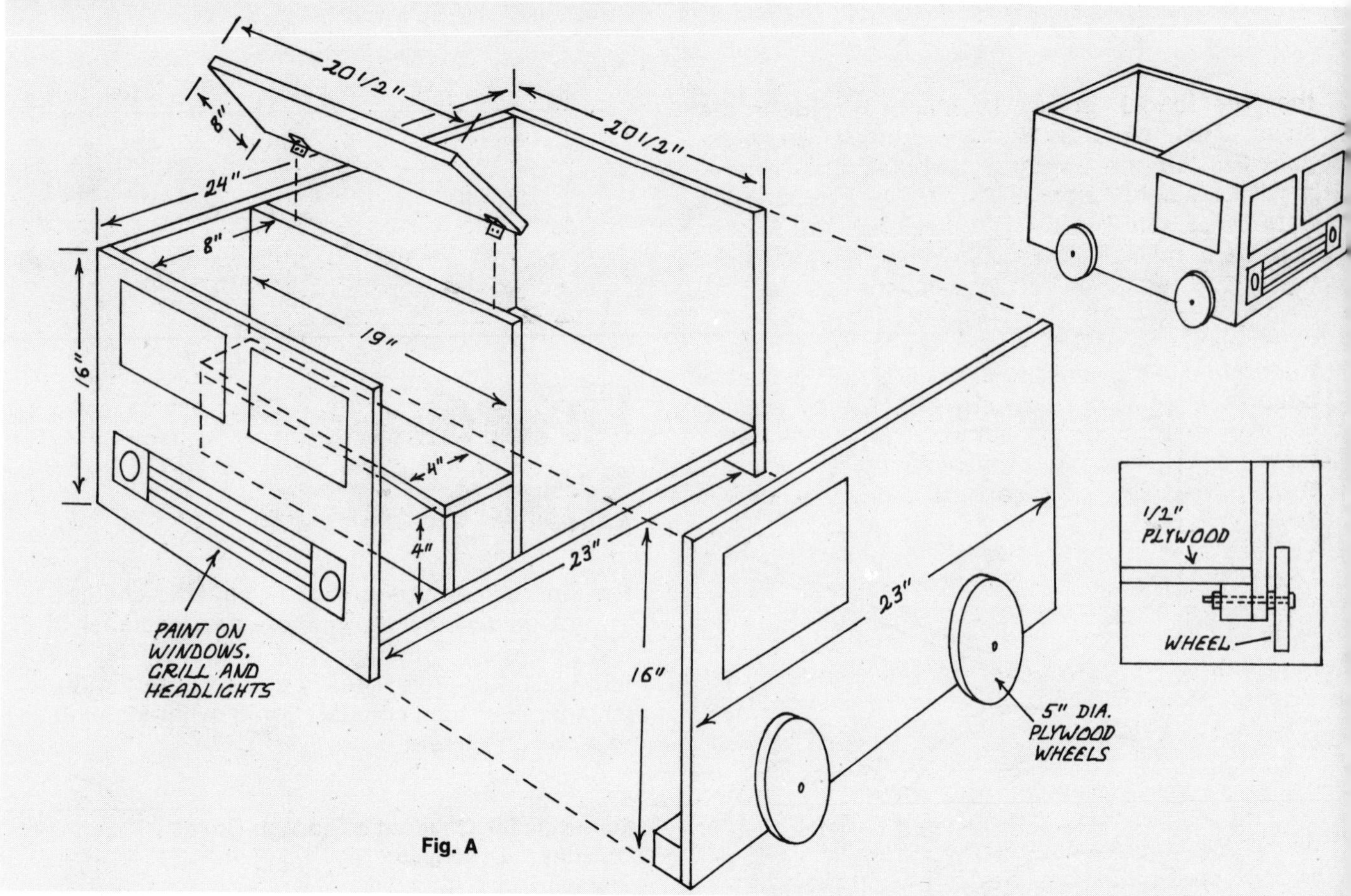

Fig. A

Cutting. Lay out and cut all parts from ¾" plywood as shown in Fig. A, including four 5"-diameter wheels. The box can be assembled with butt joints. However, the units are liable to take a beating during use, and dadoing should be considered as an alternative.

Assembly. The 2"x2"x23" axle supports are glue-nailed to the bottom edges of both 16"x23" sides

Fig. B

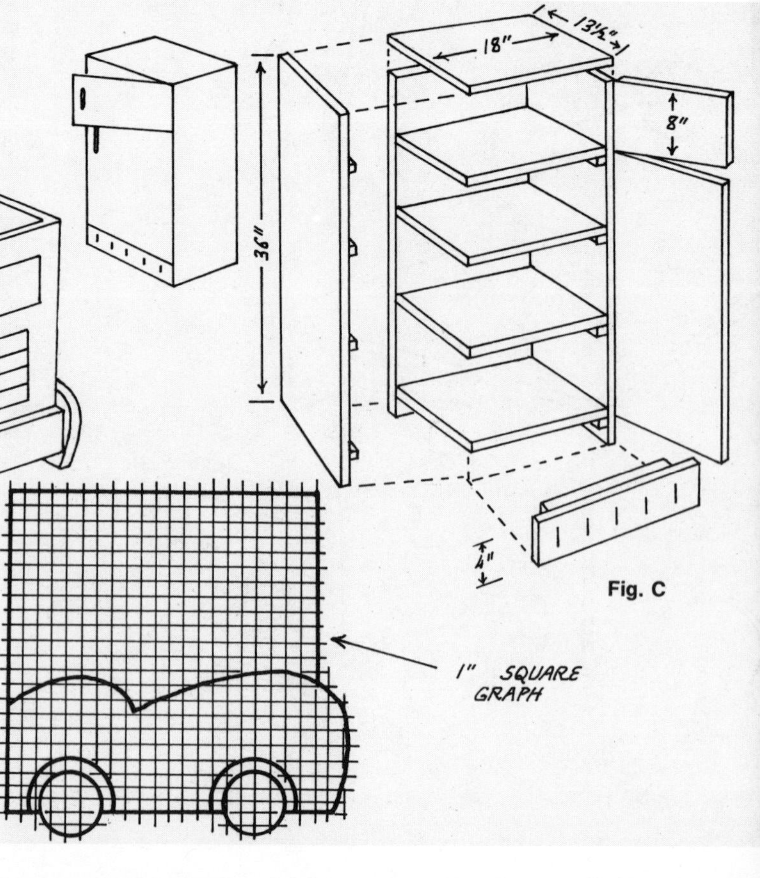

Fig. C

then the 19"x23" bottom is attached between the sides. The 16"x20½" front and back are glue-nailed to the end edges of the sides. The 19"x14" partition is set 8" from the front. The bench, made from two 4"x19" pieces, is attached to the bottom and the partition. The 8"x20½" lid is hinged to the top of the partition. The wheels are attached by drilling through the 2"x2" supports for the ½"x4" bolts, as shown in Fig. A.

Decoration. With a little paint, the box can now become a delivery truck (Fig. A). Or, by adding wooden fenders cut from plywood, it can be transformed into a moving van (Fig. B). If there are two trucks, they can be "garaged" under a simple table-garage.

Variations. Given the idea of decorated storage boxes, there are all sorts of possibilities. Leave the wheels off, make the box a little taller with plenty of shelves inside and it becomes a "refrigerator" (Fig. C). Another compatible unit is the "range" shown in Fig. D. Still another possibility is Noah's Ark (Fig. E), which is 4' long by 2' wide by 2' high, and can hold three box-animals such as a camel, a swan and an elephant. The boxes are 20" long by 15" wide by 20" high, and all three of them have wheels. One side of the ark is hinged to fold down and become a ramp leading into the ark.

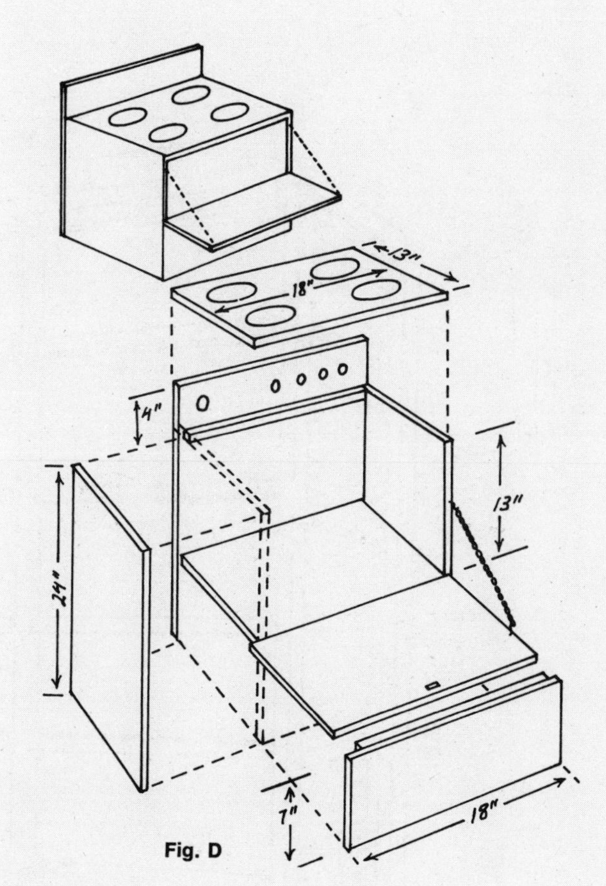

Fig. D

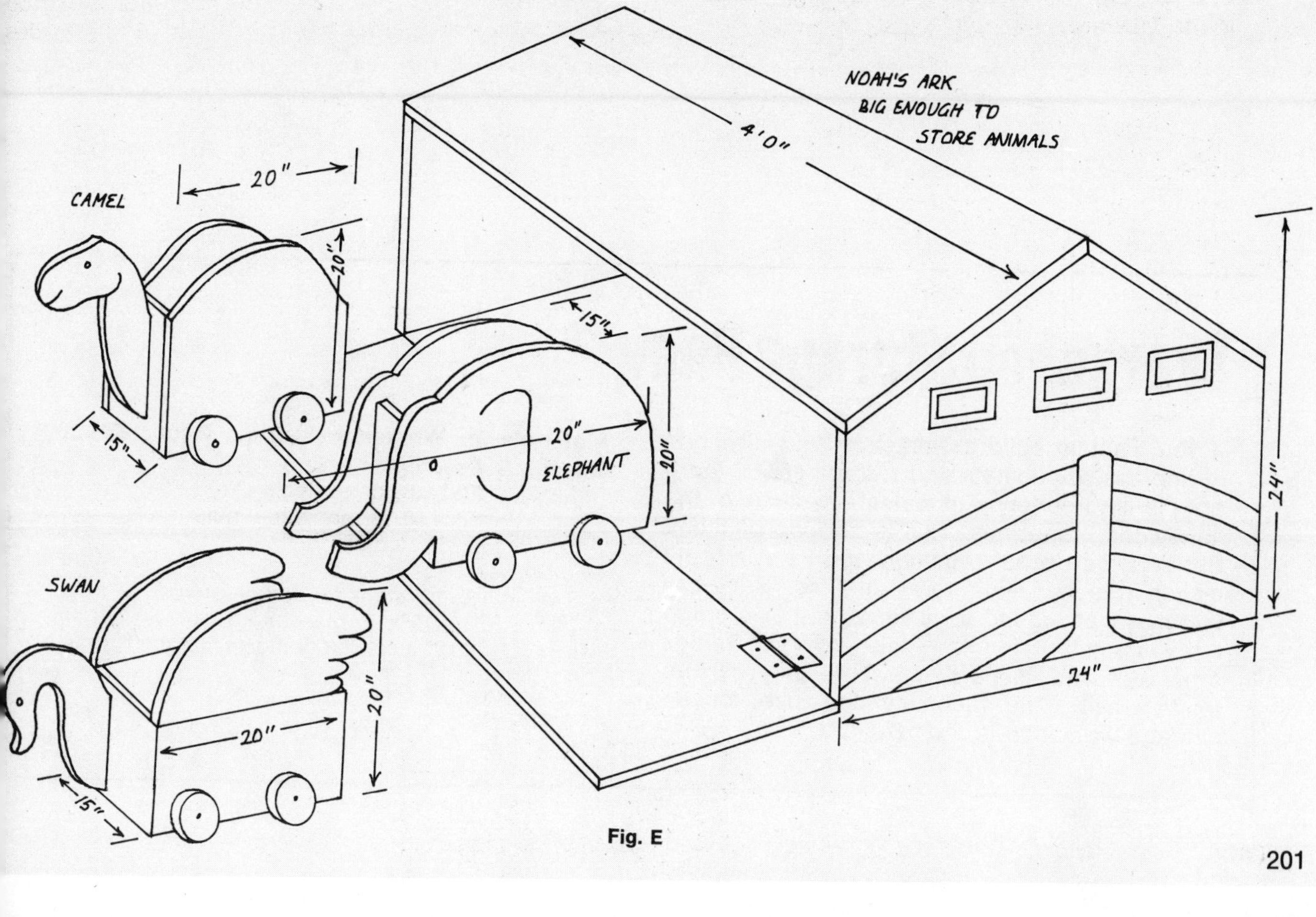

Fig. E

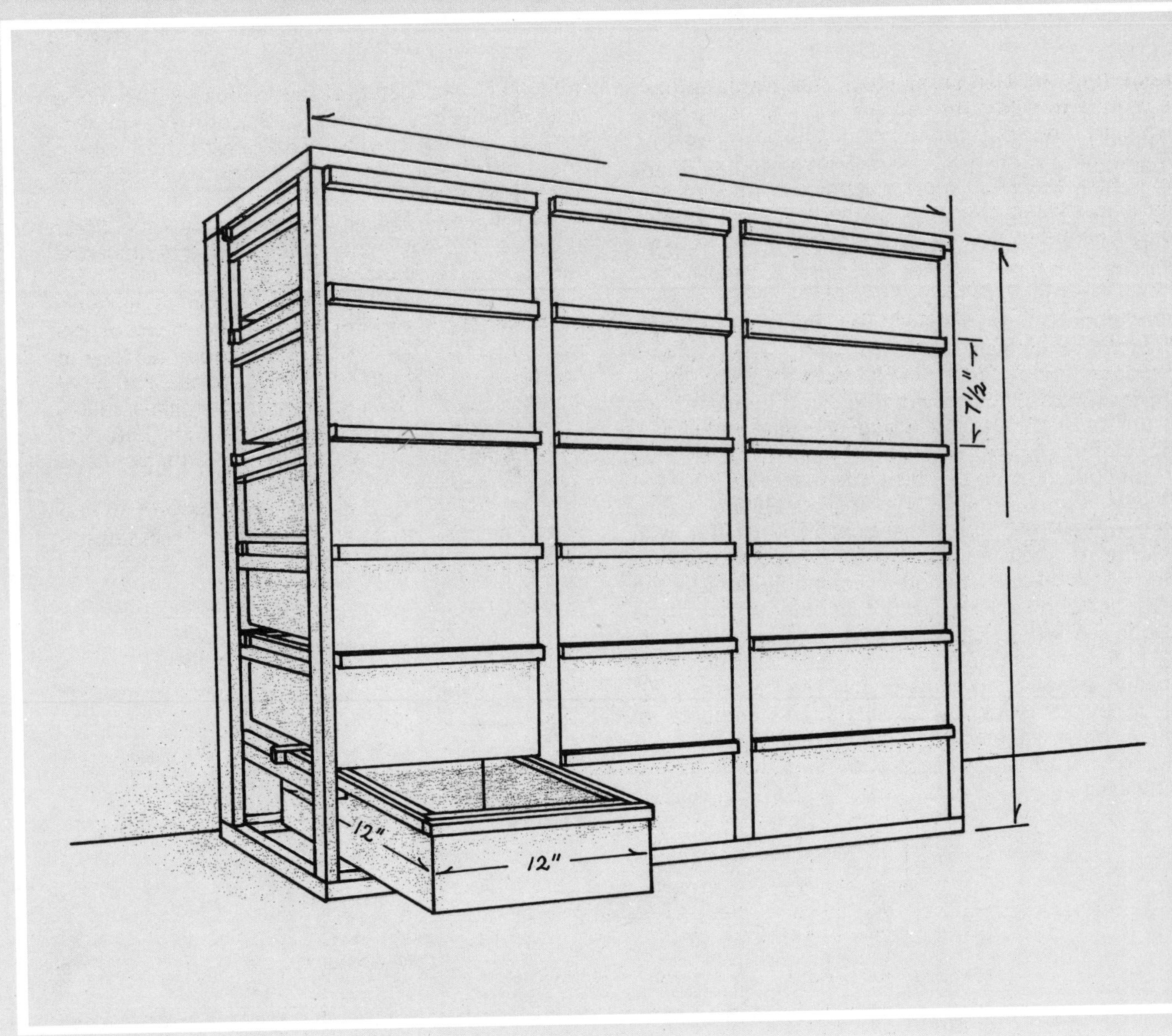

Workshop Storage Rack

If you want to build a workshop with all kinds of impressive cabinets and storage areas, there are plans to be found in almost any issue of the handyman magazines. This is not one of them. But it is fast to put together, and its very bulk makes it serviceable for a lifetime. Someday you may get around to making prettier storage for yourself but for now, this unit gets things organized and keeps them where they can be found again. The recommended size for an average workshop is 2′x6′x8′.

Materials for Workshop Storage Rack (2′x6′x8′)

Quantity	**Description**
12	2″x3″x6′ for verticals
4	2″x3″x8′ for horizontal rails
200′	2″x3″ stock for spacers
One Drawer	
4′	1″x12″ stock for drawer sides
1	¼″x12″x12″ Masonite for drawer bottom
5′	1″x2″ stock for guides, stop and handle

Frame (Fig. A). Use scrap stock that would either lie around the shop for years or have to be thrown away. If there are not enough 2"x3"s or 2"x4"s for the frame, boards will do. But ideally, 2"x3"s, 6' high, work best. Assemble a frame with the 6' verticals positioned every 16' on center in all directions. The frame can be as long as you wish, but the verticals should have 2"x3" cross-braces between the sides and across the back with 8" between tiers. A 2"x3" top plate frame is nailed to the top of the verticals.

Drawers (Fig. B). The drawers are made from 1"x8" scrap, and measure 12" square. Butt-join the front and back between the sides and nail a ¼" Masonite bottom to the underside of the frame. Nail 1"x2" strips along the top edge of both sides and the front. The back has a similar rail that extends 2½" beyond the drawer sides and acts as a stop. The 1"x2"s ride on the 2"x3" horizontals in the frame; the front piece is a handle. More importantly, the front 1"x2" has a strip of tape stuck to it which is marked with the contents of the drawer—screws, sanders, router, saw blades, hammers, plumbing tools, electrical supplies, pliers, screwdrivers, power saw, etc.

Embellishments. Drive a few nails into the 2"x3" frame, and on it hang things like circular saw blades, roofing angles and handsaws.

Nail a 1"x8" board across the top of the verticals so that it extends beyond the front of the frame (Fig. C). Tack a row of baby-food jar tops to the board by driving a nail through the center of each top; then fill the jars with screws, nails, tacks, drill bits and similarly small items. To store the jars, screw them into the tops and let them hang from the board.

Put a plate of plywood across the top of the frame and store scrap wood on top of the storage unit.

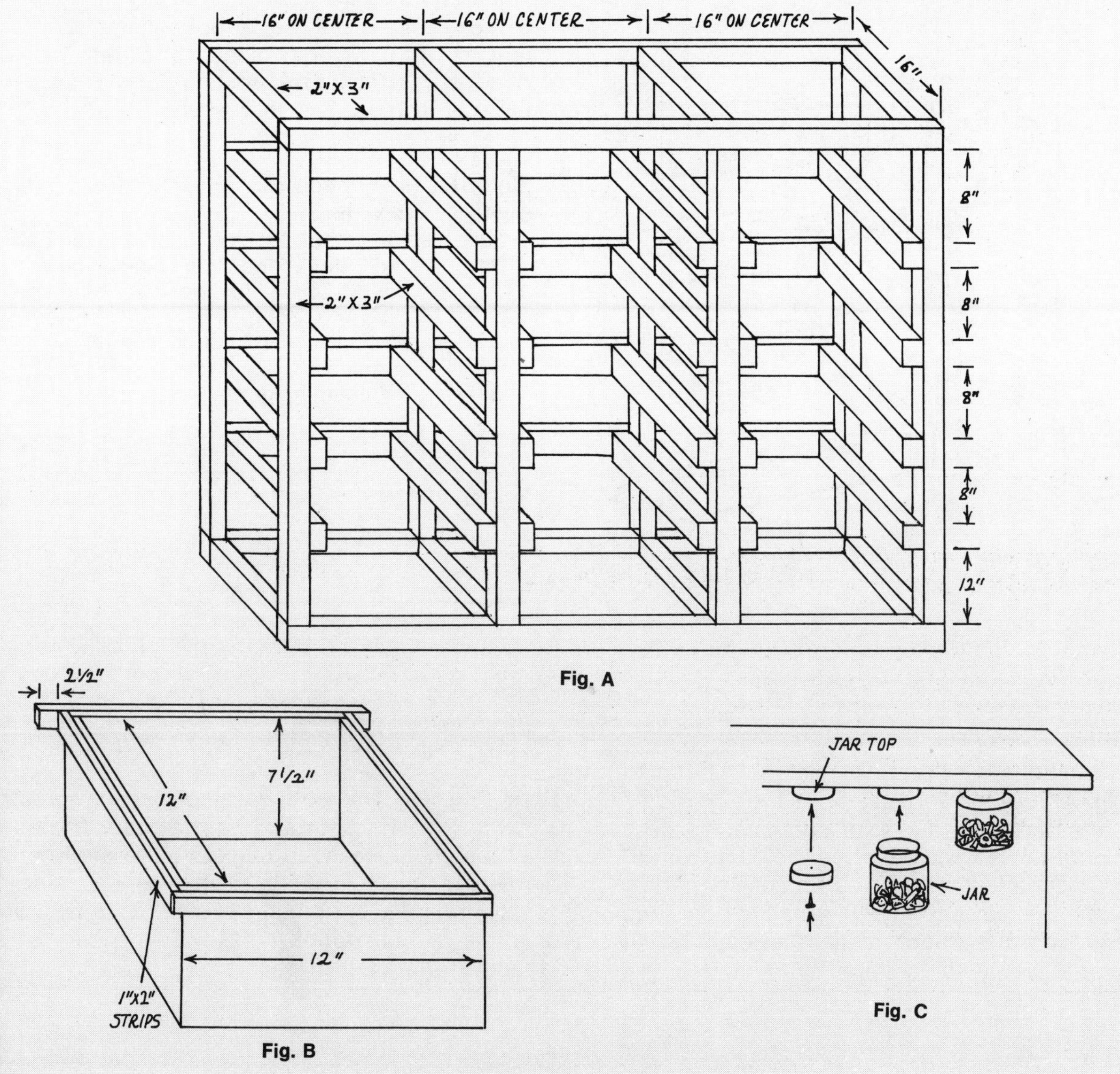

Fig. A

Fig. B

Fig. C

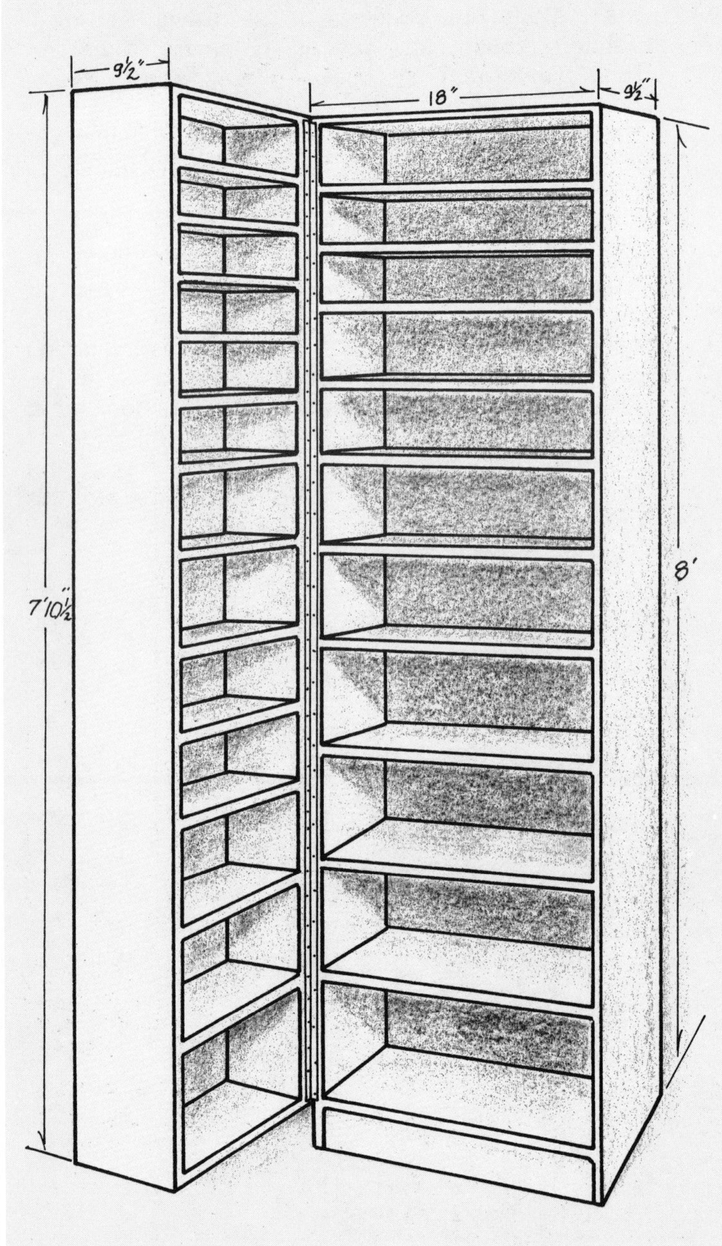

Kitchen Staple Cabinet

The double cabinet is designed to fill in a dea corner between a door and the nearest wall. A though it is ludicrously simple to build, if yo make the cabinet big enough you will be hard pressed to ever completely fill it. The dimen sions shown here are 17" deep by 18" wide b 8' high, but the unit could be any size up to tw feet in width. Over two feet, and the door w need a treaded caster for support; a door th large is also subject to warping problems.

Materials for Kitchen Staple Cabinet

Quantity	Description
32'	1"x9" stock for base and door verticals
30'	1"x9" stock for door and base shelves
2	3'x7' ⅛" or ¼" luan for door front and base backing
1	1"x2"x1½" stock for kick plate
1	large handle
8'	¾" piano hinge

Base (Fig. A). Cut the verticals from 1"x9"x8' stock. Rabbet the top and dado for the shelves. The shelves ought to have a variety of heights from 8" to 18" to accommodate any size box of dry goods. The bottom shelf is dadoed 1½" from the floor, and supported by a 1"x2" kick plate. Glue-nail ⅛" or ¼" luan or Masonite to the back.

Door (Fig. B). The door is also made from 1"x stock and is 1½" shorter than the base. The fram is rabbeted at each corner, and the shelves a dadoed in place. The door shelves can also b random heights, depending on what is to be store on them. As an option, a 2"-wide lip can be a tached to the front of each shelf, but with a 7½

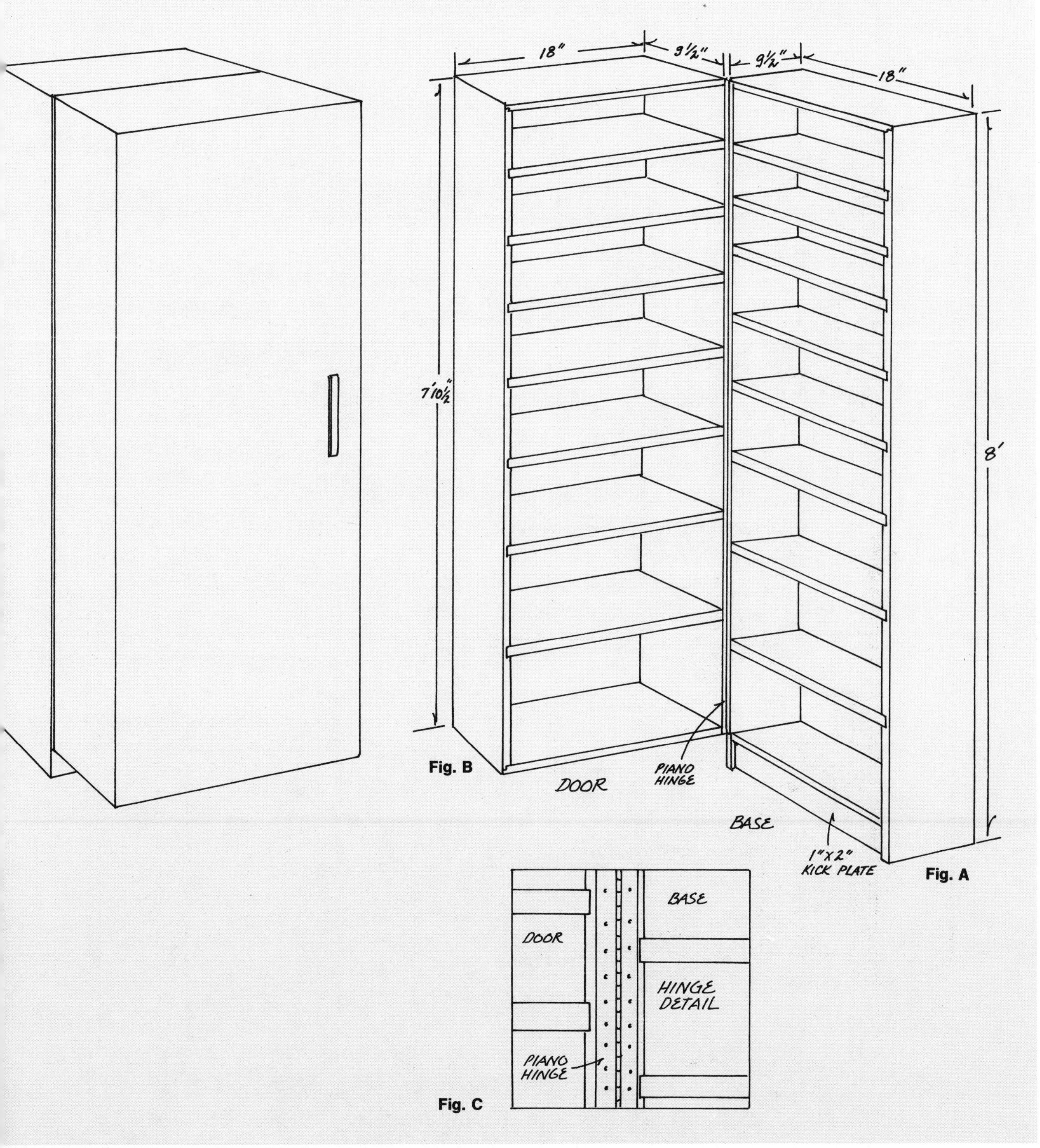

Fig. B

Fig. A

Fig. C

deep door the lips are not critical. The lips can be cut from ⅛" luan, and are glue-nailed across the front of the shelves. The front of the door is covered with either ⅛" or ¼" luan which is glue-nailed to the back of the shelves as well as to the frame. The door is attached to the base with a full-length piano hinge (Fig. C).

The handle attached to the front of the door should be a large one and because of the size of the door, mechanical, rather than magnetic, catches should be used. The door and visible side of the cabinet can be decorated with molding or trim compatible with the rest of the kitchen decor. Secure the cabinet to the walls to prevent its tipping over.

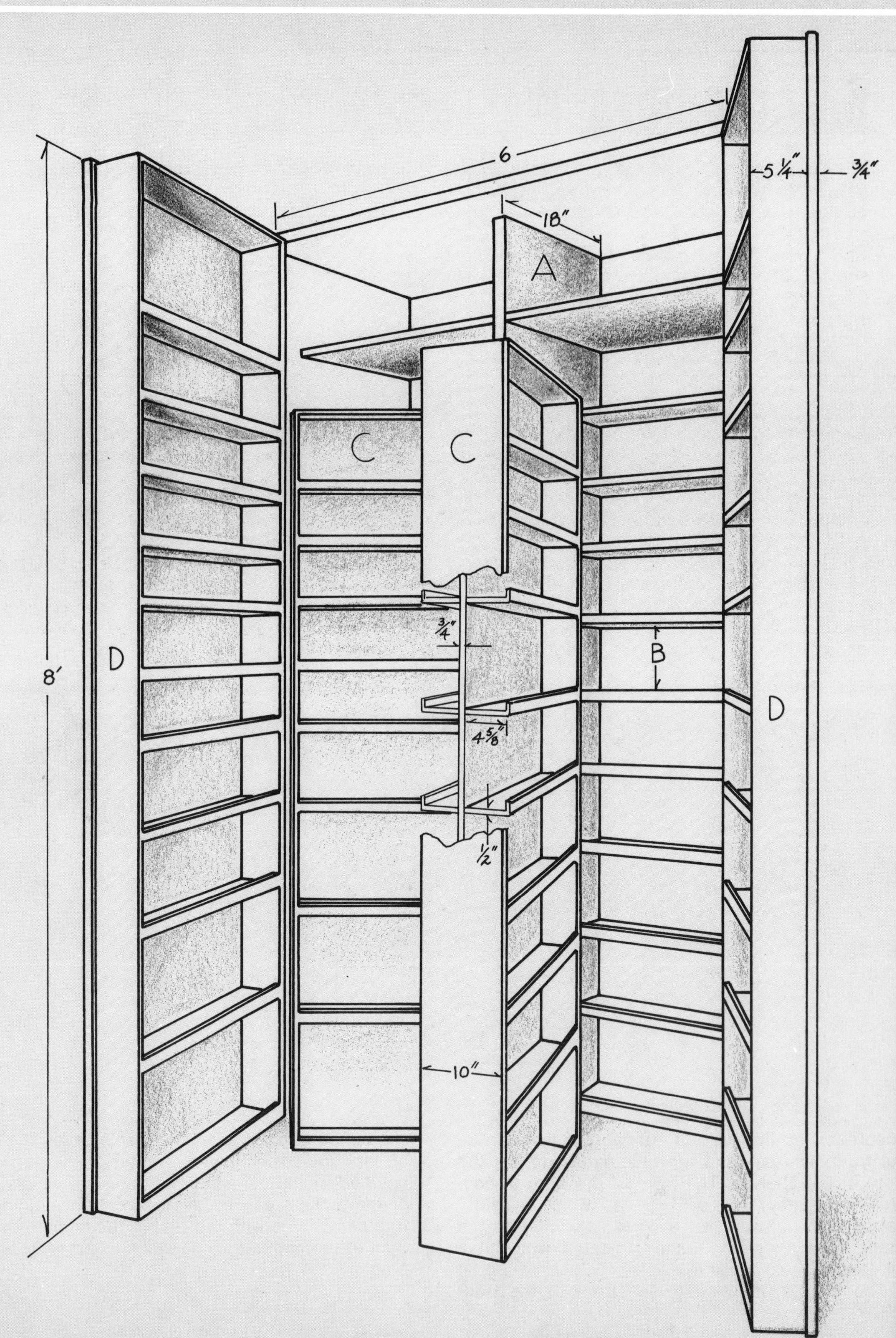

6
5 1/4″
3/4″
18″
A
C
C
D
8′
3/4″
B
4 5/8″
1/2″
D
10″

Double Pantry

Whether you can take full advantage of the space this huge kitchen pantry provides depends on the area you have to work with. An optimum size would be 6′ wide by 8′ high by 2′ deep, which would make available no less than 80 shelves of varying widths, or 240′ of storage space in what amounts to the size of an average-sized closet!

Materials for Double Pantry (6′x8′x2′)

Quantity	Description
4	¾″ plywood good on both sides
3	½″ plywood good on both sides
60′	1″x8″ common stock
4	6′ piano hinges
	4d finishing nails, glue, screws (as needed)

Frame assembly. Whatever width you are working with, first divide it in half by partition A. The partition must be at least 1½″ thick, so glue-screw two pieces of ¾″ plywood together. Assuming the depth of the pantry is 2′, place a series of ¾″x8″-wide plywood shelves (B) against the back wall on both sides of the partition.

Swing shelves. Now build the two inner swing-shelf sections (C), using ¾″ plywood for the 10″-wide frames. The frames are divided by a ¾″ plywood panel which supports ½″-thick shelves on both sides. The swing shelves are attached to opposite sides of partition A with piano hinges, as shown.

Doors. The pantry doors (D) are also made of ¾″ plywood, and are 6″ deep with ½″-thick shelves. The doors are hinged to the outsides of the pantry, as shown, with either piano hinges or 3″ door butts.

Variations. As an option, consider glue-nailing a ¼″x1″ lip across the front of the ½″ shelves. The outside of the doors is finished to match other cabinets in the kitchen.

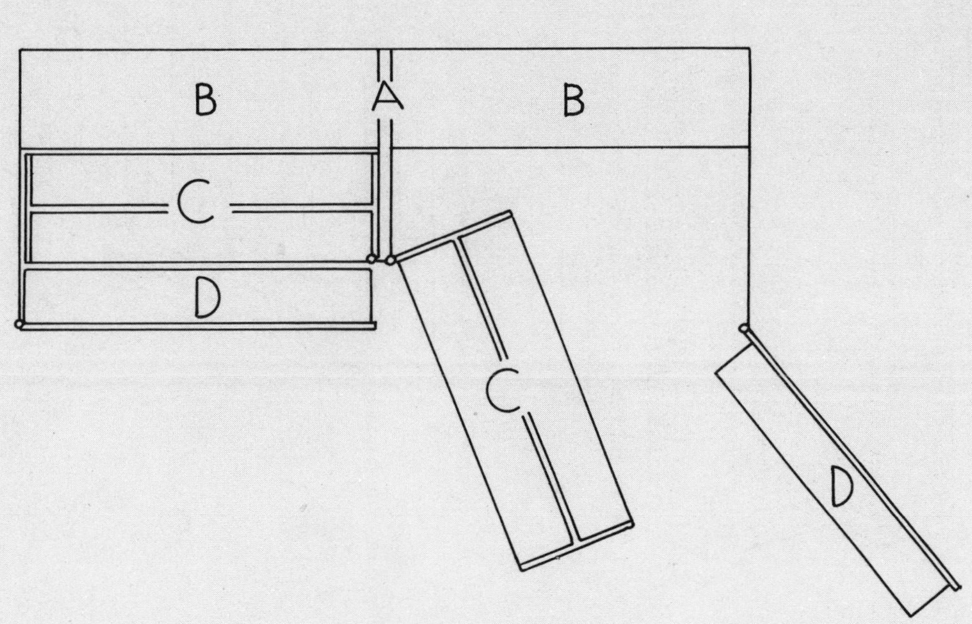

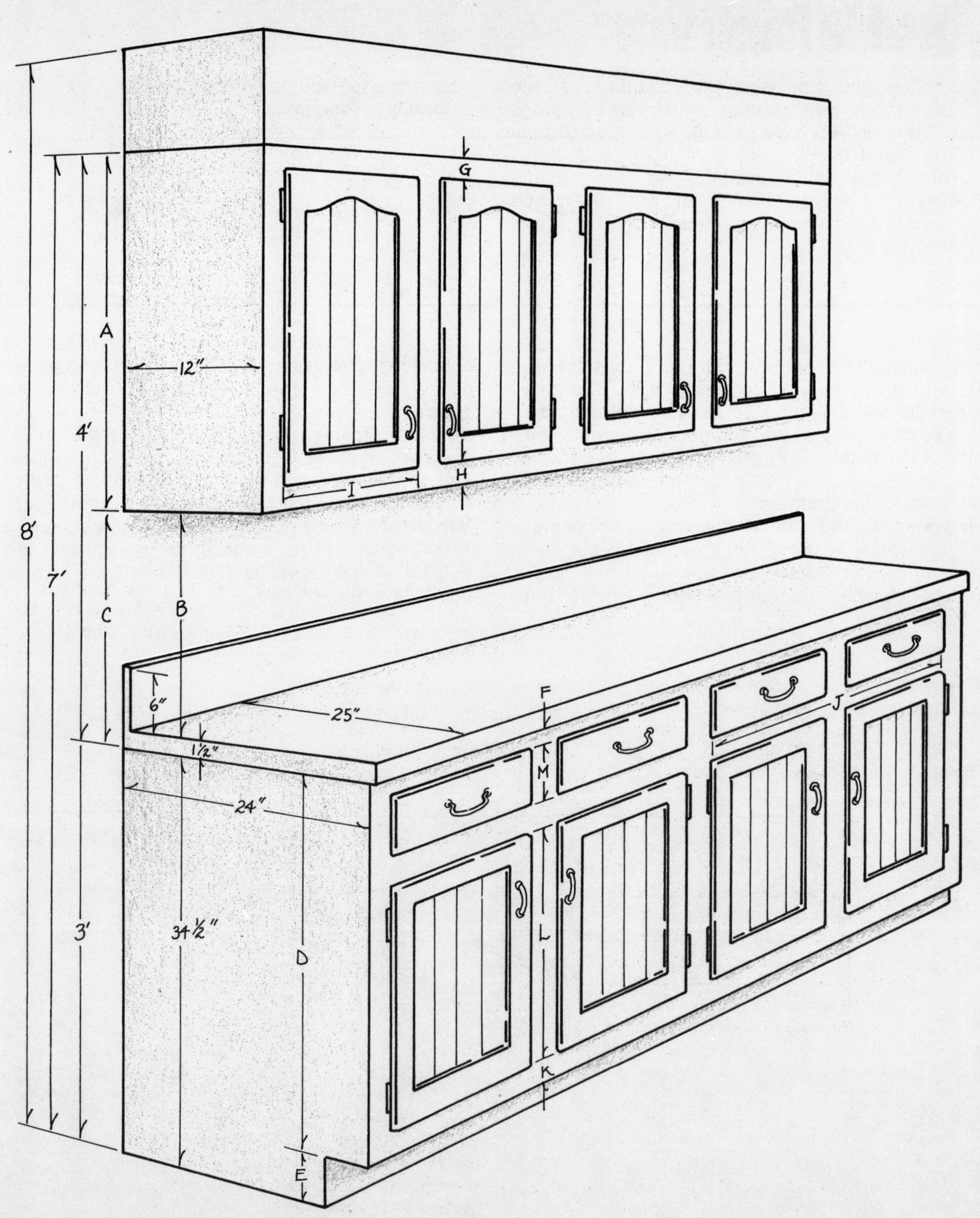

8'
7'
4'
3'
A
B
C
D
E
F
G
H
I
J
K
L
M
12"
6"
25"
1½"
24"
34½"

Standard Kitchen Cabinets

The measurements used in constructing built-in kitchen cabinets have become so standardized that it is almost impossible to change them without encountering problems. For example, if the height of the counter is set below the normal 36", no dishwasher will fit under it. If it is higher, no range will come up to the same level unless it is put on a base, so that the end of the counter will be level with range. Thus, any built-in kitchen cabinets made in the home shop must conform literally to the measurements shown in Fig. A.

Materials for Standard Kitchen Cabinets

Quantity	Description
Hanger	
2	½"x11⅝"x31" plywood for sides
2	¾"x2"x31" stock for side face stiles
1	¾"x2½"x26¾" stock for center face stile
1	¾"x2¼"x26½" stock for top face rail
1	¾"x2"x26½" stock for bottom face rail
2	¾"x1¼"x29" stock for mounting rails
2	¾"x11"x30" stock for top and bottom
2	¾"x10¾"x29" plywood for shelves
1	⅛"x30"x30" plywood for back
10'	shelf track for adjustable shelves
27'	½"x2" stock for door panels
12'	¾"x2" stock for side and bottom door frame stiles
2'	¾"x4" stock for top door frame stiles (to be shaped)
Base	
2	½"x23⅝"x34½" plywood for sides
2	¾"x2"x31" stock for face stiles
1	¾"x2"x26¾" stock for center stile
1	¾"x2¼"x26" stock for top rail
1	¾"x2"x26" stock for bottom rail
2	¾"x2"x12" stock for drawer rails
1	⅛"x29½"x31" plywood for back
1	¾"x1¾"x29½" stock for top back support rail
1	¾"x11¼"x29½" plywood for shelf
1	¼"x21¼"x29½" plywood for bottom
2	¾"x2¼"x21¼" stock for top support rails
Bottom Frame	
1	¾"x5"x30" stock for kick plate
2	¾"x5"x20½" stock for bottom end support
1	¾"x1½"x29" stock for back support
1	¾"x1½"x19¾" stock for center support
Base Doors	
27'	½"x2" stock for door panels
12'	¾"x2" stock for door frames
Base Drawers	
9'	½"x3½" stock for drawer sides
2	¼"x11"x20" plywood for drawer bottoms
2	¾"x4"x14" stock for drawer fronts
1	2"x3"x20¼" stock for center drawer guide support
2 sets	18" drawer guides
Counter Top	
1	¾"x25"x30⅜" plywood, pressboard or pine board for top
9'	¾"x2" stock for counter top doubling frame

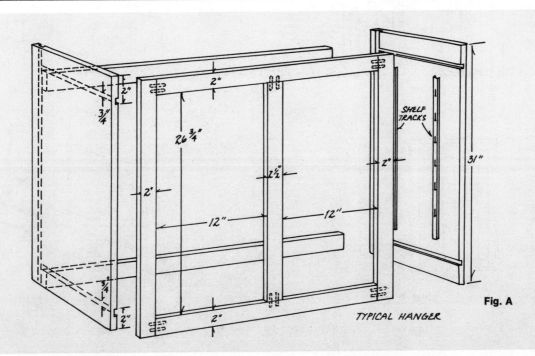

TYPICAL HANGER

Fig. A

Measurements.

A—The height of the tallest cabinet is usually from 30" to 34", with a depth of 12".

B—As a rule, the top of the cabinet is placed 4' above the bottom of the counter top. This makes measurement B the difference between the combined heights of the base cabinets and the hangers and 84". B, therefore, is between 14" and 18".

C—This is measurement B (14" to 18") plus the thickness of the counter top, (in recently built homes almost always 1½", since ¾"-thick counter tops are seldom installed today). Thus, measurement C becomes something between 14" and 18", + 1½", or between 15½" and 19½".

D—Most kitchen cabinetmakers have standardized their products so that measurements A and D are identical. In other words, the manufacturers are making their hangers and base cabinets the same height, so measurement D is between 30" and 31".

E—Since D is 30" to 31", the dimensions of the kick plate must be between 3½" and 4½". This gives the counter cabinet an overall height of 33½" to 35½".

F & G—The top facing rails are always the same width if the two cabinets are made by the same manufacturer and they will be around 1½" to 2½".

H & K—The bottom face rails are usually identical, too, ranging between 1¾" and 2". The width is determined by H so that it can create a narrow recess under the hangers for a thin fluorescent light. The light usually can be hidden behind a 1¼" facing.

I—Cabinet facings are normally worked out so that the doors are an even number of inches in width.

J—Where large double doors come together, the space above J is often divided on center to take a pair of drawers.

L & M—L is usually divisible by four spaces, each equal to the height of the drawers cavity, M. This is done by making all the rails in the facing the same width. Eliminating the rail between two adjacent spaces will leave enough room to accommodate a deep drawer, a hamper or a standard metal breadbox.

Counter top. With a 24"-wide cabinet, a 25"-wide top is attached with a ¾"- to 1"-thick splashboard, 6" high. The top overhangs the front of the cabinets by 1", but the splashboard reduces its surface to 24", give or take ¾".

Done in knotty pine for the doors or facing, or a handsome veneer, the "standard kitchen cabinet" can provide decorative storage space in the family

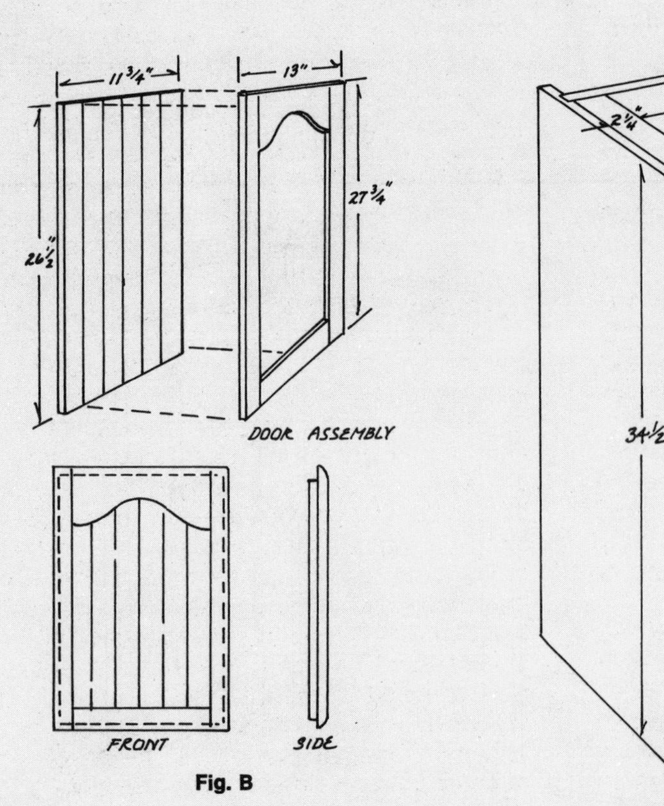

Fig. B

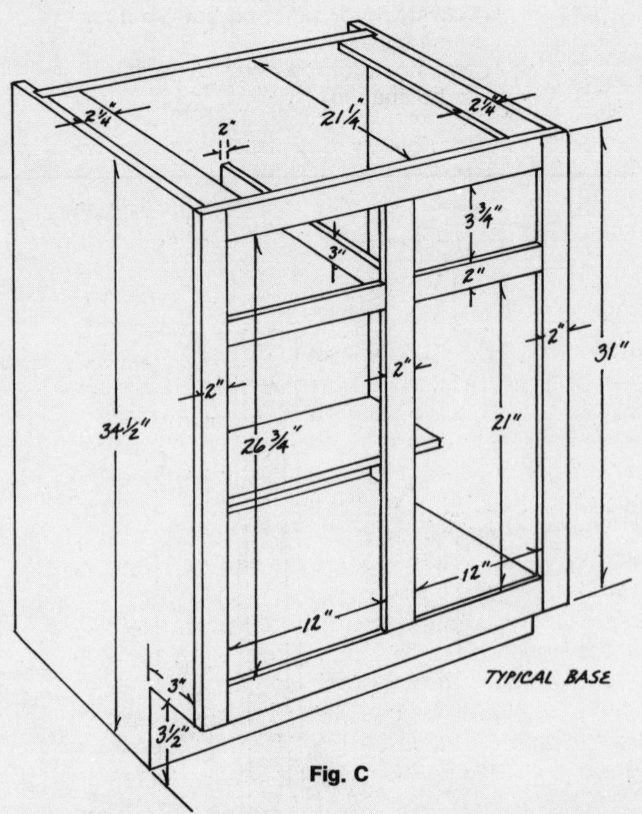

Fig. C

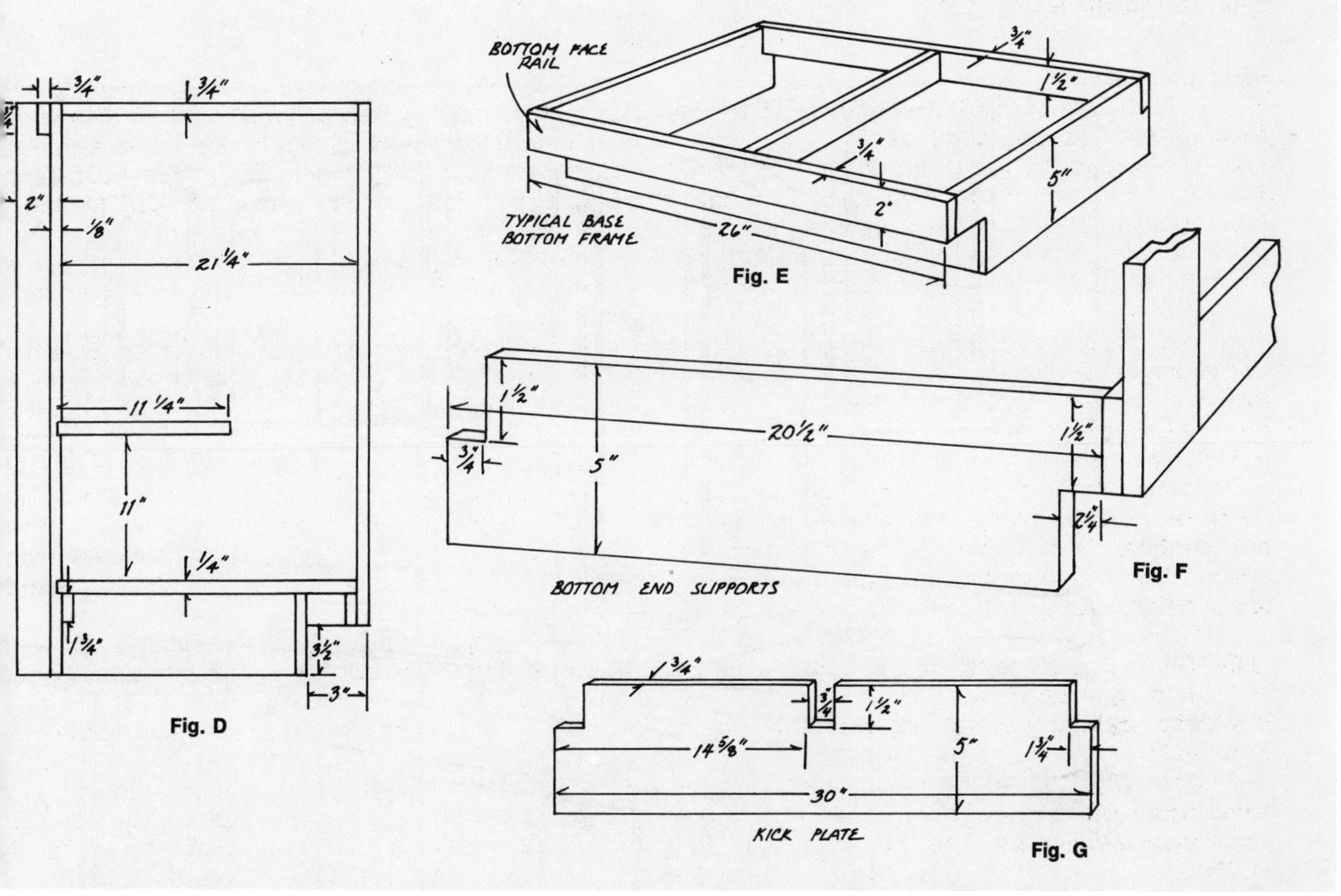

r recreation room, as well as in the kitchen, or even the bathroom. The design here is for 30"-wide units, but they could easily be extended the length of an entire wall or two.

Hanger assembly. Cut all pieces in the materials list. Rout both cabinet sides 2" from the top and bottom edges; glue-screw the top and bottom between the sides. Attach the back, then position the mounting rails under the top and bottom as shown in Fig. A. Assemble the face stiles either with dowels or mortise and tenon joints. Glue-screw the completed frame to the front edges of the cabinet. The doors are frame-and-panel construction (Fig. B). The panels are ½"x2" stock, tongue and groove, spline or rabbeted together to form a panel 11¾"x26½". The frame is ¾" stock, mortise-and-tenon joined, and measures 13"x27¾". When the frame is glue-screwed to the panel, it extends ¼" on all sides to form a lipped door. The doors are hinged to the cabinet facing. Adjustable shelf tracks are nailed to the inside of the cabinet.

Base assembly. The sides are notched at the bottom front corners for the kick plate, and are ¼"-dadoed 3½" from the bottom edges. Both sides also have stopped dadoes 11" from their bottom edges for the half-shelf (Fig. D). The sides are ploughed ⅛"x¼"x2" inside their back edges in order to accept the back (Fig. D). The bottom, back and shelf are glue-screwed in place. The 2¼"-top and 1¾"-back support rails are glue-screwed along the top edges of the sides and back (Figs. C and D). The face frame and drawer rails are assembled as shown in Fig. C, then glue-screwed to the front of the cabinet. The bottom frame end supports are notched as shown in Fig. F, and the kick plate cut according to Fig. G. The frame is assembled and glue-screwed to the underside of the cabinet. The frame-and-panel doors are made in the same manner as the hanger doors. The panels measure ½"x11¾"x20¾"; the frames are ¾"x13"x22". The 2"x3"x20¼" center-drawer guide support is glue-screwed between the center facing stile and the back of the cabinet. Drawer guides are attached to both sides of the center guide support and the sides of the cabinet before the two drawers are assembled. (See Chapter 6 for construction techniques.)

The counter top can be made of pine, plywood or pressboard. The top measures ¾"x25"x30⅜"; the doubling frame is glue-screwed on its underside, around its perimeter, then the entire unit is glue-screwed to the cabinet.

Optional. If a splashboard is desired, it can be either 6" high, or the full 14" to 18" between the counter top and bottom of the hanger.

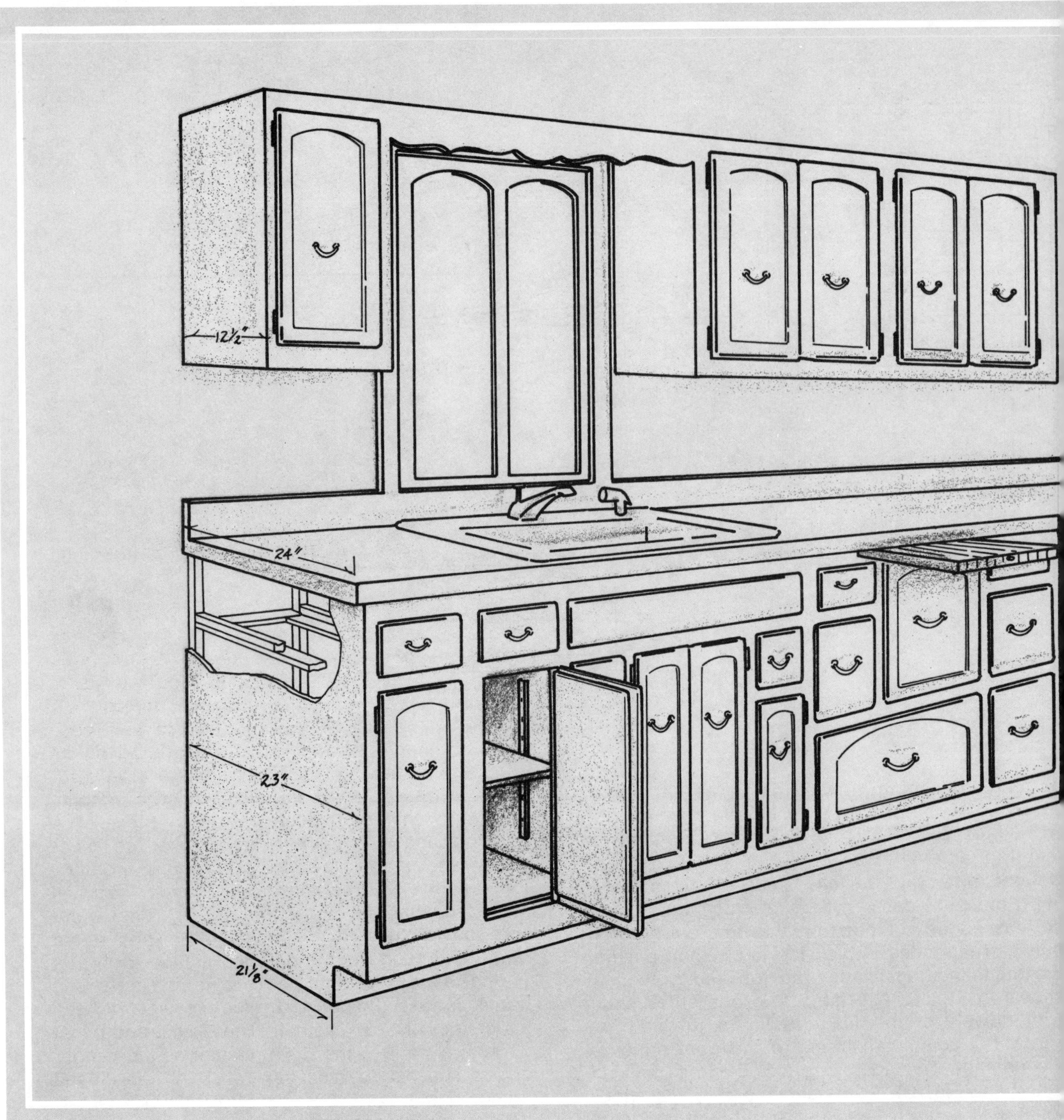

Framing. Starting with the floor, frame out the counter cabinet base using 1"x 6" stock (#1), dadoing the spacers at equal distances, and rabbeting the ends. The counter cabinets themselves can be assembled separately, or built on-site.

The outside walls of the cabinets are usually ½" plywood, and the interior partitions should be at least ¼" plywood. Every cabinet is given four walls (#2), and there are rarely any butt joints. Joinery is usually rabbets and dadoes. Where there are to be drawers, the guide rails are made from 1"x2" or 1"x1" stock. It is also a good idea to brace the top edges of the cabinets with a 1"x2" stock backing, not only for general support, but also because it makes attaching the counter easier. Framing in the front of the cabinets can be either 1"x2" or 1"x3"; obviously every door and drawer must have some kind of frame around it as should the bottom or floor of each cabinet.

Kitchen wall cabinets are constructed in the

Kitchen Cabinetry

If you decide to redo a kitchen, or build a new one, and you want to incorporate any special storage units, it is almost impossible to find them ready-made on the market. You will have to make things like swing-out spice racks, on-end drawers and corner cupboards by yourself. The construction plans here are offered as a guide to putting basic kitchen storage together; any variations and/or specialty storage should be planned for in advance.

same manner as the counter. Their backs are given frames, and so are their fronts and bottoms. Because of the frames and the smaller dimensions of wall cabinets, ¼" plywood usually can be used at bottom shelves. Shelves may be fixed in the wall cabinets, but it is simpler, and in the long run more convenient for everybody, if adjustable shelf tracks are used as much as possible.

Finishing. Wall cabinets are usually hung from 15" to 18" above the counter, and are attached to the walls with any means possible. The doors may or may not be hung before the cabinets go up on the walls. The simplest method for both the drawer and door fronts is to make them overlap their frames. (Overlapping hides a lot of errors.) The drawers should all be built before their frames are completed. The counter top can be made from any of several materials including butcher block, stainless steel, flakeboard or plywood and one of the plastic laminates.

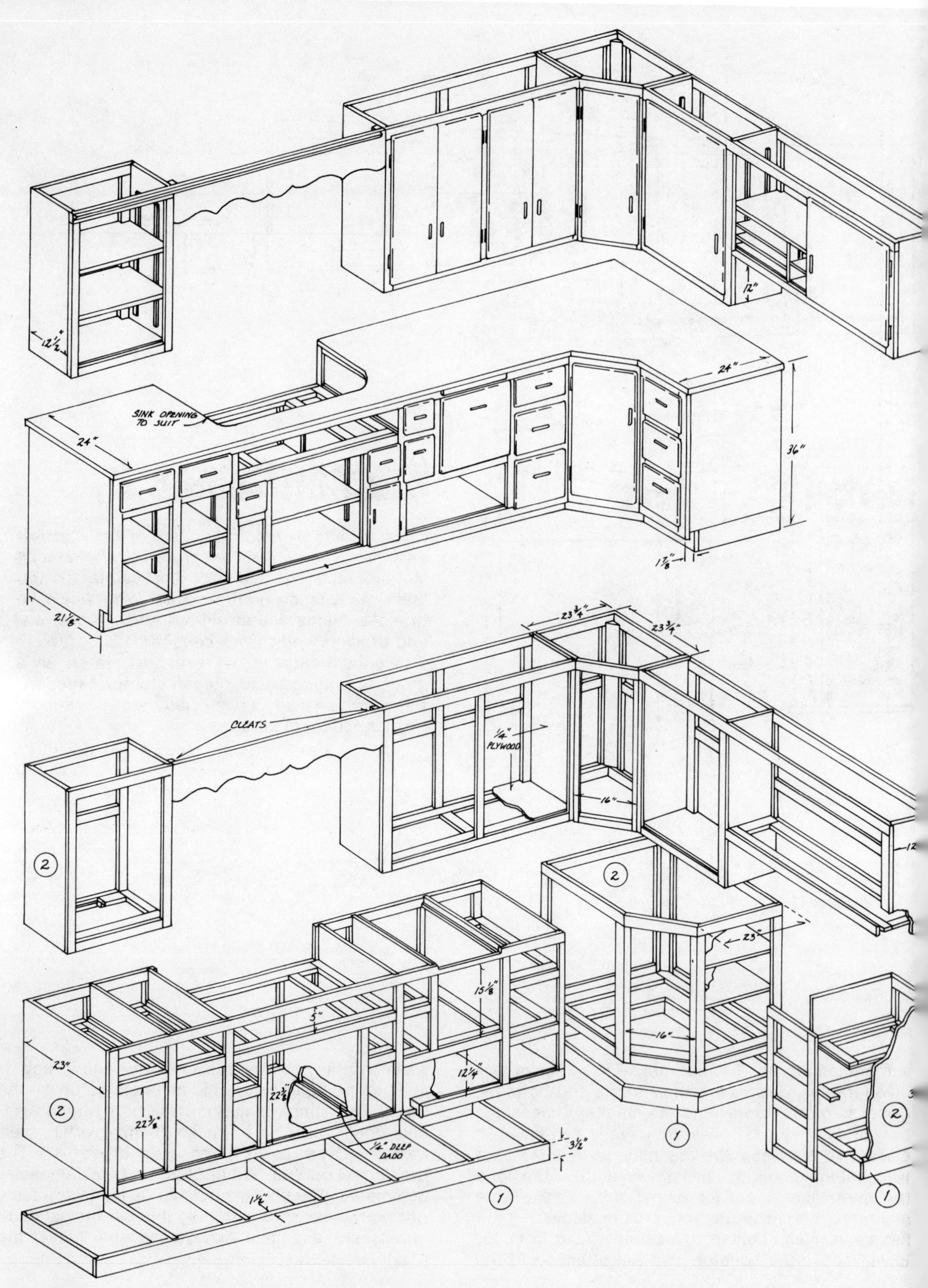
12½"
12"
SINK OPENING TO SUIT
24"
24"
36"
1⅞"
21⅛"
23¾"
23¾"
CLEATS
¼" PLYWOOD
16"
2
2
23"
15⅛"
5"
23"
12¼"
22⅞"
2
22⅞"
¼" DEEP DADO
3½"
1½"
1
16"
1
2
1

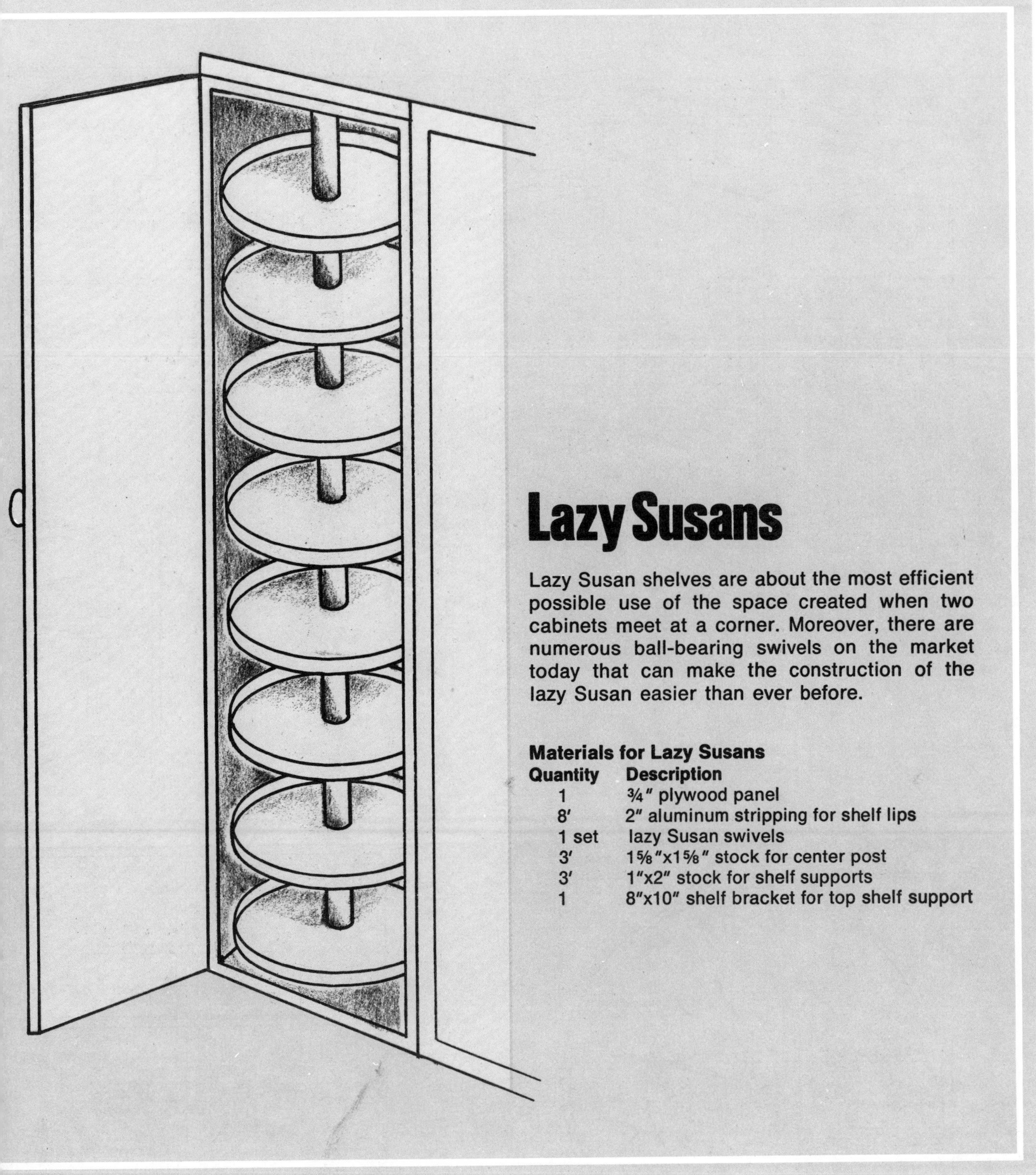

Lazy Susans

Lazy Susan shelves are about the most efficient possible use of the space created when two cabinets meet at a corner. Moreover, there are numerous ball-bearing swivels on the market today that can make the construction of the lazy Susan easier than ever before.

Materials for Lazy Susans

Quantity	Description
1	¾″ plywood panel
8′	2″ aluminum stripping for shelf lips
1 set	lazy Susan swivels
3′	1⅝″x1⅝″ stock for center post
3′	1″x2″ stock for shelf supports
1	8″x10″ shelf bracket for top shelf support

Cabinets. The standard kitchen counter cabinet is 24″ deep and about 35″ high. By the time the thickness of the walls, braces and supports are taken into account, there is roughly an area 36″ in diameter by 26″ high inside an average corner. The cabinet kick plate is about 3½″ high and 2″ to 3″ deep. It is this height that positions the bottom shelf in the lazy Susan. The kick plate can be extended to brace the center post of the unit as shown in Fig. A. Or, the center post can be planted with its base swivel directly on the floor. Beveled faceplates must be attached to the

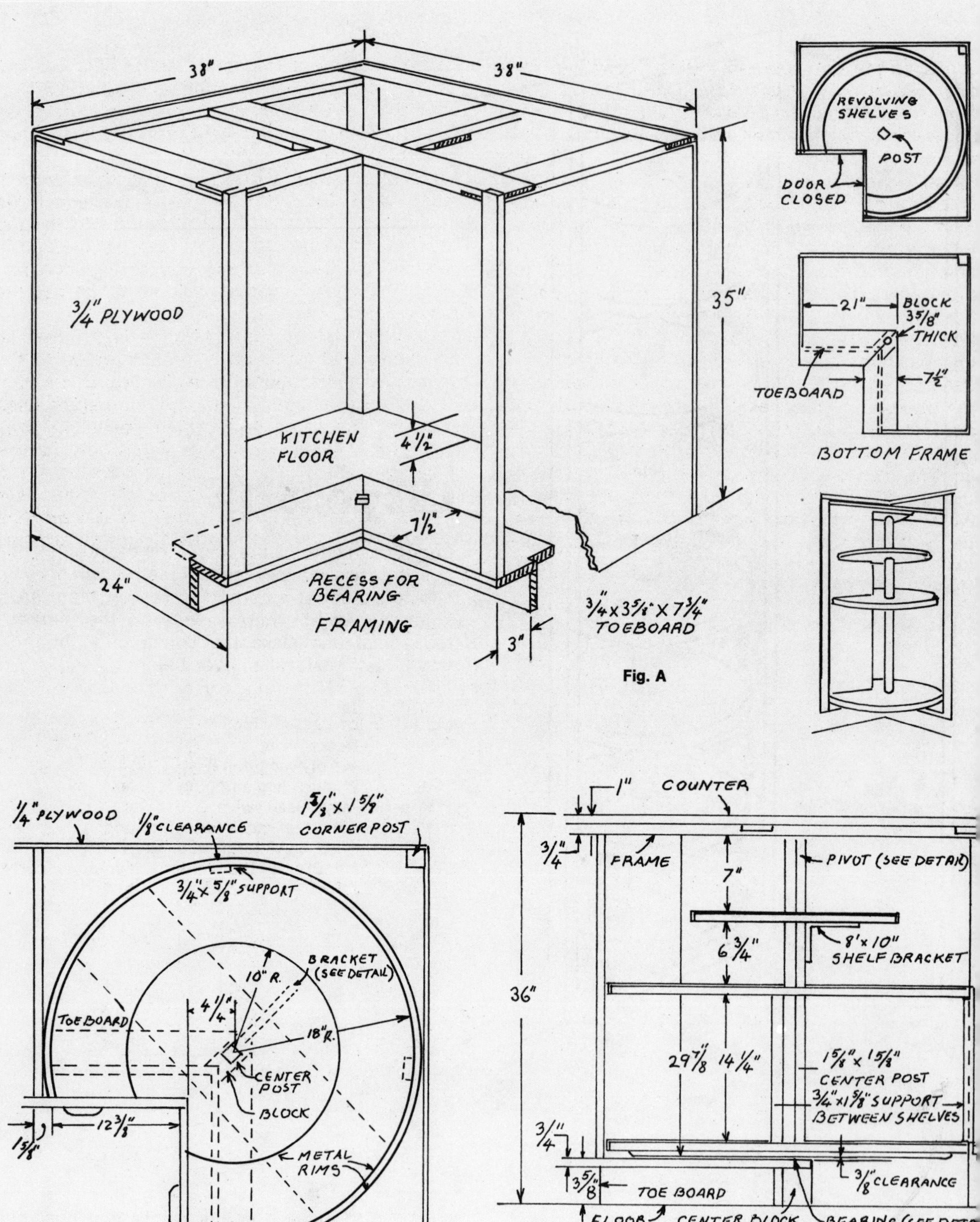
38"
38"
3/4" PLYWOOD
35"
KITCHEN FLOOR
4 1/2"
7 1/2"
24"
RECESS FOR BEARING
FRAMING
3"
3/4 x 3 5/8" x 7 3/4" TOEBOARD
REVOLVING SHELVES
POST
DOOR CLOSED
21"
BLOCK 3 5/8" THICK
TOEBOARD
7 1/2"
BOTTOM FRAME
1/4" PLYWOOD
1/8" CLEARANCE
1 5/8" x 1 5/8" CORNER POST
3/4" x 5/8" SUPPORT
BRACKET (SEE DETAIL)
10" R.
4 1/4"
TOEBOARD
18" R.
CENTER POST
BLOCK
12 3/8"
1 5/8"
METAL RIMS
BEVELED FACE PLATE
3"
4 1/2"
24"
1"
COUNTER
3/4"
FRAME
PIVOT (SEE DETAIL)
7"
6 3/4"
8" x 10" SHELF BRACKET
36"
29 7/8
14 1/4"
1 5/8" x 1 5/8" CENTER POST
3/4" x 1 5/8" SUPPORT BETWEEN SHELVES
3/4"
3 5/8
TOE BOARD
3/8" CLEARANCE
FLOOR
CENTER BLOCK
BEARING (SEE DETA
SCREW FLANGE TO BOTTOM OF REVOLVING SHELVES
SET IN RECESS IN BOTTOM FRAME
BEARING

Fig. A

Fig. B

Fig. C

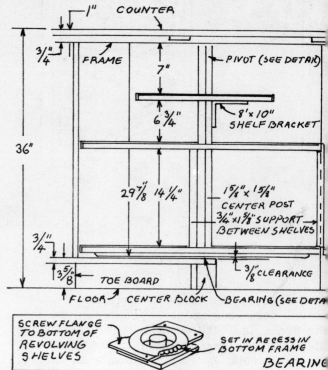

edges of the cabinets (Fig. B) to complete the door quarter of the lazy Susan, but this is best done after the unit has been installed. If the floor under the cabinet corner is at all weak, nail a ¾" plywood plate to it to give these revolving shelves as much stability as possible. The existing facings or doors of the cabinets may be reused on the Susan, so remove them from the cabinets carefully.

Revolving shelves. Everything about this shelf unit must reside completely inside the cabinet, preferably with a ⅛" clearance on all sides so that the unit swings freely. The dimensions shown in Figs. B and C are arbitrary and should be used only as approximate guides. The construction procedure begins by cutting two large circles from ¾" plywood, in this case with an 18" radius, and one smaller circle with a 10" radius. Mortise the centers for the 1⅝"x1⅝" center post (Figs. B and C). The 12⅜"x12⅜" facing quarter is cut out of the two big shelves with an appropriate amount removed from the smaller shelf. The curved edges of the shelves are given a 2" aluminum lip, and the shelves are assembled on their center post. Place two 1"x2" support braces between the two bottom shelves at their outer edges (Figs. B and C). The top shelf can be reinforced with an 8"x10" shelf bracket attached to the center post (Fig. C). Glue-screw the facings or doors to the notched sides of the shelves.

Installation. Attach the top and bottom swivels to the cabinet floor (or kick plate) and under the counter top. Screw the swivel flanges to the top and bottom of the center post and put the unit in the cabinet. Bevel cut and attach the edge facings to the sides of the cabinets to fill out the Susan facing.

Variations. The concept behind a lazy Susan is, once again, to bring hard-to-reach space to the user, and the variations are many. Fig. D is a half-Susan/half-shelf form of storage that can be used under a straight counter cabinet, or in any wall unit. Fig. E is what happens if a whole narrow closet is fitted with an 8' lazy Susan tower. Fig. F is just one way of using a lazy Susan. Other uses might be for tools in the corner of a workshop cabinet, for cosmetics and medicines or to store records.

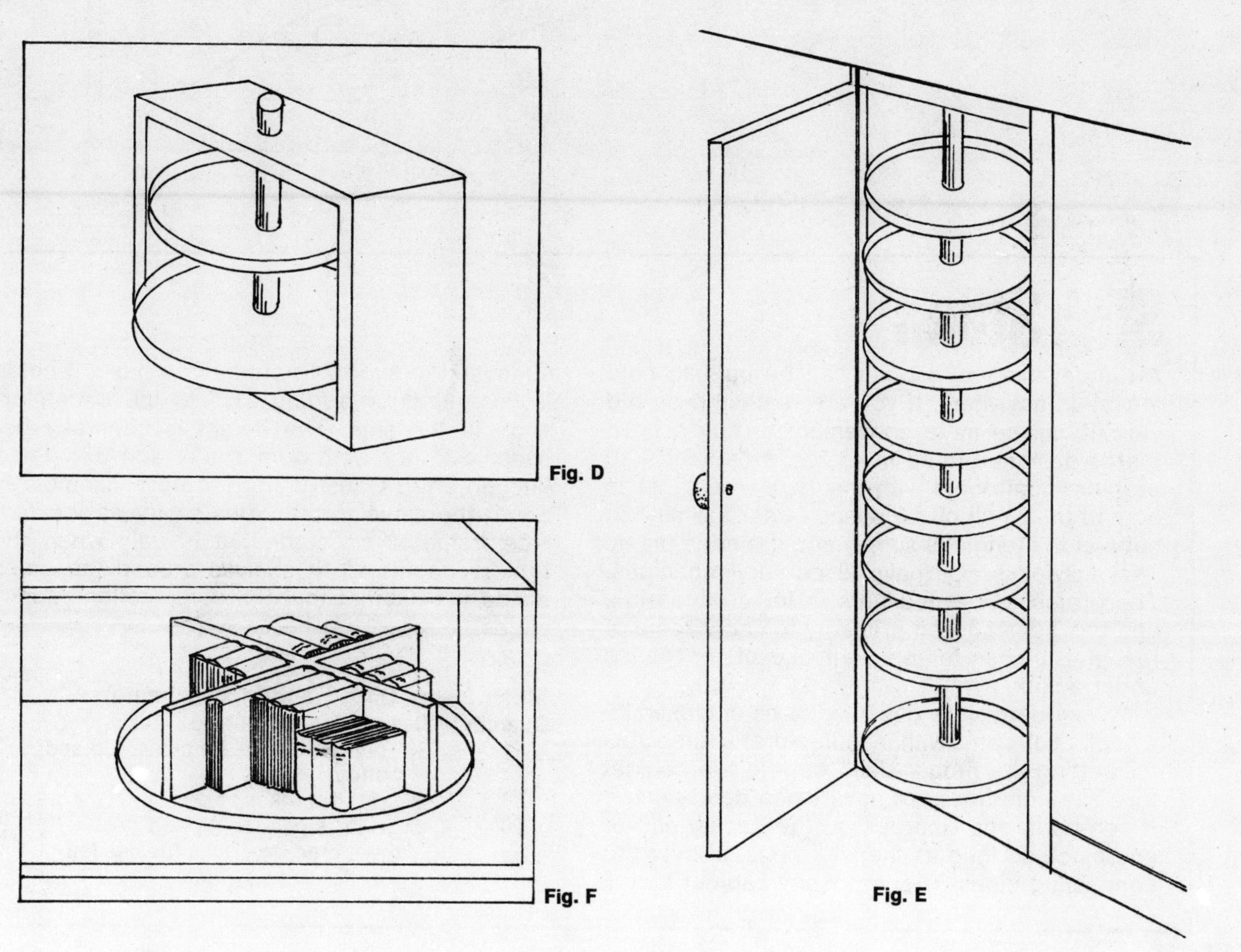

Fig. D

Fig. F

Fig. E

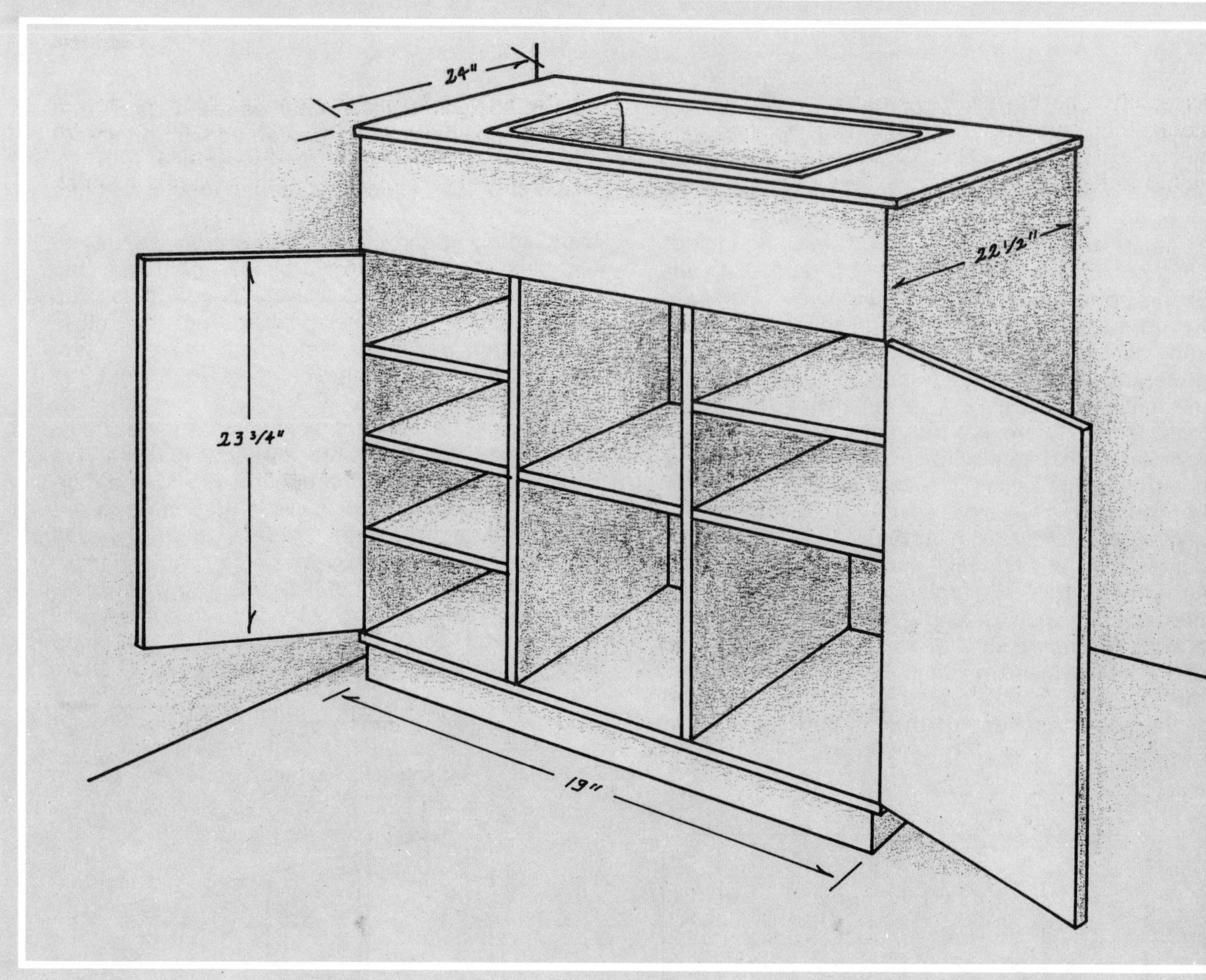

Sink Stand

An under-the-sink cabinet can be built to hold any sink, anywhere. If you are replacing an old sink, it will be more convenient to buy a bowl that is designed to be fitted into a cabinet. The problem confronted with this type of cabinet is how to utilize all of the space under the sink in spite of the tangle of supply and drainage pipes. The answer is, you have to be very ingenious. The project presented here is for a wide sink, and has been chosen primarily to show some of the possibilities for efficient use of the space under a sink.

The modern sinks designed to be enclosed by a cabinet all come with manufacturer's templates for cutting the proper-sized hole in the cabinet top. The hole does not have to be dead-center. It can be at one side or the other, at an end or any place so long as the sink remains over the connecting pipes. The top of any cabinet that is supposed to simply fit around the basin it holds is computed by adding 2½" to the circumference of the sink. The height is generally between 33" (for bathroom sinks) and 37" (for a kitchen unit). Construction of these cabinets is about the same for all types so far as the outside frame is concerned; it is only when the builder begins to fit shelves around the pipes inside the cabinet that the construction usually varies.

Materials for Sink Stand (approximate)

Quantity	Description
1	¾" plywood panel for sides, top and bottom
8′	¾"x3½" stock for base
20′	¾"x1½" stock for support rails
	hinges, brackets, pulls (as needed)

Assembly. The base is constructed with ¾"x3½" stock; this particular project, when finished, will measure 19"x21¾". The ¾" plywood bottom is nailed to the top of the frame. The sides, notched for the kick plate, are then nailed to the sides of the frame. If at all possible, a ¼" back should be attached to the rear edges of the sides and bottom frame. In all probability, if there is to be a back

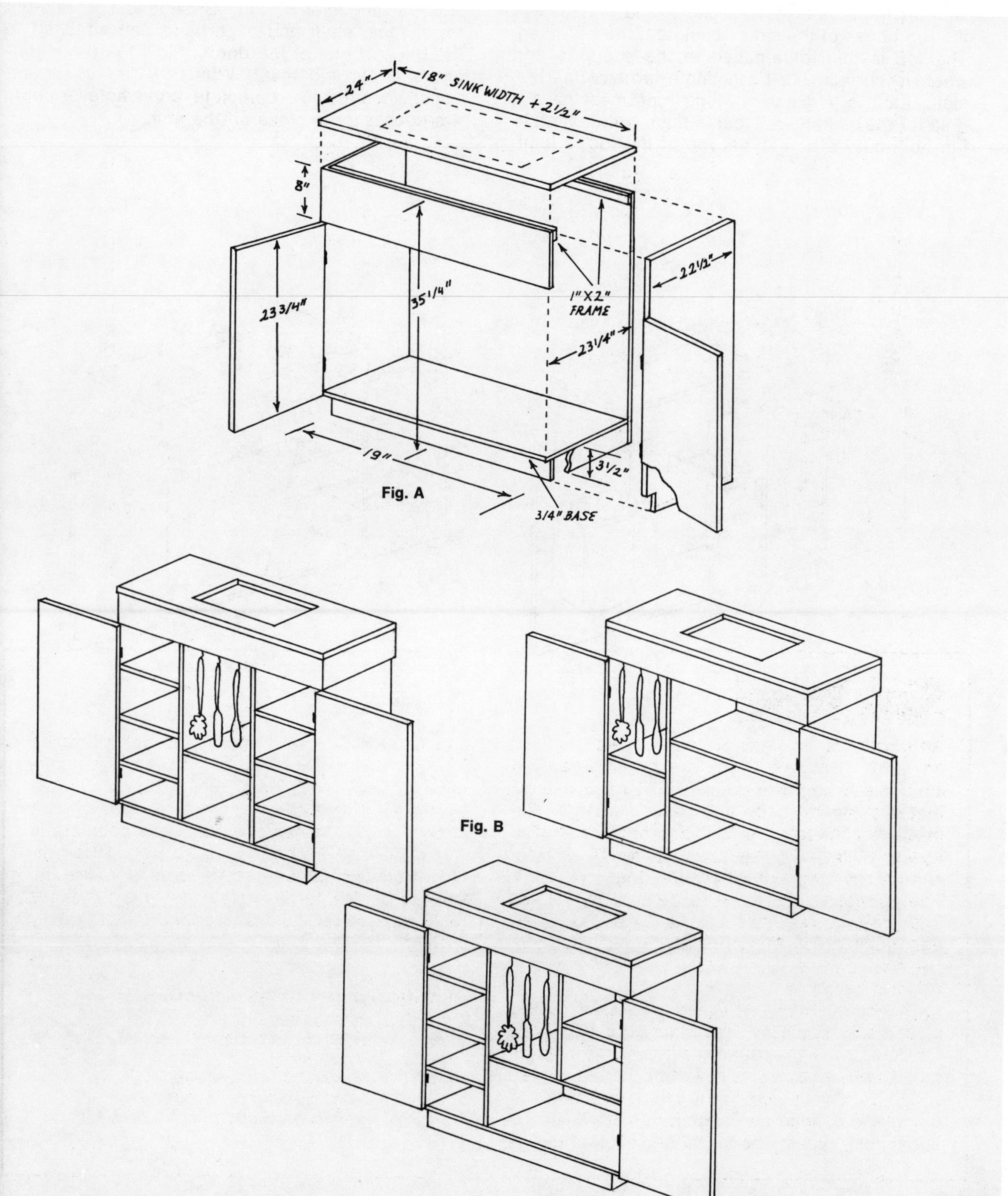

Fig. A

Fig. B

several holes for the pipes will have to be drilled through it. Sometimes, this presents so many problems that it is easier to skip the back altogether. The interior frame is made from 1″x2″ stock and is placed about 8″ from the top of the sides, or slightly lower than the bottom of the sink. The top support frame is also 1″x2″ stock and is nailed to the top edges of the sides, back and the 8″ facing. The top is then glue-nailed to the supports and whatever surface (plastic laminate, terrazzo, marble, slate, etc.) is laid down. Stone tops must have a hole for the sink already cut in them, with a matching hole cut in the cabinet top. If the top is laminated, the hole is cut out of the top with a sabre saw. The cabinet is then put in its place around the pipes, and the sink hooked into the house water-supply system.

Inside the cabinet. There are numerous ways of using the space under a sink. Fig. B shows some shelf arrangements. Fig. C suggests a pull-out towel rack, shelf and a garbage pail attached to the back of one of the doors. Fig. D is a hamper-and-shelf arrangement. Whatever the configurations, when they are complete, add whatever doors are necessary to close off the unit.

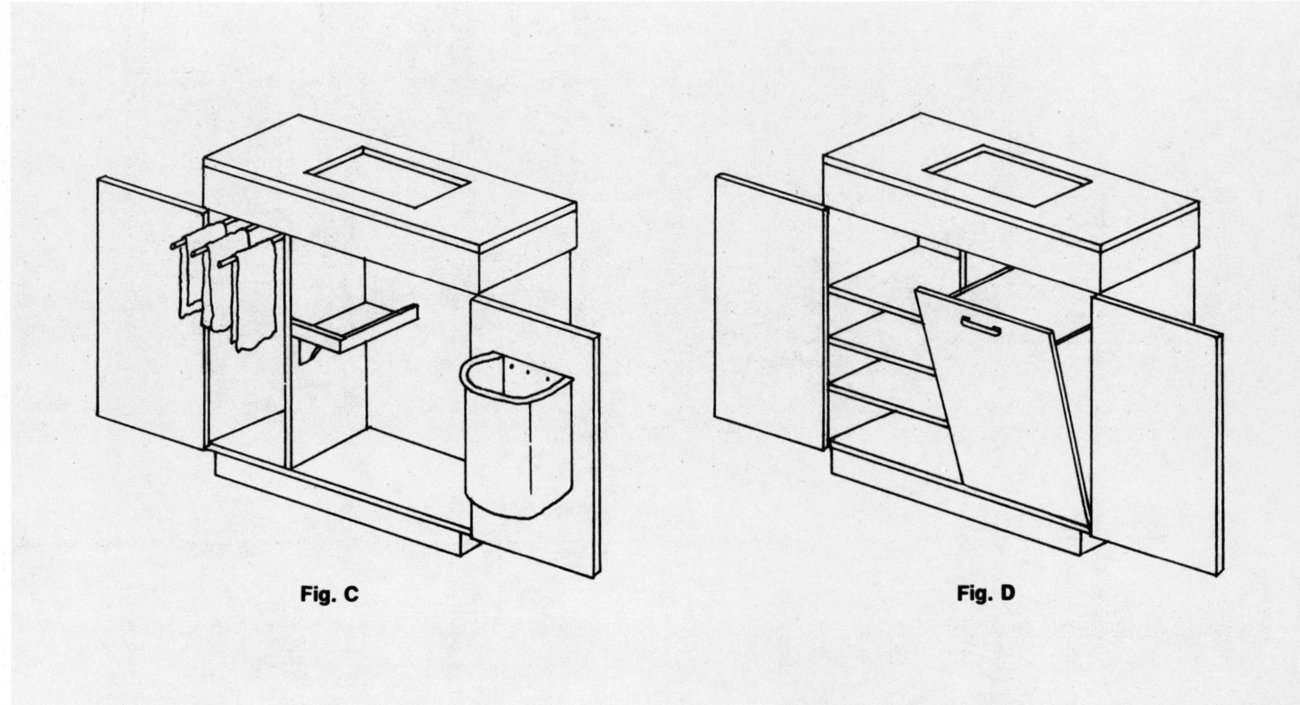

Fig. C

Fig. D

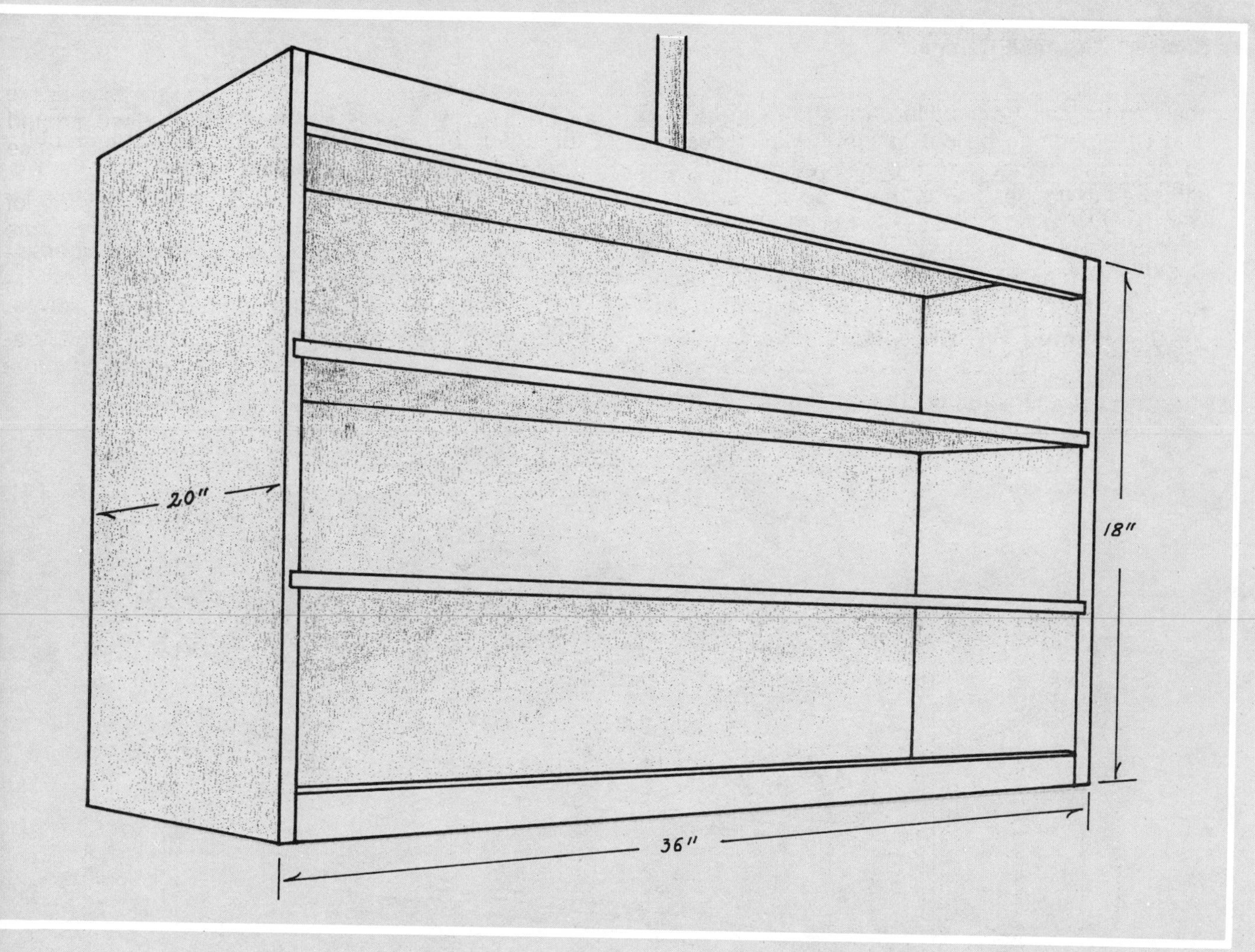

Open Hanger

The exact dimensions of this open hanger cabinet are determined by the width and length of the counter below it. The hanger could, for example, be 3′ wide and accessible from either side of a 3′-wide island. Or, as shown here, it could be 20″ wide over a 24″-wide peninsula. Clearance between the counter and the hanger is also a matter of preference. At least 18″ is recommended, but the bottom of the hanger could be as high as 6′ to provide standing clearance. The finish of the cabinet can be anything from veneer, to a plastic laminate, to a hardwood plywood, or just plain plywood. The dimensions shown in the drawing are completely arbitrary.

Materials for Open Hanger

Quantity	Description
1	¾″ plywood panel
2	2″ pipes and 4 flanges for hanging

Cutting. The sides are ¾″ plywood, cut 18″x20″ and dadoed for the three shelves and top, as shown in Fig. A. The two 5″-wide top rails and two 3″-wide bottom rails are cut 34½″ long. The three shelves and top are ¾″x20″x35¼″.

Assembly. Glue-screw the shelves and top in their dadoes; attach the top and bottom rails. Tape or add trim to the visible edges of the plywood on the sides, shelves and bottom of the rails.

Installation (Figs. B and C). Two ways in which

the hanger can be installed are shown in Figs. B and C. Pipes can be cut to the length necessary to hold the hanger at the desired height, and attached to flanges bolted to the top of the cabinet (Fig B). A 2"x6"x16" spacer is nailed between the ceiling joists to hold the cabinet in place. Or, if you are fortunate enough to have a joist running exactly where the cabinet is to hang, the pipe flanges may be screwed directly into it. A third system of hanging is shown in Fig. C; this uses a threaded rod, rod coupling and ⅜" hanger bolt. The rod assembly is attached to the joist, then a pipe or tubing is slipped over it, and the cabinet is bolted in place.

Variations. Either sliding glass or hinged wooden doors can be attached to both sides of the cabinet. If the hanger is low over its counter, glass shelves will extend its "open" look.

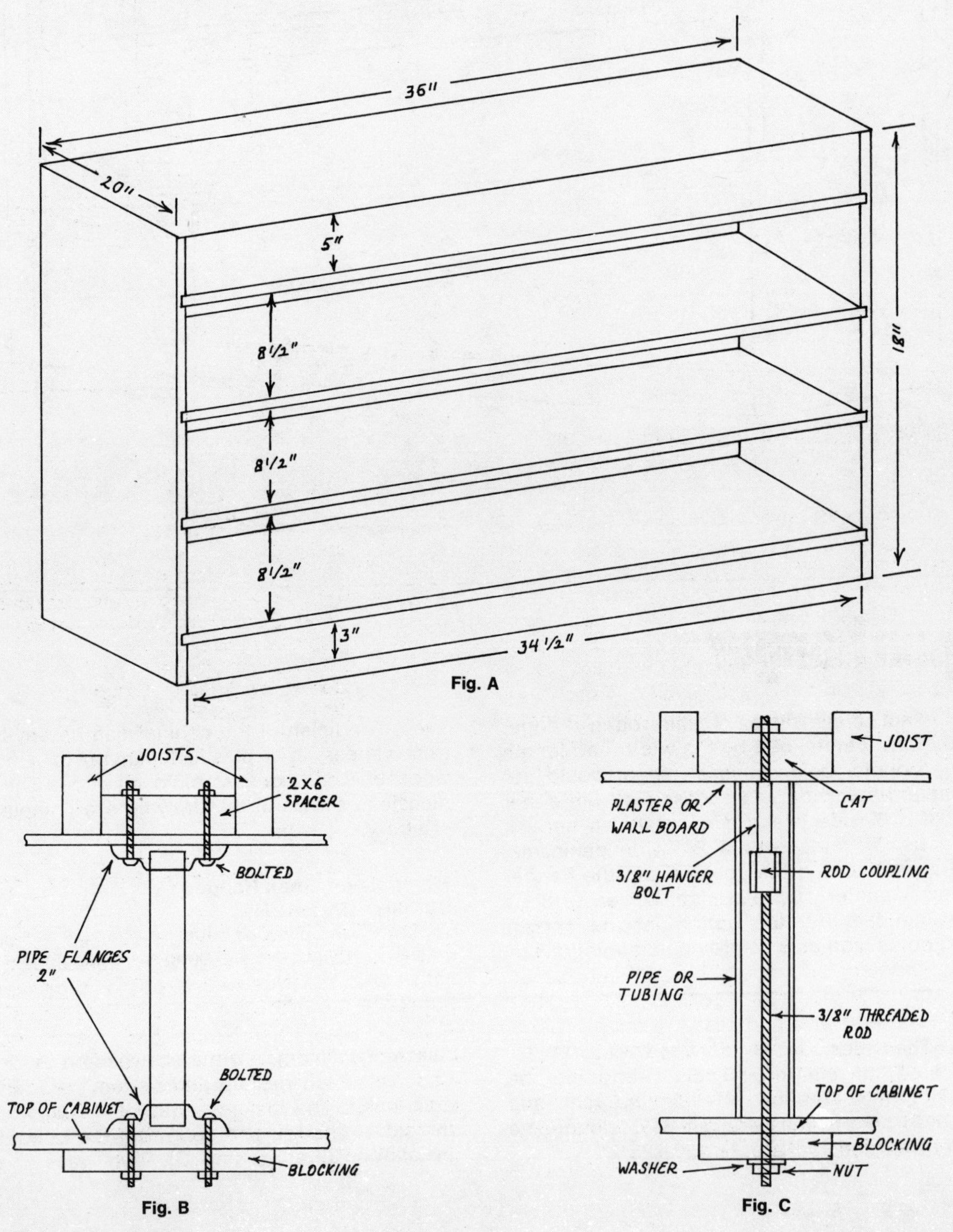

Fig. A

Fig. B

Fig. C

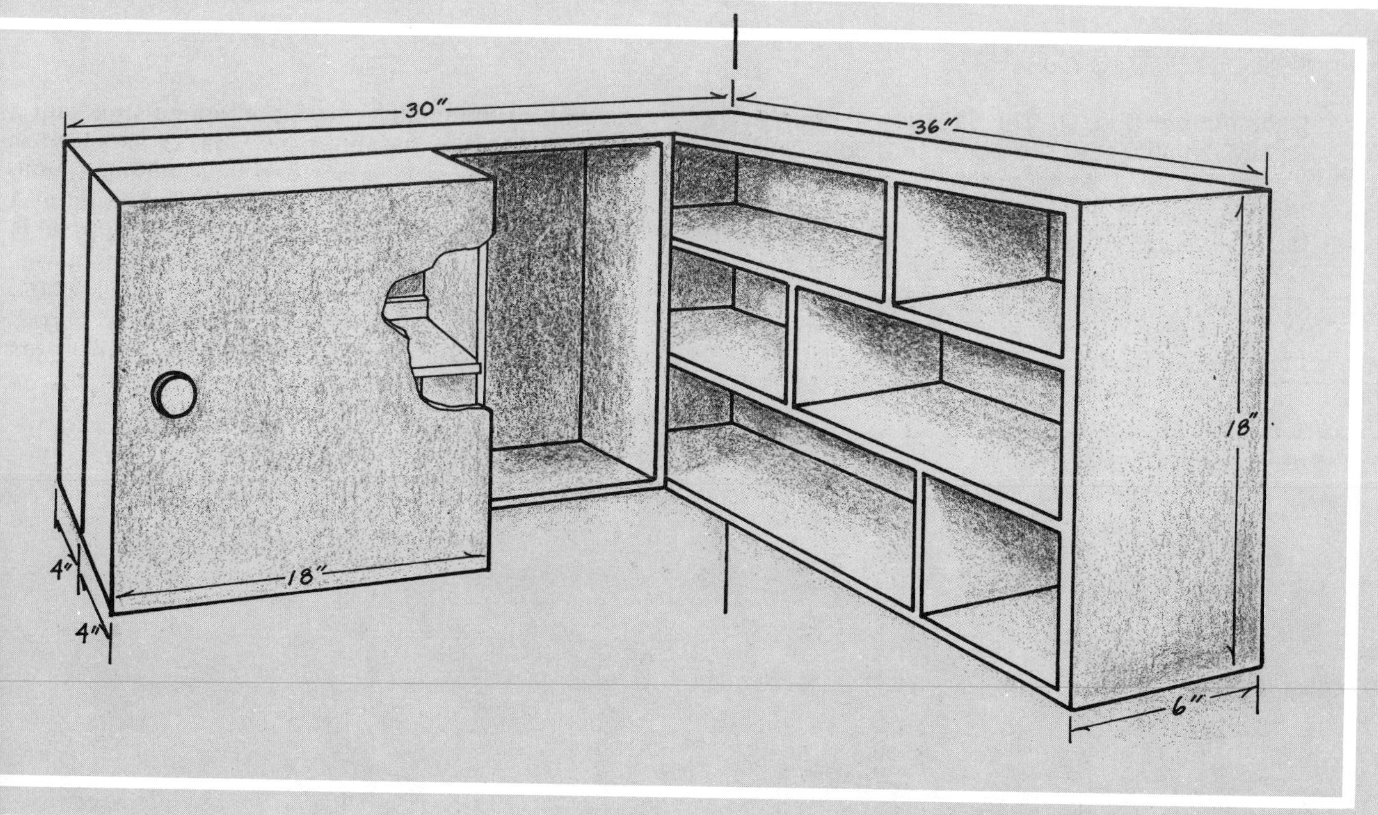

Cosmetic Corner

The cosmetic corner is actually two separate units hung on adjacent bathroom walls. Their dimensions, of course, depend on the amount of wall space available, and whether they are right- or left-angled is guided by whichever corner is being used. The shorter, doored cabinet is a total of 8" deep because that is the depth of a toilet tank which it can very nicely hang over.

Half-inch plywood will do for making the project, but ½" stock is somehow more delicate in looks. The ½" stock may have to be purchased as one wide board, then ripped to the desired widths.

Materials for Cosmetic Corner

Quantity	Description
16½'	½"x6" stock for shelf frame and shelves
19'	½"x4" stock for cabinet and cabinet door
½	⅛"x3'x7' luan for door front, backs of shelves and cabinet
1	18"x½" piano hinge
1	door pull or knob (optional)
1	latch or magnetic catch

Side shelves (Fig. A). Cut four pieces of ½"x6" in 36" lengths for the top, bottom and two shelves; rabbet the ends of the top and bottom pieces. Cut two pieces of ½"x6" to a length of 18"; rabbet them at each end and dado for the shelves. The shelves are set at 7", 6" and 5". Cut vertical dividers to be placed somewhere near the center of each shelf. These can be placed in a straight line, or staggered. Glue-nail the assembly and attach ¼" Masonite to the back.

Cabinet (Fig. B). Cut and rabbet two ½"x4"x24" pieces for the top and bottom horizontals and dado both at the 18" mark to accept the hinge partition. Cut two ½"x4"x18" verticals and dado one of them at the 9" level for the shelf. Both pieces are rabbeted at each end. The hinge-vertical is ½"x4"x 17½" with a dado at the 9" mark for the shelf. The shelf is ½"x4"x17½". Assemble the frame, hinge-vertical and shelf, and glue-nail ¼" Masonite to the back.

Cabinet door (Fig. C). This is a box 4″ deep by 18″ square, so all pieces are cut accordingly. Dado the verticals every 6″ to accept the shelves, and rabbet the top, bottom and sides of the frame. Glue-nail the assembly and attach ⅛″ luan over the front. Cut three strips of ¼″ luan, 1½″ wide by 18″ long, and glue-nail them along the front of the shelves to act as lips. Cut strips of ½″-wide luan to fill in the edges of the frame between the lips.

The door should exactly match the 18″-square section of the cabinet, and is attached to it with a ½″ piano hinge as shown in Figs. C and B. The opposite side of the door can have either a latch or magnetic catch. A pull or knob is optional.

Hanging. The wall shelves should be hung first, then the cabinet is attached to the adjacent wall and butted against the front of the shelves. Because the walls may not be absolute, a certain amount of shimming may have to be done to get everything level.

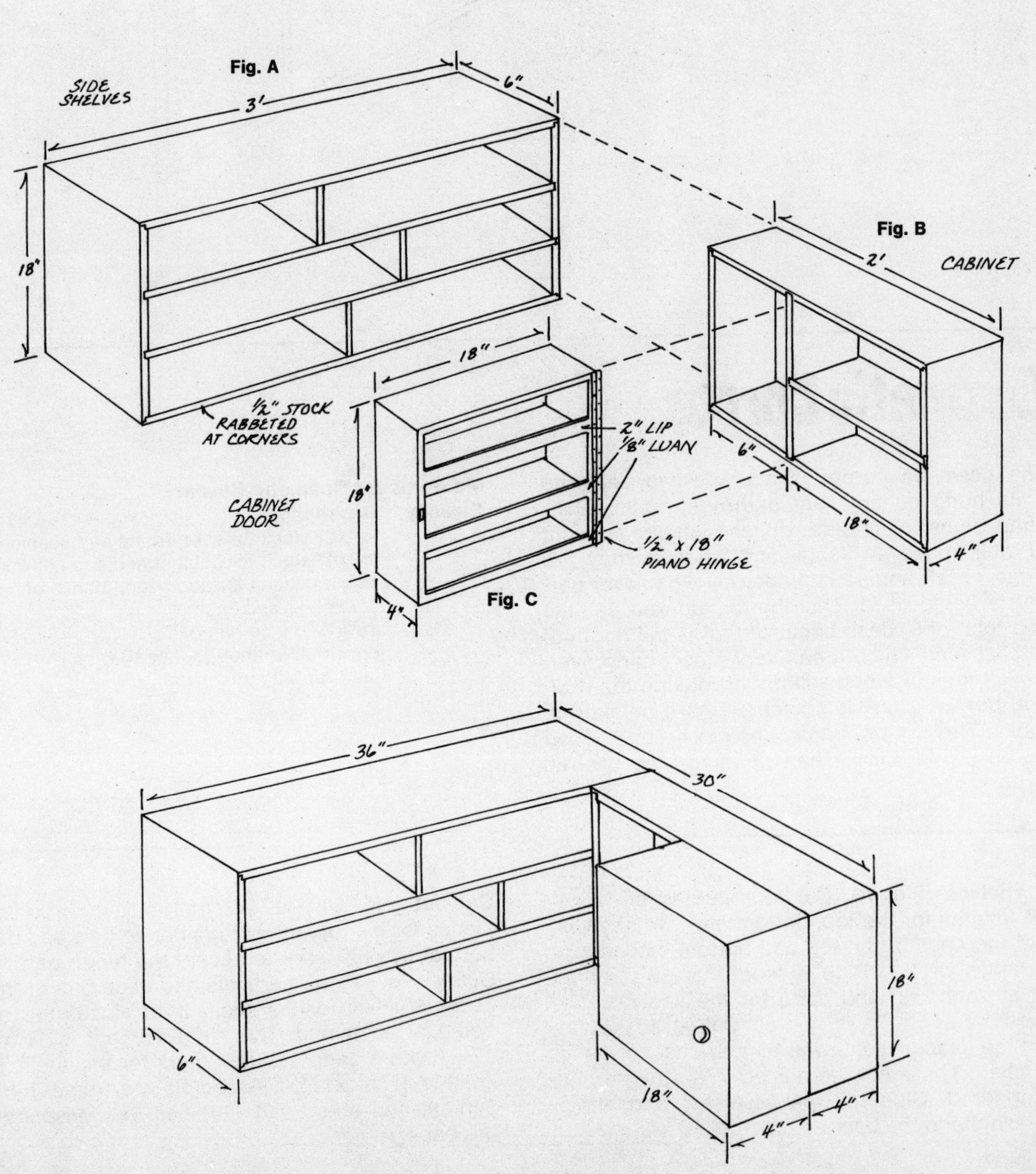

Bathroom Catchall

Take one basic cabinet with sliding doors, combine it with five more like it, hang them in a bathroom, and most of the medicines, cosmetics and notions in an average household can all be stored in one place, 7″ deep by 24″ wide by 48″ in length.

Materials for Bathroom Catchall

Quantity	Description
20′	1″x8″ stock for top, bottom, sides and shelves
½	¼″ plywood panel for back and doors
20′	hardwood sliding door track

Sides. The two sides are 1"x8" stock, cut 3⁄8"x3⁄4"x 48", and rabbeted at each end. They are dadoed on center at 9", 18", 27" and 35¼".
Shelves. All shelves are 1"x8" stock, cut 23¼" long.
Doors. The ten sliding doors are ¼"x9⁵⁄₁₆"x11⅝". Three-quarters-inch holes are drilled into one end of each door to act as pulls.
Top and bottom. The top and bottom are both 1"x 8" stock cut 23¼" long, and will fit into the side rabbets without being rabbeted themselves.

Assembly. Glue-nail the shelves in their dadoes and the top and bottom into their rabbets. Attach the ¼"x24"x48" back, glueing and nailing it to all sides and shelves. Glue-nail the door tracks along the top and bottom edges of the shelves, and insert the doors. Hang the cabinet.
Variations. All of the doors could be hinged. Decorative molding and trim could be added. The cabinet could become the top or bottom 4' of an 8'-high set of shelves.

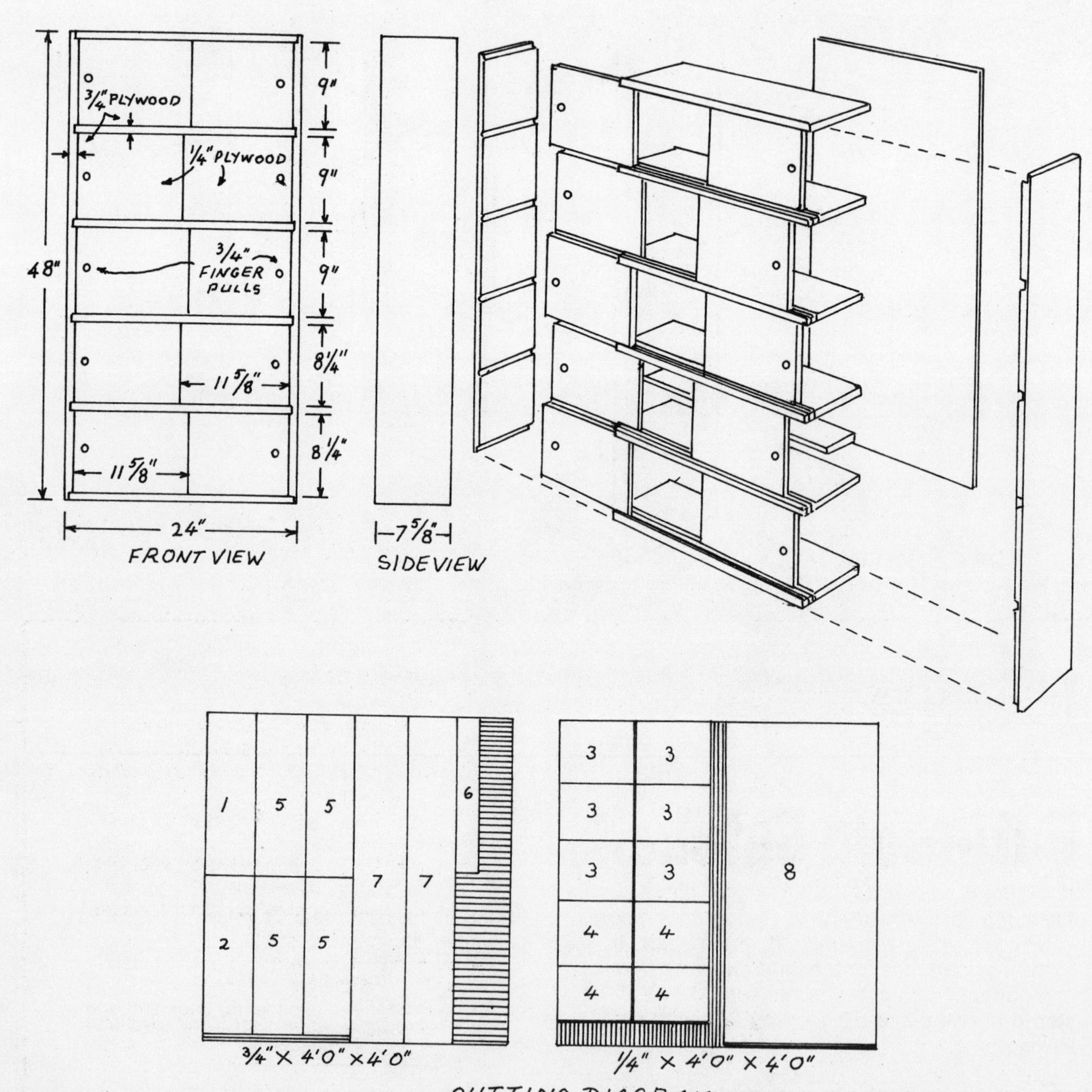

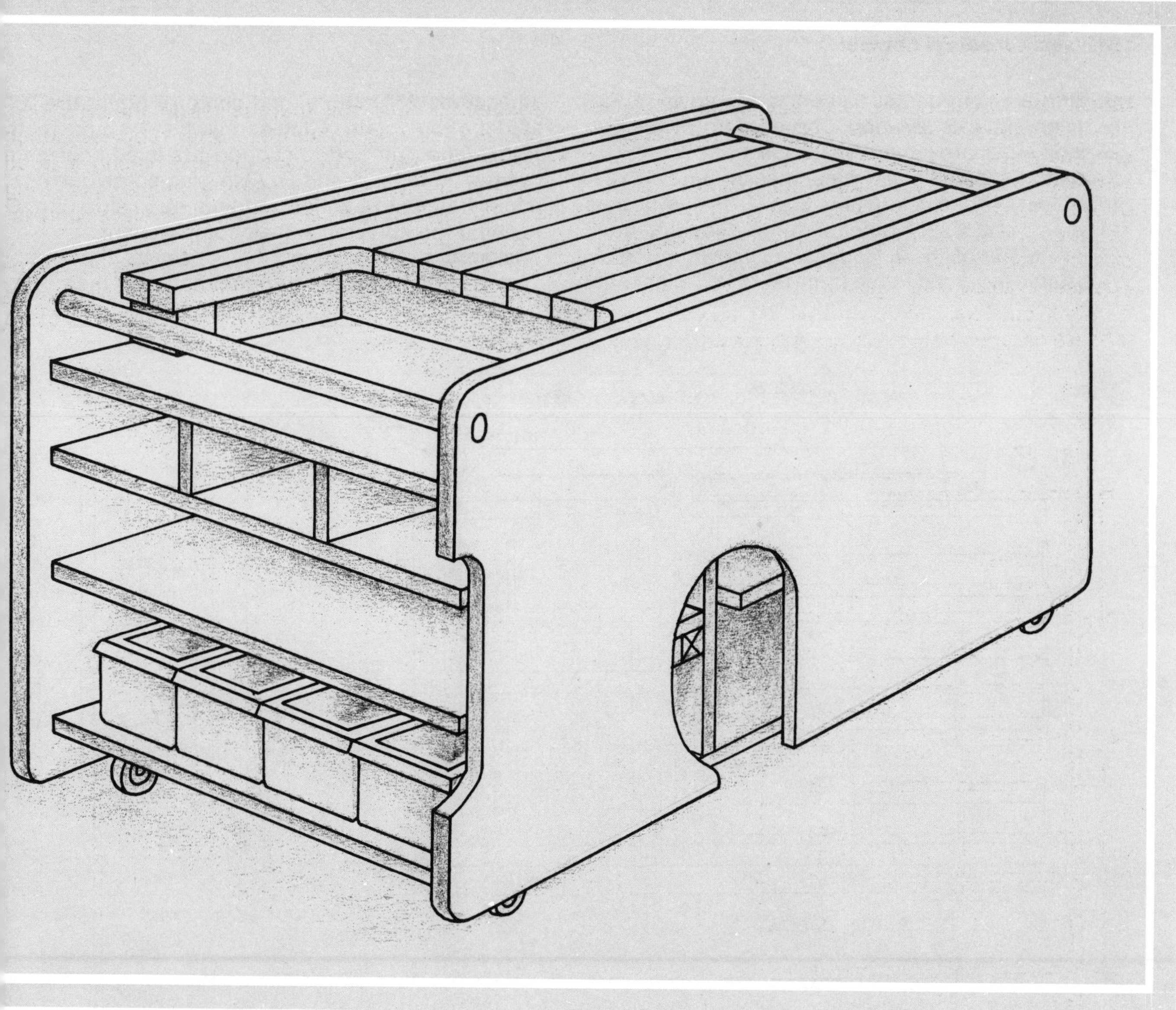

Rolling Modules

There are numerous ways of devising a serving cart, and each can have a specific use: for storage, for cooking, for serving, as a portable bar. The fundamental unit shown here is composed of plywood and laminated butcher block, and measures 39″x26½″x31¹¹⁄₁₆″.

Materials for Rolling Modules

Quantity	Description
2	¾″ A-B plywood panels for sides, bottom, doors and shelves
15′	1⅝″x1⅝″ stock for bottom and butcher block framing
1	1½″x25″x30″ laminated butcher block for fixed top
1	1½″x24½″x15″ laminated butcher block for sliding extension
20′	1″x1″ stock for shelf and door framing
4	pivot hinges for doors
4	2″ casters
4½′	1⅝″ dowels for handles
2	door pulls
1	drawer pull for butcher block extension
8′	adjustable shelf track

Cutting. Lay out and cut all parts as shown in Fig. E, using ¾" A-B plywood. The corners of the two 28"x39" sides are curved on a radius of 2¼".

Framing. Assemble a frame measuring 6½"x25" from 1⅝"x1⅝" stock. Glue-screw it to the bottom of the 1½"x25"x30" butcher block, positioning it ½" from one of the 25" edges, as shown in Fig. A. Assemble a second frame from 1⅝"x1⅝" stock that measures 25" square, and center it under the 25 36" bottom plate. Glue-screw 1"x1" strips to t sides and partition to support the fixed shelves shown in Figs. A and B. Also glue-screw the 1"x door frames to the back edge of each side (Fig. C behind the adjustable shelf compartment.

Assembly. Glue-screw the sides to the botto frame, and insert the partition between them (Fig

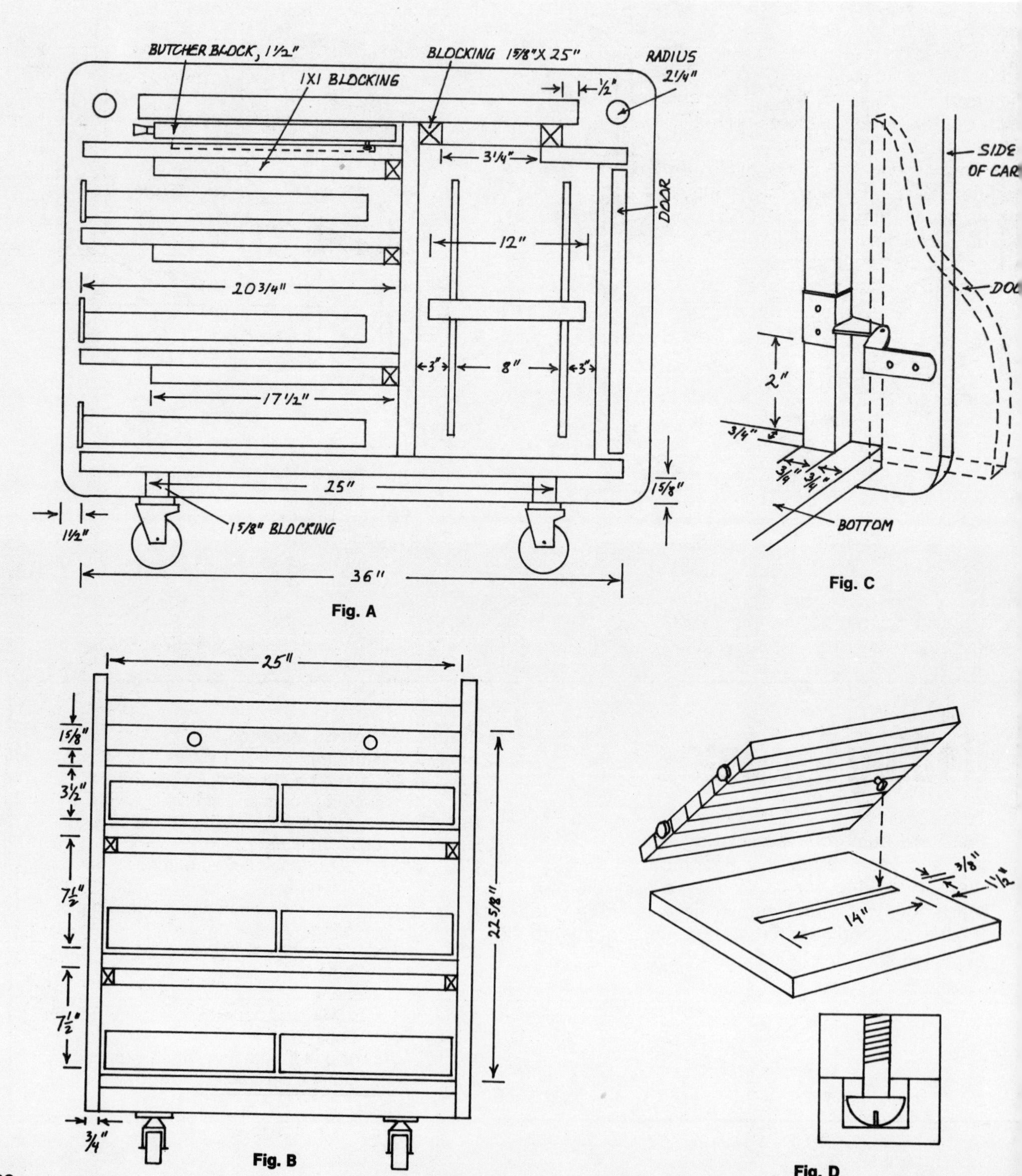

Fig. A

Fig. C

Fig. B

Fig. D

A and B). Attach the three fixed shelves to their supports and glue-screw the 4⅛"x25" top section of the door frame across the top of the sides at the back of the cart. The top fixed shelf has a ¼"x ⅜" stopped dado to accept a stopper screw in the bottom of the sliding 1½"x24½"x15" butcher block extension (see Fig. D). Insert the butcher block extension screw in the dado, and position the fixed butcher block over it, with its 1⅝" stock frame resting on the door top frame. Glue-screw the frame to the top door frame section, sides and partition of the cart. Attach the adjustable shelf tracks to the sides of the cart; hinge the doors as shown in Fig. C. Attach the four casters to each corner of the bottom frame, and insert the two 1⅝" dowels (Fig. A) for handles.

Variations. Using the same basic dimensions, the module can be redesigned to function as a bar unit as shown in Fig. F. Or, it can become a cooking unit as shown in Fig. G. The cutout in the butcher block top is approximately 18"x10½", and will contain a liquid propane burner unit.

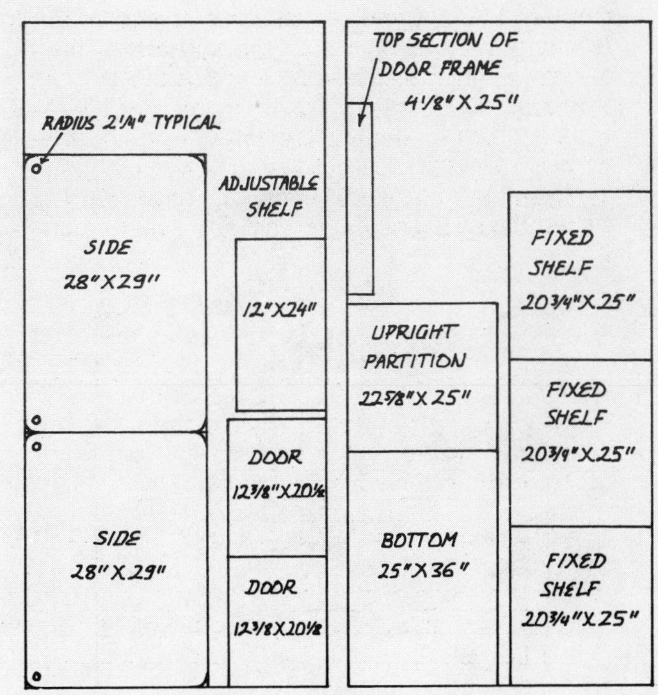

Fig. E

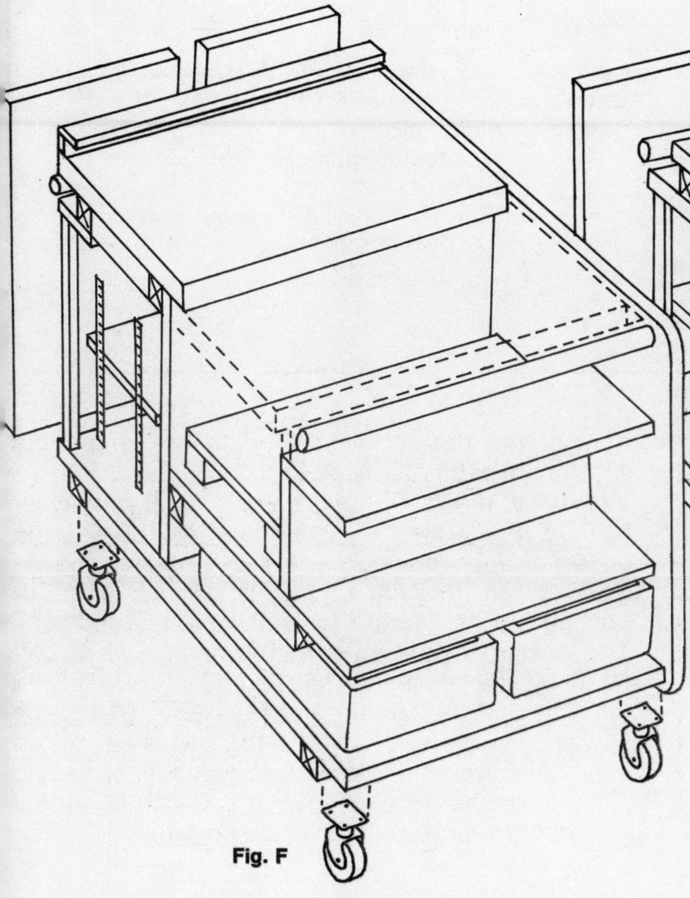

Fig. F

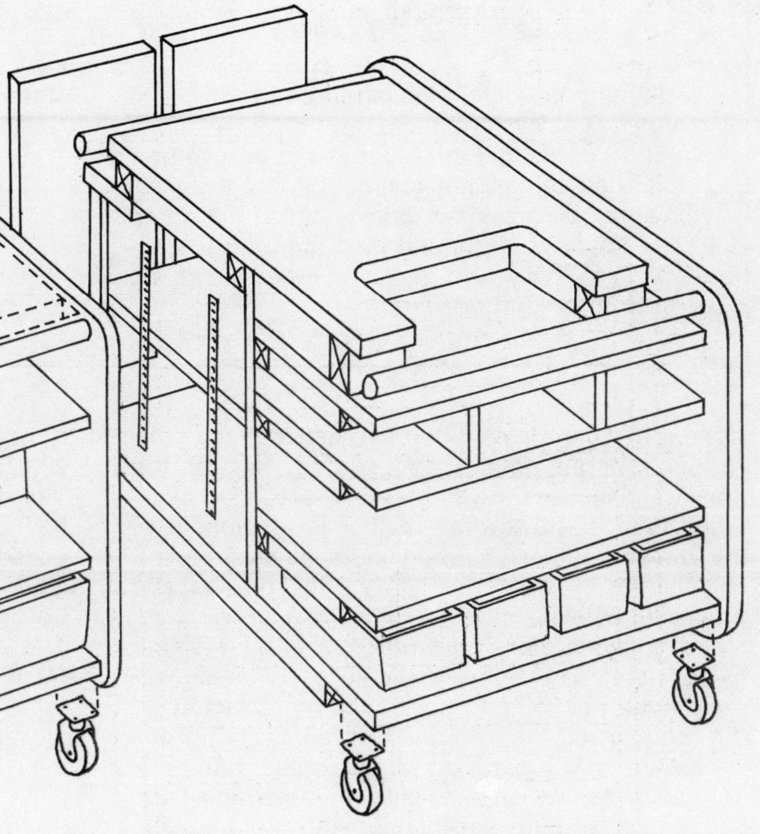

Fig. G

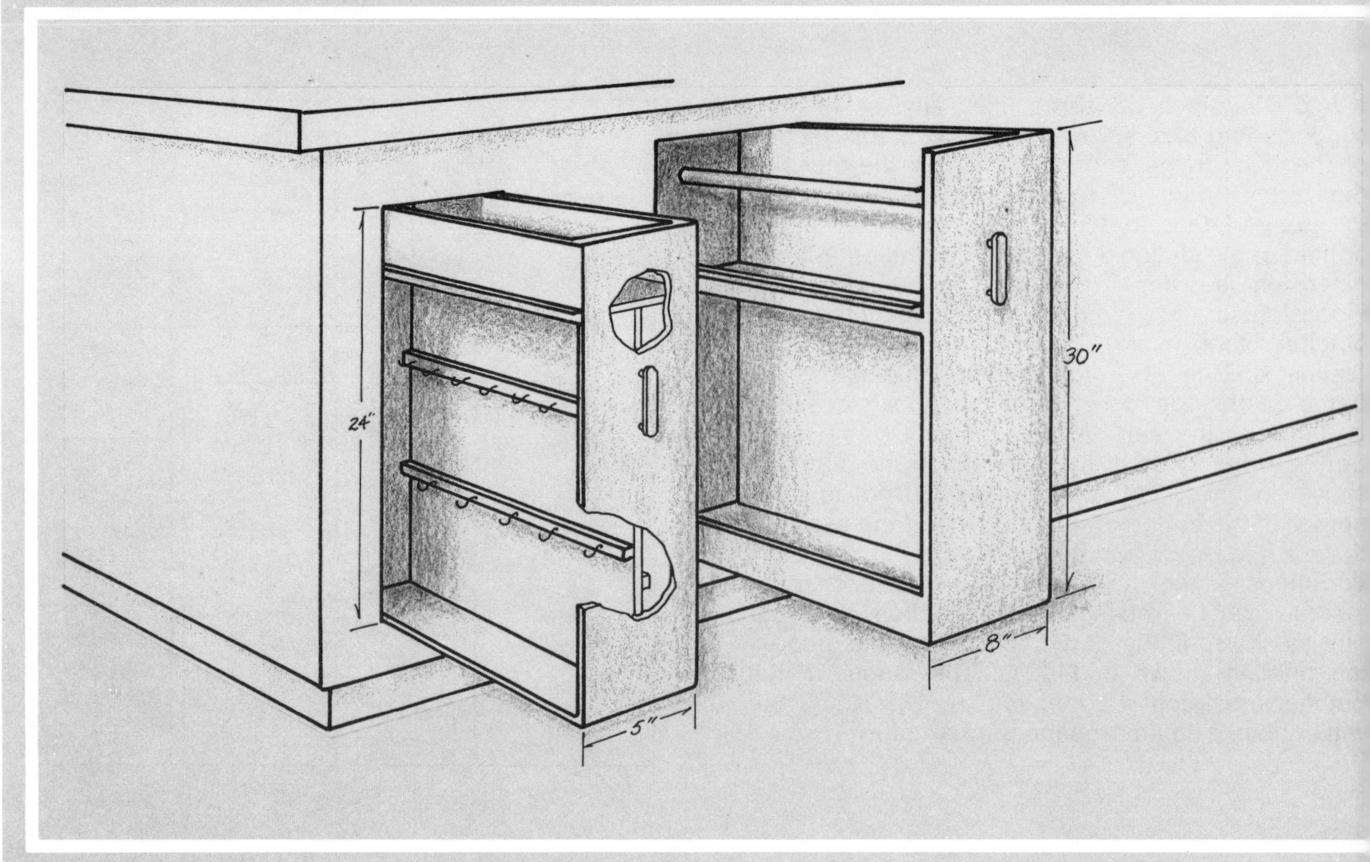

On-End Drawers

Particularly in kitchens, often in bathrooms and sometimes elsewhere, there are narrow sections under counters that are too small to be used for much of anything. They can become useful storage areas by making a drawer that is as deep as the space is wide, and then hanging it sideways. Practically any group of objects can be hung from on-end drawers.

Materials (for a drawer 6"x24"x24")

Quantity	Description
½	¼" plywood panel for partitions and shelf lips
8'	1"x6" stock for horizontals
1 set	24" drawer guides

Assembly. There is no difference between the construction of an on-end drawer than any of the drawers discussed in Chapter 6. There is an additional feature, however, and that is placement of the drawer guides. These should always be put somewhere in the upper third of the drawer and will require some kind of support to screw into. Fig. A shows a utensil drawer 5" wide by 24" high by 22" long. The top of the unit is a 5"-wide, 4"-deep knife pocket, and the tracks are attached to the bottom of the pocket. Centered under this pocket is a ¼" partition which holds four ¾"-square strips, two on each side, which support cup hooks used to hang various cooking utensils. The front of the drawer is finished to be compatible with other cabinets in the kitchen.

Variations. In Fig. B, the drawer is wider and lower to hold heavy cleaning materials, including large boxes of soap powder. The top of the unit is divided by an irregular grid of ½" dowels to partition off storage space for small bottles and jars. The design of any on-end drawer is always dictated by the allowable space and the objects to be stored. For example, pot tops (Fig. D) can be stored in a drawer no more than 6" wide, and if their pulls are small, in as narrow as 4" of space. A paper drawer (Fig. C) must be at least 8" wide if it is to hold large rolls of paper toweling.

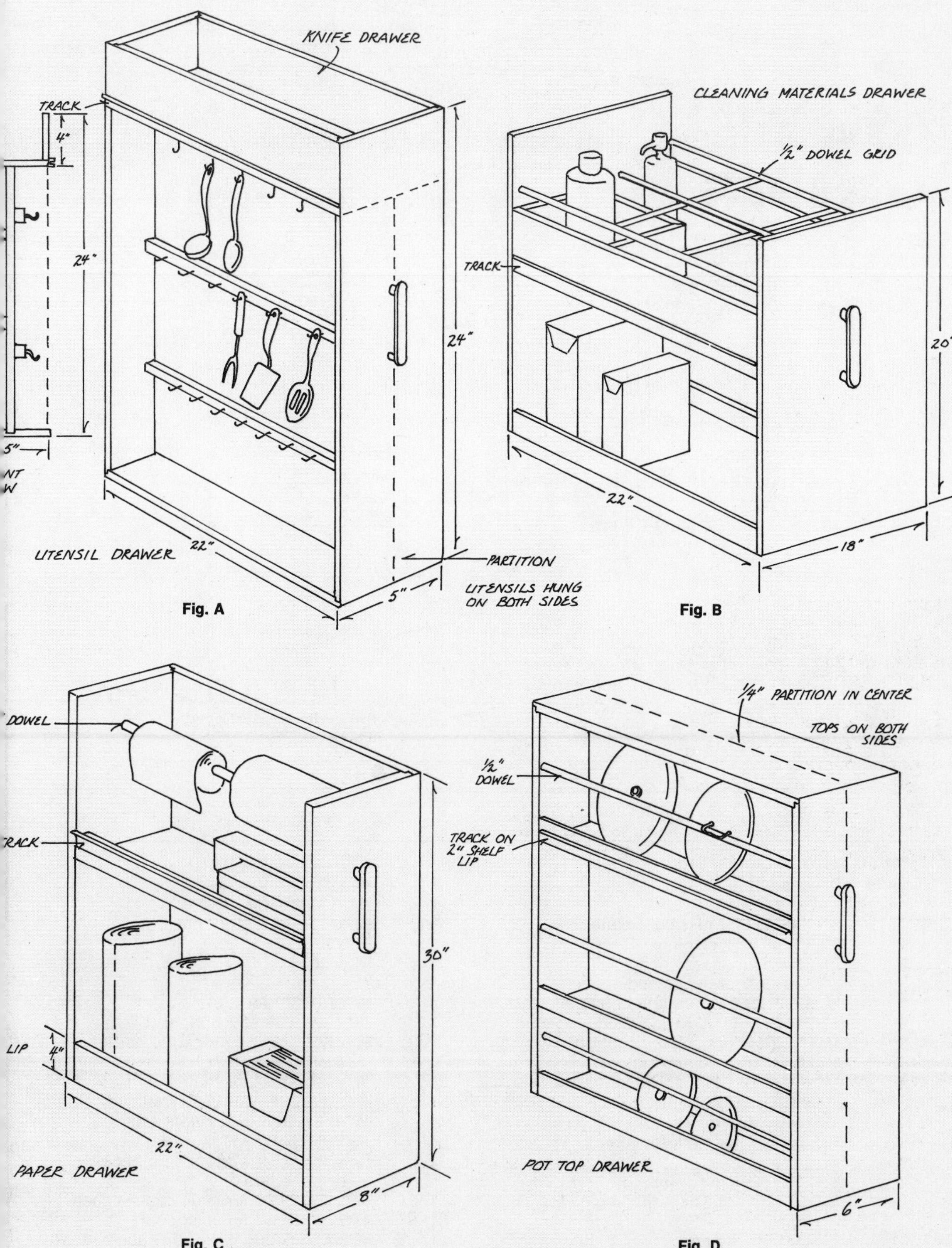
KNIFE DRAWER
TRACK
4"
24"
24"
5"
NT
W
UTENSIL DRAWER
22"
PARTITION
5"
UTENSILS HUNG
ON BOTH SIDES
CLEANING MATERIALS DRAWER
½" DOWEL GRID
TRACK
20"
22"
18"
DOWEL
TRACK
30"
LIP
4"
22"
PAPER DRAWER
8"
¼" PARTITION IN CENTER
TOPS ON BOTH
SIDES
½"
DOWEL
TRACK ON
2" SHELF
LIP
POT TOP DRAWER
6"

Fig. A

Fig. B

Fig. C

Fig. D

Workbench/ Storage Units

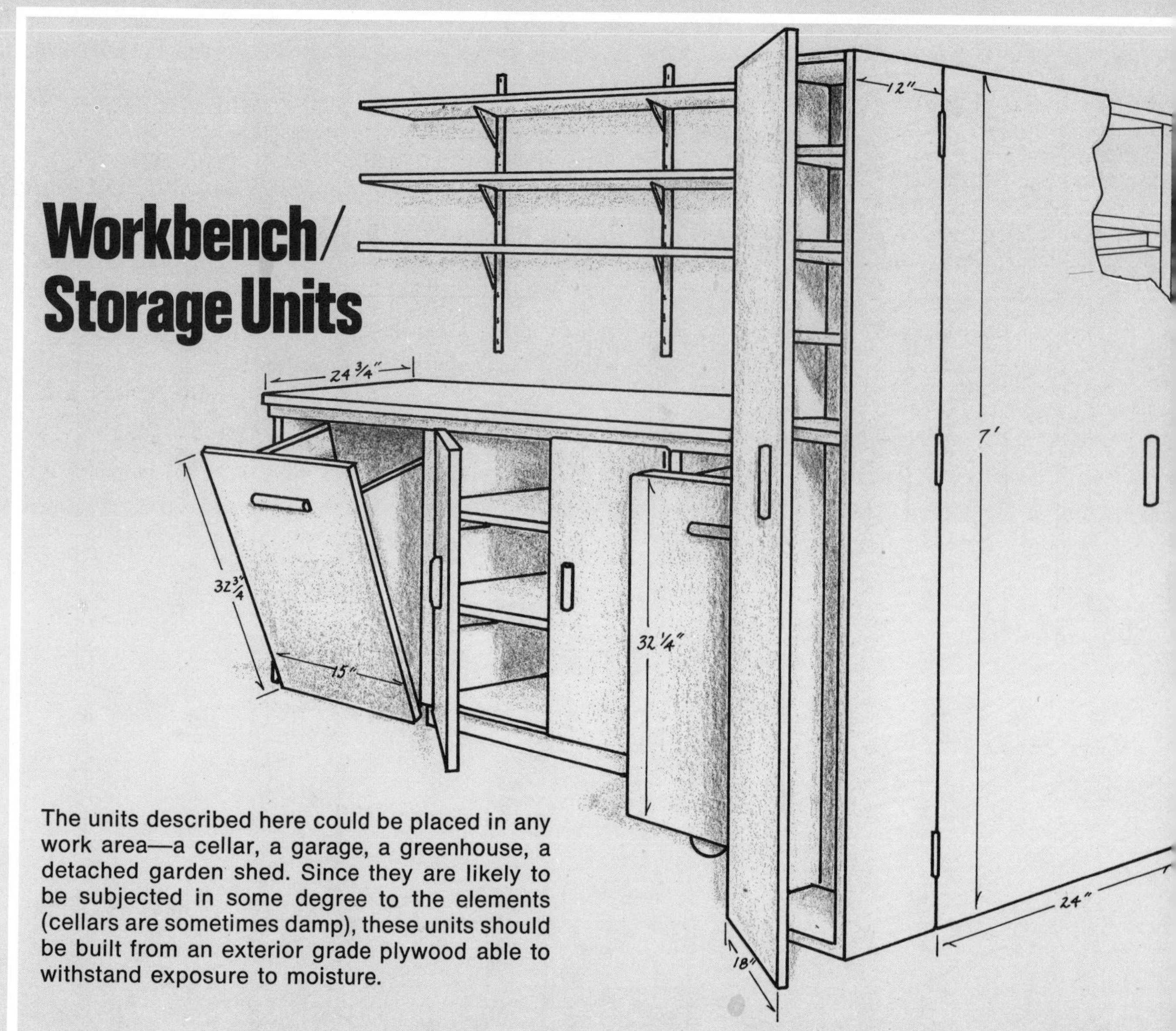

The units described here could be placed in any work area—a cellar, a garage, a greenhouse, a detached garden shed. Since they are likely to be subjected in some degree to the elements (cellars are sometimes damp), these units should be built from an exterior grade plywood able to withstand exposure to moisture.

Materials for Workbench/Storage Units

Quantity	**Description**
Workbench	
1	2"x3"x52½" for rear base plate
1	2"x3"x24" for kick plate
2	2"x3"x17" for base spacers
2	2"x3"x18½" for bench end-spacers
3	¾"x2'x2' for cabinet bottom and shelves
4	1"x2"x22½" for side and divider spacers
1	1"x2"x52½" for back top support
1	1"x2"x54" for front top support
4	¾"x24"x35¼" for cabinet sides and bench ends
1	¾"x24¾"x54" for top
1	¼"x36"x54" for back (optional)
Hamper	
1	¾"x15"x32¾" for front
2	¾"x22"x31" for sides with angled top edges
1	¾"x13"x22" for bottom
1	¾"x11¼"x29" for back
1	15"x1¼" dowel for pivot
Bin	
2	¾"x22"x30" for sides
1	¾"x13"x22" for bottom
1	¾"x11½"x29¼" for back
1	¾"x13"x32" for front
4	3" casters
Storage Unit	
1	¾"x18"x36" for top
1	¾"x17"x35¼" for bottom
1	¾"x17¾"x82½" for center partition (shelf-back)
1	¾"x12"x83½" for front-shelf side
1	¾"x12"x83½" for back-shelf side
1	¾"x17¾"x83¼" for right side
4	¾"x16½"x12" for shelves
1	¼"x23¼"x84" Masonite for back (or pegboard)
1	¾"x17"x22½" for main cabinet shelf
1	¾"x18"x83½" for shelf door
1	¾"x23¼"x83½" for main cabinet door

Workbench assembly. This can be as long as available space allows; the accompanying drawings are for a workbench measuring 54"x24"x36". The base is assembled as shown in Fig. B, and the ¾"x24"x24" cabinet bottom nailed flush with the sides of the center spacers. The two ¾"x24"x35¼" cabinet sides have 1"x2" cleats nailed at the 18¼" and the 33" marks, as well as along their top edges. The two 24"-square shelves are placed on their cleats. The ¾"x24"x54" front top support is nailed across the front top edges of the four sides. The back top corners of the cabinet sides are notched to accept the 1"x2"x52½" back top support; the ¾"x24¾"x54" top is then nailed to the top supports. The unit may have a ¼" back, if desired; it may be nailed directly to a wall; or it may simply be left open and freestanding.

Hamper. The hamper is constructed as shown in Fig. C, with all joinery consisting of either rabbets or dadoes. The 1¼" pivot dowel is positioned so that the ends rest on top of the base plates.

Roll-out bin. The bin is 13"x22"x30" (Fig. D), and rolls on 3" casters. The ¾"x22"x30" sides are butted to the outside of the ¾"x11½"x29¼" back; the ¾"x13"x32" front is butted to the front edges of the sides, as shown in Fig. D.

Storage-unit assembly. The top, bottom, sides and partitions are butted together, then glue-nailed (Fig. E). The back edge of the ¾"x18"x83¼" right side is rabbeted ⅜"x¼" to accept the ¼"x23¼"x

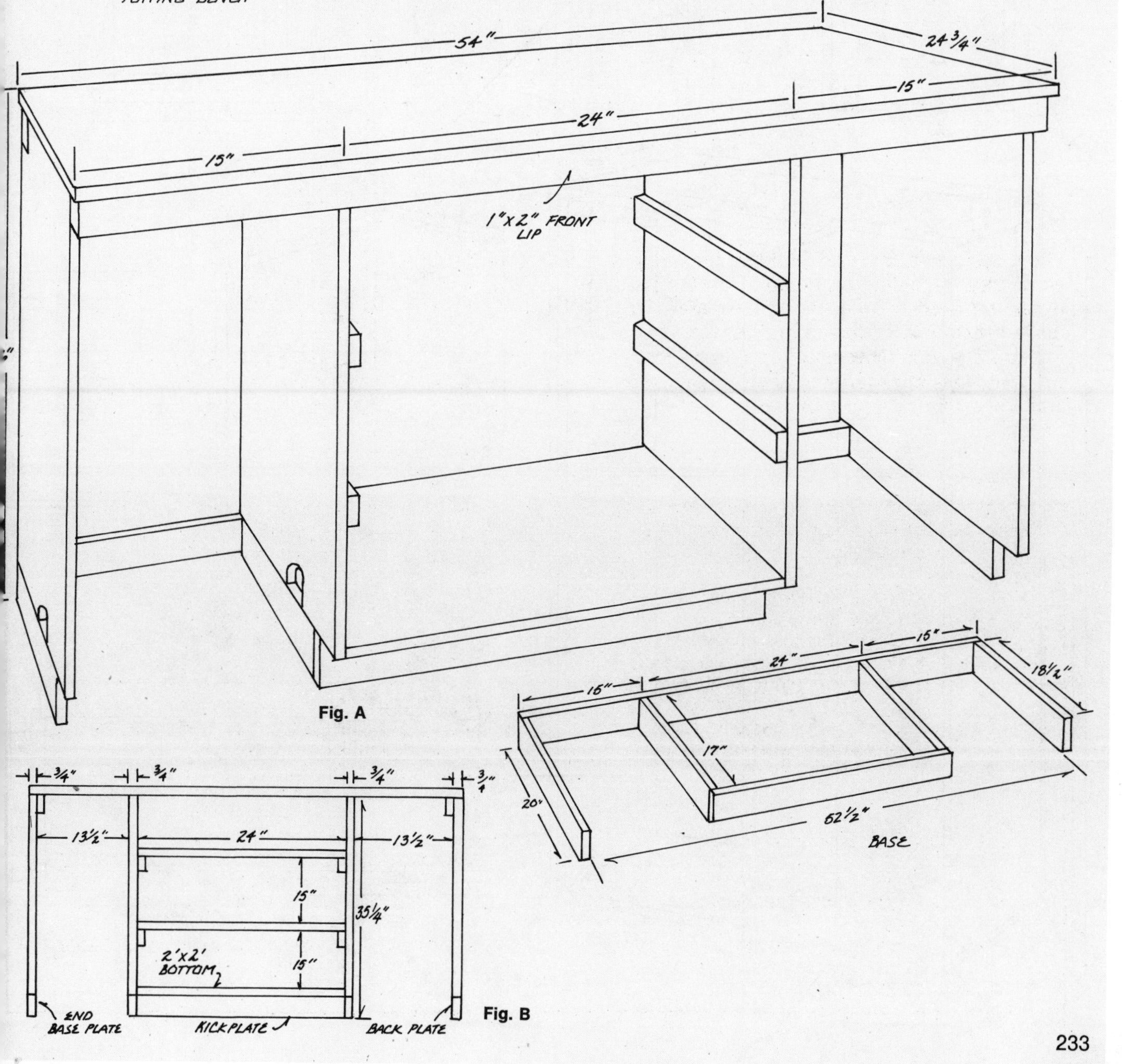

Fig. A

Fig. B

84" back, as is the outside back edge of the rear shelf side. The large compartment shelf is cleated to the right side and partition 18" below the top. The four ¾"x12"x16½" shelves are cleated between the shelf sides with 12" between each shelf. A ¾"x18"x83½" plywood door may be attached to the front of the shelves; it is hung from the center partition on three 3½"x3½" butt hinges.

Variations. Depending on how the units are arranged, shelves can be hung on the wall behind and above the workbench. The back of the storage unit can be made from ¼" pegboard, and either or both of the shelf sides can be faced with pegboard as well. Shelves or hooks for holding tools and equipment can be installed on the inside of the big cabinet door.

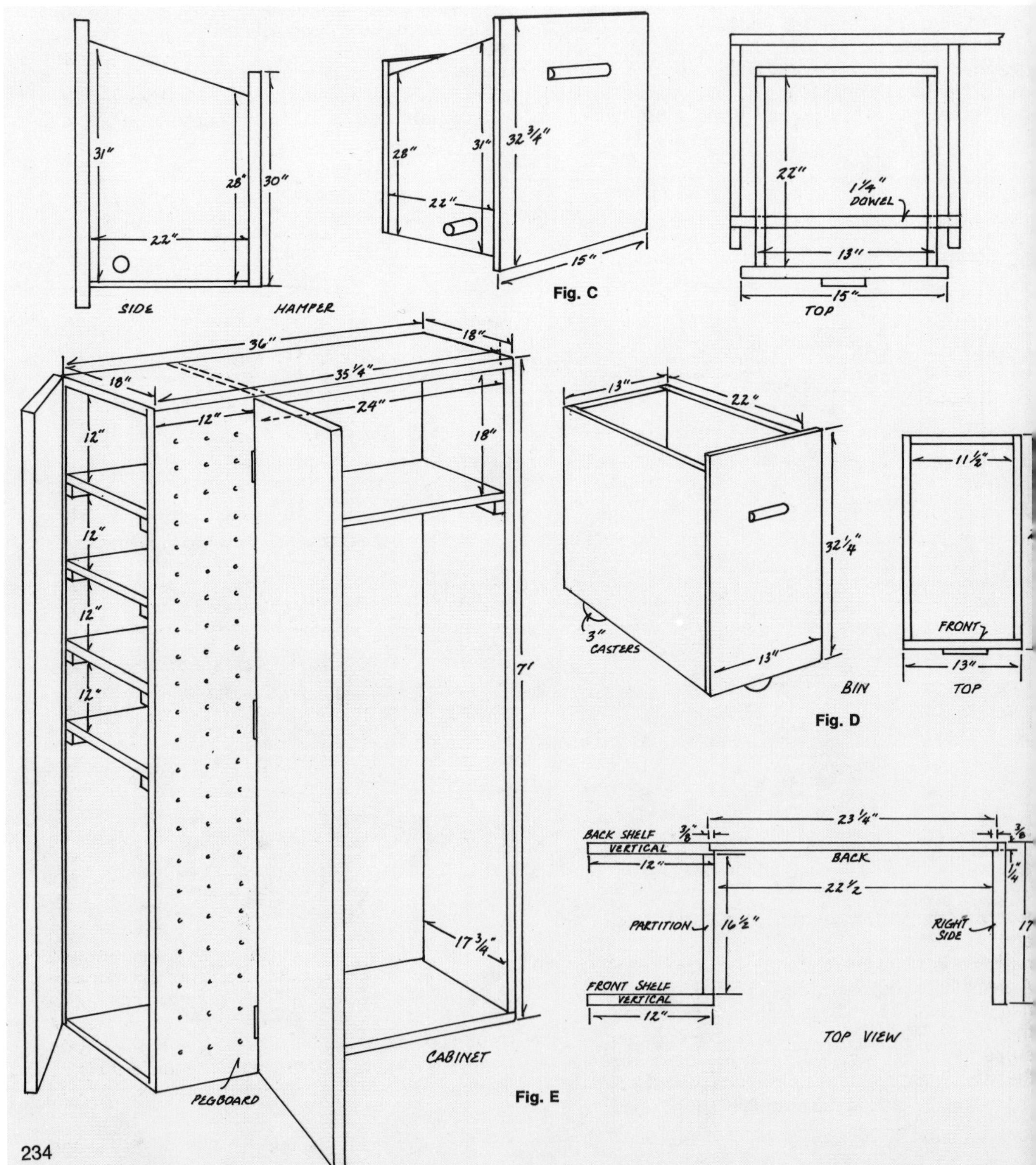

Fig. C

Fig. D

Fig. E

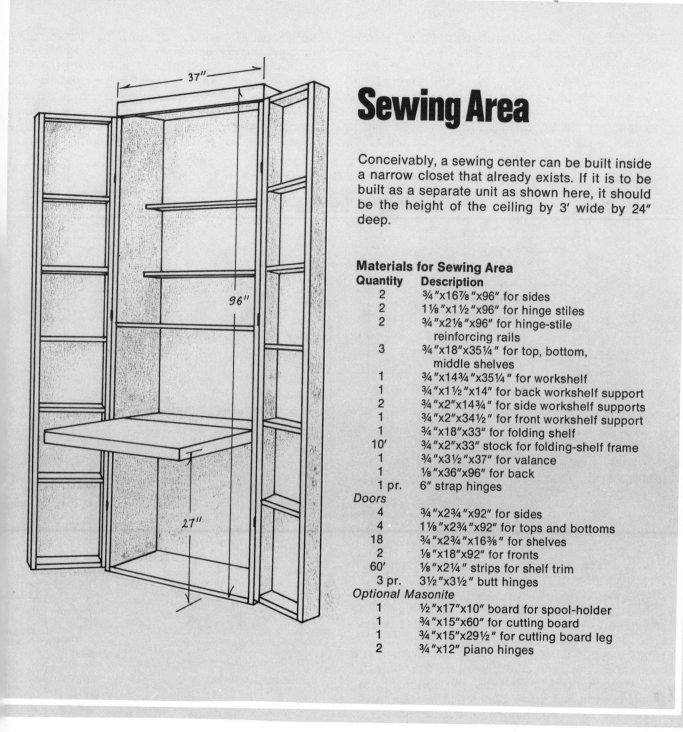

Sewing Area

Conceivably, a sewing center can be built inside a narrow closet that already exists. If it is to be built as a separate unit as shown here, it should be the height of the ceiling by 3′ wide by 24″ deep.

Materials for Sewing Area

Quantity	Description
2	¾″x16⅞″x96″ for sides
2	1⅛″x1½″x96″ for hinge stiles
2	¾″x2⅛″x96″ for hinge-stile reinforcing rails
3	¾″x18″x35¼″ for top, bottom, middle shelves
1	¾″x14¾″x35¼″ for workshelf
1	¾″x1½″x14″ for back workshelf support
2	¾″x2″x14¾″ for side workshelf supports
1	¾″x2″x34½″ for front workshelf support
1	¾″x18″x33″ for folding shelf
10′	¾″x2″x33″ stock for folding-shelf frame
1	¾″x3½″x37″ for valance
1	⅛″x36″x96″ for back
1 pr.	6″ strap hinges
Doors	
4	¾″x2¾″x92″ for sides
4	1⅛″x2¾″x92″ for tops and bottoms
18	¾″x2¾″x16⅜″ for shelves
2	⅛″x18″x92″ for fronts
60′	⅛″x2¼″ strips for shelf trim
3 pr.	3½″x3½″ butt hinges
Optional Masonite	
1	½″x17″x10″ board for spool-holder
1	¾″x15″x60″ for cutting board
1	¾″x15″x29½″ for cutting board leg
2	¾″x12″ piano hinges

Box assembly. The sides are dadoed at the 27″ and 48″ levels for full 16⅞″ shelves. The three narrower shelves have stopped dadoes every 10″. Assemble the shelves and sides (Fig. A), glue-nail the top and bottom plates in place and add the back. Glue-nail the ¾″x2⅛″x96″ reinforcing strips along the front edges of the sides, and put the 3½″ valance across the top. The workshelf (Fig. B) is supported by a frame made of ¾″x 1½″ rails glue-nailed under it to the sides and back of the box. The rail under the front edge of the shelf is 2″ wide. The folding half of the workshelf is 18″x33″, and is framed on its underside by 2″-wide rails. Mortise the top of both shelves to accept 6″ strap hinges (Fig. B), placing them as far apart as possible. When the workshelf is in

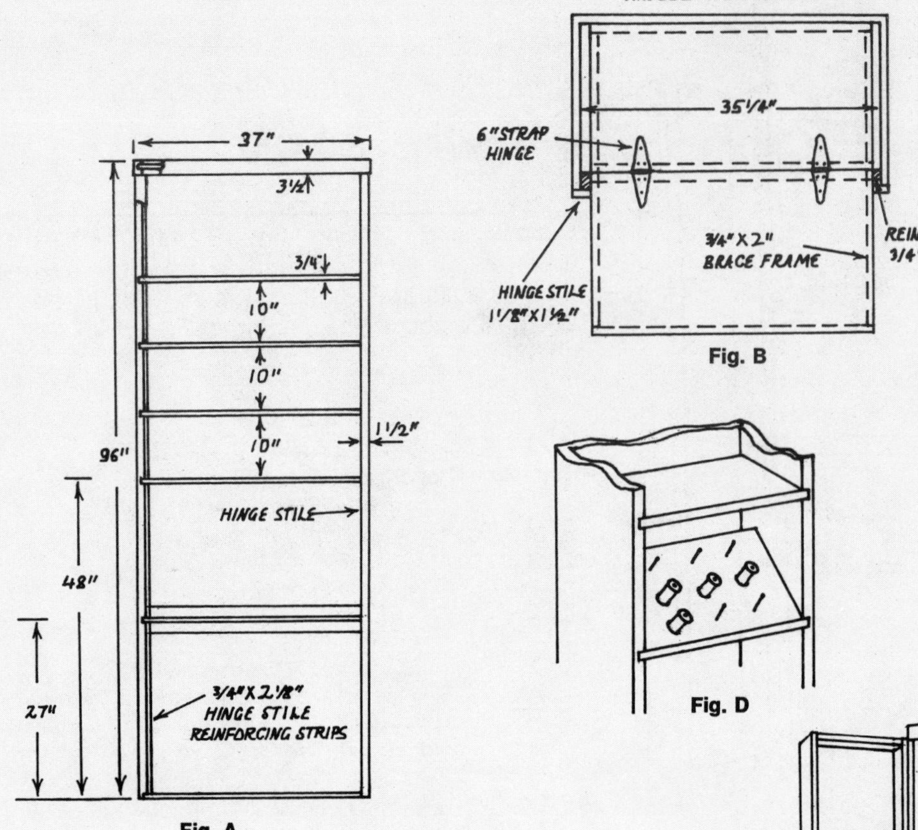

Fig. A

Fig. B

Fig. D

Fig. C

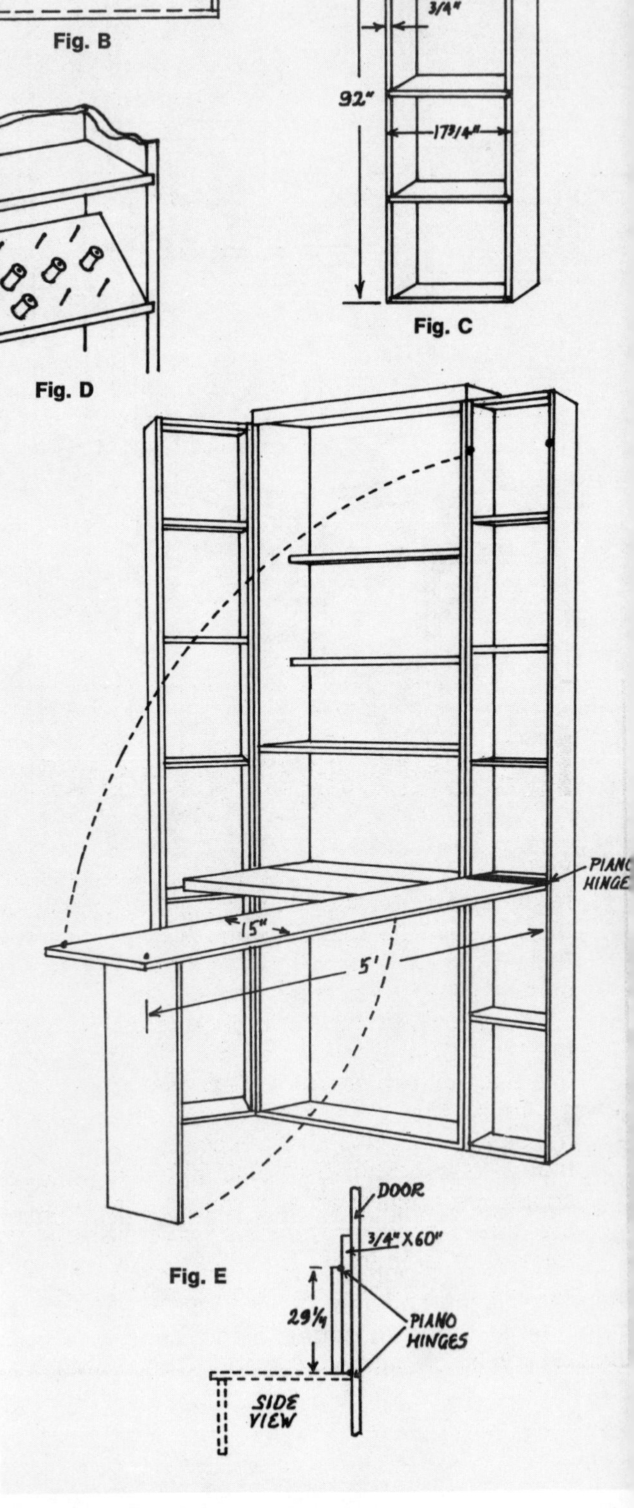

Fig. E

place, attach the door-hinge stiles to the front of the sides (Fig. B).

Door assembly (Fig. C). Both doors are 2¾" ladder frames, with the shelves dadoed into the sides and the top and bottom rabbeted in place. The doors both measure 18"x92". Glue-nail the front sheet of ⅛" Masonite to the door frames and edge-trim with a router. Glue-nail the 2¼" strips of ⅛" Masonite around the sides and bottoms of the shelves, and hang the doors on the box using three 3½"x3½" butt hinges for each door.

Optional accessories. Fig. D is a spool-holder rack. The piece is cut from ½" stock to fit inside any of the shelves. Finishing nails are driven into the board every 1½", and the board is nailed in the door shelf at a slight angle.

Fig. E is a ¾"x15"x60" fold-up cutting table, hinged at the 30" level to either of the doors. If the table is used, the full shelf above the workshelf must be made at least 1" narrower so that the door will close properly. The shelf is held against the door by pressure catches; when it is pulled down, it rests on the ¾"x29¼"x15" folding leg.

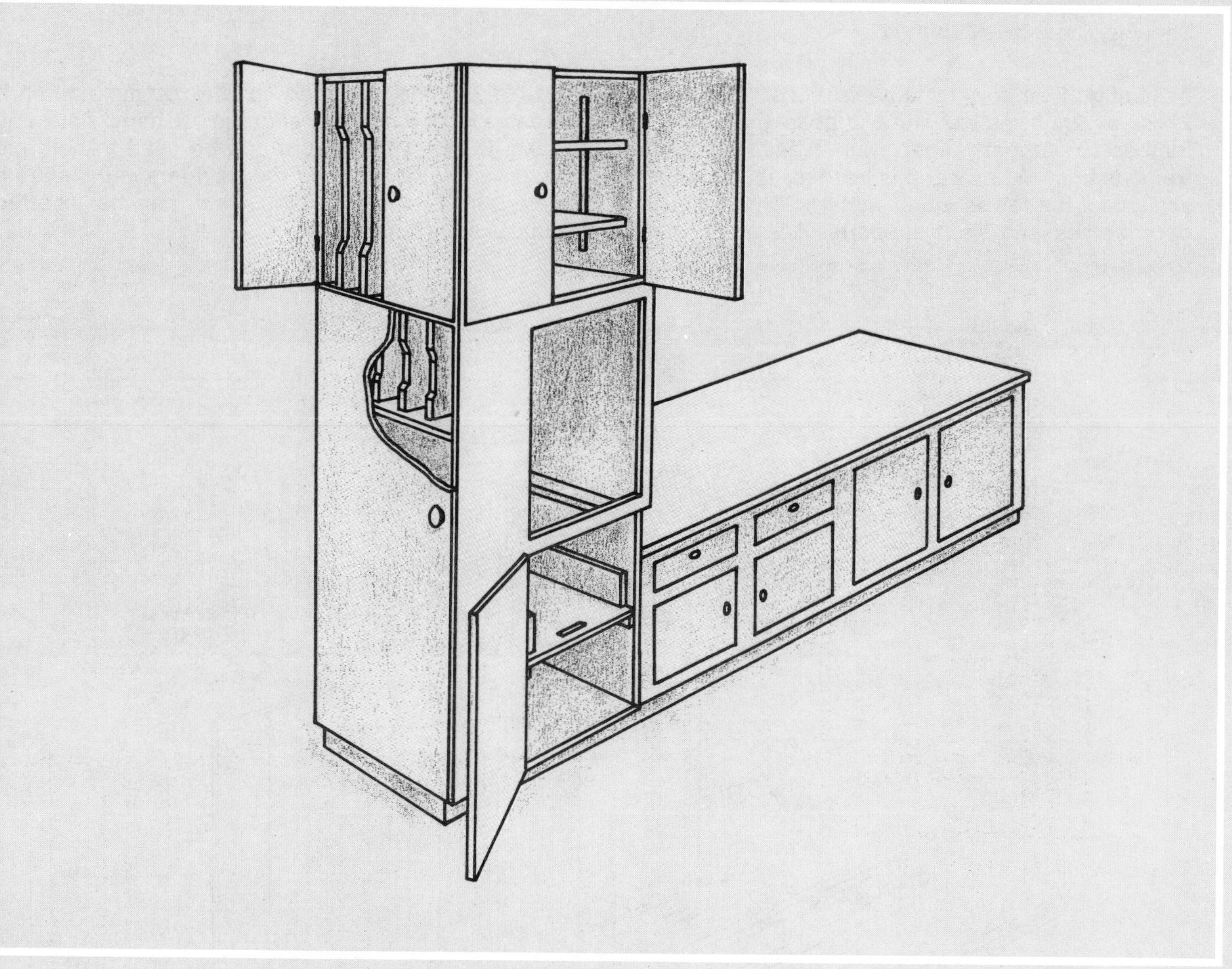

Kitchen Storage Center

Wall ovens normally end up in bulky walls that rarely make the best use of storage space. But there is no rule that says the wall cannot have two, three or even all four sides available for storing pots, pans, trays and so on.

The oven will consume about 6 cubic feet in the tower. But if the tower is 8′ high by 2′ by 3′, the possibilities for storage come from all directions. The oven will require some specific framing with 2″x4″ stock, shown in the manufacturer's diagram that accompanies it, and it should be positioned at a height convenient to the user. Assuming the tower is to stand at the far end of a counter, the accompanying Fig. A suggests possible storage compartments.

Materials for Kitchen Storage Center

Quantity	Description
60′	2″x4″ stock for framing
50′	1″x2″ stock for framing doors and shelf supports
4	¾″ A-D plywood for sides, shelves and doors

Assembly. The tower frame is constructed from 2″x3″ or 2″x4″ stock, since that is the required lumber to support most wall ovens. Once the frame is built ¾″ plywood is used for the sides and shelves of the tower, along with 1″x2″ stock for the door frames and shelf supports. Adjustable shelf tracks can be attached in any of the compartments. Hooks can be situated to hang pots and pans. Dividers (¼″ each) can be used to hold pie plates or pot tops; still other dividers can separate trays and baskets. Sliding trays can be inserted almost anywhere.

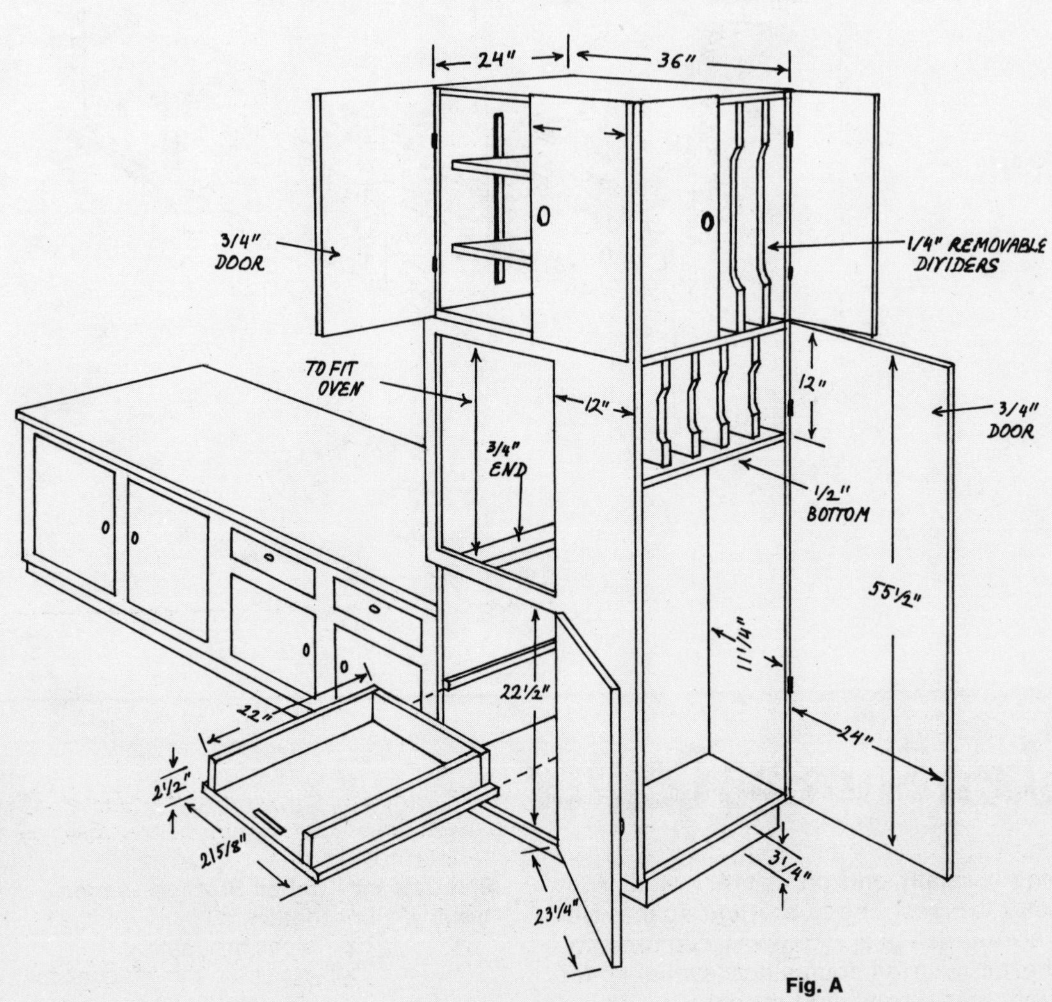

Fig. A

Sports Cabinet

Sports equipment, like anything else, should be carefully organized in its own storage space, and although it might seem that such space must change dramatically according to the sport involved, that is not really true. Presented here is a basic sports equipment cabinet that can be organized to handle the equipment for any of a dozen sports. Its outside measurements are 17¾" deep by 24" wide by 7½' high, and it can meet the needs of skiing, golf, tennis, baseball, lacrosse, hockey, badminton, croquet, softball, canoeing and squash.

Materials for Sports Cabinet

Quantity	Description
2	¾" plywood panels for sides, door, shelves
1	¼" panel for back and shelf lips
2 pr.	3½" hinges

Cutting. Lay out and cut all pieces shown in Fig. A from ¾" plywood, except for the four-door shelf lips and the back, which are made from ¼" stock.

Assembly. Attach the top, sides, partition, bottom and base, then glue-nail the ¼" back to them. The partition is situated 9" from the right side of the cabinet, and a 9"x13" shelf is positioned 48" above the bottom. The opposite side of the partition has a drop bar as shown in Fig. A. The inside of the door has a 20½"x78¾" frame made from 3½" stock, and contains three narrow shelves with 3"-high lips. Holes are drilled through the top member of the frame to hold various small tools, and wires can be strung between the frame sides to

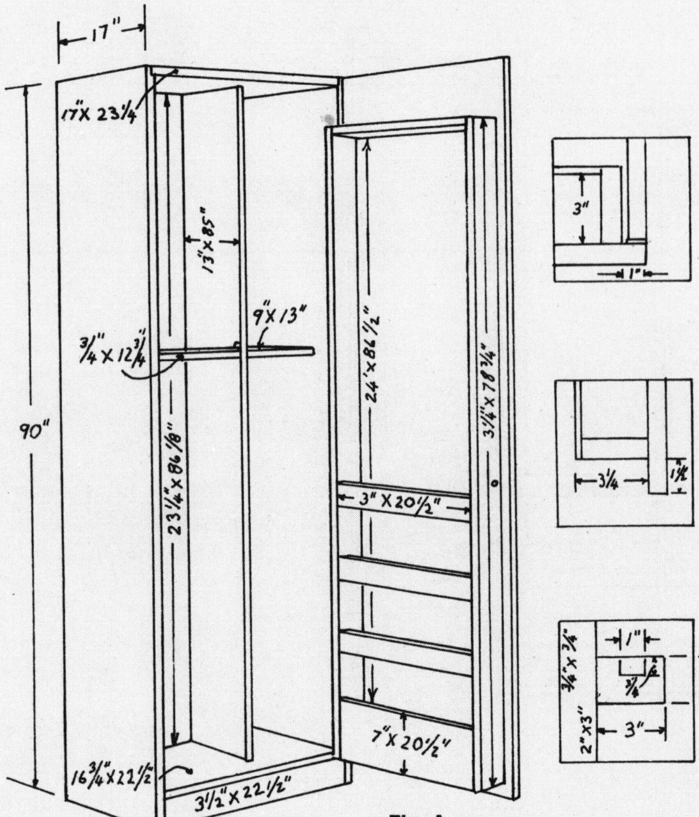

Fig. A

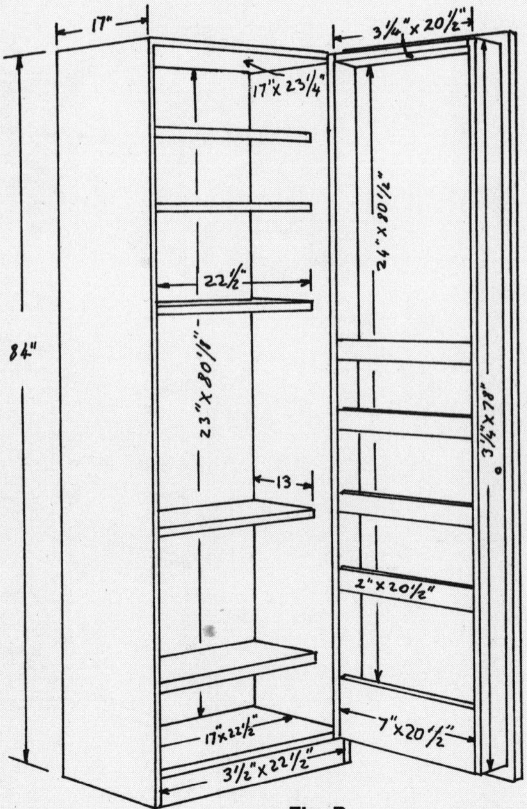

Fig. B

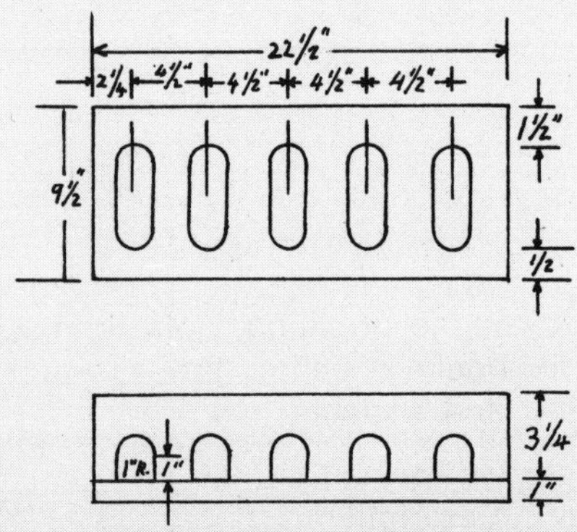

Fig. C

hang such things as gloves and mittens. The door is hinged to the cabinet with four hinges.

Variations. Two suggestions for altering the above sports cabinet are shown in Figs. B and C. Fig. B is designed for camping, hiking, climbing or sailing equipment. Fig. C is specifically for hunting and fishing, football, basketball or volleyball.

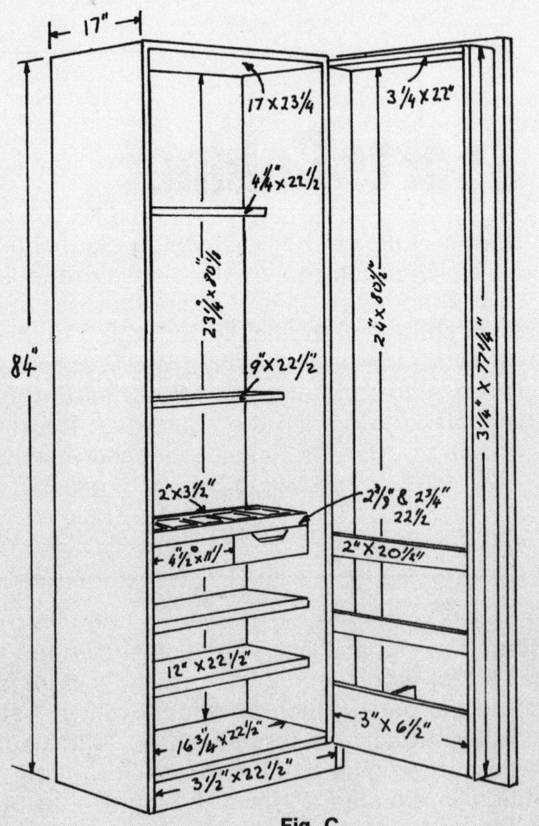

Storage Towers

Storage Towers

The intention of this project is to create related, but compartmentalized, storage space that offers as much versatility as possible. In response to the need for compartments plus versatility, one idea is to construct a series of narrow cabinets that can be hung on a wall. Another approach is to connect several 6′ 6″ high towers with hinges; this enables them to be folded into a design of their own, as well as placed in a straight line. Still another possibility is a tower of step shelves that are different heights and widths.

Materials for Storage Towers

Quantity	Description
4	¾″ hardwood panels for hanging towers
1	½″ plywood panel for hanging tower back
6	¾″ hardwood-faced plywood panels for tops, bottoms, sides and doors of tower cabinets
2	¼″ plywood panels for tower cabinet backs
4	¾″ hardwood-faced plywood panels for storage steps
2	¼″ plywood panels for backs of storage steps

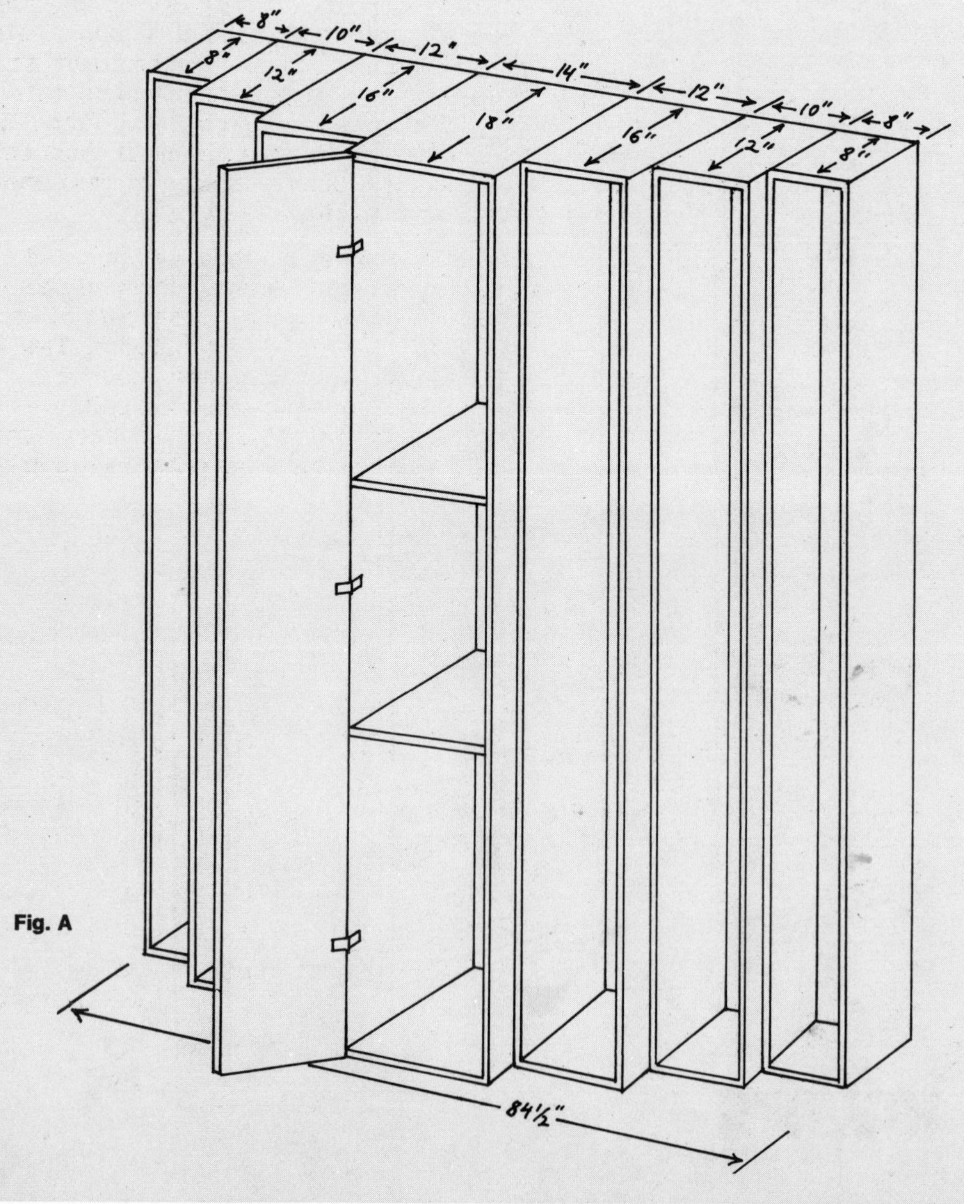

Fig. A

Hanging towers. The back of the unit is ½" plywood. Everything else is ¾" hardwood-faced plywood; the finished unit can be any length, width and depth desired. With the exception of the center cabinet, there should be two cabinets of each size chosen so that the finished project retains a symmetry.

Cutting. Cut all of the sides at the same time. The drawings shown here call for four sides measuring 8"x60", four sides that are 12"x60", four that are 16"x60", and two center cabinet sides that measure 18"x60". Now cut an identical top and bottom for the unit. Each is 84½" long and 18" wide at the center, then stepped down at regular intervals to 8"-wide ends. The reduction for each cabinet width is shown in Fig. B; both top and bottom are dadoed to accept the sides. The back is ½"x84½"x60" and the doors are all 60" high. The bottom half of the opening edge of each door is beveled to act as a finger grip. The center door is 18" wide, then there are two doors 16" wide, two that are 12", and two 8" wide.

Assembly. Glue-screw the sides into their top and bottom dadoes and glue-screw the back to the cabinet. Hang the doors so that each one swings away from the center cabinet. The center cabinet door can be hung either left or right. The insides of the cabinets should have shelf tracks; drawers and/or small interior cabinets can also be added.

Hanging. The unit can be hung in any suitable manner. Because of its weight, however, it is recommended that the split-rail hanger method (Fig. C) described in the introductory notes be used.

Tower cabinets. A variation on the hanging cabinet is a series of eight (or any number) 6' 6" high variable-depth (but narrow) towers that are all hinged together at their backs. The intriguing aspect of this is the angle of the doors. The front edges of each cabinet must be beveled so the door will close flush, as shown in Fig. E. Here again, the cabinet dimensions vary, and can really be any size you wish.

Cutting. Cut the sides, top and bottom for each cabinet from hardwood-faced plywood. The front edges of the cabinets must be beveled, and the bevel angle will vary according to the width of the particular cabinet. As shown here, the smallest cabinet is 8" wide on one side and 11" on the other, while the largest is 15" at its narrow side and 18" at its wide side. In between, the cabinet widths should progress by one or two inches. Thus, if the short sides are 8", 9", 10", 11", 12", 13", 14", and 15", the long sides will become 11", 12", 13", 14", 15", 16", 17" and 18". To find the exact angle of their bevels, stand a pair of sides up at exactly their proper distance apart and lay a straight edge from outside corner to outside corner, then mark the angle on each edge. This will have to be done with each set of sides since the width of the cabinet will also progress one or two inches at a time from 7" up.

Assembly. Rabbet the tops, bottoms and sides of each cabinet and glue-nail them to their backs. Hinge the doors on the narrow side of each cabinet, using hidden cabinet hinges. The cabinet interiors can have any shelf, cabinet or drawer arrangement you wish. When the units are finished, they are hinged together at their back edges with three 3½" door butts between each cabinet.

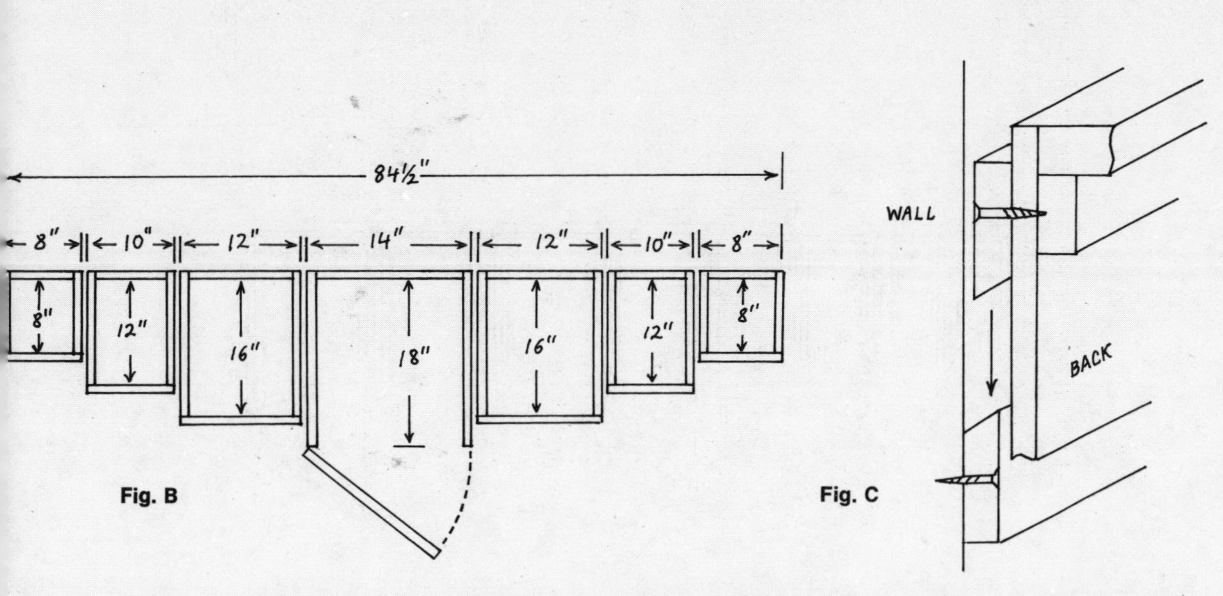

Fig. B

Fig. C

7"
8"
9"
10"
11"
12"
13"
14"
6'8"
6'6"

Fig. D

7"
8"
9"
10"
11"
12"
13"
14"
8"
11"
9"
12"
10"
13"
11"
14"
12"
15"
13"
16"
14"
17"
15"
18"

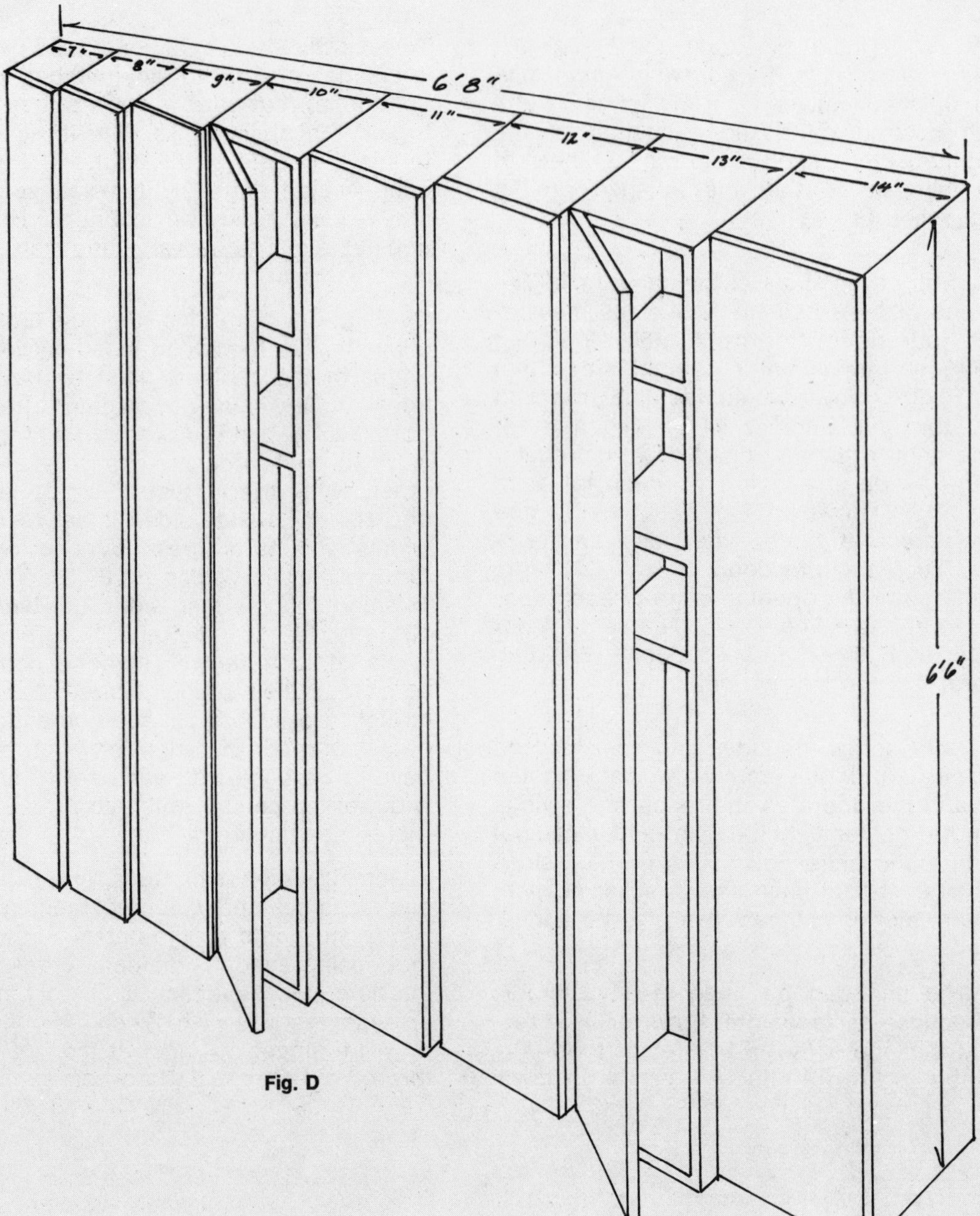

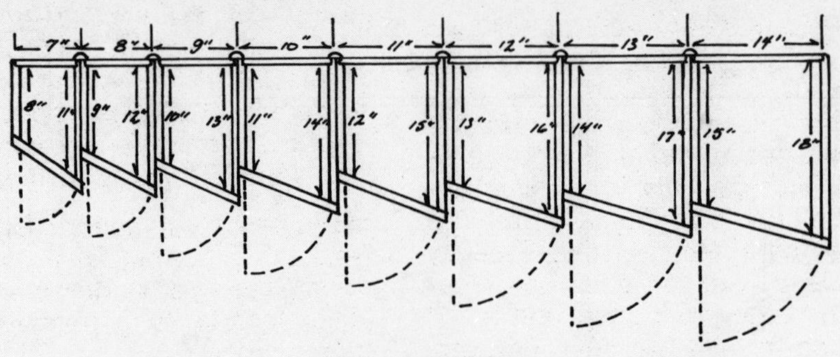

Fig. E

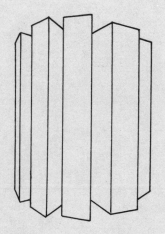

Fig. F

Variations. The internal arrangements of the cabinets are almost limitless; some of the ways they can be arranged as a standing unit are shown here. (see Fig. F).

Storage steps. Still another version of the storage tower theme is simply a pile of boxes with shelves, drawers and a door. Two storage steps side by side that offer compatible storage units are ideal for a couple's bedroom; designed carefully, these units will hold a great deal of clothing neatly. This is also an excellent storage idea for youngsters, and of course can be built to any dimensions. The twin units suggested here are each 30″ wide by 6′ 6″ high and 15″ deep. The top shelf box measures 9½″ wide by 16″ high; the bottom unit is 30″ wide and high enough to hold two deep drawers. The entire cabinet is faced with a single door, although it could have individual doors closing off one or more of the storage areas (see Fig. G).

Cutting. Measure and cut all shelves, verticals, sides and doors from ¾″ hardwood-faced plywood. Cut the back from ½″ or ¼″ plywood so that it follows the steps; the door is cut in the same manner. The flat side of each unit is 15″ wide by 6′ 6″ high and should be dadoed to accept the shelves. Dado the tops of each shelf to hold the vertical support for the shelf above it.

Assembly. Glue-nail the shelves to the side wall and to each other, then glue-nail the back to the unit. Assemble the drawers (if there are to be any). The door is hung from the long side with a 6′ piano hinge.

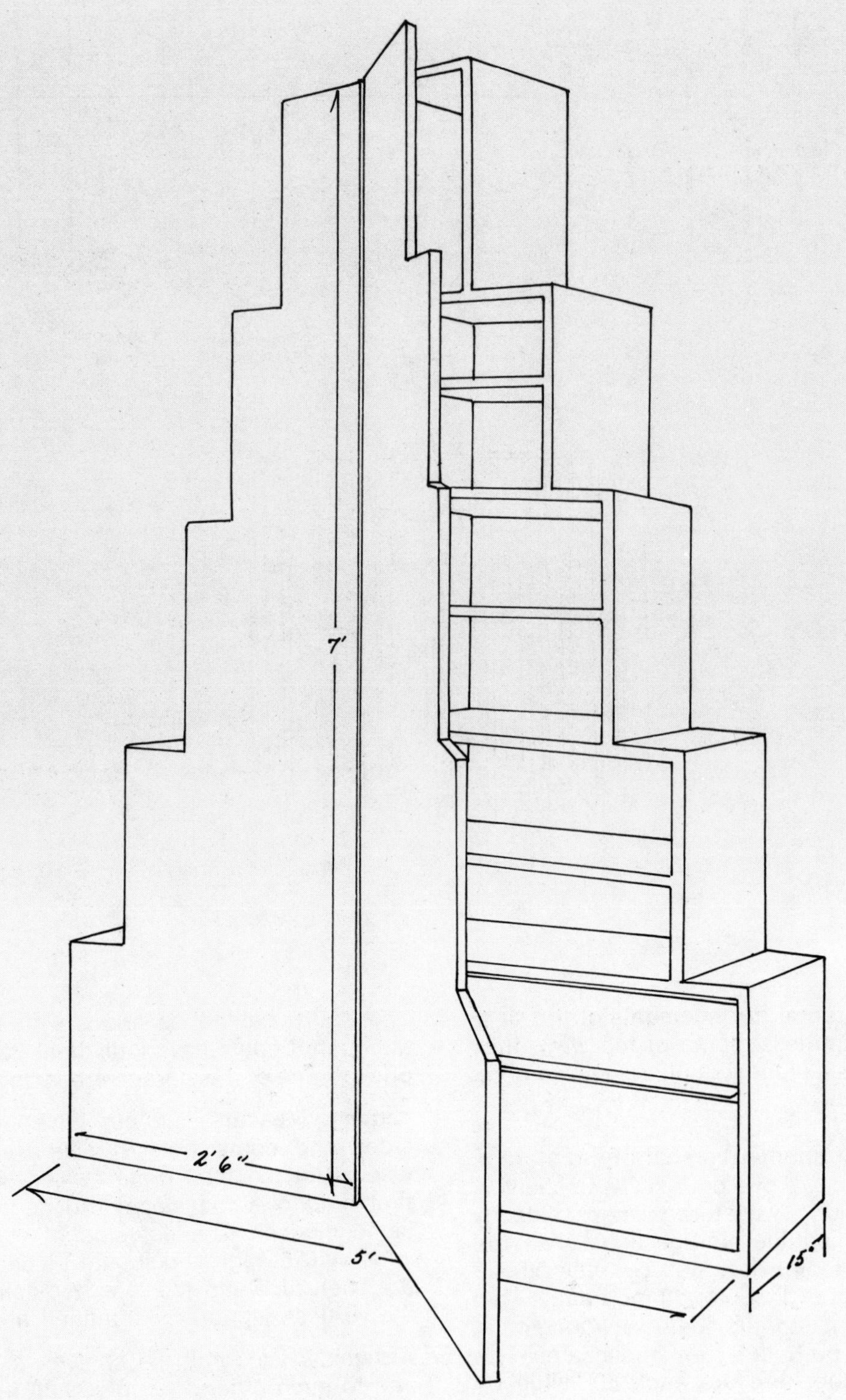
7'
2'6"
5'
15"

Pull-Out Pantry

Many times, there is a narrow space between a refrigerator and the cabinets around it. There is an easy way of utilizing that dead 6″ of space—not by trying to reach into the slot, but by bringing that space *out* to the user. The height, width and depth of a pull-out storage depends on the size of the slot; the measurements used here are 7′ high by 6″ wide by 24″ deep. The entire unit can be made of plywood, or 1″x6″ common pine. If you decide to use pine, there will be no ripping involved, but it may cost a little more for materials.

Materials for Pull-Out Pantry

Quantity	Description
30′	1″x6″ stock for frame and shelves
1	¼″ plywood panel for back and optional shelf lips
2	2″ casters
1	6″x7′ piece of ¾″ or ½″ stock for faceplate

Cutting. The two end verticals are cut 6′ 11″ long, and rabbeted at the top. All shelves are cut 22½″ long, with the top 24″ long and a ⅜″ rabbet at each end. The verticals are dadoed for the shelves, at varying heights. The narrower shelves are at the bottom, the wider ones at the top, so that heavy canned goods can be put close to the floor and the larger, lighter products like cereal are at the top. The bottom shelf is positioned 1″ from the bottom of the verticals to support a set of 2″ casters. The faceplate is exactly 6" wide by 6' 11¾" long. It can be made from ½" or ¾" stock or plywood.

Assembly. Glue-nail the shelves in the dadoed verticals and add the rabbeted top. Glue-nail the ¼"x 2'x6' 10" back to all verticals and shelves. Position a caster at each end under the bottom shelf and add the faceplate, glue-nailing it from the inside. The back of the faceplate is flush with the edge of the ¼" backing, and extends ¼" beyond the front of the shelves. Lips, ¼"x2", may be glue-nailed to the shelf fronts, if desired.

Alternatives. From the basic box-on-wheels design, the pull-out storage can be redesigned to accommodate a variety of objects. Fig. B shows how the back of the frame might be made with a pegboard so that cleaning materials and other objects can be stored in the unit. A lipped shelf or two at the bottom can provide storage for soap powders, detergents, etc.

Fig. C is another possibility, if the space is wide enough. In this instance, a partition is inserted off-center in a wider unit. Shelves on both sides of the partition can be either the same height on each side, or can vary.

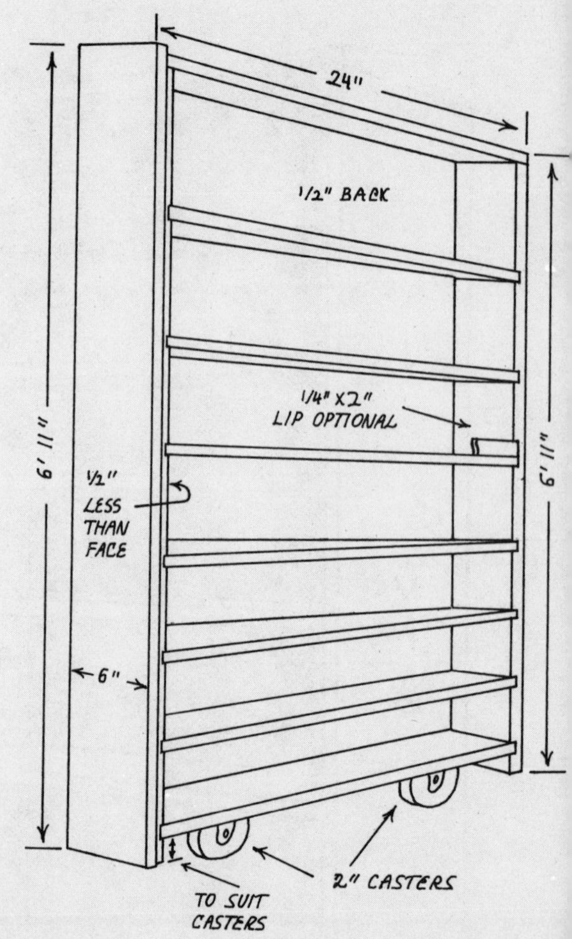

Fig. A

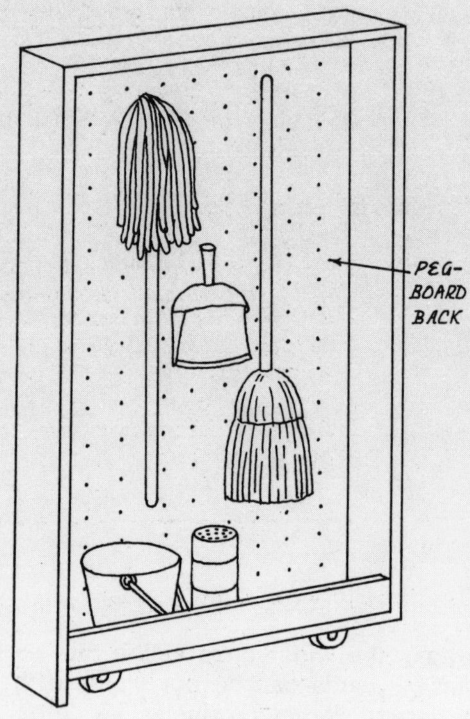

Fig. B

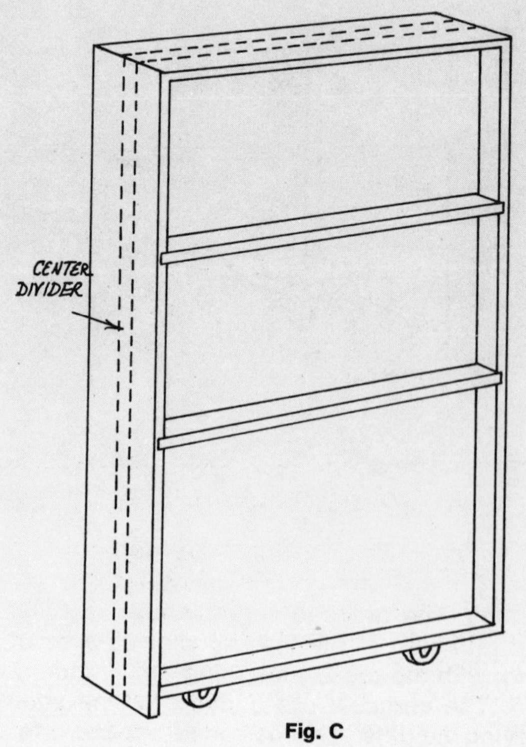

Fig. C

Study Center

Here again is a project that can be constructed to suit any amount of space available. It can be hung on any wall, can be larger or smaller and has a whole range of design variations. The basic unit divides into three 3′ sections, and is made entirely of pine shelving, with the exception of the desk.

Materials for Study Center

Quantity	Description
27′	1″x10″ for brace, shelves and doors
39′	1″x12″ for brace, partitions and shelves
9′	1″x8″ for doors and shelf lip
1	3′x3′ piece ¾″ A-D plywood for desk top and bottom
8	3″ hinges for doors
1	2′x3′ piece fiberboard or cork for bulletin board (optional)

Right shelf unit. The right side partitions (Fig. A) are 1″x12″x45″ and rabbeted at the bottom. They are dadoed every 10½″ to accept three 1″x12″x 35¼″ shelves. The bottom shelf is 1″x12″x36″, rabbeted at both ends, and has a 1″x8″x36″ lip with a gentle curve that is 3½″ at its lowest point. The shelves are glue-nailed in their dadoes; the bottom is fitted into its rabbet, and the lip glue-nailed across its front edge.

Left shelf unit. The two 1″x12″x45″ partitions are stop-dadoed 4½″ in from each end. The dadoes are 9½″ long to hold the 1″x10″x35¼″ horizontals that serve as the top and bottom for the cabinet. Shelf tracks are attached to the partition walls between the dadoes; the two shelves are 1"x10"x 33½". The double folding doors are made up of two 1"x10"s and two 1"x8"s, all 36" long. The 1"x10"s are hinged between the cabinet walls and the 1"x8"s (Fig. A).

Desk unit. The top and bottom of the desk are ¾" plywood, cut 18"x36". The sides are 1"x8"x18", butted between the plywood.

Assembly. Lay the right and left units face down on the floor. They are connected by a 1"x10"x9' brace positioned flush with the top of the partitions. A 1"x12"x9' brace is glue-nailed across the bottom of the units. The desk is inserted between the two shelf sections, and nailed to their inside partitions and to the 1"x12" brace. The entire unit is hung on a wall by either nailing the braces into the studs, or by using toggle bolts, or lead anchors if the wall is brick or concrete. A cork or fiberboard bulletin board can be attached to the braces above the desk.

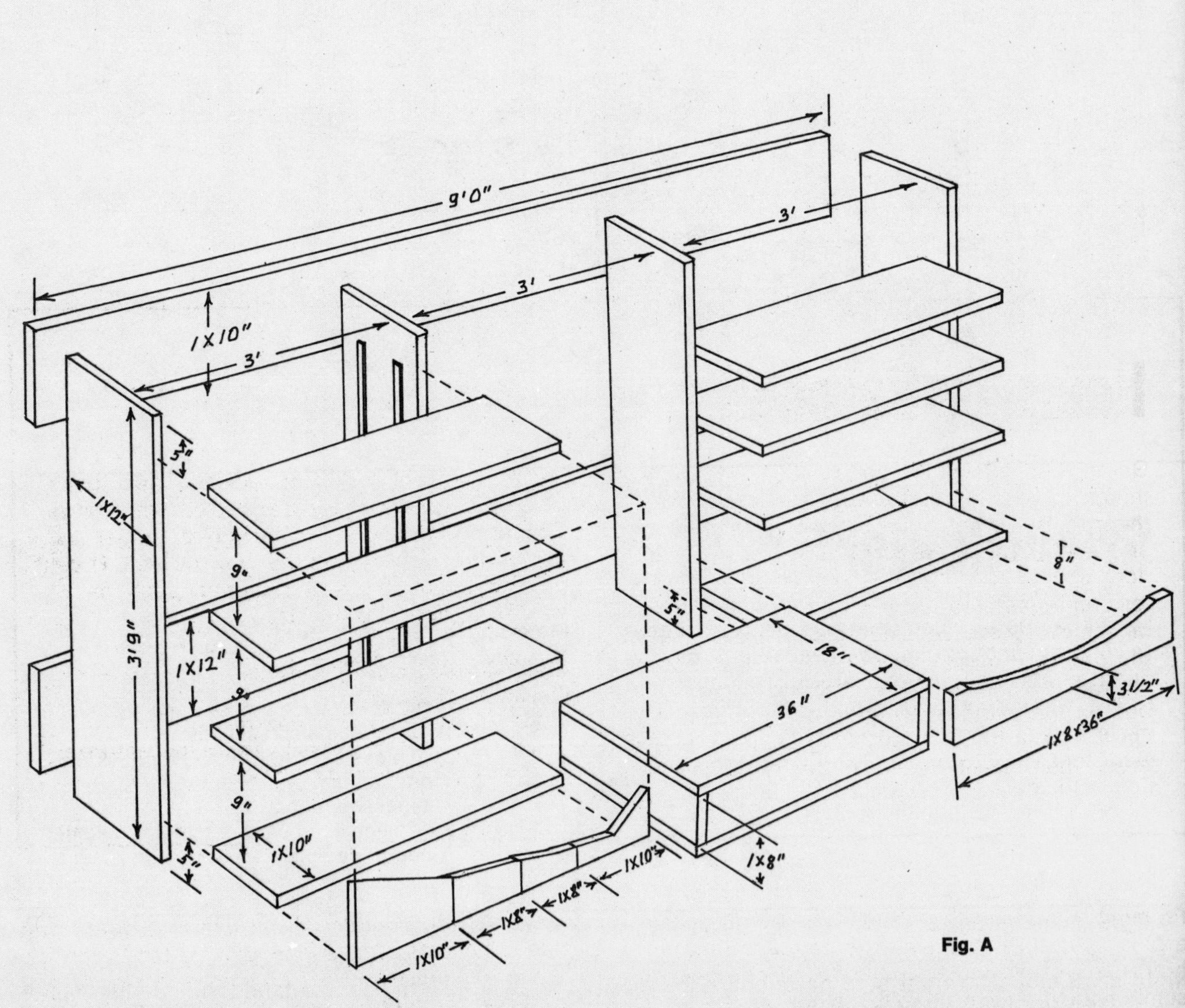

Fig. A

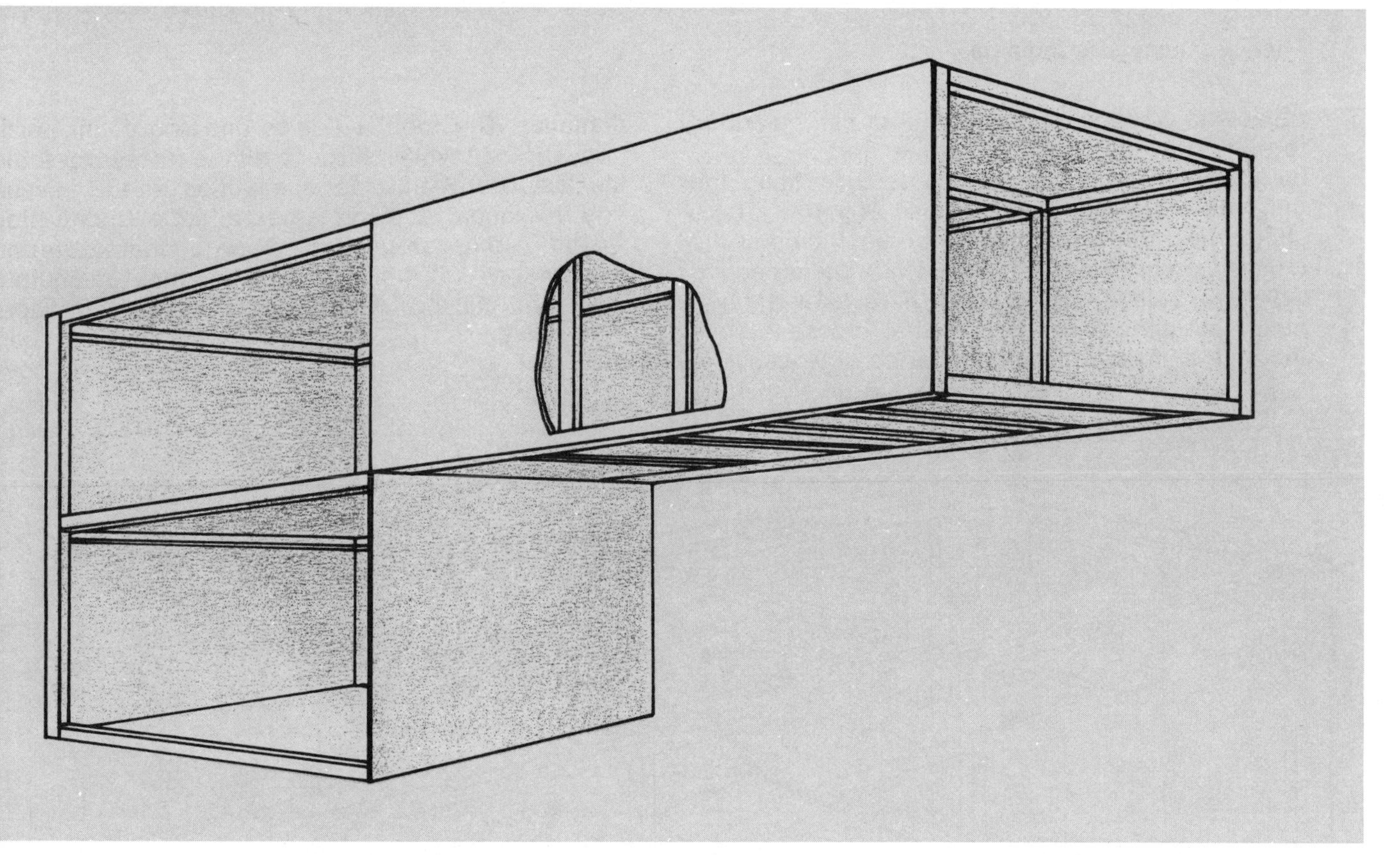

Hoist-Up Catchall

Garages never seem to be big enough for all the things that must be stored in them, along with the car. The problem, of course, is that the car and the storables keep fighting for the same floor space, and often the car loses. Nevertheless, garages tend to be 8′ or more high, which means they have considerable air space above the car for storage. One way to get at all that storage area is to cover the walls with pegboards and hang everything in sight on hooks. On the other hand, "everything in sight" means more than small items; it can include lawn chairs, bags of fertilizer, mowers, gas tanks, ladders, all sorts of awkward-sized belongings. The hoisting catchall is designed to get this miscellaneous array off the floor as well. It can be just about any size required, such as 11′ long by 2′ deep by 4′ wide.

Materials for Hoist-Up Catchall

Quantity	Description
130′	2″x2″ stock for framing
4½	¼″x4′x8′ Masonite panels (or pegboard)
12	⅝″ pulleys and rope

Framing. Assuming that the unit will hold considerable weight, the frame should be assembled with both screws and metal angles at all corners. Assemble the frame from 2″x2″ stock as shown in Fig. A, by first making the top frame, then building the unit upside down. The bottom cross-braces are 19½″ on center under the 7′ section, and 14″ on center under the 4′ section. The half-shelf at the back of the 4′ section is optional.

Assembly. The bottom of the unit is covered first with ¼″ sheets of Masonite, glue-nailed to the top of the framing members, as shown in Fig. A. The Masonite is notched to go around the verticals in the frame. The sides and top of the unit are covered on the outside of the frame, also with ¼″ Masonite. In addition, the sides of the 4′ cube section and the front of the 7′ can be covered with pegboard, which will allow a number of tools and objects to be hung on hooks. A door can be added to either or both open ends, if desired.

Installation. The more pulleys used to hang the unit, the easier it will be to raise or lower. There should be at least four pulleys on each side of the unit, situated near the frame joints and attached with eye bolts (see Fig. B). There should be a pulley strapped to every joist that crosses above the unit, and the rope used must be at least ⅝" in diameter. The rope is tied to one end of the unit (Fig. C), then woven through all the pulleys so that the last one it threads is attached to the joists. The free end of the line is tied to a cleat bolted to a stud in the garage wall. Given enough pulleys, the catchall will hold over 500 pounds of equipment and still be hoisted to the ceiling with very little effort.

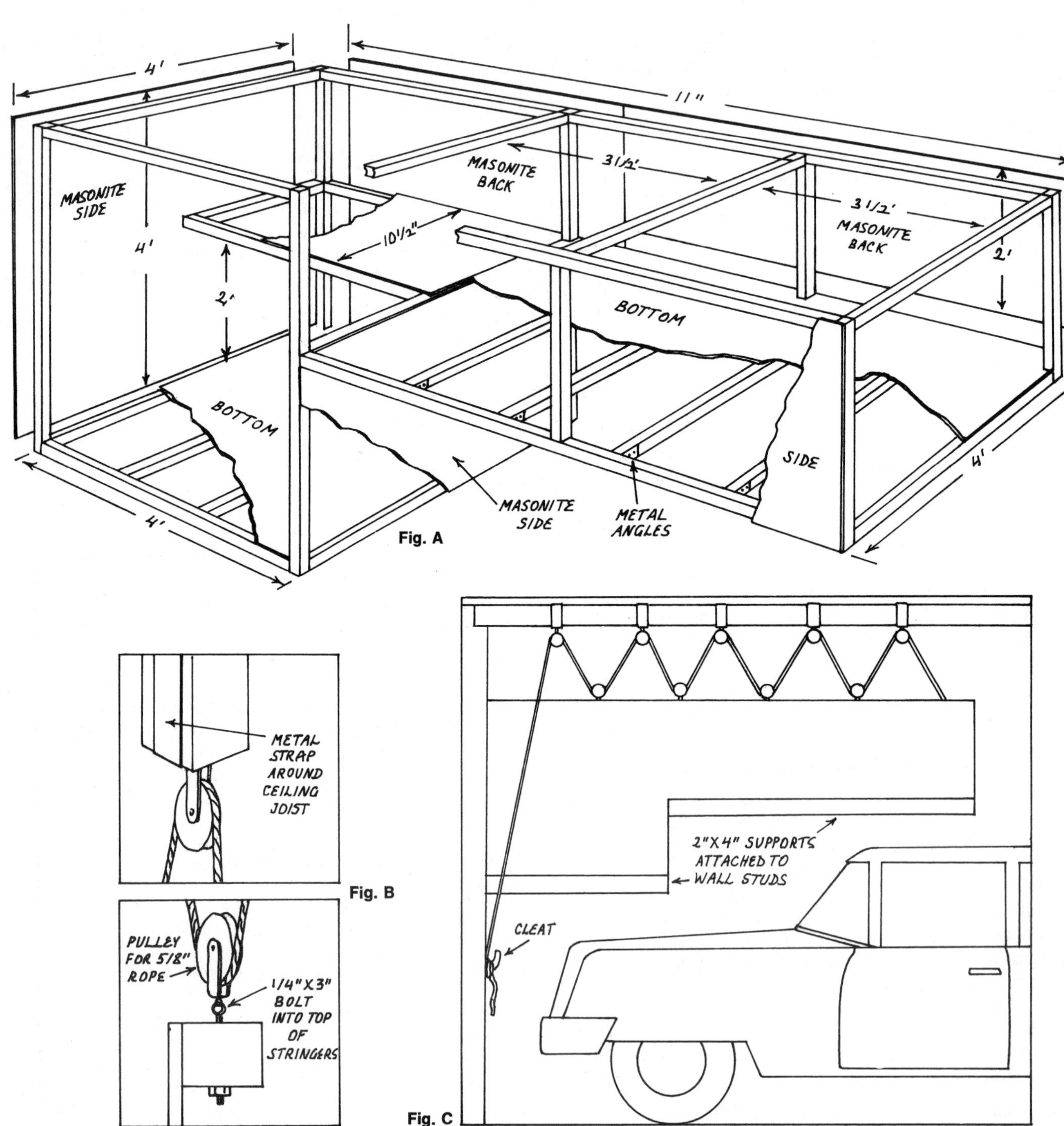

Fig. A

Fig. B

Fig. C

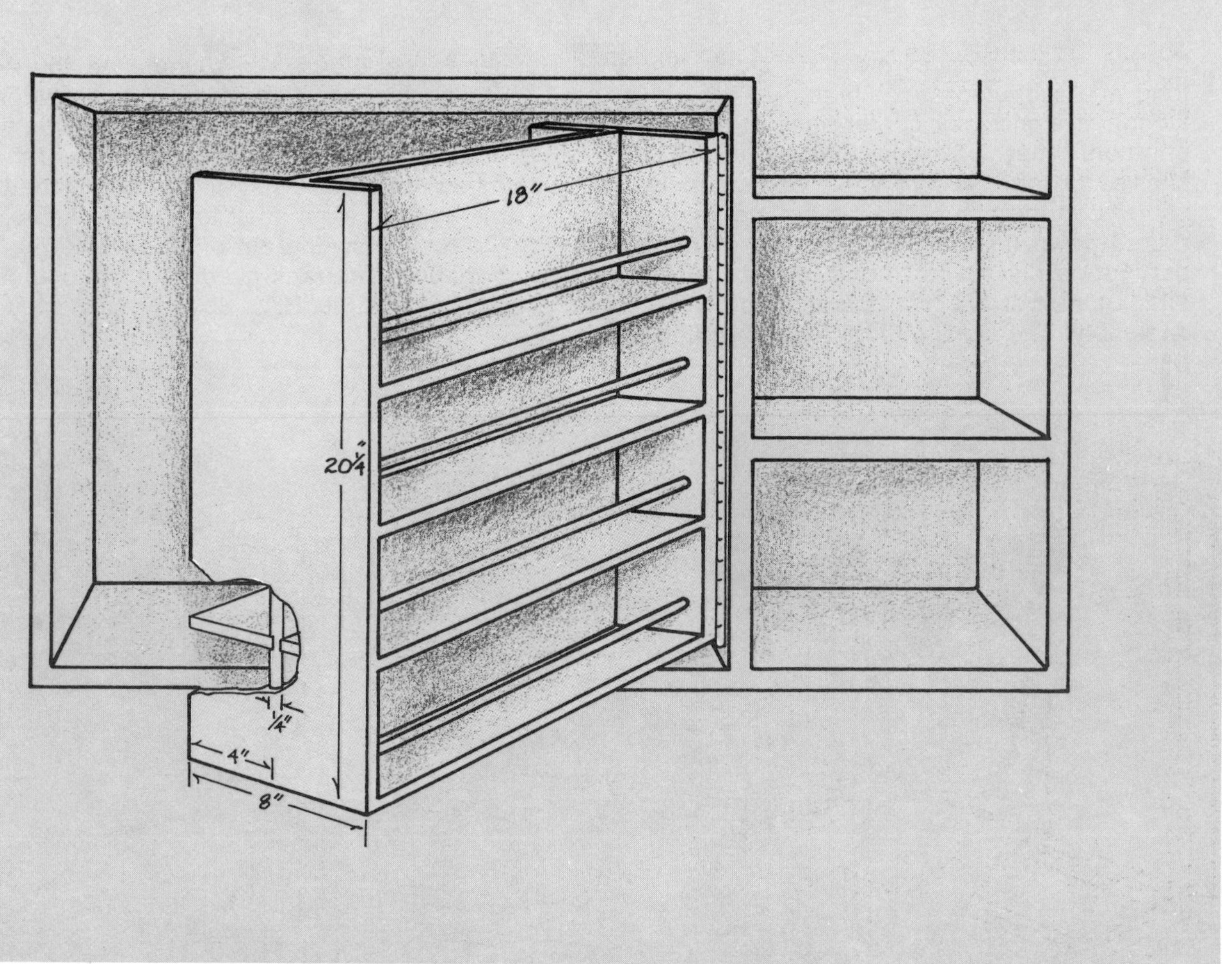

Swing-Out Spice Rack

Spices usually come in small containers and more often than not they get jumbled together on a normal shelf. At the same time, if they are lined up so they can all be seen, they can consume several feet of shelf space. The swinging spice rack shown here is an answer to the problem of keeping spices arranged so they can all be seen at a glance, and still not take up yards of shelving. A further advantage of the swinging spice rack is that it resides behind a cabinet door, so the jars cannot collect the kitchen grease that would coat them if they were stored on one long, open shelf.

The rack shown was designed to fit into a normal cabinet which had one of its shelves removed, leaving a cavity 20" wide by 10" deep by 24" high. The rack itself is 18" wide by 8" deep by 20¼" high. It is hinged to the interior partition of the cabinet, and is constructed from ½" and ¾" stock with a ¼" divider that supports shelves on both sides.

Materials for Swing-Out Spice Rack

Quantity	Description
5′	¾"x8½" stock for sides and bottom
9′	½"x4" stock for shelves
20"	¾" piano hinge
1	¼"x20¼"x18" piece plywood for center partition
10½′	½" dowel for retainers (optional)

Cutting. The rack sides are 1″x9″ stock, cut 20¼″ long and rabbeted at the bottom. Both sides are ploughed along their center lines to accept a ¼″ partition. They are also dadoed for three ½″ shelves on one side of the divider, and two ½″ shelves on the other. The ¾″ bottom shelf is also routed down its center line for the partition. The partition is cut 18″ long, and is rabbeted at each end. All shelves are ½″x4″, and are cut 17¼″ long.
Assembly. The sides and bottom are glued to the center partition, then glue-nailed to each other. The shelves are glue-nailed in their dadoes; a ¾″x 20″ piano hinge is attached to the right front edge of the rack and the interior partition of the cabinet. As an option, ½″ dowels can be inserted 1″ above the edge of each shelf to contain the spices when the rack is swung out of its cavity.
Variation. The rack need not have double shelves, as shown in Fig. B.

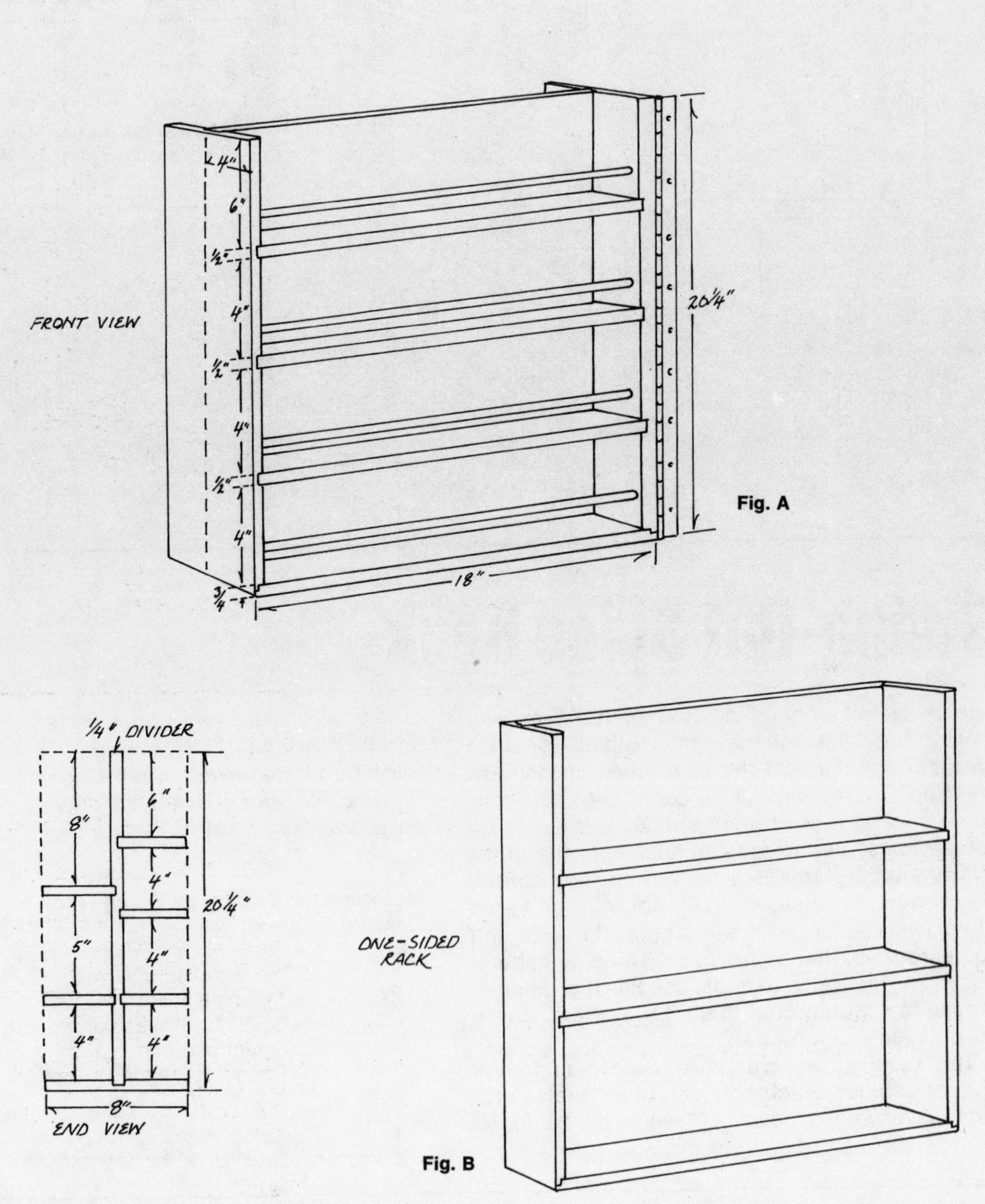

Fig. A

Fig. B

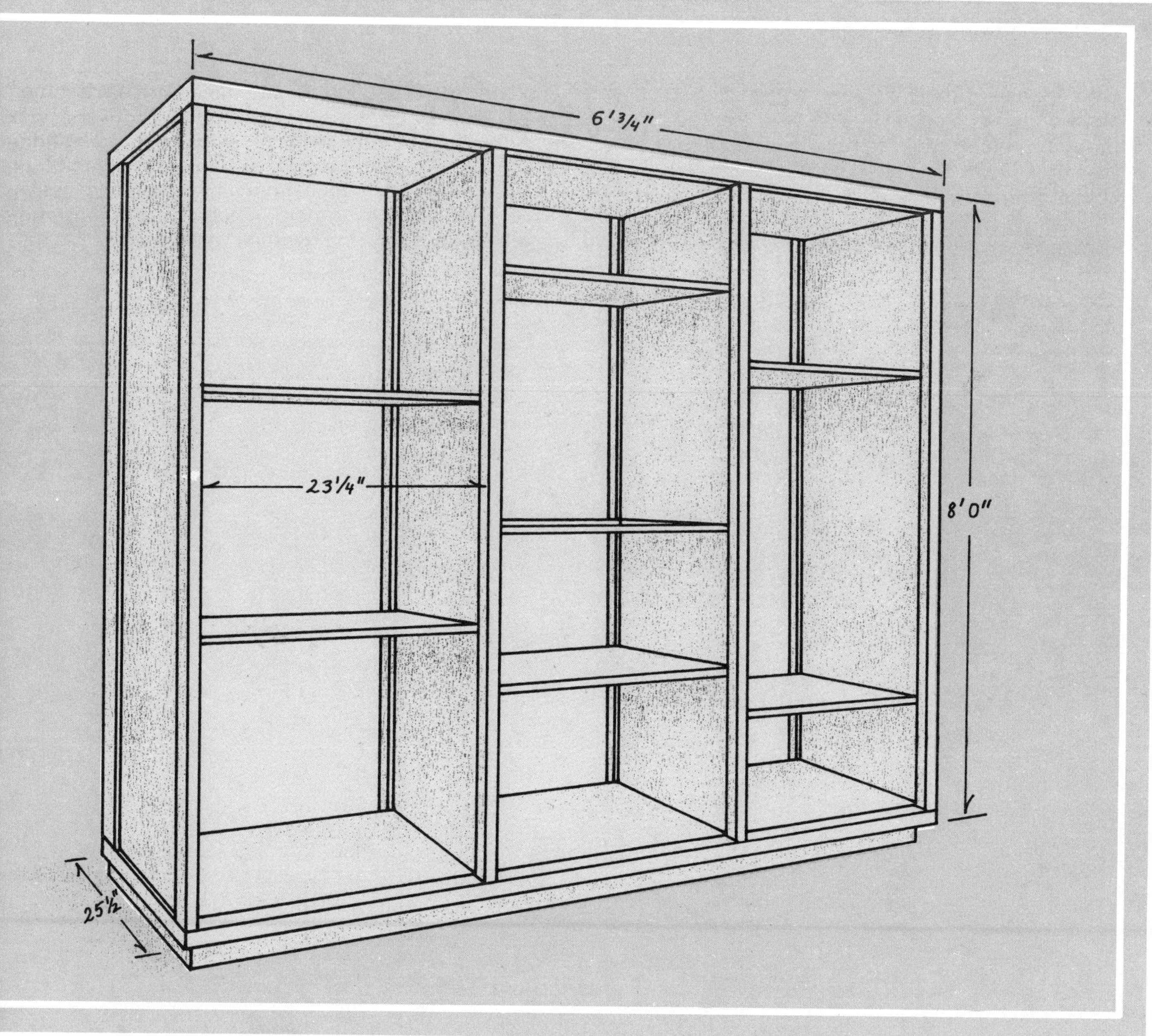

Wall Divider

There are all kinds of wall dividers that can be dreamed up for whatever space you want to divide. As a basic pattern that offers endless flexibility, the one shown here can be any size and contain all sorts of shelves, cabinets, drawers, closets—even tables. It can also be smaller or larger than the 6'x8'x2' suggested.

Materials for Wall Divider

Quantity	Description
1	¾"x24"x70½" for bottom
2	1½"x1½"x6' stock for bottom side frames, ploughed
2	1½"x2½"x22½" for bottom end frames, ploughed
2	¾"x3½"x70½" stock for base sides dadoed 24" on center
2	¾"x3½"x23¼" stock for base spacers
2	¾"x3½"x22½" for base ends, rabbeted
2	¾"x24"x64¼" for dividers
2	¾"x24"x63⅝" for unit ends
4	1½"x1½"x62⅞" for end framing on unit ends, ploughed
2	¾"x3½"x73½" for sides of soffit, mitered
2	¾"x3½"x25½" for ends of soffit, mitered
8'	¾"x¾" stock for divider cleats
108'	adjustable shelf track

Framing. The base is made from ¾"x3½" stock (Fig. A) and measures 22½"x70½", with the two spacers dadoed 24" on center. All of the 1½"x1½" stock is ploughed ¾"x¾" down center to fit around the sides, dividers and bottom panels (Fig. B). The bottom piece is fitted with 1½"x1½" framing on each of its long sides and 1½"x2½" ploughed pieces at its ends (Fig. C). The two unit ends (¾"x 24"x63⅝") have 1½"x1½" framing that is 62⅞" long and glue-nailed to the side edges, beginning 3½" below the top edge. The two dividers are ¾"x24"x62⅞" long, with ¾"x¾" notches cut out of their bottom corners. Their 1½"x1½" framing also begins 3½" below their top edges.

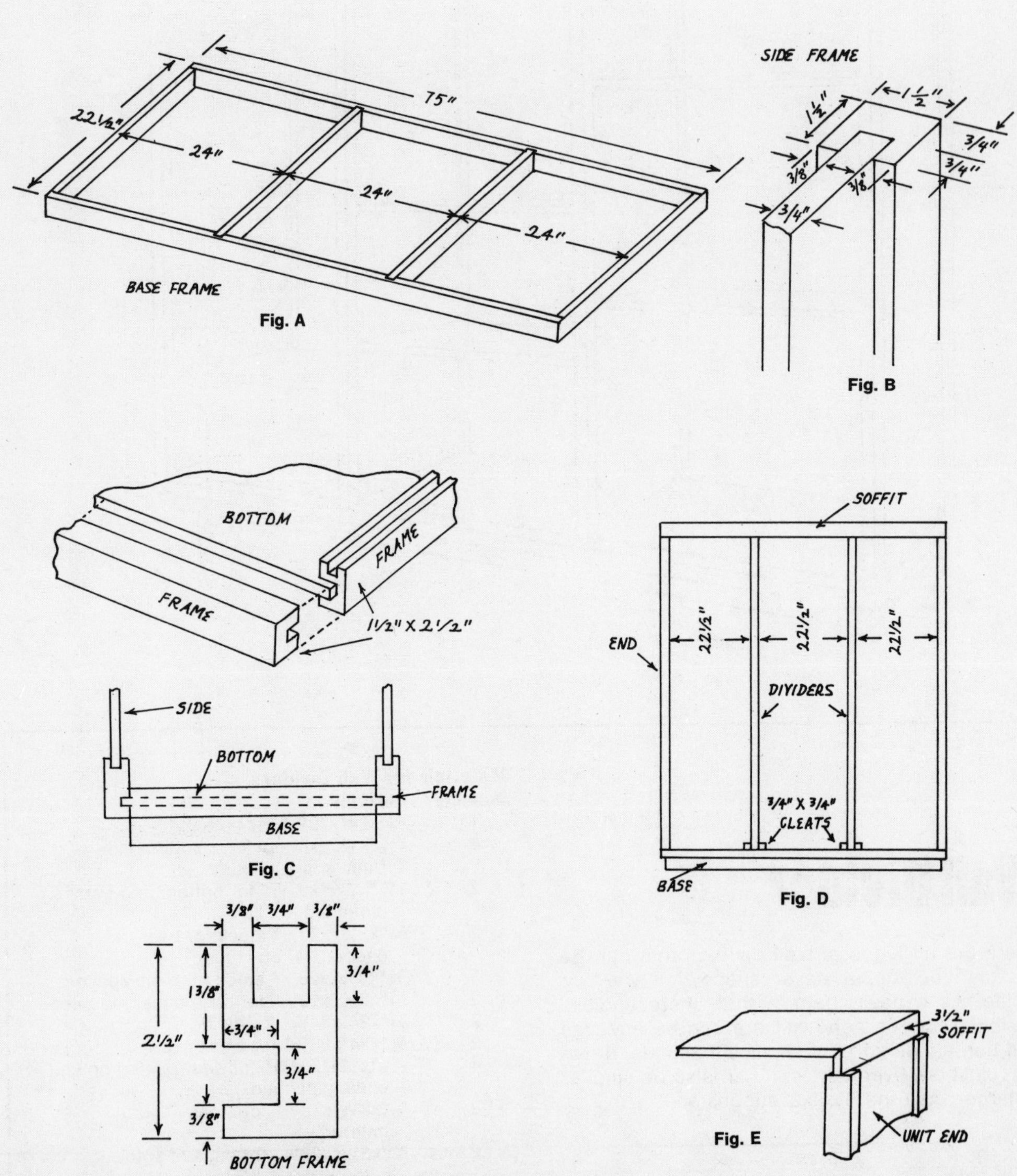

Fig. A

Fig. B

Fig. C

Fig. D

Fig. E

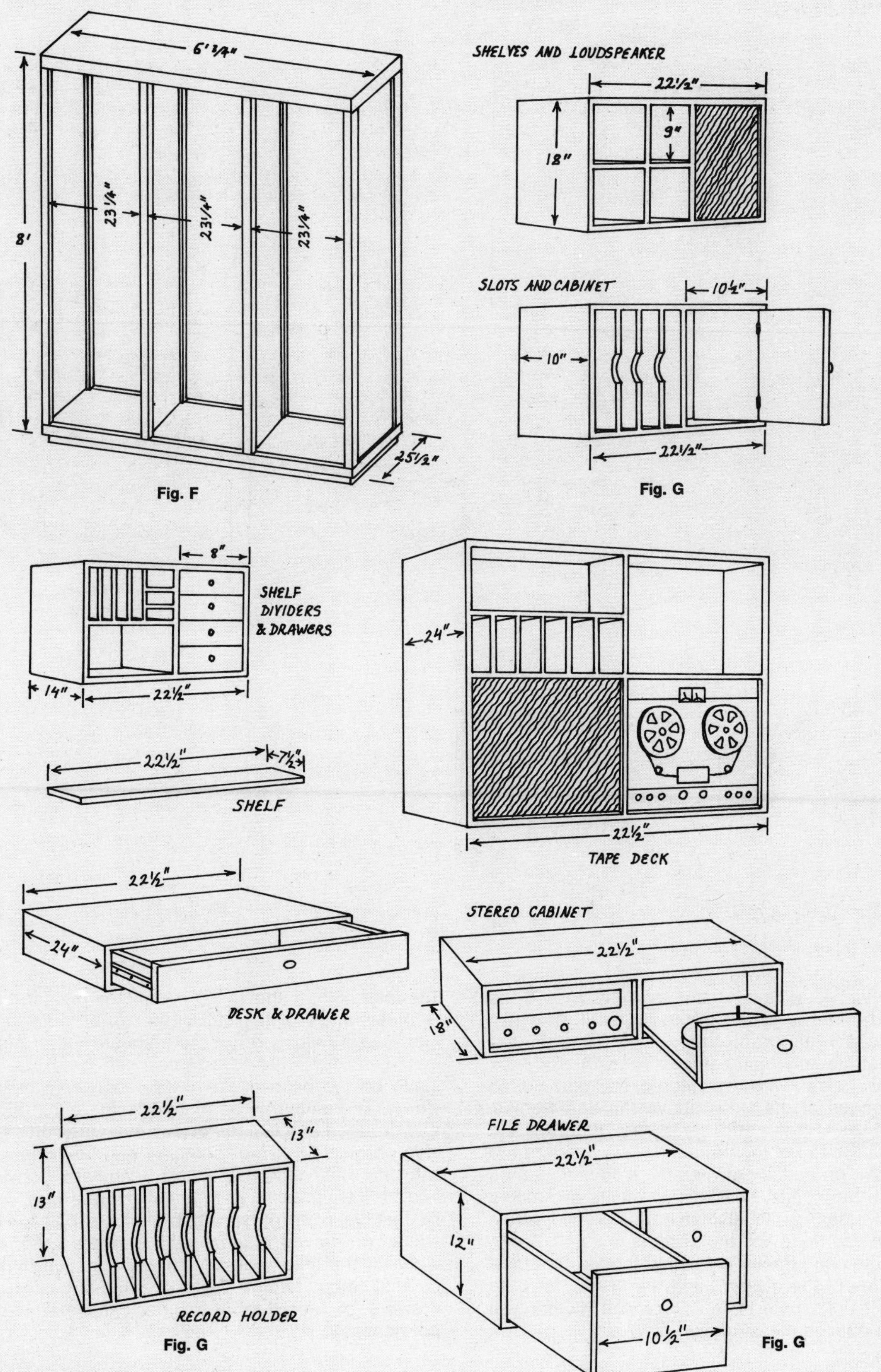

6' 3/4"
8'
23 1/4"
23 1/4"
23 1/4"
25 1/2"
Fig. F
SHELVES AND LOUDSPEAKER
22 1/2"
9"
18"
SLOTS AND CABINET
10 1/2"
10"
22 1/2"
Fig. G
8"
SHELF
DIVIDERS
& DRAWERS
14"
22 1/2"
24"
22 1/2"
7 1/2"
SHELF
22 1/2"
TAPE DECK
22 1/2"
24"
DESK & DRAWER
STEREO CABINET
22 1/2"
18"
22 1/2"
13"
13"
RECORD HOLDER
Fig. G
FILE DRAWER
22 1/2"
12"
10 1/2"
Fig. G

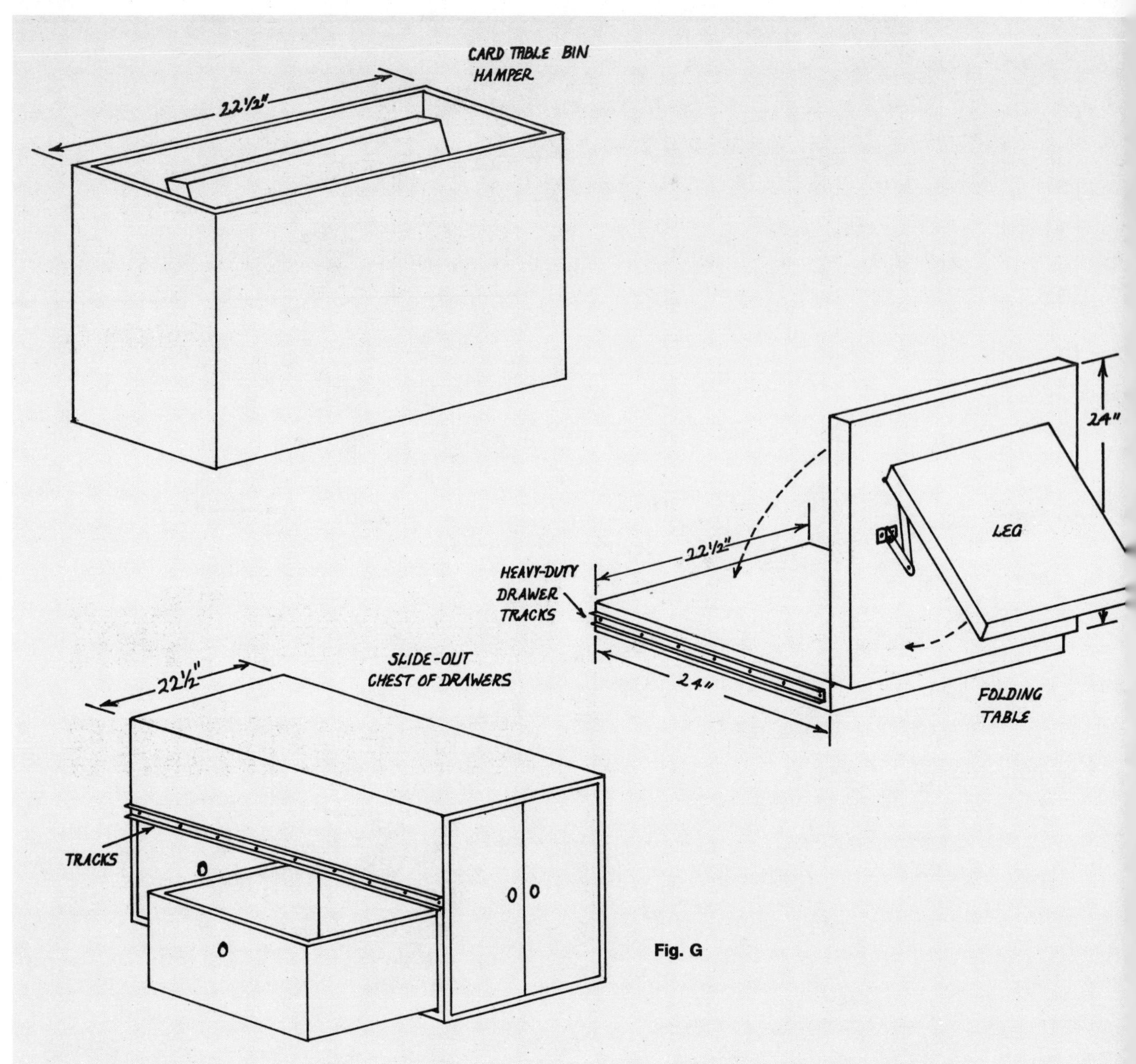

Fig. G

Assembly. The base is assembled (Fig. A) and the framed bottom is nailed to the top of it. The two ends are glue-nailed into the plough along the top of the bottom end frames (Figs. C and D). The ¾"x 3½"x73½" side soffits are mitered, and glue-nailed to the edges of the sides above the end frames. The ¾"x25½"x3½" end soffits are mitered and nailed to the top of the unit ends. The dividers are placed 24" on center between the side soffits, then nailed to the soffits. The ¾"x¾" cleats are nailed on both sides of the divider bottoms. The space between each end and the dividers is 23¼". Three adjustable shelf tracks are nailed the full length of both sides of the dividers and the insides of both ends. All units built to fit in the wall divider will have an outside measurement of 22½".

The units. Fig. F shows the completed divider. Fig. G shows a few of the units that can be built to fit into a wall divider. All of the units are either hung in the divider with adjustable shelf brackets, or stand on the base of the divider between the dividers. The units can be placed facing either side, and grouped in any manner desired. One complete side of the wall divider could be just bookshelves, with the other side made up of cabinets, drawers and hi-fi equipment. Permanent fixtures may also be installed, of course. Other fixtures can be installed on drawer guides. (If guides are used, the width of the units will remain 22½".) Such things as a slide-out folding table, or slide-out chest of drawers, or a card-table hamper can be attached permanently.

CHAPTER 13

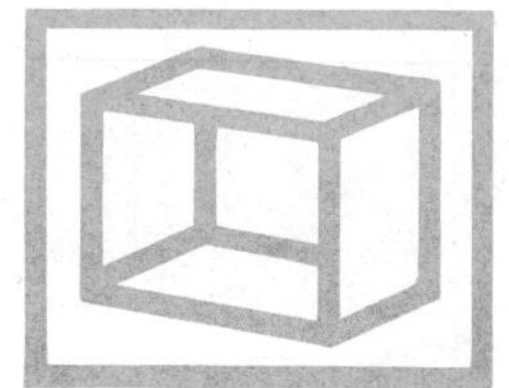
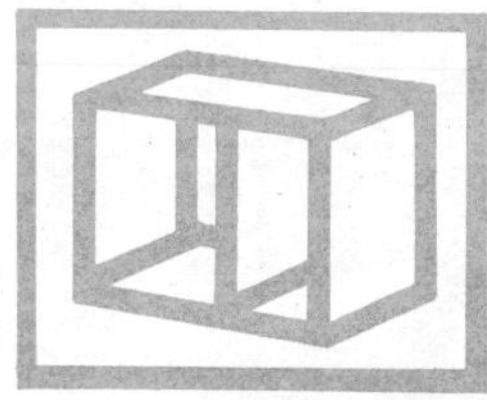
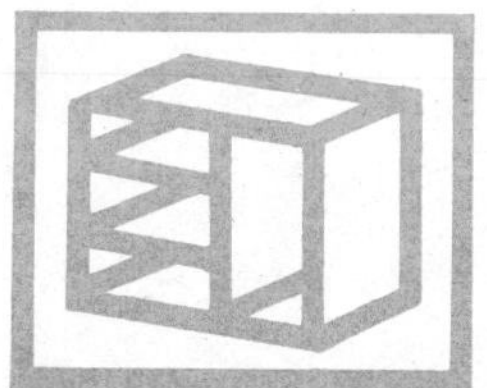

Cabinets That Are Furniture

Cabinets That Are Furniture

So far as the professional cabinetmaker is concerned, the real work begins *after* the veneer is laid down. Only then can the long and sometimes tedious process of finishing begin—and finishing always takes more time to complete than actual construction.

There is a furniture company now producing exact replicas of an 18th-century Chippendale desk that stands in the diplomatic reception room of the U.S. State Department in Washington, D.C. The original is heralded as America's finest example of a Chippendale desk, and for the manufacturer to reproduce it, complete with hand-carvings and precise duplication of every other detail, requires between five and six months, and hundreds of man-hours. The building of each reproduction is time-consuming enough, but, in this effort to recreate the exact finish that John Townsend gave the original in 1765, there are 25 separate stages of finishing, all of which are executed *by hand!* The price of the replica, by the way, is $4,800.

If the veneer is just the beginning for a professional, he still has several advantages over the home craftsman. To begin with, professionals are likely to have access to huge steam ovens that allow them to bend woods under constant pressure, as well as hydraulically controlled presses that can hold a piece of wood in its exact curve while it dries. Then there is the nature of the wood itself. The artisans who make a living at making furniture buy specially kiln-dried, grade A-1 cabinet woods not readily found in neighborhood lumberyards. They plane it and shape it and sand it on high-powered, accurate equipment. If they want to mold it, they have industrial molders, planers and shapers that rarely get out of line, each of which costs a small fortune. The radial arm saws they use are $1,500 gems, calibrated as if they were surgical instruments. Their bench saws are set up with mammoth support tables, with guide fences that are cranked toward the blade on tracks that always keep them 100% accurate.

"The professionals have it easy." But to

make a living, cabinetmakers must have more than the biggest, most accurate, timesaving tools and equipment available. They also work in space that is probably larger than the entire square footage of the average home. That is why to the professional cabinetmaker, the real work begins after the last piece of veneer is in place; his machinery is of no use during all the different stages of finishing that must be done with bare hands.

The projects offered on the next few pages are admittedly a challenge to anyone working with only the tools found in a home workshop. But they are not impossible projects, for exactness is not totally dependent on the precision of any one tool. Exactness is dependent on the standards a person sets for himself. If the saw cuts 1/32" off line, a few minutes of planing will correct the imprecision—provided the person who is doing the work has the patience and willingness to make the correction. Since professionals have machines that rarely err, they rarely have to go through those extra steps of correcting mistakes, and can therefore work more quickly and efficiently. In the end, however, both professional and amateur must achieve that same straight line, that same measurement. How they each arrive at that measurement, or how long it takes them, or how many steps they must go through, is not important.

And, having both gone about the task of building the same cabinet, there comes a point when each must put aside his machines and rely on only his hands and his patience to apply the finish. The final sanding goes swiftly, for some of it can even be done by machine. But then come the many applications of whatever is to be the finish. Between each coat there is rubbing and polishing and smoothing. It is long and slow labor that shows results only in minute changes in the texture and looks of the wood, and often there is no discernible difference from one rubbing to the next. But there is a reward. In the end, when the project at last can be smoothed and polished no more, when the grain of the wood seems to be three-dimensional as it is examined through the depth of many layers of finish, there is that ultimate satisfaction of having achieved a near-perfection. There is that physical proof that the secret beauty wrought by nature has been highlighted and brought into sharp focus.

If the finish on a cabinet becomes an obvious expression of the builder's patience and skill, there are other demonstrations as well. Not only are all the joints perfectly formed, but there is a gentle "whoosh" that can be heard each time the drawers and doors in the cabinet are closed. Such a whisper of noise comes from precisely fitted drawers that ride on carefully fitted drawer guides, previously waxed to provide a smooth sliding action. With the doors, each must be exactly formed to seat itself between the stiles of its frame with equal amounts of space around all its edges. It is a time-consuming business to fit doors and drawers like that. But it should—and will—be done by a careful craftsman.

Still another proof of the craftsman's skill is his choice of woods and the way he matches their grains. Fine cabinet-grade woods such as maple, cherry, birch and pine can combine both warmth and beauty in any richly finished cabinet, but the lumber you use must be selected carefully. Each piece must promise interesting grain configurations, free from distortion, mineral streaks or any other natural defects. Then they must be cut and assembled so that their grains seem to flow into each other at a corner, for example, or complement all the other grains visible even to the casual viewer.

If you are not a professional, if you do not have to produce dozens of projects each year in order to make a living, then you have a tremendous advantage. You have time on your side, time to spend seeking not only the right woods, but also new ones. Each wood has its own special properties and peculiarities, and each wood must be handled in a slightly different way. Some need always to be drilled or they will split. Others will not accept certain finishing materials. Still others are inherently weak and require special bracing during construction. Find the most suitable woods for your project. Buy them and work with them. Experiment with their grains, finishes they will accept, and their construction, for each species presents its own challenge, and its own special rewards.

To work with some new wood that can be formed into a cabinet presents one nagging question: What should be used as a trim? It would be ludicrous, for example, to spend weeks assembling a magnificent cabinet using Honduras mahogany, and then trim it with pine molding. Most of the molding that is sold in lumberyards today is shaped from pine or fir and, as such, is usually painted. Even if it is not painted, it is extremely difficult to stain and finish pine so that it looks exactly like mahogany. So you are faced with the problem of making your own molding for furniture you create from any of the rich cabinet woods available.

Here again, the professional has an advantage. His molders, shapers and joiners are all large, precision instruments. They can be adjusted in order to shape according to the most complicated of jigs, and allow the operator to stand before them and shove fine pieces of cabinet wood past their blades with the confidence that every piece will come out with exact curves and coves. But the amateur lacks the space, the money or even the need to possess such equipment. All he has is time and patience. Happily enough, he needs nowhere near as much of either as his forebears did. Fortunately, the machines to be found in every well-equipped home workshop are quite sufficient to make the task of molding and shaping a relatively quick and easy chore.

There is the molding head, which will fit on the arbor of any bench or radial arm saw. Because the act of molding usually involves ripping long strips of wood, the molding blade tends to be somewhat easier to use on a bench saw. There is also the router, with its complement of some 35 to 50 different bits. The hand router will do many chores very well; when you are shaping a long, thin piece of wood, it is easier to control the bits if they are used in a drill press or even on a radial arm saw. No matter how the shaping is done, it is easier to do than in the "old days," when molding and trim were shaped by hand, with hand tools.

There are two projects in this section that specifically require the dishing of a base plate. How to perform that dishing with a bench saw is shown, step by step, in the sportsman's cabinet project. What is not explicitly stated anywhere else in this section is that, depending on the wood used, all of the molding and trim for each of the projects should probably be made in the workshop. How to approach that procedure is specifically shown in the console project. This requires the use of three different molder blades, only one of which is used to create several different curves in the same piece of trim. There is also an entire page of molding shapes and how to achieve them in Chapter 7.

It is heartily recommended that, having found a new and different wood to work with, you experiment first before plunging into any project. Take a scrap of the wood and cut it, drill it, screw it, nail it—and mold it. You may discover that this wood is too brittle to respond to a molding cutter; it may have to be shaped with carbide-tipped router bits. Or it may be easy to shape, providing it is fed past the blade at an exceedingly slow rate. There can be any number of idiosyncrasies peculiar to a wood species that must be learned and then mastered. Molding is always a new adventure, particularly if some new combination of curves has been invented. Each shape will have to be cut with a different blade setting, and so each setting must first be tested. The wise craftsman always practices what he is about to do on a piece of scrap wood before he does the real cutting.

It is somehow easier to create a cabinet by matching straight lines. Who can question your taste if everything about a project is a straight line? The moment the curves appear, however, there arrives a host of "experts" who wag their heads and cluck their tongues and wonder aloud whether the curves in the door panels are not too broad, or if the molding is not too ornate, or not ornate enough. There is always somebody who sniffs and suggests that the builder must be a French Provincial, trained by Greek Revivalists and confused by Queen Victoria, in order to have cut such a gross bunch of curves and miscellaneous doodads for his cabinet.

Let them rant and rave, or lead them tactfully to your bench saw, and tell them either do better, or keep still. Whatever you elect to do, for whatever reasons, the choices *you* make are the correct ones. They have to be correct because it is your project, conceived by you, and executed with your hands. If you deem that a cabinet is enhanced by the particular molding, trim and finish you put on it, then the choices are perfect for the project. If someone else proceeds to make a similar cabinet, then that becomes *his* project, and however *he* sees the trim and the finish is perfect for what he is doing.

By some modern standards, John Townsend's 1765 version of a Chippendale desk is rather overdone. It has too many flutes and coves and curves and carvings. By Mr. Chippendale's standards it is probably a poor copy of what the master's hand could have wrought. But Townsend created a desk that his patron also happened to appreciate to the extent he paid for it. And down through the centuries, others have also appreciated the craftsmanship and artistry that the desk represents until at last, late in the 20th century, it is being paid the highest of all compliments—it is being not copied, but duplicated, curve for curve, straight edge for straight edge. Presumably, if the duplicators discover a structural error hidden somewhere within its recesses, they will faithfully reproduce that, too, for they want no criticism of their ability to exactly recreate the desk. And no one will criticize them for the ornate carvings or molding, either. They might criticize Townsend, but not them. So they are taking no risks at being laughed at, for they are doing nothing more than painstakingly reproducing another man's creativity.

You, too, can be a faithful reproducer. You can painstakingly reproduce all the curves and furbelows suggested in the furniture projects in this section. And when you are criticized for being too "heavy-handed" with your molding, or for not trimming the piece enough, you can say, "I did it because that's what the plans called for." That is a fair response, if you were faithful to the plans because what the final plans called for was exactly to your liking in every detail in the first place. But if there was a single element in those plans that you did not whole-heartedly believe was an absolutely perfect expression of what it should be, and you did not make the necessary changes, you have been untrue to yourself as a craftsman.

There must be no quarter given in the construction of any project, and having dedicated untold hours of labor and skill and time to creating a piece of furniture of which you have every reason to be proud, it is then placed on display for everyone to see in your living room. Sooner or later that hard-earned finish will be inadvertently marred, or scratched, or spotted. Here are a few of the techniques that can be employed to repair minor scratches, burns, blemishes and stains:

Minor scratches: Use a wax stick to match the color of the finish and fill in the scratch. Rub the wax in well, then wipe with a soft, dry cloth.

White spots (cause unknown). Dip a cloth in wax, lubricating oil, vegetable shortening, lard or salad oil, and then in cigar or cigarette ashes. Rub the blemish until it disappears, then immediately wipe the wood surface with a dry cloth.

Candle wax. Hold an ice cube against the wax until it hardens. Crumble off as much wax as possible using your fingers. Then scrape the wax gently with a dull knife and rub the area briskly with a clean cloth dampened with a liquid wax. Wipe the area dry and repeat the rubbing until the candle wax is gone.

Milk spots. If milk, or anything that has milk or cream in it, remains on furniture for very long, it has the effect of a mild paint or varnish remover. So wipe up spilled milk as quickly as possible, then use either of the two methods listed under alcohol spots to remove the stain.

Alcohol spots. Either of these methods can be followed: 1) Rub the spot with a finger dipped in paste wax, silver polish, linseed oil or moistened cigar or cigarette ash. 2) Put a few drops of ammonia on a damp cloth and rub the spot until it disappears. Polish the area immediately with lemon oil.

Water marks. 1) Dampen a pad of fine steel wool with furniture polish or liquid wax and rub the spot gently until it disappears. 2) Place a clean, thick blotter over the spot and press a warm iron to the paper. Keep repeating until the ring disappears.

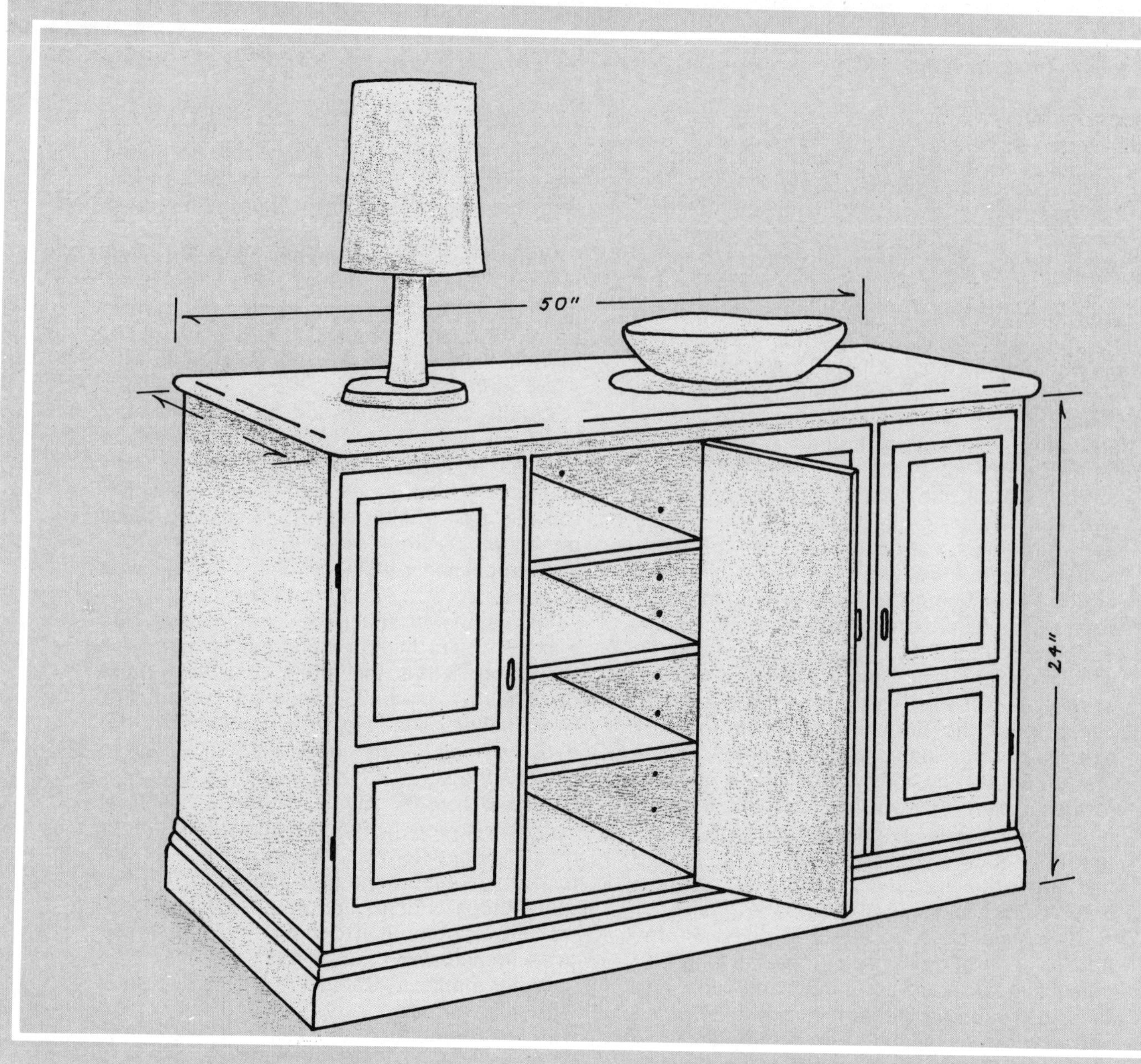

Basic Credenza

The difference between a credenza and a standard counter cabinet is the kind of finish applied to a high-grade cabinet wood. The decorative touches and face designs are endless, and so are the dimensions; the credenza here is 26" high by 16" deep by 50" long.

Materials for Basic Credenza

Quantity	Description
1	¾"x16"x50" for top
2	¾"x15¼"x23" for sides
1	¾"x14⅞"x23" for partition
2	¾"x14⅞"x23" for bottoms
3	¾"x1½"x46⅛" for top and base rails
1	¼"x21½"x46⅞" for back
2	¾"x14"x22⅜" for shelves
4	¾"x¾"x12⅝" for top battens
2	¾"x3¼"x16" for base
1	¾"x3¼"x49⅞" for base
8′	⅝"x¾" nose-and-cove molding for base
4 pr.	hinges
4	pulls
8	shelf brackets
3′	¼" dowels for joining

Assembly. All parts are cut according to the sizes given in the materials list. The sides and partition are dadoed so that the top of the bottom shelf will be 4½" from the floor. The back inside edges of the sides are rabbeted ¼"x⅜" to accept the back. The top rear corner of the partition is notched ¾"x1½" for the back top support rail. Assemble the sides and partition by glue-screwing the two bottom plates into their dadoes. The front and back top support rails are glued and doweled to the sides and partition, as is the front base rail. The sides and partition are drilled (Fig. A) to accept shelf brackets. The baseboards are mitered and glue-screwed to the sides and front of the credenza (Fig. A), then topped with nose-and-cove molding. The credenza top can have either a beveled or a rounded front and edge. It is glue-screwed to ¾"x¾" battens which are attached to the sides and partition (Fig. A).

Doors. These are panel-and-frame assemblies with any face decoration desired. Each door is lipped and measures 1¼"x12½"x21".

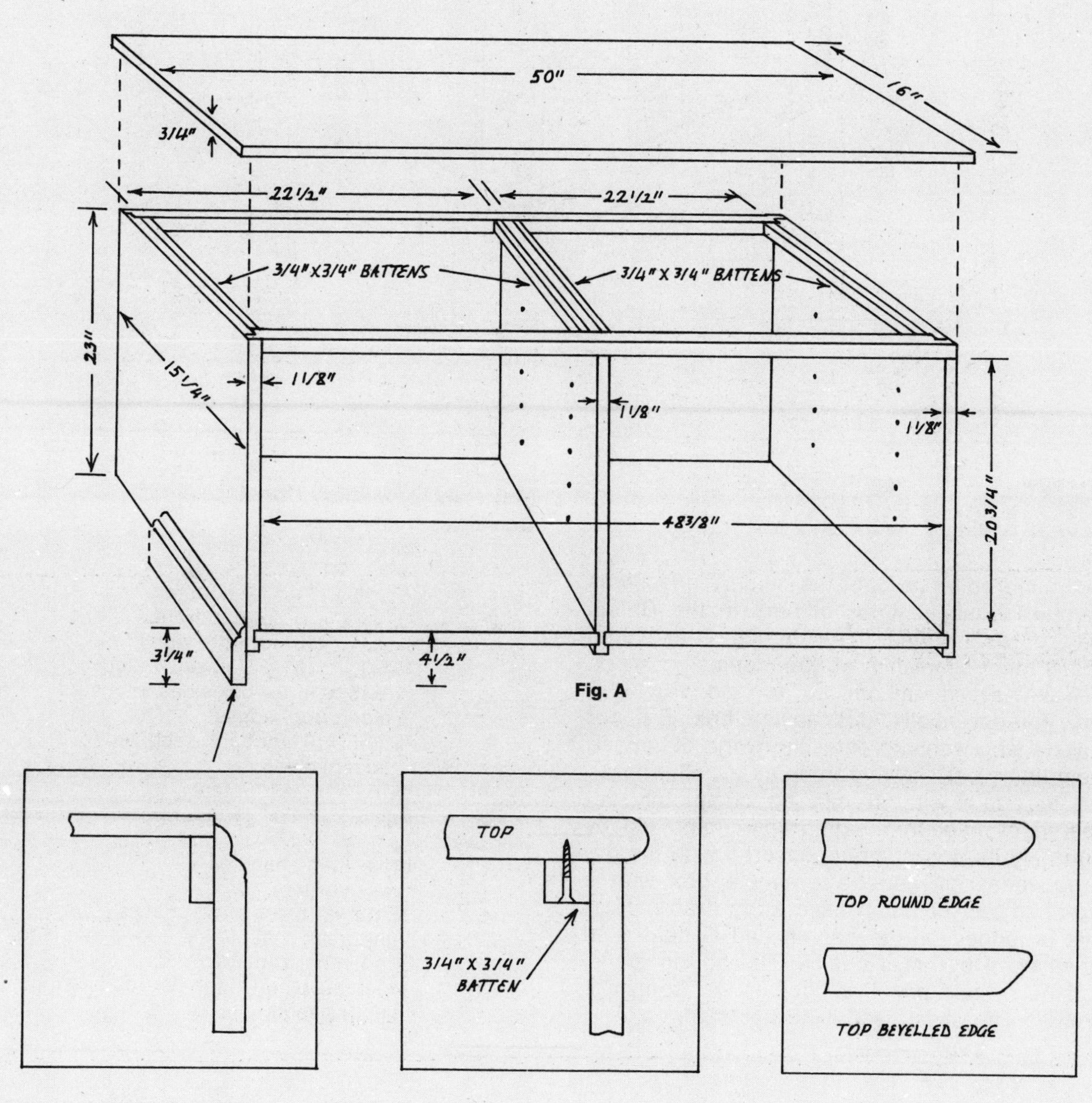

Fig. A

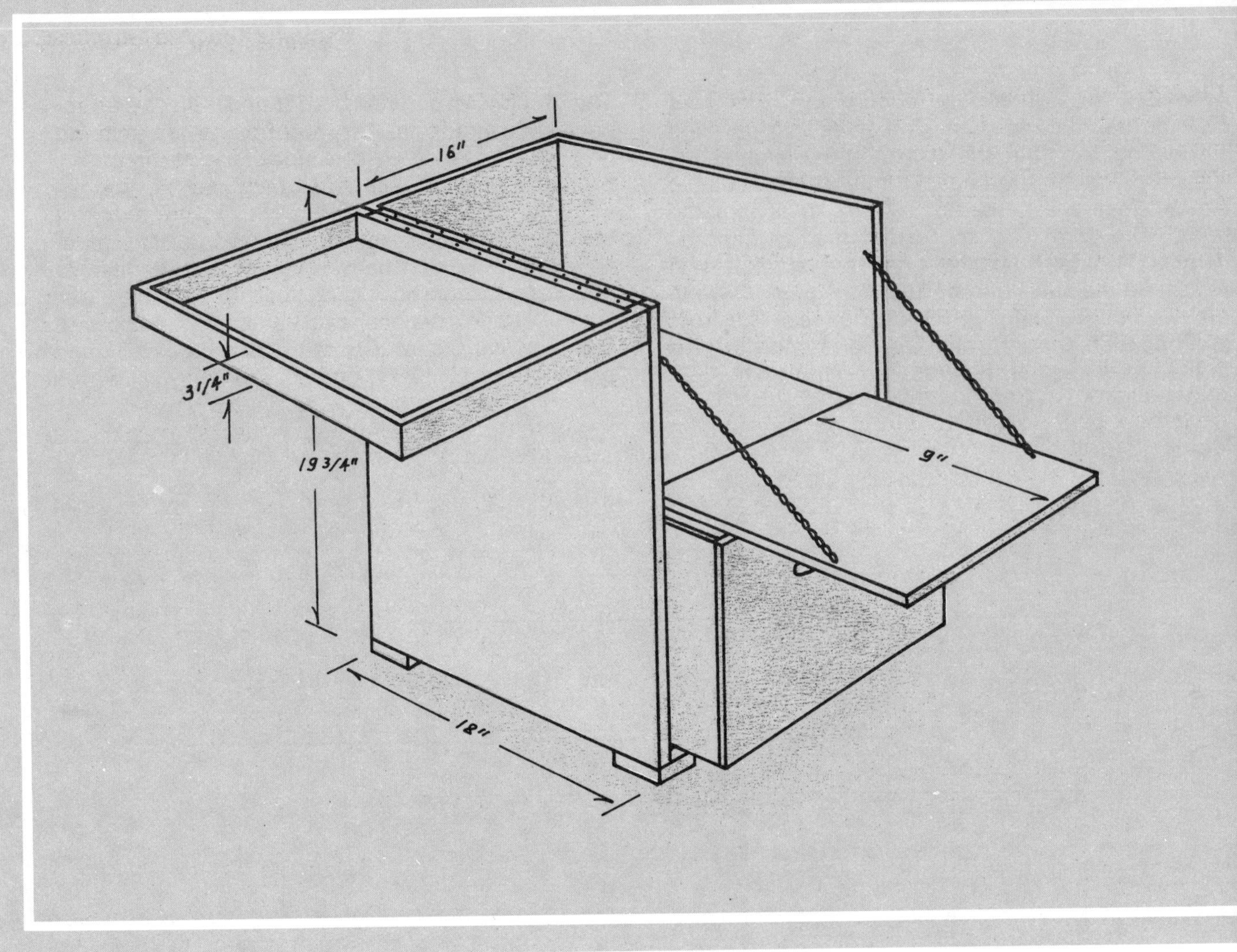

Military Chest

Two hundred years ago, the military chest was standard equipment for officers in the British Empire, who carted them all over the world. Today, the simplicity of the campaign chest makes it as streamlined as any modern furniture, for essentially, it is just a box. But, for anyone who wants to enter the world of veneer, the military bar shown here is an excellent project to begin with. It can be completely veneered, or made from high-grade cabinet woods with only its drawer fronts covered with the desired veneer. It can be a simple box with a flip-open top, or it can have a top drawer front that is hinged on the bottom and is held level when open by brass chains. The bottom panel can be a fixed panel, a door or the front of a drawer. The chest itself is 16"x18"x23".

Materials for Military Chest

Quantity	Description
1	½"x15"x17¾" for top
1	½"x15"x17¾" for shelf
1	½"x15"x17¾" for bottom
2	½"x3¼"x15" for top, front and back
1	¾"x3¼"x18" for right side of top
1	¾"x3⅛"x18" for left side of top
2	¾"x15"x19" for box sides, rabbeted along front edges
1	¾"x15"x19" for back, rabbeted to accept sides
4	¾"x3¼"x3¼" for feet
2	¾"x8⅞"x14⅞" for door panels
Hardware	
2	brass lifting handles
4	brass corners
4	½"x2"x2" brass angle braces
3'	light brass chain (if top door panel is to open horizontally)
3'	¾" brass piano hinge (for top and top door panel)

Cutting. Cut all pieces according to the sizes given in the materials list. The front edges of the sides have a ¾"x½" rabbet which forms the stop for the front panels. There is also a ¼"x½" dado in each side for the shelf. The back is rabbeted to accept the sides.

Top. Cut the four sides and top (see materials list for sizes) and rabbet the edges of the sides as shown in Fig. B. When assembling the top, note that the left side is ⅛" narrower than the other sides to accommodate the piano hinge. The hinge may be inset ⅛" and hidden by a ⅛" filler block, or it can be allowed to show as part of the decoration.

Assembly. The sides and back are assembled (Fig. A) by glueing the shelf in its dadoes. The bottom is butt-joined to the bottom of the sides, and ¾"x 3¼"x3¼" feet are glue-screwed under each corner. If the front panels are only panels, they are glued into the rabbets in the front edges of the sides. If the top panel is hinged, attach a piano hinge along its bottom edge and the shelf. Add a light brass chain to each side to hold the door horizontal. If the bottom panel is to be a drawer front, make the drawer as discussed in Chapter 6. Alternatively, the bottom panel can be a door hinged either at the side or on the bottom.

Attach the brass lifting handles, corner and angle braces.

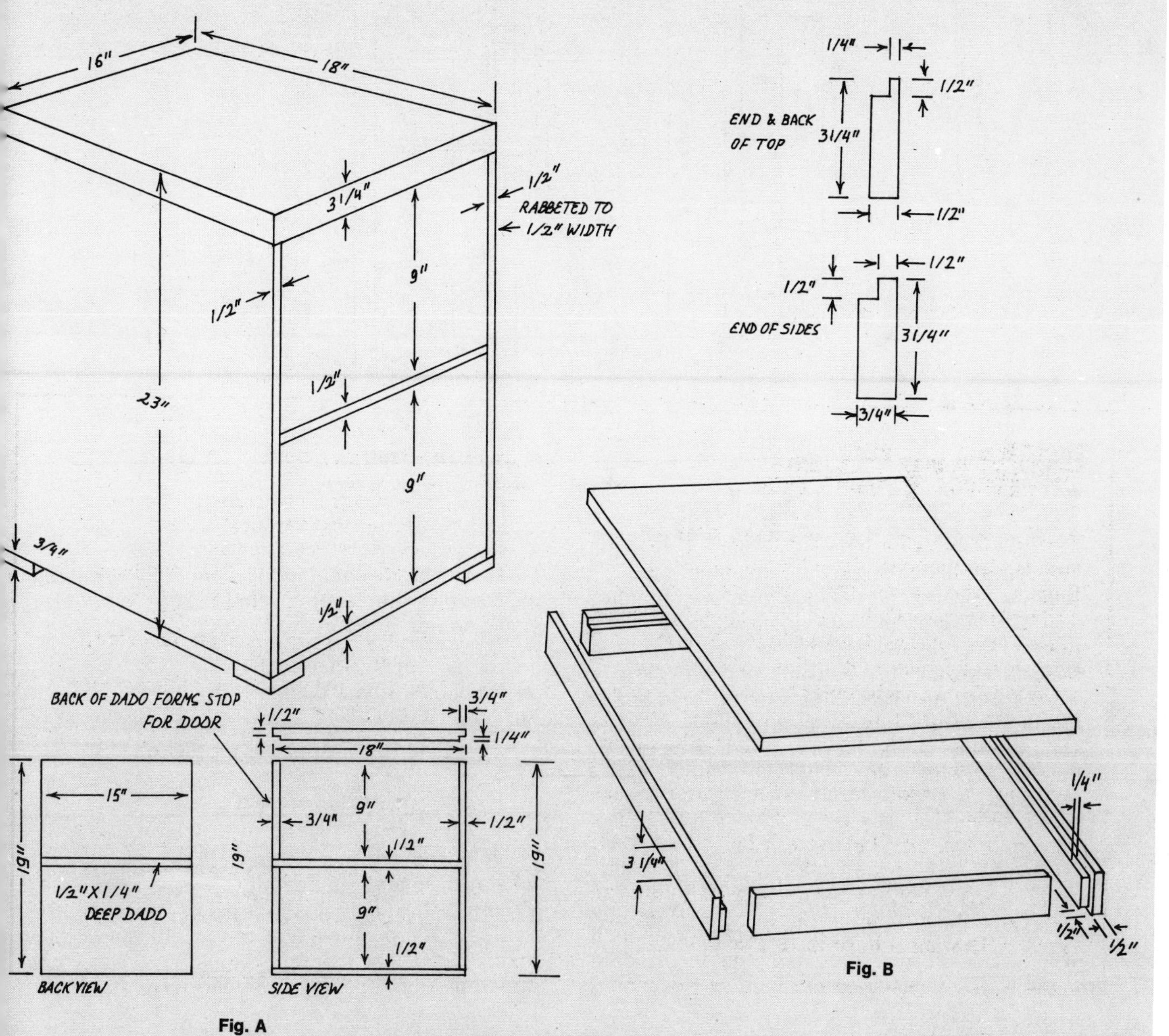

Fig. A

Fig. B

Decorative Shelves

The mere bulk of these shelf columns forms an imposing divider, particularly in a room that has a 10′ or 12′ ceiling. Here again, it is the idea, rather than the design, that is important. The shelves between the columns can be glass or wood; there can be cabinets, as well as space for hi-fi components or a television set. The columns themselves can be starkly modern, or be topped with a crown molding; they can be faced with hardwood flooring, veneered plywood, or covered with exotic veneer, such as rosewood or Honduras mahogany.

Materials (for one 8′ column)

Quantity	Description
2	½″ plywood panels for sides
9′	1″x2″ stock for spacers

Columns. Each column is 3″ wide by 12″ long, and is made from two pieces of ½″ plywood. A ¾″x 1½″x11″ spacer block (Fig. A) is positioned every 12″ on center between the sides. Half-inch plywood, 12″ wide, is rabbeted and inserted in both ends. The columns are as long as the ceiling is high, and are placed opposite each other with whatever spacing is desired.

Facings. The columns need not be unadorned verticals. A crown molding can be attached around them (Fig. C) at the top. Similarly, a base, constructed from one or more strips of baseboard trim, can be attached to the bottom of the columns. The corners of the columns can also be faced with corner molding.

Shelves. If glass shelves are used between the columns, they should not be more than 18" wide; the insides of the columns can be dadoed to hold each shelf. If ¾" wooden shelves are used, they can be held by blind dadoes, mortise and tenons or simple shelf brackets. The shelves might be faced with 1"x2" stock or made from 1½" stock, to carry out the bulky theme of the columns.

Light box (Fig. B). If light boxes are desired, the box is made from 1"x2" stock with ¼" plywood covering the bottom, and drilled to accept the lights. The front and back of the housing is given a lip high enough to conceal the lights. Wiring for the lights (or any other equipment) can be run up the inside of the columns by drilling through the spacers so that the cable can go wherever it is needed.

Mirrors. If mirrors are to be installed between columns, attach a ½" plywood backing to the back of the columns and glue mirrors to this backing. The mirrors, in conjunction with glass shelves and a light box, form an excellent indoor terrarium for houseplants.

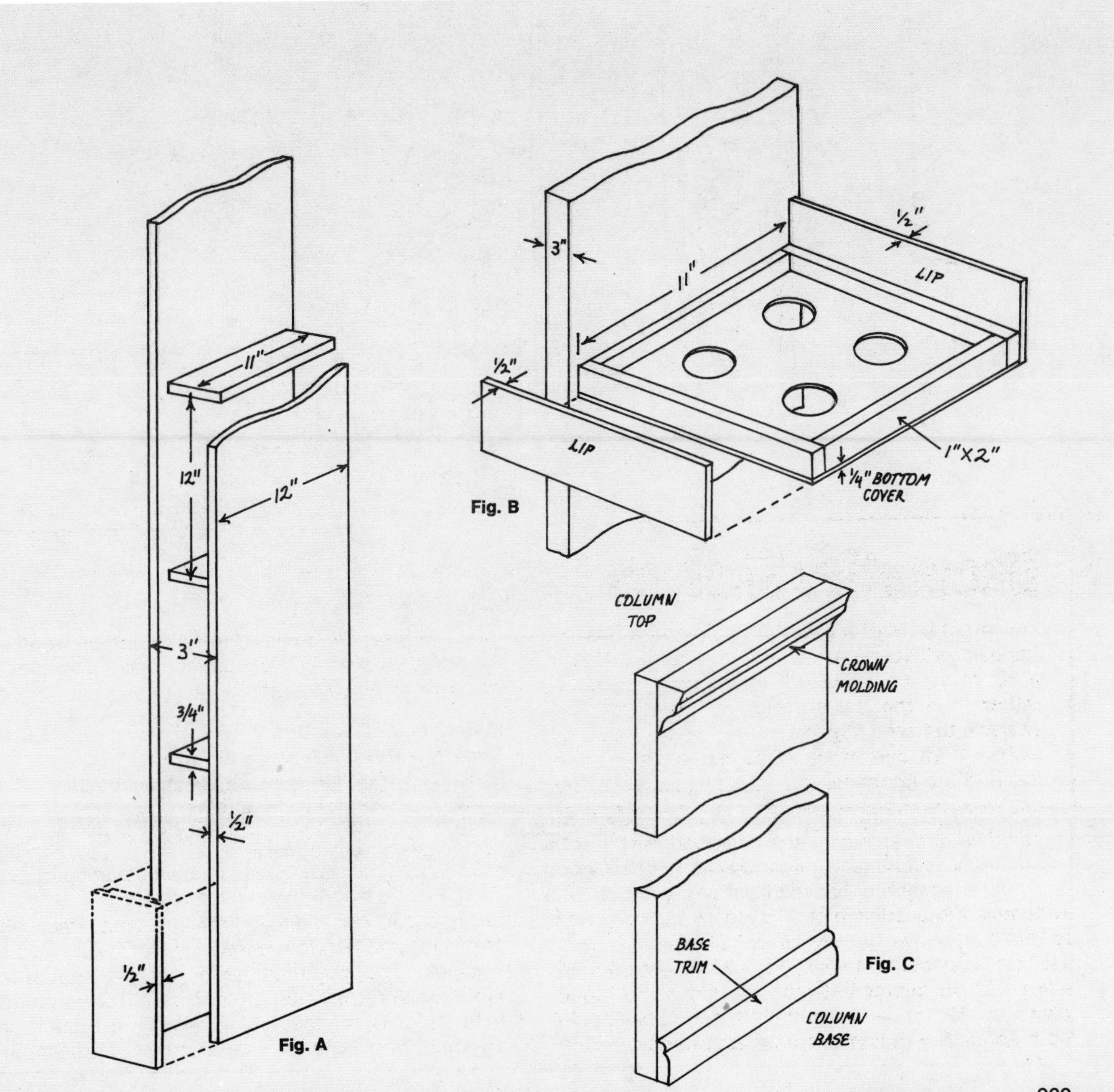

Fig. A

Fig. B

Fig. C

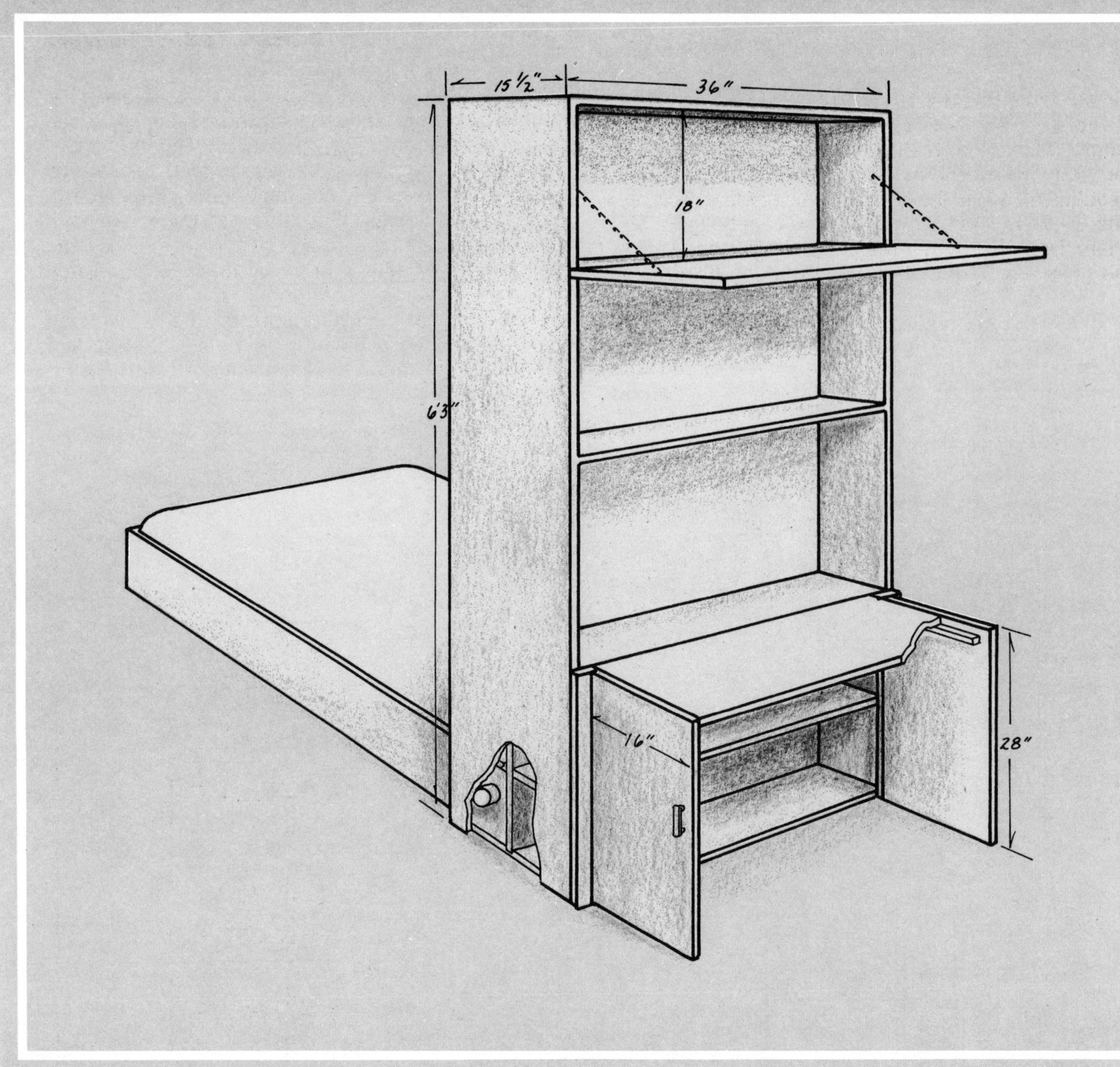

Desk-Bed

This is an attractive bookcase, desk and bar on one side, and hides a single bed in the other. But despite its many uses, the desk-bed is still not a difficult assembly. It might be made of plywood and be veneered, or built from any good cabinet wood, or just plain pine.

Materials for Desk-Bed

Quantity	Description
12′	1″x8″ for shelves and cabinet bottom
18′	1″x8″ for bed frame
18′	1″x15½″ stock for top, bottom and sides of case
1	¼″x3′x6′ plywood for center partition
1	¾″x3′x6′ plywood for bed plate
1	3′x2½′ stock for desk doors
1	1½′x3′ stock for cabinet door
8′	¾″ piano hinge
2′	light chain to retain cabinet door

Sides. The sides are 75" long by 15½" wide. They are rabbeted at both ends and ploughed their full length, 7½", from their front edge. The plough is for a ¼" plywood partition. The sides are also dadoed 18" from the top, for the cabinet bottom. The dado is 7½" long, and ends at the plough. There is a similar dado 29" from the bottom, for the desk top. Two or three shelves can be placed between the cabinet and the desk, depending on personal choice. They can either be dadoed or installed with shelf tracks.

Horizontals. The top and bottom pieces are 15½" wide by 36" long and are rabbeted at both ends. The cabinet bottom and desk-top shelf are 7½" wide by 35¼". The shelves will be the same length if they are dadoed in place. If they are to reside

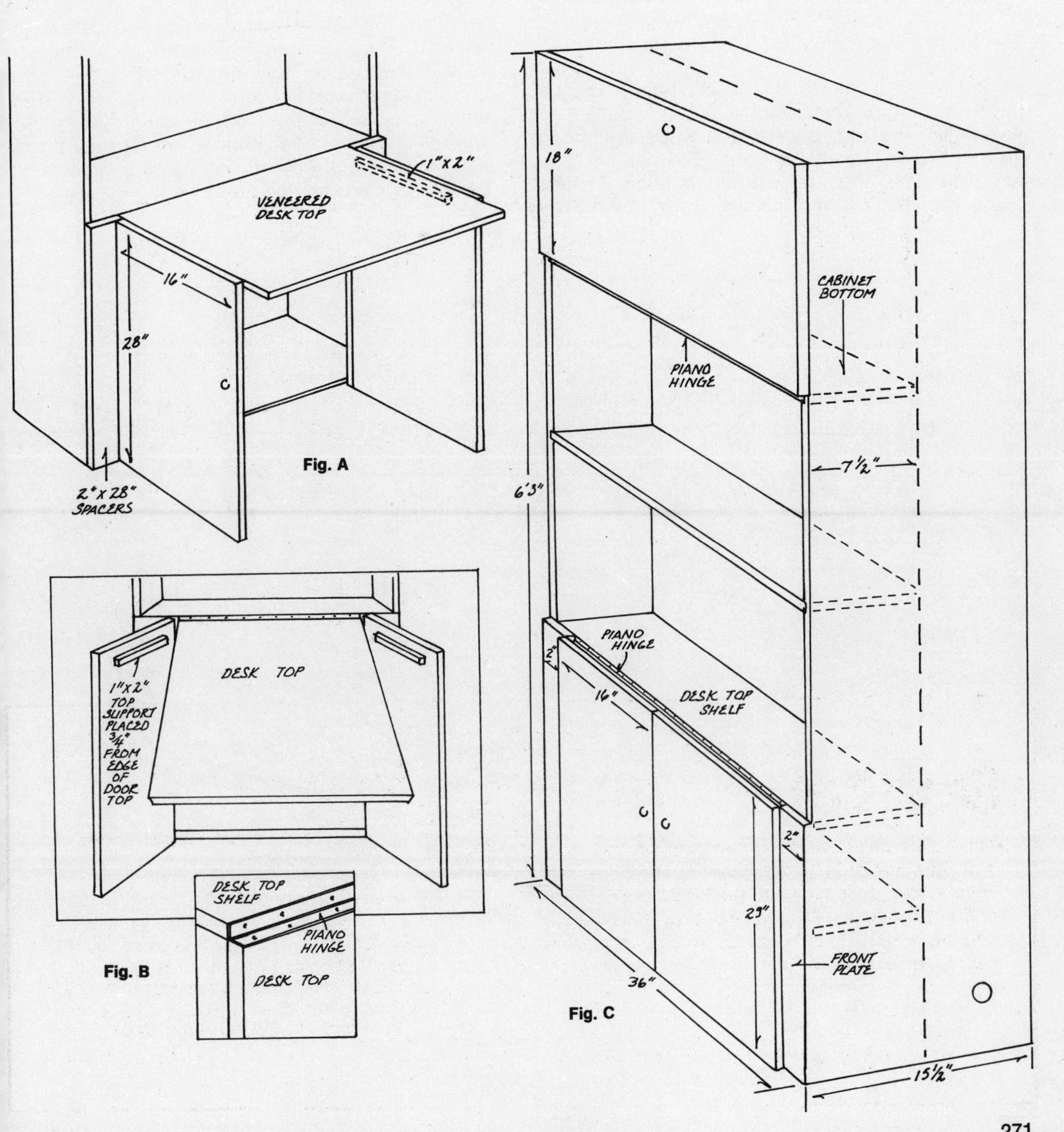

Fig. A

Fig. B

Fig. C

on tracks they will be approximately ½" shorter, or 34¾" long.

Doors. The liquor cabinet door is 18" high by 36" wide, and will be hinged along its bottom edge. The desk doors are 16" x 36". All three can be a solid construction or frame-and-panel. The backs of the desk doors have a 1" x 2" x 24" desk-top brace glue-screwed ¾" below their top edge (Fig. A). All doors must be attached with piano hinges.

Bed. The bed is a simple frame made of ¾" x 7½" stock. The frame is 34" wide by 74" long, and each side has a 2" plough, ¾" from its top edge to receive a ¾" x 33¼" x 73¼" plywood platform.

Center partition. This is ¼" luan or plywood, 35¼" x 74¼".

Desk top. At least ¾" x 32" x 26", but it can be given an edging, 2" or thicker.

Assembly. The top, bottom and sides are glued around the ¼" center partition. The cabinet bottom and desk top are inserted in their dadoes along with the shelves (if they are dadoed). The cabinet door is attached with a piano hinge across its bottom edge (Fig. B), and held closed with magnetic catches. Two chains, each 1' long, are used to hold the door level when it is open. The desk top is attached to the desk-top shelf with a piano hinge and the 2"-wide front pieces are glue-screwed to each side of the desk as shown in Figs. B and C. The desk doors are hinged to the spacers using piano hinges. When they are open, the desk top should rest on their 1" x 2" supports, as shown in Fig. A.

The bed frame is glue-screwed around its platform and pivoted to the back of the cabinet as shown in Fig. D. The desk-shelf-cabinet can be veneered or given any finish desired. The bed and its foam rubber mattress will normally stand inside the back of the cabinet against a wall and will not be seen very often. The unit may be put on small casters. Any trim or molding desired can be used to decorate the project.

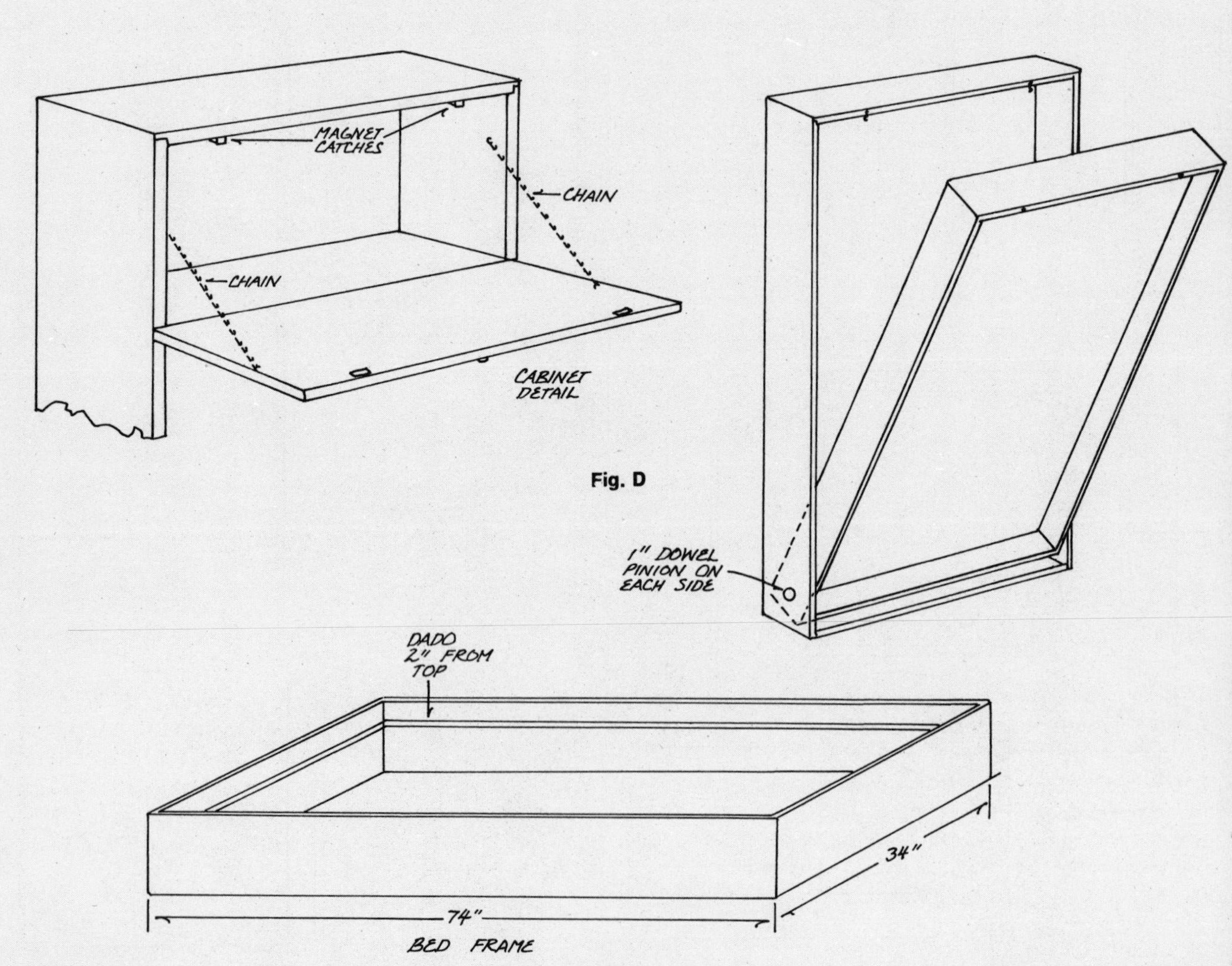

Fig. D

Library Corner Shelves

The "dead" corner problem rears its annoying head all over the house, and it cannot always be solved by building a closet. Sometimes it is preferable to fill the space with a set of corner shelves or a combination of shelves and cabinets. Even so, there is always that unnecessarily deep space in the corner that is seldom put to complete use. The combination of shelves and cabinets here assumes a corner that is 5′ by 5′ although the unit could be either larger or smaller. The project can be constructed from plywood and pressboard, although a hardwood plywood or veneering is recommended if the unit is to stand in any of the "living" rooms of the house.

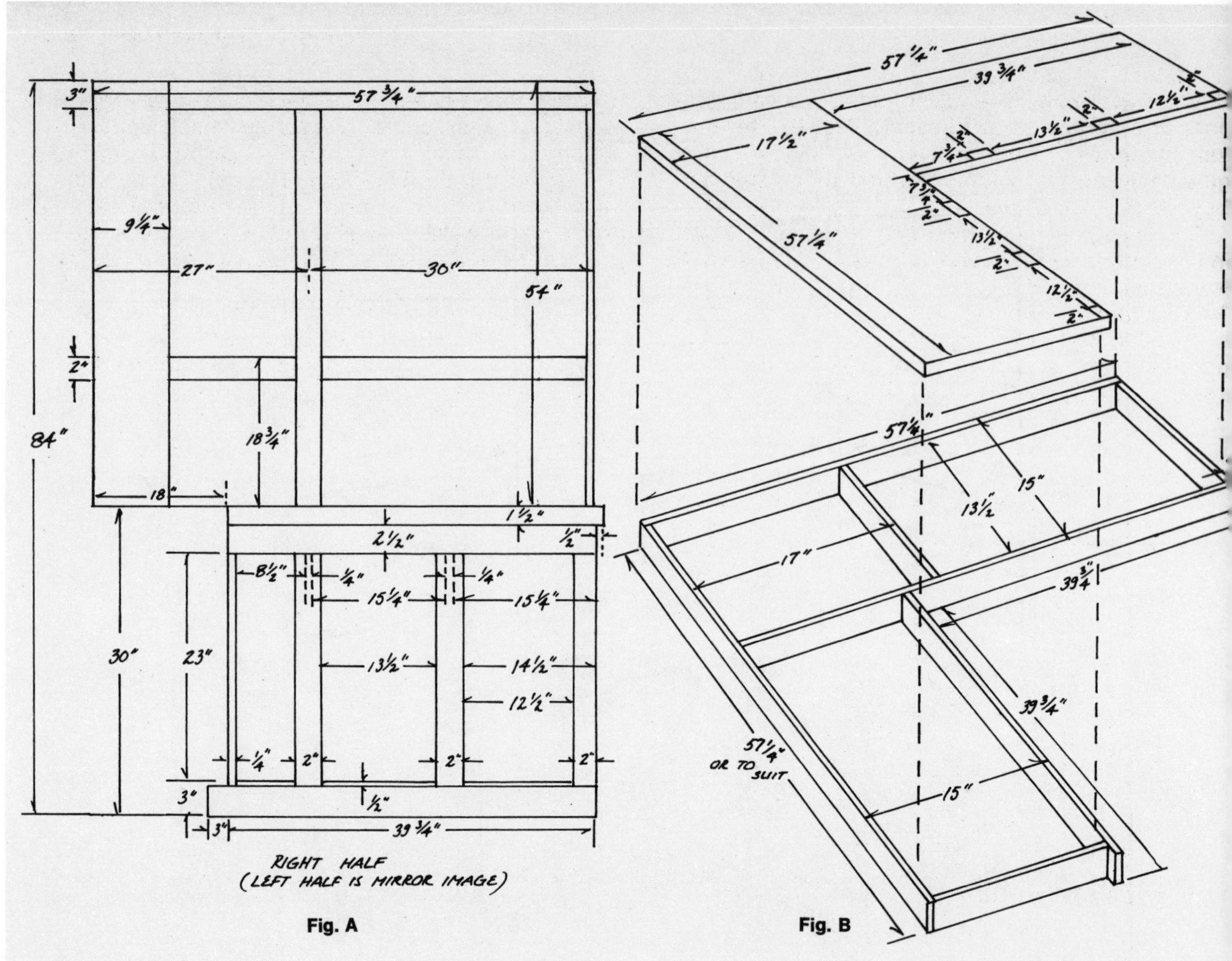

Fig. A

Fig. B

Materials for Library Corner Shelves

Quantity	Description
Cabinet	
1	¾"x3"x57¼" for back member
1	¾"x3"x56¾" for back member
3	¾"x3"x13½" for spacers
1	¾"x3"x56½" for right kick plate
1	¾"x3"x39¾" for left kick plate
1	½"x17½"x57¼" for left platform
1	½"x17½"x39¾" for right platform
2	½"x17¼"x28½" for ends
2	½"x17"x25" for partitions
6	¾"x2"x25½" for stiles
1	¾"x2"x39¾" for rail
1	¾"x2"x39" for rail
1	¾"x2"x57¼" for back top support rail
1	¾"x2"x56½" for back top support rail
2	¼"x28½"x57¼" for cabinet backs
Doors	
4	½"x14½"x22¾" plywood for wing doors
1	½"x8¾"x22¾" plywood for right cover door
1	½"x7⅞"x22¾" plywood for left corner door
4	¼"x15¼"x23¼" veneer panel for door fronts
1	¼"x8¾"x23¼" veneer panel for right corner door
1	¼"x7⅞"x23¼" veneer panel for left corner door
5	½"x20" piano hinges
5	door pulls (optional)
Shelves (optional)	
4	¾"x14"x30" for shelves for cabinet
16′	Adjustable shelf rack for cabinet
Top	
1	¾"x27⅜"x27⅜" piece for center with 6′ radius cut from front corner
2	¾"x10"x30⅝" pieces for wing tops
	veneer and veneer edging tape (as needed)
Shelves	
6	½"x9¼"x54" for shelf sides and partitions
4	¾"x27¼"x27¼" for top and corner shelves
9	¾"x9¼"x29" for top and wing shelves
1	¾"x5½"x52" for rear center shelf support
32′	¼"x1¼" plywood strips for shelf and top lips
2	¼"x30⅜"x54" for backing on wing shelves
2	¼"x28"x54" for backing on corner shelves

Cabinet assembly. The seven ¾"x3" frame members are assembled as shown in Fig. B. The bottom platforms are cut and notched (Fig. B), then glue-nailed to the platform so that they extend 4" beyond the kick plates.

Cut all cabinet parts according to the sizes given in the materials list. The two wing-ends are notched for the kick plate (Fig. C); the partitions have a ¾"x2" notch for the back rail. The sides are glue-screwed to the end plates of the bottom frame. The partitions are set 30" from the inside of the ends (Fig. C), then braced by the back top support rails. The six facing stiles are set in their platform notches and held vertical by the top rails, set in ¼" rabbets in the stile tops. The cabinet back is glue-nailed to the rear edges of the sides and back top support rails. Nail adjustable shelf tracks to the partitions and sides, if shelves are to be put in the cabinet.

Doors. The doors are cut from ½" plywood and attached to the face of the facing frame with piano hinges (Fig. D). The two corner doors are hinged

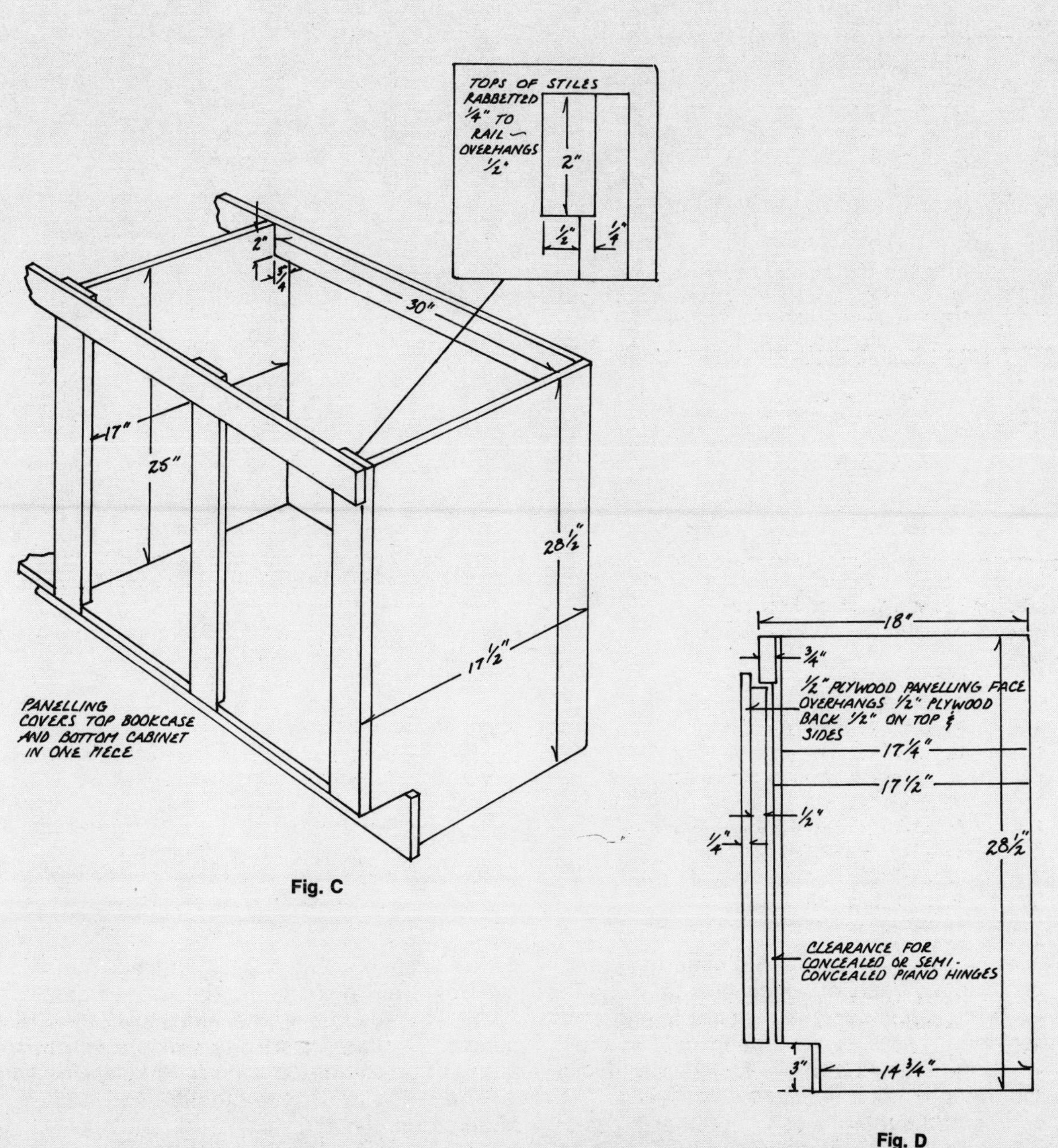

Fig. C

Fig. D

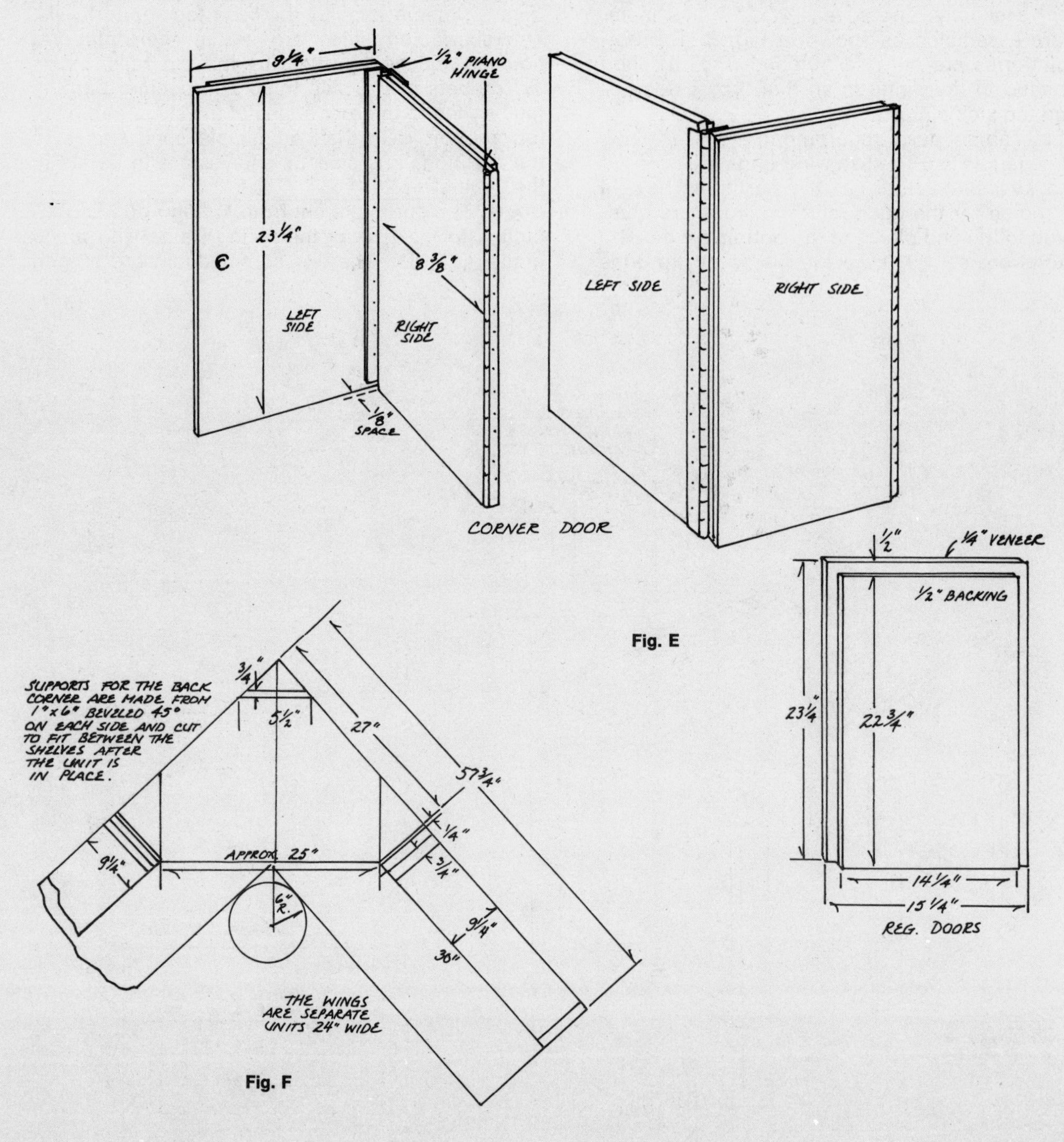

Fig. E

Fig. F

as shown in Fig. E. A ¼"-veneered panel is glue-nailed to all doors, each of which overhangs ½" on the top and sides. The ¼"-veneered facing on the corner doors has a ½" overhang only at the top. The bottom and sides of the facing are flush with the door edges.

The top is cut in three pieces from either pressboard or plywood, and is veneered (Fig. G). The center section is 27⅜"x27⅜" with a 6' radius curve cut from the front corner. The two wings are 19"x 30⅝", and overhang the sides by ½". The top pieces are glue-screwed to the top support rails, and butt on top of the wing partitions. The veneer is then glued in place on the top and edges.

Shelf assembly. The six 54"x9¼" sides are dadoed for the shelves as desired. If the bottom shelf in the center section is placed 18" above the cabinet top, the average television set will fit under it. Cut the four corner-shelves, and assemble the corner unit as shown in Fig. H. The backs of the shelves are glue-nailed to a ¾"x5½"x52" back support board, which has been beveled 45° on both its rear edges. The ¼" shelf backing is glue-nailed to the shelves, sides and back-shelf support. The wing shelves are dadoed and assembled with their backs; the ¼"x1¼" strips are glue-nailed to the front edges of all shelves and tops. The completed unit is then veneered. The shelves can be attached to each other, once they are standing on the cabinet top, by pinning the partitions together with no more than two or three screws.

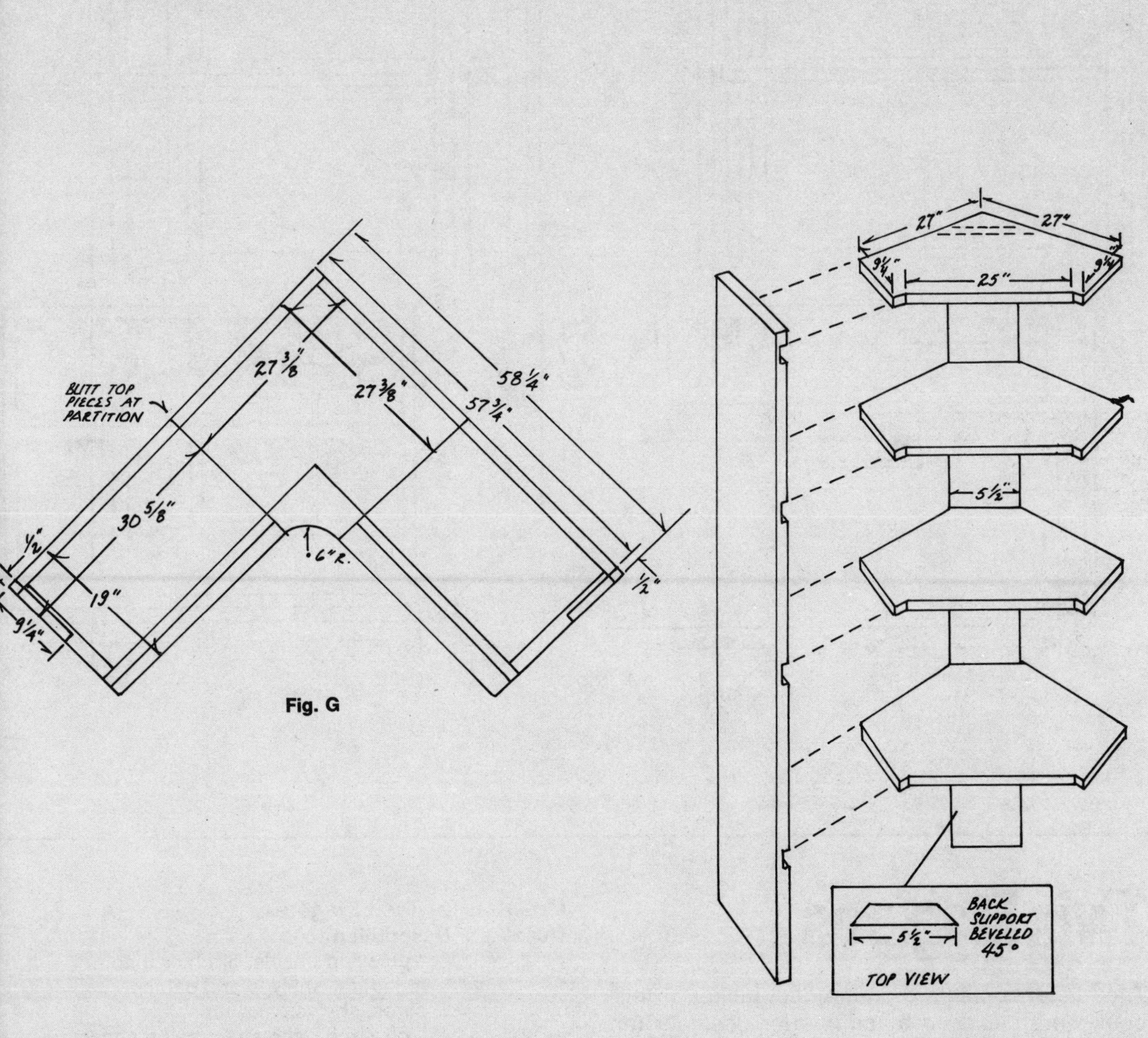

Fig. G

Fig. H

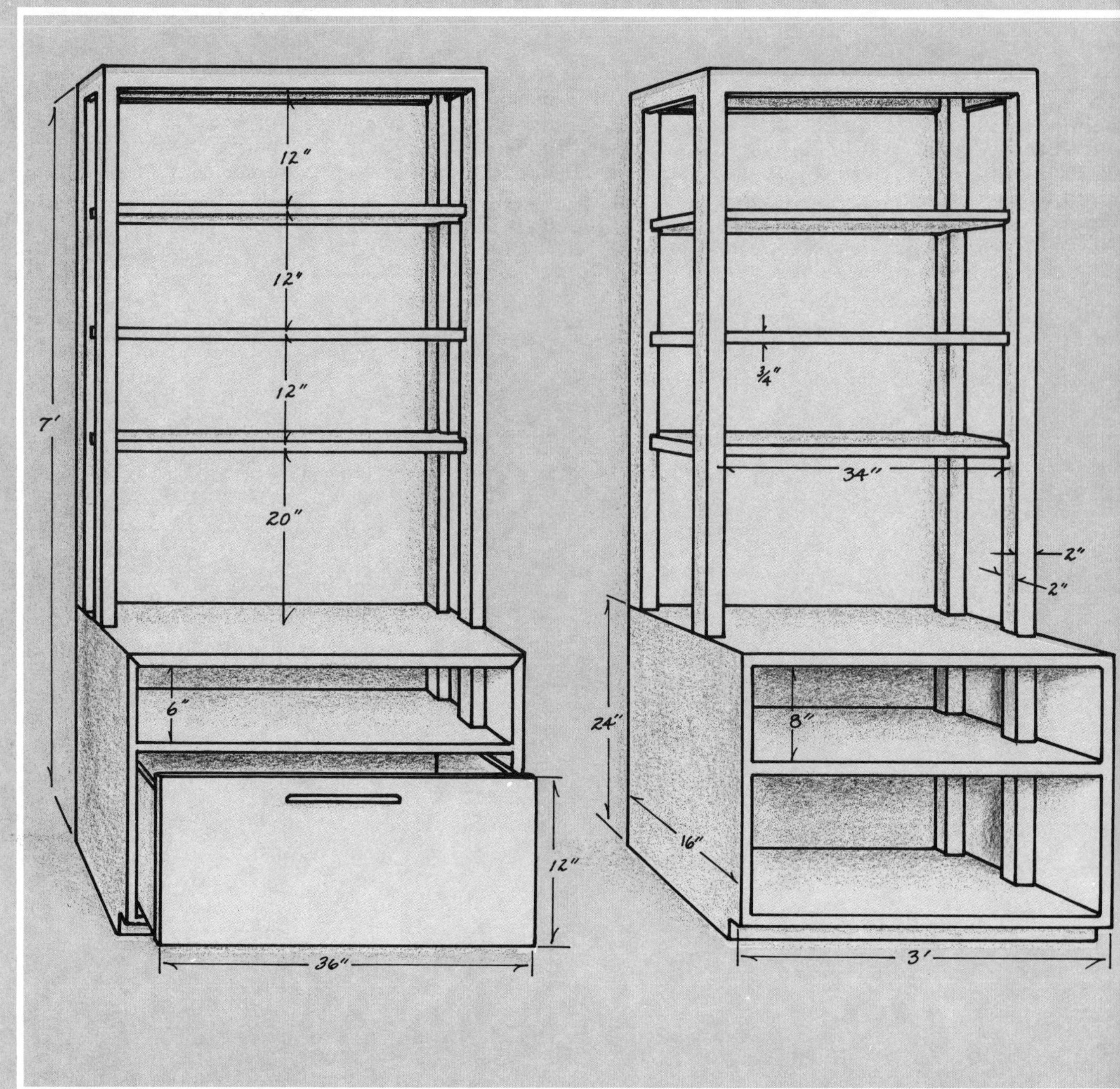

Twin Etagères

The étagères pictured on the dust jacket of this book were designed by an interior designer for the specific purpose of housing a television set and hi-fi unit, as well as files and books. The two units are identical, except that one has a file drawer and the other does not. Both are constructed from birch or maple-faced plywood.

Materials for Twin Etagères

Quantity	Description
2	¾" plywood panels, birch or maple faced, for shelves and cabinet sides, shelves and tops
2	½" plywood panels for shelf standards and cabinet bottoms
½	¼" A-B grade plywood panel for cabinet backs
1 set	14" drawer tracks

1/2" PLYWOOD FOR SHELF STANDARDS — 16 1" STRIPS 16 2" STRIPS

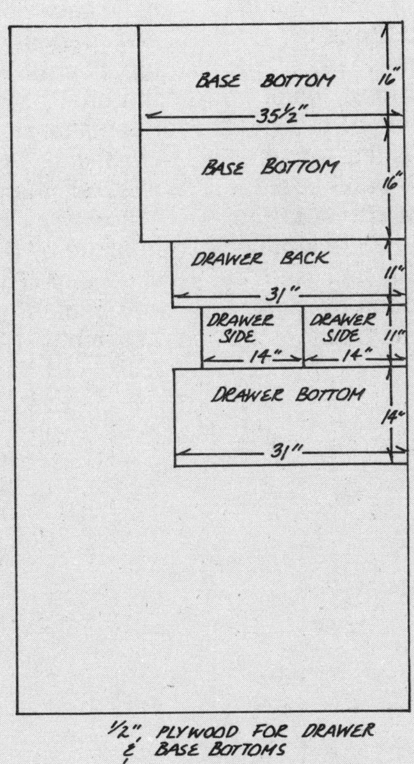

1/2" PLYWOOD FOR DRAWER & BASE BOTTOMS

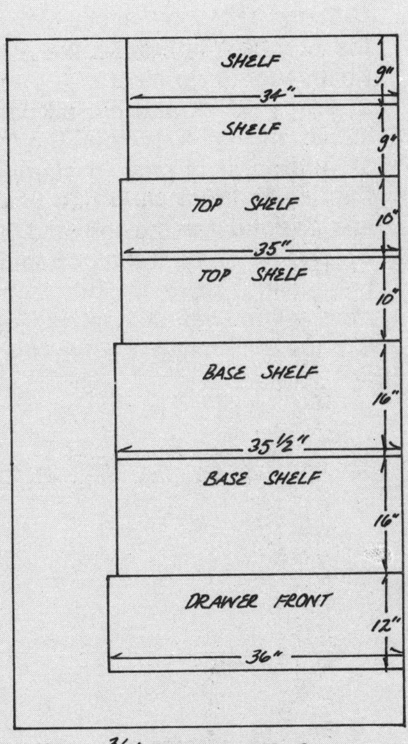

3/4" PLYWOOD FOR SHELVES & DRAWER FRONT

Fig. A

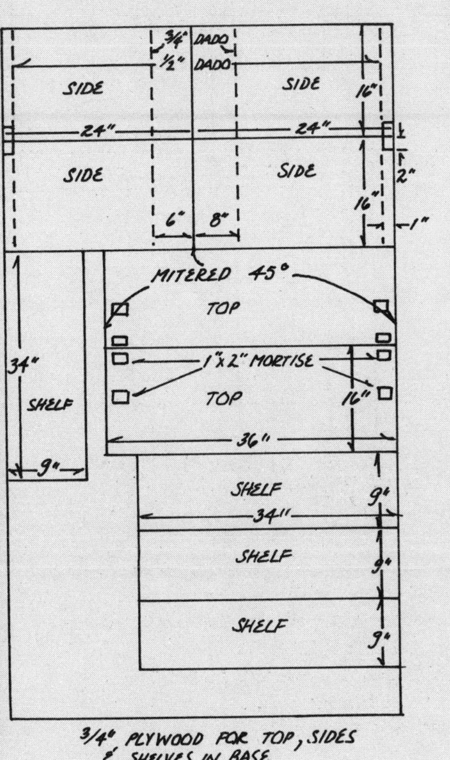

3/4" PLYWOOD FOR TOP, SIDES & SHELVES IN BASE

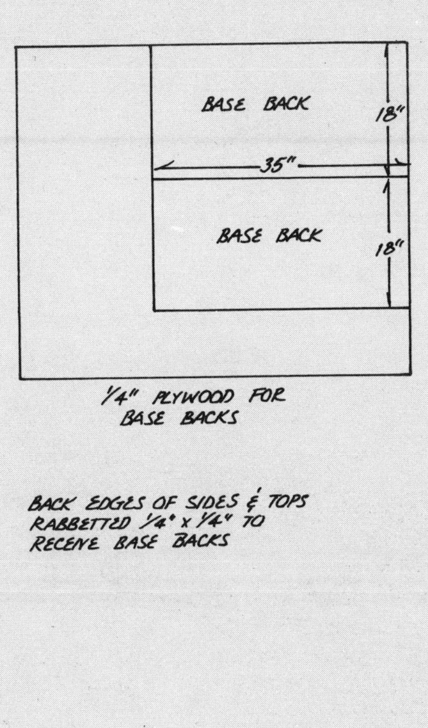

1/4" PLYWOOD FOR BASE BACKS

BACK EDGES OF SIDES & TOPS RABBETTED 1/4" x 1/4" TO RECEIVE BASE BACKS

TOP VIEW OF SHELVES & CABINET

Cutting. The most laborious part of constructing the étagères is cutting the plywood, because it is necessary to rip most of the ½" panels into 1" and 2" strips. Mark and cut all parts for both units as shown in Fig. A. In notching the sides of the shelf standards, it is best to clamp the sides together, then dado them all at one time. The cabinet sides are dadoed for the top and bottom shelves (Fig. B), and notched at the bottom for the 2" kick plate; the cabinet top and shelves must be mortised to receive the shelf standards. This is done by clamping the cabinet parts together, then placing the fully assembled shelf units against the top shelf and marking the square holes. Cut the holes in the top, push the shelves through them until they touch the shelf, then mark the shelf and mortise them. Push the standards through the cabinet top and shelf until they butt the bottom shelf and can be marked, then mortise the bottom. The shelf units will always be removable, and will be held tightly in place by only the four sets of holes the shelves slide into. The shelf units are flush with the sides and back of the base (Fig. D).

Assembly. The ½"x1" sides of each standard are

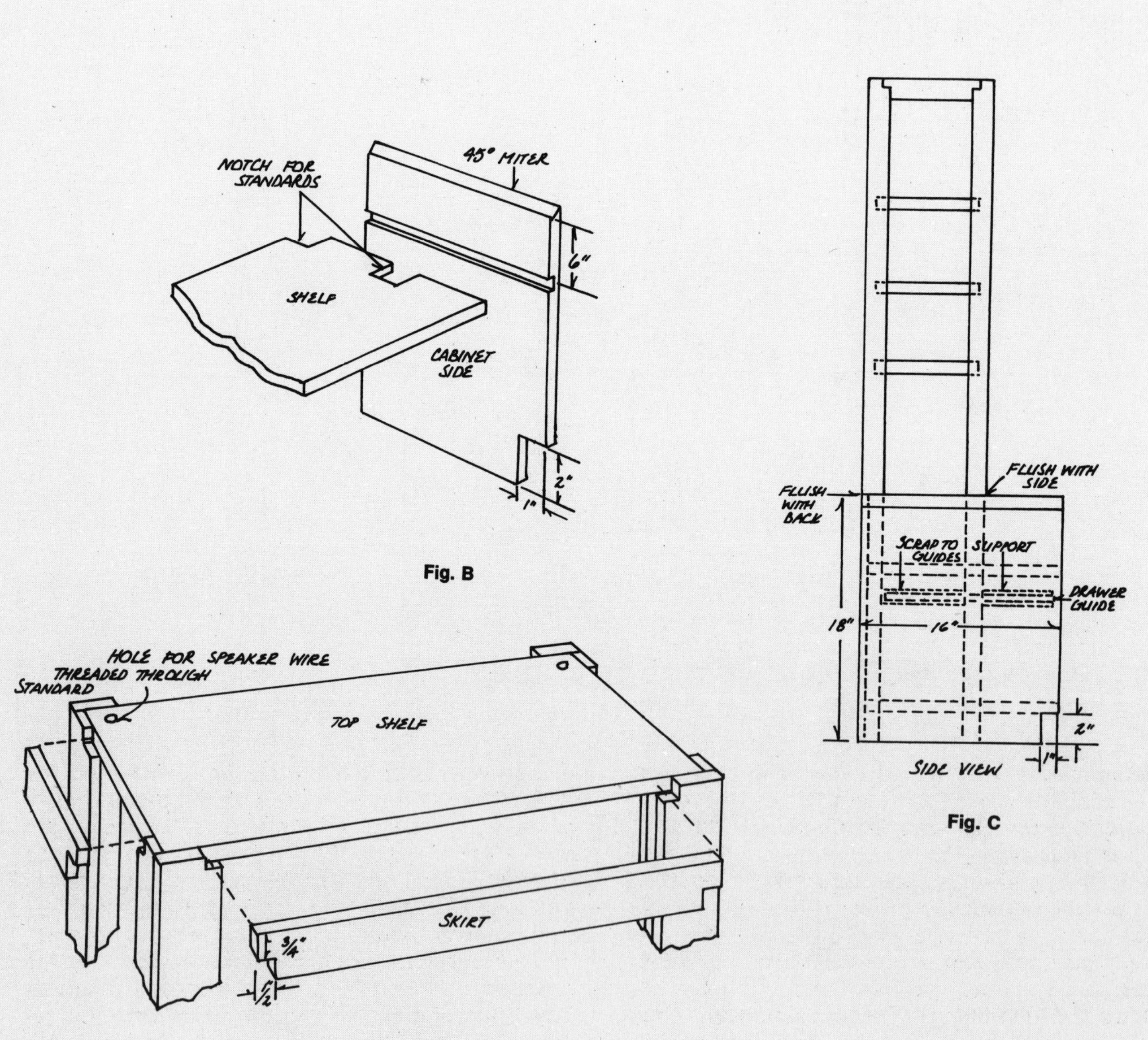

Fig. B

Fig. C

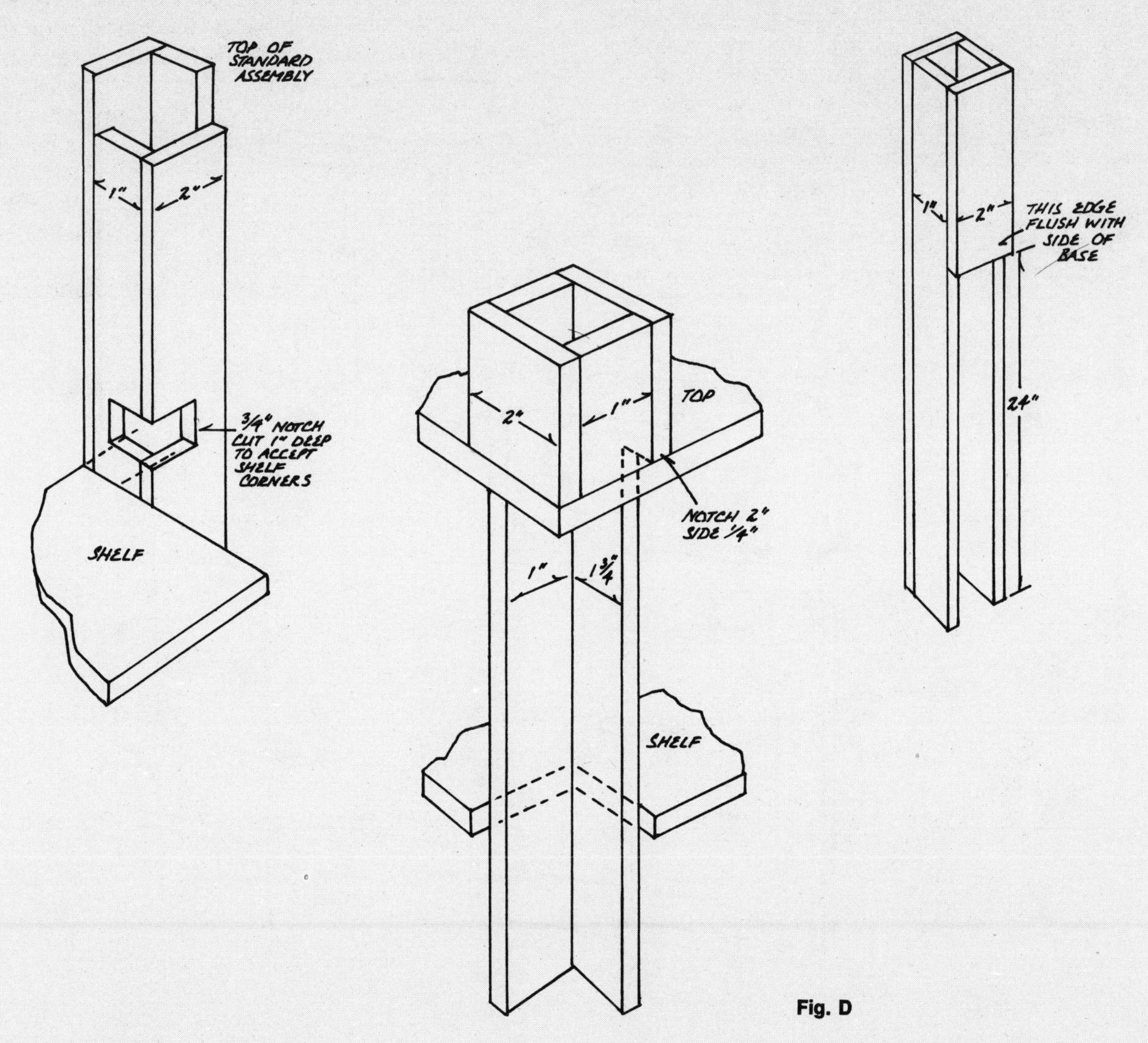

Fig. D

butted between the two 2″ sides, and are glue-nailed together. See Figs. C and D for side lengths and positioning. Be sure that each of the shelf notches lines up so that the shelves can fit tightly into them. The shelves are inserted into their slots and are glue-nailed in place, using 1½″ screw panel board nails that are countersunk. The skirt around the top shelf is glue-nailed as shown in Fig. B.

Once the mortising is completed, the base shelves are glue-screwed in their side dadoes, and the mitered top is glue-screwed through both the sides and the top. The 2″ kick plate is attached to the underside of the bottom shelf between the sides. The file drawer must slide on metal drawer guides, but the guides have to reside inside the shelf standards (Fig. C). The guides are attached to scrap pieces built up 1½″ around the standard holes, so that the standards fit between the side of the cabinet and the back of the slide. The ¼″ cabinet backs are placed in the rabbets along the sides and the top, and are glue-nailed in place. The back of the unit (which holds the hi-fi receiver) is bored to give the receiver proper ventilation. All plywood edges must be either filled or taped.

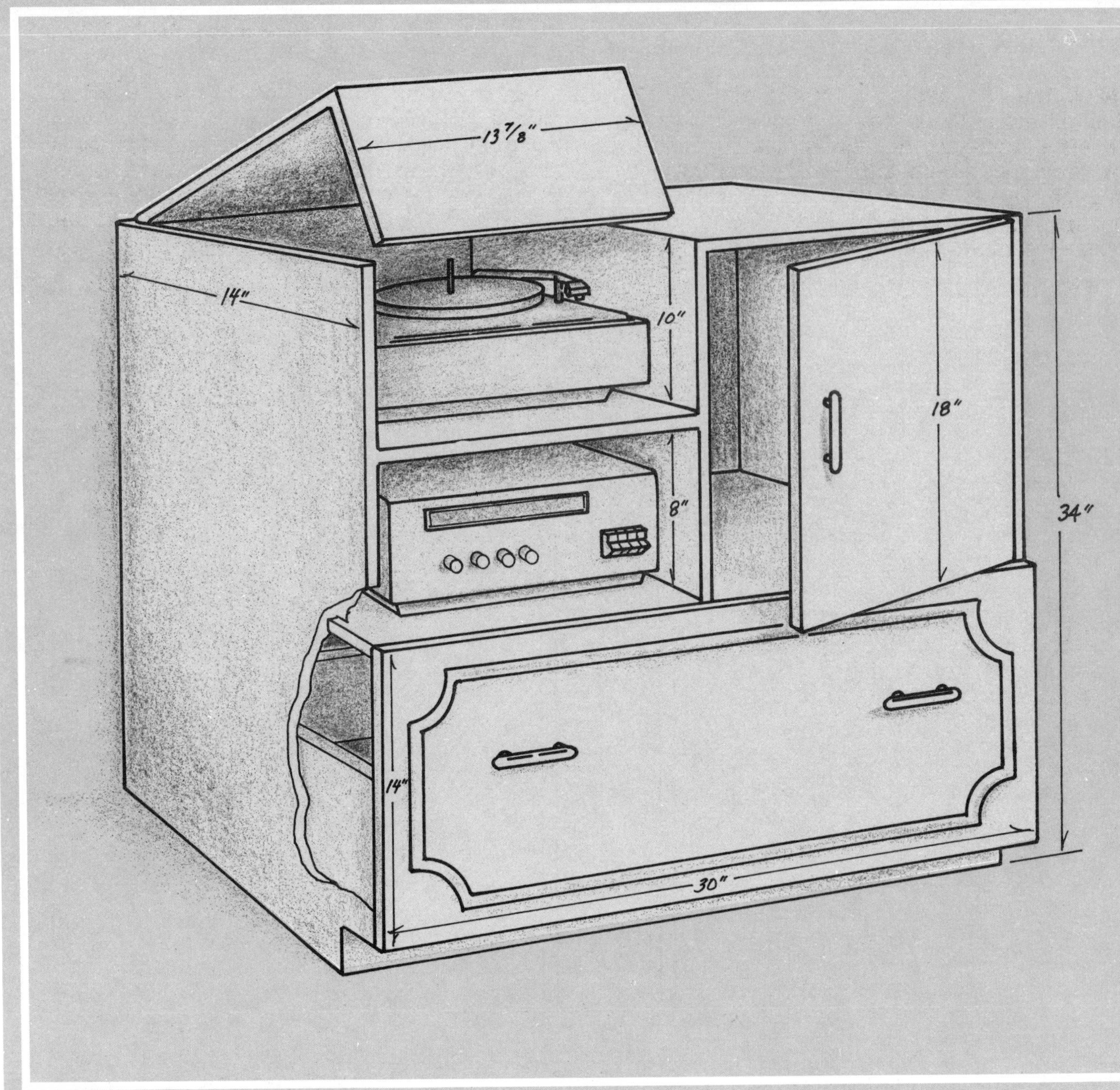

Hi-Fi Center

The hi-fi unit could be made from ¾" plywood and then veneered. A hardwood ply or a good cabinet wood might also be used. The unit can also be trimmed in any manner compatible with other furniture in the room. The basic cabinet is 34" high by 14" deep by 30" long, but it has numerous options, including the addition of a record cabinet.

Materials for Hi-Fi Center

Quantity	Description
2	¾" plywood panels, preferably with hardwood veneer
1 pr.	14" heavy-duty drawer guides
2	1' ¾" piano hinges

utting. The two sides are 14"x34" with a 2"x2" otch cut out of the bottom front corners for the ick plate. Both are dadoed ¾"x⅜" on center 3⅝" from the bottom, and also 2" from the bottom edge (Fig. A). The right side is rabbeted on its op edge; the left side has a third dado 10" down om the top edge.

The partition is 18" x 14". Its left side is dadoed 10" down from the top edge. The right side of the top edge is rabbeted. The right-side top is 13⅞"x14" and is rabbeted on both 13⅞" edges. The left-side top is 12½"x13⅞" and its front edge is rabbeted. The lid front is 10"x13⅞" and is also rabbeted on its top edge. Two of the shelves are

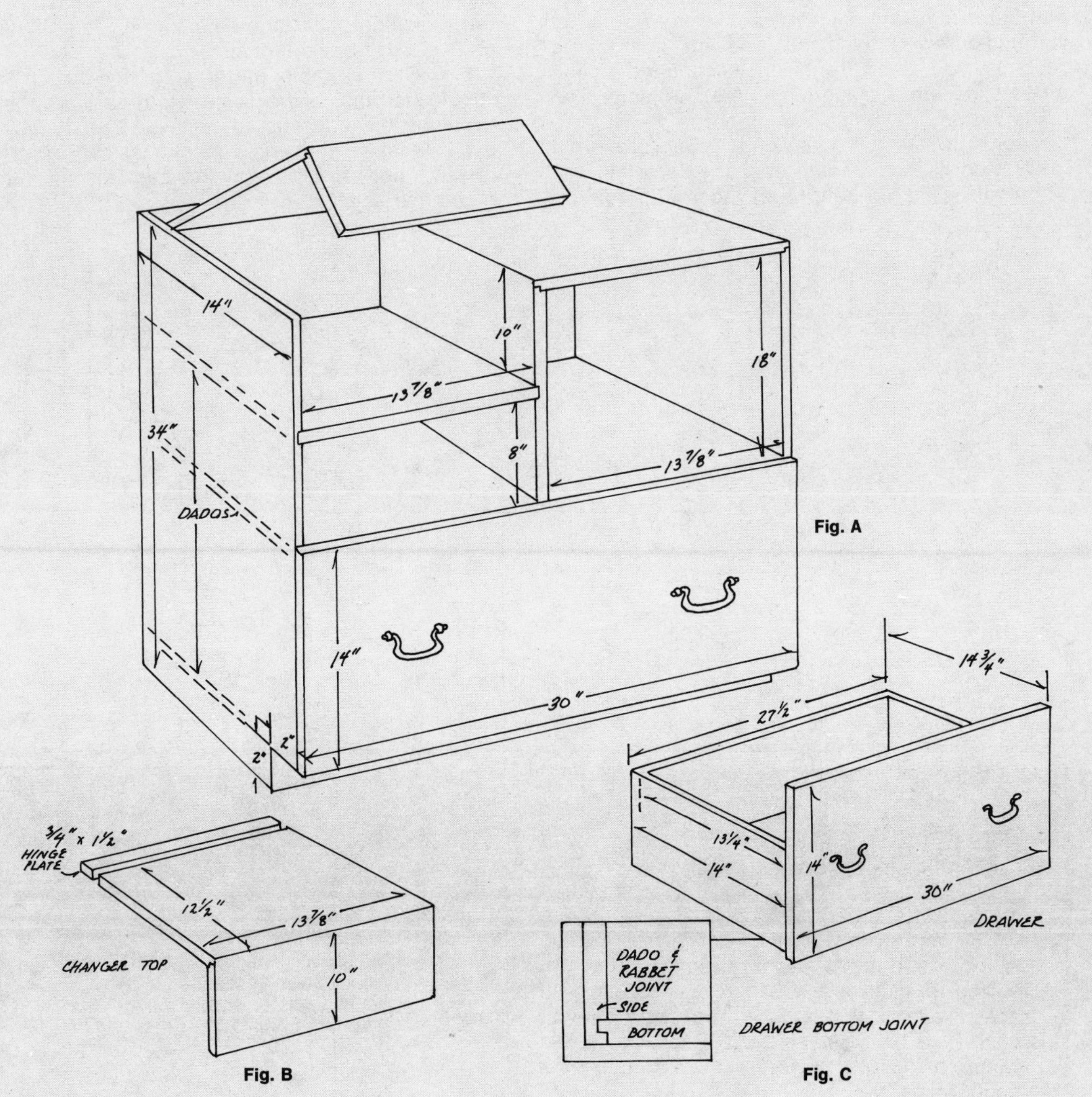

Fig. A

Fig. B

Fig. C

14"x29¼"; the third measures 14"x13⅞". The record cabinet door, if it is used, is 18"x13⅞". The back is ¼"x34"x30".

Assembly. The bottom and center shelves are glued in the side dadoes; the 2"x28½" kick plate is glue-screwed to the underside of the bottom shelf. The third shelf is glue-screwed in the left side and partition dadoes. The partition is butt-joined to the top of the second shelf. The ¾"x 1½"x13⅞" lid hinge plate is positioned at the back, between the partition and the left side, as shown in Figs. A and B. The back is attached to the partition, sides and shelves, and the right-side top is glue-screwed in place. The left-side top is rabbeted to the lid front and is attached to the hinge plate with a piano hinge. A piano hinge also holds the record compartment door in place.

Drawer. The drawer is designed to hold a great many records, so it should be made completely of ¾" wood. The ¾" bottom is dado- and rabbet-joined to the sides, as shown in Fig. C. The drawer is installed with heavy-duty drawer guides. The drawer front stops against the front edges of the shelves and sides.

Variations. Fig. D redesigns the basic cabinet to allow the unit to act as an end table. The open-side shelves can be on one or both sides, and are positioned so that they are level with the arm of the chair or sofa with which the cabinet will be juxtaposed. The top of the unit can be solid, provided the hi-fi changer-drawer is installed with drawer guides. The doors closing off the changer and receiver are optional.

Fig. E is variable in terms of its design but should be built to the same width as the cabinet it stands on, and should be high enough above the cabinet so that the changer lid can be completely opened. Doors on the cabinet can either be hinged or sliding.

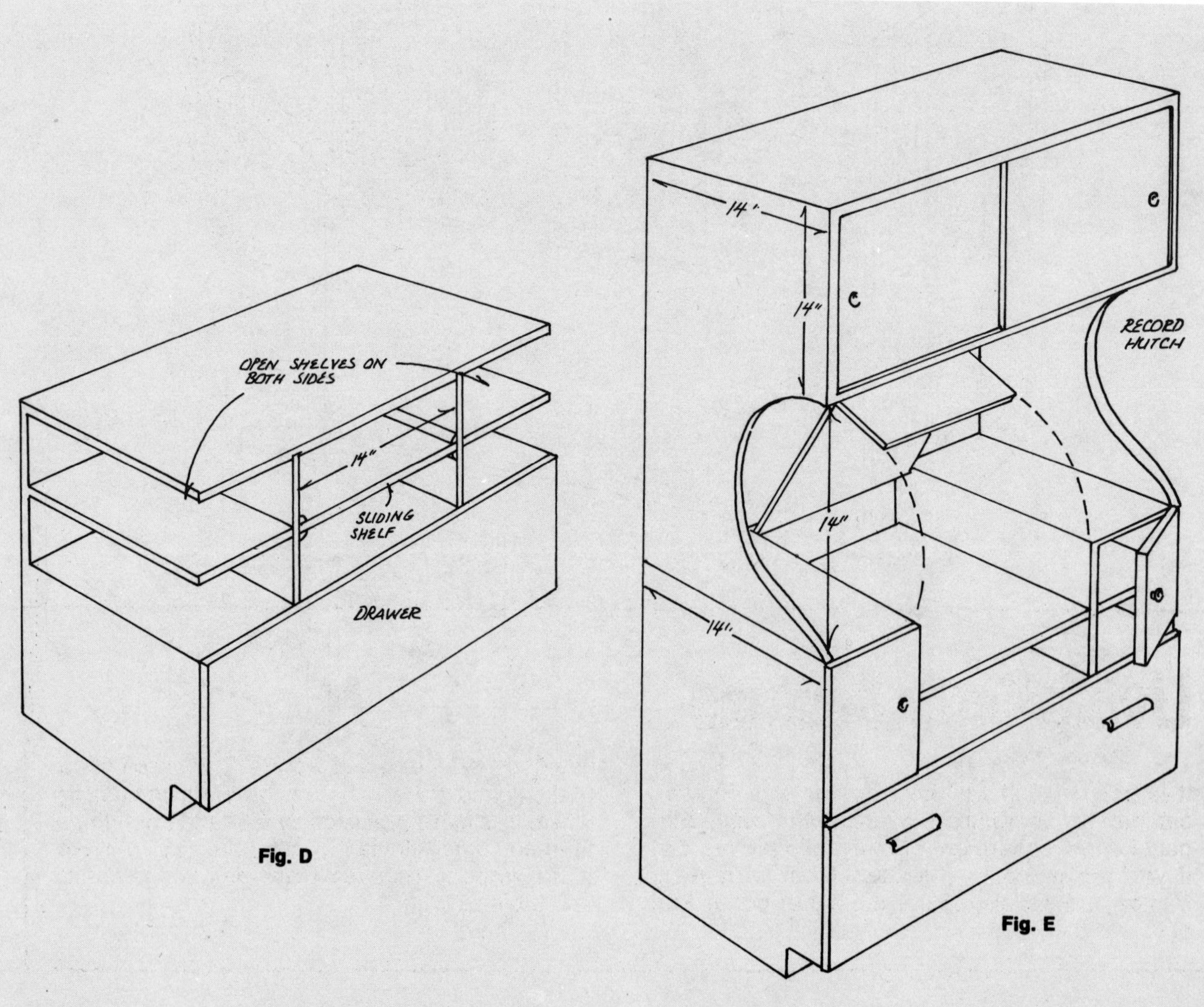

Fig. D

Fig. E

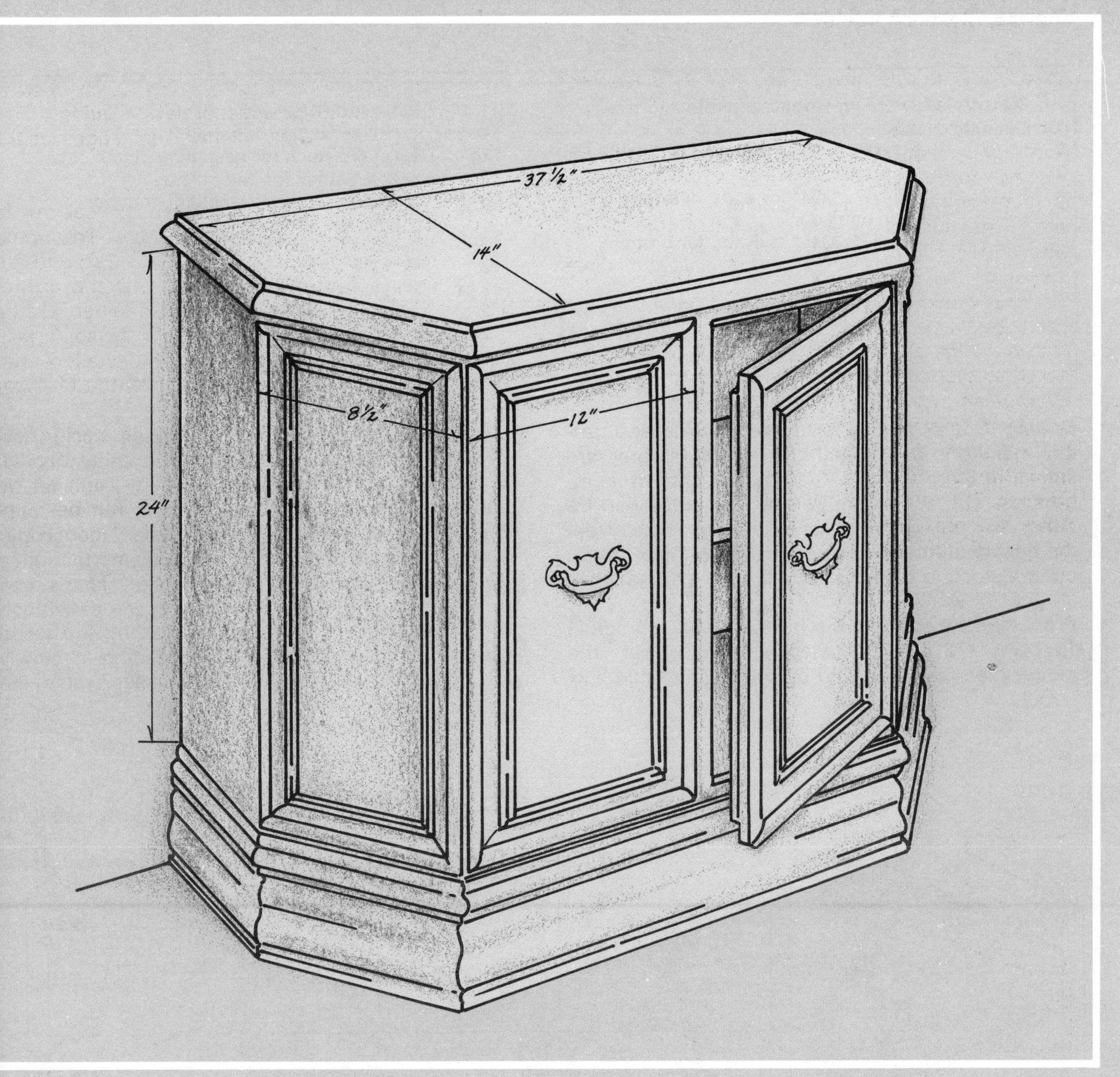

Living Room Console

It is not unusual for the sides of a decorative cabinet to be entirely made with frame-and-panel construction, rather than solid pieces. But if you are going to the extra labor of making frames and panels, spend the extra money and use good cabinet-grade woods. The assembling of the console shown here is hardly a challenge; it requires more precision to make the moldings than any other element of the unit, and to make them properly requires a molder head, router and table saw.

Materials for Living Room Console

Quantity	Description
2	½"x11⅞"x33¾" plywood for inside top and bottom plates
2	1⅛"x7¼"x24" for ends, mitered 45° on one edge
1	¾"x13"x33¾" plywood for bottom
1	¾"x14"x37½" for top, molded on three edges
72"	1⅛"x3¼" stock to be molded for base plate
1	¼"x24"x35" plywood for back
1	¾"x11¼"x33½" for shelf
72"	¾"x1¼" stock for base mounting blocks
2'	¾"x¾" stock for shelf cleats
23'	1⅛"x1⅝" stock for molding into door and side frames
2	¼"x9¾"x21¾" for door panels
2	¼"x5¼"x21¾" for fixed side panels
2 pr.	2"x1½" mortise hinges
2	magnetic catches
2	cabinet door pulls

Cutting. Cut all pieces for the top, inside and bottom members, back, shelf and bottom, as they are shown in Fig. A. The inside top and bottom members are cut from ½" plywood. The sides can be either ¾" plywood or stock. The top is cut from the best cabinet-grade wood available. Also rough-cut the stock to be molded for the base, fixed sides and door frames.

Procedure for molding the base. The base stock is 1⅛"x3¼"x72", the first step is "dishing out" the center (see Fig. B). Begin by setting the table saw blade ⅜" above the table. The blade will be too wide at its base to cut the 2⅛" dish shown in Fig. B. Therefore, a diagonal fence is set, so that by cutting the wood at an angle it will remove only 2⅛" of wood inside the dish. When the proper fence angle has been established, clamp the fence tightly to the saw table, keeping the clamps well out of the way (Fig. C). Next, lower the saw blade to $\frac{1}{16}$" and make the first pass, holding the wood firmly down on the table and feeding it slowly through the saw. After the first pass, raise the

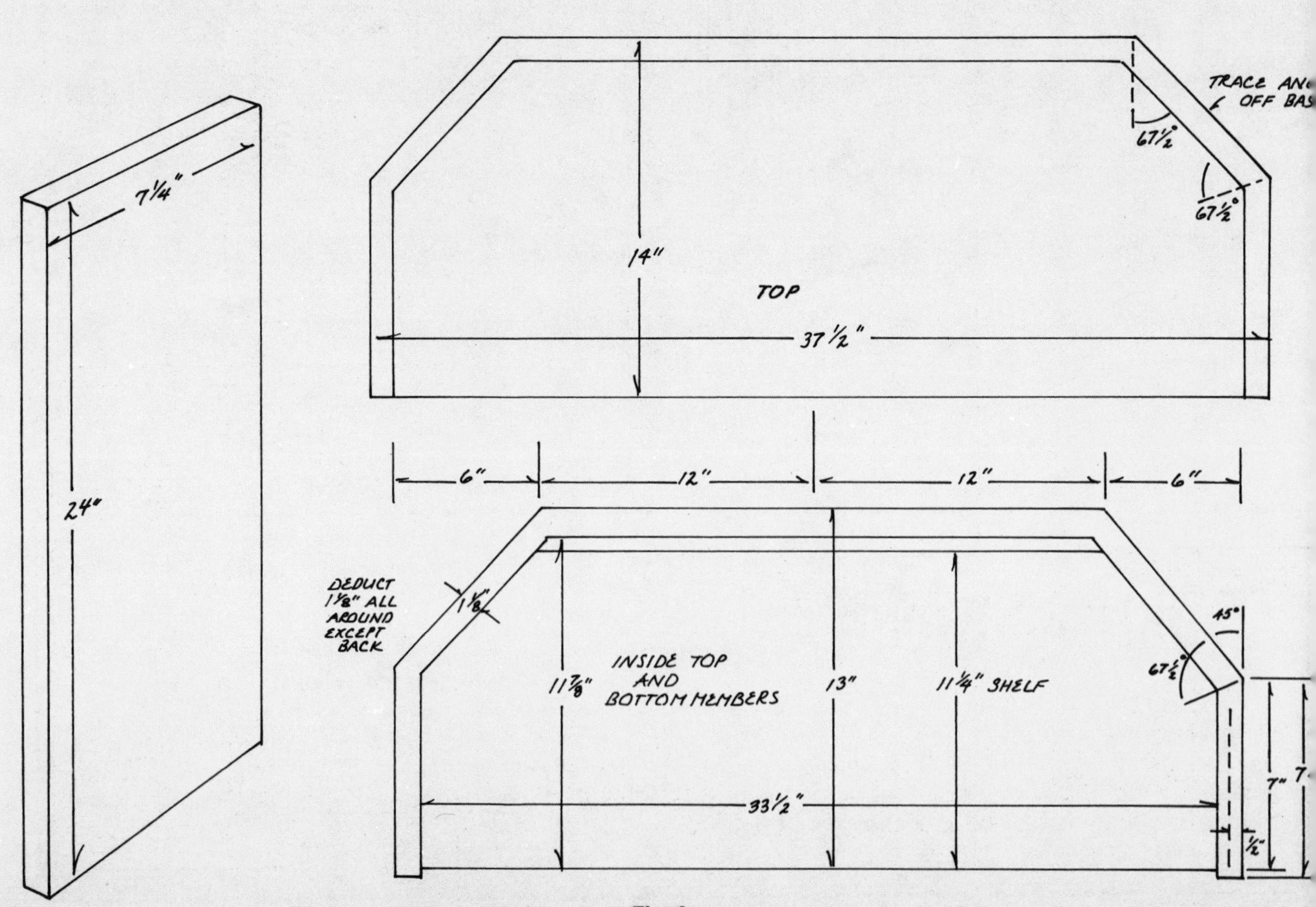

Fig. A

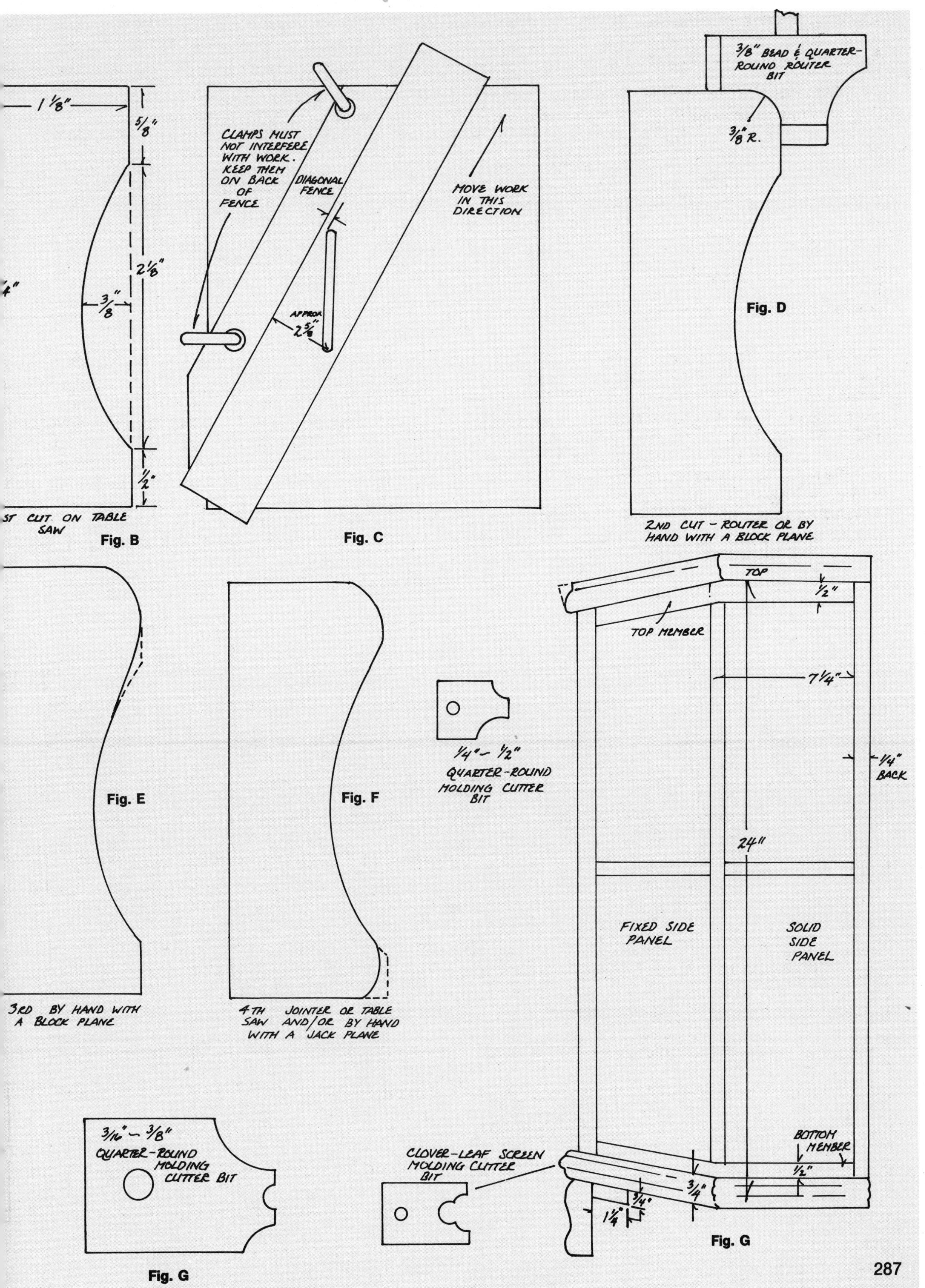
1 1/8"
5/8"
2 1/8"
3/8"
1/2"
ST CUT ON TABLE SAW
CLAMPS MUST NOT INTERFERE WITH WORK. KEEP THEM ON BACK OF FENCE
DIAGONAL FENCE
APPROX 2 5/8"
MOVE WORK IN THIS DIRECTION
3/8" BEAD & QUARTER-ROUND ROUTER BIT
3/8" R.
2ND CUT - ROUTER OR BY HAND WITH A BLOCK PLANE
3RD BY HAND WITH A BLOCK PLANE
4TH JOINTER OR TABLE SAW AND/OR BY HAND WITH A JACK PLANE
1/4" - 1/2" QUARTER-ROUND MOLDING CUTTER BIT
TOP
1/2"
TOP MEMBER
7 1/4"
1/4" BACK
24"
FIXED SIDE PANEL
SOLID SIDE PANEL
BOTTOM MEMBER
1/2"
3/4"
3/4"
1 1/4"
3/16" - 3/8" QUARTER-ROUND MOLDING CUTTER BIT
CLOVER-LEAF SCREEN MOLDING CUTTER BIT

Fig. B

Fig. C

Fig. D

Fig. E

Fig. F

Fig. G

Fig. G

Fig. G

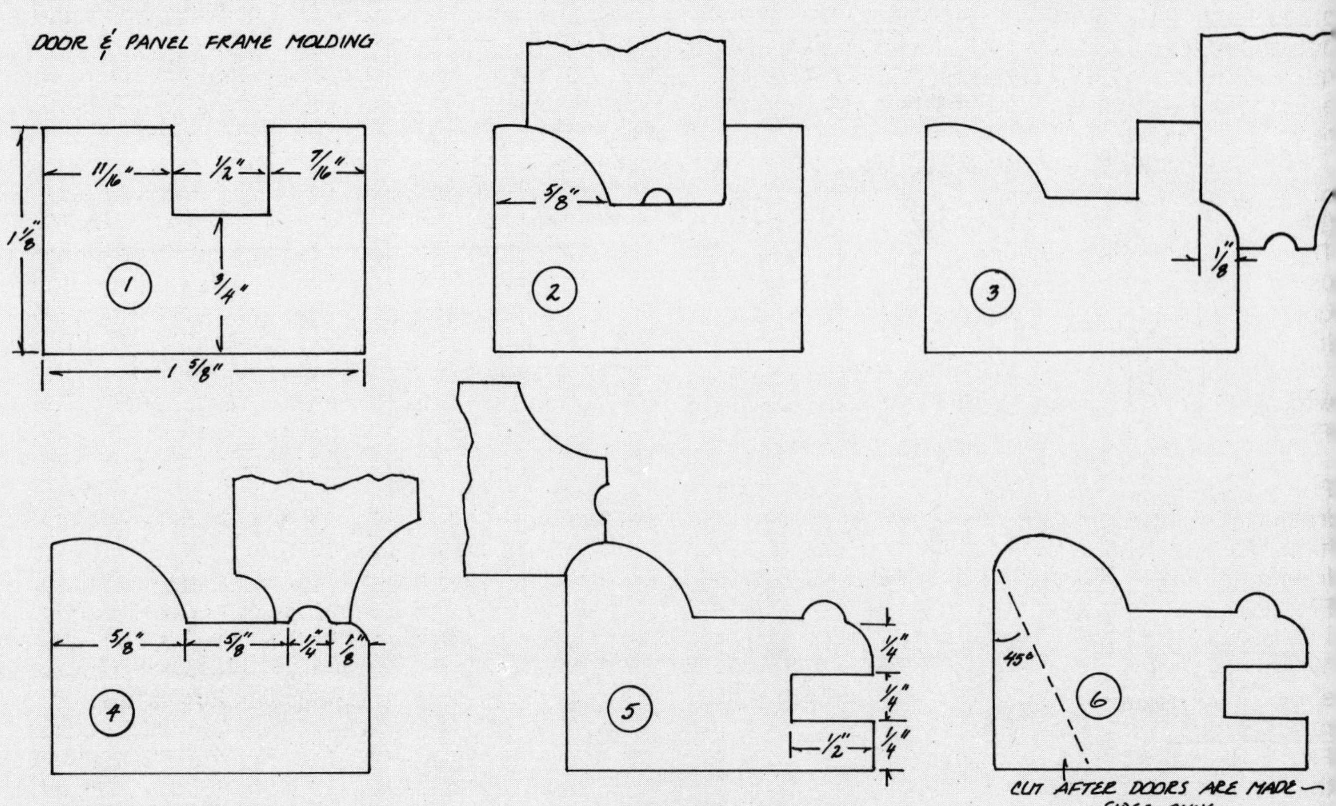

DOOR & PANEL FRAME MOLDING

11/16"
1/2"
7/16"
1 1/8"
3/4"
1 5/8"
1

5/8"
2

1/8"
3

5/8"
5/8"
1/4"
1/8"
4

1/4"
1/4"
1/4"
1/2"
5

45°
6
CUT AFTER DOORS ARE MADE—
SIDES ONLY

Fig. H

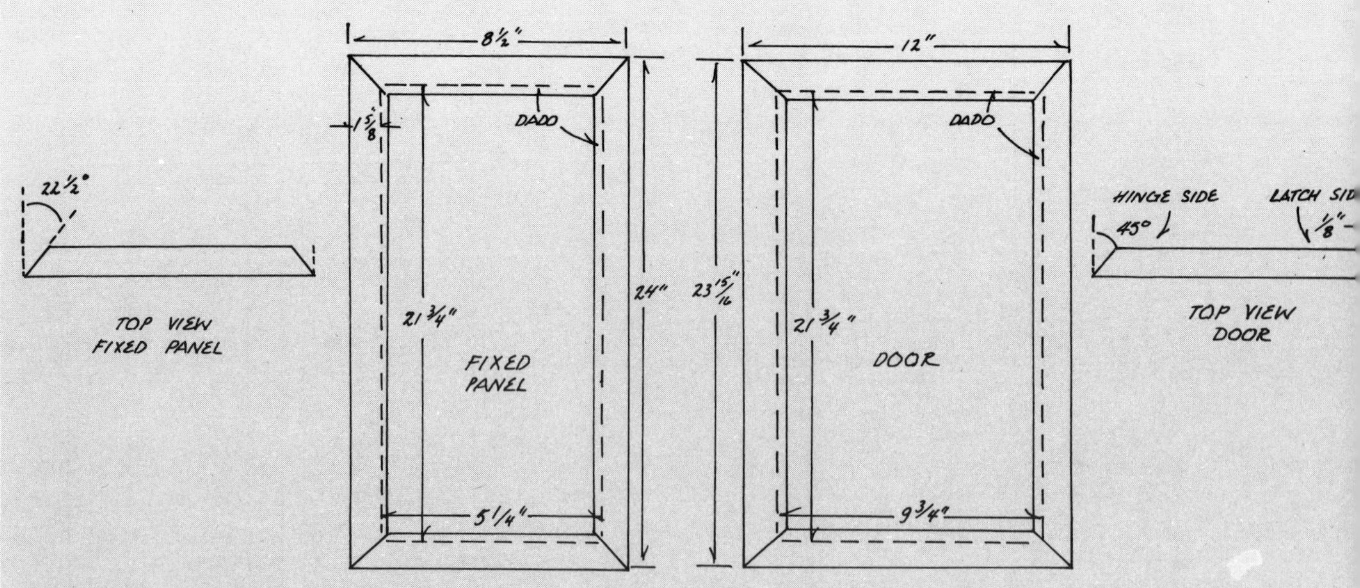

Fig. I

blade about 1/8" and check to be sure the channel is coming out in the right location. Continue raising the blade no more than 1/8" at a time for each pass until the channel has reached the correct depth (3/8") and width (2 1/8").

The second step is to round off the top corner of the piece to a 3/8" radius, using either a router (Fig. D), or working by hand with a block plane. Then round off the other side of the curve (Fig. E) using a block plane. Finally, the bottom corner is beveled either with a jack plane, table saw or jointer (Fig. F).

The base crown molding is 3/4"x1/2" stock shaped with a cloverleaf screen molding cutter bit (see Fig. G).

Procedure for molding the fixed side and door frames. The two fixed sides are 8 1/2" wide by 24" high. The doors measure 12"x23 15/16" (Fig. I). The frames for all four units are molded as shown in Fig. H.

The 1 1/8"x1 5/8" stock is ploughed 1/2" wide by 3/8" deep. The plough is in the exact position shown in Fig. H #1. Using a 3/16" to 3/8" quarter-round molding cutter bit, mold the frames as shown in Fig. H #2-#5. When the molding is complete, rout the inside edge of the frames 1/2"x1/4" to accept the panels (Fig. H #5).

The fixed side frames are assembled around their panels with mitered corners joined with either tongue and groove or dowels. The door frames and panels are joined in the same manner (Fig. I). The hinged side of each door is beveled 45°; the latch side is planed so that the front side is 1/8" narrower than the back (Fig. I).

Assembly. The front edges of both 1 1/8"x7 1/2"x24" end pieces are beveled 45° before they are glue-screwed to the back edges of the 1/2"x11 7/8"x33 3/4" top members. The 1/2"x11 7/8"x33 3/4" bottom member is glued to the 3/4"x13"x33 3/4" bottom (with the back edges flush); these are glue-screwed flush with the bottom of the end pieces (Fig. G). The back is glue-screwed to the rear edges of the sides, top and bottom members and bottom. The 3/4"x3/4" shelf cleats are attached to the sides, and the shelf is put in place. The two 1 1/8"x8 1/2"x24" fixed panels are beveled 45° along both inside edges (Fig. H #6 and Fig. A), and are glue-screwed to the top member and bottom.

The 3/4"x1 1/4" mounting blocks are glue-screwed under the front and side edges of the bottom (Fig. G). The base plate is mitered at the front corners, then glue-screwed to the base mounting blocks. The cloverleaf screen crown molding is also mitered and glue-nailed around the top of the base. The front and side edges of the top are molded with a 1/4" to 1/2" quarter-round molding cutter bit, and the top is glue-screwed to the top member. The doors are hung with 2"x1 1/2" mortised hinges and have magnetic catches.

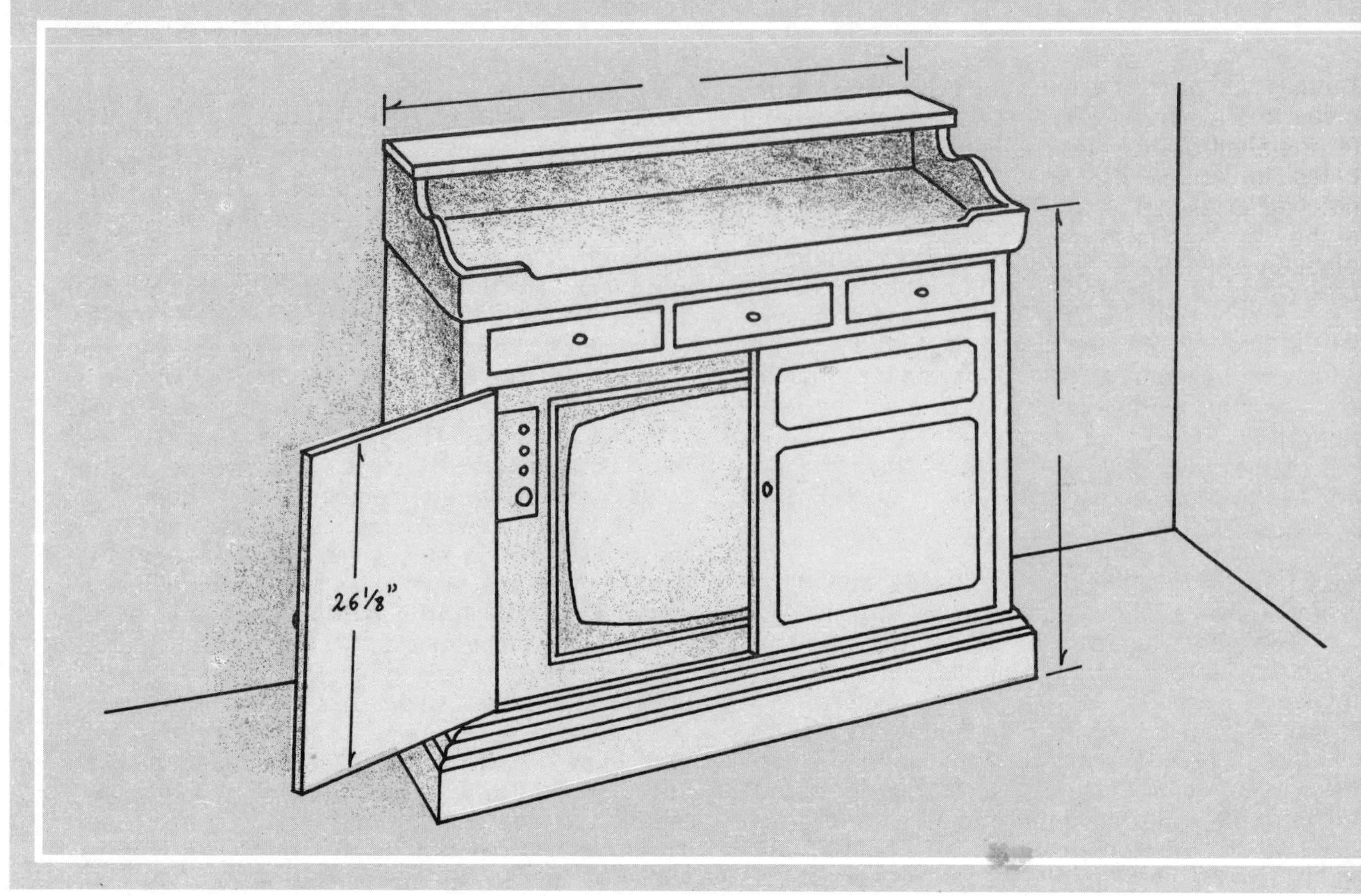

TV Cabinet

You can go out and buy a television set in any number of cabinet designs. But there is a high price tag attached to all of them. Or you can make a cabinet that continues the decor of your house, which is not to say that the design shown here will suit everyone's taste. But the notion of constructing a cabinet that can serve several purposes in addition to housing the family TV set is an idea worth considering. In this case, the cabinet also serves as a buffet and storage unit. It can be made of pine or any fine cabinet wood—even plywood if it is veneered on the top and sides.

Materials for TV Cabinet

Quantity	Description
Cabinet	
1	¾"x24"x42" for top
2	¾"x23⅝"x31⅛" for sides
2	¾"x2"x31⅛" for front rail
1	¾"x2"x38" for top rail
1	1⅛"x2"x40½" for drawer rail
1	¾"x3"x38" for bottom rail
2	1⅛"x1½"x5" for short stiles between drawers
1	⅛"x31½"x41¼" for back
1	½"x23⅝"x41¼" for bottom
1	¼"x22½"x41¼" for bottom of drawer section
3	¾"x2"x40½" for top, drawer shelf and bottom support members
Base	
1	1⅛"x4¼"x44¼" for front (molded)
2	1⅛"x4¼"x25⅛" for sides (molded)
Dry Sink Top	
1	¾"x6"x42" for back
2	1⅛"x6⅞"x25¼" for sides
1	1⅛"x7¼"x44½" for top
1	1⅛"x5"x43" for front
Drawers	
3	½"x2 15/16"x11¼" for backs
6	½"x2¾"x20" for sides
3	¾"x2 15/16"x11⅞" for flush drawer fronts
3	¼"x20½"x11¼" for bottoms
3	¾"x1"x21" for guides
Doors	
4	¾"x2½"x21¾" for frame sides
4	¾"x2½"x18¾" for frame tops and bottoms
2	½"x16¾"x19¾" for molded panels
2 pr.	3½" hinges
2	magnetic catches
3	drawer pulls
2	door pulls

Cutting. All parts are cut according to the sizes given in the materials list. The sides are dadoed for the shelf divider and cabinet bottom, then rabbeted to accept the back. The drawer rail is notched at each end as shown in Fig. B. The top of the 4½"-high base rail is molded with any combination of molder blades or router bits desired (Fig. C).

Assembly. Glue-screw the sides and back to each other, and insert the shelves and cabinet bottoms in their dadoes. Glue-screw the face frame, the drawer rail and the three drawer stiles in place. The three ¾"x1"x21" drawer guides are set 12" apart between the back and front face (Fig. A). Glue-screw the molded base around the front and sides of the bottom of the cabinet (Fig. C). Glue-

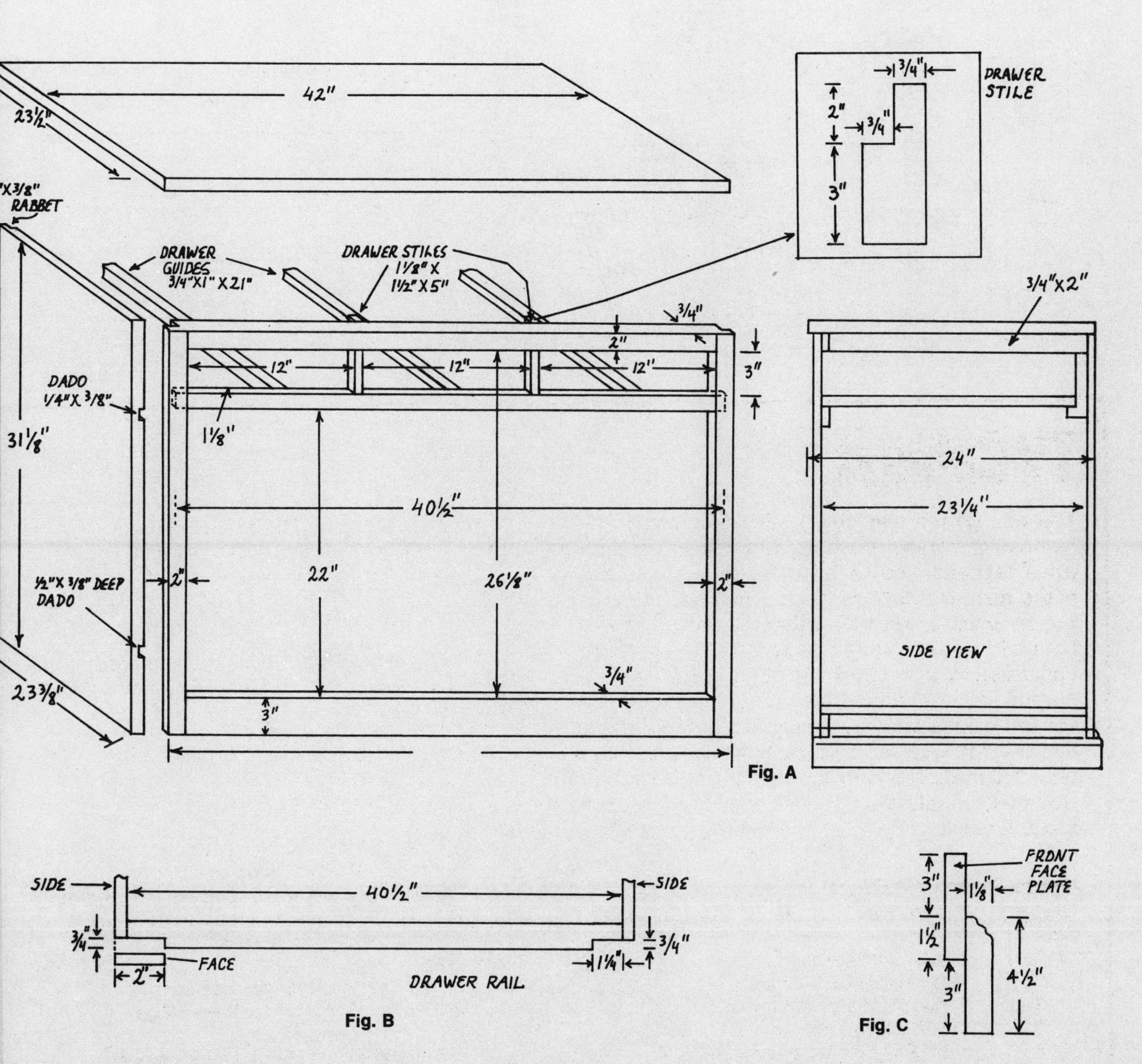

Fig. A

Fig. B

Fig. C

screw the top to the top edges of the sides. The screws will be hidden by the splashboard. Both the back and the bottom of the cabinet should have several holes drilled through them, so that the TV set will have proper ventilation. The drawers are each 11¾" wide by 20" long by 2¾" high. The curved sides of the cabinet splashboard can be any design desired. The board itself is assembled and attached as shown in Fig. D. The two cabinet doors are a standard frame and raised-panel construction, closing flush inside the 22"x38" opening in the front of the cabinet. (See Chapter 6 for construction suggestions.)

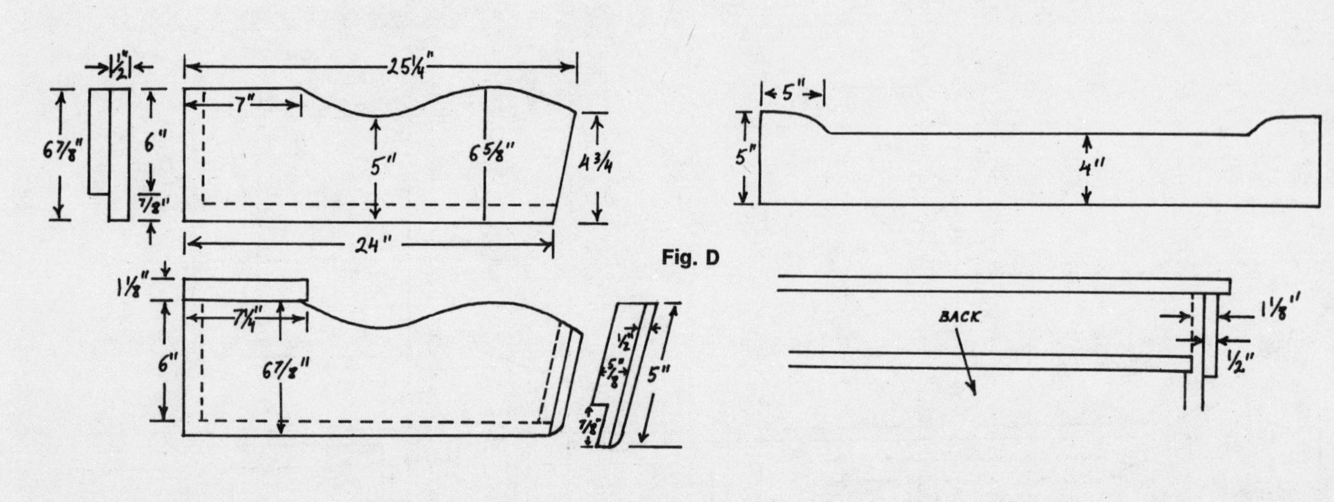

Fig. D

Sportsman's Cabinet

Sportsman's Cabinet

In order to construct this corner gun cabinet it is necessary to make a detailed plan of both the top and base, so that the exact angles and dimensions can be determined. The outside of the cabinet is made with cabinet-grade woods; the inside pieces are plywood.

Materials for Sportsman's Cabinet

Quantity	Description
Base Cabinet	
1	¾"x35"x35" plywood for base top
1	¼"x30"x30" Masonite for base top
1	¼"x3½"x80" plywood for base top edge
1	¼"x1"x80" solid stock for base top trim
1	¾"x33"x33" for base bottom
10′	¾"x¾" for base top cleats
2	¾"x2¼"x20" for face stiles
2	¾"x2"x21" for rails
1	¾"x3"x26" for base valance (front)
2	¾"x7"x23" for base side valance
2	¾"x10"x23" for base side valance
2	¼"x20"x29" for back
1	1⅛"x1⅛"x18½" stock for back corner post
15′	⅝"x¾" nose and cove for base trim
30′	¼"x⅝" stock for splines
Top Cabinet	
2	¾"x30"x30" for top and bottom
2	¾"x2"x62" for face stiles
1	¾"x2"x20" for bottom rail
1	¾"x3"x20" for top rail
2	¾"x8"x62" for sides
2	¾"x7"x62" for sides
2	¼"x25"x62" for backs
1	1⅛"x1⅛"x60½" back corner post
1	¾"x4½"x26" for front crown
2	¾"x2½"x9" for side crown
2	¾"x2½"x8" for side crown
Gun Rack	
2	¾"x24" diameter plywood for gun rack base
1	¾"x14" diameter plywood for gun barrels
1	1¼"x35" pipe for lower spool
1	1¼"x19" pipe for upper spool
3	1¼" pipe flanges
1 set	heavy-duty lazy Susan hardware
Doors	
8′	1⅛"x2¼" stock for door frames
2	½"x7"x12" stock for base cabinet door panels
1	¼"x17"x54" glass for top cabinet door

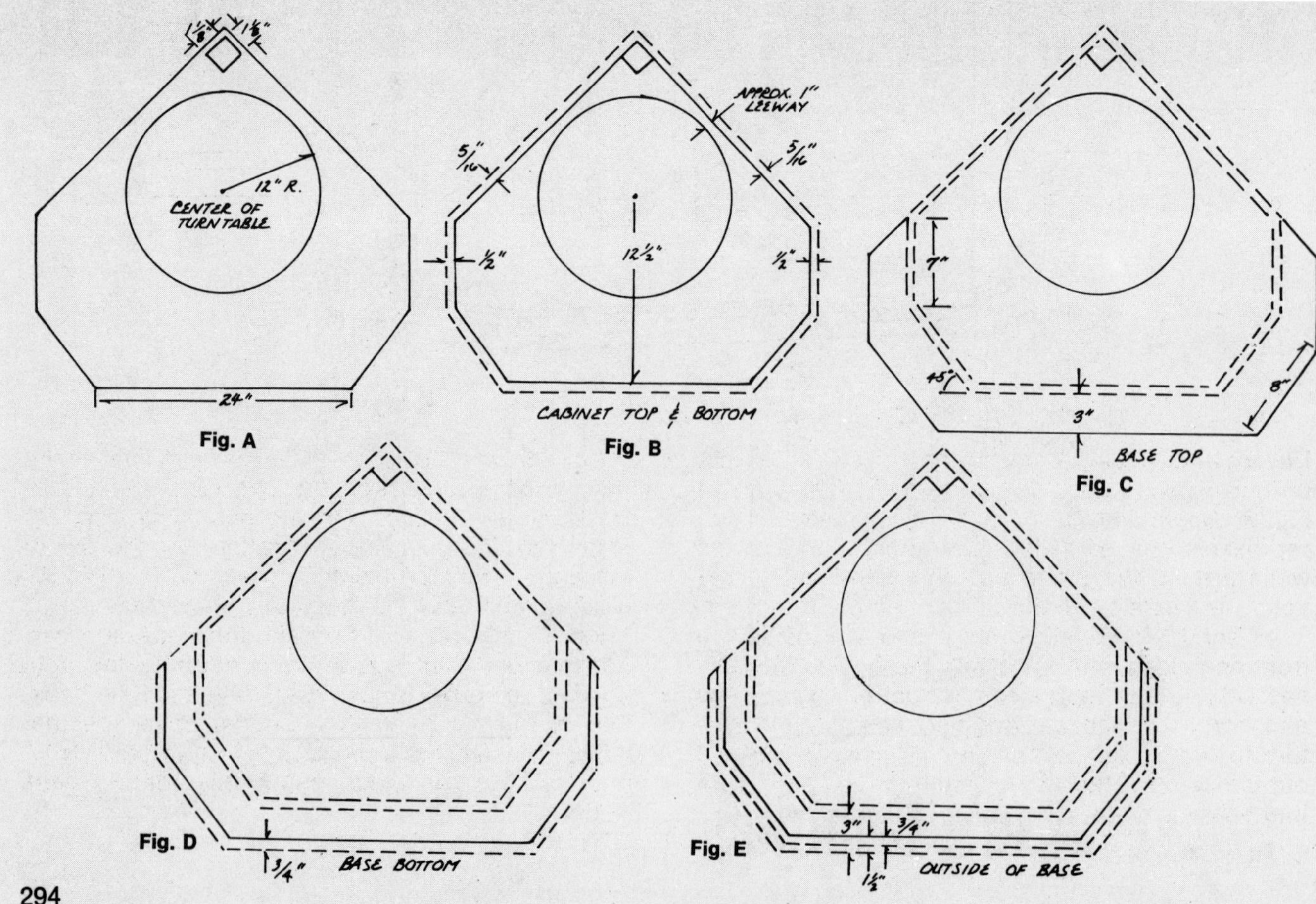

Fig. A

Fig. B

Fig. C

Fig. D

Fig. E

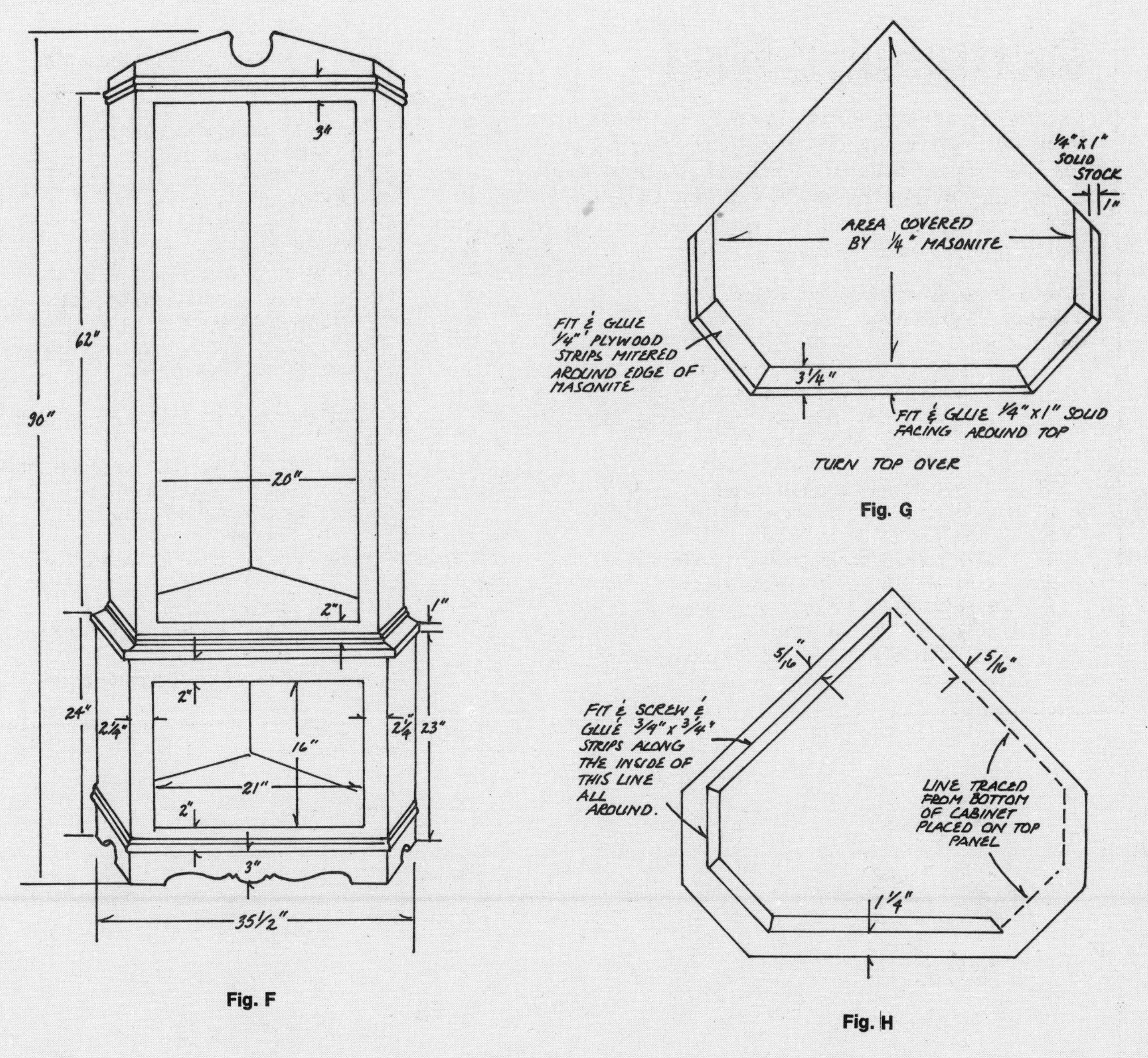

Fig. F

Fig. G

Fig. H

Layout and cutting. Lay out the full-scale cabinet on heavy kraft paper, following the dimensions in Fig. A. Begin with a circle 24″ in diameter, which represents the revolving gun rack. The cabinet walls around the circle are approximately 1″ beyond the circle at all the points nearest the circle.

As shown in Fig. B, draw a line ½″ inside the front and sides, and 5⁄16″ inside the backs. It is this second line that represents the pattern for the top and bottom of the top cabinet. Transfer the pattern to two ¾″x30″x30″ pieces of plywood and cut out the pieces. Mark them "cabinet top" and "cabinet bottom."

Now draw a line 3″ outside the first line at the front and sides. Extend the two outside lines at the back to intersect with the new lines (Fig. C). This third line becomes the pattern for the top of the base. Transfer it onto a piece of ¾″x35″x35″ plywood and cut it out. Mark this piece "base top."

Fig. D deducts 1¼″ from the third line and carries this fourth line across the front and sides, until it meets the outside lines extending from the back. This is the pattern for the bottom of the cabinet base. Transfer it to a piece of ¾″ plywood 33″x33″ and cut out the piece. Mark this piece "base bottom."

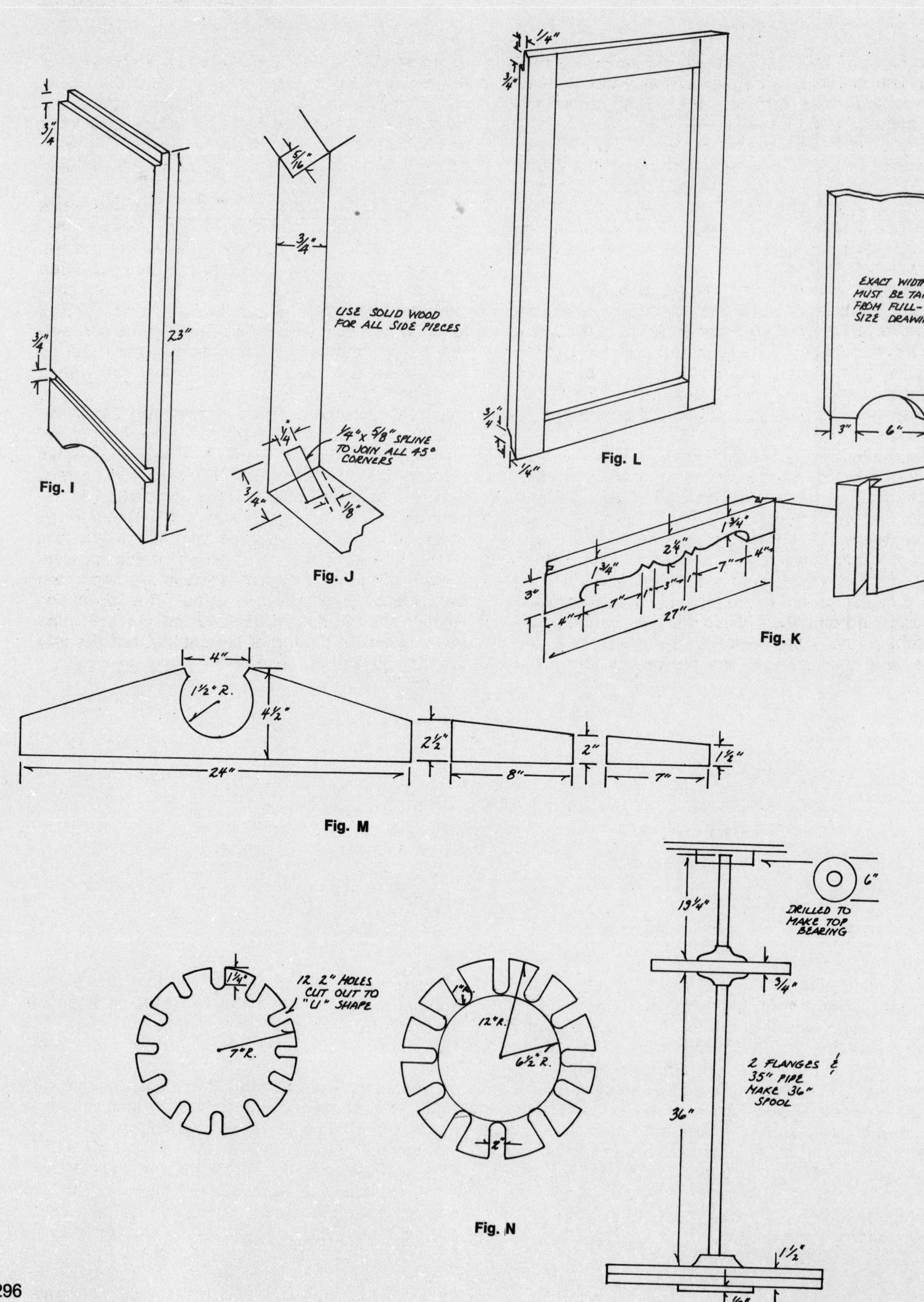

3/4"
3/4"
23"
Fig. I
5/16"
3/4"
USE SOLID WOOD FOR ALL SIDE PIECES
1/4"
1/4" x 5/8" SPLINE TO JOIN ALL 45° CORNERS
3/4"
1/8"
Fig. J
1/4"
3/4"
3/4"
1/4"
Fig. L
EXACT WIDTH MUST BE TAKEN FROM FULL-SIZE DRAWING
1 1/4
3"
6"
3"
1 3/4"
2 1/4"
1 3/4"
3"
4"
7"
1"
3"
1"
7"
4"
27"
Fig. K
4"
1 1/2" R.
4 1/2"
24"
2 1/2"
8"
2"
7"
1 1/2"
Fig. M
6"
19 1/4"
DRILLED TO MAKE TOP BEARING
3/4"
1 1/4"
12 2" HOLES CUT OUT TO "U" SHAPE
7" R.
1" R.
12" R.
6 1/2" R.
2"
2 FLANGES & 35" PIPE MAKE 36" SPOOL
36"
1 1/2"
1/8"
Fig. N

In Fig. E, a fifth line is drawn ¾" inside the outside line in the drawing, and is extended across the front and along the sides. This line represents the outside of the base.

Trace the base top onto a piece of ¼"x30"x30" Masonite (Fig. G). Then reduce the front and sides by 3¼" and cut out the piece. Glue the Masonite and base top together, with their back edges flush. Cut the ¼"x3½"x80" plywood strip according to Fig. G, mitering each piece at the corners. Now cut the solid ¼"x1"x80" stock following the same pattern and glue it around the edges of the top.

Turn the base top over and place the base bottom over it, 5⁄16" from the back edges and 1¼" from the front and sides. When the bottom is in position (Fig. H), trace it on the underside of the base top. Cut and glue-screw ¾"x¾" cleats along the inside of the line. The cleats are to hold the base top to the sides.

Base assembly. Cut the face stiles, rails, sides and backs according to the sizes in the materials list. Each of the sides is rabbeted at the top and dadoed at the bottom (Fig. I). The sides are mitered approximately 22½" and ploughed ¼"x⅜" at a right angle to the miter to accept ½"x⅝" splines (Fig. J). The valances are scrolled according to the dimensions shown in Fig. K. These are also mitered and ploughed for splines, with each piece matching the side it fits under. Assemble the sides and face stiles to the bottom and top front of the base. The 1⅛"x1⅛"x18½" back corner post is glue-screwed in place (Fig. A), and the backs are glue-screwed to the top, bottom, post and sides. The nose-and-cove trim is added to the top of the valance. The lipped doors are frame-and-panel construction (see Chapter 6 for building suggestions).

Top cabinet assembly. The face stiles and sides are cut, mitered, splined and assembled in exactly the same manner and angles as the bottom. The side pieces may be dished, if desired. (See console project in this chapter for dishing procedure.) The crown is scrolled as shown in Fig. M. When the complete top cabinet is glue-screwed to the top of the base, nose-and-cove trim is added to its base and top. The door is a frame with a glass panel inserted in dadoes.

Gun rack assembly. Three pieces, two 24" in diameter and one 14" in diameter, are cut from ¾" plywood. The smaller circle has twelve 2" holes drilled around its edge (Fig. N) for the gun barrels. One of the larger bottom circles is notched to accept the gun butts (Fig. N), and is then glued to the other 24" circle. The rack requires heavy-duty lazy Susan hardware that is attached to the top and bottom of the cabinet. The shelves are separated by 1¼"x35" pipe to form a spool. The top of the smaller shelf is flanged to hold the 1¼"x19" pipe that reaches to the top of the cabinet and fits into the lazy Susan hardware.

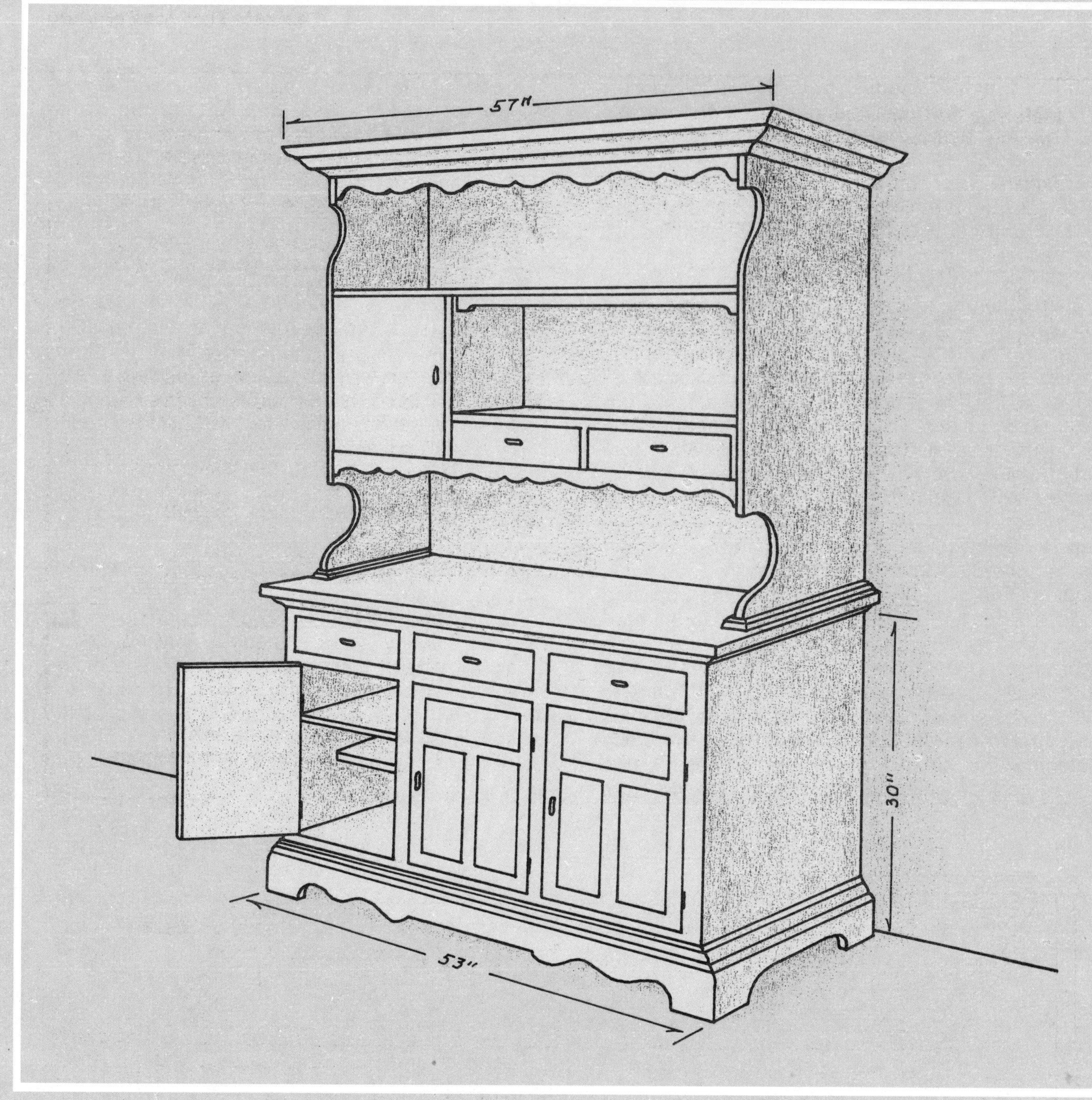

China Cabinet and Buffet

The traditional buffet and china closet has a long history that reaches back to the beginnings of many countries. There are numerous versions of the unit shown here; countless variations can be made from these drawings alone by adding or subtracting doors, drawers and shelves, almost at will within the basic structure. Cutting dimensions are listed in the materials list; the stock can be any cabinet wood or pine seasoned enough to accept a gracious finish.

Materials for China Cabinet and Buffet

Quantity	Description
Buffet	
1	1⅛"x202"x57" (made from two 1¼"x 10"x53" pieces splined together) for top
1	1⅝"x20" solid crown for top front lip
2	½"x17⅝"x30" for sides
1	¾"x2"x51½" for top frame back rail
5	¾"x2"x17¼" for top frame sides and spacers
2	¾"x2"x30" for face frame sides
1	¾"x2"x49" for face frame top rail
1	¾"x2"x25" for face frame verticals
1	¾"x3"x49" for face frame bottom
3	¾"x2"x15" for drawer spacers
2	¾"x3⅜"x19⅞" molded skirt for front feet
1	¾"x3⅜"56¾" molded skirt for side feet (mitered)
2	1⅛"x1½"x58¼" molding for front of base (mitered)
2	1⅛"x1½"x18" molding for side of base
2	1⅛"x1½"x53" for front base rail
2	1⅛"x1½"x18" for side base rails
1	½"x16"x51¾" for drawer dust shelf
1	⅛"x30"x51½" for back
Drawers	
3	½"x3 15/16"x14¼" for drawer backs
6	½"x3¾"x16½" for drawer sides
3	¾"x4⅝"x15½" for drawer fronts
3	½"x¾"x18¼" stock for drawer guides
Doors	
6	1"x2"x20" for top and bottom rails
12	¾"x2"x16" for side and center rails
9	¾"x6"x8" for raised panels
China Cabinet	
1	¾"x14"x57" for top
8'	3½" crown molding for top
1	¾"x5¼"x49¼" stock for top valance
1	¾"x2½"x49¼" stock for shelf valance
1	¾"x2"x32¼" stock for shelf valance
2	1⅛"x11¼"x50" for sides
1	1⅛"x10¾"x18¼" for cabinet partition
1	¾"x10¾"x49¾" stock for shelf
1	¾"x10¾"x32¾" stock for shelf
1	¾"x10"x49¾" for shelf
1	4½"x10¾" for drawer partition
2	¾"x2¾"x12" stock for base plates
Drawers	
2	½"x3 15/16"x15" for backs
4	½"x3¾"x10½" for sides
2	¾"x4½"x16¼" for fronts
2	¼"x15"x10¼" for bottoms
Door	
7'	¾"x1½" stock for door frame
10'	¾"x¾" stock for door frame dividers

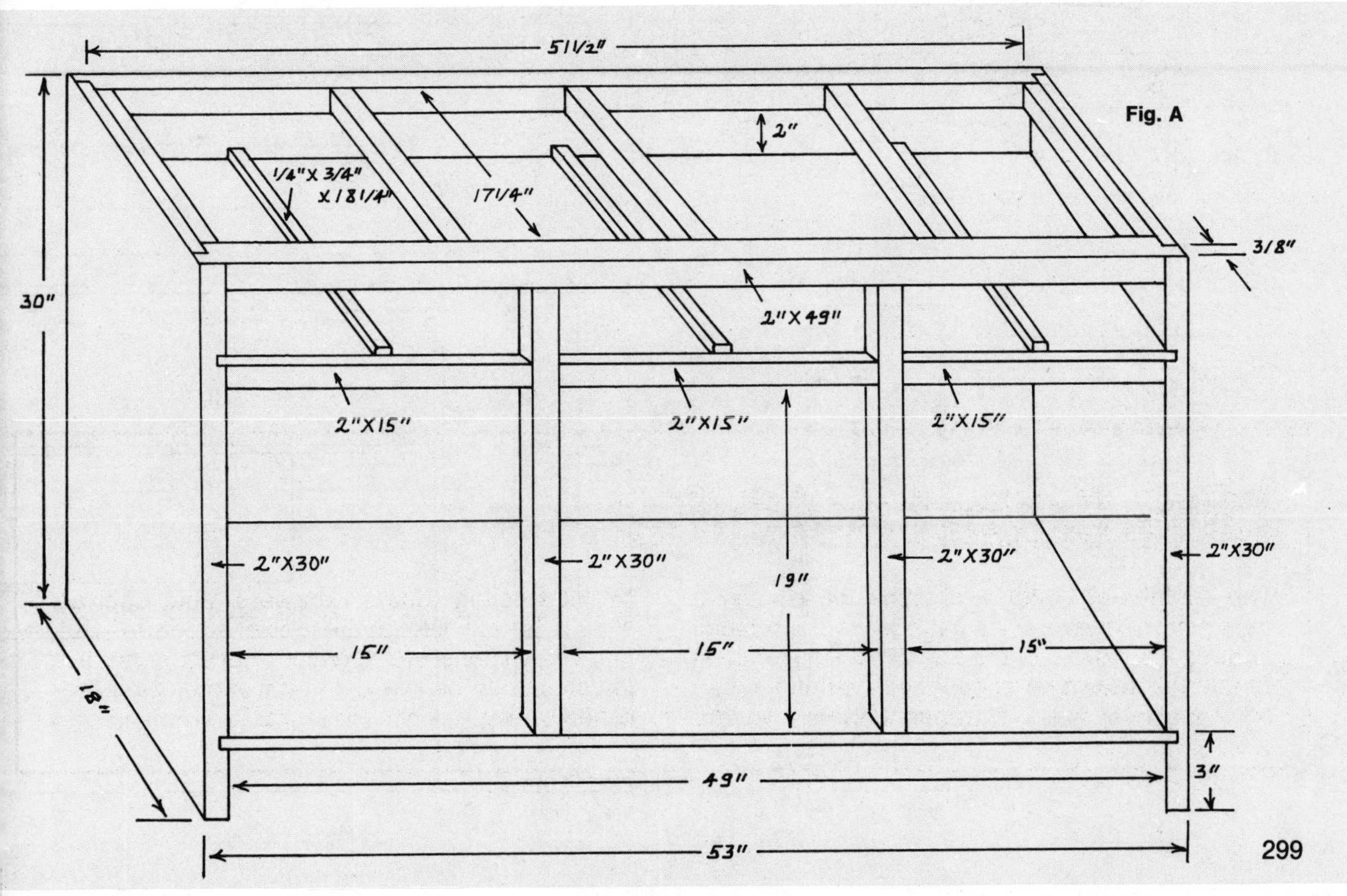

Fig. A

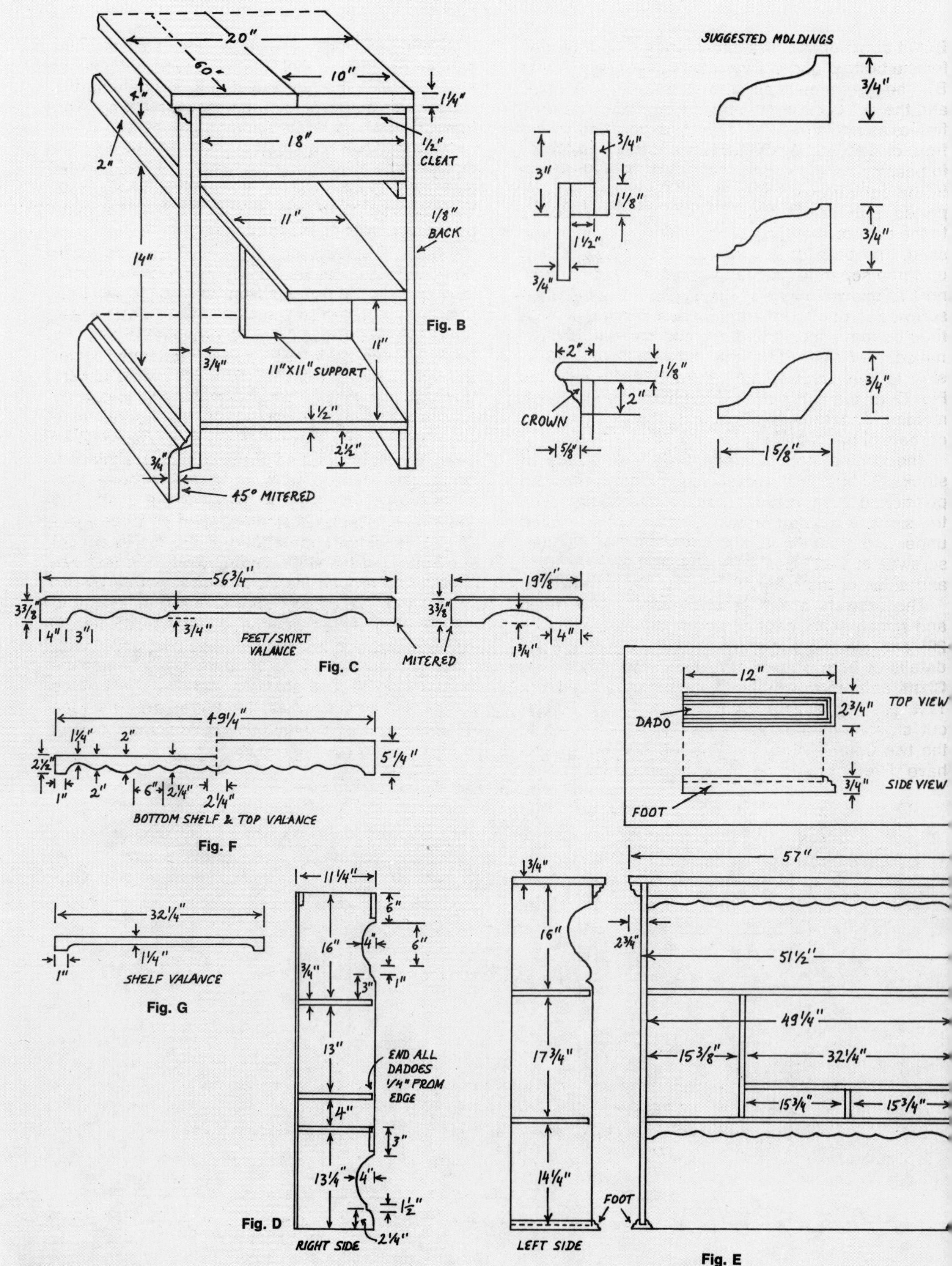

20"
60"
10"
1 1/4"
1/2" CLEAT
18"
2"
11"
1/8" BACK
14"
3/4"
11" X 11" SUPPORT
11"
1/2"
2 1/2"
3/4"
45° MITERED
Fig. B
SUGGESTED MOLDINGS
3/4"
3"
1 1/8"
1 1/2"
3/4"
2"
1 1/8"
2"
CROWN
5/8"
1 5/8"
56 3/4"
3 3/8"
4" 3"
3/4"
FEET/SKIRT VALANCE
MITERED
19 7/8"
3 3/8"
1 3/4"
4"
Fig. C
49 1/4"
1 1/4"
2"
2 1/2"
5 1/4"
1"
2"
6"
2 1/4"
2 1/4"
BOTTOM SHELF & TOP VALANCE
Fig. F
12"
2 3/4"
TOP VIEW
DADO
3/4"
SIDE VIEW
FOOT
32 1/4"
1 1/4"
1"
SHELF VALANCE
Fig. G
11 1/4"
6"
16"
4"
6"
3/4"
3"
1"
13"
END ALL DADOES 1/4" FROM EDGE
4"
3"
13 1/4"
4"
1 1/2"
2 1/4"
Fig. D
RIGHT SIDE
3/4"
16"
17 3/4"
14 1/4"
FOOT
LEFT SIDE
57"
2 3/4"
51 1/2"
49 1/4"
15 3/8"
32 1/4"
15 3/4"
15 3/4"
Fig. E

Buffet construction. The sides are cut and dadoed for the bottom and drawer dust cover (Figs. A and B). The top frame is assembled between the sides, and the ⅛" back is glue-nailed in place. The face frame, as shown in Fig. A, is glue-screwed to the front of the cabinet; the drawer guides are placed in position on the drawer dust shelf. The half-shelf in the cabinet section is ¾"x11"x52", and is supported at its center by a ¾"x11"x11" piece tacked to the bottom shelf and cabinet back as well as the shelf. The base of the buffet is made by building up three separate pieces, mitered at the front corners as shown in Fig. B. The 1⅛"x1½" rail is glue-screwed around the front and sides, flush with their bottom edges. The 1½"x1⅞" molding is glue-nailed over the top of the rail and the ¾"x3⅜" skirt is glue-screwed to the front of the rail. See Fig. C for the curve design cut from the skirt. The molding and skirt are both mitered at both front corners of the cabinet.

The cabinet top is made from two pieces of stock, 1¼"x10"x53", which are spline-joined and positioned flush with the back of the cabinet and the sides. A molded crown ¾"x1⅝" is glue-nailed under the front lip of the top. The top is glue-screwed to 1"x2" cleats attached to the front, back and sides of the cabinet.

The drawers are 14¾"x16½"x3¾". The frame and raised-panel cabinet doors measure ¾"x16"x 20" and overlap their frames. See Chapter 6 for details of both drawer and door assembly.

China cabinet assembly. Cut and shape the 1⅛"x 11¼"x50" sides as shown in Figs. D and E, and cut stopped-dadoes for the shelves as shown in the two figures. Note that the left and right sides have different dado positions because of the cabinet and drawers. Assemble the shelves and cabinet partition in their dadoes (see front view in Fig. E). Attach the top, allowing it to overhang the sides and front to accept the crown molding. The top valance is cut according to Fig. F, and is attached between the sides, across the front of the cabinet. The crown molding is then secured to the valance and the top (Fig. E). The back is a ⅛"x 44½"x48" scored panel, although it may be made by rabbeting ½"x6" stock together. Either way, the back is glue-nailed to the top, shelves, partition and sides. The valance under the bottom shelf is shaped in the same pattern as the top valance, and is glue-nailed to the front of the shelf under the drawers and cabinet. The straight-cut valance under the top shelf (see Fig. G) is attached under the front edge of the shelf. The 36" railing is centered at the front of the top shelf, and joined by inserting ¾" shaped dowels in the bottom of a piece of rounded ¾"x¾" stock (see Chapter 2 for suggestions on lathing dowels with a stationary power saw). The dowels are glued in holes partially drilled into the top edge of the shelf. The feet are ¾"x2¾"x12" stock shaped on three sides (Fig. E), molded and dadoed at the top to accept the bottom of the sides. Alternatively, the feet can be built up around the sides with separate pieces of molding. The cabinet door is ¾"x15⅞"x17", and can have glass or wooden panels inside its 2"-wide frame. The two drawers are 3¾"x15½"x10". They are divided by a ¾" partition between the bottom and second shelves, and are constructed in the same manner as the buffet drawers. See Chapter 6 for construction suggestions on making both the drawers and doors.

Index